AMERICA
in the
TWENTIETH CENTURY

Fourth Edition

George Donelson Moss
City College of San Francisco

PRENTICE HALL
Upper Saddle River, New Jersey 07458

Library of Congress Cataloging-in-Publication Data

Moss, George,
     America in the twentieth century / George Donelson Moss. — 4th
  ed.
       p.   cm.
    Includes bibliographical references and index.
    ISBN 0-13-083370-3
     1. United States—History—20th century. 2. United States—
  Politics and government—20th century. I. Title.
  E741.M67 2000
  973.9—dc21   99-13326
                                      CIP

Executive Editor: Todd R. Armstrong
Editorial Assistant: Holly Brown
Production Editor: Jean Lapidus
Copy Editor: Michele Lansing
Manufacturing Buyer: Lynn Pearlman
Interior Image Specialist: Beth Boyd
Cover Design: Bruce Kenselaar
Cover Photo Credits:
Left: Charles Lindberg and the Spirit of St. Louis.
    Courtesy Library of Congress.
Middle: Civil Rights March on Washington, D.C.
      8/28/63. Courtesy Archive Photos.
Right: Vietnam War Memorial, Washington, D.C.
    Photographer: Marc Anderson, Courtesy PH Archives.

To Linda, who knows why, and to Morris, who doesn't.

This book was set in 10/12 Palatino by BookMasters, Inc.
and was printed and bound by R R Donnelley & Sons Company.
The cover was printed by Phoenix Color Corp.

Printed in the United States of America

10 9 8 7 6 5 4 3 2 1

ISBN 0-13-083370-3

PRENTICE-HALL INTERNATIONAL (UK) LIMITED, *London*
PRENTICE-HALL OF AUSTRALIA PTY. LIMITED, *Sydney*
PRENTICE-HALL CANADA INC., *Toronto*
PRENTICE-HALL HISPANOAMERICANA, S.A., *Mexico*
PRENTICE-HALL OF INDIA PRIVATE LIMITED, *New Delhi*
PRENTICE-HALL OF JAPAN, INC., *Tokyo*
PEARSON EDUCATION ASIA PTE. LTD., *Singapore*
EDITORA PRENTICE-HALL DO BRASIL, LTDA., *Rio de Janeiro*

Contents

12 Reform, Rebellion, and War   *417*

13 The Nixon Era   *456*

14 An Era of Limits   *494*

APPENDICES

Preface

For the better part of four decades, I have been telling the story of modern American history to my students and to anyone else who showed an interest in the subject. This textbook derives naturally and inevitably from my vocation as one of the professional keepers of the nation's collective memory of itself. It represents my best efforts over many years to write a comprehensive narrative synthesis spanning the years of the twentieth century.

This book focuses on the public life of the American people. Historically, Americans have come together in the public sphere to compete and cooperate with one another; it is where the action has been. It is within the public sphere that the great decisions for war and peace, for reform and reaction, which shaped the democratic life of the American people, have been determined. It is within the public arena that powerful contending ideologies and interests have sought allegiance, and economic and cultural forces have shaped the destiny of the nation and forged the character of its people.

This narrative also incorporates much demographic, social, and cultural history to bring the experiences of all Americans into the mainstream of history. It is an inclusive account that records the historical experiences of those groups that used to be ignored or neglected in conventional history. Special attention has been given to the history of women, African Americans, Hispanics, Asians, Native Americans, and other Americans who have come together to create the most successful multicultural society in the history of the planet.

I also have devoted a lot of space to describing the major role that the United States has played in world affairs in the twentieth century. Such a focus is particularly appropriate for the half century following World War II, when the United States has been the preeminent national power in the world and forged a network of global interests.

I am delighted to have an opportunity to offer this fourth edition of *America in the Twentieth Century*. During the many years that this book has been available to students and teachers, I have received a surprisingly large number of letters, phone calls, and faxes from readers. Most have written to tell me that they found the book informative, enjoyable reading. They also have included many constructive criticisms and suggestions for improving the book. My correspondents will be pleased to discover that I have incorporated many of their suggestions into this new edition: suggestions that have tightened the organization of the book, strengthened its analyses, clarified some of the writing, and generally improved the story of America that I have been telling.

This book has been thoroughly revised. Each chapter has been carefully reworked and in some cases restructured and revamped. In some chapters, new material has been added; in others, material has been abbreviated or deleted.

In my view, confirmed by the testimony of readers, the strengths of this book are the following: it is well written and well organized. I employ a clear, concise style that avoids social scientific jargon, psychobabble, and esoteric intellectual constructs. This book is accessible to anyone who wants to understand the major contours of modern U.S. history. It is a good place to begin one's study of modern and postmodern America. This book also is well organized. The story of *America in the Twentieth Century* unfolds chapter by chapter in carefully structured and coherent categories. Each chapter carves out a chronological segment. Within each time frame, the particular topics that define an era and give it its historical significance are developed.

The master themes of modern American historical development undergird the events and personalities treated in individual chapters. These themes provide the story of America with its underlying coherence and continuity. They include: the growth in the size, cost, power, and scope of authority of the national government; the expanding role the United States plays in world affairs that often involves fighting in wars; the development and application of new systems of technology; the development of the consumer economy; the continued growth of a vital popular culture and systems of mass communication; the increasing plurality and diversity of American social life; and the continuing commitment of nearly all Americans to democratic values and practices.

This book was written for use in survey courses in twentieth-century U.S. history taught in high schools, community colleges, and the lower divisions of four-year colleges. It can also be used in upper-division courses at four-year colleges and universities in classes for students who are not history majors, or who do not have extensive backgrounds in U.S. history.

My stance toward my subject is serious, detached, and objective, if slightly ironic. I have no interest in imposing my political affiliations or ideological allegiances, disguised as historical interpretation, on my readers. My goals are *to help you learn how to think about modern American history and to provide you with a vocabulary for engaging in conversations about the endlessly fascinating story of America.*

ACKNOWLEDGMENTS

Mark Twain once said that he could remember anything, whether it happened or not. Alas, professional historians are not permitted the luxury of mythic invention, nor even of inadvertent error. Fortunately, I have had a tremendous amount of help in creating and revising this book. That help has eliminated errors and brought forth a far better book than I could have created on my own.

One of the greatest pleasures of historical scholarship is that it is so much a collective enterprise. Scores of friends, students, colleagues, and other scholars have shared in the challenging task of producing a comprehensive narrative history of twentieth-century America. I want them all to know that I am exceedingly grateful and beholden to them. I also cherish their encouragement and support while revising this book three times.

I also want to acknowledge my deep gratitude to many outstanding people affiliated with my publisher, Prentice Hall, those who managed the mysterious and magical task of transforming an ungainly manuscript into a beautiful book. Todd Armstrong, Executive Editor, made the decision to revise the book for a fourth edition. Jean Lapidus took charge of the book's production process, kept it on schedule, and kept me informed of its progress with unusual efficiency and tact.

Lastly, special thanks go to two special people: Mary Chatelier, who used her skills as a historian/detective to retrieve dozens of original photographs from the confines of the not-entirely-user-friendly National Archives photo collections, which have greatly enriched this book; and the lovely Linda, who reminds me daily of what is truly significant and beautiful in the life we share.

George Donelson Moss

1

Prologue: A Society in Transition

MODERN America emerged during the last thirty years of the nineteenth century. During those decades, a predominantly rural nation, whose people inhabited small towns and villages, evolved into an urban industrial giant. As late as the 1860s, most Americans had earned their livings as farmers, skilled mechanics, shopkeepers, and small manufacturers, or as employees of farmers, merchants, and small businessmen. By the end of the nineteenth century, large industrial corporations increasingly dominated the American economic landscape. Amidst the clamor and tumult of relentless social change, these corporations powerfully influenced what millions of Americans owned, where they worked, and what kind of work they performed, and produced the commodities that they used, from baby food to tombstones. Three historical forces transformed America as the nineteenth century ran its course: industrialization, urbanization, and massive immigration. Behind these powerful forces lay the application of new technologies. The last decades of the nineteenth century represented a crucial stage of U.S. development, during which an older America was destroyed and a newer nation was created by the modernizing forces of technological change and social upheaval.

A DEMOGRAPHIC PORTRAIT

The population of the United States grew from 60 million in 1890 to more than 76 million by 1900. As the twentieth century began, America was the fourth most populous nation in the world (after China, India, and Russia) and contained the most rapidly growing population of any large nation in the world. The rapid rate of population growth was a function of both a high birthrate among the

1

native-born population and the unprecedented massive inflow of immigrants. During the decade of the 1890s, over 6 million immigrants traveled to America, 75 percent of whom comprised the "new" immigration, people coming from the countries of southern and eastern Europe, principally Poland, Italy, and Russia. According to the census of 1900, 26 million of the nation's 76 million inhabitants were either immigrants or the sons and daughters of immigrants. In addition to the inflow of new immigrants, two other major population movements characterized fin de siècle America: People, especially farmers, continued to trek westward to farm new lands in Texas, the high plains, and California. Millions more moved from rural areas to the large towns and cities, especially in the northeastern regions of the nation. As the twentieth century began, three-fourths of the American population inhabited the eastern third of the nation, residing east of the Mississippi River.

Even though the census of 1900 showed that nearly two-thirds of American families still resided in towns of fewer than 2,500 people, the nation had undergone a rapid growth in urban population during the 1890s. The rapid urbanization of American society during the last decades of the nineteenth century was its most salient demographic trend. Population growth within the surging metropolises of America had been nothing short of spectacular. New York City, the commercial and cultural capital of the nation, had grown from 1.5 million people in the 1870s to 3.5 million by 1900. Chicago, which had only become a city during the Civil War, was approaching 2 million people by 1900. Other large cities showed similar dramatic increases. It was in the growing large cities of America during the 1890s where one could see the population diversity and cultural pluralism that was creating the world's first genuinely multicultural society.

ECONOMIC GROWTH

Economic growth characterized all regions of America during the late nineteenth century, although it was most extensive in the northeastern and Great Lakes regions. Within a generation, America had developed the world's largest industrial economy. Economic growth influenced the lives of nearly all Americans. Geographic and social mobility were enhanced. American manufacturing flourished during the decades of the late nineteenth century for many reasons. New natural resources were being discovered and exploited. The nation also expanded geographically as the West was wrested from the Plains Indians. Western expansion added to the size of national markets, which also were protected from foreign competitors by tariff walls erected by congressional legislation. Additional ingredients composed the recipe for economic growth. America raised a class of bold, skillful entrepreneurs, many from poor backgrounds, who organized and built large industrial corporations. The dominant values of the age promoted and celebrated economic growth and material acquisition as well. Manufacturing flourished too, because it was a time of rapid advancement in basic science and technology. New machines that increased productivity appeared, and engineers harnessed new power sources.

Constructing the nation's industrial infrastructure, particularly the transportation revolution wrought by the building of the railroads, made an essential contribution to the industrial revolution. Railroads formed the most important element in American economic development, for several reasons. They constituted an important industry in themselves, the nation's first big business. During the 1880s, 7,000 miles of track were laid annually. By 1890, feeder lines, regional roads branching off of the main east-west trunk lines, linked most cities and towns in the country. As the century ended, the nation's railroads owned 193,000 miles of tracks, more than half of the world's total trackage. As the nation's railroad industry expanded, it also became concentrated. By 1900, seven giant interregional railroad combines (including the New York Central, the Baltimore and Ohio, the Pennsylvania, and the Southern Pacific) controlled 90 percent of the nation's railroad mileage.

Railroads also stimulated the growth of a large-scale manufacturing economy. Before the national system of railroads was in place, manufacturing was largely confined to small businesses that sold to local markets. The railroads created the modern U.S. market economy and the modern stock exchange that enabled railroad operators to raise the vast sums of money required to build the railroad lines, purchase rolling stock, and hire thousands of employees. Industrialists in other fields borrowed money, bought new machines, purchased raw materials in large quantities, hired more workers, and employed salespeople. Branch offices and new factories were opened.

Rapid, large-scale expansion of manufacturing enterprises formed an integral part of the American industrial revolution. In 1900, the American Gross Domestic Product (GDP) reached $40 billion, a sixfold increase in twenty years. The most impressive advances in manufacturing during the late nineteenth century occurred in the steel industry. Inventors discovered an inexpensive means of mass-producing steel that transformed iron manufacturing during the 1860s. The United States, which had no steel industry at the time of the Civil War, became the world's largest steel manufacturer in 1880. The steel industry was centered in Pittsburgh because of its nearness to iron and coal deposits and its easy access to both railroad and maritime transportation. Andrew Carnegie, who came to America as a penniless immigrant boy, became the steel master of America. When he retired from business in 1901, his Carnegie Steel Company was the world's largest. His personal fortune was estimated at $500 million. He devoted the rest of his life to giving away most of his vast fortune to support various philanthropic enterprises such as libraries, public buildings, and foundations.

The American petroleum industry also grew rapidly during the late nineteenth century. The first producing oil well was drilled in western Pennsylvania in 1859. As the oil industry mushroomed during the 1860s, its most important product was kerosene, used mainly to light people's homes at night. One giant firm

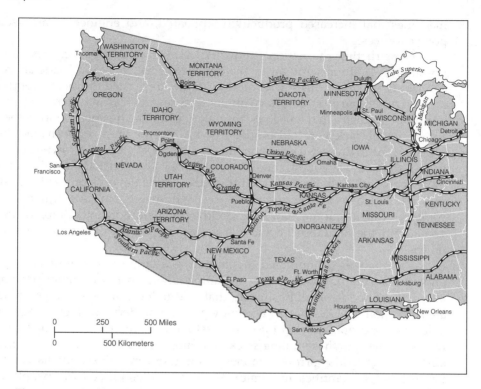

Figure 1.1   Railroad network, 1885.   *Source:* George D. Moss, *The Rise of Modern America* (Englewood Cliffs, NJ: Prentice Hall, 1995), p.3.

emerged to monopolize the oil refining industry in America, the Standard Oil Company, headed by John D. Rockefeller. Rockefeller had entered the oil business in 1863, when it was competitive and chaotic. Within a few years, Standard Oil's efficient operation made it the largest refiner. Standard Oil forced railroads to grant it rebates, giving it a tremendous competitive advantage over rival refineries. It then proceeded to buy up its competition. Competitors who initially refused to sell were driven to the verge of bankruptcy and forced to sell. The Standard Oil Trust, formed in 1882, controlled 85 percent of America's oil refining capacity, and Rockefeller had become the nation's first billionaire. He too retired from business and gave away huge sums of his money to various philanthropic enterprises.

Two other important industries evolved during the late nineteenth century, the telephone industry and the electric utility industry. Alexander Graham Bell invented the telephone in 1876. Two years later, the first commercial telephone exchange was installed in New Haven, Connecticut. During the last two decades of the nineteenth century, telephone use spread rapidly. By 1900, Americans were using over 800,000 telephones, mostly for commercial purposes. In that same year, the American Telephone and Telegraph Company acquired its monopoly. Thomas Edison, the most famous inventor in American history, played a key role in the emergence of both the telephone and electric utility industries. He vastly improved telephonic transmission, but his most significant achievement was his perfection, in 1879, of the incandescent lamp (what we now call the electric lightbulb) at his Menlo Park, New Jersey, laboratory. At Christmastime, he decorated his lab with a few dozen of the new lights. People traveled long distances to see this miraculous invention of the "Wizard of Menlo Park." Here was an invention that promised to obliterate the dark, to transform the way people lived and worked.

In 1882, Edison's company built the first power station in New York, which supplied the city with electric current for lighting for eighty-five customers. By 1898, there were 3,000 operating power stations in the country. The Edison system employed direct current at low voltage, which limited the distance electric power could be transmitted to about two miles. George Westinghouse, another versatile inventor of the era, understood that alternating current, stepped up to high voltages by transformers, could be transmitted cheaply over long distances and then reduced to lower voltages for safe use by consumers. He formed the Westinghouse Electric Company in 1886 to compete with Edison's company. Westinghouse soon surpassed Edison as a supplier of electricity.

While entrepreneurs and inventors developed the new corporate forms of organization and the new technological systems that created the American industrial infrastructure, other business leaders built extensive marketing organizations of their own. The first advertising agencies appeared during the 1870s. Ad writers created copy and devised images to promote national sales of brand names such as Quaker Oats and Kellogg. By the end of the century, Proctor and Gamble, Colgate, Kodak, Campbell Soups, and Pillsbury Flour had become household words. Large department stores such as Macy's in New York and Wanamaker's in Philadelphia made their appearance. "Chain stores" such as the Atlantic and Pacific Tea Company (the A & P grocery) and F.W. Woolworth's "five and dimes" proliferated. As the major department and chain stores plied their urban customers with a cornucopia of goods, Sears, Roebuck and Montgomery Ward sold to rural customers through mail-order catalogues. The origins of the modern American consumerist culture can be located among the web of rapidly expanding ad agencies, department stores, chain stores, and mail-order houses.

As industries physically expanded, they also tended to become concentrated: fewer and fewer firms of a larger and larger size were controlling production in most of the important sectors of the economy. One major reason for the concentration of so many industries during the late nineteenth century was that only through concentration could the new technological systems be fully utilized. Another important reason was falling prices. As prices fell, profit margins decreased, and competition intensified. Rival concerns lowered their prices to retain or increase market shares; successful firms either destroyed or absorbed their beaten rivals.

Railroads responded to price competition and its adverse consequences by reorganizing through mergers and takeovers; they combined lines into giant interregional systems during the 1880s. During the severe depression of the early 1890s, some of these combines went bankrupt. Bankers, led by J.P. Morgan, intervened to

Figure 1.2   J.P. Morgan (American banker & philanthropist)(born: Hartford, CT, 4/17/1837; died: Rome, Italy, 3/31/1913).   *©Patoli Bros. 1908. Source: Pack Bros.*

refinance and restructure the railroad systems. The financiers saved the railroads from bankruptcy and stabilized the nation's primary transportation system. The price paid for an orderly operating environment for the industry included higher rates for freight and passengers, banker control of many of the nation's largest railroads, and interregional monopolies.

At this time, most Americans were committed to economic individualism and the philosophy of free enterprise. In theory, they opposed governmental regulation of the economy. In practice, they accepted considerable governmental activity in the economic sphere—protective tariffs, internal improvements, and land grant subsidies to the railroads—because these governmental actions promoted geographical expansion and economic growth. They also generated jobs.

By the 1880s, many Americans had been frightened by the emergence of large industrial corporations such as the giant railroad systems and Standard Oil Trust. Farmers, craftsmen, and small businessmen feared that these large corporate enterprises had become too big, too powerful. Big businesses were seen as posing threats to society. Lacking competition and unrestrained by government, they could charge their customers whatever they wanted. Even worse, monopolists were destroying economic opportunity and threatening democratic institutions. Thoughtful citizens worried about the survivability of democracy in a society increasingly characterized by a widening gap between the rich and poor.

The first to act were Midwestern farmers and merchants who pressured state legislatures to regulate railroad rates. These state efforts were generally ineffective because railroads were large regional businesses whose operations spanned several states. The U.S. Supreme Court, after initially approving such state efforts, declared state regulatory efforts unconstitutional in 1886. In 1887, Congress enacted the Interstate Commerce Act to provide a measure of railroad regulation. It called for rates to be "reasonable and just," outlawed rebates, required railroads to publish and stick to their rate schedules, and outlawed some monopolistic practices. Most important, it created the Interstate Commerce Commission (ICC), the first federal regulatory agency to supervise railroads, investigate complaints, and enforce the law. In practice, the ICC proved no more successful than the state regulatory commissions. The ICC's chief weakness was its lack of power to set rates; it could only take the railroads to court and try to persuade the courts to order the railroads to reduce their rates.

At the same time that some states and the federal government were trying unsuccessfully to regulate the railroads, attempts also were made to tame the trusts. As with railroad legislation, the first antitrust laws originated in the states. Federal action came in 1890, when Congress enacted the Sherman Antitrust Act. The act declared any trust or other combination found to be "in restraint of trade" illegal. Persons forming such trusts could be fined and jailed. Individuals and businesses found to have suffered losses caused by illegal actions could sue in federal court for triple damages. The Supreme Court quickly emasculated the Sherman Act. In the case of *United States v. E. C. Knight Company* (1895), it was found that a sugar trust that controlled 98 percent of all domestically refined sugar was not in restraint of trade. The Court held that the E. C. Knight Co. had been formed to manufacture sugar, not to trade sugar, and therefore was a commercial activity, exempting it from prosecution under the Sherman Antitrust Act.

LABOR

Wage earners were affected in many ways by industrialization and the rise of big business. Some effects were beneficial, others damaging. More efficient production methods enabled industrial workers to increase their output. Real wages rose 25 percent between 1870 and 1890. Work became physically less arduous, and the average work day was shortened from eleven to ten hours.

But as machines replaced human skills in shops and mills, jobs required less skill and became repetitive and monotonous. As manufacturing units grew larger, employee-employer relations became impersonal. The bargaining leverage of workers declined, and opportunities for workers to rise from the ranks of laborers and to become manufacturers themselves decreased. Industrial work often proved dangerous. Nearly a million workers were injured annually in work-related accidents. In an age where laissez-faire attitudes dominated, there were no safety regulations or compulsory worker compensation programs. Workers and their families received no compensation, even for crippling or fatal accidents that occurred on the job. Industrialization also caused more frequent and larger swings in the business cycle. Periods of expansion would be followed by periods of depression and high unemployment.

The only labor organization to establish itself during the Gilded Age was the American Federation of Labor (AFL), organized in 1886. It took a pragmatic, businesslike approach to unionism, eschewing radicalism and politics, concentrating on organizing skilled workers and fighting for "bread and butter" issues such as better wages and shorter hours. Its chief weapon was the strike. It grew steadily and had 1 million members by 1900. Samuel Gompers and other AFL leaders fought hard to establish their union and to win important gains for their members. In so doing, however, they abandoned the vast majority of American workers for whom they could do nothing and had no intention of doing anything. The AFL craft unions wanted nothing to do with black people, recent immigrants, women, or unskilled workers, generally.

Worker frustration and discontent mounted in the late nineteenth century. Workers felt threatened by the huge size of large corporate employers, by technology, and by periodic recessions and depressions, which meant unemployment in a laissez-faire economy. Most of all they were frightened and angered by the stubborn arrogance of corporate employers, nearly all of whom opposed trade unions, fired workers for joining unions, and refused to bargain with union representatives. Strikes, which became frequent during the 1880s and 1890s, often became bitter, violent confrontations.

Figure 1.3   Striking steelworkers at the Carnegie mills in Homestead, Pennsylvania prepare for a clash with armed Pinkerton detectives hired by Andrew Carnegie to break the strike.
Source: Library of Congress.

A savage railroad strike in 1877 convulsed the nation. For a time, about two-thirds of the nation's railways were shut down. Violence erupted in several locations in Illinois, Maryland, and Pennsylvania. Workers were shot, railroad properties were sabotaged, and hundreds of people lost their lives. Federal troops were called out to keep order, in effect breaking the strikes and protecting the property of the railroad operators. A troubled President Rutherford Hayes, who had ordered the federal troops to intervene, wrote in his diary of his fear that the federal government had become a "government of corporations, by corporations, and for corporations." In 1892, a strike occurred against Carnegie's steel factory in Homestead, Pennsylvania. During the strike, a fierce battle erupted between armed strikers and company guards, a battle that claimed seven lives. The strike lasted for months before the company won, fired many of the strikers, and crushed their union.

The most important strike occurred in 1894, when workers at the Pullman Company, near Chicago, went on strike to protest wage cuts during a severe depression. Some Pullman employees belonged to the American Railway Union, led by Eugene V. Debs. They refused to work on trains with Pullman cars. The resulting strike tied up rail traffic in and out of Chicago. The railroad companies appealed to President Cleveland to send troops, and he did, on the pretext that they were required to ensure the movement of mail. When Debs defied a federal injunction, he was jailed for contempt of court, and the strike was broken. The crushing of the Pullman strike demonstrated the power of the courts to break strikes. In 1897, Debs converted to socialism and later ran for president five times on the American Socialist Party (SDP) ticket.

IMMIGRANTS

The industrial revolution stimulated a huge increase in immigration to America and tapped new population sources. Most of the immigrants who had come to America before 1890 had emigrated from the British Isles or the countries of western and northern Europe. After 1890, large numbers continued to emigrate from these traditional sources, but the majority arrived from the countries of southern and eastern Europe (Italy, Poland, Russia, and the Balkans), countries that had previously furnished few, if any, immigrants. These southern and eastern Europeans made up the new immigration. They were a predominantly peasant population pushed out of their homelands by decaying feudal economies and political and religious persecution.

Their first experiences were often harsh. They braved an uncomfortable, sometimes dangerous sea voyage and worried through inspections at Ellis Island and other immigration depots, often arriving in America with few possessions, little money, no education, and no job skills. They crowded into immigrant neighborhoods in large cities. There they found living quarters and the company of their ethnic brethren.

Although most of these new immigrants had come from peasant backgrounds, few went into agriculture in America. They lacked the capital and knowledge required to farm in America, which was a specialized business. Also, the economic possibilities and cultural attractions of the cities were more inviting than those of rural areas. The new immigrants were fed into the urban, industrial workforce, living in tenements near the factories that employed them. Many went into construction work, digging sewers, installing utilities, and paving the streets of expanding metropolises, in which the only constant appeared to be ceaseless growth. They worked hard, often long, hours, six days a week.

Even so, these harsh living and working conditions were better than what most of them had left behind. They worked no harder and earned no less than the native-born workers who were doing the same kind of work. Many immigrants acquired the income and knowledge to leave the ghettos. If they could not, their children, benefiting from educational opportunities, often achieved middle-class occupations, income, and status. There were many victors as well as victims among the immigrant groups pouring into the United States during the 1890s.

However, the oppressive living conditions prevailing in the immigrant slums and the failure of many of the newcomers to assimilate into the mainstream of American life angered and alarmed reformers. One of them, Jacob Riis, called attention to the immigrants' plight in an influential book, *How the Other Half Lives*, published in 1890. The book consisted of sketches of life in New York's immigrant ghettos, drawn from Riis's years as a reporter. Photographs accompanied the articles in his book. He piled one pathetic case upon another, his prose full of anger and shock. He declared the slums to be the children of "public neglect and private greed."

A year before Riis published his spirited book, Jane Addams opened a settlement house in a slum in south Chicago, where she and her fellow social workers provided services to the residents, who were mainly new immigrants. She called it Hull House, which became the largest, most famous of the hundreds of settlement houses opened in American cities during the last fifteen years of the nineteenth century. Hull House offered its clients a day care center, arts and crafts, counseling, playgrounds and baths for children, cooking classes, schools, an employment referral service, and access to medical and dental care. It also brought middle-class social workers into contact with immigrants, giving those professionals an opportunity for firsthand observation of immigrants' problems.

The tremendous influx of new immigrants also provoked a nativist backlash on the part of some old-stock, native-born Americans. Nativists resented what they perceived to be a flood of poor, illiterate, and unskilled people who could never become productive citizens. A body of pseudoscientific studies attempted to prove that immigrants from southern and eastern European countries belonged to races that were "inferior" to northern and western Europeans and their American descendants. During the 1880s and 1890s, nativists organized for action and became a potent political force. The most influential nativist organization was the American Protective Association (APA), founded in 1887 primarily to promote Americanism and Protestant religions, which members equated with American national culture. Their chief targets were Roman Catholics, the Catholic Church, and

Catholicism itself. During the 1890s, the leaders of organized labor called for the adoption of literacy tests to screen out immigrants. Congress moved to bar "undesirable" immigrants from entering the country; at various times, it excluded convicts, insane people, contract laborers, paupers, anarchists, and people with serious illnesses.

CITIES

The enormous expansion of industry was the chief cause of urban growth during the late nineteenth century, when modern American metropolises appeared. A steadily increasing proportion of the American urban population was made up of immigrants. By 1900, immigrant populations composed the majority of the population in several of the largest American cities. According to the 1900 census, first- or second-generation immigrants made up over 80 percent of New York City's nearly 3.5 million inhabitants.

These immigrants often got blamed for all of the problems that afflicted American cities of the late nineteenth century, but this accusation was both exaggerated and unfair. The main cause of urban problems was the rapid expansion of cities. Cities suffered from acute growing pains; city services could not begin to keep pace with the rate of urban growth. Severe problems with water supplies, sewage, garbage disposal, and police and fire protection arose. Crowded, substandard housing was the worst problem, with its attendant physical discomfort, psychological stress, juvenile delinquency, vice, and crime. Slums spawned street gangs, epidemic diseases, and high infant mortality rates.

Gradually, the basic facilities of urban living improved. Streets were paved, and electric lights pushed back the dark after nightfall. Major improvements were made in urban transportation. The major innovation was the electric trolley. These "streetcars" changed the character of urban life, extending the range of the traditional "walking city" from two and a half miles to more than six miles, which meant that the geographic areas of cities expanded enormously. Population shifts occurred as the affluent classes fled from the inner cities to the outer neighborhoods, the suburbs. They left the immigrant working classes clustered in the downtown areas. Segregated residential patterns emerged in every city, separating people by income and economic class, which correlated with ethnic and racial divisions.

WOMEN, CHILDREN, AND WORK

During the last decades of the nineteenth century, 6 million American women entered the workforce. Many entered manufacturing industries, such as shoemaking, food processing, and textiles, and became factory workers. By 1890, over 300,000 women worked in textile factories, comprising over half of the labor force. They also took clerical jobs in business as typists, bookkeepers, and salespersons. Employers were willing to hire millions of women because they could pay them

Figure 1.4   Women workers in one of the nation's "sweatshops" during the Gilded Age.   *Source:* Library of Congress.

less, substantially less, in most cases, than men. Women worked for about a third to a half of what men received for comparable work. In 1900, about 90 percent of working women were young and single. Prevailing attitudes barred married women from the workplaces of America. When a young working girl married, she usually had to quit her job. Female workers sometimes organized their own unions, carrying out successful strikes and achieving higher wages. Working women forged the first broad-based women's union in this country, the Women's Trade Union League (WTUL), founded in 1903. Women also entered most of the professions, albeit in small numbers. By 1900, most public school teachers and librarians were women.

Most working children labored on their parents' farms, but they also flooded into industrial occupations in the late nineteenth century. Children under age fifteen worked in coal mining, textiles, and other industries. Other children worked in the streets, selling newspapers and shining shoes.

NATIVE AMERICANS

During the 1870s and 1880s, as the American economy expanded and the building of the railroads opened the West for economic development, the Plains Indians became victims of the westward expansion. They were killed and conquered, their cultures fragmented, and they lost about 86 million of the 138 million acres that had been given to them earlier in the nineteenth century. The surviving remnants were tucked away on arid reservations to endure a life of poverty and isolation.

Indian resistance was heroic; they held off the encroaching whites for years, but they inevitably succumbed to overwhelming firepower and vastly superior numbers. It was the destruction of the buffalo herds that fatally undermined the ability of the Plains Indians to resist the U.S. Army. Two vast herds had roamed the prairies, furnishing the Indians with food, clothing, shelter, and tools. By the 1880s, these herds had been hunted to the verge of extinction. Fierce and proud warriors were exterminated or reduced to begging for whiskey in front of saloons. The great chiefs died or fled; Sitting Bull, the great military strategist who defeated Colonel George Custer's Seventh Calvary in the most famous battle of the Plains War, ended up as an exhibit in a sideshow. General Philip Sheridan, the Civil War hero who commanded U.S. Army forces conquering the Plains Indians, understood why the Indians fought and expressed sympathy for the people his soldiers were destroying. He wrote:

> We took away their country and their means of support, broke up their mode of living, their habits of life, introduced disease and decay among them and it was for this and against this they made war. Could anyone expect less?[1]

Plains Indians also suffered at the hands of civilian agencies entrusted with administering Indian affairs. Government agents were political appointees. They often were incompetent, corrupt, and indifferent to Indian welfare, exploiting the people they supposedly served. There were cases of crooked agents selling food supplies intended for reservation Indians to miners and pocketing the money, leaving the helpless Indians to starve.

In 1887, Congress passed the Dawes Act, which was designed to eliminate tribal life and convert the surviving Plains Indians to the white man's way of life. Reservation lands were divided into small units, with each head of an Indian household allotted 160 acres. Indians who accepted the allotments and "adopted the habits of civilized life" were granted U.S. citizenship. A clause in the Dawes Act prevented Indians from selling their allotted lands for twenty-five years. Funds also were appropriated to provide education for Indian children. Intended as a reform to help Indians, in practice, the Dawes Act proved disastrous. It shattered the remnants of Indian culture without enabling them to adopt the white man's ways. Most of the land allotments ended up in white hands, and the Indians remained dependent on government aid.

The last Indians to abandon the unequal struggle against the whites were the Chiricahua Apaches, who inhabited the desert of the Southwest. They waged a savage guerrilla struggle against the U.S. Army in Arizona Territory. In 1886, the Army succeeded in capturing their chieftain, a resourceful warrior named Geronimo. The

---

[1]Thomas C. Leonard, "The Reluctant Conquerors," *American Heritage*, XXVII:5 (August 1976), pp. 34–40.

Apaches finally yielded, and the nearly 300-year cycle of genocidal warfare waged by the European invaders of North America against Native Americans came to an end.

There was a horrible, final chapter to the Euro-American conquest of the Native American people, written in the blood-stained snow at Wounded Knee, South Dakota, in December 1890. A Paiute shaman, Wovoka, had developed a religion based on a ceremonial rite known to whites as the Ghost Dance. He converted the Lakota Sioux to his new faith. Fearful that Wovoka might lead an armed uprising, authorities sent the U.S. Calvary to suppress the religious movement.

When they saw the soldiers, about 350 Ghost Dancers fled into the wilderness in the dead of winter. The pursuing troopers caught up with them at Wounded Knee Creek. The Indians surrendered, and nervous soldiers disarmed them. Suddenly someone fired a shot, and all hell broke loose. Cavalrymen firing rifles and artillerymen firing cannons from the surrounding hills massacred the Indians as they tried to escape. Before the carnage ceased, an estimated 200 of the 350 men, women, and children had been killed. "We tried to run," a survivor recalled, "but they shot us like we were buffalo."

As the nineteenth century ended, a Native American population that had numbered in the millions and consisted of hundreds of intact cultures that inhabited a vast region at the time Europeans established their first permanent settlements on the Atlantic seaboard had been reduced by centuries of warfare, epidemic disease, and oppression to perhaps 50,000 individuals. Social scientists predicted that these degraded remnants would soon die out, that the early twentieth century would bear witness to the extinction of the Amerindians. These scientists proved to be poor prophets. Native Americans and their descendants would make an amazing recovery as the twentieth century unfolded. According to the 1990 census, there were more Americans of Indian descent inhabiting the United States than lived in the region at the time the English, French, and Spanish colonized North America.

HISPANIC AMERICANS

Native Americans were killed, died of disease, starved, or ended up on reservations. In California, Texas, Colorado, and the southwestern territories of Arizona and New Mexico, people of Hispanic descent fared little better than the Indians. As U.S. judges repeatedly ruled, *rancheros* held legal title to millions of prime acres in California. But a legal document was useless when Anglo squatters cut down orchards, destroyed vineyards, slaughtered cattle, plowed the soil, and refused to leave when ordered off lands they did not own. Much of the land ended up in the hands of Anglo lawyers and judges as payment for legal fees and court costs. Some small *rancheros* survived in New Mexico territory by holding grazing lands in common. In South Central Texas, Hispanics held title to lands as family estates rather than giving individuals the right to sell shares as he or she might wish. But Anglo-Texan cattle barons controlled the courts and legal system in this region of Texas.

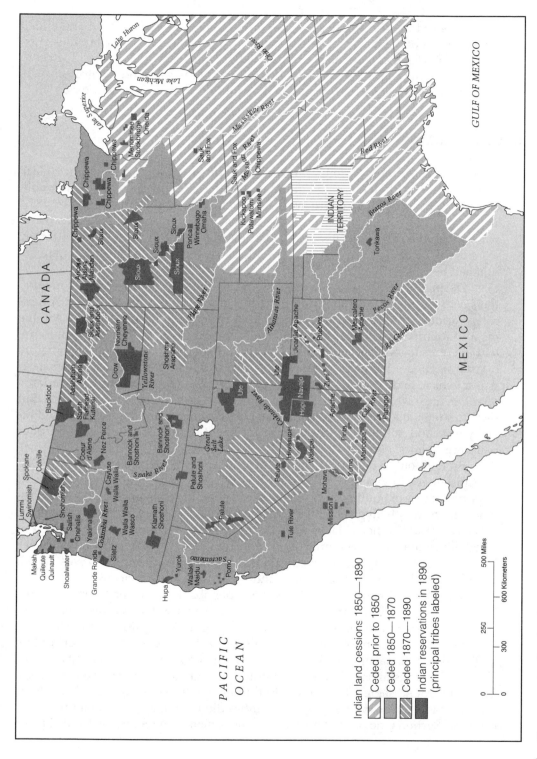

Indian land cessions 1850—1890

Ceded prior to 1850

Ceded 1850—1870

Ceded 1870—1890

Indian reservations in 1890
(principal tribes labeled)

0	250	500 Miles
0	300	600 Kilometers

Figure 1.5 Indian land cessions, 1850–1890. *Source: Moss, The Rise of Modern America, p. 16.*

They imposed the fee simple system of individual ownership of land and ended up with most of the land previously owned by Hispanics. Hispanic families often ended up working as *peons* on lands they had previously owned. As the nineteenth century ended, thousands of Hispanic families in the states and territories of the West and Southwest had dropped into the ranks of migrant farm workers.

AFRICAN AMERICANS

While Native Americans fell victim to Western expansion, the status of black people in the South deteriorated in the aftermath of Reconstruction. The Republican Party abandoned Southern blacks in exchange for the presidency in 1877. Throughout the decade of the 1880s, the status of African Americans in the South was ambiguous. They retained legal and political rights and still voted, but they were deprived of effective political power because the Republican Party organization had been destroyed.

During the 1890s, with Mississippi leading the way, Southern states rewrote their constitutions to include provisions that disfranchised most African Americans. Various subterfuges were used to circumvent the Fifteenth Amendment, the most common of which was the "understanding clause." This clause required potential voters to read and understand any section of their state constitution before registering, and it left enforcement of this rule to voter registrars. Registrars used it as a vehicle to disfranchise African Americans by imposing stringent standards on them, meanwhile allowing illiterate whites to register by taking their word that they "understood" the state constitution. Other exclusionary devices included literacy tests and poll taxes. Black disfranchisement ensured Democratic control of Southern politics.

By 1900, only 5 percent of eligible African Americans voted in the South. Disfranchisement also opened the door for the enforcement of legal segregation in all important areas of Southern life. Elaborate segregation ordinances evolved everywhere in the South, depriving black people of equal access to public accommodations. By 1900, Southern blacks were disfranchised, segregated, and deprived of equal educational and economic opportunities. There was a tremendous increase in the amount of violence directed against black people during the 1890s. Lynch mobs roamed the South, murdering hundreds of African Americans.

The application of Jim Crow had been possible because the Supreme Court had retreated from its commitment to racial democracy in the aftermath of Reconstruction. In 1883, the Court nullified the Civil Rights Act of 1875, which had outlawed segregation of public accommodations. In 1896, the Supreme Court put its seal of constitutional approval on segregation. In a notorious case, *Plessy v. Ferguson*, the Court sustained a Louisiana statute that segregated the races on railroads. The Court found segregation to be constitutional if "separate but equal" facilities were provided. "Separate but equal" facilities did not violate the equal protection clause of Section One of the Fourteenth Amendment. One Supreme Court justice vigorously dissented from the majority decision: John Marshall Harlan, a Southerner and conservative, wrote that the Court "had inflicted a terrible blow to the principle of equal protection before the law."

Plessy v. Ferguson resolved a conflict between American professions of equality and institutionalized racism when the Court also held that segregation did not imply that black people were inferior. The timing of *Plessy v. Ferguson* also was important; it removed the last barrier to the general drive to deprive African Americans of rights. Segregation would be constitutional for the next fifty-eight years. The color line spread to Northern towns and cities.

Out of this era of decline and danger for African Americans emerged Booker T. Washington, who became the foremost spokesman for black people. Deeply concerned about the ability of African Americans to survive in racist America, he developed a strategy that he hoped would lead to racial harmony and common progress. In a speech delivered at an Atlanta exposition in 1895, he preached self-help, economic progress, thrift, and racial solidarity. He told black people that if they learned to advance themselves by receiving agricultural or vocational training, saving their money, and acquiring property they would earn the respect and acceptance of whites. Washington assured white leaders that African Americans accepted disfranchisement and segregation in order to concentrate on economic gains. In return, he asked Southern white business leaders and politicians to support black education and to hire black workers.

Figure 1.6   Booker T. Washington, born a slave, rose to become a prominent leader in education and the foremost spokesman for African Americans during the 1890s. *Source:* Hampton University.

Washington's proposed accommodationist strategy made him popular among whites, enabling him to raise millions of dollars from Northern philanthropists for black technical and vocational training. Washington was a realist. He was not naive, and he was not in the service of Northern philanthropists or Southern white leaders. He chose the least bad of only bad options that were available to Southern blacks during the 1890s. Nor was Washington an apologist for injustice. He once wearily told a group of supporters, "I am not deceived. I do not overlook the wrongs that often perplex and embarrass this country."

Other African American leaders, rejecting Washington's accommodationist strategies, proposed that blacks challenge racism and legal segregation, that they demand full equality now. The most prominent African American scholar in 1900, William E.B. Dubois, told blacks that they should demand the best university educations available and that they should demand the right to vote in order to battle the segregation system through the political process. Dubois' proposals appealed to the tiny black elite but had little relevance to the lives of the mass of African Americans still residing in the rural South.

During the 1890s, over 90 percent of African Americans resided in the South, most living outside of the boundaries of industrial society. Most were forced to live within the confines of an oppressive environment without political power and with inferior legal rights. African Americans were bound by a rigid and stringent caste system that deprived blacks of equal opportunities, indeed forbade any expression of equality. In many regions of the South, African Americans were entrapped in a kind of economic bondage. They worked as sharecroppers or tenants, perpetually in debt, caught up in a credit system that enabled landowners, merchants, and bankers to hold them in virtual peonage.

Despite their difficult lives within an oppressive social system, many capable, hardworking African Americans achieved considerable successes, enjoying strong, stable family lives. They established strong communities, built around black churches and schools, and black-owned businesses. Thousands of black farmers were able to acquire their own farms. According to the census of 1900, African Americans owned about 12 million acres of land in the South.

ASIAN AMERICANS

Chinese people first emigrated to the United States during the 1840s, when they came to California to mine gold. Initially, they were welcomed. These immigrants were mostly young men who came as sojourners to make their fortunes in the region they called "Gold Mountain" and then planned to return to their villages and families in China. Many came from the Toison district of the Canton Province in southern China. During the 1860s, perhaps 25,000 Chinese were working in California's gold fields. As the gold ore played out, former miners went to work building railroads.

During the 1860s, about 12,000 Chinese worked for the Southern Pacific railroad, constructing the western half of the first transcontinental railroad, which was completed in 1869. During the 1870s, Chinese immigrants in California worked in agriculture, in the fishing industry, and in service businesses such as restaurants and laundries. They were ineligible for American citizenship under a 1790 law that limited that privilege to white people. Many prospered, despite encountering considerable, often violent, anti-Chinese prejudice. In 1882, about 30,000 Chinese immigrants entered the country, bringing the national total to 150,000, mostly concentrated on the West Coast.

Many white Americans had resented the Chinese for years. Anti-Chinese prejudice was especially strong among working-class whites. They viewed the Chinese as economic competitors who took their jobs, worked for lower wages, and could be used as strikebreakers. In 1871, white mobs in Los Angeles rampaged through Chinatown, smashing windows, ransacking homes, and stabbing and shooting Chinese people at random.

Pressure from West Coast politicians prompted Washington to conclude an agreement with China that restricted immigration. Congress implemented the ban by enacting the Chinese Exclusion Act in 1882, signed by President Hayes, which barred most Chinese immigration to the United States for ten years. It was renewed in 1892 and made permanent in 1902. The Chinese were the first national group to be formally barred from emigrating to America.

Japanese emigration to America began during the late 1880s on a small scale. By 1900, about 3,000 Japanese immigrants had reached America, most settling in California. They also encountered prejudice, which hindered their opportunities. White Californians began a drive to exclude Japanese immigrants, which would continue intermittently until World War II.

FARMERS

The economic position of many farmers declined during the late nineteenth century. Ironically, one of the major reasons for agricultural decline lay in the fact that the American industrial revolution had enabled American farmers to mechanize, to farm larger acreages and increase productivity. Both American and world agricultural production increased, and the European market, the American farmers' major overseas outlet, shrank. Farm commodity prices tumbled. As farm commodity prices fell and farm income dropped, individual farmers responded by increasing production. Increased production further depressed prices, and farm income continued to spiral downward.

Farmers also had to pay more for equipment and other supplies because manufacturers, protected from foreign competition by tariff barriers, had raised their prices. Good land was increasingly expensive in many areas, either because it was growing scarce or because the railroads and large land companies controlled it. Flour milling and meat-packing industries forced farmers and stock owners to sell their grain and beef at lower prices. Railroads, especially in regions where they enjoyed a transportation monopoly, often charged farmers exorbitant rates to haul their crops.

Figure 1.7   Harvesting wheat on one of the "bonanza farms" in western America, ca. 1890.   *Source:* Library of Congress.

Midwestern farmers organized to try to improve their economic situation. During the 1860s and 1870s, they formed Granges. These groups organized purchasing cooperatives and also lobbied state governments to regulate railroads, particularly to limit the shipping rates that railroads charged farmers. These efforts were generally futile. By the late 1870s, many farmers were in serious economic difficulty. Farm income continued to fall, and many farmers were deeply in debt for equipment and land that they had purchased previously.

In their distress, some farmers turned to currency inflation to rescue them from economic disaster. During the Civil War, the government had issued "greenbacks"—hundreds of millions of dollars of paper money that was not redeemable in silver or gold. Farmers, joined by small merchants and other hard-pressed groups, called for the government to issue more greenbacks. They reasoned that currency inflation would cause price levels to rise, that their income would increase, and that they could pay their debts. In 1880, they formed the Greenback-Labor Party, a single-issue alternative party that attracted 300,000 votes. It faded thereafter, but the idea of easing farmers' debt burdens through currency inflation did not.

POLITICS

Politics during this era was characterized by passive presidents and strong senators. The Senate dominated the federal government. Many of its members were either political bosses preoccupied with forging alliances, winning elections, and controlling patronage, or they were pawns of corporate interests. The House of Representatives was more responsive to the public interest, but it was too unstable to play an effective legislative role. Frequent, close elections meant a constant turnover in House membership, and neither party was able to control the House long enough to enact a legislative agenda.

It was an era of strong local governments and a relatively weak national government. At the local and state levels, corrupt political machines frequently controlled the government. Political machines stayed in power by turning out the voters on election day to support the organization's candidates. Control of elections meant power—power to distribute city jobs to supporters, to award franchises to companies for providing city services in exchange for bribes, and to award building contracts to construction companies willing to pay for them. Corrupt contractors often profited excessively from these contracts by overcharging the taxpayers and using cheap, substandard materials.

Immigrant neighborhoods formed the popular base of big city political machines. It was common for individuals to register illegally in several precincts and to vote many times on election day, and in exchange for votes, a voter often benefited from machine favors—a job, a cheap rental, help if there was trouble with the police, and assistance in acquiring citizenship. The political boss and many of his henchmen were often immigrants themselves, and newcomers could identify with their success and power. The machine also ran ethnically balanced tickets to appeal to a broad range of immigrant nationalities and to give members of immigrant groups an opportunity to achieve political office and participate in politics. Political machines often sponsored dinners, fairs, and picnic outings for their immigrant constituents. These events not only entertained the voters but also ensured their continuing political support.

Presidential elections were invariably corrupt, and close. The two major political parties were evenly matched. There were few significant issue differences between them, and no ideological differences. Usually Republican presidential candidates won narrowly. Grover Cleveland was the only Democratic president to hold office during the 1880s and 1890s. Elections were not decided by the issues. Voters generally voted a straight party ticket; occasionally they were attracted by the personal qualities of a candidate.

THE PEOPLE'S PARTY

By the late 1880s, continuing hard times meant that farmers continued to organize in an effort to solve their economic problems. Farmers' Alliances appeared in the Midwest and South. During the late 1880s, the Alliances claimed a membership of white and black farmers that approached 2 million. They formed cooperatives and entered politics at the local level. Alliance members, encouraged by local political successes and angered by both major parties which had continued to be unresponsive to their concerns, met in St. Louis in February 1892 to form a new national third party, the People's Party, also called the Populist Party or the Populists. They gathered again in Omaha, Nebraska, on July 4, 1892, to choose their candidate for president and to adopt a platform. In a noisy, emotional gathering that resembled a religious revival, they denounced bankers and business leaders who exploited the farmers and workers of the country.

The major plank in their platform called for currency inflation. But it was no longer a call for more greenbacks, which the farmers had abandoned as an unrealistic goal. They wanted the free and unlimited coinage of silver to gold at a ratio of 16:1. They wanted to inflate the currency, expanding the money supply by requiring the U.S. Treasury to buy and to coin free of charge all silver brought to it. They wanted silver dollars to contain sixteen times as much silver, by weight, as gold dollars would contain gold. That 16:1 ratio would ensure that silver would be more valuable as money than it would be as a precious metal, given the prevailing prices for gold and silver. Therefore, silver would remain in circulation as money, and the currency would become inflated. This money plank appealed to Western silver miners as well as farmers, and it appealed to some small business owners who saw inflation as a cure for their economic woes. Free silver also had symbolic uses: it represented the liberation of the toiling masses from economic bondage to banks and railroads. Other Populist planks called for government ownership of railroads and telephone lines, an income tax, a single term for the president, and the direct election of senators. Populists tried to attract the support of labor by calling for an eight-hour day, by denouncing contract labor (importing aliens as workers who took jobs from American workers and who could be used as strikebreakers), and by demanding an end to the use of Pinkerton detectives to break up strikes.

At the time of the Populist movement, there was a great deal of discontent among the urban working classes. Strikes and unemployment marches were symptomatic of the unrest seething in the land at the time of the Populist revolt. Some of these angry workers made common cause with the populists. In 1894, Jacob Coxey led an "army" of about 600 unemployed workers in a march from his home in Ohio to the nation's capital. Middle-class Americans were alarmed by the growing signs of social instability in their increasingly frayed society.

The Populists nominated James B. Weaver, a former Civil War general and Greenback-Labor leader, for president. Running as a third party in 1892, the Populists waged an energetic campaign. They had able leaders such as Mary E. Lease, an attorney and a powerful orator, who exhorted Kansas farmers to "raise less corn and more hell." The Populists attracted a diverse constituency of malcontents in the South and West. On election day, the Populists gathered over 1 million votes, or 8.5 percent of the total. They showed strength in two regions: the Old South and the newer states of the Midwest. They won many local elections, elected some representatives and a few senators, and won control of the Kansas legislature. They also picked up twenty-two electoral votes. The Populists did well enough in a few regions to alarm the established parties in the South and Midwest. But the Populists never established beachheads in any cities and most farmers east of the Mississippi and north of the Ohio Rivers rejected Populist causes.

The big winners in the election of 1892 were the Democrats. They controlled both houses of Congress, and Grover Cleveland was once again ensconced in the White House. It was the first time since before the Civil War that the Democratic Party controlled both the presidency and the Congress.

During 1893 and 1894, the nation was mired in the worst depression in its history. Banks and businesses failed by the thousands. Railroads controlling about one-third of the trackage in the country went bankrupt. Farmers, unable to meet mortgage payments, lost their farms. Millions of industrial workers were unemployed. Late in 1894 the U.S. Treasury faced a desperate financial crisis. Its gold reserves dwindled to $41 million, not enough to pay debt obligations that would soon come due. Only an emergency bond issue, which was floated by a banking syndicate headed by J. P. Morgan which raised $62 million, saved the American government from bankruptcy.

Because of the economic crisis gripping the nation, the 1894 elections brought unmitigated disaster to the Democratic Party. In most Northern states, all Democratic incumbents were turned out of office. The North became solidly Republican and would remain so for the next twenty years. The Populist vote showed modest increases in the 1894 elections as they continued to demand the unlimited coinage of silver to gold at a ratio of 16:1. The depression and President Cleveland's failure to solve it discredited his administration.

The Republicans met to nominate a candidate in St. Louis in 1896 and chose an Ohio congressman with a good record, William McKinley. The Republicans adopted a platform maintaining the gold standard and a protective tariff.

At the Democratic Convention held in Chicago in July 1896, President Cleveland lost control of the delegates, and they rallied to the candidacy of a thirty-six-year-old Nebraska attorney, William Jennings Bryan. Bryan won the nomination with a dramatic appeal for silver, ending his speech, "You shall not press down upon the brow of labor this crown of thorns; you shall not crucify mankind upon a cross of gold." The Convention promptly adopted a platform calling for the "free and unlimited coinage of both gold and silver at the present legal ratio of 16:1" and nominated Bryan for president.

The Democrats' actions confronted the Populists with a Hobson's choice. If they supported Bryan and free silver, they risked losing their identity as a political party. If they ran their own candidate, they ensured McKinley's election and the defeat of the silver issue. Most Populists ended up supporting Bryan and the Democrats. After 1896, Populist support declined rapidly. The Democrats had co-opted the Populists' major issue and most of their followers.

In the contest between Bryan and McKinley, issues did matter. The Republicans had many advantages that they could exploit during the campaign. The Democrats were saddled with Cleveland's discredited depression presidency and were on the defensive. Mckinley ran a well-organized, well-financed campaign orchestrated by an Ohio businessman, Marcus A. Hanna. Hanna's campaign organization flooded the nation with millions of pieces of campaign literature and 1,500 speakers. Hanna's electoral strategy called for McKinley to stay home, conducting a dignified "front porch" campaign. Selected delegates representing various national constituencies would be brought to his home. McKinley would greet them and make a speech calculated to appeal to their interests.

The Democrats had little money, weak organization, and few prominent supporters. But they had Williams Jennings Bryan, who waged an energetic one-man campaign. He traveled over 18,000 miles and made over 600 stump speeches. He had a powerful voice—loud, clear, and eloquent. He spoke, without amplification, to crowds as large as 10,000. Bryan's campaign speeches were dominated by a single theme—silver. His was mainly a single-issue campaign in contrast to McKinley's pluralistic, nationalistic approach.

In November, McKinley won decisively. He received over 7 million votes to Bryan's 6.5 million and 271 electoral votes to Bryan's 176. The Republicans also rolled up large majorities in both houses of Congress. Organization and money had beaten eloquence. Pluralism had defeated silver. Nationalism had bested sectionalism. The silver issue carried the South and Midwest, but it did not travel well outside of these regions. Bryan also failed to reach industrial workers. The Republicans got the support of most urban voters, most business voters, and most middle-class voters, and they carried the farm vote in several Midwestern states such as Illinois and Ohio, which ensured their victory. Bryan was at heart a moralist and rural reactionary, a spokesman for a vanishing, older America. The outcome of the election confirmed the triumph of the new urban industrial order and McKinley as the voice of that emerging economic order.

IMPERIALISM

For much of the Gilded Age, Americans were preoccupied with internal events such as industrialization, the building of railroads, and the settlement of the West. But toward the end of the nineteenth century, the United States turned outward. It became much more involved in world affairs, built a modern navy, expanded its overseas trade, fought a war with Spain, and acquired a colonial empire. By 1900, the United States had emerged as a world power.

Many forces converged to revive American expansionism and direct American attention overseas. Powerful economic forces stemming from industrialization played a major role. Industrialization diversified and increased American exports, creating a search for new overseas markets and a drive to expand existing ones.

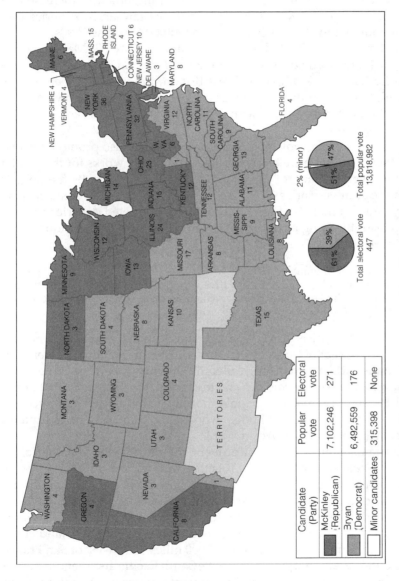

Candidate (Party)	Popular vote	Electoral vote
McKinley (Republican)	7,102,246	271
Bryan (Democrat)	6,492,559	176
Minor candidates	315,398	None

Total electoral vote 447
61% 39%

Total popular vote 13,818,982
51% 47%
2% (minor)

Figure 1.8 The election of 1896. *Source:* Moss, *Rise of Modern America,* p.25.

Andrew Carnegie discovered that he could sell a ton of steel to an English railway cheaper than English steel manufacturers could. John D. Rockefeller's Standard Oil monopoly soon dominated the European market for kerosene. Other American business leaders looked to Latin America, which was long a market for British manufacturers, for increased sales. American imports also increased, and many came from American-owned enterprises in foreign lands. American investment capital poured into Canada, Mexico, and Cuba during the 1890s.

Other forces promoted expansion. Captain Alfred T. Mahan, an avowed expansionist, urged Congress to modernize and expand the U.S. Navy. In books and essays he used the example of Great Britain, the world's preeminent power, to prove his contention that sea power undergirded all great powers. He linked together expanding sea power with expanding commercial ties and overseas colonial possessions.

The missionary movements of many churches also promoted overseas activity. In their earnest desire to save souls and do good works for the greater glory of God, they were servants of expansion, particularly in Asia. By the 1890s, hundreds of American missionaries lived and worked in China. Reverend Josiah Strong, a Congregational minister from Ohio, actively promoted American missionary expansionism. Blending a concept of religious mission with nationalism and racial ideologies, he prophesied that

> This race of unequaled energy, with all the majesty of numbers, and the might of wealth behind it—the representative, I hope, of the largest liberty, the purest Christianity, the highest civilization . . . will move down upon Mexico, down upon Central and South America, out upon the islands of the sea.[2]

Social Darwinists also advocated American expansionism. They applied the Darwinian concept of "struggle for survival" to international power politics. They were confident that what they called the mighty American "Anglo-Saxon race" was destined to acquire colonies and to expand its influence until it dominated the world. Social Darwinist foreign policy ideas also influenced men such as Theodore Roosevelt and Henry Cabot Lodge, who helped forge America's expansionist foreign policies from 1898 to World War I.

An amalgam of powerful economic, strategic, and ideological forces provided an expansionist dynamic. Together they turned a hitherto inward-looking and parochial continental power into an expansionist and international power during the last decade of the nineteenth century.

American expansion initially focused on the South Pacific. As the century came to a close, the United States gained ownership of two island chains, Samoa and Hawaii. Samoa, which lay some 4,000 miles southwest of San Francisco, commanded important shipping lanes in the South Pacific. Its splendid natural harbors of Apia and Pago Pago were desired as way stations for America's growing trade with New Zealand and Australia.

[2]Josiah Strong, *Our Country,* ed. Joseph Herbst (Cambridge, MA: Belknap Press, 1963), reprint of the 1891 revised edition. See chap. 14, "The Anglo Saxon and the World's Future," pp. 213–18.

In 1878, the United States concluded a treaty with the Samoans that gave the United States rights to a coaling station at Pago Pago. The Germans and British also negotiated treaties with Samoa, and the three nations disputed each other's interests in the archipelago. All three nations sent warships, and for a time war threatened among them. The three imperialistic powers resolved their conflicts diplomatically at a conference held in Berlin in 1889. They created a three-power protectorate that proved inherently unworkable as conflicts over economic and strategic interests continued. In 1899, the Samoan archipelago was divided between Germany and the United States, with Britain gaining territory elsewhere. Germany got the two largest islands and America the remaining islands, including Tutuila, with its harbor at Pago Pago.

American involvement with the Hawaiian Islands dated from the 1820s, when New England missionaries settled there to convert the population. American influence had become dominant in the Islands by mid-century, and some expansionists were calling for annexation. A reciprocity treaty signed between Hawaii and the United States in 1875 permitted Hawaii to ship sugar duty free to the United States, causing the Islands' sugar industry to boom. It also tied the Hawaiian economy to mainland markets. Economic dependency became a strong force for political union with the United States.

By 1890, planters of American descent controlled the sugar industry and owned about two-thirds of the land. During that year, changes in American tariff laws favoring domestic sugar growers caused mainland demand for Hawaiian sugar to drop sharply, plunging the Hawaiian economy into depression. Hawaiian sugar planters favored annexation with the United States to regain their lost markets. There were additional motives for annexation. In 1891, Queen Liliuokalani became the Hawaiian monarch. Resenting the growing influence of Americans, she abolished the existing constitution that had granted Americans control of the Islands' political life. She tried to reassert the prerogatives of the traditional Hawaiian monarchy, but her actions provoked an American-led coup that overthrew her government. The planter revolutionaries turned to the American minister to Hawaii, John Stevens, for help.

On January 16, 1893, Stevens, a strong advocate of annexation, arranged for 150 marines from the USS *Boston*, then in Pearl Harbor, to take up stations near Queen Liliuokalani's palace. The next day, Stevens officially recognized the new revolutionary regime. Two weeks later, he declared Hawaii an American protectorate and advised Washington to proceed with annexation: "The Hawaiian pear is now fully ripe, and this is the golden hour for the United States to pluck it." A delegation from the new Hawaiian government came to Washington to negotiate an annexation treaty. In mid-February, less than a month following the coup, President Harrison submitted an annexation treaty to the Senate for approval.

The Senate had not yet voted on the proposed treaty when a new president, Grover Cleveland, took office. Cleveland, who opposed annexation, withdrew the treaty from Senate consideration. He sent a special commissioner, former Congressman James Blount, to Hawaii to find out if the native Hawaiians favored annexation. Blount reported to Cleveland that the coup against the Queen could not have succeeded without U. S. complicity, and that the Hawaiians both opposed annexation and wanted their monarch restored. The president blocked annexation and tried to restore the Queen to her throne, but the American planters now controlling the Hawaiian government refused to step down.

In 1897, President William McKinley came to office favoring annexation. Another treaty was negotiated and sent to the Senate, which failed to approve it. It took the outbreak of the Spanish-American War to provide the necessary votes for the annexation of Hawaii. Advocates argued that Hawaii was needed to send supplies and reinforcements to American soldiers in the Philippines. Captain Mahan argued that the United States should take Hawaii, lest it fall into the hands of a hostile power such as Japan. The annexation treaty passed. On July 7, 1898, Hawaii became an American territory.

Another major area of American interest was the Caribbean. In 1895, U.S. attention focused on Cuba, when the Cubans rose in rebellion against Spanish rule. The fighting between the rebels and the Spanish troops was vicious. The Spanish commander, General Valeriano Weyler, in an effort to deny the guerrillas popular support, herded the Cuban people into concentration camps. Thousands of Cubans perished from disease, starvation, and mistreatment. Americans, who mostly sympathized with the rebels, were appalled by General Weyler's notorious *reconcentrado* policy and its ghastly results. American newspapers also carried exaggerated and distorted accounts of Spanish activity in Cuba, further inflaming public opinion against the Spanish. Two large New York City dailies, Joseph Pulitzer's *New York World* and young William Randolph Hearst's *New York Morning Journal,* competing fiercely for readers, ran many sensational, inaccurate accounts of the war.

Irresponsible journalism may have stirred the people, but it did not cause the United States to go to war in Cuba. Other forces were at work. Anti-Spanish sentiment was intensified in early February 1898 when Cuban rebels released a private letter that had been written by the Spanish Ambassador to the United States, Enrique Dupuy de Lome. In the letter, de Lome had criticized President McKinley, calling him "weak and a bidder for the admiration of the crowd."

A week after the publication of the letter there occurred the event that probably made war inevitable. On the evening of February 15, the American battleship USS *Maine* was blown up in Havana Harbor, killing 260 sailors. The cause of the blast has never been determined, but at the time, Americans held the Spanish responsible. Political pressure built for America to go to war against Spain. People marched through the streets chanting, "Remember the Maine! To hell with Spain!" The most fervent pro-war advocates in Washington were Democratic and Populist members of Congress who invoked the "spirit of 1776," calling for a war to liberate the Cuban people from Spanish colonialism.

President McKinley, wishing to solve the Cuban crisis by diplomacy, tried to avoid a war that he did not believe served the national interest. He tried to moderate the press and public responses to avoid being forced to war. He was particularly concerned about the popular "rush to judgment" after the sinking of the

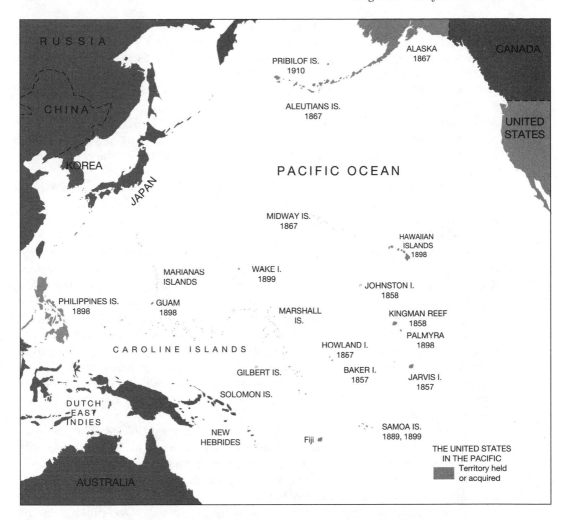

Figure 1.9   The United States in the Pacific.   *Source:* Moss, *Rise of Modern America,* p. 29.

Maine. Most businessmen strongly opposed going to war with Spain; they feared it would disrupt trade with Cuba and imperil the recent economic recovery. Backed by Wall Street bankers and business leaders, Mckinley demanded that Spain revoke the *reconcentrado* policy and grant an armistice to the rebels. In early April 1898, Spain, desperately wishing to avoid a war it could never win, agreed to these terms.

But Spain's concessions were too little too late. McKinley had decided to grant Congress the war it and the American people demanded. Internal political pressures had forced McKinley's hand. On April 11, he sent the most halfhearted war message any president ever sent to Congress, in which he noted that negotiations with the Spanish leaders were working and a war was not necessary. But on

April 18, Congress, in a jingoistic frenzy, issued an ultimatum directing the Spanish to vacate Cuba and ordered a naval blockade of the island. Four days later, Congress followed these acts of war against Spain with a formal declaration of hostilities. The United States stumbled into a war it could have avoided.

Although all eyes were on Cuba, where the crisis in relations between Spain and the United States had brought war, the opening battle of the Spanish-American War occurred on the other side of the world in Manila Bay in the Philippines. On May 1, Commodore George Dewey's squadron destroyed a Spanish fleet trapped in the bay. In August, U.S. Army forces occupied Manila, the capital of the Spanish colony.

In May, the Spanish sent a fleet of seven ships to Cuba. They anchored in Santiago Bay at the southeastern tip of the island. An American fleet, discovering their presence, hovered outside of the bay, waiting until the U.S. Army arrived to attack the city of Santiago and force the Spanish ships out of the bay. On June 22, about 17,000 American troops landed. This expeditionary force included the "Rough Riders," a cavalry unit whose second-in-command was Lieutenant Colonel Theodore Roosevelt. The Army sent to fight in Cuba also included three regiments of African American soldiers. The Army encountered stiff resistance from the Spanish defenders but succeeded in capturing the heights above the city and bay. Roosevelt led one of the assaults. The forces under his command included not only his Rough Riders but one of the black cavalry regiments as well. The Spanish fleet then tried to run past the American ships, but the much more powerful American squadron destroyed it. Two weeks later, the city surrendered. A few weeks later, another American force occupied the ancient Spanish colony of Puerto Rico; it would soon become an American territory.

The Spaniards sued for peace in August, and the war ended. The Spanish-American War was one of the most popular wars in national history. It lasted only four months, and the United States won every battle at a slight cost in lives and dollars. There was no draft, the economy boomed, and the civilian population suffered no shortages or deprivations of any kind.

At a peace conference that met in Paris from October to December 1898, the victorious Americans forced Spain to cede Guam, the Philippines, and Puerto Rico to the United States, for which the Americans paid the Spanish $20 million. The Spanish also ceded Cuba to the United States, but Cuba soon became an independent republic. The Platt Amendment, forced on the Cubans in 1901, made Cuba an American protectorate and curtailed Cuban sovereignty in numerous ways. What had begun as a war to liberate Cuba from Spanish colonialism turned into a war for an American empire.

Ironically, before it could impose its colonial rule, the United States had to fight a war in the Philippines from 1899 to 1902 to crush a Philippine nationalist insurgency. Filipino insurgents, led by Emilio Aguinaldo, already in rebellion against their Spanish overlords before the arrival of Dewey's fleet, had helped the Americans defeat the Spaniards. Aguinaldo, who believed that American leaders, including Dewey, had promised his country independence if he joined American forces in defeating the Spanish, felt betrayed by the Paris treaty. He organized a government at Malalos, wrote a constitution, and proclaimed a new independent Philippine republic in January 1899.

One month later, fighting erupted between his and American forces. The war Americans called the "Philippine insurrection" lasted nearly three years and claimed the lives of over 4,000 U.S. troops and perhaps 220,000 Filipinos, most of them civilian casualties of American counterinsurgency warfare. The conflict was one of the ugliest in American history; both sides committed atrocities.

Following the suppression of the insurrection, the United States established a colonial administration in the Philippines. American teachers, engineers, nurses, and doctors flocked to the islands to modernize Filipino society. English was made the official language. In 1908, the University of the Philippines opened to train a

Figure 1.10　The Spanish-American War: Caribbean Theater. *Source:* Moss, *Rise of Modern America,* p. 31.

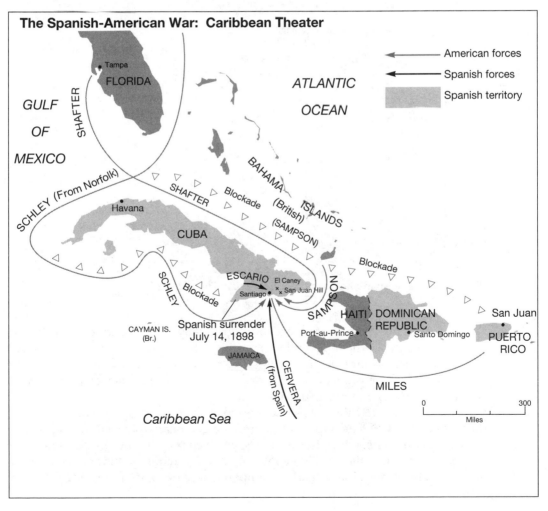

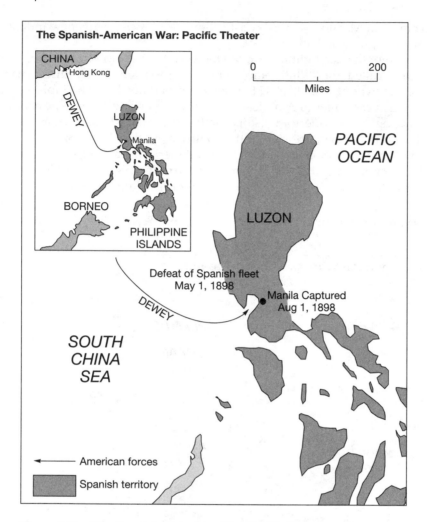

Figure 1.11   The Spanish-American War: Pacific Theater. *Source:* Moss, *Rise of Modern America*, p. 33.

pro-American governing elite that would gradually implement political democracy and prepare for the independence promised for the future. Linkages between American business interests and Filipino planters and merchants provided the foundation for forty years of U.S. colonial rule in the islands as well as a growing commerce between the two countries.

In 1898 and 1899 there was much opposition to colonial imperialism within the United States. Senate opponents of imperialism nearly blocked the ratification of the Treaty of Paris, which transferred Spanish colonies to the United States. The Democratic presidential candidate in 1900, William Jennings Bryan, back for another try at the White House, made antiimperialism a major issue. President McKinley easily won reelection in a dull, one-sided contest. The return of good times, a popular war, and McKinley's personal popularity probably were the main causes of Bryan's electoral defeat, but if the 1900 election can also be taken as a referendum on imperialism, a large majority of Americans enthusiastically embraced it.

A major reason the United States acquired the Philippines was to enhance its strategic and trading interests in the Far East, particularly in China. American traders had long dreamed of a vast China market, and U.S. missionaries had talked excitedly about winning millions of Chinese souls for Christ. During the 1890s, Americans had to watch from afar as powerful European nations and Japan carved China into spheres of influence following its disastrous defeat in the Sino-Japanese War.

With the annexation of the Philippines, and with growing trading and missionary interests in China, the United States became more actively engaged in Chinese affairs. In September 1899, Secretary of State John Hay announced a new American policy toward China, which he named the "Open Door." The Open Door policy called for equal trade in China's ports. Hay's approach endeavored to secure American commercial opportunities in the various spheres of influence without having to use military force. The Open Door fixed itself in the American mind as the guiding principle of American foreign policy in regard to China.

Figure 1.12   U.S. troops fighting Filipino nationalists.   *Source:* Library of Congress.

At the time that Hay was promulgating the Open Door, the decadent Chinese government under the Manchus could not resist the foreign invaders dominating and exploiting China. In 1900, nationalistic Chinese, resentful over the sad state that had befallen their once mighty kingdom, led by a secret society called the *I-ho ch'uan* (the "Boxers"), rose up to try to throw out their imperialist oppressors. The Boxers murdered thousands of Christian missionaries and their Chinese converts. They also laid siege to the foreign legations in Beijing. Responding to the Boxer Rebellion, the United States sent 2,500 troops to join an international expeditionary force of 15,000 soldiers that lifted the siege of the Beijing legations within a few weeks.

Following the suppression of the Boxers, Secretary of State Hay issued another note dated July 3, 1900. It reaffirmed the Open Door and called for the preservation of Chinese territorial integrity. Hay hoped to preserve American trade opportunities in China by keeping the country intact. The Open Door policy was not completely successful because Japan and the European powers with spheres of influence in China, particularly the Russians, did not always respond to American concerns. Hay's Open Door notes reinforced the growing notion in American minds that the United States had become a world power with vital interests in Far Eastern affairs.

As the twentieth century began, the United States had become an imperial democracy and one of the great powers of the globe. It held colonies in the vast Pacific basin, the Far East, and the Caribbean. It had become the overlord of the Caribbean region and had pledged itself to preserve the Open Door in China. Its overseas investments were expanding, and it had developed an export trade amounting to $1.5 billion annually. Its economy had become the largest in the world. It had built a navy that annihilated the Spanish fleet and ranked sixth in the world. Many Americans were proud of the new role the United States played in world affairs. Some were distressed by the contradictions between America's democratic professions and its imperial conquests. But most Americans believed that the United States had an imperial destiny and arrogantly assumed American imperialism would benefit its victims.

SOCIAL DARWINISM

The American industrial revolution had a profound effect on the way Americans felt and thought during the Gilded Age. Technological innovations revolutionized the communication of ideas. Materialistic values impinged upon literature, art, and public education. Darwin's evolutionary theories influenced American philosophers, social scientists, lawyers, and most educated people. Simultaneously, Americans clung to older ideas of romantic individualism and Jeffersonian democracy. American thinking during this era remained diffuse, a mixed bag of old and new forms.

While American enterprise was expanding and consolidating, fashionable intellectual currents encouraged the exploitative drives of the people. Charles Darwin's *Origin of Species,* first published in England in 1859, had begun to influence public opinion in the United States during the late nineteenth century. Herbert Spencer, a formidable English scholar and philosopher, applied Darwin's evolutionary ideas to social institutions. The idea that nature had ordained inevitable progress governed by the natural selection of individuals best adapted to survive in a competitive environment appealed to many Americans. "Let the buyer beware" intoned sugar magnate Henry O. Havemeyer. "You cannot wet-nurse people from the time they are born until the time they die. They have to wade in and get stuck, and that is the way men are educated." Havemeyer's views represented efforts to apply evolutionary theory to the marketplace. Survival of the fittest and the elimination of defectives guaranteed social progress.

The key tenets of Social Darwinism were derived from classical economics and were as old as Adam Smith. Individuals would compete fiercely within a laissez-faire economy. A few would succeed and grow rich; most would fail and remain poor. Social Darwinists wanted a minimalist state, a "night watchman" that only prevented crime and enforced contracts. Government had no regulatory or welfare functions. The poor were responsible for their fate and were, by definition, unfit. Government interference in economic affairs would be futile and would impede progress. Trade unions had no social or economic roles to play according to the logic of Social Darwinism. Andrew Carnegie counseled all who would heed him: "Leave things as they now are." The foremost American Social Darwinist, Yale sociologist William Graham Sumner, told his students, "It's root, hog, or die." It was each against all, struggling to survive in an economic jungle.

While the tough-minded aphorisms of prominent Social Darwinists appealed to many Americans, and there were plenty of success stories that appeared to confirm its principal tenets, late-nineteenth-century social realities mainly contradicted the formalistic abstractions of the Social Darwinist ideology. Most people born poor in late-nineteenth-century America remained poor their entire lives. The children of the poor rarely attended school long enough to acquire a decent education. Full-time work often yielded only enough income to buy subsistence. Racial and nativist prejudices and gender inequalities presented formidable barriers to advancement for the large majority of the population that did not happen to be white or male. In 1890, 75 percent of the national wealth belonged to about 300,000 families. At the other end of the wealth spectrum, the poorest 90 percent of American families owned about 10 percent of national wealth. In a society in which family, ethnic, gender, and class ties bestowed privileges on an elite few and condemned millions of Americans to struggle for survival, the homilies of the Social Darwinist rugged individualists were both unrealistic and unfair.

RELIGION

The transformations in American social life and culture accompanying the industrial revolution had a major impact on organized religion in the late nineteenth century. The most obvious effect was a rapid secularization of American life. Churches found themselves playing less important social roles and saw their influence decline. The mainstream Protestant and Roman Catholic leaders in America had largely lost their capacity to critique or even fundamentally analyze the new economic and social order created by the industrial revolution. Even so, religious institutions continued to thrive in urban industrial America. Most churches increased their memberships, especially the Catholic Church. The "new" immigration brought millions of Catholics to America during the 1890s.

Darwin's theory of evolution challenged the traditional religious conception of human origins. If humans evolved from apes by natural processes, then the Biblical account of creation was false, and the idea of humans being formed in God's image also was untrue. A bitter controversy pitted biological science against revealed religion. But evolutionary theory did not undermine the religious faith of most Americans. They either did not learn of evolutionary theory, or they dismissed it. Some theologians reconciled the two views, arguing that evolution was God's way of ordering the universe.

Traditional Protestant churches in the late nineteenth century were made up primarily of middle-class congregations. Ministers preached the Protestant ethic and personal responsibility for sin. Even though many of their communicants were slum dwellers, leaders of the Catholic Church also echoed the social conservatism of the Protestant ministry. Even evangelists such as Dwight Moody, the foremost preacher of the time, who endeavored to reach the urban masses by establishing mission schools in slum neighborhoods, concentrated on convincing individuals to give up their sinful ways and come to Christ. All of these religious institutions and individuals focused on the Christian drama of sin and redemption at the personal level. They were unconcerned about the causes of urban poverty, vice, and crime.

But within religious ranks, some ministers tried a different approach. These "social gospelers" tried to improve living conditions instead of saving souls. They advocated economic and social reform. The most influential social gospel minister was Washington Gladden. He supported trade unions, the regulation of industry, and other reforms. Some of these Christians also called for slum clearance, public housing, and the nationalization of industry.

SCHOOLS AND COLLEGES

The modern American system of public education was forged during the era of the industrial revolution. Americans had long held a commitment to public education, but it was only during the decades following the Civil War that the growth of large cities provided the population concentrations necessary for economical mass education. Only then did industrialization generate the increase in wealth required to finance such a vast undertaking as providing education for everyone.

During the Gilded Age, school attendance increased from 6.8 million children in 1870 to 15.5 million in 1900. Public spending on education rose from $63 million in 1870 to over $214 million in 1902. During these years the number of secondary schools increased from perhaps 100 to more than 6,000. By 1900, it was possible for youngsters living in cities to attend high school if their economic circumstances permitted. National illiteracy declined from 20 percent to 10 percent between 1870 and 1900. The goal of universal education, however, was only partially achieved during the late nineteenth century. About two-thirds of school-aged children received a few years of formal education by the 1890s. School sessions were often short, and many students dropped out after a few years of spotty attendance. Most states did not have compulsory attendance laws, which meant that school attendance was voluntary. The census of 1900 showed the median national educational attainment to be five years of schooling.

Institutions of higher learning also multiplied during the Gilded Age. Between 1870 and 1900, the number of colleges and universities in America doubled, from about 500 to almost 1,000. Curricula expanded and diversified. Harvard's president, Charles W. Eliot, introduced the elective system, added many science and engineering courses, and experimented with new teaching techniques. Much of the expansion in college enrollments occurred as a consequence of the Morrill Land Grant Act of 1862, which created state universities in the Midwest and South.

Women attended college in growing numbers. By the end of the nineteenth century, they accounted for about one-third of the 300,000 students enrolled in the nation's institutions of higher learning, with one-third of these female students attending women's colleges. In the South, college life was segregated, and African Americans, both young men and women, continued to suffer from inferior opportunities to achieve a higher education. During the Gilded Age, on many college campuses in all parts of the nation, intercollegiate athletics had become a central feature of student social life.

There was a tremendous demand for popular education outside of the schools and colleges in the late nineteenth century. The Chautauqua movement developed to fill an important cultural gap. Started in upstate New York in 1874 as a summer course for Sunday School teachers, it grew into a massive popular education system. It offered traveling lecturers speaking on hundreds of topics, as well as correspondence courses and a monthly magazine. Speakers often were chosen for their celebrity status or for their skill as entertainers. Teachers could vary from distinguished experts to assorted phonies and incompetents. To quote historian John Garraty, "Chautauqua reflected the prevailing tastes of the American people—diverse, enthusiastic, uncritical, and shallow."

MASS MEDIA

Newspapers and magazines proliferated during the Gilded Age. Technological innovations in printing made possible the mass production of attractive, cheap periodicals. Increasing population and rising levels of literacy created a larger demand for printed matter. Joseph Pulitzer created the modern style of journalism and the mass circulation daily newspaper. He built up the *New York World* until its circulation during the 1890s reached more than 1 million, the largest in the world.

Pulitzer hired talented journalists and paid them well. He went in for sensational headlines. He often sent his investigators nosing around city hall looking for scandals. He launched crusades and held banquets and carnivals to raise funds for the poor. His paper was the first to have comics. For educated readers, he included plenty of hard political, economic, and international news. He also kept the price low. The *New York World* was a good value at 2 cents an issue. Pulitzer was later imitated by an ambitious young journalist, William Randolph Hearst, who soon outdid Pulitzer when it came to sensationalism in his *New York Morning Journal.* Because of innovations in printing technology, publishers also produced high-quality weekly and monthly magazines. By the end of the nineteenth century, magazines such as *The Saturday Evening Post,* and *McClure's* enjoyed mass circulation.

ARCHITECTURE, LITERATURE, AND PHILOSOPHY

Frank Lloyd Wright, the greatest American architect of the modern era, burst upon the scene as the nineteenth century ran its course. Until Wright appeared, American houses and office buildings were boxy, banks resembled Greek temples, and government buildings looked as though they belonged in ancient Rome. His buildings exemplified key American characteristics. His work emphasized the importance of space and the natural frontier environment. He built structures that followed the contours of the land and harmonized with the environment. Dubbed the "prairie style," his houses were not boxy and rooms were not artificially separated by walls. Inside a Wright-designed home, room flowed into room, space into space, like the rolling prairie outside. He also was one of the first architects to make use of some of the new building technologies created by the industrial revolution.

In literature, a new age of realism developed during the 1870s and 1880s, influenced by the same forces that were transforming all other aspects of American life—industrialization, the rise of cities, and evolutionary science. Novelists wrote about social problems, depicted realistic settings, and created more complex characters. They took their characters from a wide range of classes and regions. One expression of the new realism was the local color school. Regional writers looked to the areas they knew best for their stories and novels. During the 1880s, Joel Chandler Harris published his *Uncle Remus: His Songs and His Sayings,* which accurately reproduced the speech dialects of blacks in rural Georgia.

Mark Twain (Samuel Langhorne Clemens) was the first great American realist and writer from the West. The story that brought Twain his first national recognition was "The Celebrated Jumping Frog of Calaveras County," and the book that made him famous was *Innocents Abroad*, published in 1869. The latter was a travelogue that made fun of Gilded Age Americans traveling abroad. Twain was both a participant and chronicler of the Gilded Age. The 1873 novel that he coauthored with Charles Dudley Warner, *The Gilded Age,* gave the era its enduring name. *The*

Adventures of Tom Sawyer came out in 1876, and his masterpiece, *The Adventures of Huckleberry Finn,* was published in 1884. No one surpassed Twain in creating characters, writing dialogue, and depicting a scene. He possessed a comic genius. Inside Mark Twain, the funnyman who made Americans laugh uproariously at themselves and their culture, beat the heart of a serious moralist. Twain was outraged, disgusted, and anguished by his age's untrammeled greed, prevalent political corruption, and heartless exploitation of the poor.

One of Twain's finest short stories is called "The Man That Corrupted Hadleyburg." It opens with a portrayal of a quiet, peaceful town. The people are not rich, but they are contented; they care for each other. One day a stranger rides into town, deposits a sack of money in front of the post office, then dashes off. He is never seen again. The rest of the story describes what happens to the townspeople as they discover the money, try to decide what to do with it, and end up quarreling over it. As the tale ends, Hadleyburg has become a hellish place. Its inhabitants are all quarreling and fighting over the money. Twain's story served as a parable for the age.

By the end of the nineteenth century, some writers had moved beyond realism to naturalism. Naturalists concentrated on industrialization and the social disintegration and destruction of individuals that it caused. They served up stark, pessimistic portrayals of the human condition—individuals trapped in deterministic environments that degraded and often destroyed them. Naturalistic writers depicted human beings as animals governed by instincts and base passions. One of the finest naturalistic novels was Theodore Dreiser's 1900 classic, *Sister Carrie.* Many readers were shocked and outraged by naturalism, by its pessimism and moral nihilism, and by its portrayals of individuals as passive victims of powerful natural and social forces.

Figure 1.13   Mark Twain, 1835–1910, the most famous writer in American history. Photo by Matthew Brady. *Source:* National Archives.

There also developed in this era a new kind of American philosophy called pragmatism. Pragmatists asserted that ideas were true only if they worked in the world, if they achieved practical results. Experience, not logic, proved the truth of an idea. The main creators of philosophical pragmatism were Charles Peirce, William James, and John Dewey. Pragmatism inspired much of the reform spirit of the early twentieth century. James subverted Social Darwinism and laissez-faire capitalism by proving that social changes came about because of the willed actions of reformers, not from impersonal environmental forces. Educational reformer John Dewey and social worker Jane Addams embraced pragmatic approaches to social change.

CIVILIZATION AND ITS DISCONTENTS

As the Gilded Age ended, the majority of Americans, especially comfortable middle-class Americans, residents of small towns, shopkeepers, many farmers, and skilled workers, remained confirmed optimists, uncritically admiring of their civilization and proud to be citizens of America. However, millions of African Americans, Asian Americans, Native Americans, Hispanic Americans, immigrants, hard-pressed Western and Southern farmers, and all of the other people who failed to achieve the good life found little to celebrate and much to protest in their increasingly industrialized, urbanized society. Giant monopolies flourished, the gap between rich and poor was widening, and poisonous slums infected every city. Industrialists worshiped the almighty dollar and made getting it their religion. America's greatest poet, Walt Whitman, famed for his poetic celebration of democracy, called his fellow Americans the "most materialistic and money-making people ever known."

Many thoughtful, well-informed middle-class people, whose own lives were comfortable and prosperous, recoiled in horror at the social consequences of industrialization, urbanization, and massive immigration. They were alarmed by social instability and outraged at both the greed of businessmen and the degraded lives of the struggling masses. Many indulged a romantic nostalgia for a vanished America of small, homogeneous communities and tranquil, orderly lives. As the nineteenth century ended, the voices of discontent with the new industrial way of life formed a rising chorus. Calls for reform resounded across the land.

IMPORTANT EVENTS

1874	The Chautauqua movement is founded
1876	Alexander Graham Bell invents the telephone
1877	The Great Railroad Strike occurs
1879	Thomas Edison perfects the incandescent lamp (electric light)

IMPORTANT EVENTS *(continued)*

1882	Congress enacts the Chinese Exclusion Act
1883	Joseph Pulitzer takes over the *New York World*
1884	Mark Twain's *The Adventures of Huckleberry Finn* is published
1886	The American Federation of Labor is organized
1887	Congress enacts the Interstate Commerce Act
	Congress enacts the Dawes Act
1889	Jane Addams opens Hull House in Chicago
1890	Congress enacts the Sherman Antitrust Act
1892	The People's Party (the Populists) is founded
1894	The Pullman strike occurs
1895	Booker T. Washington delivers his "Atlanta Compromise" speech
1898	The Spanish-American War is fought
	Hawaii is annexed
1899	War breaks out in the Philippines
	John Hay announces the Open Door policy

BIBLIOGRAPHY

There are many fine books available that cover various aspects of late nineteenth-century U.S. history. They have been written by scholars whose learning is vast and who possess genuine literary talent. Many have achieved the stature of classics in their fields. Most libraries will have these books, and they are available in paperback editions. Robert H. Wiebe, in *The Search for Order,* has written a brilliant account of the transformation of American life in the late nineteenth and early twentieth Centuries, and how middle-class intellectuals understood and reacted to this transformation. See also Samuel P. Hays' *The Response to Industrialism, 1885–1914.* A well-written account of the Gilded Age is Ray Ginger's *The Age of Excess.* Mark Wahlgren Summers' *The Gilded Age,* or *The Hazard of New Functions,* is a fine general history of late-nineteenth century America. Summers writes well, has a balanced account that incorporates recent scholarship on his subject, and makes excellent use of primary source materials. Nell Irvin Painter's *Standing at Armageddon: The United States, 1877–1919* is another fine recent addition to the general literature of this crucial era. Sam Bass Warner, Jr., in *A History of the American City,* offers the best account of the rise of American cities in the late nineteenth century. The best-written book about the politicians and business leaders who dominated the Gilded Age remains the classic work of Matthew Josephson, *The Robber Barons.* The best social history of the American industrial revolution is Thomas C. Cochran's and William Miller's *The Age of Enterprise.* Herbert Gutman's *Work, Culture, and Society* in *Industrializing America* is a collection of essays reflecting the new labor history that focuses on the culture of work. Nick Salvatore's *Eugene V. Debs: Citizen and Socialist* is the finest biography yet rendered of the greatest figure in American socialism. Oscar Handlin's *The Uprooted* is a famed account of the new immigrants who flooded into America from 1890 to 1914. A fine recent study is Alan Kraut's *The Huddled Masses: The Immigrant in American Society, 1830–1921.* In Jane Addams' *Twenty Years at Hull House,* the pioneer social worker and humanitarian tells the story of the most famous settlement house in the United States. C. Vann Woodward's *The Strange Career of Jim Crow* is a brilliant history of the rise of legal segregation in the South. Louis R. Harlan has written a splendid two-volume biography of Booker

T. Washington. A fine book on the conflict between Europeans and Native Americans is S.L.A. Marshall's *The Crimsoned Prairie.* Justin Kaplan's *Mr. Clemens and Mark Twain* is a good biography of America's most famous writer. Two histories of reform in broad perspective are Eric Goldman's *Rendezvous with Destiny* and Richard Hofstadter's *Age of Reform.* Ernest R. May, in *Imperial Democracy,* provides a brief account of the emergence of the American empire at the turn of the century.

2

The Progressive Era

AMERICANS have been infatuated by quantitative measures as indicators of progress. At the turn of the century, publicists boasted about growing American industrial might as measured by statistics of production: tons of steel produced, miles of railroad trackage lain, and barrels of oil refined. Other boasters bragged about the huge geographic size of the country, its large cities, and its ranking as the fourth most populous nation on the planet. More thoughtful Americans concerned themselves with issues pertaining to the quality of American life. They worried about some of the negative consequences of industrialization, such as corporate domination of the economy, pervasive political corruption, and the presence in all large cities of masses of impoverished immigrants. For these "Progressives," as they called themselves, progress would be better measured by their success as reformers, as problem solvers who restored the promise of American life to all people during the years between the Spanish-American War and the American entry into World War I. The combined efforts of many reformers working at all levels of government and among most groups who comprised the most diverse population on the planet shaped the age that historians label the Progressive Era.

MODERN SOCIETY

Progressive Era America was a time of rapid social development. Prosperity had returned after the depression and disorders of the 1890s. Farms and factories were once again prospering. In 1901, the economy approached full employment, and economic growth spurted. Farm prices rose almost 50 percent between 1900 and 1910, as farmers entered a "golden age." In 1900, the median industrial wage was

$418 a year. By 1915, it was about $800 a year and rising. A Boston newspaper in 1904 enthused, "The resort to force, the wild talk of the nineties are over. Everyone is busily, happily getting ahead."

Americans were excited by the prospects abounding in the new century. Wild celebrations everywhere had marked the beginning of the twentieth century. Americans had faith in the capacities of business enterprises and new technologies to shape a more abundant future. "New" became a favorite buzzword of the times. Everywhere there was talk of the new city, the new art, the new democracy, and the new morality.

Another favorite theme was "mass." Americans celebrated the quantitative aspects of their national experience. They were proud of the size and scale of America—its massive economy and large population. They flocked to mass entertainment, read mass-circulation magazines and newspapers, and took mass transit from the suburbs to central cities. They even boasted about the large crowds that turned out to watch major league baseball and college football games, as if they believed national virtue resided in population statistics.

Cities grew rapidly and on a colossal scale compared to earlier eras. Downtown areas became clusters of tall buildings, large department stores, warehouses, and hotels. Strips of factories radiated out from the center. As streetcar transit lines spread, American cities assumed their modern patterns of ethnic, social, and economic segregation, usually in the form of concentric rings. Racial minorities and immigrants were packed into the innermost ring, circled by a belt of crowded tenements. The remaining rings represented increasing status and affluence, radiating outward toward posh suburbs where the rich and elite classes lived. The largest cities were New York, Chicago, and Philadelphia whose factories and shops churned out every kind of product used by American farmers, merchants, and the growing legions of consumers.

Los Angeles passed a series of ordinances in 1915 that created modern urban zoning. For the first time, legal codes divided an American city into three districts of specified use: a residential area, an industrial area, and an area open to both residences and light industry. Other cities quickly followed suit. Zoning gave order to urban development, ending the chaotic, unplanned growth of cities that was characteristic of the Gilded Age. Zoning not only kept skyscrapers out of factory districts, and factories out of suburbs, it also had important sociological and political consequences. In Southern cities, zoning became another tool to extend segregation. In Northern cities, it was a weapon that could be used along with others against blacks and ethnic minorities—against Jews in New York City, Italians in Boston, and Poles in Detroit. In Chicago, New York, and Detroit, zoning laws helped confine rapidly growing black populations to particular districts, creating ghettos.

The consumer economy of the 1920s originated in the prewar era. As factories produced more consumer goods, they also spent more money for advertising. Ads and billboards promoted sales of cigarettes, perfumes, and cosmetics. Advertising agencies grew, and market research began. The first public opinion polls began as efforts to sample consumer preferences in the marketplace.

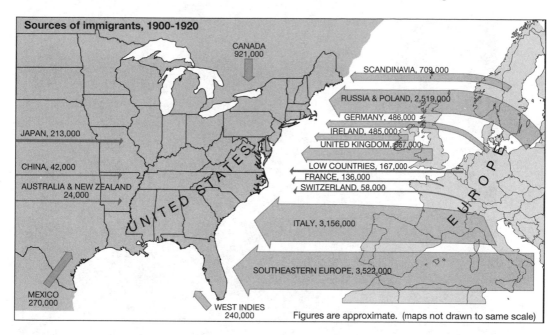

Figure 2.1   Sources of Immigrants, 1900–1920.   *Source:* George D. Moss, *Rise of Modern America,* p. 43.

Between 1900 and 1910, almost 10 million immigrants entered the country, more than those who came in any other decade in American history. These newcomers continued the trend established during the late nineteenth century. Most of them were "new" immigrants from southern and eastern European countries. The largest number emigrated from Italy, Poland, Russia, and Austria-Hungary. About 1.5 million were eastern European Jews, mainly from Poland and Russia. A large number of immigrants returned to their native lands after a stay in America, either because they were disillusioned or because they had never intended to stay permanently. Those who came with their families, such as the Jews, rarely returned. Many Serbs and Poles, who tended to come as single, young men, worked to earn money to buy a farm or business back home.

Nativist sentiment, which had accompanied earlier waves of immigration, intensified in the wake of the massive influx of new immigrants. Old-stock Americans looked down their noses at the newcomers' appearance, behavior, and language. Racial theorists stressed the superiority of northern European "races" over those from the south and east of Europe. Some hostility toward the new immigrants reflected anti-Catholic and anti-Semitic prejudices. Nativism crystallized into anti-immigration movements of growing strength. These movements aimed to restrict the new immigration, but they failed to do so before World War I brought almost all immigration to a halt. Nativists would achieve their goal of restriction during the mid-1920s.

Figure 2.2   Mulberry Street, New York City—the heart of the immigrant area of the Lower East Side in the early 1900s.   *Source:* Library of Congress.

POPULAR CULTURE

Major signs of progress in early twentieth-century American life included rising wage levels and growing leisure for American workers. The average workweek for manufacturing workers had shrunk to fifty hours by 1914. By the first decade of the new century, white-collar workers worked nine-hour days Monday through Friday and a half day on Saturday. People had more money to spend and more time to enjoy spending it on play and recreation. Increasing income and leisure promoted a flourishing mass culture in the cities.

Spectator sports were attracting large crowds. Baseball entrenched itself as the national pastime. In 1903, the pennant winners of the two major leagues met in the first World Series to determine the national champion. The Boston Red Sox, winners of the American League title, beat the National League champions, the Pittsburgh Pirates, 5 games to 3. College football was another popular spectator sport. Crowds of 50,000 or more often gathered to watch powerhouse Ivy League and Midwestern teams play. On New Year's Day, 1902, the first Rose Bowl game was held in Pasadena, California. The University of Michigan overwhelmed an upstart team from Stanford, 49 to 0.

Attendance at "movies" rose even faster than for spectator sports. Thomas Edison and a young assistant, William Dickson, had invented a process for making motion pictures in 1889. Commercial movies made their appearance during the 1890s. These early films were crudely made, their audiences recruited mainly from the ranks of immigrant populations, who were crowded into the large Eastern cities. Early movie houses were store fronts and parlors called "nickelodeons," a name derived from combining the price of admission with the Greek word for theater. After 1900, the new industry expanded rapidly.

By 1910, there were 10,000 theaters in the country showing motion pictures, attracting a weekly audience of 10 million. The most popular films were about fifteen to twenty minutes long and featured comedy, adventure, or pathos. The early center of American filmmaking was New York. In 1909, the largest companies formed a trust to control the production and distribution of films. In 1910, a group of independent filmmakers discovered Hollywood, a sleepy farming community near Los Angeles. In Hollywood, they could escape the movie trust and take advantage of the sunshine and mild weather abounding in southern California. Also, within a few miles of the studios, outdoor scenes could be found that could substitute for almost any locale a plot might call for, whether the deserts of Arabia, Sherwood Forest, or the Old South.

Before 1910, band concerts were the country's most popular mass entertainment. Thousands of amateur bands offered free concerts in parks on Sunday afternoons. The Marine Corps Marching Band, the most popular band in the land, led by John Philip Sousa, the "March King," toured the nation, attracting large crowds everywhere. Sousa also was a composer and wrote the famed *The Stars and Stripes Forever* in 1896. This robust, patriotic march became wildly popular during the Spanish-American War, making its author rich and famous.

By the end of the first decade of the new century, recorded music was taking much of the audience away from public band concerts. Phonograph and recording companies were selling millions of "records." Record players became fixtures in homes that could afford them. Early recordings usually featured vaudeville skits. The first orchestral recording was made in 1906. As record sales increased, families sang less and listened more.

Ragtime, a musical idiom featuring fast, syncopated rhythms, became popular, especially after 1911 when Irving Berlin wrote *Alexander's Ragtime Band.* Ragtime set young people to dancing fast, replacing traditional waltzes and polkas. The new dances often had animal names—Fox Trot, Bunny Hop, Turkey Trot, and the Snake. The "fast set," enjoying some of these new dances, ran afoul of the moralists, who worried about partners' getting too close and becoming sexually excited.

Vaudeville, increasingly popular after the turn of the century, flowered in the decade preceding World War I. Drawing from the immigrant experience, it featured skits, songs, dances, comedy, magicians, and acrobats, all expressing the color and variety of polyglot American urban life. Vaudeville performers also expanded the limits of what was permissible in public entertainment. Vaudeville dancers bared their legs and later their midriffs. Vaudeville comics told "dirty" jokes and got away with it. The leading impresario of vaudeville, Florenz Ziegfeld, produced his famed "Follies," featuring elaborate dance numbers by beautifully costumed "Ziegfeld girls."

Popular fiction flourished along with vaudeville. Genteel novels centering around family life, often set in rural New England, were popular. Westerns also sold well. The most popular western story was Owen Wister's "The Virginian," whose gunman hero became a prototype for later "Westerns," both novelistic and cinematic. Readers also enjoyed detective thrillers and science fiction, which featured tales set in the future about spaceships, ray guns, and gravity neutralizers.

Fiction for young people sold widely. Edward L. Stratemeyer applied mass-production techniques to the business of publishing popular fiction for young people. He formed a syndicate that employed a stable of writers who turned out hundreds of books in series, featuring Tom Swift and the Rover Boys for boys, and the Bobbsey Twins for girls. Gilbert Patten created the character of Frank Merriwell, a wholesome college athlete attending Yale.

Horatio Alger's books continued to sell well during the Progressive Era, although Alger had died in 1899. Alger, like Patten, wrote fiction for adolescent boys. In more than 130 novels, Alger stressed the same theme: how poor boys rise from the streets of cities to become successful businessmen. The secret of success in Alger's books is always the same—moral character. Alger heroes succeed because they are good, have self-discipline, and work hard. A little luck often aids the hero as he makes his way up in the world. Alger's novels sold by the millions during the years preceding World War I. Today's media frequently call attention to "Horatio Alger heroes" who rise from "rags to riches."

LITERATURE AND ART

Serious art also fared well in Progressive America, along with the simplistic sentimentalities of popular culture. Isadora Duncan and Ruth St. Denis transformed modern dance. Abandoning traditional ballet, both dancers stressed emotion, the human body, and individual improvisation. Duncan danced "the way she felt," giving expression to inner emotion and communicating ideas. Her ideas and innovative techniques swept the country.

Greenwich Village, a seedy district of New York City, became a haven for young artists, writers, and poets committed to experimenting with new forms of expression. A group of painters, including Robert Henri, John Sloan, and George Bellows, was named by its critics the "Ashcan School" because of its interest in social realism. These artists preferred to paint the subjects they found in the Village and other parts of the city-street scenes, colorful crowds, slum children swimming in the East River, the tenements, and portraits of ordinary people.

In 1913, a show at the New York Armory introduced American viewers to European modernist paintings, sculptures, and prints. Americans got their first exposure to the works of Picasso, Van Gogh, Gauguin, and Cezanne, among many others. The Greenwich Village crowd was dazzled and excited by the show. Traditionalists attacked the exhibits as being worthless and wicked, but the artists featured in the exhibit would have a profound effect on the direction American art would take in the twentieth century, and many future American painters' works would reflect their influence.

Chicago was the center of a flourishing new poetry. Harriet Monroe started *Poetry* magazine in Chicago in 1912. Many of America's most promising young poets published some of their poems in her magazine, including Ezra Pound and T.S. Eliot. Other poets experimenting with new techniques were Robert Frost, Edgar Lee Masters, and Carl Sandburg.

The culture of the early twentieth century, both in its popular and highbrow forms, foreshadowed developments in the 1920s. Changes were underway before World War I. Evidence of ferment and change could be found everywhere—in the movie houses, in popular music, in art galleries, and in the new literary magazines. The Progressive Era was the seedtime of modern American culture.

THE ROOTS OF REFORM

Progressivism sprang from many impulses. Its immediate origins lay in the 1890s, when many people responded to the transformation of American life and the social problems that it generated, particularly the many undesirable consequences of industrialization. Progressive reform mainly began in the cities of America, where large industrial corporations dominated their industries, controlled prices, and exploited their workers and customers. Corruption corroded government at all levels; from two-bit ward heelers on the streets to the upper echelons of the federal government. The cities, filling with a rising tide of immigrants, threatened to become home to a permanent underclass. Monopoly, corrupt politics, and mass poverty challenged the central promise of American life; they suggested that equality of opportunity for all was a myth. The American dream appeared beyond the reach of millions of American families. Reformers, as they set out to solve massive and often interrelated problems, did not form a coherent movement or a unified national crusade. Rather, progressivism constituted a remarkably diverse aggregation of many, often unrelated, even mutually antagonistic, efforts to achieve a broad range of economic, social, and political reforms.

Progressives sought to solve these problems by ending abuses of power and eliminating unfair privilege. They intended to replace the wasteful, competitive, anarchic industrial society with one that was efficient, orderly, and based on cooperation between business and government. Acting partly out of nostalgia, they wanted to restore the orderly American community that they believed had prevailed in preindustrial times. Progressives wanted to redeem traditional American values such as Christian ethics, political democracy, individual opportunity, and the spirit of public service. But if their goals were traditional, their means were distinctly modern. Progressives employed the systems and methods of the new industrial order—the latest techniques of organization, management, and science.

Progressives stressed volunteerism and collective action. They drew on an organizational impulse that was bringing Americans together to combat the ills afflicting modern industrial society. When voluntary action did not achieve desired goals, Progressive reformers turned to government to protect the public welfare. Progressives distrusted legislators who were often controlled by business interests or corrupt political machines, so they worked to strengthen the executive branch by increasing the power of mayors, governors, and presidents. They then made these executive officers accountable to the electorate whenever they could. Progressives also tapped into the deep talent pool of the newly professionalized middle classes. They recruited social scientists, lawyers, city planners, and educators to staff the new agencies and commissions that were created to investigate conditions and to solve problems.

Progressivism's roots lay buried deep within American political traditions, but its proximate origins could be found in a series of unrelated reform movements that erupted in this country during the 1890s. One of these comprised the agrarian insurgents of the Midwest and South. These embattled farmers called for state intervention to curb the power of the railroads, banks, and other big businesses. Within the cities, the social strains caused by rapid, large-scale industrialization activated the Social Gospelers and other pioneer advocates of social justice. During the 1890s, a literature of protest and exposure foreshadowed the Muckrakers. Henry Demarest Lloyd wrote *Wealth Against Commonwealth* (1894), a scathing indictment of the Standard Oil Company. A new generation of social scientists joined the assault on privileged wealth and irresponsible power, and a new generation of intellectuals challenged the assumptions and precepts of Social Darwinism. Well-educated young businessmen and professionals became involved in urban reform movements during the 1890s. This concerned group of individuals was outraged by the existence of widespread monopoly, political corruption, and social distress.

SOCIAL JUSTICE

If progressivism often ended as politics, it usually began as social reform. Among the most important strands of Progressive reform were the diverse movements that have been collectively labeled the "social justice movement." Many well-educated, young, middle-class women were in the front ranks of many social justice reform activities. Ellen Richards, trained as a chemist and home economist, opened the New England Kitchen in downtown Boston, where for a few pennies a day the working poor could get cheap, wholesome food. Florence Kelly worked to bring about safer working conditions for factory workers and was a pioneer advocate of consumer protection legislation. Jane Addams, the social worker who founded

Hull House, was the most prominent woman active in social justice causes. In addition to her settlement house work, Addams worked to strengthen trade unions, abolish child labor, and achieve women's suffrage. During this period, most states enacted laws that provided for worker's compensation, limited the hours of work for women, and restricted child labor.

Progressive social reformers were the first people to undertake a scientific study of the causes of poverty in America. They sought to understand the great American paradox: the persistence of massive poverty within the richest and freest society in human history. They found that the children of the poor were likely to be poor, not because they were weak, lazy, or sinful, but because they were deprived. They discovered that poverty was a symptom of many social ills—political and corporate greed, slum neighborhoods, vice, and crime. They discovered that the pathologies associated with poor people, such as alcoholism, drug addiction, and mental illness, derived from the sordid and desperate circumstances of their lives. These pioneering studies of poverty helped Americans understand that poverty was not the fault of individuals but was rooted in social conditions.

Not all social justice reformers came from the middle-class or business ranks. Industrial workers supported progressivism in some urbanized industrial states

Figure 2.3 A young mill worker in a textile factory, ca. 1910. Child labor was a scandalous aspect of American industrial society during the Progressive Era. *Source:* Library of Congress.

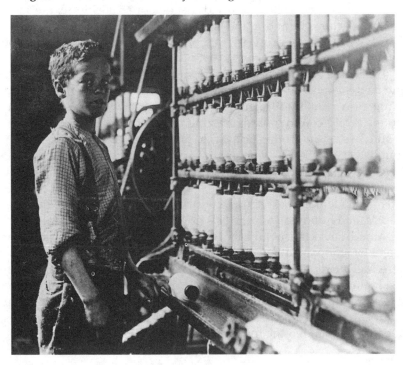

such as California and New York. They formed coalitions with middle-class reformers to press for improvements in housing and health care, for safer factories, for shorter hours, for worker's compensation, and for disability insurance. More militant members of the social justice movement moved beyond coalition politics to direct action. In 1909, the Women's Trade Union League (WTUL) and the local chapter of the International Ladies Garment Workers Union (ILGWU) waged a long, bitter strike against New York City's garment district sweatshops. After three months they gained a partial victory that resulted in the unionization of some of the sweatshops. A year later, in Chicago, Sidney Hillman led the Amalgamated Clothing Workers Union in a strike that achieved similar gains.

Immigrant and working-class neighborhoods occasionally elected Progressive reformers who had backgrounds in machine politics but were neither corrupt nor conservative. Alfred E. (Al) Smith, a Catholic and the son of immigrants, rose through the ranks of Tammany Hall to become a Progressive governor of New York. Smith worked with middle-class reformers and Progressive legislators to enact labor and social welfare legislation.

Some advocates of radical change during the Progressive Era wanted more than reform; they wanted to create a fundamentally different society. They rejected progressivism for socialism. Their ranks included some immigrant Jewish intellectuals, factory workers, former Populists, Western miners, and lumberjacks. A radical trade union, the Industrial Workers of the World (IWW), led by William (Big Bill) Haywood, tried to unite the nation's unskilled workers into one large union that would control their factories. It led a series of strikes in textile factories in Lawrence, Massachusetts, and in the West. The IWW faded into obscurity during World War I, when federal prosecutors sent most of its leaders to jail for obstructing the war effort.

Most socialists of the Progressive Era supported the American Socialist Party (SDP) and its dynamic leader, Eugene Debs. American socialism grew rapidly during the Progressive Era. By 1912, hundreds of socialist candidates had been elected to city councils and county boards of supervisors. Over fifty socialists served as mayors, and Wisconsin sent a socialist, Victor Berger, to Congress. American socialists published over 300 newspapers, one of which, *The Appeal to Reason,* claimed 700,000 weekly subscribers. Popular writers and journalists such as Jack London and Upton Sinclair were avowed socialists. Debs ran for president five times. He and his party made their best showing during the 1912 election, when he polled 900,000 votes, and hundreds of socialists got elected to local and state offices.

But American socialism and the SDP declined after 1912. Socialists opposed American entry into World War I and incurred the wrath of most patriots. Socialists suffered severe repression at the hands of the federal government. Many of its members, including Debs, were imprisoned. The party was further weakened by internal factionalism during the 1920s and lost membership to the American Communist Party. It managed to survive on the political fringes until the 1960s, when its aged leaders disbanded the remnants of a once-vital movement.

MUCKRAKERS

Progressives reformers were aided by a new breed of investigative journalists. These socially conscious writers, whom Theodore Roosevelt dubbed "muckrakers," fed their middle-class readers sensational reports covering a wide range of evils afflicting American life in the early twentieth century. Their articles appeared in *McClure's* and other slick, mass-circulation magazines. Millions of middle-class people became aware of the many ways in which American social reality contradicted the ideal image of America. Informed readers were alarmed, outraged, and anguished by muckraker revelations, and they often were motivated to support reform efforts to combat wrongdoing. Muckrakers contributed significantly to Progressive reform movements. They also established a category of reportage that became an integral part of American journalism. The popular television show *Sixty Minutes* allows electronic journalists to perpetuate the muckraking style of reportage.

Important muckrakers included Ida Tarbell, who wrote a two-volume history of the Standard Oil Company, describing the ruthless, illegal methods it had employed to forge its refining monopoly. Lincoln Steffens wrote a series of articles for *McClure's*, later published as the book, *The Shame of the Cities* (1904), which exposed the crooked ties between business and politics in several large Eastern and Midwestern cities. John Spargo's *Bitter Cry of the Children* (1903) was a fact-filled, excruciating account of child labor in factories and mines.

The most famous muckraker was a young radical novelist, Upton Sinclair, whose realistic novel *The Jungle* (1906) highlighted the brutal exploitation of workers in the meat-packing industry. His book also conveyed vividly the filthy conditions prevailing in the packing houses as they processed tainted meat for public consumption. In the following passage, Sinclair describes how sausage was prepared:

> There was never the least attention paid to what was cut up for sausage; there would come all the way back from Europe old sausage that had been rejected and that was moldy and white—it would be doused with borax and glycerine, and dumped into the hoppers and made over again for home consumption. There would be meat that tumbled out onto the floor, in the dirt and sawdust, where the workers had tramped and spit uncounted billions of germs. There would be meat sorted in great piles in rooms; and the water from leaky roofs would drip over it. It was too dark in these storage places to see well, but a man could run his hands over these piles of meat and sweep handfuls off of the dried dung of rats. These rats were nuisances, and the packers would put out poisoned bread for them; they would die, and then rats, bread, and meat would go into the hoppers.[1]

Sinclair's novel had an immediate effect. When it was published, President Roosevelt read it and promptly ordered an investigation of the meat-packing industry. Federal investigators confirmed most of Sinclair's charges. *The Jungle* also

[1] Upton Sinclair, *The Jungle* (New York; New American Library of World Literature, 1905, 1906), p. 136.

helped move out of Congress a Meat Inspection Act and the Pure Food and Drug Act, two pioneer consumer protection laws enacted in 1906. Ironically, Sinclair intended to expose the horrors of working in a meat-packing plant, to show corruption in Chicago politics, and to promote socialism as the only solution to what he termed *wage slavery* under capitalism. Most of his middle-class readership, however, reacted most strongly to his lurid descriptions of the unsanitary conditions under which the public's breakfast, lunch, and dinner meats were prepared. As Sinclair noted, ruefully, "I aimed at their hearts and hit their stomachs."

WOMEN REFORMERS

When the Progressive Era began, feminists sought liberation from domestic confines and male domination. Progressive social reform attracted a great many women who were concerned with expanding the "woman's sphere" to include involvement in public affairs. Many women joined a women's club movement. By

Figure 2.4   Alice Paul, leader of the National Women's Party, sews a ratification star on the party's flag to celebrate the ratification of the Nineteenth Amendment in 1920, which granted women aged twenty-one and older the right to vote. *Source:* Schlesinger Library, Radcliffe College.

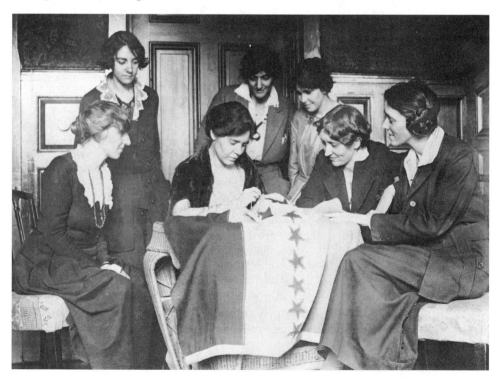

1900, the General Confederation of Women's Clubs claimed 1 million members. Because women were excluded from politics before 1920, they tended to move into social reform. They sought social goals such as the regulation of labor conditions for women and children, housing reform, and consumer protection.

Some women joined a birth control movement led by Margaret Sanger. Sanger began her career as a nurse visiting Manhattan's immigrant neighborhoods, distributing birth control information among poor immigrant women to help them prevent unwanted pregnancies. Her cause attracted the interest of middle-class women who wanted to limit the size of their families as well as control the growth of the immigrant masses. In 1921, Sanger founded the American Birth Control League. Birth control entered the realm of public discussion for the first time. Because of Sanger's efforts, many middle-class families were using contraception by the 1920s. But most states prohibited the sale of contraceptives, and most women during the Progressive Era opposed birth control because they believed it threatened their status as women.

The number of working women expanded rapidly during the Progressive Era. Perhaps as many as 7 to 8 million women were working by 1912. Charlotte Perkins Gilman became an advocate for working women. An early economic feminist, Gilman challenged the traditional satisfactions attributed to domesticity. She insisted that women, like men, could find full freedom and satisfaction only through meaningful work. At the time, Gilman's ideas applied mostly to the relatively small number of middle-class professional women. Most working-class women came from the ranks of immigrants, African Americans, and the rural poor, who worked mostly at low-paying, low-skill, and low-status jobs.

The major feminist issue of the Progressive Era was suffrage. The crusade for the vote had begun in the mid-nineteenth century as a spin-off from the Abolitionists' insistence that all Americans, regardless of sex or race, were equal and deserved the same rights. But male resistance and female apathy made the struggle for women to get the vote long and hard. The U.S. Supreme Court, in *Minor v. Happersett* (1875), ruled that women could not vote, even though they were citizens. Victories came first in the West, where women and men had already forged a more equal partnership to cope with the hardships of frontier living. By 1912, nine states, all of them in the West, had granted women the vote in local and state elections. The National American Women's Suffrage Association (NAWSA), the most important suffragist organization, claimed 85,000 members in 1912.

In 1915, a talented organizer, Carrie Chapman Catt, took over the leadership of NAWSA, and the women's suffrage movement quickly gathered momentum. She refocused suffragist energies away from state-by-state campaigns and toward achieving a constitutional amendment in order to place all women's right to vote beyond the reach of restrictive Supreme Court decisions. Many different groups worked for the cause. Some moderates relied on propaganda campaigns. Militants such as Alice Paul, influenced by radical English suffragists, used direct action tactics. In March 1913, Paul organized 5,000 women to parade in protest at President Woodrow Wilson's inauguration. A near-riot ensued, and the police hauled Paul and hundreds of her followers to jail, where they were stripped naked and thrown into cells with prostitutes. One year later, Paul aligned her forces with the radical National Women's Party. When the United States entered World War I in April 1917, Paul and her followers picketed the White House. Arrested and jailed again, she and other imprisoned women went on a hunger strike. Prison guards force-fed them. Public outrage over the abusive treatment of women suffrage militants coupled with the need for wartime unity moved the House of Representatives to propose a woman suffrage amendment in 1918. Another decisive factor was women's participation on the home front during World War I. Women worked in factories and as medical volunteers. The Nineteenth Amendment, ratified in 1920, extended the vote to adult women (age twenty-one or older). The 1920 presidential election was the first in which all women were eligible to vote.

Because so many women had fought so hard and so long for the vote, they had come to believe that achieving women's suffrage would bring the dawn of a golden era in American political life. Voting women would put a quick end to boss and business domination of politics. The moral tone of the nation's civic life would be uplifted. Those women, who expected a rapid transformation of the public life of the nation, were quickly disillusioned. Women did not vote as a unified movement. No women's agenda emerged, and only about one-third of eligible women voters voted during the election of 1920. Most of these newly enfranchised women apparently voted the way their fathers, brothers, and husbands did. Feminists, to their dismay, found that the vote did not bring empowerment for women; they did not attain the influence required to enact the programs they favored or to change the way politics and government worked.

Nevertheless, attaining the suffrage for women was a great victory, an overcoming of powerful and stubborn obstacles. The Nineteenth Amendment represented a great democratic advance, one of the crowning political achievements of the Progressive Era. Very quickly, women's voting came to be accepted as a given, a normal part of the political life of the nation. And very quickly it was forgotten that women's suffrage took seventy years of hard struggle to achieve, and that virtually to the day that it carried, powerful men denounced women's suffrage and rhetorically prophesied the end of the republic.

AFRICAN AMERICANS

The Progressive reform impulse rarely extended to the 10 million African Americans, over 85 percent of whom still lived in the South in 1910. Southern blacks were victimized by a repressive system that disfranchised, segregated, and frequently brutalized them. In 1910, fewer than 1 percent of high-school aged blacks attended high schools. Southern white political leaders, many of them Progressives, perfected demagogic politics based on the rhetorical denunciation of blacks, keeping them at the bottom of the socioeconomic pyramid. During the first decade of the twentieth century, white Southerners extended and refined the systematic legal segregation of blacks and whites. Between 1910 and 1914, white mobs lynched scores of African Americans. White Progressives shared the prevailing racist view that African Americans were inherently inferior and incapable of full citizenship. Most Southern blacks resided in rural areas, working as sharecroppers and tenants and earning a median annual income of approximately $100. Many were tied to the land by labor contracts and perpetual indebtedness to local merchants and planters. Institutionalized racism and segregation also afflicted African Americans residing in northern cities. The oppression of blacks was not only a regional problem but a national one in Progressive America.

Booker T. Washington remained the most prominent spokesman for black people, and he continued to advocate accommodation as a policy during the Progressive Era. Most white reformers welcomed Washington's accommodationist strategy because it urged African Americans to not protest and to remain in their places. But to a few black Progressives, Washington appeared to be favoring second-class citizenship for African Americans. In 1905, a group of black leaders met near Niagara Falls to endorse a more militant strategy. They called for equality before the law, voting rights, integration, and equal educational and economic opportunities for African Americans. The chief Niagara spokesman was Dr. William E. B. Dubois, who could not accept Washington's submission to white dominance.

Dubois demonstrated that accommodation was a flawed strategy, but his militant protest strategy was ineffective. He believed that a highly educated African American elite, whom he called the Talented Tenth, would lead the way by impressing whites and setting an example for blacks. Such a strategy appealed to some white middle-class Progressives, but DuBois' elitist strategy held little meaning for the African American masses who were mainly sharecroppers and unskilled workers. When Dubois and his allies formed the National Association for the Advancement of Colored People (NAACP) in 1909, with its objective of attacking racial discrimination through the courts, its leadership consisted mainly of white Progressives.

Whichever strategy they pursued, accommodation or protest, African Americans during the Progressive Era faced continued oppression. During the presidency of Woodrow Wilson, who was a Southern Progressive Democrat, the federal civil service was resegregated. African Americans struggled against long odds to achieve their portion of the American dream. However, their pride made it difficult for blacks to celebrate their American identity in a country dominated by racist whites who oppressed African Americans.

ASIAN AMERICANS

Progressive reformers were generally no more concerned about the welfare of other nonwhite minorities than they were about African Americans. Chinese Americans and Japanese Americans, mostly clustered on the West Coast, continued to experience discrimination and hostility. In 1902, Congress made the Chinese Exclusion Act permanent. In October 1906, the San Francisco school board ordered all Asian children to attend a segregated Oriental school. The Japanese government, concerned about the treatment of Japanese in foreign lands, protested this action in Washington. President Roosevelt, concerned about maintaining good relations with a rising power in Asia, intervened to persuade the school board to repeal its offensive order. An informal agreement, the Gentlemen's Agreement of 1908, was worked out. According to its terms, the school board rescinded its order against the children of Japanese subjects, and the Japanese government, for its part, agreed to restrict the emigration of Japanese peasant laborers to the United States.

Other acts against the Japanese in California occurred. In 1913, Progressives in the state legislature enacted an alien land law that forbade aliens to lease land for periods greater than three years. Such laws were ineffective in practice because Japanese farmers leased land in the names of their American-born children. In 1924, Congress, responding to political pressure from California representatives, prohibited further Japanese emigration to the United States. This irrational act profoundly insulted and angered the Japanese government, and it was, in the long run, a contributing cause of World War II in Asia.

NATIVE AMERICANS

Native Americans were almost completely ignored by Progressive reformers. American Indian policy during the Progressive Era was officially guided by Dawes Act principles. Officials in the Bureau of Indian Affairs continued to pay lip service to assimilation, but under the cover of the Dawes Act, they expropriated allotment lands, neglected schooling for Indian children, and tried to keep Indians confined to working as cheap farm laborers and domestic servants at the margins of society.

One remarkable Indian spokesman, Carlos Montezuma, became an advocate of Native American rights during the Progressive Era. A full-blooded Apache, he had been reared by an itinerant Italian musician, who treated him as a son. He went to the University of Illinois and became a prominent physician. Wealthy, learned, and articulate, Montezuma criticized the Bureau of Indian Affairs' policies. He formed organizations and raised funds for Indian causes. He urged Indians to help themselves, leave the reservations, and stop being "papooses," dependent on the white man for survival. Proud of his Indian heritage, Montezuma also urged Native Americans to honor and retain their traditional culture and Indian identity.

MORAL REFORM

Many Progressive reformers were determined to not only improve institutions, but also to improve human behavior. They set out to purge society of drinking, prostitution, and gambling.

Their campaign to outlaw alcohol was their most important moral crusade. The formation of the Anti-Saloon League in 1893 marked the beginning of the prohibitionist drive that eventually forced abstinence upon the entire nation. The

Figure 2.5   Prohibition brought many changes to the American scene. Here the former bar of a New York hotel has been converted to a library after the advent of the Eighteenth Amendment.   *Source:* Library of Congress.

League joined forces with the Women's Christian Temperance Union to portray alcoholism as a social menace that ruined lives, destroyed families, and robbed the economy of productive work. Women made up a disproportionate number of alcohol reformers. In some ways, the temperance movement reflected the growing feminist impulse to storm male bastions, in this instance, the neighborhood saloon, and to curb male violence, particularly child and spousal abuse associated with drinking. The drive against booze also was linked to the drive to clean up city politics, because political bosses often were saloon keepers, and saloons served to connect the political machines with the mass of male voters. Between 1893 and 1900, many states, counties, and cities outlawed or restricted the sale and consumption of alcoholic beverages. After 1900, prohibitionists concentrated their formidable energies on achieving a national law forbidding the manufacture, sale, and use of alcoholic beverages.

The enemies of drink got their chance during World War I. The government forbade using grain to manufacture whiskey in wartime in order to conserve food. Prohibitionists pressured the government into forbidding sales of alcoholic beverages near military bases and training camps. Citizens were encouraged to abstain from drinking as a patriotic sacrifice in support of America's soldiers fighting in France. Because Germany was the enemy and many American breweries were owned by German American families, prohibitionists urged Americans to boycott beer. Prominent industrialists called for prohibition. Henry Ford enthused, "A sober worker is an efficient worker." Prominent national political leaders became converts to the cause in wartime, and Congress proposed a constitutional amendment outlawing booze. The Eighteenth Amendment was ratified in 1919 and implemented by the Volstead Act in 1920. Prohibition would be the law of the land for nearly fourteen years. Not all prohibitionists were Progressives, and not all Progressives were prohibitionists, but the Eighteenth Amendment symbolized the Progressive urge to use governmental power to improve the nation's morals.

Progressives also attacked prostitution. No urban vice worried reformers more than prostitution; in their eyes, it threatened young city women with a fate even worse than death. The Chicago Vice Commission issued a report in 1910 estimating that there were 15,000 prostitutes plying their trade in the Windy City. Muckrakers exposed the operations of "white slavery" rings that kidnapped young women and forced them into prostitution. Sensational journalism spread rumors of a vast and profitable "white slave trade." Jane Addams wrote about the pressures of poverty that forced immigrant and black women into prostitution.

As real abuses got intermixed with lurid fantasies, Congress responded to public pressure in 1910 by enacting the Mann Act, which prohibited transporting women across state lines for "immoral purposes." By 1915, every state had outlawed brothels and public solicitation of sex. Most states also banned gambling and closed casinos.

EDUCATIONAL REFORM

Progressive reformers envisioned education as an important means for improving society. Before it could do so, however, Progressive educators demanded that schools abandon traditional nineteenth-century curricula that stressed moralistic pieties and rote memorization. John Dewey, the foremost Progressive educational reformer, believed that environmental factors shaped the patterns of human thought. He stated that the chief role of public schools in a democratic society was to prepare children for productive citizenship and fulfillment of personal lives. In Dewey's view, the classroom was an embryo of community life. In two influential books, *The School and Society* (1899) and *Democracy and Education* (1916), Dewey expounded his theories of Progressive education: Children, not subject matter, should be a school's focus. Schools must cultivate creativity and intelligence. From kindergarten through high school, children learned from experience, and curricula must be tailored to those experiences. The school should be a laboratory of democracy.

During the Progressive Era, the percentage of school-aged children enrolled in public and private schools expanded rapidly. By 1920, 78 percent of all five-to-seventeen-year-old-children attended school. Administration and teaching were

Figure 2.6   The public school system expanded rapidly during the early twentieth century, providing clerical training to meet the demand for growing numbers of office workers.   *Source:* Metropolitan Life Insurance Company.

professionalized, and salaries were raised. These gains reflected the Progressive commitment to education as well as taxpayers' willingness to fund the costs of an expanding public school system.

College curricula and enrollments also expanded rapidly during the Progressive Era. By 1910, there were over 1,000 colleges and universities in America. Much of the growth in college enrollments occurred at public colleges and universities. The first community colleges appeared during this era, products of progressive educational theories. The enrollment of women at colleges and universities expanded greatly; most of them attended coeducational institutions. By 1920, women accounted for almost half of those enrolled in college.

POLITICAL REFORM

Traditional Jeffersonian notions of limited government eroded during the late nineteenth century because of industrialization. Corporate executives, paying lip service to laissez-faire slogans, aggressively sought government aid and protection. Angry farmers called for government takeover of railroads and monopolies. Urban representatives demanded government action to correct social problems. By the dawn of the Progressive Era, middle-class reformers believed that the use of government power was necessary to counter corruption and exploitation. But before reformers could use political power, they would have to reclaim government from the political machines and corporate interests that controlled it. So Progressives turned first to politics to root out corruption and favoritism from government. They sought to gain control of the political process to reform society.

Progressive reformers had a strong aversion to party politics. They wanted to scrap political machines and bosses. To improve the political process, Progressives wanted to nominate candidates through direct primaries instead of party caucuses. They called for nonpartisan elections to bypass the corruption that party politics bred. To get people directly involved in the democratic process, Progressives advocated three reform devices: the initiative, which enabled voters to propose new laws; the referendum, which allowed voters to accept or reject laws; and the recall, which permitted voters to remove incompetent or corrupt officials from office before their terms expired. All these reform mechanisms aimed to make politics more rational, efficient, and accountable to the electorate. Progressive reformers also achieved a major political victory in 1913, when the states ratified the Seventeenth Amendment, providing for the direct election of senators. Senators had been elected by state legislators since the Constitution was adopted. The legislative selection of senators had often been corrupted by corporate interests and manipulated by political bosses.

Some business executives became Progressive reformers. They supported federal regulation of industries as a means of protecting themselves from more radical proposals, such as trust-busting or nationalization, and a bewildering variety of state regulations. Corporate leaders also saw advantages to federal regulation that created a stable operating environment for business by eliminating cutthroat competition and boom-and-bust cycles. The U.S. Chamber of Commerce and the National Civic Federation, both business and trade associations, favored limited government political and economic reform.

They started in the cities. Reformers created the city manager and city commission forms of urban government, which employed trained administrators instead of political cronies to staff municipal agencies. They bought up public utilities so that gas, water, streetcar, and electrical companies could not corrupt city governments and exploit customers. Soon, Progressive reformers expanded their horizons, moving from local to statewide reform efforts. They formed political coalitions to elect state legislators and governors. Reform aims varied regionally. In the urban-industrial East, Progressives concentrated on breaking corrupt political machines and enacting labor reforms. In the Midwest and West, they focused on railroad regulation and direct democracy. The most successful state progressive reform leader was Wisconsin's governor, Robert La Follette. He and his supporters implemented a broad reform program, including direct democracy, a fair tax system, railroad regulation, labor reform, and social welfare. Wisconsin Progressives also generously supported the University of Wisconsin, making it a leading public university. In turn, the university furnished many experts to staff state agencies and to study problems, enabling the government to use the resources of modern science and technology. After serving three terms as governor, La Follette was elected senator and took his Progressive crusade to Washington.

California also featured vigorous Progressive reform. Hiram Johnson, a San Francisco attorney, led the California Progressives. He won the 1910 gubernatorial election on a promise to curb the power of the Southern Pacific railroad, which dominated the state politically and economically. In office, Johnson and his supporters regulated the railroad. They also created a Public Utilities Commission empowered to set rates for utilities companies operating in the state.

State Progressive reformers also enacted a range of labor protection and social welfare laws that affected industrial workers more directly than did political reforms. Many states enacted factory inspection laws, and most implemented compulsory disability insurance to compensate victims of industrial accidents. They also enacted employer liability laws; they passed laws establishing minimum ages of employment, varying from ages twelve to sixteen. They also prohibited employers from working youngsters more than eight to ten hours a day. Most states enacted legislation that limited the workday for women to ten hours. In 1914, Arizona became the first state to create pensions for the elderly. But all of these laws proved difficult to enforce: many employers refused to comply with them, and the courts often weakened or nullified them.

THE ADVENT OF THEODORE ROOSEVELT

Suddenly, in September 1901, a deranged anarchist murdered President McKinley, vaulting young Theodore Roosevelt into the White House. As governor of New York, Roosevelt had angered Republican Party boss Thomas Platt by supporting regulatory legislation. Platt got rid of him by getting his good friend, President William McKinley, to offer him the vice presidency in 1900. Platt and McKinley never dreamed that they were giving the nation its most forceful president since Abraham Lincoln, a man who would revitalize the office, give it much of its twentieth-century character, and make it the most powerful branch of the national government.

Roosevelt lived on inherited wealth. He also inherited a sense of civic responsibility and morality from his father. Unusual for a man of his social background, Roosevelt became a professional politician. A Republican Party partisan, he held various New York State offices during the 1880s and 1890s. In 1897, President McKinley appointed him Assistant Secretary of the Navy. Nearly forty years old and rearing a large family that included six hyperactive children, Roosevelt resigned his office to fight in Cuba during the Spanish-American War. He returned from that war a hero and was elected governor of New York, and then vice president in 1900.

President Roosevelt became a reform leader. He shared the Progressive view that the Jeffersonian ideal of small government was obsolete in an age of giant industries and large cities. He was a Hamiltonian economic nationalist, calling for a powerful central government to regulate big business. His presidency began the

Figure 2.7   Theodore Roosevelt.   *Source:* Library of Congress.

federal regulation of economic affairs that has characterized much of twentieth-century American political history. He moved against monopoly at a time when giant trusts controlled every important economic sector. Though Roosevelt acquired a reputation as a trust-buster, he believed that consolidation was the most efficient means to achieve economic and technological progress. He had no quarrel with bigness or monopoly as such. He distinguished between "good" trusts and "bad" trusts. Good trusts did not abuse their power and contributed to economic growth. Bad trusts were those few combines that used their market leverage to raise prices and to exploit consumers. Roosevelt made it his goal to stop the bad trusts from resorting to market manipulations. If necessary, he would use antitrust prosecutions to dissolve bad trusts. At heart, Roosevelt was an old-fashioned moralist who demanded that corporations operate within the law and who believed that Christian ethics should govern the marketplace.

Roosevelt's first successful antitrust action came in 1904, when the Supreme Court agreed with his contention that a railroad holding company, the Northern Securities Company, had been formed mainly to exploit customers, thus violating the Sherman Antitrust Act. The Court ordered it dissolved. But Roosevelt preferred a cooperative relationship between big government and big business. He directed the newly formed Bureau of Corporations to work with companies when they proposed mergers. He hoped through monitoring and investigation to exert pressures on business to regulate itself.

Roosevelt pushed for regulatory legislation, especially after he won election in his own right by a landslide margin in 1904. He displayed impressive political skill in steering the Hepburn Act through a reluctant Congress in 1906. The Hepburn Act strengthened the Interstate Commerce Commission and imposed stricter controls on the nation's railroads. Roosevelt also supported consumer protection legislation. The outcry against fraud and adulteration in the patent medicine and processed meat industries intensified after the publication of Sinclair's muckraking novelistic exposé in 1906. Roosevelt supported the Pure Food and Drug Act and the Meat Inspection Act, both enacted by Congress in 1906.

Roosevelt also took a progressive stance toward labor-management relations during his presidency. In 1902, the United Mine Workers struck against coal companies in the anthracite fields of Pennsylvania. The Mine Workers wanted a 20 percent pay raise, an eight-hour day (a reduction from the then ten-hour day), and recognition of their union as the miners' bargaining agent. Company officials refused to negotiate with union leaders, and the strike dragged on. Roosevelt intervened, offering the progressive services of investigation and arbitration. Company officials rejected his offer, refusing to meet with union representatives. George Baer, spokesman for the mine owners, pompously proclaimed that

> the rights and interests of the laboring man will be protected and cared for—not by the labor agitator, but by the Christian men to whom God in his infinite wisdom has given the control of the property interests of this country.[2]

With winter approaching and city dwellers facing the prospect of acute fuel shortages, Roosevelt rallied public opinion in support of government arbitration of the coal strike. He appointed a commission to arbitrate a settlement and pressured both sides into accepting its recommendations. The commission granted the miners a 10 percent pay increase and a nine-hour day. It did not force the companies to recognize the United Mine Workers, and it permitted them to raise their

---

[2]George Baer, quoted in Henry F. Pringle, *Theodore Roosevelt* (New York: Harcourt, Brace, 1931), p. 186.

prices to cover their increased labor costs. The strike ended. Roosevelt, pleased with the outcome, observed that everyone got a "square deal." Roosevelt's enlightened role in the coal strike contrasts powerfully with Democratic President Cleveland's performance during the Pullman Strike of 1894. Cleveland used the powers of the federal government to break the strike and destroy the American Railway Union. Roosevelt also extended the Progressive concept of federal regulation to labor-management relations to protect the public interest.

Roosevelt's most enduring contribution to Progressive reform came on the issue of conservation. He added 150 million acres of Western virgin forest lands to the national forests and preserved vast areas of water and coal from private development. He also strongly backed his friend, the Interior Department's chief forester Gifford Pinchot, who shared Roosevelt's conservationist goals. In 1908, Roosevelt hosted a Washington gathering of governors and resource managers called the National Conservation Congress. Roosevelt favored national planning for resource management and ordered growth. He was not a strict preservationist, but he sought to balance the needs of economic development with the desire to preserve the nation's wilderness heritage of forests, open land, lakes, and rivers.

In 1907, a financial panic forced some large New York banks to close in order to prevent depositors from withdrawing money. Financial titan J. P. Morgan stopped the panic by providing funds to rescue some imperiled banks and by persuading financiers to stop selling securities. Roosevelt, grateful to Morgan for preventing a possible recession, allowed Morgan's U.S. Steel Corporation to buy its main competitor, the Tennessee Iron and Coal Company, giving the gigantic company monopolistic control of the steel industry.

During his last year in office, Roosevelt became more progressive, straining his relations with conservative business interests within the right wing of the Republican Party. He attacked corporate leaders, whom he called "malefactors of great wealth," calling for stricter governmental regulation of business and increased taxation of the rich. Having promised in 1904 to not seek reelection, Roosevelt decided to back his good friend and political ally, Secretary of War William Howard Taft, as his successor. Roosevelt was confident that Taft would continue his reform efforts. The Democrats nominated William Jennings Bryan for the third time. Taft, aided by Roosevelt, won easily.

TAFT VERSUS PROGRESSIVISM

Taft was an intelligent, experienced politician and was committed to Progressive causes. He also retained good relations with conservative and moderate Republicans. He appeared to be the ideal successor to the energetic Roosevelt. But he lacked Roosevelt's stamina and love of politics. At the outset of his presidency, Taft aggressively pursued a Progressive agenda: he enforced the Sherman Antitrust Act vigorously and added millions of acres of land to national forests. He signed the Mann-Elkins Railroad Act in 1910, increasing the regulatory authority of the Interstate Commerce Commission over the railroad industry. He supported labor legislation. He also called Congress into a special session in 1909 to lower tariff rates, an issue that Roosevelt had avoided.

Taft favored lowering tariff rates, and the House passed a bill reducing tariffs on most imports. The Senate, dominated by protectionists, eliminated the cuts in the House bill. A group of Progressive senators, led by Wisconsin's Robert La Follette, denounced the protectionist changes, using statistical data to show how many proposed tariff rates were unreasonably high. But Taft signed the new tariff, named the Payne-Aldrich Tariff, calling it "the best tariff the Republican Party ever passed," even though it raised tariffs on many important imports. Taft's actions outraged La Follette and other Senate Progressives, who accused him of betraying the cause of tariff reform.

The Republican Party was splitting into progressive and conservative factions. Following the tariff battle, House Progressives challenged the autocratic power of Speaker Joseph "Uncle Joe" Cannon, a conservative Republican whose control of committee assignments and debate schedules allowed him to determine the fate of most House legislation. Taft initially backed the insurgents, then changed his mind and supported Cannon. His reversal angered House

Figure 2.8   Roosevelt's greatest achievements and most enduring legacies were his conservation efforts, represented here by the magnificent trees preserved in Roosevelt National Forest, located on the eastern slope of the Rocky Mountains in northeastern Colorado.   *Source:* National Archives.

Progressives, and they joined their Senate colleagues in denouncing the president as an apostate reformer.

Taft also alienated Progressive conservationists when he permitted Secretary of the Interior Richard A. Ballinger to open 1 million acres of forest and mineral lands for development. He also fired Gifford Pinchot for protesting Ballinger's sale of some public water power sites in Alaska to private interests. Taft was not opposed to conservation; he was mainly backing Ballinger in a political feud with Pinchot, but Progressives viewed Pinchot's dismissal as an ominous sign that Taft was betraying the conservationist cause. Without consulting Taft, Roosevelt sided with Pinchot, angering the president, who resented his former friend's lack of confidence in his presidency.

As the split within Republican ranks widened, Taft cast his lot with the conservatives with whom he was personally more comfortable, and Roosevelt sided with the Progressives. Roosevelt denied any presidential ambitions, but he did speak out on the issues. He was easily the most famous living American, and his speeches made headlines. Speaking at Osawatomie, Kansas, in August 1910, Roosevelt came out in favor of a comprehensive progressive program he called the "New Nationalism." He attacked "lawbreakers of great wealth" and called for a broad expansion of federal power.

THE ELECTION OF 1912

On January 11, 1911, Progressive Republican leaders met in the nation's capital to form the National Republican Progressive League. They elected Senator Bob La Follette of Wisconsin to head their new organization. At a conference held in Chicago later in the year, the new Progressive league chose La Follette as their favored candidate for the Republican presidential nomination in 1912.

Paralleling the growing Republican Party split between progressives and conservatives, there occurred a break between Taft and Roosevelt in October 1911, when the president ordered an antitrust suit against U.S. Steel, forcing the giant company to sell off its Tennessee Iron and Coal Company. Roosevelt reacted angrily because he thought the suit was unwarranted. Also, he had approved U.S. Steel's acquisition of the Tennessee Iron and Coal Company during the financial panic of 1907. Taft's actions made Roosevelt appear to be either a supporter of monopoly or, worse, a dupe of big business. He attacked Taft's action publicly, and early in 1912, he announced that he would be a candidate for the Republican presidential nomination. He denounced Taft for betraying the reform cause. Progressive leaders rallied to Roosevelt's banner.

Roosevelt threw himself into the campaign. He was clearly the choice of the Republican Party rank and file. He was victorious in all states that held presidential primaries and even beat President Taft in his home state of Ohio. But Roosevelt could not win the nomination through the primaries, because not enough states held primaries in those days. President Taft's forces controlled the party machinery and came to the Republican Party Convention in Chicago with a small majority of the delegates. Roosevelt's forces challenged the credentials of 254 of Taft's delegates, some of whom had been chosen under dubious circumstances. The fate of Roosevelt's candidacy, the fate of the Republican Party, and the outcome of the 1912 presidential election depended on the selection of those 254 contested delegates. The Taft-controlled credentials committee awarded 235 of the disputed delegates to Taft and only 19 to Roosevelt. Having won control of the Convention, Taft's forces secured his nomination on the first ballot.

Roosevelt, outraged, was convinced that the nomination that was rightfully his had been stolen from him by the political bosses. He bolted from the Republican Convention and took Progressive Republicans with him. He decided to run for president as the head of a third-party organization. In August, delegates gathered in Chicago in the same convention hall where Taft had emerged victorious six weeks earlier to create the Progressive Party. In an emotional atmosphere that resembled a revivalist camp meeting, on the evening of August 6, delegates, who were mostly Republican Progressives, nominated Theodore Roosevelt as their presidential candidate and adopted his New Nationalism as the party platform. The delegates also chose California governor Hiram Johnson as Teddy's vice presidential running mate. Roosevelt, in a rousing acceptance speech, told the delegates that we "stand at Armageddon and battle for the Lord." Teddy, proclaiming himself "as strong as a bull moose in the rutting season," urged adoption of the New Nationalist program, including regulation of corporations, a national presidential primary, the elimination of child labor, a minimum wage, women's suffrage, and many other progressive reforms. Roosevelt's candidacy made it official: The Republican Party had split. Conservative Republicans supported President Taft's bid for reelection. Progressive Republicans, now formed into the Progressive third party, supported Roosevelt's candidacy.

The Democrats meanwhile had held their convention in Baltimore, jubilant over the divisions within the Republican Party that gave the Democrats their first realistic chance of winning the presidency in twenty years. The leading candidate for the Democratic presidential nomination in 1912 was Champ Clark of Missouri, a veteran Democratic leader and current Speaker of the House. Clark won most of the delegates during the primaries and came to the convention heavily favored to win the Democratic nomination. But Clark was challenged by a political newcomer, Woodrow Wilson, the Progressive reform governor of New Jersey, who for most of his adult life had been a college professor and an administrator.

When the Baltimore convention began on June 25, 1912, Wilson appeared to have no chance against Clark. On the initial ballot, Clark won a large majority of delegates, but he failed to get the required two-thirds vote needed for nomination. (The Democratic Party retained the two-thirds rule adopted in 1836 to give Southern delegates extra clout in choosing the Party's presidential nominees.) On many ballots the Wilson delegates held firm to deny Clark the nomination. On the fourteenth ballot, Clark made a deal with Tammany Hall to win the votes of the New

York delegation. Outraged, William Jennings Bryan, still the most popular leader in the Democratic Party, switched his support from Clark to Wilson. For three more days, the candidates continued to battle fiercely for delegates. Finally, on the forty-sixth ballot, Wilson won the nomination. He chose a political nonentity, Governor Thomas R. Marshall of Indiana, to be his vice presidential running mate.

The Socialist Party nominated its perennial candidate, Eugene Debs. The stage was set for one of the most important elections of the twentieth century, one in which the American system was subjected to a thorough evaluation, and an election in which alternative public policy options were rigorously debated and offered to the voters.

There were four significant candidates in the race: on the Right was the Republican candidate incumbent President Taft; on the Left was Eugene Debs, who ran on a socialist slate calling for the nationalization of monopolies. In the center stood two candidates—the Democratic nominee Woodrow Wilson, and the Progressive Party leader, former President Theodore Roosevelt, both of whom claimed the mantle of progressive reform. Taft had no chance of winning reelection because of the split within Republican ranks. Debs, although he too had no chance of winning, waged a spirited national campaign, exhorting voters to make "the working class the ruling class." The outcome of the 1912 election turned on the epic battle between Wilson and Roosevelt, two of the most capable leaders ever to seek the presidency.

Roosevelt ran on his New Nationalism program. Wilson countered with a progressive program he called the New Freedom. Both candidates embraced Progressive principles, and there were similarities in their appeals; however, there were significant differences between them because they represented different varieties of progressivism. The candidacies of Roosevelt and Wilson revealed a deep, ideological cleavage that had evolved within national progressivism. Their most important difference expressed a philosophical division within Progressive ranks over the fundamentals of Progressive government. Roosevelt would not destroy the trusts, which he saw as an efficient means to organize production. He favored establishing regulatory commissions staffed by experts who would protect consumer rights and ensure that concentrations of economic power performed in the public interest.

Wilson, whose New Freedom program drew heavily upon the ideas of Progressive legal reformer Louis Brandeis, believed that concentrations of economic power threatened liberty and foreclosed economic opportunity. He wanted to break up trusts to restore competition, but he did not want to restore laissez-faire, which he believed to be obsolete. He favored what Brandeis called "regulated free enterprise." Also, Wilson did not favor the cooperation between big government and big business, inherent in Roosevelt's New Nationalism. He spoke passionately of the need to emancipate the American economy from the power of the trusts. The Democratic platform, which had been largely drafted by Bryan, also called for structural reforms to make the political system more democratic and for a downward revision of tariff schedules.

But on the central issue of the 1912 campaign, the role of the federal government in promoting the economic security and social welfare of the American people, Wilson and the Democrats were mostly silent or took refuge in vague generalities. The absence of social justice planks in the Democratic Party's platform derived mainly from the Party's ancient Jeffersonian allegiances. Democrats still adhered to states rights doctrines and a general policy of modified laissez-faire at the federal level. Wilson was suspicious of both big business and big government, regarding them both as potential threats to liberty. If regulation were necessary, Wilson would have the states do it. In 1912, the Democratic Party position was that if laws were needed to protect working people, they would come from state governments, and not from Washington.

As he traveled the campaign trail in search of votes, Wilson highlighted the major themes of his New Freedom program. He would unleash the entrepreneurial energies of the American people by abolishing special privileges and restoring competition to the American system of free enterprise capitalism. He would achieve these goals by lowering tariffs, reforming the banking and currency systems, and strengthening the Sherman Antitrust Act.

Roosevelt dismissed Wilson's prescription for economic renewal as being hopelessly reactionary and infeasible. Roosevelt reminded his audiences that big business was here to stay. Large corporations were more efficient and more productive than small enterprises. They contributed greatly to national wealth and gave America a competitive edge in world markets. Roosevelt insisted that efforts to destroy large corporations would undermine national prosperity. He accepted a corporate-dominated economy, but one that was strictly monitored and regulated by a powerful central government in order to prevent trusts from abusing their power. Roosevelt called for the creation of a federal trade commission to regulate the nation's large corporations. He hedged on the tariff by calling for the creation of a nonpartisan tariff commission to make "scientific adjustments in rates," which could be either up or down. Roosevelt, in keeping with the spirit of his New Nationalism, called for a host of social justice measures protecting farmers, women, children, and workers.

On election day, voters across the nation gave progressivism a resounding endorsement. Together, the two Progressive candidates amassed 70 percent of the votes cast. Wilson won the presidency with only 42 percent of the popular vote—he was a minority president, but he carried forty states and captured 435 of 531 electoral votes. The Democrats also won control over both houses of the new Congress that would convene in 1913. Two-thirds of the gubernatorial elections held in 1912 also went to Democratic candidates. Roosevelt got about 27 percent of the popular vote, carrying six states with 88 electoral votes. Taft finished a distant third, with 23 percent of the vote and 9 electoral votes. Debs, campaigning nationally, pulled down 902,000 votes.

The Republican Party split, and the failure of Theodore Roosevelt to win over the Democratic Progressives and thus forge a majority coalition of reform forces made Wilson's electoral victory possible. Had the Republican Party been united

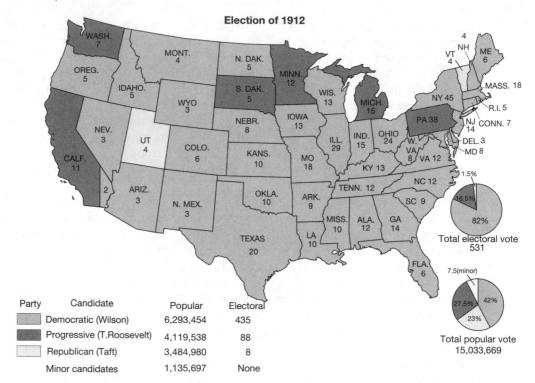

Figure 2.9   Election of 1912.   *Source:* Moss, *Rise of Modern America,* p. 85.

behind a Roosevelt candidacy, he would have won handily. Wilson, however, was able to maintain traditional Democratic constituencies, and his New Freedom program also kept Democratic Progressives within the Party's fold. Partisan political alignments, more than the issues, determined the outcome of the 1912 election.

WILSONIAN PROGRESSIVISM

Wilson made an unlikely president. After obtaining a law degree and becoming an attorney, he opted for an academic career. He received a Ph.D. from Johns Hopkins University and became a professor of history and political science. During a lengthy and distinguished academic career, Wilson taught at several different colleges and universities. From 1885 until 1902, he was a professor of history and government at Princeton university. He became an authority on the U.S. Constitution and one of the most eminent American scholars of his generation.

Wilson entered politics in middle age. In 1902, he became president of Princeton University, where he upset traditionalists with curriculum reforms. He resigned his presidency in 1910 during a dispute over university policy, intending to return to the classroom. But in 1910, the New Jersey Democratic Party needed a candidate for governor, and Wilson consented to run. The Party bosses who secured his nomination needed his respectability, and they assumed he could be managed if he won. After winning the governorship, Wilson repudiated the bosses and embraced progressivism enthusiastically. He directed the passage of a host of legislative reforms in a state notorious for boss rule and corporate domination. His accomplishments as a Progressive reform governor in New Jersey made it possible for him to win the Democratic Party presidential nomination in 1912.

Wilson proved to be an effective, even a charismatic, political leader. He took control of his party in Congress. He was a brilliant speaker; he could inspire support and intense loyalty with vivid religious imagery and ringing evocations of American principles in which he devoutly believed. Because he was steeped in the democratic and Judeo-Christian ideologies that undergirded progressivism, he could espouse reforms in moving, compelling, and irresistible phrases. More than his energetic predecessor Theodore Roosevelt, he shaped legislation and government policy on key issues.

In a brilliant inaugural address, the new president spelled out his Progressive reform agenda to the American people. His top priority was tariff reform, long a Democratic Party staple and long a failed promise. Wilson called the new Congress into special session to revise the tariff. Breaking with tradition, the new president then went in person to deliver a forceful message to a joint session of Congress, urging the quick passage of the tariff bill. Wilson was the first president to address a joint session of Congress and the first to focus public attention directly on the lawmakers.

Tariff rates had been rising for years and had appreciably increased living costs for millions of Americans. Farmers had complained for years that protective tariffs raised their operating costs and lowered their commodity prices. All previous efforts at tariff reform had been blocked by Senate protectionist forces, for example, Taft's ill-fated effort at tariff reform in 1909. Oscar Underwood, Chairman of the House Ways and Means Committee, steered the administration's tariff bill through the House. It substantially reduced duties on hundreds of items and placed many more on the free list. The measure passed easily by a vote of 281 to 139, with Progressive Republican support.

In the Senate, like so many Furies, once again the lobbyists for special interests descended on the senators to press their amendments to maintain the protectionist rates. But unlike the lethargic Taft, President Wilson was prepared to battle the lobbyists. He made a dramatic appeal to the American people. He told them that, "The public ought to know the extraordinary exertions being made by the lobby in Washington. Only public opinion can check it and destroy it." Voters strongly responded to his appeal, and the Senate passed the measure with the reductions intact. Wilson kept Party discipline and mobilized public opinion to pressure the Senate into enacting tariff reform.

Wilson signed the new law, the Underwood-Simmons Tariff Act, on October 3, 1913. It reduced average import tax rates from about 40 to 29 percent, an 11

Figure 2.10 Woodrow Wilson, the "schoolmaster in politics," was an eloquent champion of progressive reform causes. He is shown here making a campaign speech during the election of 1912.   *Source:* National Archives.

percent reduction across the board. The costs of living and of doing business for millions of Americans declined immediately. Imports to America increased dramatically. Reduced rates also meant that tax revenues declined sharply. Because tariff fees were the federal government's principal source of revenue, the new tariff bill levied a graduated income tax to replace its lost income, an option made possible by the recent ratification of the Sixteenth Amendment. The tax was small by today's standards. Incomes under $4,000 a year were excluded, which exempted over 90 percent of American families in 1914, the first year the tax was in effect. The income tax was originally intended to be a tax only on the affluent and wealthy. People in the $4,000 to $20,000 income brackets had to pay 1 percent income tax. The rate rose gradually to a top rate of 7 percent on incomes exceeding $500,000 per year. The income tax had made its debut. Passage of the tariff reform was a major political victory for the rookie president. It gave him great leverage over Democratic leaders in Congress and won him the trust and respect of most Americans, who sensed that an effective leader was in power who could keep the Progressive faith and fulfill his campaign promises.

Wilson next turned his attention to another salient Democratic campaign promise—reform of the nation's banking and currency systems. Again, the new president intervened directly in the legislative process; he worked closely with key Democratic leaders in the House and Senate to ensure passage of the kind of measure that he wanted. Carter Glass of Virginia, Chairman of the House Banking Committee, introduced the federal reserve bill in early September. The House approved it quickly, but there was a long and tough battle to get the administration's bill through the Senate relatively unscathed. Wilson persisted, and the Senate approved the measure the day before Christmas.

The Federal Reserve Act constituted the most important Progressive reform measure of Wilson's presidency. The law created the nation's first centralized banking system since Andrew Jackson had destroyed the Second Bank of the United States. It created twelve regional banks to hold the reserves of member banks throughout the nation. These district banks had the authority to lend money to member banks at low rates of interest, called the "discount rate." By adjusting this rate, the regional banks could adjust the amount of money a bank could borrow and thereby increase or decrease the amount of money in circulation. In response to national need, the banks could either loosen or tighten credit by lowering or raising the discount rate. More elasticity was structured into the money supply, and interest rates for farmers and small business owners would be lower. A Federal Reserve Board made up of five members appointed by the president with the approval of the Senate ensured that the banking industry would be regulated in the public's interest. The nation still uses the Federal Reserve system, although its powers have been significantly changed by subsequent legislation. The head of the Federal Reserve Board has the power to determine interest rates and the rate of monetary growth, and is the most powerful nonelected official in Washington.

Following his victories on the tariff and banking bills, Wilson went after Congress to achieve his third and final major reform commitment, strengthening the

Sherman Antitrust Act. Three measures, including one introduced by Henry Clayton of Alabama, cleared the House. The Clayton Act amended the Sherman Antitrust Act by outlawing monopolistic practices such as discriminatory pricing (the practice of a company's trying to destroy a smaller firm by lowering its prices in that company's market, meanwhile keeping higher prices elsewhere) and interlocking directorates (the management of two or more competing companies by the same executives). Officers of corporations convicted of antitrust violations could be held individually responsible. The Clayton Act also contained provisions that exempted trade unions and agricultural organizations from antitrust laws, and it curtailed the use of court injunctions during strikes.

These acts, especially the Clayton Act, encountered serious opposition from the business community, including many small businessmen who had supported Wilson and the Democrats. They thought that these antitrust measures went too far; besides, it was proving to be impractical to try to prohibit by law every conceivable method of restraining trade. Facing both a practical and a political problem, the Wilson administration executed a major ideological shift. Wilson dropped his support for antitrust legislation and supported instead a measure introduced by Congressman Raymond Stevens of New Hampshire, which created a federal trade commission. Wilson signed the Federal Trade Commission Act on September 26, 1914. The Federal Trade Commission Act created the Federal Trade Commission (FTC), which replaced the Bureau of Corporations. The FTC was empowered to study corporate practices and issue cease-and-desist orders against unfair trade practices. The chief purpose of the new agency was to monitor business practices and proscribe unfair practices before they had put their competition out of business and ripped off their customers.

Ironically, Wilson had been forced to abandon a key plank in the New Freedom program, antitrust, in favor of a New Nationalist plank, a federal trade commission, which had been pushed by his arch political rival, Theodore Roosevelt. By 1914, corporate mergers were so extensive that restoration of free enterprise was impossible, short of drastic antitrust actions that were unthinkable to Wilson and his key domestic adviser Brandeis, who favored the trade commission concept. Wilson and Brandeis accepted economic concentration and embraced Rooseveltian concepts of expanding the government's regulatory powers to prevent harm to the public interest.

During the first two years of his presidency, Wilson had been unconcerned about social justice legislation designed to provide federal protections for the disadvantaged classes of industrial America. Wilsonian progressivism was not responsive to the concerns of poor, weak, or helpless Americans. The president had no interest in helping African Americans, in fact, Wilson supported the resegregation of the federal civil service. Gradually, his interests turned toward labor and social reform. His shift toward the New Nationalism and his embracement of the Federal Trade Commission Act signaled a change in direction. He realized that the national government had a positive role to play in promoting social welfare and enhancing economic security. Wilson also understood that he faced defeat in the 1916 election unless he supported a vigorous slate of New Nationalist reforms. The

Democratic Party was still the minority party; unless Wilson could attract a large number of Roosevelt Progressive Republican voters, he would lose to the Republican Party candidate, who would be backed by a reunified party.

In 1916, Wilson supported a whole range of social justice measures. He advocated the passage of the Federal Farm Loan Act, which created banks to lend money at low interest rates to farmers. He also supported the Adamson Act, which gave all railroad workers an eight-hour day and time-and-a-half for overtime. Soon after signing the Adamson Act, Wilson signed a progressive tax measure that raised income tax rates, created a federal estate tax, and imposed excess profits taxes on large corporations. The tax measure represented the first effort in American history to use the tax powers of the federal government to effect a redistribution of wealth from the "haves" in the direction of the "have nots." Wilson further courted Progressive social reformers by backing laws outlawing child labor and granting federal employees worker's compensation. He also appointed Louis Brandeis to the Supreme Court. It was a controversial appointment, because Brandeis was an outspoken critic of big business and also the first Jew ever appointed to the Court.

As Wilson approached the election of 1916, his presidency had been one of the most significant and successful in American political history. His reform ideas set the direction of federal economic policy for much of the twentieth century. All major Progressive reform initiatives were enacted. Ironically, a major reason for the decline of progressivism that occurred after 1916 was that it was a victim of its own success. Its agenda was implemented—and exhausted. The "schoolmaster in politics," with scant prior political experience, in the judgment of many historians, turned out to be the greatest president since Abraham Lincoln.

PROGRESSIVISM IN PERSPECTIVE

A generation of reform had brought major changes. Late-nineteenth-century political, economic, and social institutions had been transformed. Laissez-faire had vanished. Both state and federal governments established their right to regulate the actions of private corporations for the public good. Public concern for poverty and injustice had reached intense levels, yet by 1920, for every underprivileged American at least three enjoyed material comforts and freedoms unprecedented in human history.

Progressivism was characterized by a jumble of reform movements that lacked unifying characteristics. There was no such thing as a Progressive movement, only movements. Often Progressives worked oblivious to one another, even at cross purposes to one another. Reform occurred at all levels, from neighborhood cleanup committees to national programs such as the New Freedom. Progressivism's diversity of aims, means, and achievements was its most salient characteristic. Its diversity reflected the pluralism of contemporary American society and culture.

Many Progressive initiatives failed or only partially succeeded. Sometimes failure came from strong opposition, sometimes from inherent flaws in the reform movement. The courts struck down key Progressive reforms, most notably laws abolishing child labor. Political reforms such as the initiative and referendum failed to encourage greater citizen participation in politics and were exploited by special interest groups. Federal regulatory agencies lacked the resources to perform their investigative and monitoring functions thoroughly. They often obtained their data from the companies they were supposed to police, and they were staffed by people recruited from the industries they were supposed to monitor. Some political machines survived Progressive assaults, and business influence at all levels of politics remained powerful. For all of its claims of sweeping change, progressivism left the American political and economic systems intact. Progressives of all stripes, whether Rooseveltian New Nationalists or Wilsonian advocates of the New Freedom program, wanted only to make middle-class democracy more righteous and more inclusive, and to make market capitalism more efficient.

Progressive reformers were all too often indifferent to the terrible problems and obstacles that African Americans, Asians, and other minorities faced as they struggled to survive and, in a few cases, prosper. Progressives attempted to Americanize all recently arrived immigrants rather than accepting the contributions of their cultures.

Even so, Progressives compiled a solid record of achievement. They addressed and often solved many of the problems facing a modern, urban industrial society. Progressivism refashioned the nation's future. Big business became more sensitive to public opinion. The power of political autocrats was diluted. Progressive reforms protected consumers against price fixing and dangerous products. Social reforms alleviated injustice and human misery. Expanded school opportunities enabled the children of immigrants to achieve successful careers and fulfilling lives.

Progressives challenged conventional ways of thinking. They raised urgent questions about the goals and qualities of American life and provided both a new mode of public discourse and a method for solving public problems. They proved that concerned citizens could make a difference, that they could bring the promise of American life closer to fulfillment for millions of their fellow citizens. According to historian James West Davidson, "Under progressive leadership, the modern state, active and interventionist, was born."

IMPORTANT EVENTS

1901	President McKinley is assassinated; Theodore Roosevelt assumes presidency
1902	The government sues the Northern Security Company for antitrust violations and wins
	Anthracite coal miners strike in Pennsylvania
1903	The first power-driven airplane flies at Kitty Hawk, North Carolina
	The first World Series takes place

IMPORTANT EVENTS

1904	Ida Tarbell publishes her exposé of Standard Oil
1905	The National Education Association is founded
1906	Upton Sinclair's novel, *The Jungle,* is published
1907	William James publishes *Pragmatism*
1908	Henry Ford manufactures the first Model T
1909	U.S. Marines go to Nicaragua
1910	The NAACP is founded
	The Mann Act is enacted
1911	Irving Berlin writes *Alexander's Ragtime Band*
1912	New Mexico and Arizona are added to the Union
1913	Henry Ford installs the first moving assembly line
	The Sixteenth Amendment establishes the income tax
	The Seventeenth Amendment provides for direct election of senators
1914	World War I begins
	The Panama Canal is completed
1915	D. W. Griffith produces the first movie spectacular, *Birth of a Nation*
1916	Margaret Sanger founds the New York Birth Control League
1917	Congress enacts a literacy test for new immigrants
1918	World War I ends
1919	The Eighteenth Amendment, establishing prohibition, is ratified
1920	The Nineteenth Amendment, enfranchising women, is ratified

BIBLIOGRAPHY

The Progressive Era has been a favorite of historians, and it has a vast and rich historical literature. Some of the most readable and accessible books include the previously mentioned studies of reform by Eric Goldman and Richard Hofstadter. David M. Chalmers' *The Social and Political Ideas of the Muckrakers* is the best study of the reform writers of the era. The role of women in the Progressive Era has been documented by William L. O'Neill in *Everyone Was Brave.* A first-rate biography of Margaret Sanger is David Kennedy's *Birth Control in America: The Career of Margaret Sanger.* Aileen Kraditor's *Ideas of the Woman Suffrage Movement* is an original study of the drive to win the vote for women. A fine, recent study of the U.S. woman suffrage movement has been done by Suzanne M. Marilley in *Woman Suffrage and the Origins of Liberal Feminism in the United States, 1820–1920.* Ruth Rosen's *The Lost Sisterhood: Prostitutes in America 1900–1918* is a fascinating study of this group of women. Elliot M. Rudwick's *W. E. B. Dubois: A Study in Group Leadership* is the best book about the most important black Progressive. A classic study of national progressivism is George Mowry's *The Era of Theodore Roosevelt.* The best intellectual history of progressivism remains Morton White's *Social Thought in America: The Revolt Against Formalism.* Lawrence Cremin's *The Transformation of the School: Progressivism in American Education* is the best study of an important era in education by the foremost American historian of education. An imaginative comparative study of the two greatest Progressive reform leaders, Theodore Roosevelt and Woodrow Wilson, is John M. Cooper, Jr.'s *The Warrior and the Priest*. Anyone who wants to know how Prohibition came to be the law of the land should read J. H. Timberlake's *Prohibition and the Progressive Movement*.

3

The United States and the World

IN the aftermath of its war with Spain, the United States pursued an interventionist foreign policy. It fought a war to crush a nationalist rebellion in the Philippines and joined other imperial powers to suppress the Boxer uprising in China. It sent its troops into many Latin American nations: Cuba, Panama, the Dominican Republic, Nicaragua, Haiti, and Mexico. Progressive foreign policy aimed to promote overseas trade and investment, maintain regional order, and fulfill the imperatives of the American missionary impulse to redeem the world. The foreign policy elite who formulated Progressive foreign policy believed that northern Europeans and their American descendants belonged to a superior race destined to dominate and "civilize" the darker-skinned people of Latin America, Asia, Africa, and the Pacific islands. In 1917, the United States intervened in Europe to ensure an Allied victory over Germany. World War I was a transforming experience for the United States, and it opened a historic opportunity for America to assume primacy among the world's nations.

MANAGING THE AMERICAN EMPIRE

U.S. foreign policy during the Progressive Era was determined mainly by American expansionism during the 1890s and the acquisition of an overseas empire. Progressive diplomatists were concerned with the opportunities and problems encountered in managing, protecting, and expanding the American empire, which reached from the Caribbean to the Far East. The American empire during the period between the Spanish-American War and World War I faced threats from restless nationalists, commercial rivals, and other expansionist nations.

Although Cuba did not become an American colony after the war with Spain, the United States dominated the new nation. American troops remained in Cuba until 1902, and Cuba was governed by General Leonard Wood, formerly the commander of the Rough Riders. To get rid of the American forces, Cubans were forced to accept the Platt Amendment, which was incorporated into the new Cuban constitution and later ratified as a treaty. The amendment conceded American hegemony over Cuba and impaired Cuban sovereignty. Cuba could make no treaties with another nation without U.S. approval. Cuba granted the United States "the right to intervene to maintain order and preserve Cuban independence." Cuba also had to lease a naval base at Guantanamo to the United States. When a rebellion occurred in 1906, President Roosevelt intervened to reestablish a U.S.-controlled provisional government, supported by 5,000 American troops, which ruled for twenty-eight months. Over the next fifteen years, whenever political instability occurred in Cuba, the United States sent the Marines ashore to maintain order and to protect American lives and property.

The long American protectorate left its mark on Cuba. Americans helped Cubans improve their infrastructures, develop a public school system, create a national army, increase sugar production, and raise public health levels. American investments in Cuba reached $220 million by 1913, and American exports to the island reached $200 million by 1917. Most of the Cuban sugar crop, the island's only important export, was marketed within the United States. The Cuban nation developed with a colonial mentality. Cuban patriots nurtured a resentment toward the United States that in time became anti-Americanism.

Expanding American interests in the Caribbean and Asia at the turn of the century made building an interoceanic canal across Central America an urgent U.S. priority. A possible route lay across the Colombian province of Panama, where a French organization, the New Panama Canal Company, owned the right-of-way, having inherited it from the failed De Lesseps Company, which had attempted to construct a route during the 1880s. After ten years and the loss of over 20,000 men to yellow fever and accidents, the bankrupt De Lesseps Company was forced to abandon the project. Only fifty miles separated the two oceans along this route, but the steamy, jungle-covered terrain was rugged and posed serious health hazards. Another possible route traversed Nicaragua. It was 200 miles long, but it would be an easier challenge because much of it included Lake Nicaragua and other natural waterways.

President Roosevelt considered both sites and chose the Panama route. His decision was influenced by the lobbying of Philippe Bunau-Varilla, a French engineer living in Panama, who formerly had directed the defunct French canal project. On January 18, 1903, a U.S. commission agreed to pay the New Panama Canal Company $40 million for its right-of-way and equipment. Congress subsequently approved the Panama route. On January 22, 1903, Secretary of State John Hay negotiated a treaty with Tomas Herran, the Colombian *charge d'affaires.* By its terms, the United States received a ninety-nine-year lease on a six-mile-wide zone across the isthmus of Panama; in return, the United States granted an initial payment of $10 million to Colombia and $250,000 in annual rental. But on August 12, 1903, the Colombian senate unanimously rejected the Hay-Herran treaty because the sena-

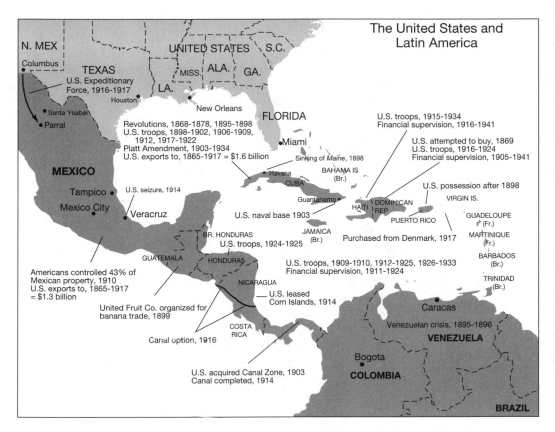

Figure 3.1   The United States and Latin America.   *Source:* George D. Moss, *Rise of Modern America,* p. 95.

tors wanted more money and because the agreement, which infringed upon Colombian sovereignty, was unpopular with the Colombian people. The senators wanted an initial payment of $15 million from the United States, and they also tried to extract $10 million from the New Panama Canal Company.

President Roosevelt could have negotiated an agreement with the Colombians, who were eager to have the United States build the canal, but he angrily denounced the Colombians, broke off negotiations, and sought to get the canal right-of-way through other means. Panamanians, also eager for the Americans to build the canal, having learned of the Colombian rejection and urged on by New Panama Canal officials, rose in rebellion on November 2, 1903. Roosevelt had previously given Bunau-Varilla indications that the United States would accept a Panamanian revolt.

That same day, an American fleet, led by the cruiser USS *Nashville,* arrived in Colon, Panama's Caribbean port. When Colombia landed 400 troops at Colon on November 3 to suppress the rebellion, the U.S. Navy did not interfere. The failure of the U.S. Navy to intervene disappointed the Panamanian rebels, who had hoped for American help. Forced to rely on their own resources, the Panamanians out-maneuvered the Colombians, bribing their leader into taking his troops back to Colombia. With the soldiers gone, the revolution succeeded. Joyous Panamanians declared their independence on the evening of November 3. At noon the next day, Secretary of State John Hay extended official U.S. recognition of the sovereign Re-public of Panama. On November 18, Hay and the new Panamanian minister plenipotentiary, the resourceful Philippe Bunau-Varilla, negotiated a treaty, the Hay-Bunau-Varilla Treaty. The agreement granted the United States a zone ten miles wide "in perpetuity" across the isthmus for the same money that Colombia had previously rejected. The New Panama Canal Company then received its $40 million for its right-of-way and properties. On February 24, 1904, the U.S. Senate overwhelmingly approved the new treaty. The American public also overwhelm-ingly approved the new treaty.

Construction of the canal began in 1904, and the fifty-mile-long canal opened to seafaring traffic on August 15, 1914. From opening day, the merchant ships of many nations and vessels of the U.S. Atlantic and Pacific fleets traversed the big ditch. Americans celebrated the opening of the canal by staging a world's fair hon-oring it, the Panama-Pacific Exposition, held in San Francisco in 1915. Building the canal was a tremendous engineering feat that served the national interest economi-cally and strategically. The United States fortified the Canal Zone, and guarding the canal and its approaches became a vital U.S. strategic interest. The terms of the treaty negotiated by United States and Panamanian officials made the Canal Zone an American colony. Panama was a sovereign nation in name only because of American control of the canal and a strip of Panamanian soil stretching across the heart of that small country.

Following his acquisition of the Canal Zone, Roosevelt turned the rest of the Caribbean into an "American lake." He was aided in these actions by the British, who were eager to improve relations with the United States. London, perceiving the shifting power balance in the Western Hemisphere and having major foreign policy concerns in other parts of the world, accepted Ameri-can hegemony in Latin America. British acceptance of American dominance in the Caribbean area signaled a growing Anglo-American accord that cleared the way for U. S. regional expansionism without fear of British opposi-tion. The new Anglo-American accord blossomed into a full-fledged Anglo-American alliance during World War I. Both world powers benefited from their "great rapprochement."

The Panama Canal gave the United States a commanding position in Western Hemispheric affairs. The Monroe Doctrine promulgated in 1823 had proclaimed U. S. opposition to further European colonization of the Western Hemisphere, but in the early twentieth century, the chronic indebtedness of Latin American govern-ments invited European intrusion. Roosevelt liked to quote the old African proverb, "Speak softly and carry a big stick." He often used the stick, but he seldom curbed his noisy rhetoric. In 1902, he pressured the British and Germans to submit a debt dispute with Venezuela to arbitration. Two years later, when the Dominican Republic defaulted on it's debt payments, he added the, "Roosevelt Corollary" to the Monroe Doctrine. It warned Latin American countries to put their governments and finances in order to forestall European intervention in their affairs or

> Chronic wrongdoing . . . may in America, as elsewhere, ultimately require intervention by some civilized nation, and in the Western Hemisphere the adherence of the United States to the Monroe Doctrine may force the United States, however reluctantly, in flagrant cases of such wrongdoing or impotence, to the exercise of an international police power.[1]

The Roosevelt Corollary to the Monroe Doctrine transformed that hallowed prohibition upon European intervention in the Western Hemisphere into a firm assertion that the United States henceforth would arrogate to itself the role of regional policeman.

Roosevelt and his Progressive successors, Taft and Wilson, frequently implemented Roosevelt's corollary. Between 1900 and the entry of the United States into World War I, American troops intervened in Cuba, Panama, Nicaragua, the Dominican Republic, Haiti, and Mexico. American officials took over customs houses to control tariff revenues and government budgets, renegotiated foreign debts with American banks, and trained national armies; and they conducted elections. Frequent U. S. interventions into Nicaraguan affairs between 1907 and 1933 made that small and poor Central American country a U. S. protectorate.

Mexico appeared especially threatening to the Progressive managers of U. S. foreign policy. In 1910, revolutionaries overthrew Porfirio Diaz, an aged dictator who had maintained a politically stable environment for U. S. and other foreign investments for forty years. Revolution plunged Mexico into a decade of turmoil. The Mexicans changed governments several times as revolutionary factions struggled for power. At various stages of the Mexican revolution, American lives and property appeared to be imperiled.

But President Wilson appeared less concerned about protecting the U. S. Mexican investment of $1 billion than he was about guiding the Mexicans to establish an American-style political democracy. In the summer of 1913, Wilson attempted to remove General Victoriano Huerta from power and to replace him with a government led by Venustiano Carranza, the leader of the liberal "Constitutionalists." When an arms embargo failed to work, Wilson sent American naval vessels to the Mexican gulf ports of Vera Cruz and Tampico.

On April 21, 1914, Wilson, learning that a merchant ship carrying arms for Huerta's forces was arriving at Vera Cruz, ordered a force of 800 U. S. sailors and Marines to enter the city and seize the customs house to interdict the arms shipment. Local Mexican forces fought the American invaders in the streets of Vera Cruz. Nineteen Americans and 126 Mexicans died in the battle. Although the U. S.

---

[1]Theodore Roosevelt, quoted in Henry F. Pringle, *Theodore Roosevelt* (New York: Harcourt, Brace, 1931, 1945), p. 207.

invasion was intended to overthrow General Huerta, the American actions offended Mexicans of all political persuasions who viewed the U.S. actions as an affront to their nationalism and a threat to their independence. Appalled at the bloodshed that he had provoked and not wanting a war with Mexico, a chastened Wilson permitted mediation of the U.S.-Mexican dispute by Argentina, Brazil, and Chile. Mediation failed, but Huerta's rivals defeated him in battle and forced his abdication in July 1914. Carranza took power. Wilson withdrew American forces from Vera Cruz and extended diplomatic recognition to the new leader.

The Mexican revolution soon turned violent again when Carranza tried to crush one of the leading generals who had helped him achieve power, Francisco "Pancho" Villa. Sporadic fighting occurred between Carranza's and Villa's forces during 1915. On March 9, 1916, General Villa, who perceived Wilson to be an ally of Carranza, led his forces across the border and attacked the American town of Columbus, New Mexico, killing nineteen Americans and torching the town.

Wilson reacted to Villa's daring raid by ordering the U.S. Army under the command of General John J. "Black Jack" Pershing to invade Mexico and capture Pancho Villa. A force of some 10,000 U.S. soldiers eventually found themselves 350 miles into Mexico without ever spotting Villa's elusive forces. Instead, Pershing's soldiers found themselves fighting two pitched battles with Carranza's federal troops.

On February 5, 1917, only when it became evident that the United States would soon enter World War I did Wilson withdraw the U.S. Army from Mexico. Impending war in Europe forced Wilson to abandon his futile efforts to direct the political destiny of Mexico. Even so, U.S. cavalry units continued to patrol the U.S.-Mexican border regions until 1920, when Alvaro Obregon overthrew Carranza's government and the Mexican revolution finally ran its course. During the decade that revolution tore Mexico apart, U.S. efforts to influence the course of the upheaval served merely to increase Mexican animosity toward the United States.

The United States policed the Caribbean region during the Progressive years for several reasons. Washington would not tolerate disorders that might threaten its new canal across Panama or its growing commerce and investments in Latin America. Between 1900 and 1917, American exports to Latin American increased from $132 million to $309 million. Imports from Latin America increased even more. American investments in Caribbean countries in sugar, tobacco, bananas, coffee, transportation, and banking expanded rapidly. Progressive diplomats also projected their reform urges outwardly. They wanted to remake Latin American societies in the image of the United States. Progressive idealists assumed all people, if given the chance, wanted to be like Americans; and if they could be like Americans, they would be greatly improved. President Woodrow Wilson asserted that "every nation needs to be drawn into the tutelage of America."

A salient characteristic of American foreign policy between the Spanish-American War and U.S. entry into World War I was insensitivity to the nationalism of other people. Americans did not take seriously the Filipino resistance to American colonial domination, Cuban anger over the restrictions of the Platt Amendment, Colombian outrage over U.S. support of the Panamanian insurrection, or

Mexican resentment over Wilsonian interventionism. The American empire that evolved during the first fifteen years of the twentieth century consisted of few colonies. It was an informal empire mainly, characterized by economic and political control instead of formal annexation and governance. The informal American empire, administered by paternalistic military officers, bankers, and reformers, many of whom displayed a contempt for the native people's culture, wounded their national pride and infringed upon the sovereignty of their governments—all in the name of national security, profits, democracy, efficiency, progress, public health, and saving souls.

U.S. foreign policy toward Europe during the Progressive Era was governed by three principles: (1) Europeans should not intervene in Western Hemispheric affairs now that American military force backed the Monroe Doctrine; (2) America should stay out of European affairs. When Roosevelt intervened to mediate a conflict between France and Germany over Morocco in 1906, he was criticized for entangling the United States in a European problem; and (3) American interests were best served by cooperating internationally with the British, the world's preeminent power.

The possession of the Philippines and the implementation of the Open Door policy had thrust the United States into Asian affairs. In the Progressive Era, American policy toward Asia was dominated by relations with Japan, a rising Asian power. When imperial conflicts over Manchuria and Korea provoked Japan and Russia to war in 1904, Japan scored quick victories. President Roosevelt mediated an end to the war at a conference in Portsmouth, New Hampshire, in 1905, trying to preserve the balance of power in the Far East. He failed. Later that year, the Taft-Katsura Agreement conceded Japanese control of Korea in exchange for a Japanese promise to not attack the American colony in the Philippine Islands. Roosevelt sent the American "Great White Fleet" on a world tour in 1907 and 1908 to impress the Japanese with American naval might. The Japanese were duly impressed, gave the Americans a lavish welcome, and began building larger ships as soon as the Americans left. In 1908, the Root-Takahira Agreement recognized Japanese interests in Manchuria in exchange for another Japanese pledge to respect American colonial possessions in Asia.

Despite these agreements, American-Japanese relations were not harmonious. The Japanese were offended by the racist mistreatment of the Japanese in California during the Progressive years. American economic activities in China also alarmed the Japanese, who worked to increase their economic concessions in that country.

EUROPE GOES TO WAR

War erupted in Europe in August 1914, to the surprise and horror of most Americans. There were many causes, including decades of imperialistic rivalries over trade and colonies. By the first decade of the twentieth century, the great powers of Europe had joined two rival coalitions, each armed to the teeth. The Triple Alliance joined together Germany, Austria-Hungary, and Italy. The Triple Entente combined Britain, France, and Russia. All members had economic and territorial ambitions that involved them in the affairs of unstable countries and provinces in the Balkan peninsula. A series of crises in the Balkans caught the great powers of Europe in a chain of events that propelled them to war. Within the Balkans, Slavic nationalists sought to build a major power by prying territories from the Austro-Hungarian Empire and adding them to Serbia. One of these territories was Bosnia, which contained a large Serbian population. On June 28, 1914, at Sarajevo, in Bosnia, the heir to the Austrian throne, Archduke Franz Ferdinand, was assassinated by a Serbian terrorist, Gavrilo Princips.

Austria, backed by Germany, delivered an ultimatum to Serbia. Serbia appealed for help from its major ally, Russia. When Austria declared war on Serbia in late July, Russia began mobilizing her vast armies. Germany asked Russia to stop her mobilization. The Russians refused, and the Germans, convinced that war was coming, declared war on Russia on August 1, and on Russia's ally, France, two days later. Germany quickly followed these declarations of war with an invasion of neutral Belgium that was part of a preconceived plan to attack the French in order to defeat them quickly and avoid fighting a two-front war against France in the west and her ally, Russia, to the east. Germany's attack on Belgium brought the British into the war on August 4. Later, Turkey and Bulgaria joined Germany and Austria-Hungary. Japan joined the Entente powers, as did Italy, after being freed from the Triple Alliance, in 1915. (Germany and the nations allied with it were called the Central Powers. The nations allied in the Entente were called the Allies.) Six weeks after the assassination at Sarajevo, Europe was at war.

UNNEUTRAL NEUTRALITY

When the war began, nearly all Americans assumed that the United States would never become involved. There appeared to be no vital American interests at stake; it was a European war over European issues. As one American put it, the war was "none of our business." No one expected the war to last more than four to six months; it would be over by Christmas, predicted the pundits.

President Wilson's response to the outbreak of war was an effort to isolate America from its effects; he declared America to be neutral. In a speech delivered before the Senate, he urged his countrymen to be neutral in their thoughts as well as their acts. The United States, he asserted, would stand as an inspiring example of peace and prosperity in a deranged world. He also believed that the United States had to remain neutral; otherwise, he feared that its "mixed populations would wage war on each other." The war, he said, was one "with which we have nothing to do, whose causes cannot reach us."

Wilson's appeal for neutrality and unity at home proved impossible to attain. Ethnic groups took sides. Many German Americans and Irish Americans sided with

Figure 3.2   World War I, 1914–1918.   *Source:* Moss, *Rise of Modern America*, p. 101.

the Central Powers. Americans of British, French, and Russian ancestry cheered the Allies. A large majority of Americans was drawn to the Allied side. They viewed the war as a struggle between democracy and autocracy. Germany's invasion of neutral Belgium at the outset of the war convinced many Americans that Germans were international outlaws, barbarian defilers of helpless innocents. Clever British propaganda reinforced this view of Germans as enemies of civilization.

America's economic ties to the Allies also made genuine neutrality impossible. War orders from France and Britain flowed in to American farms and businesses, promoting a roaring wartime prosperity. In 1914, U.S. exports to the Allies totaled $753 million; in 1916, that figured soared to nearly $3 billion. During that same period, trade with Germany tumbled from $345 million to $29 million. Much of the war trade with the Allies was financed with credit extended by U.S. banks. They loaned the Allies $2.3 billion during the neutrality period; the Germans received only $27 million. Wilson understood that the Allied war trade had become important to the American economy. If credits were not made available to the Allies, their purchases of American goods would fall sharply, hurting manufacturers, farmers, and workers in this country.

Germany viewed the commercial and financial ties between the United States and the Allies as giving its enemies access to supposedly neutral American arsenals and credits. Wilson responded to German complaints by insisting that if America cut its ties with the Allies that that would be an unneutral act favoring the Germans, since under international law the British, who controlled the seas, could, at their own risk, trade with neutrals. He maintained that it was Germany's responsibility to stop the trade with an effective blockade of the Allies. Wilson's view that American neutrality policy accorded with international law was true; British control of the seas turned this policy in favor of the Allies.

Wilson and nearly all of his leading advisers were pro-Ally in the general sense that they preferred an Allied to a Central Powers victory. They believed that American interests and ideals would fare better in a postwar world that was dominated by the British rather than one that was dominated by the Germans. Wilson envisioned a postwar world made safe for Progressive foreign policy principles of free-market capitalism and political democracy. He believed that only a free and prosperous world order could ensure perpetual peace.

Although it is accurate to say that popular pro-Ally sentiments, economic and financial ties to the Allies, and Wilson's pro-Ally preferences made genuine neutrality impossible, it is important to stress that Wilson did not seek to bring the United States into the war. He wanted desperately to avoid war, and he crafted a foreign policy that avoided war for nearly three years at the same time it protected vital American interests and national honor. Repeatedly, Wilson sent his personal representative, Colonel Edward House, to Europe to try to mediate an end to the conflict. In early 1917, Wilson cried, "It would be a crime against civilization if we went in."

But Americans got caught in an Allies-Central Powers conflict. The British were determined to use their sea power to cripple the German economy and to undermine its war machine. An integral part of the British naval war against Germany was to sever its trade with neutrals like the United States. Britannia, ruling the waves, declared a loose, illegal blockade of Central Powers ports. The British defined contraband broadly to include foodstuffs and strategic raw materials.

(Contraband was trade with belligerents forbidden to neutrals, traditionally arms and munitions.) They also harassed neutral shipping. American ships hauling goods to Germany seldom reached their destinations. To neutralize German submarines, the British violated international law by arming their merchant ships, hauling armaments in passenger ships and flying the flags of neutrals.

President Wilson frequently protested British violations of American neutral rights. He told English leaders that neutrals had the right to ship noncontraband goods to all belligerents and pointed out, correctly, that the British definition of contraband was contrary to an international agreement that the British themselves had signed. The British defused American protests by easing their blockade periodically and by paying American companies for confiscated cargoes. Two other factors prevented American-British relations from deteriorating seriously because of British violations of American neutral rights. First, expanding Allied purchases of American goods more than made up for the lost Central Powers markets; the American war economy continued to expand. Second, the Germans violated American neutral rights by sinking ships and killing people, which made British offenses appear mild by comparison. British violations of international law were annoying, sometimes outrageous, but the English never sank any American ships or killed any American citizens.

Germany, for its part, was determined to sever Allied–American trade. The German navy had conceded control of the seas to the British navy at the outset of the war. To try to cut the commercial links between the United States and the Allies, Germany resorted to submarine warfare. In February 1915, the German government announced that it was creating a war zone around the British Isles, a submarine counter blockade: All enemy ships entering the war zone would be sunk. They also warned all neutrals to avoid the war zone, lest they be attacked by mistake, and they told passengers from neutral nations to stay off enemy passenger ships. President Wilson reacted to this edict quickly and firmly. He told the German leaders that if any American property or lives were lost in the war zone, Germany would be held to "strict accountability." His message amounted to an ultimatum, a threat of war if the German attacks killed Americans.

International law in force at the time required commerce destroyers to warn merchant or passenger ships before attacking them in order to allow the passengers and crew to disembark safely. Such rules assumed that passengers and merchant crews were civilians, innocent noncombatants, therefore exempt from attack. These rules predated the development of the submarine. Wilson refused to acknowledge the limitations of submarines that made it impossible for them to warn their intended targets and still function effectively. If submarines surfaced to warn ships, they would lose their chief advantage—surprise. Any merchant or passenger ship could easily outrun a surfaced submarine and avoid its torpedoes. A surfaced submarine was an easy target for deck gunfire and was vulnerable to ramming, and the time it took for the crew and passengers to debark usually gave a ship's radioman the opportunity to call in nearby destroyers to attack the waiting U-boat. To Germans it appeared that Wilson's strict accountability policy denied them effective use of the one weapon they possessed that could disrupt the

Allies' ties with American producers. Engaged in a brutal struggle for national survival, the Germans deeply resented Wilson's strict accountability policy with its dated, legalistic views of submarine warfare. Here lay a conflict between Germany and the United States that had ominous potential.

AMERICA GOES TO WAR

Since the Germans promised to not attack American ships in the war zone, an agreement they honored until the spring of 1917, the issue became the right of Americans to sail and work on belligerent ships. Germany's sinking of the British luxury liner HMS *Lusitania* forced the issue. The 785-foot-long ship had left New York on May 1, 1915, with 1,257 passengers and a crew of 702 on board. The ship's manifest for its last voyage reads like a contraband shopping list. The *Lusitania* was hauling 4,200 cases of rifle ammunition, 1,250 cases of shrapnel, and 18 boxes of percussion caps. Before the liner set sail, New York newspapers carried announcements from the German embassy, warning passengers that Allied ships were "liable to destruction" in the war zone. Passengers ignored the warning, confident that the giant luxury liner could outrun any German submarines or torpedoes. At 2:10 P.M. local time, on May 7, about twelve miles off of the southern Irish coast, a German submarine, U-20, torpedoed the *Lusitania*. The ship sank quickly in the dark Celtic Sea, carrying 1,195 people to their deaths, including 123 Americans.

Most Americans were horrified and outraged by the attack. Wilson angrily dismissed the idea that because the ship was hauling contraband, the Germans were justified in killing nearly 1,200 innocent people. But neither the American people nor Wilson wanted war over the incident. Wilson steered a middle path between Secretary of State William Jennings Bryan, who wanted to forbid Americans from traveling on belligerent ships and to prevent Allied passenger ships from hauling ammunition, and Theodore Roosevelt, who was ready for war with Germany over the incident. Wilson sent a note to the German government, insisting on the right of Americans to travel on belligerent ships. He also demanded that German submarines protect passenger ships and pay for U.S. losses. When Wilson refused to consider banning American travelers on Allied passenger ships, Bryan resigned. His replacement, Robert Lansing, supported Wilson's position.

At first the Germans refused to apologize for the sinking of the *Lusitania* or to curb their submarines. Further notes were exchanged. To avoid war with America, the Germans eventually expressed regret for the loss of life and agreed to never again attack a passenger ship without warning. To charges from his critics that he was pursuing a double standard that favored the Allies, Wilson replied that the British were only violating property rights, whereas the Germans were violating human rights and murdering civilians.

On August 30, 1915, a German submarine torpedoed another British liner, the *Arabic;* two Americans were killed. The Germans hastened to apologize and pledged to never again attack passenger liners without warning. The *Arabic* incident fueled a debate in this country over the propriety of American passengers riding on belligerent ships. Critics of Wilson's "strict accountability" policy wanted the president to require American passengers to travel on American ships in the war zone. They believed that such an order would avoid further incidents and the risks of war. They sponsored a congressional resolution prohibiting Americans from traveling on armed merchant ships or passenger ships hauling contraband, but the resolution failed to pass in either house.

In March 1916, a German submarine attacked a French channel steamer, the *Sussex*, mistaking it for a minesweeper; four Americans were injured. An angry Wilson ordered the Germans to restrict their submarines, or he would sever diplomatic relations. The Germans, embarrassed by the incident and not wishing to go to war with the United States, pledged to not attack merchant ships without warning. They observed the "*Sussex* pledge" for the rest of the year. Relations with Germany stabilized during 1916. "Strict accountability" was working. Meanwhile, the British stepped up their blockade activities, and their violations of U.S. neutral rights escalated. Relations between the United States and the British deteriorated, as relations with the Germans improved.

Wilson had to seek reelection in November 1916. He faced a formidable challenge from the Republicans. The Party was reunited, its Progressive Party insurgents having returned to the fold. Republicans nominated an able candidate, Supreme Court Associate Justice Charles Evans Hughes, formerly a reform governor of New York. The 1916 presidential campaign was bitter, revealing deep divisions within America. Hughes attacked Wilson's social policies and accused him of not defending American neutral rights adequately against German assaults. The Democrats accused Hughes of being pro-German, and Wilson implied that anyone who thought that he was pro-British was disloyal. The key issue in the campaign was American foreign policy toward the warring powers. The Democratic Party campaigned on the slogan, "He kept us out of war," referring to Wilson's policy, which had extracted the "*Sussex* pledge" from the Germans. Also, Wilson's admirable record of achievement as a domestic reformer appealed to Progressive voters in both parties.

Hughes was favored to win when the campaign began, but he inadvertently offended California Progressive Republican leaders and thereby lost the presidency. In a close election, California, normally Republican, went for Wilson, giving him a narrow victory. A difference of fewer than 4,000 votes in California would have removed Wilson from the White House. The Democrats retained a narrow majority in the Senate, but in the new House there would be 216 Democrats, 210 Republicans, and 6 Independents. It was not clear at election time which party would control the new Congress.

Despite the campaign slogan, Wilson knew that American neutrality was precarious as long as the war continued. A German submarine skipper could provoke a crisis any time he was tempted to ignore the "*Sussex* pledge." Wilson sent Colonel House on another mission to European capitals to find a formula that could serve as a basis for a cease-fire. Wilson also appealed directly to the heads of the warring governments for "a peace without victory." His peace efforts failed because of events that were rapidly moving beyond his control.

The German government made a fateful decision to resume unrestricted submarine warfare on February 1, 1917. Henceforth, all ships, belligerent or neutral, warship or merchant, would be attacked on sight in the war zone. The Germans had decided to take a calculated risk, what they called their "gambler's throw," because their situation had grown desperate. The British blockade was severely pinching the German and Austro-Hungarian economies.

Inflation was rampant, and starvation was widespread in both countries. The Germans gambled that an all-out submarine war would enable them to cut off shipments of vital foodstuffs and ammunition to the Allies, permitting Germany to win the war before American troops could be mobilized and ferried across the Atlantic in enough strength to affect the outcome. They knew that their decision would provoke American entry into the war, but they assumed that they would win the race against time. They also believed that they were fated to lose a long-running war of attrition, for the Allies had superior resources—more people, more manufacturing capacity, and Allied sea power gave them access to their overseas colonies and the American arsenal.

Wilson, as expected, promptly severed diplomatic relations in response to Germany's direct challenge to American neutrality. But he did not ask Congress for a declaration of war immediately. British Prime Minister Lloyd George and Senate Republican leader Henry Cabot Lodge accused Wilson of cowardice. The Germans began sinking American ships. During February and March 1917, German submarines sank scores of Allied merchant ships. On April 1, the British had only a six-week supply of grain on hand. Once mighty lords of international banking, the British, by the spring of 1917, had mortgaged themselves heavily to American creditors because of their purchases of huge quantities of ammunition. The British treasury was approaching bankruptcy. Lloyd George feared a combination of hunger, bankruptcy, and submarine warfare might force the British to accept Germany's peace terms, enabling them to win their "gambler's throw."

The French also were suffering during that spring of 1917. General Robert Nivelle had tried to break the stalemated slaughter in the trenches with a spring offensive against the Germans at Champagne. The French fell into a trap set for them by the German commander, General Ludendorff, and they were slaughtered. After sustaining two weeks of massive losses under hellish conditions, the French soldiers mutinied. Nivelle was dismissed in disgrace. The French, exhausted and demoralized, appeared incapable of continuing the war much longer without help.

Spring 1917 was also a fateful season for the other major Allied power, Russia. After nearly three years of war, the Russians had lost millions of men; Czarist generals had herded unarmed peasants into fierce battles, only to have them slaughtered like sheep. The civilian population also had been subjected to severe privation and suffering. The Czar's government, aloof from the Russian people, could neither provide moral leadership nor organize the war effort efficiently. Having lost control of his army, the Czar abdicated on March 15. Two days later, Russia became a republic for the first time in its history; a provisional government led by Alexander Kerensky came to power. Kerensky pledged to honor Russian treaty and commercial obligations, and to continue the war.

The German Chancellor, Theobald von Bethmann-Hollweg, watched Russian political developments closely. Aware that Russia was riven with factionalism, he decided that Germany ought to support the most extreme groups within Russia to promote chaos and cripple the Russian war effort. He arranged for a small group of radical Russian exiles living in Switzerland to return to Russia. The radicals, led by a man calling himself V.I. Lenin (his real name was Vladimir Ilich Ulyanov), traveled across Germany on a sealed train, and they were forbidden to get off of the train while it was in Germany. Bethmann-Hollweg wanted to make sure that the radical political virus would infect only Russia. In mid-April, Lenin and his small band of "Bolsheviks" got off of the train at St. Petersburg's Finland Station. In November 1917, he led a rebellion that toppled Kerensky's fragile government and took Russia out of the war. Lenin's goal was to establish a Communist state in Russia and to promote a socialist revolution, which would sweep across Europe in the wake of war.

In late February, the British gave President Wilson a secret telegram they had intercepted and decoded, which was addressed to the German minister in Mexico from the German Foreign Secretary Arthur Zimmermann. The telegram instructed the minister to tell the Mexican government that if Mexico joined a military alliance against the United States, Germany would help the Mexicans recover their territories of "Texas, New Mexico, and Arizona," lost to the United States in 1848 in the Mexican-American War. Wilson took the Zimmermann note seriously. At the time, United States-Mexican relations were severely strained because Wilson had twice ordered American troops into Mexico during the Mexican revolution, and the two countries had verged on war. Soon after learning of the note, Wilson went before Congress seeking what he called an "armed neutrality." He hoped to forestall war by arming American merchant ships. As Congress debated his request, he released the Zimmermann note to the media. A wave of anti-German sentiment swept the country.

But a group of antiwar senators, including Robert La Follette, filibustered Wilson's armed neutrality proposal to death. Furious, Wilson excoriated them as a "little group of willful men, representing no opinion but their own, who have rendered this great nation helpless and contemptible." He then armed the ships on his own executive authority. But his action could not prevent German submarines from sinking American merchant ships.

Since the German decision to resume submarine warfare in mid-January, Wilson had hesitated to take the country to war. He confided to a friend, "It was necessary for me, by very slow stages indeed and with the most genuine purpose to avoid war to lead the country on to a single way of thinking." Since the war began, Americans had disagreed about America's relationship to it and what course of action the nation should take. Also, in the spring of 1917, America stood at the end of nearly two decades of divisive political and social upheaval. The concentration of economic wealth and power, the many Progressive efforts to tame the trusts, the serious strikes, and the arrival of over 12 million immigrants since 1900 had opened deep social fissures. Wilson did not want to burden American society further with the strains of a major war effort. He knew what the war was doing to the political and social structures of the European belligerents. He asserted that, "Every reform we have won will be lost if we get into this war." The president also feared the problems posed by the presence of millions of foreign-born residents in the country. He was particularly worried about the loyalty of those who had recently emigrated from Germany. If America went to war against Germany, could it count on the loyalty of its citizens who had come from the Fatherland?

But the momentum of events moved a reluctant nation and its leader inexorably toward war. The time for a decision had come. On March 20, Wilson met with his cabinet; its members unanimously favored war with Germany. The next day, Wilson called the newly elected 65th Congress to a special session, to receive his war message. He went before a hushed Congress on the evening of April 2, 1917, to deliver a solemn, subdued speech. He recounted the many German violations of international law and American rights. He condemned German sabotage and spying within the United States and denounced the proposed German alliance with Mexico.

Wilson then informed the assembled legislators what war would mean and what he intended to do. He planned to lend billions of dollars to the Allied nations already at war with Germany, to increase taxes to finance the costly American war effort, and to implement conscription. He also made it clear that he would insist more than ever on the preeminence of a strong executive. Although he acknowledged the loyalty of most Americans of German birth, he warned, "If there should be disloyalty, it will be dealt with a firm hand of repression." As he neared the end of his speech, Wilson explained American war aims:

> The world must be made safe for democracy. Its peace must be planted upon the tested foundations of political liberty. We have no selfish ends to serve. We desire no conquest, no dominion. We seek no indemnities for ourselves, no material compensation for the sacrifices we shall freely make. We are but one of the champions of the rights of mankind. . . .
>
> It is a fearful thing to lead this great peaceful people into war, into the most terrible and disastrous of all wars, civilization itself seeming to be in the balance. But the right is more precious than peace, and we shall fight for the things which we have always carried nearest our hearts—for democracy, . . . for a universal dominion of right, . . . and make the world itself at last free. To such a task we can dedicate our lives and our fortunes, everything that we are and everything that we have, with the pride of those who know that the day has come when America is privileged to spend her blood and her might for the principles that gave her birth and happiness and the peace that she has treasured. God helping her, she can do no other.[2]

Wilson asked Congress to commit the country to a distant war that had already butchered 7 million men and promised to add millions more names to the ledger of death before it ended. He had called for high taxes and the drafting of

[2]Taken from a copy of Wilson's War Message, printed in Armin Rappaport, *Sources in American Diplomatic History* (New York: Macmillan, 1966), pp. 211–12.

millions of young Americans who would be sent into that war. He had asked Congress to accept the expansion of presidential power, and he had called for the enforced loyalty of all Americans in a cause to which millions of his fellow citizens were hostile or indifferent.

Wilson's request for a war resolution provoked an extended debate among members of Congress that lasted four days. The outcome was a foregone conclusion. The proponents of war knew that they had an overwhelming majority of the votes. But that reality did not inhibit the enemies of war who spoke against the resolution. The supporters of the resolution shared Wilson's view of the war as a struggle between the forces of democracy and the forces of autocratic tyranny, with America aligning itself on the side of virtue in a profound ideological conflict to make the world a safe place for democratic nations.

Opponents of the resolution considered it hypocritical to demand war in the name of democracy. They considered the European conflict a contest between rival imperialisms. As they saw it, only territory and markets were at stake, not democratic principles. They also pointed out that many ardent supporters of the war were among the most determined opponents of Progressive reform efforts to make American institutions more democratic. Some Midwestern Progressive opponents of war viewed the conflict as benefiting the rich at the expense of ordinary citizens. Republican Senator George Norris of Nebraska passionately declared:

> War brings no prosperity to the great mass of common patriotic citizens. . . . We are going into war upon the command of gold.[3]

Norris's Progressive colleague, Senator Robert La Follette also charged the Wilson administration with having forced the war upon America by pursuing a pro-British neutrality policy. Other foes of war adhered to traditional isolationist views; they believed that intervening in a European war was contrary to American interests and values. Jeannette Rankin, the first woman ever to sit in Congress, spoke with tears coursing down her cheeks: "I want to stand by my country, but I cannot vote for war."

Six senators and fifty representatives finally voted against American entry into the war. There were others who opposed the war but voted for it anyway. But all opponents of the war resolution made it clear that their opposition would cease once war was officially declared.

Wilson took the United States to war in the spring of 1917 for many reasons: to defend democracy, international law, morality, and the nation's honor. Wilson stressed these idealistic war aims in his stirring peroration. The United States also went to war to protect its commerce and national security. Further, Wilson and his advisers feared that the Allies could lose the war if the United States did not enter on their side. Another reason for entering the war was to ensure an American role at the peace conference. Wilson hoped to be a major influence in shaping the

[3]Quoted in David Kennedy, *Over Here: The First World War and American Society* (New York: Oxford University, 1980), p. 19.

postwar world along Progressive lines; he perceived that unless America participated in the war, it would be excluded from the peace conference.

The decisive event which brought the United States into World War I was the German decision to resume unrestricted submarine warfare in early 1917. This decision nullified Wilson's neutrality policy based upon "strict accountability" and forced him to choose between war and appeasement. Wilson's critics have cited his rigid conception of international law, which did not fit the reality of submarine tactics. They also have faulted his unyielding defense of the right of Americans to travel on belligerent ships, even those hauling contraband. But most Americans supported his neutrality policy, and when he told the people on April 2, 1917, that "neutrality was no longer feasible nor desirable," most supported his request for war.

OVER THERE

The United States had been preparing for possible combat during the years of neutrality. As early as 1915, President Wilson began planning a large military buildup. His proposals triggered a great debate within the nation over preparedness. Many congressmen and senators opposed the buildup. Pacifist Progressives led by Jane Addams formed an antiwar coalition, the American Union Against Militarism. Businessmen like Andrew Carnegie, who in 1910 had established the Carnegie Endowment for International Peace, helped finance peace groups. Henry Ford spent half a million dollars in 1915 to send a "peace ark" to Europe to urge the European powers to accept a negotiated settlement.

Despite opposition from pacifists both in and out of government, Congress enacted the National Defense Act of 1916, which increased the size of the National Guard and established summer training camps for soldiers. The Navy Act established a three-year naval expansion program. To finance these expensive preparedness measures, Congress enacted the Revenue Act of 1916. It was a progressive tax increase, calling for a surtax on high incomes and corporate profits, a tax on large estates, and increased taxes on munitions makers. Despite these preparedness activities, the United States was not ready for war in the spring of 1917. The U.S. Army was small and equipped with obsolete weapons.

Soon after the United States entered the war, Congress enacted a Selective Service Act implementing conscription. Antidraft forces challenged the constitutionality of the draft, but the Supreme Court quickly upheld it as a proper exercise of the "implied powers" principle. It required that all males between the ages of twenty and thirty register for the draft. By war's end, 24 million men had registered for the draft, nearly 5 million had been conscripted, and 2 million had been sent to fight in France. Millions of draft-age men received deferments because they worked in war industries or had dependents. Over 300,000 evaded the draft by refusing to register or not responding when called. About 300,000 men volunteered for duty. Thousands of women volunteered for military service; they worked as clerks, telephone operators, and nurses. The typical "doughboy" was a draftee,

Figure 3.3   Black troops fought in all-black, segregated units during World War I. This photo shows troopers from the 369th Infantry Regiment, who saw heavy combat on the Western Front in 1918.   *Source:* National Archives.

twenty-two years old, white, single, and with a seventh-grade education. In a nation of immigrants, nearly one draftee in five had been born in another country, many from the European countries currently at war. Military training often aimed at educating and "Americanizing" these ethnic recruits.

About 400,000 black men were drafted or volunteered. The American military, reflecting the society from which it was recruited, was segregated during World War I. African American soldiers were kept in all-black units and were not allowed to become aviators or join the Marines. A separate officers' training program provided African American Army officers, who were never allowed to command white soldiers.

Even though the United States entered the war belatedly, and on a smaller scale than the other major combatants, its armed forces played major roles in the war. The U.S. Navy performed crucial service. In April 1917, when America entered the war, German submarines were sinking Allied merchant ships at a rate of 870,000 tons per month. American destroyers, teamed with their British counterparts, reduced, and eventually stopped, the submarine threat. American naval planners helped develop the convoy system, in which destroyers and other warships escorted merchant ships across the Atlantic, effectively screening out German submarines. American troop ships were convoyed to France, and all 2 million men arrived safely.

As American troops arrived in France, General John J. "Black Jack" Pershing, the commander of the American Expeditionary Force (AEF) refused to allow them to join Allied units. He refused to let American soldiers be fed into the mincing machine. Allied commanders had locked themselves into suicidal trench warfare, producing years of stalemate and ghastly casualty rates. Zigzag trenches fronted by barbed wires and mines stretched across the 200-mile-long Western Front, which ran from the French channel coast, curving across northeastern France, to the Swiss border. In front of the trenches lay a region called "no-man's-land," cratered by heavy artillery bombardments. Allied soldiers, upon order, would charge the German lines on the other side of this deadly frontier. Rapid-fire machine guns mowed them down, and chlorine gas poisoned them. Little territory would be gained, yet the human cost was great. Then it would be the German's turn to be ordered to die in a futile charge. The stalemated slaughter went on for over three years. Before the advent of the Americans, the blood of millions of German, French, and British soldiers had spilled over the killing fields of northeastern France.

At the Battle of the Somme in 1916, the British and the French launched their greatest offensive of the war, losing 600,000 men, killed or wounded, to gain 125 square miles of territory. The Germans lost 500,000 men defending that small piece of blood-stained ground. The Germans also tried to break the impasse in 1916 by laying siege to a crucial French fortress at Verdun. The German strategy at Verdun was simple and horrible: Besiege the fort indefinitely and bleed France dry, relying on the numerical superiority of German manpower to guarantee eventual victory. The siege ended six months later, with 350,000 French and 330,000 German soldiers dead. The front had not moved.

The entry of American men and material into World War I determined its outcome. With both sides on the verge of exhaustion, the arrival of fresh American forces tipped the balance decisively toward the Allies. American forces began combat in March 1918, when the Germans launched a great spring offensive, their armies now strengthened by the arrival of thousands of battle-hardened veterans from the Eastern Front. In late May, advance units reached the Marne River, near the village of Chateau-Thierry, fifty miles from Paris. Early in June, 27,500 American soldiers fought their first important battle, driving the Germans out of Chateau-Thierry and nearby Belleau Wood. The size of the American forces expanded rapidly. In early July, near the Marne, 270,000 Americans joined the fighting, helping to flatten a German bulge between Reims and Soissons. On July 15, the German army threw everything into one final effort to smash through to Paris, but in three days they were finished. The war had turned in favor of the Allies.

Between September 12 and 16, the American First Army, now 500,000 strong and fighting with French forces, wiped out a German thrust at Saint-Mihiel. Two weeks later, the Americans began their most important battle of the war: 1.2 million "doughboys" launched the Meuse-Argonne offensive. In forty days and nights of heavy slugging in the region of the Argonne forest, the Americans eventually

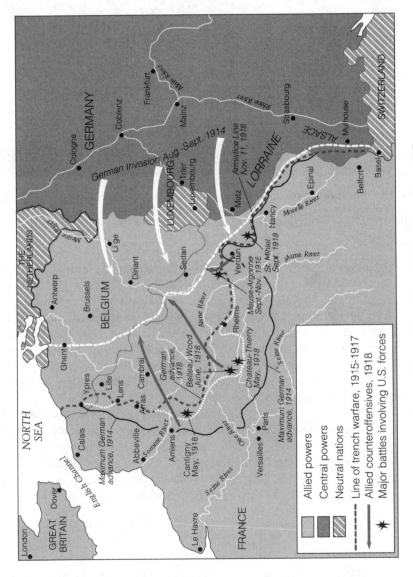

Figure 3.4 The Western Front. *Source: Moss, Rise of Modern America, p. 115.*

Map labels: NORTH SEA, GREAT BRITAIN, London, Dover, English Channel, Calais, Abbeville, Le Havre, THE NETHERLANDS, Antwerp, Ghent, Brussels, BELGIUM, Ypres, Lille, Lens, Arras, Cambrai, Somme River, Amiens, Paris, Versailles, Oise River, Seine River, Liège, Dinant, Sedan, Aisne River, Rheims, Meuse River, FRANCE, GERMANY, Cologne, Coblenz, Frankfurt, Mainz, Main River, Trier, Luxembourg, LUXEMBOURG, Metz, Verdun, Nancy, Moselle River, Marne River, Strasbourg, Mulhouse, Basel, Belfort, Epinal, SWITZERLAND, ALSACE, LORRAINE

German Invasion Aug.-Sept. 1914
Armistice Line Nov. 11, 1918
Maximum German advance, 1914
German advance, 1918
Belleau Wood June, 1918
Chateau-Thierry May, 1918
Meuse-Argonne Sept.-Nov. 1918
St. Mihiel Sept. 1918
Cantigny May, 1918

Legend:
Allied powers
Central powers
Neutral nations
Line of trench warfare, 1915–1917
Allied counteroffensives, 1918
Major battles involving U.S. forces

Figure 3.5   The most important campaign in which American doughboys fought was the Meuse-Argonne Offensive in the fall of 1918. In forty days and nights of continuous fighting, U.S. troops sustained heavy casualties on their way to victory.   *Source:* National Archives.

fought their way through the formidable defenses of the Hindenburg Line. To the West, French and British forces staged similar drives. On November 11, with German armies in full retreat and the German submarine threat neutralized by the Anglo-American convoy system, Germany signed an armistice. After four years of killing, the war had ended. The Allies were victorious. The Americans had lost 48,909 men killed, with another 230,000 wounded. Losses to disease, mainly influenza, eventually ran the death total to over 112,000.

Ten months before the armistice, Wilson had outlined a peace plan called the Fourteen Points. The first five points incorporated liberal principles upon which the peace must be based—open negotiations, freedom of the seas, free trade, disarmament, and a colonial system designed to serve the needs of subject peoples. The next eight points called for territorial transfers within Europe to implement the principle of "self-determination," which would permit all people possessing a distinct history, language, and ethnic identity to live under governments of their own choosing. The fourteenth point created an international agency to oversee the new order:

> a general association of nations . . . formed . . . for the purpose of affording mutual guarantees of political independence and territorial integrity to great and small states alike.[4]

In the final weeks of the war, Wilson lured the Germans into overthrowing the Kaiser and surrendering by promising them a peace based on the Fourteen

[4]Taken from a copy of The Covenant of the League of Nations, found in Armin Rappaport, *Sources in American Diplomacy*, p. 218.

Points. He then pressured the Allies into accepting the Fourteen Points, somewhat modified, as the basis for conducting the impending peace conference. It was brilliant diplomacy by Wilson. His efforts made him immensely popular among Europeans. He was the savior who had delivered them from a murderous war and promised a just and lasting peace.

THE HOME FRONT

The war experience had a profound effect on American lives and institutions. Government had to quickly mobilize a vast military force, gear the economy for war, and prepare the American people to meet the rigorous demands of belligerency. With sweeping grants of authority provided by Congress, President Wilson constructed a massive federal bureaucracy to mobilize the home front. The state intervened in American life in unprecedented ways, and tremendous power was concentrated in Washington. Business and government became partners for the duration of the war. Hundreds of new government agencies, staffed mostly by businessmen, came into being to manage the war effort. Many of these agencies clamped controls on the economy. The Railroad Administration took over the

Figure 3.6   During the war, thousands of women, hitherto excluded from many industrial occupations, found work in war industries. The wartime economic performance of women was a major factor in their getting the vote in 1920.   *Source:* National Archives.

operation of the nation's railroads when they had broken down under the strains of wartime usage. The federal government also took over the operation of the telephone and telegraph companies to avert strikes. The largest and most powerful wartime agency was the War Industries Board (WIB), created in July 1917. Headed by a friend of Wilson's, financier Bernard Baruch, the WIB coordinated the war economy. As the main instrument for mobilizing U.S. industrial capacity, the WIB imposed on American industry a system of production and price schedules keyed to military requirements.

Wilson proved to be a strong war leader, and America eventually delivered enough men and material to win the war. About 25 percent of American production went into the war effort. Farmers enjoyed boom years; they put more acreage into production, bought new farm machinery, and watched farm commodity prices soar. Farm income rose from $7.6 billion in 1914 to nearly $18 billion at war's end. Steel production doubled during wartime. The gross domestic product more than doubled between 1914 and 1920.

The most serious wartime economic problem was rampant inflation. One cause was the increased demand for goods created by Allied and U.S. government purchases. But the major cause was government refusal to set price controls or ration scarce commodities. The cost of living doubled between 1914 and 1920. The war cost the nation about $34 billion. The government financed one-third of its cost through taxes; the remaining two-thirds came from borrowing, including the issuing of "Liberty" bonds sold to the people.

The War Revenue Act enacted in October 1917 established a graduated personal income tax, a corporate income tax, an excess profits tax, and increased excise taxes on several items. Despite the higher war taxes, corporate profits during wartime reached historic highs. Net corporate income rose from $4 billion in 1913 to over $7 billion in 1917. The Revenue Act of 1917 effected a fiscal revolution in federal taxation. It greatly increased the importance of income taxes and made the principle of progression a permanent fixture of the national tax system. When the war began, about 25 percent of federal revenues derived from income taxes; at war's end, that figure had risen to 75 percent.

Organized labor also prospered in wartime. The president of the American Federation of Labor, Samuel Gompers, gave a no-strike pledge to the Wilson administration during wartime. He and other labor leaders also served on wartime government agencies. The National War Labor Board protected the right of workers to organize unions and to bargain collectively. Union membership rose from 2.7 million in 1916 to over 4 million in 1919. Wages rose, and many workers won an eight-hour day, but sharp inflation canceled most of the economic gains made by workers. To forestall worker discontent during the war years when labor was scarce, employers were forced to form company unions, and provide social and recreational activities for the families of their employees. In so doing, American industries moved one step closer to the welfare capitalism that would flourish in the 1920s.

Disadvantaged groups also benefited in wartime. With 16 percent of the workforce off fighting the war and with immigration curtailed, war industries turned to women, African Americans, and Hispanic Americans to fill job vacancies. The war brought about 1 million new women into the workforce. Most were young and single. Women entered many industrial trades hitherto closed to females, such as railroad engineers, drill press operators, and fork lift drivers. The movement of women into previously all-male job categories generated controversy. Women were often paid less than men for the same work and excluded from unions. When the war ended, most of the wartime gains women had made evaporated as male veterans returned to work and the country demobilized.

War-generated economic opportunities also opened up for African Americans. About 500,000 blacks fled poverty and oppression in the South, heading north for Detroit, Chicago, and New York City, where the war industries were located. Most African American migrants were young, unmarried males in search of work.

New jobs and improved living opportunities for blacks during wartime provoked a white backlash. The Ku Klux Klan revived. There were savage race riots in several cities. During the summer of 1919, race riots rocked over twenty Northern cities. The worst violence occurred in Chicago. On a hot July day, an incident at a beach started the rioting. Stabbings, burnings, and shootings went on for days. Thirty-eight people died, and over 500 were injured before National Guardsmen restored order.

PROPAGANDA AND CIVIL LIBERTIES

Civil liberties also were a casualty of war. The targets of abuse were German Americans, whose loyalty was suspect, and other Americans, who refused to support the war effort. These dissenters included pacifists, conscientious objectors, socialists, tenant farmers in Oklahoma who rebelled against the draft, and Progressive reformers like Robert La Follette and Jane Addams.

Soon after the United States entered the war, President Wilson appointed George Creel, a Progressive journalist from California, to head a Committee on Public Information (CPI). The CPI was a government propaganda agency created at Wilson's request to promote the war effort. It hired writers, scholars, filmmakers, and artists to mobilize public opinion in support of Allied war aims, and to arouse anti-German sentiments. CPI enthusiasts blanketed the country with their propaganda blitzes. CPI organizers created "Loyalty Leagues" in ethnic communities and sponsored parades and rallies in support of the war effort. CPI members also urged people to spy on their neighbors and report "suspicious" behavior to the authorities.

For a time there was vigorous debate between the supporters of the war and antiwar critics. Creel Committee speakers were the most prominent defenders of the American effort. Wilson himself provided the most potent ideological defense of the war when he called it a struggle to preserve democracy. Linking the war to democracy made it a crusade, tying it to the ancient doctrine of American mission. World War I became a war to save democracy, to save Europe from itself, and to redeem mankind. America would send its young manhood to rescue the Old World from itself. Most Americans embraced the notion of a great war to make the world a safe place for democratic governments. Against Wilson's and the Creel Committee's defenses of the war, the arguments of critics, however plausible, were ineffective. Isolationist, populist, and humanitarian arguments collapsed. The champions of war won easily the battle to define the symbolic meaning of the war and to win the allegiance of most citizens.

But their propaganda victory had its costs. Congress passed repressive legislation to curb dissent in wartime, which President Wilson strongly endorsed. The Espionage Act, enacted into law on June 5, 1917, gave the government powerful tools for suppressing opponents of war. It levied fines up to $10,000 and prison terms as long as twenty years for persons who obstructed military operations in wartime, and up to $5,000 fines and five-year sentences for use of the mails to violate the law. It also prohibited any statement intended to impede the draft or to promote military insubordination, and it gave the Postmaster General power to ban from the mails any publication he considered treasonous. Armed with the powers of the Espionage Act, Postmaster General Albert Burleson barred many German-American and socialist publications from the mails.

The Sedition Act, enacted in 1918, was more severe than the Espionage Act. It made it a crime to obstruct the sale of war bonds or to use "disloyal, profane, scurrilous, or abusive" language against the government, constitution, flag, and military uniforms. It made almost any publicly voiced criticism of government policy or the war effort a crime punishable by fines, imprisonment, or both. The Justice Department prosecuted over 2,000 people under the two acts, and many more people were bullied into silence. The most famous victim of wartime repression was Eugene Debs, the Socialist Party leader. Debs, who opposed the war, delivered a speech to a Socialist convention gathered in Canton, Ohio, on June 16, 1918. He spoke for over two hours. His speech was a general indictment of the American economic system and a call for socialism. He only mentioned the war in one passage, which follows:

> The master class has always declared the wars; the subject class has always fought the battles. The master class has had all to gain and nothing to lose, while the subject class has had nothing to gain and all to lose—especially their lives.[5]

Justice Department agents in the audience wrote down his words. Within two weeks, he was indicted by a federal grand jury for violating the Sedition Act. During his trial, Debs acknowledged the offending remarks. His defense consisted solely of having his attorneys argue that the Sedition Act violated the First Amendment and was therefore unconstitutional. His remarks were therefore within the boundaries of constitutionally protected free speech. His defense failed because the Supreme Court had previously upheld the constitutionality of both the Espionage

[5]Quoted in Ray Ginger, *Eugene V. Debs: The Making of an American Radical* (New York: Collier, 1949), pp. 376–77.

and Sedition Acts on the grounds that in time of war the government can legitimately curb free speech.

A jury convicted Debs on three counts of obstructing the draft, and he was sentenced to ten years in federal prison. His attorneys appealed the conviction. On March 10, 1919, the Supreme Court sustained his conviction. Debs began serving his sentence in April at a federal penitentiary near Atlanta, Georgia. Debs remained in jail until December 1921, when he was pardoned by President Harding. While in prison, Debs ran for president on the Socialist Party ticket during the 1920 election, campaigning from his Atlanta jail cell. He received 920,000 votes, the most votes he had ever received in his many presidential campaigns.

State and local governments also joined the war against dissent. Officials removed what they considered pro-German books from schools and libraries. Iowa refused to allow any foreign languages to be taught in its public schools. Teachers who questioned or challenged the war were dismissed.

Encouraged by government actions, vigilante groups and superpatriots went after alleged enemies and traitors. They became proficient at book burning, spying on their fellow citizens, harassing school teachers, vandalizing German-owned stores, and attacking socialists. Radical antiwar figures were frequent vigilante targets. In April 1918, a Missouri mob seized Robert Prager, a young man whose only crime was that he had been born in Germany. He was bound in an American flag, paraded through town, and then lynched. A jury acquitted his killers on the grounds that they had acted in self-defense.

The federal government, which encouraged and supported the campaign to crush dissent, concentrated its fire on the American Socialist Party and the Industrial Workers of the World, both of which openly opposed the war. By the end of the war, many leaders of both radical organizations were in jail, and their organizations were in disarray. Neither organization ever regained the following it had enjoyed before the war. President Wilson's own crusading zeal was partly to blame for the severe repression of the war years. The victims totaled 8,000 to 10,000 individuals who suffered repression, imprisonment, mob violence, or deportation. Wartime repression reached its apogee in the formation of numerous private, quasiofficial organizations to supplement official authority. The largest of these groups, the American Protective League (APL), claimed a membership in excess of 250,000. With the sanction of the Justice Department, the APL conducted private inquests into the loyalty of their fellow citizens that often veered toward vigilantism.

RED SCARE

Wartime suppression of dissent spilled into the postwar era during the Red Scare of 1919 and 1920. During this turbulent period, the targets of government prosecutors and vigilantes were Communists or Communist sympathizers, many of them aliens, suspected of plotting to overthrow the government. The Bolsheviks had come to power in Russia in November 1917. After the war, Communism did appear to be spreading westward. Communist uprisings occurred in Hungary and Germany. Americans fearfully looked at a Europe in chaos—shattered economies, weakened governments, and hungry millions struggling to survive in a world in which democracy appeared more imperiled than ever. In 1919, the Soviets established the Comintern to promote world revolution, and in that year, two Communist parties were formed in the United States. War had also disrupted American race relations and family life. Inflation and unemployment were both rampant. Nervous Americans, aware that a small, disciplined band of revolutionaries had taken advantage of mass misery, chaos, and government breakdown to come to power in Russia, feared that the Red revolution could spread to the United States.

Dramatic events occurring in this country in 1919 intensified fears of possible revolution and created the paranoid atmosphere that made the Red Scare possible. Over 3,600 separate strikes erupted during the year, idling over 4 million workers. A general strike in Seattle was particularly alarming. In May, dozens of letter bombs were mailed to prominent businessmen and politicians, although none of the intended targets were killed or injured. Police never caught the bombers, but unidentified anarchist terrorists were the prime suspects. In June, seven explosions in five Eastern cities destroyed homes, public buildings, and a rectory, killing one man. One of the explosions destroyed the downstairs front of the home of Attorney General A. Mitchell Palmer. July brought race riots in Cleveland and in the nation's capital, Washington, D.C. In September, the Boston police, who belonged to an American Federation of Labor (AFL) local, went on strike. The governor of Massachusetts, an obscure politician named Calvin Coolidge, became famous when he sent a terse telegram to the elderly Samuel Gompers, the president of the AFL, which read, "There is no right to strike against the public safety by anyone, anytime, anywhere." Coolidge also called out the Massachusetts National Guard, which restored order and broke the police strike.

Shortly after the police struck in Boston, the two largest strikes occurred—in the steel industry, when 350,000 workers walked off their jobs, and when 394,000 coal miners walked out. With two basic industries shut down, many people feared the beginning of a nationwide general strike. In reality, these strikes were not part of any master plan or conspiracy. Striking workers sought union recognition, reductions in their work schedules, and pay increases to offset the hyperinflation of the war years that had eroded their purchasing power. In both the coal and steel strikes, management refused to negotiate any of the workers' grievances and moved to break the strikes. The companies hired strikebreakers, "goon squads" to assault strikers, and launched a massive propaganda campaign in the media to convince the public that these strikes were indeed a Bolshevik conspiracy to overthrow the American government.

Attorney General Palmer stepped forward to save America from the Red revolution. Palmer was a Progressive Democrat with an excellent record of accomplishment, and he also harbored ambitions to win the 1920 Democratic presidential nomination. To combat the Red menace, Palmer hired a young attorney, J.

Edgar Hoover, to direct a newly created Bureau of Investigation. Hoover promptly placed thousands of people and many organizations under surveillance. State and local governments took various repressive measures. Vigilantes, many of them war veterans, swung into action.

In January 1920, using information collected by Hoover, Palmer ordered raids in thirty-three cities across the nation. Federal agents, assisted by local police, broke into homes and meeting halls. About 6,000 people were arrested in the raids. The Palmer raids were preemptive. Palmer and Hoover intended to catch the conspirators plotting their revolutionary actions, to seize their maps, weapons, and the plotters themselves before they could carry out their plans. There were massive civil liberties violations. Many of those arrested were not radicals, were not Communists, nor had they committed any crimes. Eventually most of those arrested during the raids were never formally charged and were released. About 550 aliens who had been picked up during the raids were deported for having violated immigration laws.

Investigators never uncovered any revolutionary plots; the Red revolution in America apparently existed only in the feverish imaginations of Palmer, Hoover, and their hard-core supporters. When Palmer's bold prediction that there would be a revolutionary uprising on May Day, 1920, proved mistaken, he lost credibility with most citizens. Some Progressive senators criticized Palmer's disregard of constitutional rights and due process. The Red Scare gradually died down as the strikes ended, the bombings ceased, the Communist threat in Europe receded, and the nation gradually returned to normal peacetime activities.

One episode from the Red Scare has endured. On April 15, 1920, a paymaster and his guard were shot dead during a robbery of a shoe factory in South Braintree, Massachusetts. Three weeks later, Nicola Sacco, a shoe worker, and Bartolomeo Vanzetti, a fish peddler, both Italian immigrants and committed anarchists, were arrested and charged with murder. During their trial, witnesses for the prosecution perjured themselves, and there were indications that the police had tampered with some of the evidence used against the two defendants. The trial judge, Webster Thayer, was biased against the defendants.

When a jury convicted them of first-degree murder and Judge Thayer sentenced them to death, many observers believed that Sacco and Vanzetti were innocent; they believed that the two men had been convicted of a capital crime because they were immigrants who held radical political beliefs. The governor of Massachusetts appointed a special commission to review the case. After a careful examination of the trial, the commissioners concluded that justice had been done.

The case of Sacco and Vanzetti assumed international proportions, engaging the passions of men and women around the globe. Despite the worldwide protests, both men were electrocuted on August 23, 1927. To this day, scholars of the case continue to argue its merits. Some believe that Sacco and Vanzetti were innocent victims of political vengeance. Others cite evidence that they believe establishes their guilt beyond a reasonable doubt. It is impossible to resolve the issue, so the debate goes on.

The Red Scare left many other casualties besides Sacco and Vanzetti. Panicky federal officials, overreacting to acts of terrorism, scapegoated groups of recently arrived immigrants. Thousands of people were sent to prison, suffered civil liberties violations, physical deprivations, severe emotional stress, or were deported. The give and take of free and uninhibited debate, essential to maintaining a healthy political democracy, was curtailed. Reformers no longer criticized institutions or proposed reforms. Radical political movements in America were badly wounded by combined wartime and Red Scare repressions. The government's vigorous campaign against its critics marred Wilson's otherwise excellent record as a war leader. He appeared to believe that free speech and radical dissent were luxuries America at war could not afford. A legacy of repression, intolerance, and conformity carried into the 1920s.

THE PEACE CONFERENCE

While the nation was in the throes of the Red Scare, President Wilson journeyed to Paris to try to implement his Fourteen Points. He faced many obstacles, some erected by his political rivals and some he created himself by making political mistakes. Wilson was the first U.S. president to travel abroad on a diplomatic mission during his term of office; his decision to go was controversial. Republican opponents suspected that Wilson desired to get all of the credit for the peace settlement; they accused him of having a "messiah complex." He also left behind some serious domestic problems.

Wilson made a serious blunder by making a blatantly partisan appeal to the voters for the election of a Democratic Congress in the 1918 elections on the eve of his departure for France. The voters, concerned mainly with domestic issues, particularly inflation, which had seriously eroded the purchasing power of the dollar, promptly elected Republican majorities to both houses of Congress. The outcome of the 1918 elections meant that any treaty Wilson brought back from Paris would have to be ratified by a Republican-controlled Senate. Wilson also lost considerable political stature in the eyes of foreign leaders with whom he would soon be negotiating. He made further political errors when he did not appoint any prominent Republican leaders to the delegation accompanying him to Paris, nor did he consult with the Senate Foreign Relations Committee before he left.

Everywhere Wilson traveled in Europe he was hailed by the people as the man who had delivered them from history's most terrible war. In Paris, 2 million people showered him with flowers. In Rome, huge crowds chanted "Veelson, Veelson." With the cheers of the crowds echoing in his mind, Wilson went to the conference, confident that he could achieve the liberal goals embodied in the Fourteen Points. But at the conference, he encountered more obstacles. The Allied leaders were determined to impose a harsh peace on the defeated Germans. The French Premier Georges Clemenceau, the British Prime Minister David Lloyd George, and

Figure 3.7 Europe after Versailles.
Source: Moss, *Rise of Modern America*, p. 128.

the Italian leader Vittorio Orlando, along with President Wilson, were the dominant voices at the peace conference. They had signed secret treaties during the war, and they came to Paris intending to enlarge their empires at Germany's expense. They dismissed Wilson's liberal war aims as being foolish and irrelevant.

Most of the conference sessions were held at Versailles, a suburb of Paris. The delegates met behind closed doors, immediately repudiating one of the Fourteen Points, which had called for open diplomacy. The victors demanded and received a clause written into the treaty, making Germany solely and absolutely responsible for causing the war and creating a reparations committee to determine the huge bill Germany would have to pay. (The commission later set the figure at $33 billion!)

Wilson fought hard for decolonization and self-determination, but he had to make many concessions to imperialism. Former German colonies were placed in a mandate system that gave the British, French, and Japanese access to their resources. Japan gained control over Germany's former sphere in China at Shantung and many of its former Pacific island colonies. France occupied Germany's Rhineland, but Wilson was able to carve several newly independent nations out of the remnants of the Austro-Hungarian empire—Austria, Hungary, Yugoslavia, Czechoslovakia, and Poland. He also helped to erect a *cordon sanitaire* of new nations—Finland, Estonia, Latvia, and Lithuania, along the western border of Russia—to contain Communism.

Wilson also fought hard for the League of Nations charter. He was willing to sacrifice many of his Fourteen Points because he believed that the League would moderate the harsh peace terms and ensure collective security in the postwar era. He wrote most of the new international organization's charter and created a League of Nations, dominated by a permanent council of the major powers, an assembly for discussion and debate among the member nations, and a World Court. The heart of the League's covenant was Article X, the collective security provision. It provided for League members to "respect and preserve as against external aggression the territorial integrity and existing political independence" of all members. Wilson also insisted that the League of Nations charter be incorporated into the body of the peace treaty, forming an integral part of it.

German representatives signed the Treaty of Versailles in June 1919 under protest, giving up huge chunks of their territory, 10 percent of their population, all of their colonies, and a large portion of their wealth. It was a vindictive, humiliating peace imposed on the defeated Germans by the victorious Allied powers. Its draconian terms violated the spirit and most of the specific terms of the Fourteen Points. Many commentators, including a young British economist John Maynard Keynes, foresaw the seeds of another war sown in the harsh terms imposed by the peacemakers at Versailles.

While the peace conference was still in session, Senator Henry Cabot Lodge, chairman of the Senate Foreign Relations Committee, circulated a resolution signed by thirty-nine senators, more than enough votes to block ratification, stating that the League charter did not protect American national interests. Wilson responded by writing language into the League covenant that exempted the Monroe Doctrine and U.S. internal matters from League jurisdiction.

FIGHT FOR RATIFICATION

As the terms of the treaty became known in the United States, criticism of it mounted from several sides. Many Progressives attacked Wilson's betrayal of so many of his Fourteen Points. Other liberals attacked the closed sessions, the concessions to imperialism, and the huge reparations imposed on Germany. Senator La Follette said the treaty's provisions confirmed his view that World War I was nothing more than a struggle between rival imperialisms. Conservative critics such as Senator Lodge feared that the League would limit American freedom of action in the postwar world. Isolationists feared that Article X would obligate the United States to provide armed forces to preserve collective security in the postwar world.

Wilson returned home to face his critics and to defend the treaty. He defended his concessions as being necessary compromises, and he pointed out that the League of Nations would eventually right all wrongs in the postwar era. Senator Lodge was unimpressed; he organized Senate opposition to the Treaty of Versailles.

He introduced fourteen reservations, modifications that he wanted made in the League charter, before he would approve the treaty. These reservations included exempting U.S. immigration policy from League decisions and giving Congress the right to approve any League resolution that implemented Article X.

The forty-nine Republican senators formed three distinct factions in the debate over ratifying the impending treaty. Twenty-three shared Lodge's view that all fourteen reservations would have to be implemented before they could support the treaty. They were called "strong reservationists." Twelve would support the treaty if some of the reservations were implemented. This group was known as the "mild reservationists." Fourteen isolationists opposed the treaty in any form and were determined to oppose it with or without reservations. These senators formed the "irreconcilables."

In the fall of 1919, President Wilson went on a nationwide speaking tour to rally public support for the treaty. In Pueblo, Colorado, a crowd of 10,000 heard one of Wilson's greatest speeches. He spoke of the thousands of American soldiers killed in France and of all the American boys whom the League of Nations one day would spare from death. That evening, utterly exhausted, Wilson collapsed in a spasm of pain. Four days later, back in the White House, he fell to the bathroom floor, knocked unconscious by a thrombosis which left him partially paralyzed. For six weeks he was incapacitated, unable to perform his duties as president, and for months after he could work only about an hour a day. His second wife, Edith Bolling Wilson, handled the routine business of government along with the president's personal secretary and doctor. The American people knew nothing of the seriousness of Wilson's condition. He slowly recovered, but never fully. Even after he had made a partial recovery, his judgment remained impaired. He refused to consider compromising with his Republican opponents in the Senate, and he demanded absolute loyalty from his Democratic supporters.

In November 1919, the Senate voted twice on the treaty. Before the votes were taken, the Senate Democratic floor leader, Gilbert Hitchcock, told the president that the treaty could not pass without reservations. He suggested that "it might be wise to compromise." Wilson responded curtly, "Let Lodge compromise!" The first vote taken was on the treaty, with Lodge's fourteen reservations attached. The Senate rejected it by a vote of 39 for to 55 against. Then a vote was taken without the reservations. It also failed by a vote of 38 to 53. The "irreconcilables" voted against it both times. They absolutely opposed American entry into the League of Nations. Senators representing Midwestern and Eastern states voted against the unamended version of the treaty. Democratic senators from the South favored it; Western senators were divided.

A third vote was taken in March 1920, with the reservations attached to the treaty. Wilson continued to insist that all Democrats oppose the treaty in amended form, refusing all efforts at compromise. Although twenty-one Democrats defied Wilson's order, the third vote fell seven votes short of the necessary two-thirds majority, 49 to 35. Had Wilson permitted Democrats to compromise with Republicans who favored mild reservations, he would have probably gotten the two-thirds majority required for passage, and the United States would have joined the League of Nations. Wilson's refusal to compromise doomed the treaty.

The fundamental conflict between Wilson and Lodge concerned two competing conceptions of the national interest. Was the national interest best served, as Wilson believed, by endorsing collective security? Or was it best served, as Lodge believed, by continuing to travel the traditional American path of unilateralism, as expressed in Washington's Farewell Address and the Monroe Doctrine? Looking out on the postwar world, many senators preferred unilateralism, which meant nonalignment and free choice over the binding commitments of collective security mediated through the League of Nations. Woodrow Wilson had a bold vision of a new world order based on internationalist collective security arrangements, but he was unable to find the arguments that would enable him to bring the requisite number of senators along with him.

Historians have speculated on the long-run historical significance of the failure of the United States to join the League of Nations. The United States emerged from World War I the preeminent world power economically and financially; it also had the potential to be the world's number one strategic power. Had the United States joined, the League of Nations would have been a stronger and more prestigious agency. During the 1930s, when aggressor nations began to disrupt the world order, the League of Nations, bolstered by American membership, might have been more effective at maintaining collective security and curbing aggression. World War II might have been avoided, or at least curtailed.

THE WAR EXPERIENCE

World War I was a brief, intense experience for the American people that had a profound and enduring effect on their lives and institutions. During the war, the federal government intervened in the economy and influenced the lives of Americans in unprecedented ways. The wartime cooperation of business and government stimulated the growth of trade associations that during the 1920s lobbied to protect their interests and minimize competition. The suspension of antitrust laws in wartime fostered the growth of monopoly that flourished during the 1920s. War accelerated the emergence of the modern corporate economy with its complex, usually cooperative, relations with the central government. The war effort was a modernizing experience that ended forever the old laissez-faire, voluntaristic order that had emerged from the nineteenth century.

The war also afforded American businessmen many world economic opportunities. They reduced the outflow of capital from this country by purchasing billions of dollars of American stocks and bonds sold on the market by foreign belligerents desperate for cash. They also reclaimed many of the dollars spent repatriating these securities by selling huge quantities of foodstuffs and ammunition to the Allies. When the Allies had exhausted their dollar accounts, American banks advanced them billions in credit, which reversed America's historic credit dependency on European investors. Americans also moved to take over markets previously dominated by Europeans, particularly in Latin America, at the expense of the British and Germans.

America emerged from the war as the world's preeminent economic power. U.S. trade accounted for about 30 percent of the world's commerce. American corporations opened subsidiaries in foreign lands. European companies, strained by the war, fell behind their U.S. rivals. America had also become the world's leading creditor. New York replaced London as the world's banking center. U.S. financiers and investors loaned billions of dollars to businesses and governments in Europe and Latin America.

Although the Versailles settlement disillusioned many Americans about the war and the United States did not join the League of Nations, the United States did not revert to isolationism after the war. American observers attended all League meetings, and America usually supported League actions. But the United States was wary about intervening in European affairs, given Europe's postwar economic and political disorder; America preserved its freedom of action.

The war changed the public mood. Photographs and films revealed the brutal, deadly reality of trench warfare, dramatically different from the soaring rhetoric of President Wilson's speeches. Veterans cared only about returning home and forgetting their war experiences. Americans quickly wearied of idealistic crusades; they became cynical about their internationalist commitments. They turned inward, closing out the larger world.

The war split the Progressive movement. Most Progressive intellectuals ended up supporting the war, sharing Wilson's belief that it was a war to save democracy. A left-wing Progressive minority, led by Jane Addams, retained its pacifistic beliefs and opposed the war. Progressivism emerged from World War I shaken and much weaker. Progressives who had viewed the war as a grand opportunity for America to reform the world—a chance to bring peace, democracy, and Progressive capitalism to Europe—also became disillusioned. Many lost their enthusiasm for crusades, both at home and abroad. Some reformers felt betrayed by European imperialists who had used the Paris conference to turn a glorious victory into a sordid settlement, perpetuating world problems and sowing the seeds of future wars. Progressivism had lost its innocence.

IMPORTANT EVENTS

1900	U.S. troops join an international force to suppress the Boxer Rebellion in China
1902	The Platt Amendment is imposed on Cuba
1903	The Panamanian revolution occurs
1904	Construction of the Panama Canal starts
	The Roosevelt Corollary to the Monroe Doctrine is announced
1905	Theodore Roosevelt mediates the settlement of the Russo-Japanese War

IMPORTANT EVENTS (continued)

1906	U.S. troops intervene in Cuba
1907	U.S. "Great White Fleet" embarks on world tour
1910	The Mexican revolution begins
1914	World War I begins
	U.S. troops intervene in Haiti
	Wilson sends U.S. sailors and marines to Vera Cruz, Mexico
1915	The HMS *Lusitania* is sunk by a German submarine
1916	Mexican general "Pancho Villa" invades the United States
	Wilson orders the U.S. Army to invade Mexico
	The *Sussex* pledge is given
1917	U.S. enters World War I
	The Russian revolution occurs
1918	Eugene Debs is jailed for violating the Sedition Act
	World War I ends
1919	The Treaty of Versailles is signed
	The Red Scare breaks out
1920	The U.S. Senate rejects the Treaty of Versailles

BIBLIOGRAPHY

John Dobson's *America's Ascent: The United States Becomes a Great Power, 1890–1914* charts the rise of the United States to world prominence during the Progressive Era. Howard K. Beale's classic *Theodore Roosevelt and the Rise of America to World Power* remains the best book on Progressive foreign policy. David McCullough's *The Path Between the Seas: The Creation of the Panama Canal, 1870–1914* is a beautifully rendered account of the Panama Canal project. David Healy's *Drive to Hegemony: The United States in the Caribbean, 1898–1917* charts the growth of the informal U. S. empire in the Caribbean area. All facets of the American experience during World War I have been written about. The best account of the causes of U.S. entry into the war is Ernest R. May's *The World and American Isolation, 1914–1917*. Ross Gregory's *The Origins of American Intervention in the First World War* is a short, lively account. A classic study of America and the war is Daniel M. Smith's *The Great Departure: The United States and World War I, 1914–1920*. Wilson's official biographer, Arthur Link, has written a good account of the president's diplomacy in *Wilson the Diplomatist*. The best military history of the American involvement in World War I is Edward M. Coffmann's *The War to End All Wars*. A. E. Barbeau and Florette Henri have written *The Unknown Soldiers: Black American Troops in World War I*. The role of women in the war has been recorded by Maurine W. Greenwald in *Women, War, and Work*. The best account of the home front in the war is David Kennedy's *Over Here: The First World War and American Society*. The attack on civil liberties in wartime is recorded in H.C. Peterson's and Gilbert Fite's *Opponents of War, 1917–1918*. The best account of the Red Scare and the man who led the attack on it is found in Stanley Coben's *A. Mitchell Palmer: Politician*. The best account of the fight over the League of Nations is by Thomas A. Bailey in *Woodrow Wilson and the Great Betrayal*.

4

The Twenties

THE 1920s were a complex, vital, and divided decade, an era of conflict and contrast. Americans during the 1920s were forward-looking and nostalgic, liberal and repressive, progressive and reactionary. A majority of Americans enjoyed a life of unprecedented material abundance and leisure. But poverty plagued millions of small farmers, unskilled workers, and nonwhite minorities.

The most important trend of the 1920s was the emergence of a new mass consumer culture that fostered changes in the ways many Americans worked, lived, and cared for one another. It brought changes in manners, morals, and personal identities as well. Consumerism also shifted the American sense of community—from communities based on shared values toward those based on shared styles of consumption. But beneath the surface unity of consumerism and mass participation in new games, sports, and recreations, cultural conflicts and tensions seethed. During the 1920s, American society was fragmented along many fault lines—urbanites versus rural folks, white Anglo-Saxon Protestants (WASPs) versus ethnics, white against black, and perhaps the profoundest divide: between those who embraced a modernist culture and those who retained traditional values.

The 1920s were a decade of great accomplishments in art, science, and technology. Creative American writers, musicians, and artists flourished. It also was a decade characterized by stunts, fads, contests, and commercial promotions. It was a time of prosperity, social change, and personal liberation. And it was an age that featured an upsurge in religious fundamentalism, the Ku Klux Klan, nativist immigration restriction, and repression of radicalism. Crime rates and church attendance both soared during this decade.

The 1920s also marked a beginning, a time when millions of Americans adapted to urban patterns of existence, centering their new urban lifestyles around ownership of automobiles and participation in the new urban mass consumerist culture. While many urbanites abandoned their former rural, agrarian ways of life, they retained some of its values. The decade was a time of transition. During the 1920s, the major historical developments of twentieth-century American life—technological change, urbanization, the growth of bureaucratic modes of organization, and the growth of the middle classes—accelerated rapidly. Between the end of World War I and the stock market crash that began in late October 1929, the shape of modern America emerged. The 1920s were the first recognizably modern decade.

A MOBILE PEOPLE

The 1920 census confirmed the major demographic trend underway in this country since the American Revolution, that a majority of American families had left the countryside and moved to the city. Of the 106,000,000 people living in America in 1920, 52 percent resided in towns and cities with populations of 2,500 of more. America had become an urban nation. That movement, from the hinterlands to the cities, accelerated during the 1920s. By 1930, 69,000,000 of the 123,000,000 inhabitants of the United States resided in urban areas, compared to the 54,000,000 who lived in the countryside.

Because the United States severely restricted immigration after 1921, and because the birth rate dropped sharply among middle-class families, the growth rate of the population during the decade of the twenties slowed to the smallest rate recorded since the nation began taking censuses in 1790. While national population growth rates slowed, the rate of urban population growth accelerated, especially in the nation's largest cities. The five American cities whose populations exceeded 1,000,000 people in 1920—New York, Chicago, Philadelphia, Detroit, and Los Angeles—collectively increased their populations by 50 percent during this decade.

During the 1920s, for the first time in American history, the nation's farm population showed a net decline. During the decade, more than 13,000,000 rural Americans left the countryside and moved to the urban frontiers. Construction of interurban highways and the advent of mass ownership of automobiles permitted rapid growth of suburban communities that sprung up around the nation's largest metropolitan centers. During the 1920s, the other great demographic trend, as old as the Republic itself, continued, as millions of families continued to move West, although during the 1920s they made that trek in cars rather than in covered wagons.

THE CONSUMER ECONOMY

The "roaring twenties" got off to a bumpy start. Americans suffered severe economic difficulties during 1919 and 1920. High inflation continued to plague consumers. As 1920 ended, recession occurred. Consumer demand fell, exports dropped as war markets closed, and farm income plunged. Unemployment

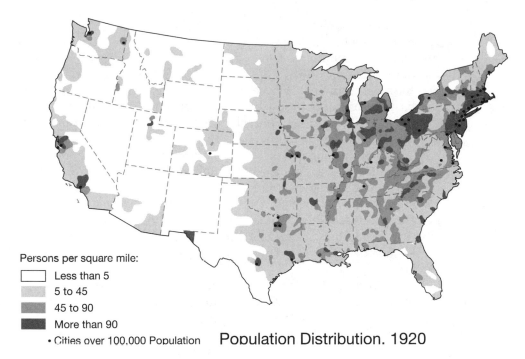

Population Distribution. 1920

Figure 4.1   Population distribution, 1920.   *Source:* George D. Moss, *Rise of Modern America*, p. 133.

soared—from 2 or 3 percent to over 12 percent, the highest rate since the severe de-pression of 1892 to 1894. Railroads went bankrupt, coal mines closed, and many New England textile mills shut their gates. Prosperity returned in 1923 and con-tinued until the collapse of the securities industry in 1929, one of the longest epochs of good times in American history.

During these seven good years, the American economy experienced a revo-lution in production. Industrial output nearly doubled and the gross domestic product (GDP) rose 40 percent. Between 1923 and 1929, the economy grew at the rate of 7 percent a year, the largest peacetime rate ever. During those years, national per capita income increased by 30 percent, from $520 to $681. Prices remained stable, even dropping for some items during the late 1920s. In an economy with no inflation and no rise in the cost of living, increased GDP meant significant increases in consumer purchasing power and rapidly rising living standards. By the mid-1920s, a typical middle-class household owned an automobile, a radio, a phono-graph, a washing machine, a vacuum cleaner, a sewing machine, and a telephone. A generation earlier, only the rich could have afforded these possessions, and they would have used technologically inferior versions.

The key to the new prosperity lay in the development and use of new tech-nological systems. The continuous flow assembly line, pioneered by Henry Ford at his River Rouge auto factory near Detroit, became standard in most American manufacturing plants. Electric motors replaced steam engines as the basic source of energy driving factory machines. By the end of the decade, electricity supplied 70 percent of all industrial power. Efficiency experts broke down manufacturing processes into minute parts in "time and motion" studies to show how men and machines could maximize output. Frederick W. Taylor, trained as a civil engineer, was the most prominent of these "time and motion" experts. Output per man-hour, the basic measure of productivity, increased an amazing 75 percent over the decade. In 1929, a workforce only slightly larger than the one employed in 1919 was producing almost twice as many goods.

Most of this explosive growth occurred in industries producing consumer goods—automobiles, appliances, furniture, clothing, and radios. Dozens of new consumer products flowed from America's factories and shops. New alloys, chemicals, and synthetics, such as rayon and cellophane, became commonplace. People bought processed, and canned foods and bought more machine-fashioned clothing. In addition, Americans discovered a whole new spectrum of products to buy—cigarette lighters, wristwatches, heat-resistant cookware, and sheer rayon stockings.

Service industries also expanded rapidly to accommodate the new affluence and leisure that middle-class Americans enjoyed. Specialty stores, restaurants, beauty shops, and movie theaters proliferated. Henry Ford's slogan, "Buy a Ford and Spend the Difference," best expressed the spirit of the New Era's rampant consumerism.

The automobile led the parade of technological marvels that made the American way of life the wonder of the world during the 1920s. During the decade, Americans bought 15 million new cars. Efficient production methods sharply dropped the prices of new cars, making what had been a plaything of the rich affordable to middle class and prosperous working-class families. Many families who could not afford a new car surely could buy a used one.

The man who put America on wheels was a Michigan farm boy who taught himself to be a mechanic. Henry Ford had two key insights: the first, in his words, was "Get the prices down to the buying power." He installed continuously moving assembly lines in his factories, which enabled him to manufacture 9,000 cars a day by 1925. During that year, a new Model-T rolled off the assembly lines every ten seconds! The second insight was to pay his workers top wages. The assembly line increased worker productivity significantly. It also simplified jobs, making them boring and fatiguing. The unrelenting and repetitious labor, driven at a furious pace by the logic of the assembly-line process, was simply more than many employees were willing to take. Absenteeism and high worker turnover became serious problems for Ford. In 1914, he raised wages to $5 a day, twice the prevailing rate in the industry. He also reduced working hours from forty-eight to forty a week, and cut the workweek from six to five days. Ford employees became the highest paid industrial workers in the world. Absenteeism and turnover dropped. Ford's sales and profits soared. Between 1922 and 1927, more than half of all new cars sold in America were Model-T's. By 1927, Ford had sold over 15 million of his famed "tin lizzies." During those years, Henry Ford became the nation's second billionaire.

A new Ford Model-T cost as little as $265 in 1925, and the joke went that you could get it in any color you wanted, as long as it was black. New or used Fords could be purchased by factory workers, who earned about $1,200 annually during the 1920s, and by office workers, who earned about $2,000 a year. For many car buyers, owning an automobile was more urgent than owning a home or the other consumer items of the era. An interviewer once asked a rural housewife why her family owned a car but not a bathtub. Her reply, "Bathtub? You can't go to town in a bathtub!"

Being a new mode of mass transportation may have been one of the Model-T's less important functions. Mass ownership of automobiles profoundly altered American culture. The automobile catered to the American desire for individual autonomy. Young people out for a drive could escape the watchful eyes of parents. Moralists feared that automobiles were becoming "bedrooms on wheels." An exasperated juvenile court judge, after hearing many cases of "sex crimes," most of

Figure 4.2   Henry Ford (right) beside the first automobile he built in 1896. His son, Edsel, inspects the ten millionth (!) "Model T" Ford car, which rolled off of the assembly line in 1924. *Source:* National Archives.

Figure 4.3   Traffic jams that clogged the streets of all large cities by the 1920s and that even began spilling into the suburbs, as shown here, were a sign that Americans had entered the Age of the Automobile.   *Source:* Michigan State Archives.

which had occurred in cars, pronounced the automobile "a house of prostitution on wheels."

Most of all, the motor car symbolized a new age of social equality. The average man could own America's most important status symbol. Henry Ford, the man who had put America on wheels, had accomplished a capitalist revolution. The son of an east European peasant could now drive along the same highways, view the same scenery, and enjoy the same trip just as much as a rich man. The car became the supreme symbol of the 1920s' version of the American dream, with its promise of mobility, freedom, and social equality.

The automobile stimulated extensive road construction and spawned many service industries that catered to drivers. Congress enacted a Federal Highway Act, which provided federal money for states to build highways. This enactment amounted to a public commitment to automobiles, trucks, and buses as the primary transportation system for the country henceforth. It also meant the beginning of a long decline in railroads, which had been the dominant transportation system since the 1860s. The Bureau of Public Roads began planning a national highway system. Service stations and a new kind of hotel, a motor hotel, later shortened to "motel," made its appearance. Insurance companies, previously concerned with life insurance, added auto insurance to their policy lines.

The oil industry, which had sold mostly kerosene to light people's homes, shifted production to gasoline, an unimportant product before the advent of the automobile, with its internal combustion engine. During the early 1920s, oil companies could not produce gasoline fast enough to meet the rapidly growing demands of a people taking to the roads. An "energy crisis" occurred. Long lines of angry motorists formed at the gas pumps. The price of a gallon of gas doubled, from 20 cents to 40 cents. The crisis faded in 1924, when Standard Oil gained access to British-controlled oil in Iraq, and once again U.S. drivers could exercise their divine right to drive wherever they wanted to, whenever they wanted to.

The automobile also altered urban residential patterns. People now drove downtown to work and to shop instead of catching a trolley. Suburbs, previously located within the outer neighborhoods of cities, now evolved as satellite cities, often ten to twenty miles away from central cities. Los Angeles was the first American metropolis to develop during the age of the automobile. It took shape as a series of neighborhoods and shopping districts, sprawling over a large geographic area, all connected by long streets and highways.

As a greater percentage of the nation's factories turned out consumer goods, prosperity hinged increasingly on consumption. The more goods consumers purchased, the more productivity would increase, at the same time bringing down costs. Lower production costs allowed lower commodity prices, thus increasing sales further. Everything in this new cycle of 1920s' prosperity depended on consumer purchases. In the new consumer economy enveloping American society during the 1920s, wives and husbands ceased to be merely homemakers and workers and became consumers. Consuming became their most important economic function. Increasing consumption produced two of the most important innovations of the 1920s, massive advertising campaigns to encourage people to buy and making credit available to help them pay for their purchases.

The most distinctive feature of the new consumer economy was its emphasis on advertising. The advertising industry, which developed during the Gilded Age, centered on Manhattan's Madison Avenue and became a big business during the 1920s. Advertisers sought to create consumer desires for new products by identifying them with the good life; sometimes they employed psychology to appeal to consumer needs, fears, anxieties, and sexual fantasies.

Advertisers viewed human beings as being infinitely suggestible. Edward Bernays, who became America's leading public relations expert during the 1920s, believed that opinions were formed by groups, not by individuals. He insisted that advertisers appeal to group leaders. Sell a new product by getting celebrities or socially prominent people to endorse it. Hire Babe Ruth to sell athletic equipment to kids. Hire a movie actress to sell cigarette smoking to women. Bernays strongly believed in the ability of an educated elite to use the persuasive power of advertising to sell the growing cornucopia of consumer goods and services to the receptive masses. He once snorted; "The average person does not know what he wants until we tell him."

An adman became a best-selling author. Bruce Barton, who wrote *The Man Nobody Knows* (1925), expounded a new gospel of business. The man nobody knew was Jesus of Nazareth. According to Barton, Jesus was the greatest salesman who ever lived and "the founder of modern business." This Madison Avenue Jesus "picked up twelve humble men and created an organization that won the world." The new consumerism was enhanced by advertising and fueled by credit. Installment buying or time payment plans flourished. In 1919, General Motors created the General Motors Acceptance Corporation (GMAC), the nation's first consumer credit organization. By the end of the decade, Americans were buying most of their cars, radios, appliances, furniture, and clothes on credit. By 1929, consumer debt had reached $7 billion, twice the size of the federal budget.

During the 1920s, a revolution in communications and the rapid expansion of advertising combined to create a consuming public that possessed up-to-date information about the latest products, services, fads, and fashions. People spent much time and energy learning about new products and the latest trends—of wanting what others had, of "keeping up with the Joneses." H. L. Mencken, one of the leading journalist-pundits of the twenties, observed that advertisers employed the new communications media to create a new human species in America, *Homo consumerins.*

National chain stores proliferated during the 1920s, at the expense of small, local businesses. Atlantic and Pacific Tea Company (A & P) and Safeway dominated the retail food market. Giant drug chains like Rexalls spread from coast to coast. J. C. Penney opened thousands of clothing stores. As the 1920s ended, chain stores in many retail fields had opened outlets in nearly every town and city in the land. They offered their customers good value and courteous service, and they generated huge profits from volume sales.

Corporations continued to be the dominant economic unit of the 1920s. Large corporations often had a million or more individual stockholders, and one individual rarely held more than a few percent of the stock. Most corporations generated large profits from volume sales during the 1920s, enabling them to finance research and expand production out of revenues, thus freeing them from dependence on bankers and financiers. A salaried bureaucracy of executives and plant managers formed a new elite. Many of these new corporate managers were college graduates, trained in the techniques of "scientific management" taught at the new schools of business that were appearing on the campuses of the nation's elite universities. Professing a new ethic of social responsibility, professional corporate managers ran their giant firms independently of any external controls or restraints.

Big business grew bigger during the 1920s. Over 8,000 mergers occurred between 1920 and 1928, as thousands of small firms, unable to compete with big companies, were taken over. As the decade ended, about 200 giant corporations owned half of the nation's wealth. In almost every manufacturing sector, huge, integrated companies were in control—in automobile manufacturing, steel milling, oil refining, meat processing, flour milling, mining, railroading, and countless other industries. They dominated not only production but marketing, distribution, and financing. Antitrust activities faded in an age of economic giants and the continuing centralization of economic activity.

Organizational activities, fostered by Progressive reformers before and during the war, flourished during the 1920s. Business and professional associations worked to protect their members' interests. Retailers and small manufacturers formed trade associations to exchange information, coordinate planning, and promote their industries. Farm bureaus and farm cooperative associations lobbied for government help and tried to stabilize declining commodity prices. Lawyers, engineers, doctors, college professors, teachers, scientists, and other professionals formed associations and societies to promote their interests. The Progressive organizational impulse had turned from reform to professionalism.

Uniformity and standardization, the dominant characteristics of modern mass production processes, became a major cultural influence. An Iowa farmer bought the same kind of car that an auto worker in Detroit or a businessman in Los Angeles purchased. He also bought the same groceries, the same health and beauty aids, and the same underwear, and listened to the same radio programs, saw the same movies, and read the same comic strips. Regional differences in lifestyles and speech accents declined. Americans began to look, act, and sound more and more alike. Consumerism fostered conformity in manners and morals.

THE NEW URBAN NATION

The census for 1920 showed that a majority of Americans lived in cities for the first time in the history of the Republic. Urbanization continued at a rapid pace throughout the decade. Millions of Americans left farms and small towns and moved to the cities. Between 1920 and 1930, cities with populations of 250,000 or more added 8 million more people. New York, America's great metropolis, grew 25 percent during the decade. Detroit, the site of America's expanding auto industry, more than doubled its population during the same period. Hordes of Iowans and other Midwestern migrants moved to Los Angeles, the burgeoning metropolis of southern California. Southerners left their farms and hamlets for Northern industrial cities. Miami was the one Southern city that grew rapidly during the 1920s. Its flourishing real estate boom attracted thousands seeking retirement or vacation homes.

African American sharecroppers fled the deteriorating Southern agricultural economy for Northern cities, continuing a trend that had begun during World War I. African American newcomers to city life were forced to squeeze into Northern ghettos as they discovered that better neighborhoods were closed to them. The black populations of New York, Chicago, and Detroit doubled during the decade.

Thousands of Northern African Americans during the early 1920s joined a black nationalist movement led by Jamaican immigrant Marcus Garvey. Garvey denounced all white people as corrupt and preached a doctrine of black separatism. He promoted racial pride and black capitalism. He also started a "back to

Africa" campaign and founded a steamship line to foster emigration. Later, Garvey's steamship company went bankrupt, and he was deported for mail fraud. His movement quickly disintegrated, but Garvey had tapped a wellspring of black grievances and aspirations.

By the 1920s, people of Hispanic descent had inhabited regions within the United States for nearly 400 years. At the turn of the century, approximately 250,000 Mexican Americans lived in California, Texas, Colorado, and in the territories of New Mexico and Arizona. During the first decade and a half of the twentieth century, *campesinos,* fleeing poverty and revolutionary upheaval, poured into the United States. During the 1920s, American farmers, facing labor shortages created when workers flocked to the cities seeking industrial jobs, opened a campaign to attract farm workers from Mexico. Hispanic emigrants also poured into America's cities during the 1920s. They emigrated to Detroit, Chicago, and Kansas City. By the end of the decade, many Northern industrial cities had thriving communities of Mexican immigrants. More Mexicans migrated to the growing cities of Los Angeles, Tucson, and San Antonio. These Mexican immigrants crowded into low-rent, inner-city districts to form their own communities, or *barrios.* In these *barrios,* Hispaniphones settled into a vibrant immigrant life of family and festivals, churchgoing, and hard work.

During the 1920s, thousands of Puerto Ricans moved to mainland America. They represented a surplus rural population attracted by economic opportunities in the states. Large Puerto Rican communities were formed in Brooklyn and Manhattan. These migrants found work in hotels, restaurants, and domestic service. Their children found their first educational opportunities in the public schools of New York.

Along with technology and consumer spending, construction was one of the booming industries that promoted economic growth during the "roaring twenties." Skyscrapers were tossed up in every large city in the country. These towering buildings of concrete and steel were uniquely American contributions to urban landscapes. The major cause of this massive building upward was a sharp rise in land values generated by industrial expansion and rapid population growth. New York led the way. Manhattan got a new skyline of tall towers topped by the Empire State Building. The skyscraper became a major symbol of the new American economy and the mighty metropolis on Manhattan Island was the dynamic center of American civilization, its commercial and cultural capital.

Residential construction grew rapidly as middle-class families moved from the big cities to the surrounding suburbs. Rising prosperity and the coming of automobiles made fringe areas surrounding central cities accessible. The greatest urban growth of the decade took place in middle- and upper-middle-class enclaves surrounding New York, Chicago, and Los Angeles. These suburbs often incorporated, developed their own city services, and resisted annexation to core cities. Suburbanites fought to preserve local control and to avoid the dirt, noise, crime, and higher taxes of the big cities. Road construction also made suburban life possible and pumped millions of dollars into the economy.

It was in the cities and suburbs of the roaring twenties that the new mass consumer culture flourished. Urbanites dined out, went to movies, and attended sporting events. They embraced fads such as crossword puzzles, mahjong, miniature golf, and marathon dancing. Most "speakeasies" (illegal bars and clubs open during Prohibition) were located in cities where patrons could drink, wear garish clothes, and listen to jazz. Cities also were the center of a growing social and cultural pluralism in American life.

WOMEN AND FAMILY LIFE

Birth control became more effective and more widely practiced during the 1920s. Birthrates and family size dropped sharply. Average family size shrunk from six or seven members in 1900 to four or five members by 1930. Divorce rates rose sharply. In 1920, there was one divorce for every eight marriages; by 1929, the ratio of divorces to marriages was 2 : 7. Young people during the 1920s were spending more years in schools, lengthening adolescence and postponing the time when they would marry or enter the workforce. High school enrollment quadrupled between World War I and 1930; by 1929, one-third of all high school graduates entered college. More women than men were going on to college as the decade ended.

Schools and peer groups played a much more important role in socializing children than ever before. Classes, sports, and social clubs brought young people of the same age together. A middle-class youth culture made its appearance with its own values, consumer preferences, and lifestyles, often conflicting with those of their parents'. Prolonged adolescence led to strains on the family, as youngsters rebelled against parental authority and their Victorian moral standards. Novelist F. Scott Fitzgerald recorded the heavy drinking, casual sexual encounters, and constant search for thrills and excitement among upper-class youth in his first successful novel, *This Side of Paradise*. The theme of rebellion characterized this generation of "flaming youth."

Improved nutrition, health care, and easier lives caused the average life expectancy to increase from fifty-four years to sixty years during the decade. The elderly were the most rapidly growing demographic group in the population. Retirement communities sprang up in the warm climes of Florida and southern California. It was also during the 1920s that median female life expectancy exceeded male life expectancy for the first time in history. Lengthened female life expectancy was caused mainly by reducing the dangers of pregnancy and childbearing. And infant mortality rates decreased by two-thirds during the 1920s.

The elderly emerged during the twenties as a large, growing population category with distinct needs and preferences. Many of the elderly were poor because of forced retirement and lack of pensions. Progressive reformers of the 1920s devised ways of meeting the economic needs of some of the elderly poor. Most states implemented old age pensions during the decade, and the principle of old age support through pensions, insurance programs, and retirement homes was firmly established.

The new lifestyles of the 1920s had a major effect on the lives of women. Middle-class women had fewer children to rear. Their houses often had central heating and hot water heaters. They used vacuum cleaners, electric irons, electric sewing machines, electric stoves, and washing machines to lighten domestic duties. They bought preserved foods, ready-made clothing, and mass-produced furniture. Women were no longer domestic producers or beasts of burden as their mothers and grandmothers had been. But labor-saving devices and ready-made products did not allow most middle-class women to become women of leisure. Performance standards were raised. Homes had to be kept immaculate. Nurturing responsibilities toward children expanded, even though there were fewer children to care for. Women also were household managers and were responsible for much of their family's consumer spending.

Although domesticity remained the most common realm of women, millions joined the labor force during the 1920s. In 1920, about 8 million women worked outside of the home. By 1930, about 11 million had jobs. But traditional patterns of gender discrimination continued during the 1920s. Women earned about half of what men did for comparable work; most women worked in "female jobs" where few males were found—teachers, nurses, typists, bookkeepers, clerical workers, department store salesclerks, domestics, waitresses, maids, and hairdressers. The largest increases in women's employment came in the general category of office work. The number of women working in factories did not increase during this decade. The number of women working in some professions even declined during the 1920s. The number of women doctors dropped by half. Medical schools imposed strict quotas, and most hospitals would not accept female interns. Although women earned about one-third of all graduate degrees awarded during the 1920s, they made up only 4 percent of college faculties. Most of the professions remained mostly all-male bastions.

Before the 1920s, most women who worked had been young, single females from poor backgrounds who had to work. A few had been middle-class careerists, mostly unmarried doctors, attorneys, scientists, or academics. During the 1920s, married women entered the labor force in significantly increasing numbers. Some married women were responding to the pressures of poverty; more were working to supplement family incomes and to enhance their family's lifestyles. Most married working women claimed that they worked because of economic necessity, but their definition of need reflected new consumer values. Their families "needed" radios, a new car, and a larger home. But most married women did not work outside of the home during the 1920s; only about 10 percent had jobs.

Feminists continued to be active during the 1920s. With the battle for the vote won, they concentrated on issues involving women in the workplace. Feminists pushed for greater economic opportunity and equal pay. Alice Paul, leader of the National Women's Party, supported an equal rights amendment introduced in Congress in 1923. Some feminists, many of whom had fought for the vote, such as the League of Women Voters, opposed the equal rights amendment because they believed that women needed special legal protections, particularly laws guaranteeing them a minimum wage and setting a ceiling on their hours of work. They were familiar with the conditions under which women worked, and they knew that the death and accident rates for working women were higher than for men. They feared that the courts would nullify these protective laws for women if the equal rights amendment (ERA) was ratified. The drive to enact the ERA during the 1920s failed. So did feminist campaigns to improve the economic status of women and to abolish child labor. Feminists succeeded in getting the Sheppard-Towner Act (1921) passed, which authorized federal aid to states to establish maternal and infant health care programs. Also, feminists continued to be involved in local and state progressive reform politics, pushing for consumer protection legislation and for the inclusion of women on juries.

A generational change had a major effect on feminism during the 1920s. New images of femininity emerged. Young women were more interested in individual freedom of expression than they were in political reform or social progress. Some adopted what H. L. Mencken called the "flapper image." Short skirts and bobbed hair, signals of sexual freedom, spread on college campuses and in offices. Young women rouged their cheeks, smoked cigarettes, swore, drank at parties, danced to the beat of "hot jazz" combos, and necked in the back seats of automobiles. Premarital sex increased as Victorian inhibitions declined.

Popular female movies stars like Clara Bow, the "It Girl," and Gloria Swanson, a passionate screen lover, became role models for young women. The mass media promoted the flapper image as a new woman whose manners and morals resembled her male counterparts. The androgynous aspects of the flapper image, particularly bobbed hair, small breasts, and short skirts, suggested that many young women in the twenties equated liberation with emulating men. Young, middle-class women were liberated from many social restraints of the prewar era. Flappers competed with men on the golf course and in the speakeasies. They expected sexual fulfillment before and during marriage.

It is important to not exaggerate the extent to which women participated in the new trends and styles of the 1920s. A contemporary survey of over 2,000 middle-class women found that only 7 percent of them had engaged in premarital sex. The typical American woman of the 1920s did not work outside of the home, and she lived in a household that could not afford most of the new labor-saving appliances of the age. The average housewife-mother spent about fifty hours a week performing household duties. According to feminist historian June Sochen, "In the 1920s, as in the 1790s, marriage was the only approved state for women."

POPULAR CULTURE

Even as they tried to preserve old values, many Americans were irresistibly attracted to the new order. During the 1920s, millions of Americans turned enthusiastically to varieties of recreation, as participants and as spectators. In 1929, Americans spent over $4 billion on play, a figure that would not be surpassed until 1955. The entertainment industry became big business as promoters hurried to satisfy the great American need for fun. Fads flowered, and ballyhoo flourished.

Fashions and fads flashed across the recreational landscape during the twenties. Early in the decade it was mahjong, a parlor game imported from China. In 1924 and 1925, crossword puzzles seized the popular fancy. Every newspaper and mass circulation magazine soon carried crossword puzzles. A new card game invented by a group of American socialites, contract bridge, became enormously popular. In the late 1920s, miniature golf became the rage. Throughout the decade, various dance crazes like the Charleston and the Black Bottom attracted millions of enthusiasts.

THE MOVIES

Americans became avid moviegoers during the 1920s. Motion pictures became a mass medium and big business. Movies also became a major American art form. Almost every community had at least one movie theater. Movie houses ranged from small-town storefronts to big city luxury palaces. In 1925, 60 million people attended movies each week. By 1930, the figure had reached 100 million, nearly twice the average weekly church attendance.

The most popular movies were grand spectaculars such as *The Ten Commandments* (1923), slapstick comedies starring Charlie Chaplin, and adventure films like *Robin Hood* (1925), starring Douglas Fairbanks. Movie romances also had large audiences. John Gilbert and Greta Garbo were the most famous screen lovers of the silent film era, their passionate lovemaking enthralling audiences everywhere. Moviegoers idolized and often identified with film stars, who ranked among the reigning celebrities of the 1920s. Mass circulation gossip magazines offered lurid details of their private lives to credulous fans.

The most ballyhooed movie star of the 1920s was Rudolph Valentino, an Italian immigrant whose passionate Latin machismo caused women in the audience to sigh and faint. Valentino's films played upon sexual fantasies and thrilling encounters with evil. In his most famous role he played an Arab sheik, a combination kidnapper and seducer, who lifted women into his arms and carried them into his tent. When he died of ulcers at age thirty-one in 1926, his New York funeral turned into a public spectacle. Police had to fend off thousands of weepy women who tried to throw themselves on his coffin.

The decade of the 1920s was the great age of silent films. The beginning of their end came when sound was introduced in *The Jazz Singer*, starring Al Jolson, in 1927, although studios continued to turn out silent films into the 1930s. Sound had its hazards, however, for some of the great silent screen stars turned out to have squeaky or harsh voices, unsuitable for talking films. John Gilbert was sound's

Figure 4.4   Rudolph Valentino was Hollywood's greatest romantic idol during the 1920s (pictured here with co-star Nita Naldi). *Source:* The Museum of Modern Art/Film Stills Archive.

most famous casualty. The great screen lover had to retire from movie-making for want of a voice.

SPECTATOR SPORTS

Spectator sports also boomed in the 1920s. Each year, millions of fans packed stadia and arenas to watch college football, major league baseball, auto racing, boxing, horse racing, and tennis. Sporting events provided excitement, thrills, and drama. Sportswriters and radio sportscasters described athletic contests and reported results. The new media information technologies such as the national wire services, radio, and film newsreels quickly disseminated box scores and outcomes of sporting events to huge national audiences. National sporting events also served to unite Americans who were divided along ethnic, racial, class, and regional lines.

Baseball was the most popular spectator sport of the 1920s. Attendance at major league games increased vastly in the early 1920s, when owners introduced a livelier ball that enabled powerful hitters to belt home runs into the stands, and sometimes out of the ballpark. More than 20 million spectators attended games in 1927. The most popular baseball player of the 1920s, the most famous celebrity athlete of his era, was George Herman "Babe" Ruth. The Babe hit sixty home runs in 1927 and led his New York Yankees to a World Series sweep over the Pittsburgh Pirates. Ruth was legendary for his off-the-field exploits as well. He was a glutton for food, drink, and women. People tended to forgive the Babe for his transgressions, since he was a remarkable athlete and spent a lot of his time visiting with youngsters and signing autographs.

Second in popularity only to Ruth was Jack Dempsey, a powerful fighter, who was heavyweight champion from 1921 until 1926. Dempsey's fights were often savage brawls, and they drew huge gates. In a fight with Luis Firpo, an Argentine slugger, Dempsey got knocked out of the ring in the first round. He managed to crawl back through the ropes and knock Firpo out in the third round. He lost his title to Gene Tunney, a skilled boxer, in 1926, through a decision. He failed to regain his title in a rematch with Tunney the following year at Soldier Field in Chicago. Dempsey's second fight with Tunney drew 145,000 fans, the largest crowd ever to attend an athletic event in the United States.

Other athletes enjoyed celebrity status in the 1920s. William "Big Bill" Tilden was a champion tennis player. Earl Sande was the finest jockey of his era. Gertrude Ederle, a seventeen-year-old schoolgirl, became the first woman to swim the English Channel, and she set a new record doing it. The greatest college football player of the decade was Harold "Red" Grange, a running back for the University of Illinois and a three time All-American. Grange was a talented broken-field runner who thrilled spectators with his long touchdown runs. He became a celebrity while still in college, receiving lucrative offers from movie studios and real estate promoters.

AN AMERICAN HERO

The greatest hero of the 1920s was a young aviator named Charles Augustus Lindbergh. In May 1927, Lindbergh flew solo nonstop across the Atlantic from New York to Paris in thirty-three and a half hours in a small monoplane named *The Spirit of Saint Louis,* which had been specially built for the attempt. Eight other flyers had died previously trying to cross the ocean. Lindbergh alone succeeded. His feat was the greatest news story of the decade. President Coolidge sent the cruiser USS *Augusta* to bring Lindbergh home. As he sailed up the Potomac, he received an honor previously reserved only for visiting heads of state, a 21-gun salute.

Lindbergh was a handsome, modest, middle-class Midwesterner who did not try to cash in on his fame. His quiet personality, at variance with the frantic hype and ballyhoo of the decade, caused Americans to honor him even more. Lindbergh's flight also represented a triumph of American industrial technology. It was

Figure 4.5 **In a hero-worshipping age, Charles A. Lindbergh was the greatest hero of all for his solo flight across the Atlantic in May 1927. Here he stands before "The Spirit of St. Louis," the plane in which he made his historic flight.** *Source:* Library of Congress.

the machine that had been specially configured for the long flight as much as the man who made the crossing possible. A contemporary observer also suggested that the intense emotional response Lindbergh provoked in this country was a reaction to his clean-cut appearance, WASP background, and moral character. In an age of ballyhoo and change, Lindbergh affirmed traditional values. Will Rogers, an actor and a humorist, said Lindbergh's flight proved that "someone could still make the front pages without murdering anybody."

THE ETHIC OF PLAY

In their heedless pursuit of fun, Americans in the 1920s became lawbreakers and supporters of organized crime. Americans had voted for Prohibition, which took effect on January 1, 1920. The law was effective initially. Per capita liquor consumption dropped sharply. By some estimates, alcohol consumption was reduced by as much as half. Prohibition was especially effective in the South and Midwest, where it had strong popular support. But from the start, enforcement was underfunded and understaffed. The Prohibition Bureau, charged with enforcing the law, had a small budget and only a few thousand agents, many of whom were inept, corrupt, or both. After 1925, enforcement declined in urban areas. Smuggling and the home manufacture of liquor increased. Many people made beer, wine, and "bathtub" gin. Foreign booze was brought across the nation's long borders and shorelines. Local police stopped enforcing Prohibition in many cities. One unintended social consequence of Prohibition brought an advancement to women's rights. Whereas saloons had discriminated against women, at least respectable women, speakeasies welcomed them.

Prohibition represented both cultural and class legislation. Support for the movement had always run deepest in particular Protestant churches, especially the evangelical Baptists and Methodists. Alcohol reformers always retained powerful antiurban and nativist biases. Traditionalists might celebrate their noble victory over demon rum, but among modern urbanites, Prohibition generated only resentment and wholesale evasion.

Illegal drinking became a big business with millions of customers. Criminal organizations moved into the illicit liquor industry. The most notorious of these crooked businesses was headed by Al Capone, whose mob seized control of the liquor and vice trade in Chicago. Capone maintained his power for years through bribery, threats, and violence. During the 1920s, more than 500 gangland murders occurred on the streets of Chicago, many involving Capone's hired gunmen. Capone's organization took in an estimated $60 million a year. He was immune from local reprisals, but he ran afoul of the Federal Bureau of Investigation (FBI). Capone was convicted of income tax evasion and sent to prison in 1931.

Americans during the 1920s were caught between two conflicting value systems. They retained the traditional ethics of hard work, thrift, and sobriety, but they also embraced the new ethic of play. They turned to mass entertainment provided by nightclubs, movies, sports, and radio. They also took up individual hobbies and amusements like photography, stamp collecting, playing and listening to music, and camping. Most such activities were neither illegal nor immoral, but millions of Americans were willing to break the law or reject traditional morality if such restrictions interfered with their pursuit of pleasure.

POPULAR WRITERS

During the 1920s, Americans read millions of books, but most did not read serious works of literature. Most critically acclaimed writers of the 1920s whose books have become classics did not sell well during the decade. The most popular writers of the 1920s, whose books sold millions of copies and who perennially topped the best-seller charts, included Geneva "Gene" Stratton-Porter, Harold Bell Wright, Zane Grey, and Edgar Rice Burroughs.

Gene Stratton-Porter became rich writing novels that affirmed traditional values during a transitional era. Her books championed the virtues of optimism, a love for nature, and triumph over adversity. Harold Bell Wright, formerly a minister, was a prolific writer, who used his novels as didactic vehicles to preach the gospel of hard work and clean living. Zane Grey was the most popular of the 1920s' novelists. His books appeared on the best-seller lists every year during the decade, and total sales exceeded 20 million copies. Grey's novels usually were set in a highly romanticized version of the Old West and many were transformed into Western movies. Edgar Rice Burroughs made his fame and fortune as the author of the Tarzan books. Burroughs' novels were purely escapist fare—he wrote about the adventures of a white man in African who had been reared by apes. Tarzan became the inspiration for cartoons, comic books, and dozens of films starring several different athletic actors playing the lead role.

Americans during the twenties also were enthusiastic readers of newspapers. The trend toward consolidation occurring in the industrial economy also happened in the newspaper business. Ownership of newspapers was increasingly concentrated in the hands of a few media magnates such as William Randolph Hearst. Even though newspaper readership increased by millions during the decade, in 1929 there were 2,000 fewer papers than in 1919. Tabloid newspapers made their appearance during the 1920s, led by the pioneer in the field, *The New York Daily News*. Tabloids sensationalized and simplified news stories—feeding their readers a steady diet of lurid stories about scandals, crime, sex, and murder.

LITERATURE

The most impressive cultural achievement of Americans during the 1920s was a vast outpouring of serious literature. America produced a generation of literary intellectuals who attacked the new consumer culture and its values. Many of the young writers had been involved in the war and came home disillusioned by the failed crusade to save democracy. The war experience shattered their lives and destroyed their Progressive idealism. They were bewildered by rapid social change and appalled by the shallow materialism of the New Era. They condemned the excesses of the new business civilization and lamented the loss of American innocence.

The new writers included Ezra Pound, who developed new forms of poetic expression. He abandoned rhyme and meter to use clear, cold images that powerfully conveyed reality. Pound called the Western world that had waged four years of destructive warfare a "botched civilization, an old bitch gone in the teeth." He wrote of the hellish experience of American soldiers fighting on the Western Front and then coming home to a society that they found empty and disillusioning.

T.S. Eliot, born in St. Louis, Missouri, moved to England, later becoming a British citizen. His greatest poem, published in 1922, is *The Wasteland*. It expressed Eliot's profound despair about modern life and its loss of faith. He evoked images of sterility and fragmentation, depicting contemporary civilization as a spiritual and moral wasteland. *The Wasteland* became an anthem for the disillusioned writers of the postwar generation.

From the depths of their profound disillusionment this generation of young writers forged a major new American literature. The symbol of this "lost generation" was F. Scott Fitzgerald. In his fine novel, *The Great Gatsby* (1925), Fitzgerald told the tragic story of Jay Gatsby, a romantic believer in the American dream who was destroyed by an unscrupulous millionaire, Tom Buchanan. Buchanan had Gatsby killed because he had fallen in love with Buchanan's wife, Daisy, a "vulgar, meretricious beauty" who did not deserve Gatsby's passion. Fitzgerald told his generation that innocent America, where the dreams of men came true, had been corrupted. Money and power had become the arbiters of man's fate.

Many young American writers and artists fled the United States. They lived and worked in Rome, Berlin, London, and especially Paris. In Paris, they resided along the Left Bank of the Seine. They lived cheaply and mixed with other writers, artists, and Bohemians. Ernest Hemingway was the best writer of the young expatriates. He had grown up in the Midwest and worked as a newspaper reporter. During the war he was an ambulance driver on the Italian Front. He was seriously wounded by an artillery shell. After his recovery and return to America, he worked for a time as a reporter. In 1922, he settled in Paris to write. *Farewell to Arms* (1929), his finest novel, portrayed the horrors and confusions of the war. Like Hemingway, the main character in the story, Frederick Henry, is wounded on the Italian Front, and Hemingway uses Henry's wound to symbolize the disillusionment and psychic damage done by a pointless war.

It was Hemingway's style—direct, terse, and simple—that evoked powerful feelings that made him the most important American writer of his generation. Hemingway was a muscular, athletic man who loved the outdoors and participated in strenuous sports. He boxed, fought bulls, and hunted lions in Africa. He survived a plane crash in Africa. The Hemingway lifestyle created a legend and made him a cult hero, the celebrity writer. Many people were more interested in the life of the artist than they were in his art.

Sinclair Lewis was the most popular serious writer of the 1920s. His first major work, *Main Street* (1920), sold well and drew critical acclaim. It depicted the ignorance, smugness, and mean-spiritedness of small-town life. Two years later, he brought forth *Babbitt,* his most famous novel. George Babbitt represented the archetypal businessman of the 1920s. Babbitt was a booster, gregarious, and narrowly conformist in his opinions. But beneath the noisy cliches hid a timid man who wanted to do better but was afraid to try. Both book titles passed into the language. "Main Street" symbolized the complacent bigotry of small-town life. "Babbitt" became a symbol of middle-class materialism and conformity. Lewis, a social satirist with great descriptive powers, masterfully depicted the sights and sounds of 1920s' American life. His scathing satire skewered the fads and foibles of his era.

H. L. Mencken was another prominent American writer of the decade. Mencken was a middle-aged journalist, who founded the *American Mercury,* a sophisticated magazine that carried modern poetry, short stories, reviews, and satire. Mencken introduced American readers to many important modernist European writers and thinkers. He also savagely satirized every aspect of American life. Anything sacred or significant to traditionalists was fair game for Mencken. At one time or another, he went after the Ku Klux Klan, Rotary Clubs, funerals, the boy scouts, motherhood, home cooking, Prohibition, democracy, and religious fundamentalism. He especially disliked religious people, all of whom he called "Puritans." He defined a Puritan as someone "who lives in mortal fear that somewhere, somehow, someone might be enjoying himself."

Mencken was at his best ridiculing politics and politicians. He regularly launched all-out assaults on the men in the White House and other prominent politicians. His readers laughed as he called William Jennings Bryan "a charlatan, a mountebank, a zany without sense or dignity." He called Woodrow Wilson a "bogus liberal." Harding was a "numskull," a "stonehead," and Coolidge was "a cheap and trashy fellow," a "dreadful little cad." Mencken's Hoover became a "pious old woman, a fat Coolidge." He once defined democracy as a form of government where people got what they wanted—good and hard. He coined a word "booboisie" to describe the complacent middle-class majority. Once, when a young woman asked him why be bothered to live in the United States, Mencken replied, "Why do people go to zoos?"

Mencken was a professional iconoclast. His satires were amusing but never profound. His chief talent was his marvelous flair for language. He appeared to believe only in his own cleverness and a good turn of phrase. Mencken also very much reflected the spirit of the 1920s. When the depression brought hard times in the 1930s, Mencken, in his accustomed way, satirized Franklin Roosevelt and made fun of his physical disability. This time, no one laughed, and Mencken faded from public view.

The literary explosion of the 1920s was broad, rich, and diverse. It included the novelists Sherwood Anderson and John Dos Passos, who showed how the new technologies had undermined traditional values of craftsmanship and community. American dramatists Eugene O'Neill, Maxwell Anderson, and Elmer Rice created the modern American theater. Women writers made major contributions to the literature of the 1920s. Edith Wharton wrote a scathing indictment of wealthy Easterners in *The Age of Innocence* (1921). Willa Cather and Ellen Glasgow wrote novels focusing on the problems besetting women in the Midwest and South.

THE HARLEM RENAISSANCE

African American writers also flourished during the 1920s. Harlem (a part of New York City), the largest black city in the world during the 1920s, became a cultural mecca, site of the "Harlem Renaissance." African American newspapers, magazines, and theater companies flourished. William E. B. Dubois was the dominant intellectual voice of Harlem. James Weldon Johnson, scholar, novelist, and poet, was another significant voice.

Figure 4.6   Langston Hughes. Harlem was almost a city in itself—consisting of over one-half million people during the 1920s. Young black writers and artists gathered to celebrate a new pride in black people and black culture. Langston Hughes was one of the most gifted of the young black writers congregating in the black mecca. *Source:* New York Public Library.

Langston Hughes, the leading poet of the Harlem Renaissance, wrote excitedly of the gathering of young African American poets, novelists, painters, and composers. Poets Countee Cullen and Claude McKay both wrote militant verses urging African Americans to challenge bigotry in all of its forms. Jean Toomer was an outstanding realistic novelist and short story writer. Alain Locke wrote of a "New Negro" coming into being who would shed his dependency and become a participant in American civilization. Zora Neale Hurston, the ablest black woman writer of the Harlem Renaissance, turned out novels and short stories. Other writers addressed the issue of black identity—how to retain pride in their African heritage and come to terms with themselves as Americans. Hughes wrote:

> We younger Negro artists who create now intend to express our individual dark-skinned selves without fear or shame. If white people are pleased we are glad. If they are not, it doesn't matter. We know we are beautiful.[1]

[1]Quoted in Norton and others, *A People and A Nation,* p. 703.

Art and music also thrived during the Harlem Renaissance. Plays and concerts were performed. All were part of the ferment. Historian David Lewis commented, "You could be proud and black, politically assertive, economically independent, creative and disciplined. . . . " Although Harlem was the center of African American intellectual and artistic life during the twenties, the new black cultural awareness spread to other cities, where theater groups and poetry circles flourished.

THE JAZZ AGE

The Jazz Age owed its name to the music created by African American musicians working in the brothels and gaming houses of New Orleans, Memphis, and St. Louis at the turn of the century. Jazz was a complex blend of several African American musical traditions, combining the soulfulness of the blues with the syncopated rhythms of ragtime music. By the 1920s, it had spread to the rest of the country. The distinctive style of jazz bands derived from a marvelous improvisation as the musicians embellished melodies and played off one another. Jazz also provided a way for African Americans to express symbolically their resentments and frustrations over the constraints imposed on their lives. It expressed their joy and a sense of community, serving as a call for freedom and rebellion. Jazz also appealed to young, middle-class whites who were rebelling against the Victorian restraints imposed on them by their parents.

Gifted African American jazz musicians, such as trumpeter Louis Armstrong, trombonist Kid Ory, and blues singer Bessie Smith, became famous during the 1920s. Phonograph records and radiocasts popularized their music. Music that was recorded by African American artists and bought by millions of black purchasers gave African Americans a distinctive place in the new consumer culture. Most important, jazz gave America its most distinctive art form.

Popular songwriters, some working in the jazz idiom or blending it with traditional musical forms, occupied a central place in the culture. Thousands of songs expressed the spirit of the age, the values, and the important personal concerns. Records, radio, and movies greatly expanded the availability of new popular music. Music could be heard everywhere. Some of the great masters of popular songwriting were active during the decade, including Irving Berlin, Jerome Kern, Cole Porter, and Fats Waller. Many of their songs have endured, providing valuable historical clues to the inner life of the era.

It was during the 1920s that popular songs took on their modern form, a subjective, personal idiom expressing the singer's private feelings. A recurrent theme of 1920s' songs was a man or woman singing of a lost love, of a lost romance still felt. Another was the hope that true love would come along someday, or of a love that was all-possessive. Many songs were upbeat and happy, expressing the gaiety and fun-loving aspects of a decade in which many people devoted themselves to the serious business of going to parties. It is the popular songs of this decade that comprise one of its richest cultural legacies.

ART AND MUSIC

In all cultural realms, the decade of the 1920s was one of the most creative eras in American history. In addition to the literary outpouring, the evolution of jazz, and the wide circulation of popular songs, Georgia O'Keefe worked to develop a distinctive American style of painting. Composer Aaron Copeland built orchestral and vocal works around native themes and folk idioms. George Gershwin blended jazz, classical, and folk musical forms in compositions, including *Rhapsody in Blue* (1924) and *Concerto in F* (1925). Midwesterner Frank Lloyd Wright continued to build homes, churches, and schools in his distinctive prairie style, in which he merged the environment and the structure.

There is a paradox at the heart of the cultural flowering of the roaring twenties. All serious writers and artists railed against the conformity and materialism of the age. They wrote scathingly of the flawed promise of American life. They attacked technology, mass production, and the forced, frantic pace of modern existence. They were oblivious to politics and to social reform. They retreated into individualism, into writing, and into other forms of artistic expression. But despite their disillusionment and their alienation, or perhaps because of them, they created a first-rate body of artistic works. Ironically, contemporary critics of the 1920s wrote some of the finest American prose and poetry ever. Despite their complaints and condemnations, American writers and artists had come of age.

THE RISE OF RADIO

Radio hardly existed when the 1920s began, but within a few years, the electronic medium enjoyed explosive growth. Over 500 radio stations were launched in 1922. The Radio Corporation of America (RCA), which had begun the first commerical broadcast station to promote the sale of its radios, organized the first national network of stations in 1926 and called it the National Broadcasting Company (NBC). In the early years of broadcast radio, music dominated the airwaves. It was radio that popularized jazz and the hit songs coming out of Tin Pan Alley.

Although musical programs continued to dominate the airwaves, radio diversified and expanded its programming as the 1920s unfolded. Radio began covering major sporting events during the 1920s, including the World Series and major college football games. Heavyweight championship fights were broadcast to the rapidly growing national radio audience. Soon, comedy shows, drama, soap operas, and quiz shows were added to the network repetoire of programs.

By the mid-1920s, most radio stations devoted a few minutes each evening to broadcasting national news. By 1930, about half of American households owned at

Figure 4.7   Radio had become a mass medium by the mid-1920s and brought urban popular culture to rural Americans.   *Source:* National Archives

least one radio. Comedian Fred Allen called radio, "furniture that talks." By the end of the decade, radio had become a mass medium, and a big business. Advertisers were paying thousands of dollars to purchase a minute's worth of prime-time advertising. The Radio Act of 1927 formally established the policy of federal regulation of the broadcast industry. The act also created the Federal Radio Commission to license stations and to assign them broadcast frequencies.

RELIGIOUS FUNDAMENTALISM

Traditionalists opposed many of the modernist social and cultural trends of the 1920s. They were threatened by the secularist, hedonistic, and pluralistic tendencies of urban Americans, and they acted to defend themselves against these offending forces.

Millions of Americans turned to religious fundamentalism. They sought certainty in a rapidly changing society by joining evangelical Protestant churches, which embraced a literal interpretation of the Bible. Unquestioning faith in the revealed word of God brought fundamentalists both a means to salvation and protection against a materialistic and skeptical social order.

Fundamentalists, who were most numerous and politically influential in Southern states, campaigned to have legislatures enact laws prohibiting the teaching of Darwinian evolutionary theory in public schools and colleges. They did not want young people learning a theory that stated human beings had evolved by natural processes over vast stretches of time from lower forms of life, a theory that contradicted the Biblical version of Divine creation. Tennessee was one state that passed an antievolutionism law.

In 1925, scientific theory and revealed religion collided in a courtroom in Dayton, Tennessee. By teaching his class evolutionary theory, John Scopes, a young high school biology teacher, deliberately violated the state's antievolutionism statute to provide a test case. The trial became front-page news in the summer of 1925, when prominent public figures involved themselves on both sides of the controversy. William Jennings Bryan, three-time presidential candidate and longtime spokesman for traditional values, joined the prosecution. Clarence Darrow, the country's most successful trial lawyer and professed agnostic, headed a defense team of civil libertarians who had volunteered their services because they believed that an important constitutional issue was at stake. It was rural Bryan against urban Darrow in a confrontation that Bryan called a "duel to the death" between Fundamentalist Christianity and evolution. Journalists descended on the small farm community in the Tennessee hills to provide sensational coverage of the "Monkey Trial." Millions more listened to their radios to the first trial ever broadcast.

The emotional highlight of the trial came when Darrow cross-examined Bryan about his beliefs. Darrow exposed Bryan's ignorance of science and his fundamentalist religious views. The old Populist insisted that Eve had been created from Adam's rib and that a whale had swallowed Jonah. He told Darrow, "If God wanted a sponge to think, a sponge could think. " He also quipped, "It's better to know the Rock of Ages than the age of rocks." Liberal intellectuals and educated, secular people laughed at Bryan's old-fashioned religious beliefs. H. L. Mencken savagely satirized the old man's views, delighting sophisticated readers on college campuses.

But Bryan and the fundamentalists won their case in court. The Tennessee state prosecutor won a conviction against Scopes on the grounds that the legislature had the right to determine what was taught in public schools within the state. The Dayton jury took only eight minutes to find Scopes guilty and to fine him $100. Darrow appealed the conviction, but the Tennessee State Supreme Court sustained the state's right to ban the teaching of unpopular theories, even if they were scientifically valid. The state supreme court also outmaneuvered the defense attorneys when it overturned Scopes' conviction on a procedural technicality and remitted the fine. These actions prevented the defense from taking the case to the U. S. Supreme Court. Tennessee's antievolutionism law remained on the books.

Additional states soon passed antievolutionism laws. Publishers removed accounts of Darwinian theory from high school biology textbooks. By 1930, 70 percent of high school biology classes did not teach evolutionary biology, far fewer than in 1920, when the fundamentalists began their crusade. Modernists might scoff at Bryan's antiquated views; Darrow might reduce the old man's ideas to intellectual rubble, but Bryan and his fundamentalist cohorts won the battle to influence young people's minds, which was the most important issue at stake in the

"Monkey Trial." If the key question in the trial was, "Should religious beliefs influence public education in a nation where church and state were constitutionally separated?" the antievolutionists emphatically answered "Yes!" and their views prevailed. In this famous clash of cultures fought in the courts, country folks scored a significant victory over urban sophisticates.

THE REVIVAL OF THE KLAN

Another reactionary movement of the 1920s, the revived Ku Klux Klan (KKK), also involved millions of Americans defending traditional values against the forces of change. The new Klan was founded in 1915 by William J. Simmons, an Atlanta insurance salesman. Simmons claimed that he was reviving the terrorist organization that had intimidated and brutalized blacks during Reconstruction in order to purge Southern culture of what he called "corrupting influences." The new Klan adopted the earlier organization's cloth hoods, mystical terms, secrecy, and vicious tactics, and it achieved a far larger membership than the old Klan.

It spread nationally, and during the early 1920s, the "Invisible Empire" claimed 5 million members. It often allied itself with Protestant church congregations and local leaders in Southern and Midwestern communities. It achieved significant political influence in various regions of the country and wielded power

Figure 4.8   The "invisible empire" of Ku Klux Klan members marching in full regalia in the nation's capital in 1926.   *Source:* Library of Congress.

within the Democratic Party in several states. The revived Ku Klux Klan was a species of reactionary populism that flourished in the early twenties, a time of economic dislocation and moral confusion.

The new Klan also sought a broader range of targets than had its predecessor. It tapped powerful nativist sentiments that asserted native, white Protestant supremacy, not only over blacks but also over immigrants, Catholics, Jews, radicals, and anyone else who violated their sense of moral order and social hierarchy. They intimidated, beat up, and occasionally murdered blacks. They administered vigilante justice to bootleggers, prostitutes, and adulterers. They campaigned against Catholic and Jewish political candidates. They forced schools to adopt Bible readings and to stop teaching evolutionary theory. They beat up trade union organizers and harassed immigrant families.

During the mid-1920s, the Klan went into decline. Some members became involved in bootlegging and racketeering. One of its leaders was convicted of murdering a young women whom he had kidnapped and raped. The economy revived, and the Klan's brand of coercive, exclusive patriotism gradually lost much of its appeal within a pluralistic society. Some analysts have defined the 1920s' Ku Klux Klan as an indigenous American Fascist movement, resembling the Italian Fascisti and German Nazis. These analysts ignore or misunderstand the ideological underpinnings of the KKK; they cherished traditional American republican values. They did not repudiate liberal democracy; they embraced a narrow, cranky, and bigoted version of it.

CLOSING THE DOOR

Another powerful reactionary current flowing through the early 1920s sprang from native-born American prejudices against the "new" immigrants from southern and eastern Europe. Since the 1880s, nativist organizations, labor leaders, and some Progressive reformers had urged an end to unrestricted immigration. Nativists complained that these newcomers were inherently inferior, with alien habits and beliefs that they did not abandon, and that they polluted native stock. They also feared that Catholic private schools would undermine the American system of public education. Labor leaders charged the "new" immigrants with lowering wage levels, raising unemployment, refusing to join unions, and working as strikebreakers. Some reformers argued that the immigrants who were crowding inner-city slums exacerbated urban problems, supported corrupt political machines, and formed a permanent underclass of unassimilable aliens.

The drive to restrict immigration gained momentum during and after World War I. Congress enacted a Literacy Test Act in 1917 over President Wilson's veto. The Red Scare heightened fears of radical aliens importing revolutionary ideologies and tactics. Industrialists, who had long been the most powerful champions of free immigration because it provided them with workers, installed assembly line technologies that decreased their need for workers and cut labor costs.

Social scientists also joined the cause of immigration restriction when they misinterpreted the findings of intelligence tests the U.S. Army had given draftees during World War I. They found that recruits from southern and eastern European countries scored much lower than soldiers whose ancestors had come from the British Isles, northern, and western Europe. The tests really measured educational levels attained and the cultural opportunities experienced, but scientists assumed that they measured innate intellectual abilities, confirming the nativist assumption that the "new" immigrants were of lower intelligence than old-stock Americans.

When immigration after the war threatened to reach prewar levels, Congress enacted restrictive legislation that reduced immigration generally, sharply curtailed immigration from southern and eastern Europe, and excluded Asians. In 1921, Congress enacted the Emergency Quota Act. According to its provisions, immigrants equal to 3 percent of the number of foreign-born residents of the United States could enter each year. This number amounted to about 350,000 people, since there were 11.7 million foreign-born Americans according to the 1910 census. Each country's portion of the 350,000 was determined by the number of its nationals already residing in the United States.

The Emergency Quota Act was a temporary measure. Following extensive study and hearings, Congress enacted a comprehensive measure in 1924, the National Origins Act, which would define U.S. immigration policy for the next forty years. The act phased in a more restrictive system that reduced the "new" immigration to an annual trickle and banned Asians altogether, but it allowed sizeable numbers of immigrants from northern and western Europe to continue to enter America. Beginning in 1925, immigration equal to only 2 percent of the foreign-born population living in the United States in 1890 could enter the country. Since that population amounted to about 7.5 million, only 150,000 people could enter annually. This law both sharply reduced total immigration and further limited "new" immigration, because most southern and eastern Europeans residing in the United States had arrived after 1890.

Congress amended the National Origins Act in 1927 to establish an immigration system that kept the 150,000 annual quota but further reduced the number of "new" immigrants allowed to enter annually. Starting in 1929, each nation's quota was based not on a percentage of the foreign-born population living in the United States but on the national origins of the entire European population of the country according to the 1920 census. For example, there were about 3,800,000 Americans of Italian descent residing in the United States in 1920, counting both those born in Italy and their descendants born in America. They composed 4 percent of the total European population in 1920 of 96,000,000. So Italy got 4 percent of the 150,000 immigration slots available in 1929, or 6,000 openings. Between 1900 and 1910, before the country adopted restrictive immigration policies, about 1.6 million Italians had come to the United States, an average of 160,000 annually. All southern and eastern European nationalities suffered sharp reductions in their quotas, similar to the Italians

In practice, the national origins quota system reduced immigration well below the 150,000 allowed annually, because it assigned large quotas to western and northern European nations that did not use all of their assigned slots each year. Great Britain had 65,000 slots annually, most of which went unused during the depression years of the 1930s. The unused slots did not transfer to other nations. Meanwhile in Italy and other southern and eastern European countries, which had small quotas, a huge backlog of potential immigrants built up.

The national origins system was designed to preserve the ethnic and racial status quo that prevailed during the 1920s. It also reflected prevailing nativist assumptions and prejudices. America sent a message to the world with its new immigration policy: If you were white, Anglo-Saxon, and preferably Protestant, you were welcome. If you were Catholic, Jewish, or Slavic, a few of you could come each year. If you were Asian, you were excluded. America, which had opened its doors to the people of the world as no nation ever had, now closed the "golden door" except to a few favored nationalities.

Religious fundamentalism, the Ku Klux Klan, and immigration restriction represented reactionary efforts by traditionalists to preserve an older, a simpler, and (from their perspective) a purer America against spreading modernism and urban-industrial values. Traditionalists attempted to sustain old values in the midst of a dynamic materialistic, hedonistic, and pluralistic society.

THE BUSINESS OF GOVERNMENT

With the upsurge in prosperity, most Americans shed their fears of big business and ceased complaining about the depredations of large corporations. Part of the new acceptance of oligopoly was attributable to the public's perception that big business contributed to rising productivity, higher wages, and improved living standards. Popular approval of big business also was encouraged by skilled public relations experts who projected a corporate image of ethical concern and social responsibility. An ethic of service replaced the older predatory, "public-be-damned" attitudes of Gilded Age buccaneers.

Both Congress and the executive branch supported business during the 1920s. Congress lowered corporation taxes in 1921 and raised tariff rates a year later. Secretary of the Treasury Andrew Mellon got Congress to slash federal spending from a high of $18 billion in 1918 to $3 billion in 1925, generating a surplus used to retire part of the national debt. He persuaded Congress to reduce income taxes in 1926. In 1921, the government returned the railroads, modernized at the taxpayers' expense, to their private owners. Government-built merchant ships were sold to private shipping companies at a fraction of their cost. Regulatory agencies, such as the Federal Trade Commission and the Interstate Commerce Commission, were staffed with businessmen who took a protective stance toward the industries they were regulating.

The federal government's role in the economy increased during the 1920s. Republicans widened the scope of federal activity, and the number of government employees nearly doubled between 1921 and 1929. Herbert Hoover led the way in the Commerce Department, establishing new federal agencies to make the housing, transportation, and mining industries more efficient. Government encouraged corporations to develop welfare programs for employees. Agencies also devised new federal machinery to arbitrate labor disputes. Despite their use of the rhetoric of laissez-faire, the Republican administrations of the 1920s expanded the apparatus of the developing federal bureaucracy pioneered by Progressive reformers. They applied Theodore Roosevelt's conception of business-government cooperation, although the 1920s' presidents viewed the role of government as a passive servant of business rather than as an active regulator that Roosevelt had championed.

Progressivism declined during the 1920s. Antitrust activities and the commitment to social justice waned. But Progressivism survived in Congress: a group of midwestern senators supported labor legislation and aid to farmers. Progressivism also survived at the state and local levels. Several states enacted workmen's compensation laws and old age pensions. City planning and zoning commissions controlled urban growth in a professional manner. Social workers provided help for the urban poor.

The 1920s were lean years for organized labor. Public opinion was indifferent or hostile to trade unions, especially when they struck. Government hostility also hindered the growth of unions. The Justice Department used court injunctions against striking unions; the Clayton Act's provisions that were designed to protect unions proved useless. The new scientific managers of industrial corporations during the 1920s stressed good relations between managers and employees, but at the same time they were hostile toward trade unions and determined to weaken them whenever they could. Some companies joined the "American Plan," aimed at ending "closed shops," factories where only union members could work. Other firms promoted a social innovation called "welfare capitalism." They built clean, safe factories, installed cafeterias, hired trained dietitians, and formed baseball teams. Some companies enrolled their workers in company unions that provided members with health insurance and a grievance procedure. They also enrolled African Americans, immigrants, and women. Company unions, profit sharing, pensions, and company-sponsored social events were all expressions of welfare capitalism. Trade unions could not compete with welfare capitalism. Union membership fell from 5 million in 1920 to 3.6 million at the end of the decade.

The U.S. Supreme Court was dominated by conservative jurists during the 1920s, headed by Chief Justice, and former President, William Howard Taft. Many of its decisions protected business from rigorous regulation, weakened trade unions, and nullified social legislation. In *Bailey v. Drexel Furniture Company* (1922), the Court nullified a law restricting child labor. In *Adkins v. Children's Hospital* (1923), the Court overturned a minimum wage law for women on the grounds that it infringed upon women's freedom of contract.

Electoral politics during the 1920s continually demonstrated the strong popular appeal of Republican candidates. At the 1920 Republican Convention, a lightly regarded candidate, Senator Warren G. Harding of Ohio, received the presidential nomination because the leading contenders were deadlocked. His genial personality and lack of strong views made him an appealing compromise choice. He conducted a clever campaign tailored to the public mood, which had turned against both domestic reform and Wilsonian internationalism. Harding coined a new word to describe public yearnings; he told an audience that Americans wanted "not nostrums but normalcy."

Harding and his running mate, Calvin Coolidge, who was made famous by his role in the crushing of the Boston police strike, easily defeated their Democratic opponents, Governor James Cox of Ohio and Franklin Roosevelt, formerly assistant secretary of the U.S. Navy and a distant relative of the late President Theodore Roosevelt. Cox was saddled with Woodrow Wilson's discredited administration, and Cox's support for American membership in the League of nations had become unpopular by the fall of 1920. Harding and Coolidge rolled to a landslide triumph. Harding received over 16 million votes, more than twice as many as any previous candidate had ever gotten. His 61 percent of the popular vote also was a historic high; his huge majority came from women voters. The 1920 election was the first in which the Nineteenth Amendment, enfranchising women, was in force. Feminists were disappointed when only about 25 percent of eligible women voted and when most voted the way their husbands did.

Figure 4.9   Election of 1920.   *Source:* Moss, *Rise of Modern America,* p. 144.

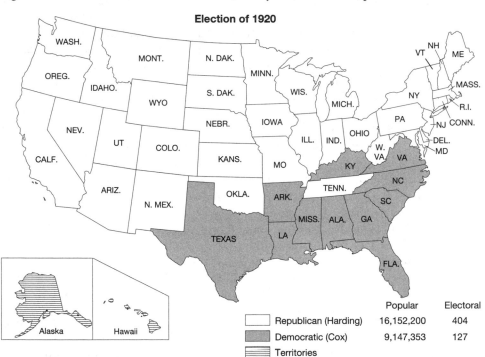

	Popular	Electoral
Republican (Harding)	16,152,200	404
Democratic (Cox)	9,147,353	127
Territories		

President Harding was a politically shrewd and hardworking man. He selected capable men to serve in key cabinet positions. These appointees included Secretary of State Charles Evans Hughes, Secretary of Agriculture Henry C. Wallace, Andrew Mellon at the Department of Treasury, and Herbert Hoover at the Department of Commerce. Harding relied heavily on his cabinet advisors. Harding's wife, Florence Kling Harding, was a formidable personality who pursued activities that ranged far beyond traditional First Lady duties as a host and a humanitarian. She was a shrewd political adviser to her husband, fought for women's rights, and sought better medical care for wounded World War I veterans.

Although a traditional Republican, Harding was responsive to some reform concerns. He established a modern budgeting system for the government, supported an antilynching measure, approved legislation aiding farmers, responded to some labor concerns, and supported civil liberties. Harding pardoned Eugene Debs, the Socialist leader imprisoned for his opposition to the war, and invited him to the White House for a visit following his release. The genial Harding implemented a moderately conservative style of governance that downplayed partisan rivalries and sought to incorporate the concerns of most Americans within a consensual framework.

Harding's administration is best remembered for its many scandals. Although honest himself, Harding inadvertently appointed many men to office who were crooks. Charles Forbes, who headed the Veterans Bureau, served time in prison for fraud and bribery. Attorney General Harry Daugherty, Harding's campaign manager in 1920, was tried for bribery but avoided conviction by refusing to testify. The most notorious case revealed that the Secretary of the Interior, Albert Fall, had accepted bribes from oil companies in exchange for his leasing public oil lands to them illegally. It is known as the Teapot Dome Scandal, named for the site of a federal oil reserve in eastern Wyoming, which had been turned over to the Mammoth Oil Company. After a congressional investigation unearthed the criminal activity, Fall was tried, convicted, fined $100,000, and sent to prison.

In the summer of 1923, neither Harding nor the American people knew about his administration's extensive corruption, although there is evidence suggesting that Harding was becoming suspicious and fearful. Harding went on a speaking tour of the West, became ill, and died in San Francisco August 2, 1923. The cause of death was a coronary embolism, a blood clot which had lodged in his brain. The sudden death of a popular president came as a great shock to the nation, and millions mourned the passage of a kindly, genial man who appeared to be the appropriate leader for a country seeking "normalcy" in the wake of world upheavals.

In the years after his death, investigations and trials exposed the corruption and thievery riddling his administration. Stories about all-night poker sessions and heavy drinking further damaged his declining reputation. The American people learned that Harding had been an energetic womanizer all of his adult life. While married, he had carried on several affairs and was the father of two illegitimate children. Florence Kling Harding, aware of some of her husband's infidelities and other scandals, joined efforts to destroy evidence, to raise money to pay off blackmailers, and to intimidate witnesses who might furnish damaging testimony against administration personnel. Socialite Alice Roosevelt Longworth, daughter of the late Theodore Roosevelt, suggested an epitaph for Harding when she said, "He wasn't a bad man. He was just a slob."

Calvin Coolidge, a laconic Puritan from rural Vermont, succeeded the affable Harding. Coolidge quickly purged the government of crooks and thieves. He replaced Daugherty with Harlan Fiske Stone, the respected dean of Columbia Law School and future Supreme Court justice. But mostly he kept the Harding administration in place and continued Harding's policies. Coolidge was devoted to the principles of laissez-faire. He observed that, "The business of America is business." He also stated, "If the federal government disappeared, the average citizen would probably never notice the difference." Coolidge also blended religious and business ideologies: "The man who builds a factory builds a temple. The man who works there worships there."

Coolidge was an able politician. He quickly took control of the Republican Party and easily gained his party's 1924 presidential nomination. His restoring of integrity to the national government and the nation's rising prosperity ensured his election. Coolidge also was aided by the Democratic Party, which nearly tore itself apart at its nominating convention. The Party was split into an Eastern urban wing and a Southern rural wing. A motion to condemn the Ku Klux Klan was ferociously debated, and defeated. Southern Democrats, dry (politicians who favored retaining Prohibition were called "drys," politicians who favored repealing Prohibition were called "wets"), anti-immigrant, and pro-Klan, rallied to the candidacy of William Gibbs McAdoo. Eastern big-city Democrats supported Governor Alfred E. Smith, a Catholic Progressive with a background in machine politics. It took 103 ballots before the deadlocked convention could agree on a compromise candidate, John Davis, a conservative corporation lawyer associated with Morgan banking interests.

Robert La Follette, entered the 1924 presidential race as the head of a reborn Progressive Party. Progressives adopted a platform calling for government ownership of railroads, direct election of the president, and a host of labor and social reforms. His Progressive candidacy contrasted sharply with the pro-business platforms of the major parties.

The election results were predictable. It was 1912 in reverse. The two pro-business candidates got most of the votes. Coolidge won easily, defeating Davis and La Follette in the popular vote. He received 15.7 million to 8.4 million for Davis and 4.8 million for La Follette. In the electoral vote column, Coolidge got 382 to Davis's 136. La Follette carried only his native Wisconsin. In an electoral contest characterized by a low voter turnout, "Coolidge prosperity" had received a strong popular endorsement. The Republicans also retained large majorities in both houses of Congress. It was time to "keep cool with Coolidge."

President Coolidge chose not to run in 1928, mainly for health reasons. Had he sought another presidential term, he would easily have been reelected. The country was prosperous, and most people were content, convinced that the wonders of the New Era would continue indefinitely. When Coolidge stepped aside, Herbert Hoover came forward to wear the mantle of prosperity. Hoover was an apt candidate for the Republicans. He combined the traditional ethic of personal success through hard work with a progressive emphasis on collective action. Hoover was a multimillionaire mining engineer who retired from business to begin a second career in government service. During and after World War I, Hoover distinguished himself as the U.S. food administrator and head of general relief for Europe. He served as Secretary of Commerce under Harding and Coolidge. In both administrations, he was a highly visible, energetic cabinet officer.

Hoover was not a traditional Republican; he was a Progressive who expanded Theodore Roosevelt's New Nationalist concept of business-government cooperation. As Commerce Secretary, he had promoted business, encouraged the formation of trade associations, held conferences, and sponsored studies— all aimed at improving production and profits. In his speech accepting the Republican nomination for President in the summer of 1928, Hoover proclaimed that Americans would soon be the first nation in the history of the world to abolish poverty.

The Democrats nominated New York Governor Alfred E. "Al" Smith. Smith's background contrasted dramatically with Hoover's. Whereas Hoover had rural, Protestant roots and a business background, and had never run for office, Smith was from immigrant stock, was raised on the streets of a Manhattan slum, and was a professional politician. His political career was rooted in machine politics, having risen through the ranks of New York City's Tammany Hall. He also was the first Roman Catholic to run for president on a major party ticket.

Hoover ran on a platform pledging to continue Republican prosperity for four more years. Unwilling to challenge the public's complacent view of Coolidge prosperity, the Democrats adopted a similar, conservative program. Smith appointed his friend, John J. Raskob, the president of General Motors, to manage his campaign. But nothing Smith could say or do convinced businessmen or most voters that he was a better choice than Coolidge's heir apparent. Smith also lost votes in some regions because of his religious affiliation, his political machine connections, his urban background, and his attacks on Prohibition.

Smith waged a spirited campaign. He struck back at bigots who charged that his Catholicism made him a servant of the Pope. But he was overwhelmed by the prosperity wave that Hoover rode to a landslide victory. It was the prosperous economy, and not his Catholic religion, that defeated Al Smith. Hoover won the popular vote with 21 million votes to 15 million for Smith. In the electoral vote, Hoover received 444 to Smith's 87. Hoover even won a few states of the "solid South," the first Republican to carry Texas and Florida since Reconstruction. The Republicans also rolled up large majorities in both houses of Congress.

After this defeat, its third shellacking in a row, the Democratic Party appeared to be on the verge of extinction. But the epitaphs that were sounded were premature. Prosperity had defeated Smith; and, although no one in November 1928 could know, prosperity was about to end. Hoover's overwhelming victory concealed a

IMPORTANT EVENTS

1920	The first commercial radio station, KDKA, in Pittsburgh, begins broadcasting
	Prohibition goes into effect
	The Nineteenth Amendment grants women the right to vote
1921	The first Miss America is crowned in Atlantic City, New Jersey
	Margaret Sanger founds the American Birth Control League
1922	*The Wasteland,* by T. S. Eliot, is published
	Babbit, by Sinclair Lewis, is published
1923	The Teapot Dome scandal is exposed
	Time magazine is founded
1924	The National Origins Act is passed
	George Gershwin composes "Rhapsody in Blue"
1925	*The Great Gatsby,* by F. Scott Fitzgerald, is published
	The New Negro, by Alain Locke is published
	The Scopes "Monkey Trial" occurs in Dayton, Tennessee
1926	*The Sun Also Rises,* by Ernest Hemingway, is published
1927	The first sound motion picture, *The Jazz Singer,* is released
	Charles Lindbergh flies solo across the Atlantic, from New York to Paris
	Babe Ruth hits sixty home runs
	Sacco and Vanzetti are executed
1928	The Kellogg-Briand Treaty is signed
	Herbert Hoover is elected president
1929	The stock market collapses

significant political realignment taking form. Catholic working-class voters in the big cities, who were not sharing in the 1920s' prosperity, were switching from the Republican to the Democrat ranks. Coolidge had carried the twelve largest cities in 1924. All twelve had voted for Smith in 1928. Farmers in the Midwest, upset over continuing low prices for farm commodities, also voted for Smith in 1928. A new alliance of urban workers and dissatisfied farmers was in the making, a core around which the Democrats would build the most powerful vote-getting coalition of the twentieth century. This coalition waited upon the economic collapse that was just around the corner.

BIBLIOGRAPHY

The best book ever written about the 1920s is Frederick Lewis Allen's famed *Only Yesterday: An Informal History of the 1920s,* a relatively brief, entertaining account that highlights the frivolity and disillusionment of the era. William E. Leuchtenburg's *The Perils of Prosperity* is the best scholarly history of the New Era. A fine recent account is found in

Geoffrey Perrett's *America in the Twenties.* Isabel Leighton, editor of *The Aspirin Age,* offers a fine collection of essays on various events and personalities of the 1920s and 1930s. James J. Flink, in *The Car Culture,* gives us the best study we have of the impact of mass ownership of automobiles on American life. A fine study of young people in the 1920s is Paula Fass' *The Damned and the Beautiful: American Youth in the 1920s.* Kenneth S. Davis' *The Hero: Charles A. Lindbergh* is a good biography of the preeminent culture hero of the times. In *Babe,* Robert Creamer has written the best biography of the greatest baseball player of the 1920s. Nathan I. Huggins has written the finest account of black culture during the 1920s, *Harlem Renaissance.* Ray Ginger's *Six Days or Forever* is a marvelous account of the famous Scopes "Monkey Trial" that took place in 1925. Andrew Sinclair's *Prohibition: The Era of Excess* records the social consequences of the Noble Experiment. Roderick Nash, in *The Nervous Generation: American Thought, 1917–1930,* offers a fine intellectual history of the 1920s. Gilbert Seldes, in *The Seven Lively Arts,* has written the best cultural history of the 1920s. Frederick L. Hoffmann's *The Twenties: American Writing in the Postwar Decade* is the best general study of the great American writers of the 1920s. George Soule's *Prosperity Decade: From War to Depression, 1917–1929* is a fine short economic history of the 1920s. And Irving Berstein, in *The Lean Years: A History of the American Worker, 1920–1933,* presents the best 1920s' labor history.

5

The Great Depression

THE prosperous 1920s gave way to economic disaster during the 1930s. The spectacular collapse of the securities markets in this country during the fall of 1929 catalyzed the process of economic disintegration that historians label the Great Depression. The boosterism of the 1920s collapsed, along with stock values, commodity prices, and real estate prices. President Hoover, who had ridden the last wave of 1920s prosperity to an overwhelming electoral victory in 1928, found himself confronting an unprecedented national crisis. Millions of his fellow citizens faced massive unemployment and underemployment, failing businesses, and farm commodity prices so low that it did not pay to harvest the crops. The American economic collapse of the early 1930s triggered a worldwide crisis of capitalism that gripped most of the leading industrial countries and Third World producers of raw materials for years. International trade declined sharply. Most nations devalued their currencies in vain efforts to maintain their export markets. Internationalism weakened, and aggressive nations such as Germany, Italy, and Japan took advantage of the situation to conquer weak and vulnerable countries. Within the United States, American voters during the election of 1932, perceiving Hoover's vigorous efforts to combat the effects of depression as ineffective, turned to the Democratic candidate, New York Governor Franklin Delano Roosevelt, to lead them out of the morass of depression.

THE HOOVER ERA

No American presidency ever began as favorably as Herbert Hoover's did. His administration would crown one of the most successful careers in the history of the Republic. His experiences as a businessman, wartime food and general relief administrator, and cabinet officer had prepared him thoroughly for the presidency. His career combined the idealistic and the pragmatic; he was the utopian who got things done in business and government.

America in March 1929 was peaceful and prosperous. Its economy was preeminent in the world, and New Era living standards were the highest in human history. Poverty persisted in America, but Hoover had declared repeatedly during his campaign for the presidency that the United States was putting poverty on the road to extinction. He had proclaimed, "We shall soon be in sight of the day when, God willing, poverty will be banished from this nation." All families would soon have "two cars in every garage and a chicken in every pot." Hoover's inaugural address celebrated the American standard of living: "We have reached a higher degree of comfort and security than ever before existed in the history of the world." Hoover also espoused an energetic philosophy of government, firmly grounded in the Progressive tradition of Theodore Roosevelt: "The election has again confirmed the determination of the American people that regulation of private enterprise . . . is the course rightly to be pursued in our relations to business."

Some dissenters voiced concern about the rampant speculation in the stock market. Hoover himself had, at times, fretted about the speculative mania that siphoned off investment funds into unproductive channels, but he had done nothing about it. He regarded agricultural problems and tariff reform to be more pressing than reining in market speculators. He called Congress into a special session to tackle farm and tariff problems. Congress enacted the Agricultural Marketing Act that Hoover had requested, but it failed to raise farm prices. His tariff proposals failed to pass during the special session.

But Hoover did get much of his legislative program enacted during the eight months of his presidency preceding the stock market collapse, many of them Progressive measures. Congress outlawed any further leases of public oil lands to private developers. Appropriations for Native American educational and health services were increased. Hoover created a commission to study ways of abolishing poverty in America and to usher in what he called a "Great Society." These and other Progressive measures suggest the direction in which Hoover was moving and indicate what might have been if the stock market had not crashed and plunged Americans into a depression that transformed the Hoover administration into an ordeal of frustration and failed policies.

THE GREAT CRASH

During the summer of 1929, the economy slipped. Construction starts declined, as new building permits were down 65 percent. Business inventories increased sharply, as consumer spending slackened. During August, industrial production and wholesale prices dropped, and unemployment rose. The economy was sliding into a recession caused by declining consumer spending. Simultaneously, the

Federal Reserve Board raised its discount rate, hoping to gently dampen the speculative orgy in the stock market. But higher interest rates did not slow the traffic in brokers' loans; unfortunately, they did contribute to the recessionary downturn because they reduced borrowing by consumers and investors.

The stock market ignored the recession; stock prices continued to climb during August and September, as stock averages soared to historic highs. On September 3, the price of a share of General Electric was up to $396, triple its price eighteen months previously. The volume of sales on the New York Stock Exchange had quadrupled from 1923 to 1929. Other exchanges in Chicago, St. Louis, and San Francisco had registered similar gains. The motto, "buy low and sell high" had given way to "buy high and sell higher," and the Great Bull Market roared on, oblivious to the signs of impending doom. Driven alternately by the twin emotions of fear and greed, by the summer of 1929, greed reigned supreme in the stock exchanges. "Everybody ought to be rich" went the credo—and anyone could be, or so it seemed.

The Crash began on Wednesday morning, October 23, 1929, when millions of shares of common stocks were suddenly offered for sale at the New York Stock Exchange by brokers executing sell orders from their customers. Although no one panicked that day, brokers noted nervously that the market had lost $4 billion. Speculative stocks had taken a beating, and many blue chips were off by as much as five points.

No one knows for sure why thousands of investors chose that particular morning to sell their holdings. The national mood was confident. Hoover's presidency had been successful. There were no political or economic crises anywhere to frighten investors. The mild recession was not considered serious, nor likely to last long. There was no conspiracy to rig the market. There was no shortage of investment funds. Banks and corporations had plenty of money, which they were eager to lend, despite the new tight money policy. Higher interest rates had not deterred speculators.

The market had shown periodic weakness previously. In March 1929, it had dropped, causing widespread anxiety and concern. But bankers made additional loan money available, the "Fed" did not raise interest rates, and the market resumed its bullish pattern. The market faltered in September, but it had rallied. Sharp losses occurred during the first week of October, but the market again rallied. Losses occurred during the week preceding the Crash but had caused no alarm. On both October 21 and 22, the market closed on the upside. The selling and huge losses of October 23 caught everyone by surprise. That night, optimism vanished at the world's most important financial center. The bulls all became bears. The floodgates opened on Thursday, October 24. Prices fell and did not recover. Bedlam reigned on the floor. Brokers shouted themselves hoarse seeking vanished buyers. At times, there were no takers of stocks at any price. Hysteria and panic prevailed.

Although the origins of the selling wave of October 23 remain mysterious, its consequences proved catastrophic. It generated the contagion of selling that historians call "Black Thursday." That afternoon, a group of New York's leading fi-

Figure 5.1 **President Hoover, shown here on the day of his inauguration, battled the Great Depression vigorously, but ultimately his efforts failed to rid the country of depression or to even arrest the downward spiral.**
Source: National Archives.

nanciers meeting at the House of Morgan across the street from the stock exchange formed a pool to buy stocks and to stem the panic. A pool member walked on the floor of the exchange and in a loud voice bid $205 for 25,000 shares of U.S. Steel, then selling for $193. For a moment, that dramatic gesture worked. Selling stopped, and prices steadied.

A flood of reassuring statements came the next day. John Maynard Keynes, the world's foremost economist, declared the decline a good thing, for it had eliminated speculators and money would now be channeled into productive enterprises. New York Governor Franklin Roosevelt expressed confidence in the stock market. President Hoover declared, "The fundamental business of the country is on a sound and prosperous basis." These official optimists failed to restore confidence. Stock prices held for a few days only.

New torrents of selling occurred the following week. Many investors were forced to sell to cover their debts. The bubble burst on Tuesday, October 29. In one of history's greatest avalanches of panic selling, more than 16 million shares were dumped on the market. Stock averages lost almost forty points. By month's end, over $15 billion in stock values had been lost. At year's end, losses reached $40 billion, representing 60 percent of the total value of stocks listed on the Exchange when the Crash began.

As 1930 began, some businessmen still exuded optimism, because no one had yet connected the Wall Street disaster to the general economy. They believed that the market crash had merely ruined the lunatic fringe of margin speculators without harming the people who had produced and distributed goods within the economy.

CAUSES OF THE GREAT DEPRESSION

As 1931 began, the recession, which had begun during the summer of 1929, had become a depression, the first to afflict America since the terrible years of 1892 and 1893. The depression had multiple causes, including several flaws inherent in the prosperous economy of the 1920s. A fundamental defect of the 1920s' economy was the unequal distribution of wealth. Average per capita disposable income rose about 10 percent during the 1920s, but the income of the wealthiest Americans rose 75 percent during that same period. The savings of the top 60,000 families exceeded the savings of the 25,000,000 poorest families. Cuts in corporate and personal income taxes, which mainly benefited business and wealthy people, increased the inequality of income distribution. Because a rising portion of national income went to upper-income families, the economy became increasingly dependent on their spending and saving for continued growth. With wealth concentrated at the top, much income went into investments, luxury purchases, and stock speculation, instead of into spending for consumer durables. The wealthy had more money than they could spend; farmers, workers, and the bulk of middle-class families together did not have enough money to keep the economy growing during the period 1928–1929.

Because profits rose faster than wages, businessmen increased their production of goods by investing some of their profits for plant expansion at a greater rate than the slowly increasing capacity of consumers to buy the goods. The gap between production and consumption of goods widened in the durable goods industries, such as automobile manufacturing and housing construction, which had become the mainstays of the 1920s' consumer economy because so many other businesses depended on them. In 1928 and 1929, sales lagged, inventories rose, production decreased, and unemployment rose.

Farmers did not share fully in the expanding consumer economy. They never recovered from the collapse of commodity prices after World War I. Most farmers had been suffering from a kind of permanent recession since 1921. They had received 16 percent of national income in 1919; ten years later, they received only 9 percent. Because of their declining incomes, farmers' purchasing power remained weak during the 1920s.

Industrial wages rose about 10 percent during the decade, but workers also earned a smaller share of national income at the end of the decade than they did when it began. Technological unemployment caused by businessmen installing new labor-saving machinery in their factories threw thousands of people out of work each year. Unemployment remained high throughout the 1920s, averaging about 7 percent.

In the fall of 1929, about 3,000,000 people were out of work, many of them in the textiles, coal mining, lumbering, and railroad industries. These "sick industries" all suffered from overexpansion, declining demand, and inefficient management and could not compete with more efficient rivals. Impoverished, unemployed workers could not participate in the consumer economy. The closing of a coal mine or textile factory also blighted communities and regions that depended on them, creating depressed areas.

Another inherent weakness of the New Era economy lay in the realm of international economic policy. During World War I, the United States became the world's leading creditor nation because European nations incurred huge losses of wealth and borrowed billions of dollars from American banks and the U.S. Treasury. But the United States never adjusted its trade relations to accord with the financial realities of the 1920s. A debtor nation must export more than it imports to earn foreign exchange with which to pay its foreign debts. A creditor nation has to import more than it exports to provide those nations that owe it money an opportunity to earn funds with which to pay its debts. Throughout the 1920s, the United States annually ran trade surpluses with its major European and Latin American debtors. Also, America enacted higher tariffs to protect its industries and farmers from foreign competition. These higher import taxes made an equal exchange of goods between the United States and its debtors impossible. What kept these unsound commercial relations going was credit. American lenders extended credits to foreign businesses and governments to enable them to pay off debts and buy American goods.

When the Crash occurred, many American lenders refused to make new foreign loans and called in existing ones as they matured. Credit cutoffs caused foreign debtors to default and to stop buying American exports. American exports dropped sharply. American farmers suffered acutely, because many of them sold a large part of their crops abroad. Sharply declining international trade following the stock market collapse was a major cause of the Great Depression.

Weaknesses within the U.S. corporate structure also helped cause the depression. Many holding companies (corporations created to own stocks in other corporations instead of owning physical assets) had been set up within the electric power, railroad, and securities industries. Promoters used holding companies to get control of many companies in a given industry and to sell huge stock issues. A holding company was "pyramided" upon a holding company until a small company at the top of the pyramid controlled hundreds of companies at its base. Many of these elaborate holding company structures collapsed after the Wall Street panic because the operating companies at the bottom of the pyramids stopped earning dividends. When these dividends stopped, all of the other "upstream" companies in the pyramid collapsed because they had issued bonds whose interest had been paid by dividends from the "downstream" operating companies. With their bonds defaulting, the holding companies collapsed. A giant investment trust, Goldman, Sachs, and Company, sold $1 billion worth of securities in 1929. After the Crash, its portfolio dwindled to zero! Sometimes these disastrous liquidations engulfed banks that had invested heavily in these trusts. Speculative and sometimes fraudulent holding companies were a weak link in the business sector. Their collapse ruined thousands of investors and shattered confidence in the soundness of the American financial system.

Long before the Crash, bank failures had reached epidemic proportions in the Midwest and Southeast. Between 1921 and 1928, over 5,000 mostly small rural banks had failed. There were several causes: mismanagement, fraud, inadequate regulation, and economic decline in their operating regions. Often a bank failure would set off a series of devastating runs on nearby banks, as depositors scurried to withdraw their funds, ensuring the banks' failures. These panicky runs often meant that formerly sound banks went down along with the weak, crooked, and mismanaged ones. Weaknesses in the U.S. banking industry were a major cause of the depression following the stock market collapse, because there was a severe shortage of credit available at a time when businessmen, farmers, and consumers desperately needed to borrow money.

The most spectacular flaw in the 1920s' economy was the stock market itself. The Great Bull Market, which began in 1924, rose continually for five years, peaking in September 1929. The stock market came to dominate American financial life. Newspaper headlines quoted stock numbers daily; nearly everyone followed the market. It became the greatest celebrity of a hero-worshipping age, a symbol of economic health. Because the market occupied a central place in the public's consciousness, its collapse had a profoundly negative psychological effect far greater than the immediate financial disasters it caused. It confused and frightened people, shattering their confidence in the economy and the men who managed it, even though most Americans did not own a single share of stock and suffered no direct loss from the Crash.

What had kept the market rising for years had been the continuous entry of new investors who bought mostly common stocks. Money to fuel the market became abundant, and funds came from many sources, both foreign and domestic.

Institutional investors dominated, but thousands of small investors also played the market. Banks speculated with depositors' funds. Businessmen invested their profits. The easy money policy of the Federal Reserve Board kept credit readily available at low interest rates, encouraging investment in the market.

In 1928 and 1929, thousands of small speculators were lured into the market by low margin requirements. (Margin was the amount of down payment required for purchasing a portfolio of stocks from a broker.) Margins as low as 10 percent were available to clients. Brokers loans increased spectacularly as people swarmed in to buy stocks on margin. These margin-account speculators helped drive stocks to their historic highs on the eve of the Crash.

The danger inherent in the market was that the boom was always self-liquidating. It required a continuous inflow of new investors to generate the demand that bid up stock prices and created the capital gains that most investors sought. When, for reasons that are unknown and unknowable, on the morning of October 23, 1929, the customary buyers did not show up and thousands of investors telephoned in sell orders, the market dropped sharply. That day's selling was a signal for massive selling to begin, both for those who wanted to sell and those who had to sell because their stocks, purchased on credit, were no longer safely margined. The rout was on; prices plummeted because there was no one or no instrument to stop them.

In the weeks following the Crash, newspapers carried sensational stories of ruined speculators committing suicide by leaping from upper-story windows at their banks and private clubs. There was, in reality, no suicide wave in the aftermath of the collapse. More people killed themselves during the summer of the Great Bull Market than in the winter following the Crash. If the suicide rate after the Crash did not rise, the embezzlement rate did, or at least the number of trials for business crimes rose sharply. Investors, smarting from their losses, demanded audits of company books and management policies. Audits often led to indictments and trials. Embittered investors discovered that formerly admired financial wizards had often been crooks as well as incompetent or unlucky managers.

The central question is, what role did the market collapse play in causing the depression? Did the Crash cause the depression, or was the Crash only a symptom of the coming collapse? Although few could see it at the time, the panic on Wall Street was a major cause of the Great Depression, for it exposed many of the underlying weaknesses inherent in the 1920s' economy. Deep-rooted faults surfaced, compounded by foreign influences, faulty economic knowledge, political errors, and irrational behavior.

The Crash curtailed the purchasing power and investing capacity of the wealthy classes upon whom the consumer economy had come to depend for growth, because many rich people had lost money in the market. The collapse also shook their confidence in the economic system, making them less willing spenders and investors. Loans to foreign governments that had kept international trade and debt repayments flowing stopped, causing massive defaults on bond payments and loss of foreign markets for American exporters. Investors, exporters, and farmers who sold their crops abroad lost income and purchasing power. Jerry-built holding companies collapsed. Investment trusts depreciated to nothing. Bank failures escalated. Credit dried up. Financial markets were deranged. Corporations that had lost money in the stock market had to curtail investment, decrease production, and eventually lay off workers. As workers were fired, aggregate purchasing power dropped further, starting another round of cutbacks and layoffs. In sum, the stock market crash immensely damaged the economy in many ways and was both a catalyst and a major cause of the depression.

Governmental financial policy also contributed to the coming of the Great Depression. Easy availability of credit and low interest rates encouraged speculation in the market, and the government did nothing to regulate these. After the Crash, the Federal Reserve Board raised interest rates and tightened credit, which further weakened a severely deflated economy. Business confidence spiraled down with the business cycle. A nation of boosters had been transformed into a country full of anxious pessimists by a disastrous chain of events triggered by the collapse of the Great Bull Market.

THE DEEPENING DEPRESSION

As the depression deepened, statistics embodied a litany of human disaster. All of the gains made during the 1920s were wiped out in a few years. Between 1929 and 1933, about 100,000 businesses failed. Investments declined from $7 billion to less than $2 billion. Corporate profits fell from $10 billion to less than $1 billion. The gross domestic product dropped from $80 billion to $42 billion. Manufacturing also declined by half. Wholesale prices shrank by almost 40 percent. Almost 6,000 banks went under during those four years, and they took with them millions of savings accounts representing $25 billion in savings. By 1933, the Dow-Jones average for industrial stocks stood at 32 points, about 10 percent of its value on the eve of the Crash.

When the Crash occurred, unemployment stood at about 3 million. It climbed steadily thereafter as an average of 100,000 workers lost their jobs every week during the first three years after the stock market crash. Some large corporate employers laid off all of their full-time employees. By March 1933, unemployment had soared to an estimated 13 million, about one-fourth of the workforce. At least that many people continued to work part time, often for drastically reduced wages. During the depths of the depression, about half of the American workforce was either unemployed or underemployed. Labor income fell 40 percent during those four dismal years.

Public schools suffered serious damage because of depression conditions. In 1931 and 1932, about 5,000 elementary, middle, and high schools closed across the nation because of lack of funds. Thousands of other schools shortened their in-

Figure 5.2   Unemployed workers during the Great Depression selling apples for 5 cents apiece.   *Source:* Library of Congress.

structional days, shortened the school year, fired teachers, increased class sizes, and eliminated programs. Educational opportunities, especially in the rural Midwest and South, were curtailed. Across the land, thousands of teachers joined the swelling ranks of the unemployed.

Scenes of misery abounded in the industrial cities. A million unemployed men and women trudged the sidewalks of New York. Unemployed office workers sold apples on street corners for 5 cents apiece. People sat forlornly in employment offices, keeping watch for nonexistent jobs. Diets deteriorated, malnutrition became all too common, and weakened people easily contracted diseases. People stopped going to doctors and dentists. The incidence of epidemic diseases like tuberculosis, typhoid, and dysentery increased. People, unable to pay their heating bills, huddled together for warmth in unheated tenements. Many doubled up in crowded apartments. Often those who were unable to pay the rent were evicted.

Figure 5.3   Bread lines were commonplace during the Depression years of the early 1930s. Here unemployed workers wait in line for a free meal. *Source:* Library of Congress.

Homeless people built shanty towns on vacant lots, in gullies and canyons, and in forests on the edge of cities. Other wanderers slept in parks and doorways. Bread lines and soup kitchens manned by charities proliferated. People stole food from grocery stores, rummaged through garbage cans and city dumps, and begged for food. In 1932, New York City hospitals reported twenty-nine victims of starvation and 110 people dead of malnutrition. Most of these unfortunates were children.

In rural areas, long troubled by economic difficulties reaching back into the 1920s, the depression often made conditions far worse. Between 1929 and 1933, farm income, already low in many regions, dropped by one-half. Farmers responded to falling prices by producing more. Their increased productivity depressed prices further, and their troubles were compounded by the loss of foreign markets because of tariffs and economic collapse in Europe. Falling income, droughts, plagues, bank failures, unpaid mortgages and taxes, bankruptcies, and foreclosures ruined farmers. In some regions of the rural South and Southwest, the economy collapsed from a combination of economic and natural disasters, depriving the rural poor of an economic base. Many poor tenant farmers and their families became transients, hitting the roads in search of jobs or food. Those who remained on the land struggled to survive on cash incomes of $300 to $400 a year.

The depression also brought ecological disaster to the Great Plains region. Between 1929 and 1933, scores of dust storms howled across the land each year. These black blizzards brought darkness at noon and transformed an area stretching from the Oklahoma panhandle to western Nebraska into a giant "Dust Bowl." Drought-parched fields and pastures turned into sand dunes. Searing summer heat killed thousands of cattle, fish, and birds. Millions of people were forced to flee the stricken regions. Nature alone was not to blame for the Dust Bowl. The arid lands west of the 98th meridian were not suitable for intensive agriculture or livestock grazing. Sixty years of ecological abuse had stripped the Great Plains of its natural vegetation by the time the droughts struck. Denuded of its native sod, the land lay helpless when the hot, dry winds came. One-third of the Great Plains just blew away during the early 1930s. Grit from the Nebraska plains collected on window

Figure 5.4   The Depression savagely struck farm families. Farm commodity prices plunged disastrously, and it was impossible for many tenant farmers and sharecroppers to make a living. Families like this one hit the road to join the thousands of other homeless wanderers. *Source:* Library of Congress.

sills at the White House. Sailors swabbing the decks of ships in New York harbor swept away bits of Montana.

Many Americans found depression conditions difficult to understand. The nation's productive capacity was unimpaired. Factories were intact, farm productivity was higher than ever, and workers were desperately eager to work. Yet economic paralysis was everywhere. The contradiction of poverty amidst plenty made little sense to a people reared on the gospel of hard work and self-help. Farmers produced too much wool and cotton in the countryside, and yet unemployed workers wore ragged clothing in the cities. Dairy farmers poured fresh milk on the ground, and wheat farmers refused to market their crops, and yet people starved in the cities.

The Great Depression forever marked the generation of Americans who had to endure a decade of deprivation. Years later, long after prosperity had returned and most middle-aged Americans enjoyed affluent lives, many still retained vivid memories of their depression experiences. They remembered the shame, the humiliation, and most of all, they remembered the paralyzing insecurity and fear. Deep down they also worried that it could happen again, that the bottom could once more fall out, and that they would lose everything. The depression left its invisible scars.

Figure 5.5   The Dust Bowl, triggered by years of poor land management and drought, brought ecological and economic disaster to the Great Plains region.   *Source:* Library of Congress.

AFRICAN AMERICANS

Economic depression brought devastation to millions of African American families. Black people, many of whom were poor when the depression struck, sank deeper into poverty and deprivation. Most African Americans lived in the South during the 1930s, and most Southern blacks resided in rural areas. The depression exacerbated antiblack racism in the South. The Ku Klux Klan reported an upsurge in membership, and the number of lynchings trebled from 1932 to 1933. African American sharecroppers joined the Southern Tenant Farmers Union, which was organized in Arkansas in 1934. The union organized strikes in the cotton fields and attracted national support from liberal and radical political leaders.

African Americans continued to migrate North, but during the depression years, they found economic opportunities no better in Northern cities than the impoverished circumstances they left behind. Black unemployment always vastly exceeded white unemployment. Both employers and trade unions discriminated against African American workers. Black industrial unemployment rates ran between 40 and 50 percent in most cities. Hard times meant a continuing struggle for survival for many African Americans within the confines of second-class citizenship.

WOMEN AND FAMILY LIFE

The depression severely affected family life. Heads of families feared for the survival of their families and doubted their abilities to provide adequate shelter, food, and clothing for their children. Marriages were postponed. During the 1930s, the number of women aged twenty-five to thirty who never married increased 30 percent over the previous decade. Young married couples put off having children. The birth rate fell sharply. Although the divorce rate declined during the early 1930s, the desertion rate increased sharply. Young people dropped out of school and abandoned their plans to go to college. Family members, too poor to enjoy recreational pursuits outside of the home, spent more time together. People found ways of amusing themselves and of passing time without spending money. Church attendance dropped off, but public libraries were heavily utilized.

When the depression struck, most families had a one income earner who was almost always the husband. Unemployment usually meant the man, the sole provider for the family, lost his job. After a few weeks of fruitless searching for another job, men often grew discouraged, and began hanging around their homes. Many were demoralized by the experience of long-term unemployment. Traditional cultural values had defined them as society's producers and providers for their families. Unemployment deprived them of their accustomed social roles and robbed their lives of meaning and purpose. Within a culture that accentuated the traditional values of self-reliance and self-help, millions of unemployed men felt shame; they saw themselves as worthless failures. Feeling responsible for their children having to wear old clothes to school and to subsist on inadequate diets, they often suffered from intense feelings of guilt and self-hate. Under the strains caused by hard times, rates of mental illness and suicide rose.

Most of the nation's 30,000,000 homemakers stayed at home during the depression. Their daily routines were less disrupted than their spouse's, but pressures on them mounted because during hard times the role of homemakers became more important and their resources were often drastically limited. Managing a household on severely shrunken budgets often required enormous resourcefulness. Some families took in boarders, relatives, and in-laws. Some women started home businesses to supplement their meager family incomes.

The depression often affected women workers differently from male workers. Female unemployment rates during the depression were always lower than male rates because "men's jobs" in manufacturing were lost at a greater rate than were "women's jobs" in the service sectors. Assembly line workers were laid off more often than domestics, secretaries, teachers, social workers, or nurses. In a few formerly two-income families, the wife continued to work after the husband had been dismissed.

The proportion of women in the workforce rose during the 1930s from 20 to 25 percent. But traditional gender discrimination still dogged women in the depression workforce. Over half of women workers were employed as domestic servants or worked in the garment trades. The pay in these jobs was low. Working women earned about 50 cents for every dollar that men earned. Few school districts would hire married women as teachers. During the 1930s, government employers prohibited more than one member of a family from working for the civil service, and if a spouse was forced to resign, it was the woman who usually gave up her job.

POPULAR CULTURE

Popular culture flourished during hard times and also reflected the impact of depression. Americans, especially young people, still had fun amid harsh depression realities. Games, hobbies, and fads, many of them carryovers from the 1920s, continued to be popular. Along with stamp collecting, contract bridge, six-day bicycle racing, and marathon dancing came a new game, Monopoly, invented by an unemployed Atlantic City real estate salesman. Millions of Americans who had no money to invest in the real world accumulated a tidy fortune in Monopoly properties. In a generally depressed decade, Monopoly permitted vicarious accumulations of real estate and reinforced capitalistic values. Other people took a shot at the Irish Sweepstakes and got involved in chain-letter schemes.

Record sales increased during the depression decade. Classical music enjoyed new popularity. By 1939, there were more than 270 symphony orchestras in the country, and an estimated 10,000,000 people listened weekly to symphonic music and opera on radio. Popular music generally gave expression to cheerful, sentimental, and romantic themes. In the later 1930s, "swing" and "big band"

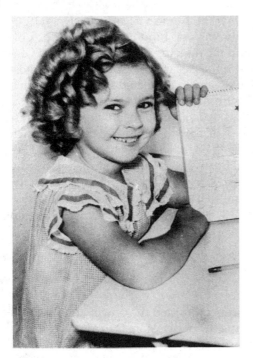

Figure 5.6   America's child sweetheart, child actress and movie star Shirley Temple, was one of Hollywood's biggest box office attractions during the Depression decade.   *Source:* National Archives.

orchestras became enormously popular. A jazz clarinet player, Benny Goodman, became known as the "King of Swing," and his concerts inevitably played to sold-out audiences. Young couples learned an acrobatic dance, the "jitterbug," to keep pace with the fast rhythms produced by Goodman's and other swing orchestras. Other dancers added exotic Latin American imports like the rhumba, the samba, and the beguin to their repertoires.

The 1930s coincided with the golden age of radio. People relied on radio for everything—news, sports, weather, music, drama, comedy, adventure, murder mysteries, religious inspiration, and advice. Daytime melodramas, called "soap operas" attracted devoted female audiences. One of the most popular radio shows for young people was the adventures of "The Lone Ranger" astride his spirited stallion "Silver." There was no more familiar phrase in all of radioland than "Hi-Yo Silver Awaaay." Radio provided some of the strongest cultural bonds holding depression Americans together. Generally, this electronic mass medium functioned as a conservator of traditionalist values in a time of grave economic crisis.

Hollywood also entered its golden age during the 1930s. Eight large studios churned out nearly all of the hundreds of feature films made each year. Technicolor made its appearance in 1935, although most motion pictures made in the late 1930s continued to appear in black and white. The major studios tended to serve up escapist fare that steered clear of depression realities and avoided raising serious social issues. Horror films such as *Frankenstein* and gangster films such as *The Public Enemy*, both made in 1931, were popular. The Marx brothers brought a kind of inspired anarchy to the cinema that entertained millions in *Monkey Business* (1931) and *Duck Soup* (1933). Mae West used bawdy Western humor to become a box-office star. Busby Berkeley's choreography and the dancing of Fred Astaire and Ginger Rodgers thrilled audiences in the best musicals of the 1930s. The two most popular movie stars of the depression years were an animated cartoon character, Walt Disney's Mickey Mouse, and a child actress, Shirley Temple.

Millions of Americans remained enthusiastic sports fans during the depression. The most popular sport continued to be baseball, the "national pastime." Each year, millions of Americans clustered around their radios to listen to the World Series. College football also was very popular. Boxing was a major attraction during the 1930s, and the most popular fighter was heavyweight champion Joe Louis, the son of an African American sharecropper. Another African American athlete, Jesse Owens, starred in the 1936 Olympic Games held in Berlin, winning four gold medals in three days.

HOOVER BATTLES THE DEPRESSION

Far more than any previous president, Hoover committed the power and financial resources of the federal government to battling the depression. Previous presidents had left fighting depressions to the private sector. Grover Cleveland confined his actions to maintaining the gold standard during the severe depression of the 1890s. Hoover, eschewing laissez-faire, accepted governmental responsibility for reviving the economy and saving the capitalist system. His actions paved the way for the New Deal of the mid-1930s; some New Deal proposals extended programs begun by Hoover.

A few weeks after the Crash, President Hoover began a series of anti-depression measures. His approach reflected his Progressive faith in voluntary business-labor-government cooperation. He held meetings with prominent business, farm, and labor leaders. These leaders complied with his request to hold the line on production and wage levels to prevent the stock market collapse from spreading to the general economy. He requested and received an income tax cut from Congress to stimulate demand. He persuaded the Federal Reserve Board to lower interest rates to stimulate borrowing. Most important, the president expanded federal public works projects to stimulate regions with slack economies. Hoover was the first president to cut taxes, reduce interest rates, and use public works projects to try to stimulate the economy and revive the business cycle. Roosevelt and his New Dealers would later make extensive use of all of these inflationary devices.

Hoover's anti-depression program, along with declining federal tax revenues caused by economic contraction, unbalanced the federal budget. Despite strong bipartisan pressure from Congress to keep the budget balanced, Hoover accepted deficit financing as being necessary to combat the economic downturn. From 1931 to 1933, Hoover's budgets ran deficits totaling $6.5 billion; the national debt rose from $16 billion to $22.5 billion. Deficit spending in peacetime was unprecedented, and Hoover incurred much criticism for his efforts. During the 1932 presidential campaign, Roosevelt repeatedly attacked Hoover for his profligacy.

Hoover's anti-depression program not only failed to generate economic recovery, it failed to even arrest the downward spiral of the business cycle. Industrialists who had pledged earlier to hold the line were forced to cut production in the face of declining sales and mounting inventories. They also cut wages and hours, and they discharged employees. Lowered interest rates failed to stimulate borrowing, and tax cuts failed to stimulate spending. Public works projects offset only a portion of the decline in the construction industry. Although Hoover had made unprecedented use of federal power and battled the depression across a wide front, there were limits to the actions he was willing to take. He opposed using federal funds for unemployment relief and insisted that relief efforts remain in the hands of local governments, with supplemental aid from private charities. Despite his refusal to authorize federal funds for relief, Hoover's unprecedented use of the powers of the central state was an advanced idea for his time. But he lacked both the political acumen and the power to turn the economy around without making use of massive deficit spending. Hoover could neither support nor get Congress to support such action, which, according to the conventional economic wisdom of the era, would only make a bad fiscal and financial situation worse.

Amidst the rising tide of depression, the 1930 elections occurred. The Democrats blamed the Republicans both for causing the depression and failing to cure it. The Democrats won control of the House, but the Republicans retained narrow control of the Senate. The Republicans were clearly weakened by the Crash and the economic downturn that followed. The Democrats made a decisive comeback from their 1920s' doldrums and realized that they could win in 1932. In New York, Governor Franklin Roosevelt won reelection to a second term and positioned himself to win the Democratic presidential nomination in 1932.

THE COLLAPSE OF EUROPEAN ECONOMIES

During the first half of 1931, economic conditions within the United States improved. President Hoover confidently proclaimed that the depression was over. But in July, the economy nose-dived again, skidding to new lows. The summer decline coincided with the collapse of European economies, which was caused largely by the withdrawal of American credits and the loss of American markets. These effects of the American depression dealt body blows to weak European economies only partially recovered from the ravages of World War I. Germany and Austria, the two weakest links of the continental economy, were the first to fail. The contagion of collapse spread to the rest of Europe, then to its colonies. Great Britain was forced to take the pound sterling off the gold standard, which destabilized all national currencies. The international free market was replaced by controlled national economies that instituted high tariffs, import and export quotas, and managed currencies. These devices were implemented to gain advantages over trading partners and to insulate national economies from the effects of worldwide deflation.

The American scene of mass unemployment, bankruptcy, and deprivation occurred on a world scale. In Britain, long lines of unemployed workers waited for relief benefits. German peasants starved in their fields. Millions of Frenchmen were reduced to one meal a day in a country famed for its abundant harvests and fine food. But in no other country were the effects of depression as severe as in America. Nowhere else did production decline so steeply, unemployment climb so high, currency deflate so severely, and recovery take so long. President Hoover, perceiving the interrelatedness of the American and European economies, moved to combat the European crisis. He persuaded Congress to grant a one-year moratorium on all intergovernmental debt payments to try to save the international credit system. He failed. Soon after the moratorium ended, Germany defaulted on its reparations payments to France and Great Britain; both in turn defaulted on war debt payments to the United States.

The effects of default were devastating financially and psychologically because Americans viewed debt repayments as moral as well as contractual obligations. To Americans, default represented betrayal by former allies whom they had rescued from the brink of defeat in 1918. The United States became more isolationist, increasingly reluctant to join cooperative efforts to solve international economic and political problems.

The European collapse further weakened the American economy, causing President Hoover thereafter to insist that the main causes of the American depression were foreign. He believed that his anti-depression program was working and that the American economy was on the road to recovery when it was derailed by the European depression. It is true that an American upturn occurred during the spring of 1931, preceding the European collapse, but Hoover failed to see that it was the loss of U.S. credits and markets that had toppled the weak European economies. The main causes of the U.S. depression were internal and can be found in the many weaknesses of the 1920s' economy exposed by the stock market collapse. President Hoover only saw half of a central truth—that the international economic crisis of the early 1930s revealed how interdependent the capitalistic economies of the Western world had become. The Great Depression of the early 1930s was a worldwide capitalist crisis.

THE DEPRESSION DEEPENS

Sharp declines in foreign trade following the European collapse devastated the already depressed American farm sector. Declines in farm prices were greatest for wheat, cotton, and tobacco, which were the major U.S. export crops. Hoover spent much time trying to solve farm problems, but he could never solve the fundamental problem of overproduction. Programs extended credit to farmers. The federal government allotted emergency funds to feed starving livestock in drought-stricken states. The Federal Farm Board purchased surplus wheat and cotton and turned the surplus over to the Red Cross. The Red Cross processed the crops and then distributed flour and clothing to needy rural families. It was a generous gesture, but farmers needed higher commodity prices, not handouts, and the Farm Board did not have the legal authority to order production cuts or make cash payments to farmers. Neither the President nor Congress was willing to devise farm programs that would curb production or increase farm income with subsidy payments as demanded by farm advocates.

As farm income fell and taxes and mortgage payments remained fixed, thousands of farmers lost their land. Government's failure to raise farm prices or to prevent foreclosures provoked direct action among militant Midwestern farmers. In Iowa, during the summer of 1932, Milo Reno formed the Farmers' Holiday Association, which organized a farmers' strike. Association members refused to ship their crops to market to force commodity prices up. They also blockaded highways to stop trucks from hauling nonmembers' produce to markets. Wisconsin dairy farmers dumped milk along the roadsides and battled with deputy sheriffs. In Storm Lake, Iowa, farmers forcibly halted a foreclosure sale. These direct action tactics signaled the growing radicalism of farmers who were facing desperate economic circumstances and ineffective government programs.

Along with farmers, industrial workers suffered the ravages of depression. Autoworkers living in Detroit were especially hard hit as the market for new cars fell drastically. By fall 1932, approximately 350,000 people, half of the city's workers, had lost their jobs. At Ford's River Rouge assembly plant, only about one-quarter of the 1929 workforce was still on the job in 1933. The Communist Party organized a march of unemployed workers to the gates of Ford's factory to ask for jobs. Company guards opened fire upon the marchers, killing four men and wounding others. Other industries sharply curtailed production and discharged workers by the thousands. Layoffs generally were by seniority. Young people, minorities, and unskilled workers were often the first fired and the last to be rehired.

By fall 1931, unemployment approached 8 million, representing about 18 percent of the workforce. As unemployment reached massive proportions, private charities and municipal relief agencies proved inadequate to meet the ever-growing demands on their limited resources. States inevitably were forced to intervene. New York, under the leadership of Governor Roosevelt, took the lead among states in accepting responsibility for unemployment relief. The New York State Legislature created an agency to help city and county governments handle their relief burdens. Other states followed. But in time, as the army of unemployed swelled to unprecedented size, state funding also proved inadequate. As 1931 ended, with the economy continuing to shrink, it was evident that only the federal government had the financial resources to provide anything like adequate relief for unemployed workers and their families.

President Hoover, beset by a deteriorating economy and rising popular discontent, launched another recovery program in December 1931. The most important measures included the Glass-Steagall Act (1932), which reformed the banking system and increased the amount of money in circulation. The Federal Home Loan Bank enabled some homeowners to refinance their mortgages and save their homes. The heart of Hoover's second-phase program was the Reconstruction Finance Corporation (RFC), a lending authority funded by $500 million from the U.S. Treasury and authorized to borrow an additional $1.5 billion from private sources. The RFC made large loans to banks, insurance companies, and railroads, many of whom were in financial difficulty during the depression. The New Dealers would later expand the RFC and use it extensively to fight the depression.

Hoover also tried to use psychological tools to fight the depression and promote recovery. He tried to use publicity releases to stimulate optimism about American economic prospects. He stated that "the worst has passed" and "prosperity is just around the corner." But, by 1932, the only thing around most corners was the lengthening breadlines of unemployed men and women. As the depression lengthened, his upbeat statements made the president appear out of touch with reality, or worse, a cynical manipulator. Had Mr. Hoover been able to engineer a recovery, these efforts at ballyhoo and prophecy probably would have worked. President Roosevelt and his New Dealers used similar techniques to promote optimism successfully because they were accompanied by some improvement in business conditions during 1933 and 1934.

But Hoover continued to resist federal aid for the unemployed. He deplored the suffering that hard times inflicted on millions of his fellow citizens, but he deplored even more what he believed would be the consequences of federal relief: mass demoralization and the creation of a large class of welfare recipients permanently dependent on government handouts. The president's ideological rigidity on this crucial matter of federal unemployment relief provoked bitter criticism from some Democrats and the opposition press. Hoover was denounced as the man who fed starving Europeans after the war but refused his countrymen funds with which to buy their families food. He could rush food to starving cattle but not to people. Hoover yielded a little in the summer of 1932, when he supported amendments to the RFC, which allowed it to lend $300 million to state and local agencies for relief purposes; but large-scale federal unemployment relief had to await the New Deal.

Many other politicians of both parties and prominent Americans shared the president's concerns about relief. Franklin Roosevelt publicly worried that direct relief would undermine the characters of working men. Congress, in 1932, voted down a measure to funnel federal relief funds to the states, with Democratic senators providing 40 percent of the votes that killed it. The traditional American view of relief yielded slowly, even in the face of massive economic decline and vast human suffering.

As the president and his critics debated the relief issue, one group of unemployed sought to dramatize their plight and seek financial aid. In May 1932, about 15,000 World War I veterans converged on Washington. They came to support a demand veterans were making of Congress for early payment of an insurance bonus due them in 1945. They needed the money in 1932 to pay debts and feed their families. As their leaders lobbied on Capitol Hill, the veterans set up camps on marshy flats across the Anacostia River. Congress refused to grant the estimated $250 million required for early payment of the bonus, contending that it was too costly.

After this defeat, most of the veterans went home, but about 2,000 people remained. They lived in the Anacostia camp and occupied vacant public buildings. They were squatters, trespassers. They were a nuisance, maybe an embarrassment, but they posed no serious threat to public health or safety. On July 28, the president ordered the police to evict all squatters from government buildings. A conflict occurred at one site, several policemen were injured, and police shot and killed two veterans. Following this violence, President Hoover ordered the U.S. Army to drive the veterans out of Washington.

General Douglas MacArthur commanded the operation. The U.S. Army deployed cavalry, infantry, tanks, tear gas, and machine guns. The soldiers cleared the buildings and then attacked Anacostia Flats. The U.S. Army forcibly dispersed the

Figure 5.7   The rout of the Bonus Marchers. In late July 1932, President Hoover ordered the U.S. Army to disperse the marchers and their families from public lands, where they had set up a shantytown in the nation's capital.   *Source:* National Archives.

veterans and their families, tossing tear gas at the defiant veterans and burning their shanties to prevent their return.

After the U.S. Army had completed its mission, General MacArthur called the veterans "a mob . . . animated by the essence of revolution." President Hoover claimed that most of the veterans were Communists and criminals. Neither a grand jury probe nor an exhaustive Veterans Bureau investigation found evidence to sustain these charges. More than 90 percent of the marchers had been veterans; 70 percent had served overseas, and one in five was disabled. What they wanted were jobs and food for their families. The Bonus Marchers were mostly poor and unemployed patriotic Americans petitioning their government for relief during hard times, hoping that their World War I military service gave them a claim for special treatment. They were at first rejected, and, later, thousands of them were attacked by their government. The *Washington News* editorialized:

> What a pitiful spectacle is that of the great American government, mightiest in the world, chasing unarmed men, women, and children with army tanks.[1]

THE ELECTION OF 1932

President Hoover's callous handling of the Bonus Marchers hurt him politically, but the deteriorating economy and the failure of his anti-depression programs did far worse damage to his reelection prospects. There was little enthusiasm for Hoover or his program at the Republican Convention, although it was tightly controlled by the president's men and gave the incumbent a first ballot nomination by acclamation. Republican congressmen and senators who did not want to be associated with an obvious loser ran independent campaigns.

The Democratic contest was much more exciting. New York Governor Franklin D. Roosevelt was the front runner for the nomination. He had formidable political assets—a famous name, a good record as a Progressive governor of the most populous state, and strong support in all regions of the country. His principal challenger was Alfred E. "Al" Smith, Roosevelt's former mentor who had preceded him as New York's governor. Smith, whom Hoover had beaten decisively in 1928, fervently sought his party's nomination again, confident that he could avenge his loss and lead the nation back to prosperity.

Roosevelt came to the convention with a majority of delegates, but short of the necessary two-thirds required for nomination. Smith's strategy was to get enough votes (along with the votes pledged to other candidates) so he could prevent Roosevelt from getting a first ballot victory. Several candidates were waiting in the wings if Smith succeeded in stopping Roosevelt and deadlocking the convention. The most important of these challengers was John Nance Garner, Speaker

[1]Quoted in Arthur M. Schlesinger, Jr., *The Crisis of the Old Order, 1919–1933* (Boston: Houghton Mifflin, 1957), p. 265.

of the House, championed by William Randolph Hearst, a Democratic party titan because of his great personal wealth and his control of a vast media empire.

Roosevelt had appeared unstoppable in the spring; he won all of the early primaries. Then Smith beat him in Massachusetts; and Garner, with Hearst's help, beat him in California. Roosevelt's momentum slowed. When the convention opened in Chicago in late June, all was uncertainty. The stop-Roosevelt coalition, led by Smith, came within a whisker of victory. Through three ballots, Roosevelt fell about 100 votes short of the two-thirds majority that he needed to nail down the nomination, and he could not break through that barrier. His support in several Southern states was wavering. The convention recessed after the third ballot. Roosevelt's backers had a few hours in which to save his candidacy if they could. During those hours, a bargain was struck that saved the nomination for Roosevelt. The key figure in the deal was Hearst. He agreed to switch California's delegation from Garner to Roosevelt if Roosevelt would accept Garner as his vice presidential running mate. James A. "Big Jim" Farley, Roosevelt's campaign manager, accepted Hearst's offer. The convention reconvened, and a fourth ballot was taken. The leader of the California delegation, William Gibbs McAdoo, rose to cast the Golden State's forty-four votes for Roosevelt. Within minutes, Roosevelt had the nomination.

He flew to Chicago to make his acceptance speech. It was an aggressive one, peppered with criticisms of the Hoover presidency. He drew his loudest applause when he proclaimed "the theory that government helps the favored few" had been discredited and that his administration would do "the greatest good for the greatest number." Roosevelt called for economy in government, a balanced budget, and lower taxes, sounding more conservative than President Hoover. He also advocated progressive measures, including expanding public works, production controls for agriculture, and federal relief for unemployed workers. He pledged to help the "forgotten man" find meaningful work and regain his lost standard of living. Near the end of his speech, Roosevelt told the delegates, "I pledge you, I pledge myself, to a New Deal for the American people." The press seized upon that upbeat figure of speech, and the New Deal became a popular slogan for Roosevelt's anti-depression program.

One feature of both conventions provides insight into the politics of depression America. Prohibition remained a major issue with both parties. Both parties contained wet and dry factions, although there were more wets among the Democrats and more drys among the Republicans. After a ferocious debate over the issue, the Republicans adopted a plank keeping Prohibition, but they also proposed another constitutional amendment that would permit each state to determine whether it wanted to be wet or dry. The Democrats also had a rousing debate on the subject before adopting a plank calling for repeal of the Eighteenth Amendment. Walter Lippmann wondered why the delegates spent so much time on the Prohibition issue instead of addressing the many urgent economic problems created by the Great Depression. Will Rogers quipped that the debate over Prohibition did not matter much anyhow, since "neither side could afford the price of a drink."

Both Hoover and Roosevelt began their campaigns in August. Both campaign organizations spent heavily for media exposure, mostly for radio time. Hoover had the support of most of the nation's newspapers and radio stations, and he had more money to spend than Roosevelt. But these advantages could not offset the fatal disadvantage of being the president in office when financial and economic disaster struck the nation.

Neither candidate succeeded in arousing the voters. Hoover's efforts failed completely. Roosevelt's speaking style was cool and priggish. He conveyed no deep understanding of the economic crisis that was imperiling Americans. His cheerful confidence and statements of faith in the capacity of American institutions to revive and prosper were superficial, uninformed by statistical data or economic theory. He appeared to lack understanding of complex economic and financial processes. He had no program to offer the American people, merely a collection of miscellaneous proposals.

Roosevelt's campaigning disappointed Progressive intellectuals, especially his habit of backing off from a position if it was attacked. A pattern emerged during the campaign: Roosevelt would attack Hoover in general terms; Hoover would strike back, refuting Roosevelt by citing statistical data; Roosevelt would beat a retreat, shifting the argument as he backed away. By the end of the campaign, Roosevelt had eaten so many of his own words that the voters had difficulty discerning any important issue differences between him and the incumbent. Hoover ridiculed Roosevelt's habit of waffling on the issues, calling him a political "chameleon." To those who sought a savior from depression in 1932, Franklin Roosevelt neither looked nor sounded like a messiah.

Roosevelt did not offer the American people a New Deal during the 1932 campaign because it did not then exist. The phrase was merely empty rhetoric. He and his advisers concentrated on winning the election; programs to combat the depression and promote recovery would come later, after victory and after he had forged his administration. It also was unnecessary for Roosevelt to offer specific programs; he knew that he was winning without them, so he played it safe. He blamed Hoover and his party for causing the depression, condemned them for failing to solve it, and promised to solve all problems if elected.

Roosevelt understood that the central issue in the campaign was Hoover's failed program. Roosevelt avoided specific commitments and resisted all efforts by journalists and the embattled Hoover to pin him down. He did, on occasion, propose a few general programs—federal unemployment relief, more public works, production controls for farmers, and expansion of the Reconstruction Finance Corporation's lending authority to include small businesses. But the main purpose of these proposals was to attract votes, not to solve depression problems. The only specific commitments he made during the campaign were ones that he never kept: balance the budget, cut taxes, and reduce spending by 25 percent. At times, his campaign utterances were contradictory, such as calling for spending for public works and unemployment relief at the same time he promised to cut taxes, reduce spending, and balance the budget. But always, Roosevelt's trump card was to deplore the effects of depression on the American people and to condemn the Republicans for letting it happen. His strategy worked brilliantly.

Compared to Roosevelt's clever performance, Hoover's reelection campaign was pathetic. No longer calm or confident, Hoover sounded harassed and peevish as he faced an increasingly skeptical and hostile electorate. He was an uninspiring speaker at best, reading his speeches in a nasal monotone that failed to arouse audiences or to even hold their attention. He failed to project much concern for the mass of ordinary citizens mired in depression miseries. He became defensive, angrily lashing back at Roosevelt, journalists, and other critics.

Hoover was a proud, stubborn man, unaccustomed to failure or defeat. He could neither acknowledge the failure of his program nor devise alternatives, bound as he was by ideological blinkers. Long before election day, it was obvious to most observers that Hoover's reelection campaign had failed. He rarely left Washington during the final weeks, and when he did, crowds frequently jeered and booed the harried leader. Much hostility toward him personally pervaded the stricken land. The Great Engineer, the Horatio Alger hero of 1928, now stood before the electorate in 1932 as the condemned killer of the American Dream. He became the butt of countless depression-spawned jokes. Vaudeville comedians, upon hearing that business was improving, asked, "Is Hoover dead?" His name became a derisive prefix—Hoovervilles were shanty towns inhabited by the homeless; Hoover blankets were newspapers the unemployed wrapped themselves in for warmth; and Hoover hogs were jackrabbits put into hobo stew. On the final day of his campaign, Hoover's motorcade was stink bombed.

On election day, the voters repudiated both Republicans and President Hoover by decisive majorities. In the popular vote, Roosevelt rolled up almost 23 million votes to Hoover's 15.8 million. In the electoral vote column, Roosevelt got 472 votes to Hoover's 59, and he carried forty-two of forty-eight states. No Republican incumbent had ever been so badly beaten except William Howard Taft in 1912; but Taft's decisive defeat had been caused by divisions within his party. The 1932 election also represented a significant party victory as well as a personal triumph for Roosevelt. The Democrats attained their largest majorities in both houses of Congress since before the Civil War, winning the House with 312 seats to 123 seats and the Senate with 59 seats to 37 seats. The 1932 election was the most dramatic reversal in American political history. Roosevelt had beaten Hoover even worse than Hoover had beaten Smith in 1928. Hoover had won forty states in 1928; he got six in 1932. Roosevelt won millions of nominally Republican votes in Northern and Western states. About 3 million first-time voters cast ballots in the 1932 election, and Roosevelt got about 80 percent of them. These new voters were mostly young urban dwellers, many of them the children of "new" immigrants coming of age. These "ethnics" became an important voting block in the emerging Democratic coalition.

The political reversal of 1932 was both historic and long lasting. The Republican Party had been the party of the normal majority since 1894 and had dominated national politics during the first three decades of the twentieth century. Since

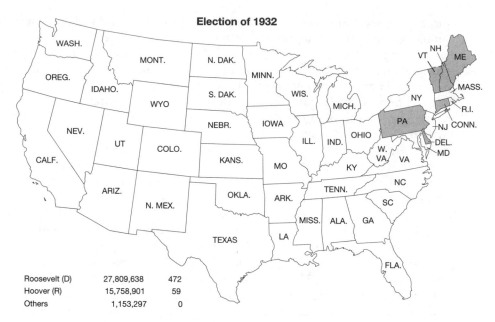

Election of 1932

Roosevelt (D)	27,809,638	472
Hoover (R)	15,758,901	59
Others	1,153,297	0

Figure 5.8   The election of 1932.   *Source:* George D. Moss, *Rise of Modern America*, p. 207.

1932, the Democrats have been the normal majority party, although their coalition has weakened since the late-1960s. Only three Congresses since 1932 have held Republican majorities. A major realignment of political parties occurred during the 1932 election, catalyzed by the Crash, the Great Depression, the Republican political failures, and demographic change.

The large majority who voted for Roosevelt and his party in 1932 could not know what programs they were voting for. Mainly they voted for an attractive political personality who expressed faith in American institutions and the American people, and who promised immediate action. Millions, including many who had voted for him in 1928, were repudiating Hoover, his party, and his failed policies; they were not endorsing a not-yet-existent New Deal. Republicans had been given three years to whip the depression, and they could not; conditions were worse than ever on election day 1932.

For the United States, it was politics as usual amidst the severest economic crisis in the history of the Republic. Most Americans, despite enduring three years of economic depression with no end in sight, remained politically passive in 1932. Organized labor was quiet. Only Communists tried to organize the unemployed masses. The Communists, partially subsidized by Moscow, staged unemployment marches, rent strikes, and hunger riots. Party membership increased between 1930 and 1932, but Communism attracted few industrial workers, however hard pressed they may have been. The Communist Party made special efforts to recruit African American workers, but it could only attract a few. Probably in the view of most African Americans, it was tough enough being black in America without being a "Red" too. Despite hard times and government failures, there was little protest or rebellion in depression America, and those few that occurred neither changed the conditions they challenged nor posed any threat to authorities. Neither the power nor legitimacy of government at any level was ever challenged by more than a handful of people. Discontent, yes, but not even the preconditions for revolution had appeared in depression America by 1932.

Both the Socialist Party and the Communists ran presidential candidates in 1932. Their candidates articulated radical indictments of the American capitalist system and offered socialist alternatives. Together the two radical parties polled fewer than 1 million votes, less than 2 percent of the votes cast. Much more expressive of popular political views in the depths of economic depression were the 16 million voters who cast their ballots for Mr. Hoover, despite hard times, his failed program, and his lackluster campaign.

Far more Americans were demoralized by economic depression than were radicalized by their searing experiences. Angry and desperate victims of economic depression overthrew governments in seven countries in Latin America during the early 1930s. But within the United States, most citizens turned their anger inward. Clinging to traditional individualistic values, they could not see economic collapse as a collective failure, as a crisis of institutions. They assumed personal responsibility for their predicaments, blaming themselves instead of the American system and its leaders for their impoverishment. Others, overwhelmed by disaster, were incapable of anger or rebellion. Dispirited, they remained at home or sat on park benches muttering to themselves. They suffered in silence, alone and isolated. Many hit the roads or rode the rails, joining 2 million other rootless individuals seeking a job, a meal, shelter, or merely a sense of motion. Along with these homeless migrants of despair there were others who, rejecting all secular saviors, awaited divine deliverance from their earthly afflictions.

INTERREGNUM

The four-month interval between Roosevelt's election in November 1932 and his inauguration on March 4, 1933, proved to be the most painful winter of the Great Depression. Unemployment climbed past 13,000,000. Each month, thousands of farmers and businessmen went bankrupt. Across the land, destitute families shivered in darkened, heatless rooms without adequate food, clothing, or medical care. Recovery appeared nowhere in sight.

As the depression continued to deepen and its miseries multiplied, the search for scapegoats escalated. Who was to blame for the economic collapse? Inevitably millions of Americans reached the same conclusion: If businessmen and Republican Party leaders were responsible for the prosperity of the 1920s, they were surely responsible for the poverty of the early 1930s. The reputations of financiers, industrialists, economists, and politicians plummeted. A senate investigating committee, chaired by Ferdinand Pecora, probed the investment practices on the New York Stock Exchange. Pecora's committee discovered that Wall Street titans had rigged investor pools and often profiteered at the expense of their customers and firms. Inside traders had frequently bought stocks below the market prices paid by the general public.

Pecora's committee failed, however, to prove its suspicion that a conspiracy of "short sellers" had caused the market to collapse, despite wide circulation of such rumors. (Selling short is an investment strategy used by speculators to profit from a declining stock market. They contract to sell stocks they do not yet own in the future at their current price. If the price of the stock drops before delivery date, speculators buy the stock at the lower price and deliver it to the buyer, who has contracted to pay the previous higher price. The short seller pockets the difference as his profit for having guessed accurately that the market would drop.) But Pecora's committee succeeded in exposing many financiers as ruthless crooks who sold out their customers and banks to save their own financial skins. The committee's investigations were one of many depression era events that destroyed the American financier as folk hero.

The social irresponsibility of some prominent businessmen also contributed to the public's disillusionment with the business community. During a time when millions of families were living in dire poverty, many businessmen continued to collect large salaries and manipulate their investments to avoid taxes. Some falsified their tax returns, while others refused to pay their taxes. Henry Ford, Detroit's largest employer and the richest man in America, refused to accept any responsibility for the army of jobless workers filling the city. A nation that had regarded its financial and business leaders with awe in 1929 turned on them furiously now that their wondrous abilities to generate wealth and good jobs had vanished.

Congressional investigations, grand jury indictments, and trials of businessmen during the depression paralleled the "witch hunts" for Communist subversives during the McCarthy era of the early 1950s. A similar need existed during the early 1930s to simplify and personify a grave disaster that, in reality, was vastly complex, and caused by a bewildering variety of forces and circumstances. It provided bleak comfort to confused, angry, and hungry citizens to believe that an evil conspiracy of greedy inside traders selling short had engineered the stock market crash for their own profit and then panicked when it got out of control, destroying the securities market and causing the depression. In fact, no one planned the Crash, and no one understood precisely why the market had fallen so sharply, why the depression ensued, or why it was so severe and seemingly interminable.

Many who angrily scapegoated businessmen also despaired of the political process, which appeared incapable of coping with economic crises. During its "lame duck" session from December 1932 through February 1933, Congress failed to enact a single important piece of economic legislation. The national government appeared to have been reduced to farcical ineptitude at a time when there was an urgent need for effective measures to rescue Americans from economic calamity.

NADIR

During that harrowing winter of 1932 and 1933, with the economy depressed and the government paralyzed, some observers feared that the American system of political economy was dying. The European depression proved that the capitalist malaise was worldwide. Only the Soviet Union, undergoing rapid industrialization during the 1930s, had an expanding economy and labor shortages. During the Great Depression, over 100,000 unemployed Americans, responding to ads a Soviet company had placed in American newspapers, applied for work in the Soviet Union. About 6,000 obtained jobs and left the stagnant American economy to live and work in the Soviet Union. Some American voices were heard calling for an end to political democracy and the creation of a directorate to make the "tough" decisions necessary to restore prosperity and order. These calls for "strong" leadership in time of crisis sounded the siren song of an American-bred Fascism fearing economic collapse and the rise of radicalism. Perhaps it could happen here?

Meanwhile, President Hoover and President-elect Roosevelt were playing a political game. The outgoing president invited Roosevelt to attend a conference on European debt problems. They meet on November 22, 1932. Hoover, believing that the main causes of the American depression were foreign, gave foreign economic policy a higher priority than Roosevelt, who saw, correctly, that the depression's main causes were domestic. Their meeting was unsuccessful. Roosevelt, suspecting Hoover was trying to get him to endorse his policies, avoided making any commitments. He did not want to be identified with the failed policies of a discredited leader. Hoover and Roosevelt had another inconclusive meeting in January 1933. Hoover believed that Roosevelt did not understand the economic situation and thought him a shallow demagogue. Both men, formerly good friends, had come to dislike each other intensely. The long delay between Roosevelt's election and his ascension to power in time of crisis brought about the enactment of the Twentieth Amendment, moving up the inauguration date from March 4 to January 20.

Roosevelt spent most of the four-month interval between his election and inauguration meeting with advisors, forming his government, and drafting his legislative agenda. He was forging what would become the New Deal. Many of his staffers were college professors recruited from the social science faculties at Columbia and other prestigious Ivy League universities. These scholars would form the "brains trust" of the Roosevelt revolution that was about to descend upon Washington.

At a time when the political leadership of the nation appeared helpless, with a repudiated leader still holding office and the President-elect without power, there occurred an event that nearly eliminated the New Deal before it could begin. On February 15, 1933, three weeks before his scheduled inaugural, Roosevelt came to Miami to attend a reception. Sitting on the top of the back seat of an open car in a city park, Roosevelt addressed a crowd of well-wishers. After finishing his informal speech, Roosevelt slipped down into the car seat. At that moment, the mayor of Chicago, Anton Cermak, came up to the car to ask a political favor of Roosevelt.

Roosevelt leaned forward to hear what Cermak was saying. A short, dark man, standing on a box thirty-five feet away, began firing a pistol at Roosevelt. Cermak was fatally wounded, and four others were hit by bullets. Roosevelt escaped the deadly assault unharmed. The assassin was instantly captured and jailed. The man who had tried to kill the President-elect was Guiseppe Zangara, a little man with a consuming hatred of all rich and powerful people.

Roosevelt shrugged off the frightening incident. He showed courage and poise, dismissing the murderous assault with jokes and smiles. Roosevelt also expressed remorse over the death of Cermak and sympathy for the others wounded during the shooting. It is sobering to reflect on what directions the history of the United States might have taken during the years of grave economic crisis at home and international disorder abroad had Zangara succeeded in killing Roosevelt.

As the spring of 1933 approached, the nation appeared to headed for financial collapse. Another epidemic of bank failures swept the land. As February 1933 ended, banks all over the country closed their doors. They were either bankrupt or had closed to avoid bankruptcy. Panicky depositors stood in long lines for hours waiting to withdraw their money. They believed that their dollars would be safer in shoe boxes, under mattresses, or in tin cans buried in their back yards than in bank vaults. By March 3, the day before Roosevelt's inaugural, thirty-eight states had shut down all of their banks, and the remaining ten states were moving to close theirs. Normal business and commerce ground to a halt. People reverted to bartering for necessary goods and services. On that same day, the New York Stock Exchange suspended all securities trading and closed down, because no one wanted to buy stocks. Financial paralysis crept across the nation.

IMPORTANT EVENTS

1929	The Great Stock Market Crash occurs
1930	The Hawley-Smoot Tariff is enacted
1931	The Great Depression begins
	Weak European economies collapse
	Hoover declares a one-year moratorium on international debt payments
1932	The Bonus Marchers descend on Washington, D.C.
	The Pecora Committee investigates Wall Street
	The Reconstruction Finance Corporation is established
	The Farmers' Holiday Association is formed
	Franklin Delano Roosevelt is elected president
1933	Guiseppe Zangara tries to assassinate President-elect Roosevelt
	Franklin Roosevelt is inaugurated
	Black blizzards create the Dust Bowl in the Great Plains states
	An estimated 13,000,000 Americans are out of work
	The Twenty-first Amendment is ratified, repealing Prohibition

1934	The Southern Tenant Farmers' Union is organized
	Hollywood implements the Motion Picture Production Code
1936	Jesse Owens wins four gold medals in the 1936 Olympic Games
1937	Joe Louis becomes the heavyweight boxing champion of the world

BIBLIOGRAPHY

Many good books have been written about the stock market crash, the causes of the Great Depression of the 1930s, and the depression's impact on the American people. Robert Sobel's *The Great Bull Market* and John Kenneth Galbraith's *The Great Crash* are two valuable short studies of the most famous financial calamity in American history. Gordon Thomas and Max Morgan-Witts have written a colorful social history of the Crash called *The Day the Bubble Burst.* The impact of the depression on the lives of people is vividly expressed in Studs Terkel's *Hard Times,* a collection of interviews with hundreds of people who recall their experiences of hard times. David Shannon, editor of *The Great Depression,* offers an excellent collection of primary sources about life during the nation's worst economic crisis. The finest economic history of the Great Depression, which explains why the depression was so severe and lasted so long, is Michael Bernstein's *The Great Depression: Delayed Recovery and Economic Change in America, 1929–1939.* Another fine account of the depression experience is Caroline Bird's *The Invisible Scar.* Two classic studies from the 1930s have endured: Robert S. and Helen Merrell Lynd's *Middletown in Transition,* a sociological study of a Midwestern city during the depression; and James Agee's and Walker Evans' *Let Us Now Praise Famous Men,* a powerful documentary in words and pictures of poverty-stricken Alabama sharecroppers. John Garraty, in *The Great Depression: An Inquiry into the Causes, Course, and Consequences of the Worldwide Depression of the 1930s,* presents a fine recent study that puts the depression into comparative perspective. Two good recent biographies of Herbert Hoover are David Burner's *Herbert Hoover: A Public Life* and Joan Hoff Wilson's *Herbert Hoover: Forgotten Progressive.* Roger Daniels' *The Bonus March* and John Shover's *Cornbelt Rebellion* are fine accounts of 1932 radical protest movements.

6

The New Deal

WHEN Franklin Delano Roosevelt assumed the presidency on March 4, 1933, the United States and most of the world was gripped by the iron hand of depression. Roosevelt himself was largely an unknown quantity, and the New Deal existed only as a species of upbeat political rhetoric. Over the next five years, Roosevelt and the New Dealers proceeded to design and implement an energetic legislative program to alleviate the effects of depression, restore prosperity, and make the federal government responsive to a broad range of circumstances affecting most Americans. Although the New Deal only partially solved the grave problems of economic depression, Roosevelt and his program achieved a resounding political success. Roosevelt became one of the most powerful and popular leaders in the history of the Republic. His overwhelming reelection victory in 1936 demonstrated that the New Deal accorded with the hopes and dreams of most Americans. Before the New Deal ran its course, the basic American approach to governance had been redefined, and the role of the federal government in the lives of most Americans had been enlarged. The American welfare state had been forged, and the federal government had committed itself to maintaining minimum living standards for those in need.

FDR

Franklin Delano Roosevelt was a professional politician from a wealthy background. He was tutored by governesses at home until he was fourteen; he then went away to Groton, a distinguished prep school near Boston. At Groton, he came under the influence of Headmaster Endicott Peabody, who implanted within young Roosevelt the Christian gentleman's ideal of service to the less fortunate and the conviction that privileged Americans should help solve national and international problems. He was much influenced by the achievements of his famous distant cousin, Theodore Roosevelt, whom he affectionately called "Uncle Ted," and Franklin apparently aspired to the presidency from an early age. After Groton, he enrolled at Harvard. From Harvard, he went to Columbia Law School. In the spring of 1905, Roosevelt married his fifth cousin, Eleanor. In 1907, he began a law career with a prominent Wall Street firm. But corporate law could never satisfy his ambitions or his exalted sense of himself as a man of destiny. He yearned for a larger arena, and he found it in politics.

He entered politics as a Progressive Democrat and worked for political reform, conservation, and aid for farmers. In 1912, he campaigned energetically for Woodrow Wilson. President Wilson rewarded his efforts by making Roosevelt Assistant Secretary of Navy, a position he held for eight years. It was the job he most wanted, for it both advanced his political career and was closely tied to his favorite pastime—sailing. Sailing was Roosevelt's passion; most vacations were spent with friends who shared his love of ships and the sea. In 1920, he was the Democratic vice presidential candidate running with James Cox on a ticket that got buried by Harding and Coolidge. This experience did no political harm to Roosevelt, however, and he emerged from the campaign a nationally known figure and party leader. In the summer of 1921, Roosevelt was suddenly felled by a severe attack of polio at age thirty-nine. The disease left him a cripple with wasted legs.

His illness slowed but did not derail his political career. He was never out of politics; he remained a party leader all through the 1920s. He supported New York Governor Alfred E. "Al" Smith's candidacy at the 1924 Democratic Convention and attracted national attention with a brilliant speech endorsing Smith's nomination. He supported Smith again in 1928 and also won election as governor of New York, succeeding Smith, who had lost his bid for the presidency to Republican Herbert Hoover. Roosevelt's gubernatorial victory instantly made him a leading contender for his party's next presidential nomination. Roosevelt's tenure as New York governor coincided with Hoover's presidency. As governor, he showed a greater commitment to unemployment relief than Hoover and a greater willingness to experiment with innovative programs in a time of economic crisis.

Roosevelt's political philosophy was anchored firmly within the Progressive tradition, and despite his association with Wilson, he was more of a New Nationalist than a Wilsonian. These views he shared with his leading advisers. Roosevelt favored a vigorous role for the federal government in regulating corporate enterprise and restoring purchasing power to farmers, workers, and hard-pressed, middle-class citizens. He favored the application of scarcity economics, that is, a reactionary policy of reducing production in order to raise prices and increase profits and wages as the best way to end the depression and restore prosperity.

Roosevelt was an experienced, confident political leader, convinced that he could provide both the leadership and the programs to lead his nation out of its greatest economic crisis. As he prepared for his inauguration, he believed he could restore both confidence and prosperity. He was prepared to act boldly and to experiment.

THE NEW DEAL BEGINS

On March 4, 1933, a man who could not walk began to lead a nation crippled by economic depression. Not since 1861 had a new president taken office amidst such ominous circumstances. With their economy mired in its longest and deepest depression, their government paralyzed, and their financial system crumbling, Americans turned to Roosevelt with desperate expectations. "First of all," declared the new president in his inaugural address, "let me assert my firm belief that the only thing we have to fear is fear itself—nameless, unreasoning, unjustified terror." Speaking firmly, a tinge of anger in his voice, he denounced businessmen and bankers who caused the depression and could find no cure for it: "Rulers of the exchange of mankind's goods have failed, through their own stubbornness and their own incompetence, have admitted their failure, and have abdicated." The heart of his speech was a promise to fight the depression with a bold program, to do whatever was necessary to restore prosperity.

His words electrified a people yearning for reassurance. In one speech he had accomplished what Hoover had failed to do in four years; he convinced Americans that an effective leader with faith in the future had taken command. As one hopeful citizen put it, "At last, a live leader in the White House!" That night, instead of attending the inaugural ball, he met with financial advisors to face the nation's imminent financial crisis. The next day he declared a four-day "bank holiday" and summoned Congress to a special session. Congress began its emergency session on March 9, just five days after Roosevelt had taken office.

His first measures revealed a streak of fiscal conservatism in the early New Deal. An Emergency Banking Relief bill, drafted with the help of Hoover's treasury officials who were still on the job, attacked the banking crisis. It outlawed hoarding and exporting gold. It also arranged for the reopening of solvent banks and the reorganization of failed banks under Treasury Department supervision. But it left the banking system essentially unchanged and with the same people in charge. Complained one Congressman, "The President drove the money changers out of the Capitol on March 4—and they were all back on the ninth." Roosevelt then sent Congress an Economy Act to trim federal expenditures by $400 million and balance the budget, mainly by cutting veterans' benefits. Another measure raised federal excise taxes. These deflationary measures made the New Deal initially appear more conservative than Hoover's program.

Roosevelt's effective leadership in time of grave economic crisis depended crucially on his ability to communicate with average citizens. He made expert use of all available mass media. He held frequent news conferences and quickly mastered the format. Journalists, even those who worked for papers that attacked Roosevelt and his New Deal, liked the man. He had a keen sense of humor and a master politician's sense of timing. No one has ever been better than FDR at delivering a speech from a prepared text. He used radio to demonstrate a talent for explaining complex socioeconomic policies in simple language intelligible to ordinary citi-

Figure 6.1 A *New Yorker* cover featuring a gloomy Hoover and a buoyant Roosevelt en route to the inauguration ceremony on March 4, 1933. *Source:* Franklin D. Roosevelt Library.

zens. His demeanor, captured best by the newsreels shown in the nation's movie houses, reflected that of an optimistic, energetic, and capable chief executive who held a special concern for the welfare of those Americans hardest hit by the Great Depression.

Early in his presidency, he developed one of his most successful communicatory devices: a radio address directly to the American people, the "fireside chat." On Sunday evening, March 12, Roosevelt gave the first of many fireside chats he would deliver over his long presidency. He spoke informally to an estimated 60 million Americans gathered around their radios across the nation. He talked about the banking crisis and the measures his administration had taken to solve it. He assured his countrymen that the banks were once again sound and "would take care of all legitimate needs." He told them it was safe to put their money back in the banks. The next day, long lines once again appeared in front of banks, but this time customers came to put their money back in. He had told the people the banks were sound, and they had believed him. The banking crisis was over.

During his presidency, Roosevelt relied on his wife Eleanor more than any previous president had ever depended on his wife. She redefined what it meant to be First Lady. She became a political force in her own right, one of the leaders of the liberal wing of the Democratic Party. She was enormously popular with most Americans and often received higher public approval ratings than did the president. She made public appearances, gave speeches, held press conferences, and

Figure 6.2   Early in his presidency, Roosevelt hit upon one of his most popular devices—the "fireside chat," an informal radio address to the people in which he discussed important issues of the day. He conducted dozens of fireside chats during his long presidency. *Source:* National Archives.

made weekly radio broadcasts. She also wrote a newspaper column, which was nationally syndicated, and wrote articles published in mass circulation magazines. She traveled 40,000 miles a year as the eyes and ears of her husband's presidency. She would report back to him how cotton farmers were faring in Southern states, and how auto workers and coal miners were faring in Northern industrial states. She reported on the mood of the people, what they told her, and how they responded to New Deal programs. More progressive than Franklin, Eleanor functioned as a liberal conscience, as a kind of goad to take actions on behalf of the disadvantaged. He also used her as a trial balloon, to find out how far he could move on a particular issue.

THE HUNDRED DAYS

During the next few months, which became known as "The Hundred Days," the New Deal gathered momentum. Many legislative proposals were sent up the hill to the special session of Congress. These bills dealt with a wide range of depression problems. Congress quickly enacted relief measures to help unemployed Americans. One of the first measures created the Civilian Conservation Corps (CCC). Young men were taken out of the cities where there was no work for them and put to work in camps organized along military lines in national parks and forests. They planted trees, cleared campsites, built bridges, constructed dams, and made fire trails. During its ten-year lifetime, the CCC put over 2 million young men to work. The Federal Emergency Relief Act (FERA) was another early New Deal measure that allocated $500 million to state and local governments to dispense to needy families.

The Agricultural Adjustment Act (AAA) was enacted in May 1933. Its chief purpose was to raise farm income by raising commodity prices. Defining the farm problem as one of overproduction, the measure reflected Roosevelt's commitment to scarcity economics. A domestic allotment program was established for seven major commodities—cotton, corn, tobacco, rice, wheat, hogs, and dairy products— whereby the government paid farmers to reduce their acreage and produce less. Subsidy payments came from a tax levied on the primary processor for each crop. The subsidy payments were based on "parity," a system designed to allow farmers to regain the purchasing power they had enjoyed during the period 1910–1914, a time of general agricultural prosperity.

Before the "Triple A" could be put into effect, the 1933 crops had already been planted. To forestall another year of overproduction, Secretary of Agriculture Henry A. Wallace ordered farmers to plow up millions of acres of cotton, corn, and wheat and to slaughter millions of baby hogs to be eligible for the subsidy payments. These drastic actions taken at a time when many Americans went to bed hungry each night provoked furious criticisms. It also raised food prices to consumers during a time of massive unemployment and underemployment. Other New Deal programs shared this particular characteristic with the Triple A: the price of helping a special interest group was higher living costs borne by the general public. But the AAA did benefit those farmers who participated in its subsidy programs. For the first time since World War I, farm income rose.

A month after passing the AAA program for agriculture, Congress enacted a comprehensive program for industrial recovery, the National Industrial Recovery Act (NIRA). The NIRA expressed the early New Deal's commitment to economic planning and business-government cooperation as replacements for the depression-spawned cutthroat price competition raging in all industrial sectors. The NIRA set up a planning agency, the National Recovery Administration (NRA), which exempted businesses from antitrust laws. Under the NRA's supervision, competing businesses within a given industry met with union leaders and consumer groups to draft codes of fair competition that limited production, divided it among various companies, and stabilized prices by establishing minimum price levels. Section 7(a) of the NRA guaranteed workers' rights to join unions and to engage in collective bargaining. It also established minimum wages and maximum hours for workers. The NIRA, like the AAA, was based upon the principles of

Figure 6.3   The Civilian Conservation Corps (CCC) was one of the most popular early New Deal programs, and it was Roosevelt's favorite. Begun in 1933, it took unemployed young men off of the streets where there was nothing for them to do and put them to work in the countryside. Here workers check farmland erosion. *Source:* Franklin D. Roosevelt Library.

scarcity economics, designed to promote industrial recovery by curbing production and raising prices that would generate higher profits and wages. The NRA failed to promote much industrial recovery. Production increased slowly, and companies did not hire many additional employees.

The New Deal's first large-scale public works program was an integral part of the NIRA. Called the Public Works Administration (PWA), it carried a $3.3 billion price tag to build roads, public buildings, airfields, ships, and naval aircraft. Its purpose was to let contracts to idle construction companies, put unemployed workers to work, and stimulate local economies by pumping in federal funding for the projects. It also added appreciably to the nation's infrastructure and helped modernize the U.S. Navy and the Army Air Corps.

Congress also created the Tennessee Valley Authority (TVA). The TVA was a multipurpose regional developmental program for the Tennessee River Valley running through Tennessee, North Carolina, Kentucky, Virginia, Mississippi, Alabama, and Georgia—one of the most depressed areas of the nation. The TVA spent billions of dollars constructing dams to control floods and to generate hydroelectric power. Other TVA projects reclaimed and reforested land and fought soil erosion. The TVA widened and deepened a 650-mile stretch of the river, making it navigable to river traffic. It also provided thousands of jobs for poor residents, both black and white, in the region. This striking example of Progressive enterprise was originally one of eight proposed regional development plans for the nation. But effective political opposition by power companies that charged the government with unfair competition killed all of the other projects.

Other significant early New Deal measures included the Federal Securities Act, which grew out of Senator Pecora's exposures of wrongdoing on Wall Street. The new law gave the Federal Trade Commission (FTC) the power to supervise

Figure 6.4   Tennessee Valley Authority.   *Source:* George D. Moss, *The Rise of Modern America*, p. 221.

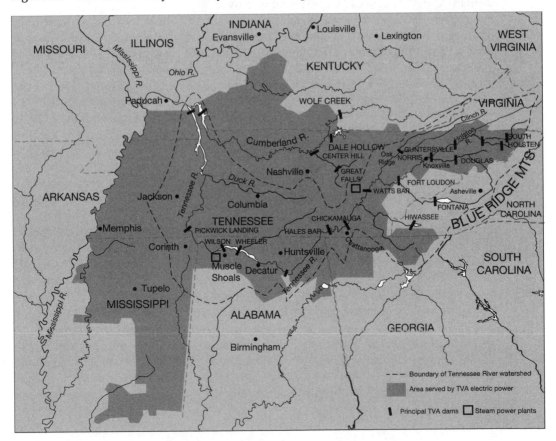

new securities issues, to require each new stock issue to be accompanied by statements disclosing the financial status of the issuing company, and to make misrepresentation a federal crime. A Banking Act created the Federal Deposit Insurance Corporation (FDIC), which ensured depositor bank accounts through the Federal Reserve System. The Home Owners' Loan Corporation (HOLC) enabled homeowners to refinance their home mortgages at lower rates of interest and with smaller payments. Roosevelt also took the nation off the international gold standard in order to inflate the currency to complement his efforts to raise domestic price levels through the Triple A for agriculture and the NRA.

Roosevelt also requested that Congress make good his campaign promise to repeal Prohibition. The lame-duck Congress meeting in February 1933 had proposed a constitutional amendment repealing the Eighteenth Amendment. While the amendment was making its way through the states, the new Congress modified the Volstead Act by legalizing beer and wine with an alcoholic content of 3.2 percent. These beverages went on sale on April 7, 1933, marking the first time in over thirteen years that it was legal to drink in America. The new amendment, the Twenty-first, was ratified in December 1933. Booze was back, although eight states remained dry. The Noble Experiment was over.

Congress ended its special session June 16. The "Hundred Days" were over. During this intensely busy congressional session, Roosevelt and his New Dealers had sent up fifteen major bills; all were enacted, with few changes. Normal partisan rivalries and debate were suspended as both houses responded positively to Roosevelt's energetic assault on a wide range of depression miseries. During the "Hundred Days," the public mood had been transformed. Americans had reclaimed their characteristically American optimism, confident that they could whip the depression and control their destiny. During the next year, many more New Deal measures became law. These laws gave further help to farmers, created additional relief projects employing thousands of workers, strengthened trade unions, aided small businessmen, and helped homeowners refinance their mortgages.

The 1934 elections confirmed the immense popularity of Roosevelt and his New Deal. Normally the party in power loses seats in an off-year election, but voters in November elected 322 Democratic congressmen to only 103 Republicans, a gain of thirteen seats for the Democrats. Never in its history had the Republicans held such a low percentage of House seats. In the Senate, the rout of the GOP was worse. The Democrats gained nine seats, bringing their total to sixty-nine, and leaving the Republicans with only twenty-seven seats. One of the new Democratic senators was an obscure county judge from Missouri, Harry Truman. Forty-one of the forty-eight states elected Democratic governors. The 1934 elections almost erased the Republican Party as a national force. They had no program and no national leader with any popular appeal. Arthur Krock of the *New York Times* exclaimed that the New Deal had won "the most overwhelming victory in the history of American politics." William Allen White noted that Roosevelt "has been all but crowned by the people."

CRITICS—LEFT, RIGHT, AND POPULIST

Although the 1934 elections demonstrated the immense popularity of Roosevelt and the New Deal, he and his programs called forth a barrage of criticism. New Deal critics spanned the political spectrum from radical left to far right, and some of them defied political categorizing. Many businessmen and conservative politicians attacked the New Deal, denouncing excessive taxation and government regulation of business. Others criticized deficit financing, public works, and federal relief payments to the unemployed. Conservatives denounced the growth in the size, power, and scope of authority of the federal government. They worried that Roosevelt might be assuming dictatorial powers, and they suggested that the New Deal state resembled totalitarian Fascist and Communist regimes. The American Liberty League, formed in 1934, served as a vehicle for corporate anti-New Deal critics. Former President Hoover and former Democratic presidential candidate Alfred E. (Al) Smith both bitterly attacked the New Deal. Despite spending over $1 million, Liberty League orators failed to inflict any serious political wounds on Roosevelt or the New Deal.

Other critics attacked particular New Deal programs as being inadequate and unfair. The National Recovery Administration attracted much criticism. Its detractors charged that corporate leaders had written NRA codes that favored big businesses' interests over the interests of workers, consumers, and small businesses. The AAA also came under attack. People were angry about the wasteful destruction of food crops to start the program at a time when millions were ill fed. Although the "Triple A" worked for landowners, it neglected tenants and sharecroppers. They rarely got subsidy money for cutting back production. Owners who took land out of production to collect the AAA subsidies often turned their sharecroppers off the land, depriving them of their economic base. Thousands of these uprooted "Okies" and "Arkies" headed for California, victims of both hard times and New Deal politics.

Many people were disappointed by the partial recovery made under the New Deal in 1933 and 1934. Even though business was up and unemployment was down, they remained well below 1920s pre-depression standards. Demagogues appealed to the dissatisfactions and frustrations of many Americans. Father Charles Coughlin, a Roman Catholic priest whose parish lay in a suburb of Detroit, developed a following of millions with his weekly radio broadcasts denouncing the New Deal. He organized a political movement called the National Union for Social Justice and preached a blend of anticommunism, anticapitalism, and anti-Semitism, which appealed mainly to Midwestern farmers and ethnic city dwellers.

Another anti-New Deal movement that called attention to its shortcomings was the Old Age Revolving Pensions plan, conceived by Dr. Francis E. Townsend, a retired dentist. Dr. Townsend proposed that everyone over age sixty receive $200 a month on the condition that they spend the money during the same month they received it. The money for the pensions would be raised by a "transaction tax," a sales tax levied each time goods were sold. He claimed that his plan would both provide for the elderly and end the depression by pumping billions of dollars of purchasing power into the economy. New Deal economists quickly demonstrated that the plan was fiscally unsound. The tax could raise only a portion of the money required to fund the plan, and it would have only a small impact on the depression. Dr. Townsend's scheme attracted a huge following. Millions of elderly, whose savings and investments had been lost during the depression, joined his movement. It also called attention to inadequate pensions and local relief for aged, retired workers. Social Security was enacted, in part, to undercut the appeal of the dentist's panacea.

The most significant challenge to the New Deal came from Huey Long, a brilliant Southern demagogue. Long, a left-wing populist, became the governor of Louisiana in 1929 and a U.S. Senator in 1932. Along the way, he forged a corrupt political machine that gave him dictatorial control of Louisiana politics. He also enjoyed an immensely popular following among workers and farmers of Louisiana because of his program of public works and public schools, which were paid for by taxes on corporations doing business in the state. Long did much to improve the quality of life for ordinary people in one of the poorest regions of the country.

Long enthusiastically supported the New Deal when it began, but turned against it in 1934 because of its fiscal conservatism. He made a bid for national leadership with a program he called "Share the Wealth," and he coined the slogan "Every Man a King." "Share the Wealth" proposed using the tax power to confiscate all incomes over $1 million and all estates over $5 million. The money raised would furnish each family with $5,000 for buying a farm or home, an annual income of $2,000, a free college education for their children, a radio, and other benefits for farmers and industrial workers. Long's plan also was fiscally unsound. The funds raised by confiscatory taxes would not begin to pay for the promised benefits. The Senate twice rejected his tax bills by large majorities. But Long's scheme appealed to the aspirations of poor people during the depression, to their resentment of the rich, and to their disappointment over New Deal efforts at recovery. Even though he was a corrupt demagogue and his distributionist schemes were fiscally unsound, Long addressed a real problem: the uneven distribution of wealth in America that allowed mass poverty in a rich country. By mid-1935, he had built a national following of millions, and he was planning a presidential bid in 1936, challenging Roosevelt. However, an assassin's bullet ended Long's career in September 1935, and his movement quickly disintegrated.

There also were many other left-wing critics of the New Deal. Both the Communist and Socialist parties attacked it. Minnesota elected a socialist governor. In California, the socialist muckraker, Upton Sinclair, captured the 1934 Democratic Party gubernatorial nomination. He campaigned for governor on a program he called End Poverty in California (EPIC), which included establishing socialist enterprises within the state. Although he was decisively beaten by a conservative Republican, Sinclair attracted over 800,000 votes.

Figure 6.5   During the mid-1930s, Huey P. Long of Louisiana emerged as the most formidable challenger to Roosevelt and the New Deal.   *Source:* National Archives.

The New Deal also came under attack from the Supreme Court. Most justices feared that many New Deal measures, which were hastily drawn up and enacted without debate or criticism by Congress, gave the executive branch too much power. On "Black Monday," May 27, 1935, the Supreme Court handed down three decisions that nullified key parts of the New Deal. In the most famous of these cases, *Schechter v. U.S.*, a unanimous court declared the NRA unconstitutional on the grounds that it gave excessive legislative power to the White House and that the commerce clause of the Constitution did not give the federal government the authority to regulate intrastate commerce. The *Schechter* decision killed the New Deal's most important program for industrial recovery. In *U.S. v. Butler* (1936), the Court also destroyed the AAA when it declared the processing tax unconstitutional. The *Butler* decision killed the New Deal's major program for agricultural recovery.

THE SECOND NEW DEAL

As 1935 dawned, the New Deal faced trouble. Critics were attacking particular programs and their failure to bring complete recovery. Demagogues were offering alternatives and luring away supporters, and the Supreme Court was dismantling some of its major programs. Roosevelt burst forth again in the spring and summer of 1935 with a flurry of legislative initiatives known as the Second New Deal. The Second New Deal differed from earlier efforts in several significant ways. The first New Deal had emphasized relief and recovery measures; the second continued relief and recovery efforts, but it was more concerned with reform. Earlier, Roosevelt had sought to cooperate with business; in 1935, he accused business of putting its interests ahead of the general welfare. He also proposed measures for increasing business taxes and tightening government regulation of some industries. The First New Deal had been most responsive to political pressures from established interests—bankers, large farmers, and big business. The Second New Deal responded to the rising power of organized labor and included measures that reflected Roosevelt's concern about the emergence of demagogic critics of the New Deal. Together, these factors combined to move Roosevelt to the Left; the Second New Deal was more progressive than the first; FDR abandoned his alliance with the business community and more directly addressed the needs of the disadvantaged and dispossessed.

In April 1935, Congress enacted the first major piece of Second New Deal legislation, the Emergency Relief Appropriation Act (ERAA). The new law empowered President Roosevelt to establish public works programs for millions of jobless Americans, including the Works Progress Administration (WPA). The WPA was the most important of the New Deal work relief programs. Before it was phased out in 1943, more than 8.5 million people were employed on more than 1 million different projects. WPA workers built over 650,000 miles of roads, 125,000 public buildings, 8,000 parks, and hundreds of bridges.

In addition to its construction projects, the WPA also funded many cultural efforts. The Federal Theater Project brought dramas, comedies, and variety shows to cities and towns across the nation. Artists on WPA payrolls painted murals in post offices and other public buildings. Dance and music projects sponsored ballet companies and symphony orchestras that performed across the country. The Federal Writers' Project hired authors such as Richard Wright, John Steinbeck, and John Cheever to write guidebooks and regional histories. The WPA even hired unemployed historians for its writer's project.

In addition to the WPA, the ERAA also funded other relief and public works measures. The Resettlement Administration (RA) moved thousands of impoverished farm families from submarginal land and gave them a fresh start on good soil with adequate farming equipment and guidance from farm experts. Later, the Farm Security Administration (FSA), which replaced the RA, granted long-term, low-interest loans to sharecroppers and tenants, enabling them to buy family farms. Another FSA program built chains of sanitary camps for migrant farm workers.

The ERAA also established the Rural Electrification Administration (REA). No other New Deal measure improved the quality of rural life as much as the REA. Until 1935, rural America lacked electrical power. Kerosene lamps illuminated homes after dark, and farmer's wives lacked washing machines, refrigerators, vacuum cleaners, and radios. The REA subsidized the building of power lines in rural America. Where private power was unavailable or private companies refused to build lines, the REA financed the creation of nonprofit, cooperative electric companies. In 1935, fewer than 10 percent of rural homes had electricity. By 1940, 40 percent were electrified, and by 1950, 90 percent.

The ERAA also authorized the National Youth Administration (NYA), the most important New Deal relief measure for young people. Its director, Aubrey

Figure 6.6   First Lady Eleanor Roosevelt was a powerful political leader in her own right and an ardent liberal advocate for the poor and disadvantaged during the Depression.   *Source:* Library of Congress.

Williams, worked to find part-time employment for more than 600,000 college students and over 1.5 million high school students so that they could continue their studies. It also found employment for over 2 million jobless young people who were not in school.

In June 1935, Roosevelt sent Congress five major bills—a labor bill, a Social Security bill, a banking bill, a public utilities bill, and a tax measure. Congress responded with a "Second Hundred Days" and enacted them all. Out of this productive congressional session came some of the most important and enduring legislation in the history of the Republic.

The first bill to pass was the National Labor Relations Act (NLRA), also known as the Wagner Act, after its principal sponsor, Senator Robert Wagner, of New York. The NLRA reaffirmed the right of workers to unionize and to bargain collectively, which had been guaranteed in Section 7(a) of the National Recovery Administration. But the Wagner Act was much stronger than the NRA, for it required management to bargain with certified union representatives. It also created the National Labor Relations Board to supervise plant elections and to issue "cease-and-desist" orders against companies that committed "unfair labor practices," such as refusing to permit union elections and firing employees engaged in union activities. The Wagner Act created a legal framework within which labor-management activities could function. It strengthened the bargaining leverage of unions and reduced the power of companies to resist unionization. Additionally, its passage showed the growing political influence of organized labor within New Deal ranks. Labor had become a core element in the evolving New Deal coalition.

After the NLRA came the Social Security Act, which created a series of programs, including a partial retirement pension for elderly workers. It also established three joint federal-state systems of unemployment insurance, disability insurance, and welfare payments to mothers with dependent children. The pension supplement was a compulsory insurance program funded by a payroll tax paid jointly by the employee and his employer.

Social Security pensions were created, in part, to deflect the challenge of the Townsendites, as well as to meet the pressing needs of the aged. Social Security also reflected the fiscal conservatism of President Roosevelt. It was the only social security system ever established that was self-funding; it was paid for not from general tax revenues but from a trust fund paid into by workers and their employers. It also was funded by a regressive tax, because the more a worker earned, the less tax he or she paid proportionally. Further, Social Security was a deflationary measure that took money out of a still depressed economy and did not return any for five years.

Compared to social insurance programs implemented by European nations which were not as rich as the United States, Social Security appeared paltry. Initially, it excluded millions of workers—farm workers, domestics, and many categories of industrial workers. Because it excluded many low-wage occupations, it necessarily excluded large numbers of women and minority workers. But, for all of its limitations, it was a historic measure. It established federal responsibility for assisting the elderly, the temporarily unemployed, the disabled, and poor mothers with dependent children. A new social contract, however narrowly defined, counterbalanced the gospel of self-help. For the first time in the history of the Republic, the federal government acknowledged the social rights of its citizens and a responsibility to protect them. The American welfare state had arrived.

Next came the Banking Act of 1935, which overhauled the Federal Reserve System and brought major changes to the nation's banking industry. The new law expanded the size of the Board of Governors of the Federal Reserve to seven members and lengthened their terms of office. It also gave the board greater control over regional banks, interest rates, and the setting of reserve requirements of member banks. Further, it gave the board control over open market operations, and it required that all state banks join the Federal Reserve System by July 1, 1942, if they wished to remain eligible for Federal Deposit Insurance Corporation (FDIC) coverage. The Banking Act of 1935 centralized the American banking system, giving the federal government much greater control over currency and credit, which was Roosevelt's aim. It was the most important banking measure since the Federal Reserve Act created the system in 1913.

The fourth law created the Public Utility Holding Company Act (PUHCA). It was the first piece of antitrust legislation enacted since Wilson's first term. Its key provision provided for the elimination of utility holding companies, and within three years of its passage, almost all of them had been extinguished.

The fifth of the major Second New Deal measures was a tax measure that proposed to redistribute wealth by "soaking the rich." It called for increased inheritance taxes, imposition of gift taxes, graduated income taxes on large incomes, and significantly higher corporate income taxes. Roosevelt also had a political motive for proposing his tax bill—to offset the rising power of Huey Long, who was trumpeting his "Share the Wealth" movement. Roosevelt's "wealth tax," the most radical of all New Deal proposals, provoked a firestorm of criticism from business and the media. Business and other interests lobbied Congress intensively to eliminate or reduce Roosevelt's tax proposals, and Congress proceeded to gut the measure. The tax measure passed by Congress eliminated the inheritance tax and reduced corporate tax rates sharply. The Wealth Tax Act of 1935 raised little revenue and did not redistribute wealth. Even though the wealth tax had little fiscal effect, no other New Deal measure provoked as much bitter criticism. Roosevelt, despite proposing the wealth tax, remained a fiscal conservative at heart.

The Second New Deal was the culmination of Roosevelt's efforts to impose a welfare state on a capitalistic economic foundation in order to bring the American ideal of equality of opportunity closer to reality. Without challenging the system of private profit or redistributing wealth, New Dealers used the power of the federal government to regulate corporations, strengthen trade unions, provide pensions for the elderly, help the disabled, maintain the poor, and provide relief to the unemployed. The New Deal represented the fullest expression of the Progressive social vision to date.

Figure 6.7   Conservation was a top New Deal priority from its be-ginnings. The New Dealers' most spectacular ecological step was the building of a "shelterbelt," the planting of millions of trees on the Great Plains states along the 100th meridian.   *Source:* National Archives.

A NEW DEAL FOR THE ENVIRONMENT

Franklin Roosevelt shared his cousin Theodore Roosevelt's love of nature and his concern to promote and develop national conservation policies. New Dealers did more to protect the American ecosystem and to develop national conservation poli-cies than any administration since Theodore Roosevelt's presidency during the first decade of the twentieth century. Conservation was a top New Deal priority from the beginning. Franklin Roosevelt's main environmental concerns were pro-tecting land and water resources.

Both the size of the U.S. Forest Service staff and its budgets were increased in 1933 and 1934, and its existing programs were expanded. Perhaps the most spec-tacular step to enhance national ecosystems taken by New Dealers was the build-ing of a "shelterbelt" on the Great Plains. Over 200 million trees were planted across a 100-mile-wide zone along the 100th Meridian. Stretching from the Cana-dian border south to the state of Texas, the shelterbelt functioned as a giant wind-break and also prevented the disastrous dust storms which had blown away much of the Great Plains topsoil during the early 1930s. Congress enacted the Soil Con-servation Act in 1935, which enabled the federal government to tackle the problem of soil erosion on a national scale. At about the same time, Congress also enacted the Taylor Grazing Act, which set strict requirements for grazing cattle on the vast Western rangelands owned by the federal government. The CCC and many WPA projects also conserved natural resources and provided jobs for the unemployed during the depression.

THE ELECTION OF 1936

Public opinion polls taken in 1936 showed that Roosevelt and his New Deal programs enjoyed broad popular support in all regions of the nation. The Republicans faced a strong uphill battle in their first campaign to oust the popular incumbent. To oppose the president, the GOP turned to Alfred M. "Alf" Landon, a former follower of Theodore Roosevelt and the current Progressive Republican governor of Kansas. He had a good civil liberties record and favored regulation of business, and endorsed many New Deal programs to the dismay of many conservative members of his own party.

Landon's campaign against Roosevelt never caught fire, even though the Republicans outspent the Democrats $14 million to $9 million, and most of the nation's newspapers and radio stations endorsed Landon. He was a colorless individual and a poor public speaker. His radio delivery also was ineffective. He tried to make issues out of Roosevelt's deficit spending and the huge increase in the size and power of the presidency, but neither carried much beyond the realm of those already converted to his political philosophy. The Liberty League was so obviously a front for wealthy critics of New Deal tax and regulatory policies that Landon asked it to not endorse his candidacy. However, the Kansan did attract a number of disaffected Democrats, including two former presidential candidates, Al Smith and John W. Davis.

There was another element in the 1936 election. Roosevelt's political advisers feared that popular demagogues might combine forces to mount a third-party challenge. Huey Long's assassination had eliminated the most dangerous threat. The major challenge came from Father Coughlin and Dr. Townsend, who tried to join with the Reverend Gerald L.K. Smith, an anti-Semitic rabble-rouser who had inherited part of Long's forces, in support of the candidacy of Congressman William Lemke of North Dakota, who was running as the candidate of the newly formed Union Party. These efforts failed, as the extremists feuded among themselves and Father Coughlin went off on his own. Coughlin's radio speeches denounced Roosevelt's New Deal in vicious terms. He sounded anti-Semitic themes, called Roosevelt "anti-God," and accused him of being a Communist. But the challenge posed by the demagogues in 1936 proved to be weak. They neither hurt Roosevelt's candidacy nor had any impact on the election's outcome.

When Roosevelt hit the campaign trail in 1936, he ran hard against the business classes. His opening speech attacked "economic royalists" who took "other people's money" to impose a "new industrial dictatorship." Roosevelt turned his reelection campaign into a liberal crusade, a clash between the "haves" and "have-nots." For the rest of the campaign, he ignored the weak challenge of Landon and ran against former President Hoover and "the interests." Hoover responded with a series of denunciatory speeches. He claimed that the New Deal philosophy rested on "coercion and the compulsory organization of men," and that it derived part of its program from Karl Marx.

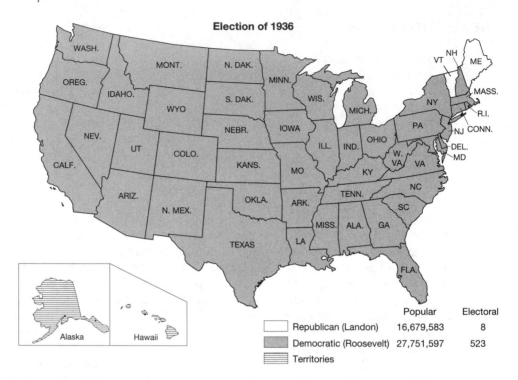

Election of 1936

	Popular	Electoral
Republican (Landon)	16,679,583	8
Democratic (Roosevelt)	27,751,597	523
Territories		

Figure 6.8   The election of 1936.   *Source:* Moss, *Rise of Modern America,* p. 237.

In his final campaign speech, delivered at Madison Square Garden to a full house cheering his every word, Roosevelt taunted his hapless Republican opponents:

> Never before in history have these forces been united against one candidate as they stand today. They are unanimous in their hate for me—and I welcome their hatred! I should like to have it said of my first administration that in it the forces of selfishness and lust for power met their match. I should like to have it said of my second administration that in it these forces met their master.[1]

Roosevelt and the Democrats swept to a landslide victory. Roosevelt received 27.8 million votes to Landon's 16.7 million. Lemke attracted only 882,000 votes, and Socialist Party candidate Norman Thomas received a mere 187,000. Six million more people voted in 1936 than had cast ballots in 1932, and most of these new voters voted for Roosevelt. Most new voters were recruited from the ranks of people on relief, the unemployed, and the working classes, who expressed their solidarity with the man who had forged the New Deal. They had perceived Roosevelt to be a candidate with a program and a conception of government that favored the common people. The Democrats carried every state in the union except Maine and Ver-

---

[1]Quoted in Leuchtenburg, *Franklin Roosevelt and the New Deal,* p. 184.

mont, and they rolled up huge majorities in the House and Senate. The people had been given a chance to vote on the performance of Roosevelt and his program, and they had responded with an overwhelming vote of approval. Some analysts thought that the Republican Party was on the verge of extinction, about to go the way of the Federalists after 1801 and the Whigs after 1852. James "Big Jim" Farley, Roosevelt's campaign manager, quipped that the election proved that "as Maine goes, so goes Vermont."

THE NEW DEAL COALITION

By 1936, Roosevelt and the Democrats had forged a new political coalition, firmly based on the mass of voters living in large Northern cities and led in Congress by a new political type, the Northern urban liberal. Whereas old-stock Americans in small towns and cities clung to the GOP, the newer ethnic groups in the cities joined the Democrats. These "ethnics" had benefited from New Deal programs and were delighted at the attention given to them by New Dealers. Hard times and New Deal programs also had attracted the votes of most farmers and the elderly. Organized labor was an integral part of the New Deal coalition, especially the new industrial unions forged by the Congress of Industrial Organizations (CIO). Black voters in Northern cities abandoned their historic allegiance to the Republicans and joined the new coalition. Many former Republican Progressive middle-class voters and thousands of former Socialists also joined the Roosevelt coalition.

A dramatic political realignment had taken place in America, as important as the one occurring in 1894 and 1896, which had made the Republicans the dominant party until the Great Depression. Now the Democrats had become the majority coalition, and they would retain their dominance for more than thirty years. A historic realignment, underway since the election of 1928 and forged in the crucible of the 1932 depression election, was completed in 1936.

ROOSEVELT ATTACKS THE SUPREME COURT

Roosevelt's Second Inaugural Address, delivered on January 20, 1937, sounded a call for more radical reforms. He spoke feelingly of the plight of the poor: "I see one-third of a nation ill-housed, ill-clad, and ill-nourished." Observers wondered if he had a New Deal war on poverty in mind. Conservatives trembled at the thought of the new tax bills and antitrust measures Roosevelt might propose. The once mighty Republican Party had been reduced to a legislative remnant in both houses of Congress, incapable of effective opposition.

As he began his second term, Roosevelt was at the height of his power and prestige; he was coming off an election in which he, his program, and his party had been given an emphatic endorsement. If he read the result as a mandate to continue on a Progressive path, who would resist? If he had in mind an assault on the prerogatives of the rich in favor of the poor, who could prevent it? But when Roosevelt sent a specific legislative proposal to Congress two weeks later, he surprised everyone. He asked not for more social reforms, but for reform of the Supreme Court, an issue which he had never raised in the recent campaign.

The Supreme Court had already nullified several important New Deal measures, including the Triple A and the NRA. Roosevelt and his advisers were afraid that it would soon invalidate recently enacted Second New Deal measures, particularly the Wagner Act and the Social Security Act. Roosevelt was angry with the Court's conservative majority which had thwarted many New Deal efforts to promote recovery and reform American society.

To prevent further damage to the New Deal, he proposed to change the Court. On February 5, 1937, Roosevelt sent Congress his Judiciary Reorganization Bill. He requested the authority to add a federal judge whenever an incumbent reached age seventy and failed to retire within six months. He proposed adding fifty federal judges, including six Supreme Court justices. He insisted that the current judiciary was understaffed, and that additional jurists were required to relieve overworked "elderly, feeble" judges. Six additional judges on the Supreme Court would help the "nine old men." Roosevelt's disingenuous proposal fooled no one. It was obvious that he would use court reform as a vehicle to liberalize the Supreme Court by appointing younger, more progressive members. At the time Roosevelt proposed restructuring the Court, its lineup included four reactionaries, who adamantly opposed the New Deal, three liberals, who usually supported it, and two moderates—Chief Justice Charles Evans Hughes and Associate Justice Owen Roberts. Hughes and Roberts were the swingmen; they sometimes upheld New Deal legislation, but more often they opposed it.

Roosevelt's controversial proposal generated much opposition. Critics quickly dubbed his proposed court reform "Court packing." Two polls showed the the public was divided on the issue. Media editorials almost universally condemned it. Most Republicans opposed it, as did many Democrats, including some liberals. Roosevelt had attacked a national symbol that gave Americans a sense of identity and unity. He also threatened the constitutional principle of checks and balances with his blatant proposal to politicize the Court and bend it to the executive will. The debate in Congress lasted for months and divided the Democrats.

As debate over the measure continued, the two swingmen, Hughes and Roberts, voted to sustain a state minimum wage law. In April 1937, in *National Labor Relations Board v. Jones and Laughlin Steel Corporation*, they voted with the majority in a five to four decision, sustaining the National Labor Relations Act. A month later, they joined with another majority in a five to four decision to uphold Social Security. The conservatives had been eclipsed.

A few days after the Social Security decision, Justice Willis Van Devanter, a conservative judge, announced his retirement from the Court. Roosevelt would now have a six to three majority on the Court willing to approve New Deal legislation. The need for drastic Court reform had vanished. Hughes's and Roberts's sudden conversions to New Deal liberalism, coupled with Van Devanter's resig-

Figure 6.9   Roosevelt's proposal to reform the Supreme Court alarmed many Americans who feared that he was trying to impose one-man rule on the country.   *Source:* Franklin D. Roosevelt Library.

nation, doomed Roosevelt's bill. In a career hitherto marked by matchless political astuteness, Roosevelt committed a costly blunder. He refused to yield and continued to battle stubbornly for what had become a hopeless cause. The Senate adjourned in July without passing his judicial reform proposal, handing Roosevelt his first major political defeat.

In later years, Roosevelt claimed that he had lost the "battle" but that he had won the "war" for judicial reform. In a sense, he was correct. He appointed a liberal, Alabama Senator Hugo Black, to replace Van Devanter. Within two and a half years after Congress had rejected his Court-packing scheme, Roosevelt had appointed four more liberals to the Supreme Court. The new "Roosevelt Court" greatly expanded the constitutionally permissible areas of government regulation of economic activity. Never again would a major Roosevelt bill be overturned. In fact, from 1937 to the present, the Supreme Court has never overturned a single piece of significant national or state social legislation. Out of the political jumble of 1937, there occurred a constitutional revolution without the enactment of any new amendments.

But FDR's success represented a Pyrrhic victory. In more important ways, Roosevelt lost the "war." The Court fight divided and weakened the Democratic Party, and it greatly strengthened the emerging conservative bipartisan coalition of Southern Democratic and Northern Republican opponents of the New Deal. The Roosevelt Court might uphold all new laws, but Congress, no longer so responsive to Roosevelt's leadership, passed few measures for the justices to consider. Shortly after the Court fight, a major administration bill to reorganize the executive branch was sent to Capitol Hill. Alarmed opponents denounced the measure as an effort to impose dictatorship on the American people. Congress rejected the bill, handing Roosevelt another stinging political defeat. Although Roosevelt would never acknowledge it, most historians date the beginning of the end of the New Deal from the repercussions of the political fight he provoked over the Supreme Court. Ironically, a constitutional breakthrough coincided with the throttling of the very liberal reform impulse, to which the constitutional barriers had been removed.

THE ROOSEVELT RECESSION

Roosevelt was also partly responsible for triggering a severe economic recession that began in 1937 and persisted until 1939. Never comfortable with deficit financing, the president decided that the economy had recovered to the point where it no longer needed stimulation from government spending and budget deficits. During the first half of 1937, Roosevelt ordered the WPA to cut its enrollment from 3 million to 1.5 million jobs. Other New Deal relief agencies slashed their enrollments drastically. To reduce the inflation rate that had reached 3.5 percent, the Federal Reserve System tightened reserve requirements and raised interest rates. The economy, deprived of billions in federal spending, declined sharply; within a year, the unemployment rate had risen five percentage points.

Confronted with the sharp economic downturn, Roosevelt quickly reversed himself and revived deficit financing. The WPA, CCC, and other work relief agencies all increased their appropriations. But it was not until the end of 1939 that unemployment returned to early 1937 levels. Leaders of both parties criticized Roosevelt for having unnecessarily subjected Americans to two years of increased hardship. The "Roosevelt recession" quickly erased gains that had taken four years to achieve, and it discouraged many people who had come to believe that the depression was behind them. The President's popularity and prestige sagged to new lows.

Occurring in the midst of a recession that Republicans could blame on the president, the 1938 elections severely damaged the New Deal coalition. Republicans picked up eighty-one seats in the House and eight seats in the Senate. Robert Taft, from Ohio, son of the former President and Chief Justice William Howard Taft, was one of the new Republican senators. Several prominent incumbent liberals went down in defeat. Roosevelt also hurt himself by intervening in several Southern elections trying to get rid of prominent conservative Senate opponents of the

New Deal. All incumbents defeated the liberal challengers backed by Roosevelt, dealing him another serious political defeat. The conservative coalition emerged from the 1938 elections as the strongest political force in Washington. From 1939 on, Roosevelt and the New Dealers were on the defensive, unable to enlarge the New Deal and at times forced to accept cuts in its programs.

THE END OF THE NEW DEAL

By 1938, Roosevelt was also increasingly involved with conflicts in Europe and Asia. Japanese aggression in China and Germany's annexation of Austria threatened to send the world skidding toward another world war. Increasingly, the outer world claimed the president's attention.

Congress enacted the last two significant New Deal measures in early 1938; one was a new Agricultural Adjustment Act to replace the one nullified by the Supreme Court. Yielding to pressure from the farm bloc, the new AAA allowed unlimited crop production and larger subsidies. The government was required to store the inevitable surplus production and sell some of it overseas at low prices. Agricultural overproduction returned, but farm income was maintained by taxpayers providing new Triple A subsidies. The final New Deal reform was the Fair Labor Standards Act (FLSA), enacted in May 1938, which established the first minimum wage at 40 cents an hour and set the standard workweek at forty hours. The FLSA forced immediate pay raises for over 12 million workers who were making less than the minimum wage at the time it became law. The act also abolished child labor and established rules for the employment of teenagers.

The New Deal had ended by the summer of 1938. It was a victim of recession, declining liberal support, political blunders by President Roosevelt, and the growing prominence of foreign affairs in a sullen world girding for war. But mainly it had been stifled by the growing assertiveness of the bipartisan conservative coalition comprised of Northern Republicans and anti-New Deal Southern Democrats. Ironically, Roosevelt's own political mistakes, especially his feckless effort to reform the Supreme Court, had created the New Deal's nemesis that stopped it in its tracks.

THE RISE OF ORGANIZED LABOR

At the outset of the Great Depression, trade unions in this country were neither strong nor militant. Only about 3 million of the nation's 46,000,000 workers belonged to unions, and most of these unionists were skilled workers who belonged to the American Federation of Labor. This AFL membership consisted mainly of members of craft unions. (Craft unions typically represented skilled workers in a particular trade, for example, plumbing or typesetting.)

The National Recovery Administration promoted union growth through its Section 7(a), which required that every industrial code grant employees "the right to organize and bargain collectively through representatives of their own choosing." The greatest increase was among industrial unions within the AFL. (Industrial unions represented all workers, skilled and unskilled, in a given industry, for example, steelworkers or autoworkers.) The United Mine Workers added 300,000 workers within a few months. After one year of NRA, over 1,700 locals had been formed in the automobile, steel, rubber, aluminum, and other mass production industries, adding 1 million members to AFL rolls. But many companies resisted unionization through the NRA codes; they prohibited unions or formed company unions. NRA officials often went along with efforts to thwart independent unions. Disappointed labor leaders complained about the "National Run Around," and a wave of strikes spread across the country in 1934.

An important strike occurred on the San Francisco waterfront in July 1934, when shipping companies rejected longshoremen's demands for union recognition, control of hiring halls, and higher wages. A violent confrontation occurred when police tried to clear 5,000 pickets from the Embarcadero, the main waterfront street, to let strikebreakers work. Shots were fired from both sides. Scores of people were injured, and two strikers were killed. The governor sent National Guardsmen to occupy the waterfront. Organized labor responded with a general strike that nearly shut down the city for four days. Federal officials intervened to facilitate a settlement granting union recognition and control of hiring halls, a major victory for labor.

In 1935, the Supreme Court nullified the NRA; a few months later, Congress enacted the National Labor Relations Act (Wagner Act), which created a more hospitable environment for unionizing activities and strengthened union bargaining leverage with employers. Union organizing efforts increased dramatically. The Wagner Act also spurred the creation of a new labor organization, which originated as a faction within the AFL that was dissatisfied with the Federation's lack of sympathy for industrial unionism. Its leader was John L. Lewis, head of the United Mine Workers, who formed a Committee for Industrial Organizations within the AFL. In 1936, AFL leaders expelled Lewis and his industrial unions, which later formed their own trade union organization, renamed the Congress of Industrial Organizations (CIO).

The CIO launched major organizing drives in mass-production industries in the late 1930s. One of its first campaigns occurred in the steel industry, which had been a bastion of nonunion shops since the failed strikes of 1919. It created a Steel Workers Organizing Committee (SWOC), under the leadership of Philip Murray, and 400 organizers descended upon the nation's major steel centers. "Big Steel," as the United States Steel Corporation was known, the nation's largest steel company, gave up without a fight. After secret negotiations, a contract was signed recognizing the SWOC as the bargaining agent and granting workers an eight-hour day, a forty-hour week, and a large pay raise. It was an astonishing settlement from a company that had been an antiunion bastion since its creation in 1901. U.S. Steel's management cut the deal with the SWOC because it did not want a strike that would disrupt its production schedules during a time of improving business.

"Little Steel," the four companies ranking from second to fifth, refused to surrender. Under the leadership of Republic Steel, the companies prepared to battle the SWOC. In May 1937, the union called a strike against the companies, and a fierce conflict occurred. "Little Steel" employed a variety of antiunion tactics, including intimidation and violence. The worst violence occurred on May 30, when Chicago police attacked picketers in front of Republic's main plant. They fired into the crowd, killing ten strikers and wounding dozens more. This brutal incident is known as the Memorial Day Massacre. It created widespread sympathy for strikers, but "Little Steel" broke the strike and defeated the CIO's organizing effort that year.

In December 1936, another CIO union, the United Automobile Workers (UAW), began a famous strike in Flint, Michigan, against General Motors, the world's largest industrial corporation. The strikers used a novel tactic, the "sit-down" strike, against the giant automaker. Instead of walking out of the Fisher Body Plant at the end of a shift, the workers took over the factory. They sat at their stations on the shop floor, shutting down the assembly line and preventing strikebreakers from working. Caught off guard by the sit-down tactic, company officials tried to dislodge the workers. They cut off the heat, letting wintertime temperatures drop to zero, but the workers built bonfires and stayed inside of the factory. Police charged the plants, but they were driven off by a barrage of coffee mugs, tools, lunch pails, and auto parts. Police then lobbed in tear gas, but the workers broke windows to let the gas out and again drove the police back, this time using company fire hoses.

General Motors' officials then demanded that the state militia be mobilized to remove the strikers, and they got a court order setting February 3 as the deadline for evacuation. The workers, who were risking fines, imprisonment, and possibly violent assaults, refused to yield. They demanded that the company engage in collective bargaining. When February 3 arrived, Michigan Governor Frank Murphy, a liberal Democrat elected with labor support, mobilized Illinois National Guard units but ordered them to preserve law and order and to protect the workers. President Roosevelt, who also sympathized with the strikers, appealed for negotiations. Faced with the prospect of class warfare and powerful political opposition, General Motors capitulated. Negotiations between company representatives and UAW leaders began. Within weeks, the UAW was recognized as the autoworkers' bargaining agent. Company and union representations negotiated a contract that provided substantial pay increases and a forty-hour week. Chrysler signed a similar agreement after a short strike. Ford, bitterly antiunion, held out until the spring of 1941, and there were several bloody encounters at Ford's River Rouge plant between UAW forces and company guards.

The sit-down strike proved to be an effective tactic, and all kinds of workers used it in the late 1930s—textile, glass, and rubber workers; dime store clerks, janitors, dressmakers, and bakers. Sometimes workers sat down spontaneously on the job and waited for CIO organizers to come to sign them up. The sit-down tactic worked and expressed the rank-and-file militancy that energized the trade union movement in the late 1930s. A liberal-dominated Supreme Court outlawed the sit-down strike tactic in 1939.

The CIO, aided by legislation, liberal politicians like Governor Murphy and President Roosevelt, and often favorable public opinion, added millions of union members during its organizing drives of the late 1930s. Hundreds of thousands of auto workers, coal miners, steelworkers, clothing workers, rubber workers, and others formed strong industrial unions. Most of the nation's major mass-production industries were organized. CIO membership reached 5 million by the end of the decade. A significant transfer of economic power had occurred. By the end of the decade, one in four workers belonged to a trade union. Unskilled workers had a major voice in the CIO. Women's membership in unions tripled. African Americans became a significant part of industrial America. Millions of union members were immigrants or the sons and daughters of immigrants; they achieved not only significant economic gains, but they and their families now found themselves launched into the mainstream of American life.

A NEW DEAL FOR WOMEN

Various New Deal programs designed during the 1930s often helped women less than men. The National Recovery Act allowed industries to structure gendered wage differentials into their codes of fair practices; women inevitably received the lower wages. Many New Deal programs resisted hiring women or hired far fewer women than men. Of the myriad of projects funded by the WPA, the largest of the New Deal public works program, perhaps 10 percent of jobs went to women, and these jobs generally were limited to clerical work, libraries, recreational activities, health and nutrition programs, and most often, sewing projects. The Civilian Conservation Corps excluded women, while providing work for over 2 million unemployed young men.

Women improved their political status during the 1930s. Arkansas elected the first woman to serve in the U.S. Senate, Hattie Caraway. Middle- and upper-middle class women, led by First Lady Eleanor Roosevelt and Secretary of Labor Frances Perkins, the first woman cabinet member, made significant political gains during the New Deal years. Josephine Roche served as assistant secretary of the treasury, and Nellie Taylor Ross became the director of the U.S. Mint. Many women joined the staffs of newly created New Deal agencies. Franklin Roosevelt was the first president to appoint women diplomats. Women became important parts of the Democratic Party political machinery and the new Democratic Party coalition. There were over 200 women delegates at the 1936 Democratic Convention. Under the leadership of Mary W. "Molly" Dewson, a close friend of Eleanor's, the Women's Division of the Democratic National Committee played a major role in orchestrating Franklin Roosevelt's landslide reelection victory in 1936.

During the depression decade, women significantly increased their influence in the nation's cultural life. The increasing cultural influence of women derived largely from the depression-generated upsurge of cultural nationalism. Government patronage of the arts was more likely to be gender-neutral than private patrons, and it involved a far larger number of women because it was publicly funded. Thousands of talented women participated in WPA artistic and cultural projects. Women writers participated in the Federal Writers Project.

Women also made their mark in the popular culture—in aviation, sports, and, above all, the movies. The greatest woman athlete of the 1930s was a young Texan, Babe Didrickson. At the 1932 Summer Olympics, held in Los Angeles, she won four gold medals. Later she became the nation's finest women's golfer. Amelia Earhart was the most famous pilot of the 1930s, the first woman to fly solo across the Atlantic, duplicating Charles Lindbergh's famed feat. Determined to prove that women aviators could equal or surpass the achievements of male pilots, Earhart set many new flying records, but she disappeared while on a flight across the Pacific Ocean.

It was through movies that women actresses exercised their greatest cultural influence on the American people: in the realms of styles of dress, speech, manners, mores, behavior, sexuality, and appearance. Women movie stars were the highest paid women in the country; in fact, the salaries of the top women film stars equaled or surpassed those of all but a few men. Each week, of the 80 million or more Americans who attended the movies, probably 60 percent were females.

During the 1930s, despite the hard times and the widespread suffering of women, they often were able to achieve greater economic independence, enter a wider range of occupations, join unions, enjoy greater personal and sexual freedom, enhance their political status, achieve greater cultural influence, and achieve a more serious and positive public image. In the words of Susan Ware, the leading historian of women during the 1930s, women "held their own," and they often made modest advances.

THE EMERGENCE OF ETHNIC AMERICANS

During the 1930s, millions of ethnic Americans, the sons and daughters of the "new" immigrants who had poured into America during the first fifteen years of the twentieth century, came of age during the 1930s. The large majority of these first-generation Americans identified with Roosevelt and the New Deal. They saw Roosevelt as both a leader who acknowledged their claims to full acceptance as Americans and their sense of entitlement to all of the opportunities and challenges of citizenship. Roosevelt cemented his hold on the loyalties of ethnic Americans by appointing their leaders in unprecedented numbers to important public offices. Nearly one-fourth of the federal judicial appointments made during the New Deal era were Catholics.

Most ethnic Americans during the 1930s resided in the large cities of the Northeast and the Midwest, especially in New York and Chicago. During his 1936 electoral sweep, Roosevelt carried 104 of the nation's 106 largest cities. By 1936,

Northern ethnic Americans had acquired enough political clout within the Democratic Party to abolish the rule requiring the party's presidential candidate to win a two-thirds majority vote at its nominating convention. This rule, in place for more than 100 years, had been used by Southern Democrats to prevent any candidate they did not accept from getting the nomination. The anachronistic two-thirds rule had nearly cost Roosevelt the 1932 nomination. Bolstered by the support of Northern ethnics, he got rid of it by the time of the 1936 convention.

Most Catholics supported the New Deal and the Democratic Party. In large Eastern cities, Irish Americans and Italian Americans flocked to Roosevelt's banner. In the Midwest, Polish Americans and other Slavic groups also joined the New Deal coalition. A large majority of American Jews, most of them the sons and daughters of Russian or Polish Jews who had come to America during the first decade of the twentieth century, enthusiastically supported Roosevelt and the New Dealers. Jews perceived the Roosevelt administration as being a special protector of Jews, determined to extend their educational, economic, and social opportunities.

AFRICAN AMERICANS AND THE NEW DEAL

African Americans benefited from many New Deal programs and rallied to Roosevelt's leadership. New Dealers were more responsive to African American concerns than any other administration since Reconstruction. Roosevelt invited many African American visitors to the White House and appointed an unofficial black cabinet to advise him on African American issues. He also appointed several African Americans to important government jobs. He appointed a prominent black educator, Mary McLeod Bethune, as Director of Negro Affairs of the National Youth Administration. The WPA hired black workers for 18 percent of its jobs at a time when African Americans made up 10 percent of the national population. The federal civil service hired thousands of black employees during the New Deal era. African American illiteracy declined, and life expectancy for black people increased about five years during the 1930s.

Several New Dealers were committed to undermining both segregation and African American disfranchisement. Eleanor Roosevelt was the leader of those New Dealers committed to equal rights for African Americans. She worked closely with Walter White, president of the NAACP, supporting its efforts to strike at the legal foundations of Jim Crow laws. In 1939, when the Daughters of the American Revolution (DAR) refused to allow an African American opera singer, Marian Anderson, to perform in Washington's Constitution Hall, Mrs. Roosevelt arranged for her to sing "God Bless America" on Easter Sunday from the steps of the Lincoln Memorial.

But President Roosevelt was never committed to black civil rights. Unwilling to risk alienating Southern whites, he never endorsed two key African American political issues of the 1930s—a federal anti-lynching law and abolition of the poll tax. He also accepted discrimination and segregation against African Americans by many government agencies, as New Dealers acceded to prevailing racist practices. Under NRA codes, employers replaced black workers with whites, or paid black workers less than white workers for doing the same work. The Federal Housing Authority (FHA) accepted residential segregation by refusing to guarantee mortgages purchased by African American families in white neighborhoods. The CCC was racially segregated, as was the TVA, which constructed all-white towns and confined African American workers to low-paying job categories. Since waiters, cooks, janitors, domestics, and farm workers were excluded both from Social Security coverage and from the minimum wage provisions of the Fair Labor Standards Act, millions of African American workers who held these low-paying jobs were denied benefits available to most white workers. One New Deal program harmed blacks. The Triple A denied crop subsidies to African American tenants and deprived thousands of black sharecroppers of their livelihoods by forcing them off of the land. Even though African Americans were worse off than whites during the depression and their needs were greater, they received fewer benefits than whites. When African Americans did benefit from New Deal programs it was more because they were economically distressed citizens than because they belonged to an oppressed racial minority.

Despite the shortcomings of the New Deal for African Americans, blacks supported it enthusiastically. African American voters abandoned their historical allegiance to the party of Lincoln and moved into the Democratic camp. Two-thirds of African American voters had voted for Hoover in 1932. In 1936, two-thirds voted for Roosevelt, joining the New Deal coalition. By the 1938 congressional elections, 85 percent of African American voters had joined the Democratic Party. Since the New Deal era, African American voters have been a loyal Democratic constituency, and the Democratic Party has been much more responsive to black concerns than the Republicans. Today, African American politicians form one of the most powerful blocs within the Democratic Party, and almost all elected black political leaders are Democrats.

HISPANIC AMERICANS DURING THE NEW DEAL

Many of the approximately 1.2 million Mexican Americans living in the Southwestern United States suffered extreme hardship during the depression, but they received little help from the New Deal. Mexican Americans had little political clout, and official America was not very concerned about their welfare. Mostly uneducated and unskilled, they toiled at the economic margins. They were either beyond the reach of or fell through the cracks of many New Deal programs. U.S. government policy during the 1930s discouraged Mexican Americans from living in the United States. The Mexican-born population declined substantially during the years of the New Deal, as many families returned to Mexico because of U.S. government pressure and declining economic opportunities.

But despite poverty, hardship, and official indifference or hostility, the members of the Mexican American population who were politically active generally voted Democratic and supported Roosevelt's New Deal. In Texas, Arizona, and California, Mexican Americans enrolled in sizeable numbers in the Civilian Conservation Corps and some of the WPA projects. One of the major reasons Hispanic Americans benefited to the extent that they did from New Deal social welfare programs and supported Roosevelt was the political influence of Senator Dennis Chavez of New Mexico, the only important U.S. political leader during the 1930s of Hispanic descent. Roosevelt frequently sought the advice of Chavez and regarded him as the national spokesman for the Hispanic American community.

During the 1920s, hundreds of thousands of Mexicans had moved to California and the Southwest. When depression struck the Golden State, Mexican Americans, who made up most of the agricultural workforce, reacted to hard times by engaging in strikes. Mexican American workers in Southern California formed a union that staged about twenty strikes from 1933 to 1936. About 18,000 Mexican American cotton pickers joined a union and struck the cotton fields of the San Joaquin Valley in 1933. Vigilantes fired on their union hall, killing two workers. The Immigration Service supported growers' efforts to break the strike by deporting workers, some of whom were legal residents.

The arrival of dispossessed white tenant farmers and sharecroppers from the Southern Plains states undermined the economic position of Mexican American farm workers in California. Between 1935 and 1938, about 300,000 "Okies" came

Figure 6.10   During the late 1930s, hundreds of thousands of farm families fled rural poverty in the southern plains states for California. This photo shows a family of "Okies" stalled by car trouble somewhere in New Mexico in 1937.   *Source:* Library of Congress.

to California's Central Valley to work in the fields. Growers were happy to hire them as strikebreakers and replacements for the Mexicans. By the late 1930s, poor whites composed 90 percent of the state's migrant farm workers, and many of the Hispanic workers they had displaced had been forcibly taken or voluntarily returned to Mexico.

During the 1930s, a sizeable number of Mexicans emigrated to Midwestern states such as Illinois, Michigan, and Ohio. Refugees from grinding rural poverty in their native land, they arrived uneducated and unskilled. They often found work as migratory farm laborers; some found their way into the lower ranks of the unskilled workers in some of the traditional industries, including railroad gangs, meatpacking, steel, and auto. Many of the *barrios* of Midwestern as well as Southwestern and Western cities were founded or greatly expanded during the depression decade.

During the 1930s, a relatively small immigration from Puerto Rico to the United States mainland continued. These Puerto Ricans, like the Mexicans, mostly refugees from an oppressive rural poverty, settled in New York, Philadelphia, and a few other large Eastern cities. Most lacked education and job skills, and they did not speak English upon their arrival. Many Puerto Ricans discovered in the depression America of the 1930s that they had traded rural poverty in their homeland for urban poverty in America.

A NEW DEAL FOR NATIVE AMERICANS

Federal Indian policy was transformed during the 1930s. Although President Roosevelt had little firsthand knowledge of Native Americans or their problems, he relied on Harold Ickes, who did. Ickes arranged for John S. Collier to become Commissioner of the Bureau of Indian Affairs (BIA). Collier, a social scientist who had been a director of the American Indian Defense Association, had long championed Native American causes. He also had edited *American Indian Life*, the most important journal devoted to Native American issues. Collier had become convinced that the federal government's integrationist policy had failed to work, and that it was destroying Native American culture. He believed that Native Americans required autonomy and self-determination to survive. During his long tenure as commissioner of the BIA from 1933 to 1945, Collier worked to promote cultural pluralism and cultural nationalism among Native Americans.

He fought for Indian tribal ownership of land and championed the Indian Reorganization Act, passed by Congress in 1934, which ended the allotment policy established by the Dawes Act nearly fifty years earlier. The allotment system had worked to transfer much Indian land to white ranchers, miners, and farmers. Since 1887, Indian landholdings had dropped from 138 million acres to 48 million. When the depression struck, Native Americans were the poorest and most depressed of all major ethnic groups in the country. Indian families on reservations earned an average annual income of about $100. Their infant mortality rate was the highest, their life expectancy was the shortest, their educational attainment was the lowest, and their rate of unemployment was the highest of any major group in the nation.

The Indian Reorganization Act restored lands to tribal ownership. Collier also tried to acquire additional lands for many of the tribes through government grants, court actions, and private efforts. Other stipulations of the reorganization act provided for Indian self-government and loans for economic development. Collier promoted efforts by Native Americans to develop their own business enterprises on reservations. Medical and educational services were expanded. Native American religious practices and traditional cultures were protected. Collier, deeply respectful of Indian ways, was committed to democratic pluralism. He stated, "The cultural history of Indians is in all respects to be considered equal to that of any non-Indian group." For the first time in its history, under Collier's leadership, the Bureau of Indian Affairs hired many Native Americans for its own staff. Of the approximately 5,000 employees of the BIA in 1938, 1,300 were Native Americans.

Native Americans also benefited from some New Deal relief programs. The Civilian Conservation Corps was especially appealing to young Native American men who received an opportunity to perform important conservation work and to earn money that was desperately needed by their families. Altogether, more than 80,000 young Indian men participated in CCC projects in fifteen Western states. During the 1930s, for the first time since Columbus "discovered" America, the Native American population showed a net increase.

Under Collier's enlightened leadership, the BIA promoted efforts by various tribes to develop governing councils to administer programs and formulate policies at the local level. At the same time, bureau officials sought to promote Native American cultural awareness and pride. Indians were encouraged to preserve their native religions, arts and crafts, languages, rituals, ceremonials, and traditions. Native Americans were urged to respect and celebrate the traditional Indian ways and to speak their native languages. Collier hoped that Native Americans would achieve both political and cultural autonomy, protected from the oppressions and depredations of Euro-American society. Collier also worked to end the practice of sending young Native Americans away to boarding schools. BIA officials built schools on reservations where Native American youngsters could both learn how to cope with mainstream America, and learn about their own culture and develop a strong Indian identity.

FDR AND THE NEW DEAL IN PERSPECTIVE

The New Deal was an extension of the commanding personality at its center, Franklin Delano Roosevelt. He began his presidency confident that he could lead the American people out of the morass of depression, that he could provide both the inspiration and the means to restore prosperity and confidence. Roosevelt loved being president; there was a remarkable fit between the demands of the office and his particular mix of temperament and talents. With the help of cooperative photojournalists, he was able to hide his disability and vulnerability from the American people. Always, he projected an image of masculine physical vitality and robust good humor.

FDR's leadership proved effective. Feelings of despair, of imminent collapse, vanished. Partial recovery occurred, and people regained their optimistic vitality. James MacGregor Burns, a Roosevelt biographer, found in Roosevelt "the lineaments of greatness—courage, joyousness, responsiveness, vitality, faith, and above all, concern for his fellow man." A poll of American historians taken in 1984 rated Roosevelt number two among all presidents, behind Lincoln and ahead of Washington. During the New Deal years, neither his popularity nor his power were seriously challenged by spokesmen for the Left or Right. His smashing electoral victory in 1936 confirmed his popularity and the political success of the New Deal programs.

But Roosevelt and the New Deal were controversial, and he provoked legions of detractors. Most newspaper and radio editorials regularly attacked the man in the White House, often vehemently. Rightist critics called him a dictator, a Socialist, a Communist, and a Fascist. They denounced the New Deal as being un-American, subverting the American way of life. They also insisted that deficit spending for New Deal relief programs would bankrupt the nation and that Roosevelt's usurpations of power would destroy democracy. None of these Rightist criticisms is literally true: they were hyperbolic rhetoric that mainly expressed the feelings of intense fear, hostility, and hatred Roosevelt aroused among corporate executives and the wealthy elite, some of whose prerogatives had been modestly curtailed by New Deal reforms.

More thoughtful critics have faulted Roosevelt for being too pragmatic, too opportunistic. They assert that he failed to formulate a coherent strategy for economic recovery and social reform. The New Deal was not planned; it evolved. It was a series of ad hoc improvisations. Roosevelt's grasp of economics was superficial; he did not understand economic processes or grasp economic theory. His ignorance of economics hindered recovery efforts.

Other critics have cited flaws in the personality, character, and intellect of President Roosevelt. He was not close to his wife Eleanor, nor was he a good father to his several children. He had a long-term affair with another woman, Lucy Mercer. He was not always truthful, nor was he particularly loyal to many political associates. He seemed to enjoy setting his advisers against one another and to have them compete for influence and power within his administrative circle. He had a petty, even a vindictive streak, and he appeared to delight in humiliating his political opponents, such as former president Herbert Hoover. He was a man of ordinary, perhaps slightly above-average, intelligence. He was poorly read and lacked the ability to think systematically or analytically about public policies and problems. He received most of his ideas and policies from picking the brains of his advisers during the New Deal era.

During the New Deal, the institution of the presidency was transformed; it vastly increased in size, power, and scope. Most New Deal agencies were created as bureaucracies within the executive branch. The national government, particularly its executive branch, became a major growth industry during the 1930s. During the New Deal era, the federal government became the focal point for civic life. People increasingly turned to Washington for solutions to problems; the importance of local and state governments withered. The New Deal was an ongoing civics lesson, educating people in the possible uses of federal power to stimulate the economy, change the money and banking systems, provide jobs, aid farmers, supervise labor-management relations, and save homes and small businesses. The New Deal spawned the American welfare state.

At a time when dictators and militarists took power in Germany, Italy, Japan, the Soviet Union, and elsewhere, the New Deal preserved and revitalized political democracy in America. Roosevelt and the New Dealers found a pragmatic "middle way" between the extremes of Left and Right that preserved constitutional democracy while making some modest changes in the American system of political economy.

Even though his conservative critics never appreciated it, Roosevelt's moderate mix of reforms probably saved the capitalist system from self-destruction or socialism during its gravest crisis. Roosevelt, himself a wealthy man, had a sense that he was saving the American system. He was annoyed at shrill attacks leveled on him by other rich people that appeared to him both misguided and unfair. Capitalism not only survived, but the New Deal brought about some modest reforms that strengthened its underlying structure. In particular, banking reform and securities legislation brought a greater degree of responsibility, safety, and stability to the American financial world. Profits and private property remained fundamental to the American system.

The wealthy survived as a class, although there occurred a modest redistribution of wealth during the New deal era. In 1929, the top 5 percent of the population received 30 percent of national income. In 1938, the top 5 percent's share had dropped to 26 percent. The income lost to the wealthy went mostly to middle- and upper-middle-income families whose share increased from 33 percent in 1929 to 36 percent in 1938. The income share going to the poorest families rose slightly, from 13.2 percent to 13.7 percent.

The New Deal also altered the distribution of political power. Business remained the single most powerful political interest, but during the New Deal it was forced to share power with other groups. Farmers gained political clout, as did trade unions. The New Deal also responded to consumers and home owners. Millions of unemployed workers benefited from New Deal relief programs. The most important political creation of New Dealers was the broker state. New Dealers responded to organizations, interest groups, lobbies, and trade associations. The web of power and influence expanded and diversified. Mediating claims of various groups pressuring the government became a complex art form. But the millions of Americans who were not organized to make claims upon the broker state were neglected. The reach of the New Deal rarely extended to minorities, slum dwellers, sharecroppers, and other poor, unorganized, and powerless people. Those whose needs were greatest received the least help from the New deal because they lacked the means to influence New Deal power brokers.

The New Deal helped create a more inclusive political order by including farmers, industrial workers, particular ethnic groups, and a new class of intellectual administrators. Yet it represented only a halfway revolution, swelling the ranks of the middle classes while continuing to exclude and marginalize millions of Americans—sharecroppers and tenant farmers, slum dwellers, most nonwhite minorities, and most women.

At its core, the Deal was an evolutionary centrist reform program. It drew upon ideologies that had been around for decades, principally the New Nationalism of Theodore Roosevelt and Wilsonian Progressivism. New Dealers rejected Socialism, Fascism, and also eschewed indigenous radicalisms like the confiscatory tax schemes of the Populist demagogue, Huey Long. Fundamentally, the New Deal tried to conserve the American capitalistic system by rescuing it from depression and incorporating a broader range of interest groups. New Dealers also were concerned about reforming the American economy to prevent a recurrence of depression and to fend off more radical reforms.

But the New Deal was only a partial economic success. It proved politically invulnerable to the challenges of both radicalism or reaction. It succeeded politically, but it failed to solve the fundamental economic problem caused by the Great Depression—unemployment. As the New Deal ended in 1938, over 10 million men and women were still without jobs; the unemployment rate hovered near 20 percent. New Dealers failed to eliminate unemployment because they never solved the problem of underconsumption. Consumers and businesses were never able to buy enough to stimulate enough production to approach normal employment patterns. Years after the New Deal had ended, massive unemployment persisted. The most serious failure of the New Deal was its inability to promote economy recovery from depression. New Dealers enjoyed great success with most of their efforts to relieve distress and to reform the American system of political economy. But they failed to revive the American economy, restore prosperity and full employment, and stimulate sufficient capital investment or promote economic growth. Programs such as the National Recovery Administration (NRA) retarded economic recovery during the period 1933–1935.

It required the gigantic federal spending and deficit financing to pay the costs of World War II to restore production, return everyone to work, and regenerate prosperity. Prosperity only returned to America years after the New Deal was a spent force, and it came about because of government spending for the largest and most destructive war in the history of the world. Long before world war restored American prosperity, many other nations had shaken off the effects of the worldwide depression. But had war not come, economic stagnation in America would have persisted well into the 1940s, perhaps longer.

IMPORTANT EVENTS

1933	Franklin Delano Roosevelt inaugurated as the thirty-second president
	The "Hundred Days" legislation is enacted; the New Deal begins
	Frances Perkins, first woman cabinet member, is appointed Secretary of Labor
	Prohibition is repealed
1934	Securities and Exchange Commission is created
	The American Liberty League is formed
	The Indian Reorganization Act is passed
1935	The Supreme Court nullifies the NRA
	The WPA is created
	The Social Security Act is passed
	The National Labor Relations Act (Wagner Act) is passed
	Huey Long is assassinated
1936	The Congress of Industrial Organizations (CIO) is formed
	The UAW initiates the sit-down strike tactic
	The Supreme Court nullifies the first AAA
	Roosevelt is reelected
1937	The SWOC organizes U.S. Steel workers
	The "Memorial Day Massacre" occurs in Chicago
	Roosevelt's efforts to "pack" the Supreme Court fail
1938	The Fair Labor Standards Act (FLSA) is passed
	The New Deal ends
1939	African American singer Marian Anderson sings at the Lincoln Memorial

BIBLIOGRAPHY

There is a vast historical literature about the New Deal era and the commanding figure at its center. The best one-volume treatment is William E. Leuchtenburg's *Franklin D. Roosevelt and the New Deal, 1932–1940.* Arthur M. Schlesinger, Jr., in *The Age of Roosevelt,* offers two lively volumes covering the period 1933–1936. Anthony Badger's *The New Deal* is a fine recent study. There are several fine biographical treatments of Franklin D. Roosevelt: James MacGregor Burns' *Roosevelt: The Lion and the Fox* is the best. Joseph P. Lash, in *Eleanor and Franklin,* presents a graceful study of the president and his extraordinary First Lady. Lois Scharf's *Eleanor Roosevelt: First Lady of American Liberalism* is a recent, first-rate biography of the great First Lady. Walter J. Stein's *California and the Dust Bowl Migration* is the best study of the uprooted "Okies," who left the Southern Plains states for California during the depression. Walter Galenson, in *The CIO Challenge to the AFL,* offers a good account of the rise of industrial unionism during the late 1930s. John Barnard's *Walter Reuther and the Rise of the Auto Workers* is a fine short study of the building of a progressive union. Alan Brinkley, *Voices of Protest: Huey Long, Father Coughlin, and the Great Depression,* presents a major study of the two most prominent New Deal critics. James T. Patterson's *Congressional Conservatism and the New Deal* charts the rise of the bipartisan conservative coalition of Southern Democrats and Northern Republicans that blocked New Deal reforms after 1938. Susan Ware's *Beyond Suffrage: Women in the New Deal* and Raymond Wolters' *Negroes and the New Deal* are excellent studies of the impact of the depression on particular groups. Kenneth Philip, in *John Collier's Crusade for Indian Reform, 1920–1954* offers an account of the New Deal for Native Americans. Richard H. Pells's *Radical Visions and American Dreams: Culture and Social Thought in the Depression Years* records the nation's artistic and intellectual life during the 1930s. A recent book by Alan Brinkley, *The End of Reform: New Deal Liberalism in Recession and War,* emphasizes the conservative nature of New Deal liberal reformism. Brinkley explains why the New Deal failed to bring a greater measure of social justice and why it failed to cure the Great Depression.

7

Diplomacy between Wars

THE United States emerged from World War I as an acknowledged world power with the most productive and prosperous economy in the world. American banks dominated the realms of international finance and investment. American diplomats understood that even if they had desired it, America could not be a bystander in world affairs. It is true that during the interwar period Americans tried to avoid foreign entanglements, but it is also true that American diplomatists pursued an activist foreign policy appropriate to that of a leading world power. During the 1920s and 1930s, American leaders sought a peaceful and prosperous world order by using nonmilitary means: treaties, disarmament conferences, moral suasion, and financial arrangements. The United States pursued isolationist policies between the wars only in the sense that it wanted to avoid war, reduce foreign military involvements, and preserve its freedom of action in international affairs. Historian Joan Hoff Wilson has characterized American interwar diplomacy not as isolationism but as "independent internationalism," that is, actively involved in international affairs but preserving independence in actions. With differing degrees of success and sophistication, all of the presidents who served between the wars pursued this uniquely American approach to international affairs.

THE SEARCH FOR PEACE

President Harding came into office in 1921, committed to returning the nation to "normalcy." In foreign policy, "normalcy" meant repudiating Wilsonian internationalism and its commitment to collective security. Harding believed that his landslide victory expressed deeply felt popular yearnings for ending overseas crusades, avoiding foreign entanglements, curtailing huge military expenditures, and healing domestic conflicts.

In November 1921, Harding presided at ceremonies burying the Unknown Soldier in Arlington National Cemetery. In a moving speech, the president resolved that "never again" would the nation be led into another foreign war, and he called for "a new and lasting era of peace." That same month, Harding signed separate peace treaties with all Central Power nations that were still technically at war with the United States because of the Senate's rejection of the Treaty of Versailles. He also opened a major international conference in Washington, hosted by the United States.

The Washington Conference, which convened in the nation's capital on November 12, 1921, was the first important diplomatic gathering of the postwar era. It was called by the United States to show America's commitment to ensuring peace in the postwar world, despite its refusal to join the League of Nations. It also was the first major international conference ever held in America, indicating the new prestige of the United States that had come out of the war as the world's preeminent power. Eight nations joined with the United States to discuss disarmament and Far Eastern diplomatic problems left by war.

Secretary of State Charles Evans Hughes seized the initiative at the Conference with a bold speech calling for naval disarmament. After intense negotiations, the major naval powers accepted Hughes' proposals. A Five Power Treaty, signed on February 6, 1922, by the United States, Great Britain, Japan, France, and Italy, established a ten-year moratorium on new capital ship construction. (Capital ships were battleships and cruisers exceeding 10,000 tons.) The treaty also required that the signatories scrap ships built or being built until their relative strength in capital ships reached a ratio of 5 to 5 to 3 to 1.75 to 1.75, in which a 5 would equal 525,000 tons of capital ships. The Americans and the British would have the highest ratio numbers of 5, allowing them 525,000 tons of capital ships each. The Japanese would have a ratio number of 3, allowing them 315,000 tons of capital ships. The French and Italians would have ratio numbers of 1.75 each. To reach treaty limits, the major powers had to scrap seventy warships totaling nearly 2 million tons. The Five Power Treaty curbed a costly and dangerous postwar naval arms race among the major powers. It was a significant disarmament agreement, but the treaty had loopholes—there were no limits applied to submarines, destroyers, and cruisers under 10,000 tons.

A second treaty worked out at the Conference, the Four Power Treaty, signed by the United States, Great Britain, Japan, and France, required those four nations to respect each other's territorial claims in the Pacific and to refer any disputes to a joint conference. This agreement bound the four powers to respect one another's island possessions in the Western Pacific. A third agreement, the Nine Power Treaty, bound all of the nations attending the Conference to observe the American Open Door policy toward China and to respect the "sovereignty, the independence, and the territorial and administrative integrity of China." The signatories formally affirmed the traditional American Open Door policy toward China, promulgated by John Hay in 1899 and 1900.

The Washington Conference represented a major diplomatic achievement for the United States. Secretary of State Hughes provided the leadership that halted a naval arms race, saving taxpayers billions of dollars and easing international tensions. In the Far East, the Open Door was given a new lease on life, and a new power balance emerged in Asia reflecting postwar realities. The Senate promptly ratified all three treaties, although isolationist senators attacked them during debates, especially the Four Power Treaty, which they saw as possibly involving the United States in a future war with Japan. As they ratified these agreements, the Senate, reflecting the sentiments of most Americans, declared "there is no commitment to armed force, no alliance, no obligation to join in any defense."

All three treaties would eventually prove to be toothless, because neither the United States nor any other signatories bound themselves to defend the agreements with force or sanctions. The treaties were gentlemen's agreements; their effectiveness depended on good faith compliance, which proved, in time, to be a frail prop. Beginning in 1931, the Japanese ultimately violated all of the agreements.

American peace societies during the 1920s advocated many strategies to preserve order in the world. They proposed cooperating with the League of Nations, joining the World Court, having additional disarmament conferences, signing arbitration treaties, curbing international business activity, and cutting military spending. The National Council for the Prevention of War kept alive ghastly memories of war carnage and reminded Americans of the suicidal folly of trying to settle international conflicts by war.

President Coolidge issued a call for another naval disarmament conference that convened in Geneva in 1927. Coolidge wanted to extend the 5 to 5 to 3 to 3 to 1.75 to 1.75 ratios to all categories of warships to end a naval arms race developing in cruisers under 10,000 tons, destroyers, and submarines. After six weeks of angry debate, the delegates failed to find a formula they could accept. The conference broke up in complete failure.

Following the failure at Geneva, peace advocates shifted their emphasis from abolishing arms to abolishing war. Americans took the initiative in the movement to outlaw war. They approached French Foreign Minister Aristide Briand, who announced in April 1927 that France was prepared to sign a joint pact with the United States outlawing war. The drive generated wide popular support in both countries. American Secretary of State Frank Kellogg suggested that the proposed bilateral agreement be expanded to include other powers, and the French agreed. The treaty was worded to permit defensive wars, but to outlaw war "as an instrument of national policy." On August 27, 1928, the Pact of Paris was signed by fifteen nations, and in succeeding months, another forty-five nations signed it, including Japan and Germany. The American public overwhelmingly supported the pact, which the Senate ratified by a vote of eighty-five to one.

The Pact of Paris amounted to merely a statement of principle, requiring neither sacrifice nor the assumption of any responsibilities for keeping the peace. The Pact reflected the delusions of Americans and others who believed that war could be eliminated by declaring it illegal. But the treaty did not outlaw war, only aggressive and declared wars. Thereafter, nations were to only fight "defensive" wars and become involved in "incidents." Even as they approved the treaty, most U.S. senators understood that the Pact was nothing more than a pious gesture. On the same day that it ratified the treaty, the Senate also voted for funds to build fifteen new cruisers.

Other disarmament conferences were held during the 1930s. The London Naval Conference (1930) extended the Five Power Treaty ratios to all categories of warships, closing a huge loophole in the previous treaty. But the French and Italians refused to accept these limits. Another disarmament conference met in Geneva in 1932 to try to reduce the size of armies. President Hoover strongly supported this conference, urging the reduction of all armies by one-third and the abolishment of all offensive weapons. The conference failed completely, mainly because of Japanese aggression in Manchuria and the rise of Hitler to power in Germany. Another naval conference met in London in 1935, but no major agreements could be reached because the Italians still refused to accept any more limits on its naval forces, and the Japanese, harboring expansionist ambitions in China and Southeast Asia, walked out. In 1936, the Japanese formally renounced all naval limitations. By 1938, all nations had abandoned them.

The League of Nations also failed to keep the peace, not only because the United States refused to join but because its members usually chose not to use it to settle international disputes. Although the United States never joined the League of Nations, Americans participated in League activities during the 1920s and 1930s, attending meetings about public health, drug trafficking, and other affairs not connected with international security. Eminent American jurists such as Charles Evans Hughes served on the World Court, even though America had never joined it either. But the League of Nations, the World Court, the Pact of Paris, and the disarmament conferences could not maintain world peace once the Great Depression of the 1930s and its disastrous economic effects undermined the fragile world order.

FOREIGN ECONOMIC POLICY

During the early 1920s, the Harding administration and Congress both promoted American business activity overseas. Secretary of State Charles Evans Hughes believed that a prosperous world would be a peaceful world, free of political extremism, aggression, revolution, and war. He understood that in the modern world, American international commercial and financial interests blended with traditional diplomatic concerns in the conduct of foreign affairs. The chief governmental agency actively promoting overseas business during the 1920s was the Department of Commerce, headed by Herbert Hoover, who had been an international businessman before going into politics.

Americans assumed a dominant role in international economic activity during the 1920s. The gigantic American economy produced nearly half of the world's manufactured goods. American traders had become the world's leading exporters

Figure 7.1   The League of Nations building in Geneva. The sphere in the foreground was a gift from the Woodrow Wilson Foundation.   *Source:* National Archives.

and American bankers the world's foremost lenders. Between 1920 and 1929, American investments abroad increased from $6 billion to almost $16 billion, most of them made in Europe and Latin America. U.S. corporate investors led the way. General Electric invested heavily in various Germany enterprises. Standard Oil of New Jersey bought into Venezuela's rich oil resources. United Fruit Company was a huge landowner in several Central American countries. International Telephone and Telegraph built Cuba's communication network.

As American companies expanded their overseas activities, the American government moved energetically to collect war debts it was owed by European nations. When war had begun in 1914, the United States was the world's largest net debtor; Americans owed foreigners $3 billion more than foreigners owed them. Huge European expenditures for war quickly transformed America from a net debtor to the world's leading creditor. By 1920, Europeans owed the U.S. Treasury $10.4 billion, of which the British owed $4.3 billion, the French $3.4 billion, and the Italians $1.6 billion. The smaller nations together owed another $1 billion.

These nations had borrowed the money mostly to buy war materials, principally ammunition, from American suppliers. The money had been collected from American citizens who had purchased Liberty Bonds. The government credited the money to European accounts opened in American banks, which in turn paid it to businesses that had sold ammunition to the Europeans. These loan funds never left the United States, and their being spent in the United States contributed significantly to the wartime prosperity that most Americans enjoyed.

During the 1920s, Europeans tried to persuade Americans to cancel these debts. They used a variety of arguments to claim that the loans were subsidies: as Europeans fought and died, neutral Americans prospered. The Allies had paid in blood, thus Americans should pay in dollars by canceling the loans. The Europeans also insisted that they could not repay the loans; they had no gold. American tourism did not begin to provide enough funds, and American tariff barriers prevented Europeans from earning export credits to apply against their loans.

Americans rejected all of the European arguments and demanded repayment. They insisted that the loans were loans and that they had been made in good faith with money borrowed from the American people. Americans also noticed that, despite their pleas of poverty, the Europeans, especially the French, were quickly rearming after the war.

Congress established a World War Foreign Debt Commission to set up repayment schedules with each of the debtor nations. The British were the first to sign up, agreeing to repay their $4.3 billion obligation in full over sixty-two years at 3.3 percent interest, a mortgage on the wealth of the next two British generations.

Several European nations refused to pay their war debts unless they could be assured of collecting reparations from Germany with which to pay them. The Allied Reparations Commission, meeting in 1921, had saddled the hapless Germans with an absurdly inflated $33 billion reparations bill. Germany could not begin to pay that amount and soon defaulted. In response to Germany's defaulting, French troops occupied Germany's Ruhr Valley, its industrial heartland, and prepared to extract reparations in kind. The Germans foiled the French efforts by mounting a campaign of passive disobedience. Reparations dried up. Angry American officials denied any connection between German reparations payments to the Allies and Allied war debt payments to the United States, and they demanded that the French and others pay up.

Even though the United States officially rejected any tie-in between reparations and war debts, an American banker, Charles Dawes, worked out an arrangement, with Secretary Hughes' unofficial approval, to ease the payments crunch. The Dawes Plan encouraged U.S. bankers to lend the Germans $200 million, and it scaled down the size of German reparations payments to 1 billion marks ($250 million) per year, an amount the Germans could pay. Assured of reparations, the French and the other debtors all negotiated repayment plans similar to the British. In 1929, the Dawes Plan gave way to a plan devised by Owen Young, Chairman of the Board of General Electric, which was a major investor in German companies. The Young Plan called for Germany to pay reparations annually for fifty-nine years, at the end of which the Germans would have paid about $9 billion plus interest, a drastic reduction of the $33 billion originally demanded by the Allies.

With repayment of the Allied war debts owed to the United States chained to German reparations payments to the Allies, a financial merry-go-round evolved. American investors loaned the Germans money; the Germans paid the Allies reparations; and the Allies in turn paid war debts to the United States. But war debt and reparations payments depended on the continuing flow of loan money from Americans. After the stock market collapsed in the United States in October 1929, American loans to Germany dried up, German reparations payments ceased, and Allied war debt repayments to the United States stopped. The financial merry-go-round slowed to a halt.

President Hoover and Congress contributed to the spreading depression by enacting the Smoot-Hawley Tariff Act (1930). Smoot-Hawley raised U.S. tariffs to historic high levels and triggered a chain reaction of economic miseries at home and abroad. Foreign traders, no longer able to sell their goods in the United States, stopped buying American exports. Twenty-six nations retaliated against the Smoot-Hawley tax schedules by raising their tariff rates, which closed their markets to American goods. Great Britain abandoned its historic free-trade policy and bound its empire more closely to its home market through an imperial preference system.

Worldwide depression wrecked international trade and finance. From 1929 to 1933, world trade declined 40 percent; American exports shrunk 60 percent during those four years. As the Great Depression deepened, economic nationalism intensified. Nations increasingly sought to insulate themselves from the virus of economic depression at the expense of other countries. Efforts at international economic cooperation failed. Autarky, a kind of international anarchy, became the rule of the day.

President Hoover tried to salvage the system of international debt payments before it completely collapsed. He declared a general moratorium for one year on all debt transactions, beginning in June 1931. Congress approved Hoover's proposal. During the one-year holiday, efforts were made to further reduce the size of both reparations and war debt payments, but these efforts proved unsuccessful. The moratorium ended in July 1932. When the first war debt payments came due in December 1932, six nations defaulted. More nations defaulted in 1933, and all were in default by 1934, except Finland. Payments were never resumed.

Resentment and disunity lingered on both sides of the Atlantic during the 1930s, facilitating Hitler's rise to power. The collapse of reparations and debt payments, the decline in trade, and the rise of economic nationalism were major causes of World War II. American efforts to use its vast economic and financial resources to promote international prosperity and peace failed in the face of international depression and anarchy.

LATIN AMERICA

By 1920, the Caribbean Sea had become a "Yankee lake." An informal American empire, including many countries within the sea and along its Central American coast, flourished. The United States maintained control of its client nations in this region through military occupation and economic domination, which American officials justified by evoking the Roosevelt Corollary to the Monroe Doctrine. In 1920, American troops occupied Cuba, the Dominican Republic, Haiti, Panama, and Nicaragua.

During the 1920s, American military occupation of Latin American countries came under fire, both at home and abroad. Senator William Borah of Idaho asserted that Latin Americans should have the right of self-determination; he also accused President Coolidge of violating the U.S. Constitution by ordering troops into Nicaragua in 1927 without a congressional declaration of war. Nationalistic Latin Americans claimed that U.S. military intervention in the Caribbean area violated both American democratic traditions and the spirit of Pan-Americanism. American businessmen worried that resentful Latin terrorists might attack Americans or their property.

President Hoover came to office in 1929, determined to improve U.S. relations with Latin America. As president-elect, he had gone on a goodwill tour of many Latin American nations, the first ever by an American leader. Many Latin Americans were delighted by Hoover's visit, especially when he stated that relations between Western Hemispheric nations should be governed by the principle of the "Good Neighbor." In his inaugural address, the new president made clear his determination to accelerate a "retreat from imperialism" in Latin America and to remove American troops. Hoover embraced a memorandum prepared in 1928 by Undersecretary of State Reuben Clark. The Clark Memorandum repudiated the Roosevelt Corollary, arguing that the many American interventions in the Caribbean had not been justified by the Monroe Doctrine, which had aimed at keeping European nations out of the Western Hemisphere and not promoting U.S. intervention in Latin America. President Franklin Roosevelt, who succeeded Hoover, embraced and enlarged the Good Neighbor policy during the 1930s.

The Great Depression severely tested Hoover's "Good Neighbor" policy. Economic hardship weakened governments and provoked rebellions in many Latin American nations. Hoover refrained from sending in the Marines in all of these uprisings, even when revolutionaries triumphed. The depression also caused large reductions in U.S. investments and trade in Latin America, "dollar diplomacy in reverse." Congress pressured Hoover to withdraw troops stationed in Latin America as an economy measure, and before he left office in March 1933, all U.S. troops were out of Latin America.

In small, poor countries like Nicaragua, Haiti, and the Dominican Republic, the withdrawal of American troops did not bring democratic governments to power. In these countries, the departing Americans trained national guards to maintain order. Dictators emerged from the ranks of these national guards to seize control of governments. In the Dominican Republic, a guard commander, Rafael T.M. Trujillo, became head of state in 1930 and ruled his country with an iron fist until he was assassinated in 1961. In Nicaragua, the head of the national guard, General Anastasio Somoza, became dictator in 1936. With American backing, he (and then his son) ruled Nicaragua like a medieval fiefdom for over forty years.

In Cuba, the scenario was somewhat different, but military dictatorships backed by the United States ruled Cuban affairs most of the time. By 1929, U.S. investments in Cuba had reached $1.5 billion. Americans owned about two-thirds of the Cuban sugar industry, the mainstay of its economy. With American troops withdrawn, Cuban rebels overthrew a military dictator, General Gerardo Machado. They installed a radical intellectual as president, Ramon Grau San Martin, in 1933. San Martin canceled the Platt Amendment and nationalized some American properties. Roosevelt, unhappy with San Martin, refrained from military intervention, honoring the Good Neighbor spirit. However, he supported a coup led by an army sergeant, Fulgencio Batista, which overthrew San Martin in 1934. Batista ruled Cuba, sometimes as president, sometimes from behind the scenes, with American backing for twenty-five years. The Batista era in Cuba ended in 1959 when the aging dictator was overthrown by Fidel Castro.

U.S. relations with Mexico during the depression years took a different turn. At the time of the Mexican revolution, from 1910 to 1917, American investments in Mexico were extensive—railroads, silver mines, timber, cattle, farmland, and oil. Over 40 percent of the capital wealth of Mexico belonged to American companies. Article 27 of the Mexican Constitution, proclaimed in 1917, stated that all land and subsoil raw materials belonged to the Mexican nation, placing in jeopardy about $300 million of U.S. investments in land and oil. In 1923, the two nations signed an agreement that permitted American companies that held subsoil rights before 1917 to keep them, and it required payment to Americans whose holdings were expropriated by the Mexican government.

In 1938, American business interests collided with Mexican nationalism when Mexican President Lazaro Cardenas nationalized all foreign oil properties, including extensive U.S. holdings. Secretary of State Cordell Hull angrily denounced the Mexican takeover. President Roosevelt suspended U.S. purchases of Mexican silver. American oil companies refused to transport Mexican oil. Standard Oil of New Jersey, whose Mexican subsidiary was the largest company to be nationalized, mounted a propaganda campaign in the United States, depicting Cardenas as a Bolshevik bent on socializing Mexico's entire economy.

Roosevelt ruled out military intervention, opting for negotiations to gain compensation for expropriated U.S. oil properties. His restraint was caused partly by his desire to observe the Good Neighbor policy and partly because Mexico threatened to sell its oil to Japan and the European Fascist powers if the American oil companies continued to boycott Mexican oil. After lengthy negotiations, the two nations reached an agreement. Mexico would retain ownership of the oil properties that it had seized, but it would pay the foreign companies for their nationalized properties. Mexico remained a major trading partner of the United States and joined the fight against the Axis powers in World War II.

Pan-Americanism also flourished during the era of the Good Neighbor. Pan-Americanism had originated with Secretary of State James G. Blaine in 1889 to promote trade and political stability among Western Hemispheric nations. Pan-Americanism later was broadened to include cultural exchanges and to encourage inter-American unity and friendship. At a Pan-American conference held in Montevideo, Uruguay, in 1933, Secretary of State Cordell Hull supported a resolution that stated; "No state has the right to intervene in the internal or external affairs of another." At the 1936 conference in Buenos Aires, Argentina, Hull again endorsed a nonintervention statement, which he understood to bar military intervention, but not political or economic pressure.

By the late 1930s, the United States was clearly worried about possible Axis inroads in Latin America. Nazi activists were present in Argentina, Uruguay, Chile, and Brazil. At the 1938 Pan-American conference in Lima, Peru, the United States stressed continental solidarity and hemispheric security. All nations attending the conference signed the Declaration of Lima, which committed them to cooperate with one another in resisting any foreign activity that might threaten them. In 1939, these nations formed a security belt around the Western Hemisphere to prevent Axis intrusions. With the outbreak of World War II, the United States led a united band of Western Hemispheric nations against the Axis powers. The United States' Latin American policy of the Good Neighbor paid off: it increased hemispheric friendship, promoted American trade and investment, curtailed revolution, allowed the United States to retain its hegemony by nonmilitary means, and promoted regional solidarity in wartime.

THE TRIUMPH OF ISOLATIONISM

Franklin Roosevelt took office in March 1933, determined to concentrate his energies on rescuing the American economy from depression. When an economic conference convened in London in the summer of 1933 to grapple with urgent international economic problems, including war debts, tariff barriers, and monetary stabilization, Roosevelt opposed any changes in tariff policy and refused to discuss war debts. When the conference tried to commit the United States to a currency-stabilization system, Roosevelt, who had recently devalued the American dollar to promote American exports, rebuked the conferees for ignoring "fundamental economic ills." Roosevelt, the leader of the world's preeminent economic and financial power, refused to commit the dollar to any stabilization program that might harm the weak American economy. His actions undermined the London Economic Conference. It collapsed shortly thereafter, its participants unable to reach an agreement on any important issues and unhappy with the economic nationalism displayed by the new American leader.

Roosevelt also sought to undo the damage done to American trade by the Smoot-Hawley tariff. His Secretary of State, Cordell Hull, was a longtime advocate of lower tariffs. Congress enacted the Reciprocal Trade Agreements Act in June 1934. The act empowered the president to negotiate bilateral arrangements with nations to reduce tariffs up to 50 percent with each nation that was willing to make reciprocal concessions. The act also granted "most favored nation" status with the United States to any nation that joined the United States in negotiating a trading arrangement, entitling both nations to the lowest tariff rates on the commodities they sold each other. Hull actively sought reciprocal agreements among Latin American and European nations. During his long tenure as Secretary of State (from 1933 to 1944), he negotiated agreements with over twenty nations, which reduced domestic tariffs covering nearly 70 percent of American imports. Smoot-Hawley tariff rates were reduced, and American exports, particularly to Latin American countries, increased significantly.

The American peace movement, active in the 1920s, increased in strength during the 1930s. Led by women, clergy, and college students disillusioned by the outcome of World War I, it claimed 12 million members and reached an audience of 50 million. As depression and international tension increased, and as disarmament conferences failed, peace advocates pushed for an arms embargo to be applied by the president in time of war against aggressors. Roosevelt supported this discretionary arms embargo, but opposition from arms manufacturers and isolationist Congressmen killed it.

The lobbying of munitions makers who opposed arms embargoes provoked a Senate investigation of the arms industry. The chairman of the committee was a progressive isolationist, Gerald P. Nye of North Dakota. Nye believed that America had been pressured into entering World War I by a conspiracy of American business interests protecting their investments in an Allied victory. Committee hearings, held between 1934 and 1936, investigated the activities of bankers and munitions makers. Staff members found many instances of business profiteering and lobbying, which made headline news. They found that the Du Pont Company had made huge profits from the war, a revelation which angered millions of Americans who were suffering from the deprivations of the Great Depression.

Senator Nye claimed that his committee investigations proved that the bankers who had lent the Allies money to buy arms, and the "merchants of death," who sold them ammunition, had conspired with President Wilson to take the country to war in 1917. In reality, his committee found no evidence to sustain his charge. Committee findings showed that munitions makers profited more during neutrality than during American participation in World War I. Nye also found no evidence that industry spokesmen had pressured President Wilson into a declaration of war, and committee investigators ignored the German submarine threat. But many Americans were willing to believe the worst about big business and President Wilson during the 1930s, and many accepted Nye's sensational charges. The Nye Committee hearings reinforced the popular conviction that American involvement in World War I had been a mistake, or worse, promoted by a sinister conspiracy of business interests and politicians. It also strengthened many people's determination to never again participate in a foreign war.

As the Nye Committee made headlines going after the munitions makers, revisionist journalists and popular historians wrote accounts of the American entry into World War I. The best of these books, Walter Millis' *Road to War* (1935), claimed that British propaganda, business and financial ties to the Allies, and President Wilson's pro-Allied bias combined to draw the United States into a war that it should have avoided. A 1937 public opinion poll found that 60 percent of Americans believed that U.S. involvement in World War I had been a mistake.

The activities of peace groups, the Nye Committee investigations, and the writings of revisionist scholars and journalists, which reinforced the idea that American participation in World War I had been a mistake, led to the triumph of isolationism in the mid-1930s. As the threat of another war increased steadily in the world because Japan, Italy, and Germany were willing to use force to achieve their expansionist aims, isolationist attitudes intensified. Americans tried to withdraw from world affairs and immunize themselves from the contagion of war. If, as many Americans believed, U.S. entry into World War I had been a mistake, they vowed not to blunder into another foreign war in the 1930s.

Isolationist sentiment was strongest in the Midwest, particularly among German Americans and Irish Americans, but isolationism cut across all regional, class, and ethnic lines, appealing to most Americans during the mid-1930s. Isolationism spanned the American political spectrum, from left-wing New Dealers to right-wing Republicans. It also included Socialists like Norman Thomas, Communists, and Fascist sympathizers. What united these disparate groups was the shared conviction that involvement in another world war would be ruinous to America, thus it must be avoided. They believed that the nation could pursue diplomatic and economic policies that would both avoid war and preserve American security and freedom. Although he remained a Wilsonian internationalist at heart, President Roosevelt expressed isolationist attitudes during the mid-1930s, as did most senators and congressmen. It was not until the late 1930s that Roosevelt and many other Americans, at last perceiving the danger of Axis aggression, cautiously distanced themselves from the noninterventionists.

EUROPE DISINTEGRATES

In 1933, Adolph Hitler came to power in Germany by promising to solve Germany's severe economic and security problems. Like Benito Mussolini, who had gained power in Italy in 1922, Hitler was the leader of a Fascist movement. Hitler headed the National Socialist Workers Party, nicknamed the Nazis. He vowed to revive German economic and military power, crush the Bolshevik threat, and purify the German "race" from the "contamination" of Jewish influence, whom he blamed for all of Germany's many severe problems.

In 1933 and 1934, Hitler withdrew from the Geneva disarmament conference, pulled Germany out of the League of Nations, and began to rearm his nation in violation of the Versailles Treaty. He began secret planning for the conquest of Europe. Neither Western leaders nor Roosevelt perceived initially the mortal danger Hitler would pose to their interests. Tragically, neither he nor his fanatical doctrines and ambitions were not taken seriously for several years.

Hitler watched approvingly as Italy prepared to invade the African country of Ethiopia in 1935. This threat of war caused American isolationists to impose a strict neutrality policy on the United States government. In August, Congress passed the Neutrality Act of 1935, which prohibited arms sales to either side in a war. President Roosevelt had wanted a law that allowed him to embargo arms sales only to aggressors, but the legislators, who recalled what they believed were President Wilson's unneutral maneuverings that had led America into World War I, wanted a law that strictly limited presidential action. Roosevelt signed the measure and kept his misgivings to himself.

In October 1935, Italy invaded Ethiopia. Roosevelt then invoked the Neutrality Act. Most Americans sympathized with the Ethiopians, who fought with spears against a modern, mechanized army using planes, tanks, and poison gas. The League of Nations imposed a limited embargo against Italy that did not curtail its war effort. Roosevelt, who wanted to curb Italian aggression if he could, called for an American "moral embargo" that would deny shipment of important raw materials to feed Italy's war machine. The moral embargo failed. American companies increased their shipments of strategic raw materials, especially oil, to the Italians. Italy conquered Ethiopia and turned it into an Italian colony. In February 1936, Congress enacted another neutrality law that tightened America's neutrality policy, adding a loan embargo to the arms embargo.

In the summer of 1936, civil war began in Spain when Francisco Franco, an army officer with Fascist beliefs, led a revolt of Spanish army units against Spain's center-left republican government. Roosevelt adopted a policy of neutrality toward the Spanish Civil War and supported French and British efforts to confine the war to Spain, even if that meant a Fascist victory. Congress responded with a third neutrality law in 1937, applying the arms and loan embargoes to the Spanish Civil War.

Most Americans were indifferent to the outcome of the Spanish Civil War, favoring neither side. But a few Americans passionately took sides, especially when the Fascist powers, Italy and Germany, intervened to aid Franco's Nationalist forces, and the Soviet Union aided the Spanish Republicans. American volunteers, many of them Communists, calling themselves the Abraham Lincoln Battalion, went to Spain to fight for the Republican cause. Franco's forces, with German and Italian help, eventually prevailed. General Franco took power in early 1939 and established an authoritarian government with Fascistic characteristics in Spain that lasted until his death in 1976.

As the Spanish Civil War raged, Germany and Japan became bolder. In 1936, Hitler sent his troops into the Rhineland, a region demilitarized by the Versailles Treaty. France, responsible for enforcing the treaty, accepted the German action. Later that year, Germany and Italy signed an agreement called the Rome-Berlin Axis. Germany and Japan united against the Soviet Union, forming the Anti-Comintern Pact. Great Britain and France responded to these moves by adopting a policy of appeasement, hoping to satisfy Germany's and Italy's expansionist appetites with territorial concessions that would avoid war.

In 1938, Hitler pressed Europe to the brink of war. In March, he annexed Austria. The democracies, pursuing their policy of appeasement, did nothing. In the fall, Hitler continued his "war of nerves" by threatening to invade Czechoslovakia when it refused to give him its Sudetenland, a mountainous region bordering the two countries, whose inhabitants were mostly ethnic Germans. The Czechs mobilized their armed forces and turned to their allies, France and the Soviet Union, for help. Both the French and the Soviets refused to honor their treaties with the only democracy in eastern Europe. Britain and France both pressed the Czechs to give Hitler what he wanted in exchange for his pledge: "This is the last territorial claim I have to make in Europe."

To a hastily called conference in Munich on September 29, 1938, came Prime Minister Neville Chamberlain of England and Premier Edouard Daladier of France. There they met with the Fascist leaders, Hitler and Mussolini, to sacrifice Czechoslovakia upon the altar of appeasement. The Czechs, isolated and vulnerable, surrendered. They demobilized their army, and Germany sheared off the Sudetenland for annexation.

Although he had doubts about the effectiveness of the British and French appeasement policies, President Roosevelt hailed the Munich agreement as an act of statesmanship that had averted war. Upon his return to England, Chamberlain proclaimed: "I believe it is peace for our time." In Parliament, Winston Churchill rose to dissent: "England and France had to choose between war and dishonor. They chose dishonor; they will have war." Churchill perceived the moral bankruptcy and strategic folly of appeasement embodied in the Munich agreement; it was merely surrender on the installment plan. Six months after Hitler solemnly promised to seek no additional territory, German columns erased the Czech remnant from the map. A month after the rape of Czechoslovakia, Mussolini's legions conquered defenseless Albania. Two more dominoes had fallen to the Fascists. The Munich agreement could only postpone war, not prevent it. And when war came, it would be more terrible than ever.

At last awakened to the Nazi peril, Britain and France abandoned appeasement. They quickly concluded security treaties with Poland, the next target on Hitler's list of intended victims. But the decisive factor in the European political equation that tense summer of 1939 was the Soviet Union. When the Western leaders rebuffed Stalin's offer of alliance against Germany, he turned to Hitler. On

August 23, the Germans and Soviets stunned the West by concluding a nonaggression pact that publicly proclaimed peace between them yet secretly divided the spoils in eastern Europe. With his eastern flank secured by this adroit agreement with the Soviets, Hitler unleashed his torrents of fire and steel on the Polish people on September 1, 1939. Two days later, honoring their commitments to Poland, Britain and France declared war on Germany. World War II in Europe had begun.

The United States, as it had done when World War I began, promptly declared itself neutral. Unlike President Wilson in August 1914, Roosevelt did not ask the American people to be neutral in thought: "Even a neutral cannot be asked to close his mind or his conscience." He made clear that his sympathies lay with the victims of German aggression, as did those of nearly all Americans. Roosevelt also told the American people: "I hope that the United States will keep out of this war. I believe that it will." Most Americans shared the president's views.

Following his speech, he called Congress into a special session to amend the neutrality legislation to permit British and French arms purchases. Isolationists loudly opposed his request and vowed to resist "from hell to breakfast." But the public supported Roosevelt. They wanted to stay clear of the war, but they also wanted to help the Allies. After six weeks of heated debate, Congress modified the neutrality laws to permit "cash and carry"; the Allies could buy American arms if they paid cash and hauled them in their own ships.

The Soviet Union posed a special problem for American foreign relations during the years when Europe lurched toward war. Starting with Woodrow Wilson in 1917, four consecutive administrations had refused to recognize the Moscow regime. They adhered to a policy of nonrecognition because in 1917 the Bolsheviks had repudiated wartime alliances and concluded a separate peace with Germany, imperiling the Allies. The Communist leaders also repudiated Czarist debts to Washington and expropriated American properties in Russia without compensation. But most other nations had recognized the Soviet Union by 1933, and America's policy of nonrecognition had neither isolated nor weakened the Soviets.

The Great Depression changed American attitudes toward the Soviets. American businessmen hoped that normalizing relations with the Soviet Union would open new markets in that vast country and reduce unemployment in the United States. Japan was threatening China, and Hitler was on the rise in Germany; Roosevelt hoped that recognition of the Soviet Union might serve to restrain those two expansionist powers.

After negotiations with Soviet representatives, the United States formally recognized the Soviet Union in November 1933. In exchange for U.S. recognition, the Soviets agreed to permit religious freedom in the Soviet Union and to stop spreading propaganda within the United States. The debt payment question and other claims were deferred.

United States' recognition of the Soviet Union proved to be a great disappointment. The expected increase in trade did not materialize. The Soviets continued their anti-American propaganda and their denial of freedom of worship within the Soviet Union. The two nations did not coordinate their foreign policies

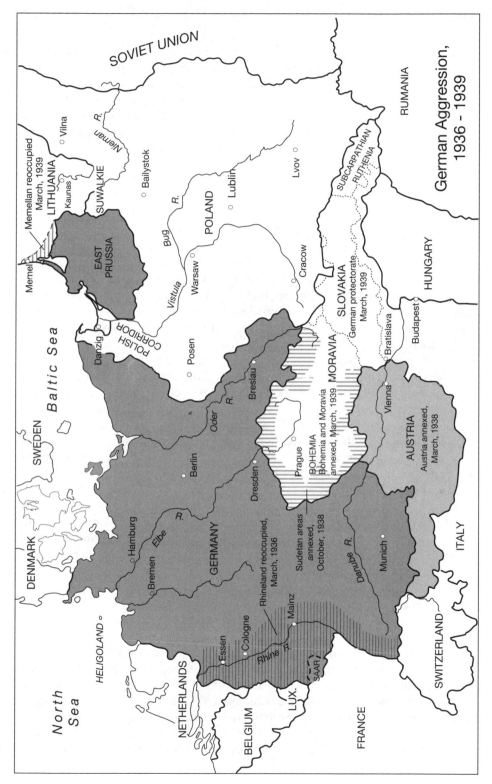

Figure 7.2   German aggression, 1936–1939.   *Source:* George D. Moss, *Rise of Modern America*, p. 287.

to curtail Japanese or German expansionism but continued to pursue independent foreign policies. Relations between the two countries were not notably friendlier following recognition. Relations with the USSR deteriorated further after the Nazi-Soviet Pact of 1939 and a Soviet attack upon its small neighbor, Finland, in 1940. As World War II began, many Americans could see little difference between the Nazis and the Communists: both appeared to be aggressive dictatorships bent on military conquest, and they were partners in aggression.

THE RISING SUN

United States–Japanese relations in the twentieth century were rarely cordial. U.S. officials viewed the Japanese as potential threats to American Far Eastern possessions, which included the Philippines, Guam, and other Pacific islands. The United States also retained a variety of interests in China—missionaries, trade, investments, and maintenance of the Open Door policy. The Japanese suspected that the United States wanted to restrain Japanese expansionism and deprive Japan of the fruits of empire that America and many European powers enjoyed. They resented U.S. criticism of Japanese imperialism, which they regarded as hypocritical and self-serving. The Japanese also were deeply insulted by the National Origins Act (1924), which excluded Japanese immigrants from the United States.

During the 1920s, despite the Washington treaties, naval competition continued between the two nations. Naval war planners in both countries conducted mock wars against the other's forces, preparing for a possible real war in the future. Trade rivalries strained relations between the two nations.

In 1931, Japanese army units took control of Chinese Manchuria. The Japanese had been in Manchuria since they had defeated the Russians in 1905. The region was valuable to them as a buffer against the Soviet Union and as a source of foodstuffs and raw materials. The seizure of Manchuria violated the Nine Power Treaty, but that treaty was toothless, having no binding enforcement provisions. The United States, powerless to force the Japanese out of Manchuria, resorted to moralistic denunciations of Japanese aggression and adopted a policy of nonrecognition. Secretary of State Henry Stimson asserted that the United States would not recognize violations of the Open Door policy. Nonrecognition was an ineffective policy that merely annoyed the Japanese without deterring them. They installed a puppet regime in Manchuria, renamed the region Manchukuo, and turned it into a Japanese colony.

In July 1937, following a clash between Japanese and Chinese troops at the Marco Polo Bridge near Beijing, Japanese forces invaded northern China. Full-scale fighting erupted between Japanese and Chinese troops. World War II in Asia had begun. Japanese planes bombed Chinese cities, killing thousands of civilians. Japanese armies occupied many urban areas. Americans angrily denounced Japanese aggression and atrocities. In an effort to help the Chinese, President Roosevelt refused to declare the existence of war in Asia so that China could buy American

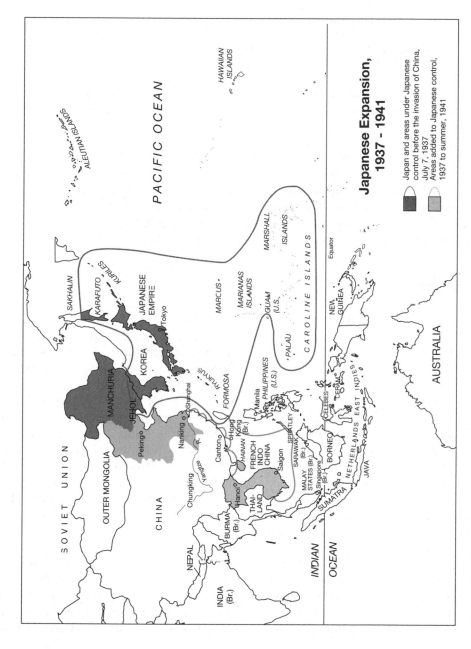

Figure 7.3 Japanese expansion, 1937–1941. *Source: Moss, Rise of Modern America,* p. 291.

arms. Roosevelt also spoke to the American people on the evening of October 5, 1937. He tried to rally the Western nations to act against aggressors.

> The peace-loving nations must make a concerted effort in opposition to those violations of treaties and those ignorings of humane instincts which today are creating a state of international anarchy and instability from which there is no escape through mere isolation or neutrality.[1]

He called for a "quarantine" to curb "the epidemic of world lawlessness." Most Americans responded sympathetically to the president's words, but isolationist leaders such as Senator Nye warned that the president was edging toward war.

Japan continued its war in China in 1938 and 1939. The United States sent military equipment to the Chinese and loaned them money. But the United States also continued its extensive trade with Japan, which included strategic raw materials. Roosevelt did not want to impose economic sanctions on Japan, lest they provoke a war at a time when the president saw the more serious threats to U.S. interests coming from Europe. When war broke out in Europe in September 1939, United States–Japanese relations were strained further.

WAR IN EUROPE

World War II began in Europe with Germany's invasion of Poland on September 1, 1939. Poland fell within a month to German forces invading from the west and Soviet forces invading from the east. Following their conquests, the Nazis and the Communists partitioned Poland in accordance with their previous pact and settled in for a joint occupation.

Following Poland's destruction, an eerie silence descended upon Europe. German and French armies faced each other from behind their fortified Siegfried and Maginot lines. Isolationist Senator William Borah sniffed: "There's something phony about this war." Soon Americans talked of a "phony war" in Europe. Three thousand miles away, Americans viewed events in Europe with considerable detachment. Once war erupted, they believed, the British navy would strangle the Germany economy, and the French army, the largest in the world, would whip its upstart foe. Europe's latest conflagration would have a quick resolution, the Allies would win, and it could never reach the United States.

The American false confidence was shattered by German offensives launched in April 1940. Hitler's "blitzkrieg" (lightning war) overran Denmark, Norway, the Netherlands, Luxembourg, and Belgium within a month. Germany then attacked France. Hitler sent his Panzers (armored divisions) crashing through the Ardennes Forest. Within two weeks, German forces had shattered French defenses and swept behind the Maginot line. Paris fell on June 16, and Germany soon occupied the

[1]Quoted in James MacGregor Burns, *Roosevelt: The Lion and the Fox* (New York: Harcourt, Brace, 1956), p. 318.

northern two-thirds of the country. The unoccupied southern third of France was permitted a rump government at Vichy. Wherever the Nazis extended what they called their New Order, they established a reign of terror. Concentration camps, slave labor, extreme repression and brutality, mass execution of civilians, and wholesale looting of governments and private citizens became common aspects of German occupations.

The fall of France stunned and alarmed most Americans. Hitler had required only six weeks to achieve what Germany had failed to accomplish in four years of attrition warfare during World War I. The fall of France erased a lot of U.S. illusions; a majority of Americans now understood that Germany posed a potential long-term threat to the United States and the Western Hemisphere. Only the British survived to carry on the struggle against the Nazis. If England fell, Germany might gain control of the British navy. The Atlantic Ocean would then no longer be a barrier shielding America from Europe's power struggles; it would become a watery highway for Nazi penetration of the New World.

The British, viewing the fall of France with dismay, prepared to battle the Nazis. Prime Minister Neville Chamberlain resigned in disgrace in May 1940, and he was replaced by Winston Churchill. Following the Allied rout on the continent, the British managed to retrieve their army, which had been fighting in France and was cut off from land retreat, by evacuating 330,000 men from the beaches at Dunkirk in the north of France. The British also possessed a formidable fleet, a modern air force, and an indomitable leader who rallied his people to face the German war machine.

In the summer of 1940, Hitler hurled his Luftwaffe (air force) at the British. His goal was to achieve air superiority over England preparatory to launching an amphibious invasion of the islands. Night after night, waves of German bombers attacked British air bases. The Germans were on the verge of winning the Battle of Britain; they had destroyed or shut down almost all of the Royal Air Force interceptor bases. One more raid would have given Hitler control of the English skies. At that moment, Hitler suddenly switched tactics. He turned his bombers on British cities, planning to bring England to its knees by terror bombing civilians. Hitler's tactical switch saved England. The British people, though badly battered, refused to break. British air defenders used this time as a reprieve to repair their damaged bases and planes. Gradually the tide of battle turned in Britain's direction. Within three months, the battle was over. The Royal Air Force had won, and Germany had lost the cream of its air force.

Hitler was forced to cancel his planned invasion of Britain, thus he turned his attention to the Balkans and North Africa, where his ally, Italy, was engaged. German troops aided the Italians, who were losing battles to Greek forces and Albanian guerrillas. During the spring of 1941, German armies conquered Yugoslavia, Greece, Hungary, Rumania, and Bulgaria. In North Africa, German forces put tremendous pressures on British armies protecting the approaches to the Suez Canal. These campaigns in the Balkans and North Africa preceded the German war to destroy Hitler's most hated foe, the Soviet Union, which began on June 22, 1941.

Following the fall of France, and with the outcome of the Battle of Britain hanging in the balance, President Roosevelt committed the United States to a policy of "all aid to the Allies short of war," abandoning any pretense of neutrality. The U.S. military buildup accelerated. In July, Congress appropriated $8 billion for rearming the nation, an unprecedented sum for a peacetime mobilization. Bidding to form a bipartisan coalition in support of his foreign policy, FDR appointed Republicans Henry L. Stimson, Secretary of War, and Frank Knox, Secretary of the Navy. At his request, Congress enacted the first peacetime conscription in American history.

U.S. industry, spurred by defense contracts, showed signs of life not seen since the late 1920s. By the end of the year, factories had produced 17,000 planes, 17,000 heavy artillery, and 9,000 tanks. Even though isolationists and peace groups denounced the military spending and draft bills, Roosevelt had committed the United States to pro-Allied nonbelligerency. U.S. neutrality amounted to no more than a legal sham. A Gallup poll taken at the time showed that a majority of citizens favored all of these measures; isolationist sentiments were losing their hold on some Americans in the face of the Nazi conquest of western Europe.

With the Battle of Britain raging, Churchill wrote to Roosevelt, requesting that the United States transfer a portion of its destroyer fleet to the Royal Navy to protect the British home islands and to escort arms convoys across the Atlantic. Roosevelt, linking American security to the survival of Britain, responded promptly. On his executive authority, he offered the British fifty old destroyers in exchange for leases to eight British military bases, stretching from Newfoundland to British Guiana. Churchill, needing the ships desperately, quickly accepted Roosevelt's proposal. Giving warships to a nation at war was clearly a violation of America's official neutrality policy, but FDR stressed the importance of guarding the Atlantic approaches to U.S. territory.

THE ELECTION OF 1940

Amidst the U.S. military buildup, the deteriorating world situation, and the destroyer-for-bases deal, the 1940 election occurred. It pitted Roosevelt, seeking an unprecedented third term, against the Republican challenger, Wendell Willkie. Willkie, a utilities magnate turned politician, was an internationalist and generally supported Roosevelt's foreign policy. But he attacked the New Deal for failing to lift the country out of economic depression. He also attacked Roosevelt's bid for a third term as being contrary to the spirit of American democracy, and he denounced Roosevelt's failure to clear the destroyer transaction with Congress as "the most dictatorial action ever taken by an American president."

In late September, Willkie was running well behind Roosevelt in the polls. His attacks on Roosevelt for failing to end the depression and to provide a proper defense had been ineffective. Desperate to find an issue that would enable him to gain ground, he abandoned his bipartisan approach to foreign policy and attacked Roosevelt as a warmonger whose policies would take the country to war. He struck a responsive chord among nervous voters in both parties. Polls taken in mid-October showed Willkie cutting into FDR's lead.

Roosevelt, who had avoided campaigning until Willkie's charges that he was a warmonger flushed him out, responded forcibly, but Willkie continued to gain. As election day approached, Democratic party officials anxiously watched the polls. On October 30, a poll showed that Willkie had closed to within four percentage points of the president. On the same day, the Republican challenger charged that reelection of Roosevelt would mean American entry into the war by April 1941. That night, Roosevelt told the mothers of America,

> I have said this before, but I shall say it again and again; your boys are not going to be sent into any foreign wars.[2]

FDR's reassurances worked. Roosevelt fended off Willkie's late surge and won reelection handily. The president received 27 million votes to Willkie's 22 million. Roosevelt had a decisive 449 to 82 margin in the electoral votes. But Willkie had gotten 5 million more votes than Landon had in 1936, and he had given Roosevelt his toughest election campaign to date. The Democrats retained large majorities in both houses of Congress, but the bipartisan conservative coalition continued to gain strength.

But neither candidate had leveled with the voters during the campaign. After it was over, Willkie confessed that his warmongering charges had been "just politics," and he strongly supported Roosevelt's policy of giving all-out aid to the Allies, short of war. Roosevelt, bowing to political pressures, had given the American people a false assurance of peace, knowing that his policies risked eventual entry into the European war. The 1940 election was neither the first nor the last in which presidential candidates dealt dishonestly with the crucial issues of war and peace.

LEND-LEASE

Once reelected, Roosevelt soon confronted a new crisis in the Atlantic. Germany, failing to subdue England by air, turned to its submarines to try to sever Britain's oceanic lifeline and starve its people into submission. Great Britain also faced another threat to its survival besides German U-boats. Its dollar reserves depleted, England could no longer pay for its American supplies.

When that problem had arisen during World War I, American bankers had advanced credits to the British. But in this war, neutrality legislation prohibited bank loans to nations at war. Roosevelt himself devised a clever program to circumvent the Neutrality Act: Lend or lease to the British the guns, tanks, planes, ammunition, whatever they needed to win the war, and they would repay or replace these materials after the war ended. In a December 29, 1940, fireside chat, he explained Lend-Lease to the American people, stating that aiding the British was the

[2]Quoted in *Ibid.,* p. 449.

best way to keep America out of the war. He also urged the United States to "be the great arsenal of democracy." It was one of his most successful speeches; over 60 percent of the public approved the Lend-Lease proposal.

Isolationists in Congress battled to defeat Lend-Lease. They were convinced that its passage would lead to entry into a war whose consequences would be ruinous to the United States. Senator Burton K. Wheeler compared Lend-Lease with the Agricultural Adjustment Administration's crop plough-up of 1933, calling it "the New Deal's Triple A foreign policy: it will plough under every fourth American boy." Although they made an all-out effort to defeat Lend-Lease, the isolationists did not have the votes. The bill passed easily, 60 to 31 in the Senate and 317 to 71 in the House. Public opinion polls showed that a broad national consensus favored the legislation. Roosevelt signed the measure, formally titled "An Act to Promote the Defense of the United States," into law on March 11, 1941.

The passage of Lend-Lease marked a point of no return for America. The United States had committed itself to the survival of Great Britain with an aid program that amounted to a declaration of economic warfare on Germany. Lend-Lease committed more than American economic resources to the British; it also expanded the naval battle in the Atlantic to include U.S. destroyers patrolling for German submarines. In April 1941, U.S. Marines occupied the Danish colony of Greenland. In August, they took over Iceland. Roosevelt also authorized U.S. destroyers to convoy British ships hauling Lend-Lease supplies as far as Iceland. At the time, fleets of German submarines were roaming the North Atlantic shipping lanes and sinking cargo ships hauling Lend-Lease supplies at the rate of one or two a day.

Roosevelt was determined to do everything necessary to ensure Germany's defeat, even though it risked American entry into the war. By the spring of 1941, he had apparently concluded that American military intervention would be necessary to achieve victory over the Axis powers. He seized Axis shipping in American ports and froze German and Italian assets in the United States. When Germany invaded the Soviet Union on June 21, 1941, Roosevelt promptly offered support to the embattled Soviets.

For four days in July, Roosevelt met with the British prime minister at a conference held off the Newfoundland coast aboard the USS *Augusta*. Their discussions focused on the means necessary to defeat Germany and to contain Japan. The meeting also produced the Atlantic Charter, a joint declaration of war aims. It reaffirmed the principles of self-determination, free trade, and freedom of the seas, and it called for the creation of a new postwar international organization to keep the peace. Roosevelt hoped that the Charter would educate Americans to what was at stake in the European war and make them more willing to intervene if conflicts with Germany escalated. The Atlantic Charter also signaled the kind of postwar world that Roosevelt envisioned: A stable international order in which all nations could enjoy freedom, equal economic opportunities, and prosperity, a world in which American power and wealth would dominate, for the benefit of all nations. Henry Luce, an influential publisher, in a 1941 editorial in *Life*, wrote of the "American century" that was dawning, exhorting his fellow citizens "to assume the leadership of the world" for the good of people in every land. The Atlantic Charter gave ideological shape to the American century.

UNDECLARED NAVAL WAR

With American destroyers convoying British ships as far as Iceland, clashes between U.S. warships and German submarines became inevitable. On September 4, 1941, a U-boat, after being chased for hours by a destroyer, the USS *Greer,* turned and attacked the destroyer, but the torpedo that the U-boat fired missed. The president used the *Greer* incident to announce an undeclared naval war in the North Atlantic. He ordered all ships engaged in escort duty to "shoot on sight" any German submarines appearing in waters west of Iceland.

But most Americans still hoped to stay out of the war. They hoped that all aid short of war would prevent American entry. Roosevelt faced a dilemma, given the public's contradictory attitudes. Seventy percent of Americans wished to avoid the

Figure 7.4   Roosevelt and Churchill first met in August 1941 off of the Newfoundland coast during the Atlantic Charter meeting.   *Source:* National Archives.

war; seventy percent also wanted Hitler defeated at all costs, even if that meant America entering the war. President Roosevelt believed that if he asked Congress for a declaration of war in the summer of 1941, he would not get it and would lose popular support. The war declaration request also would trigger an angry, divisive debate between isolationists and interventionists. He decided to build, incrementally, a consensus for war by devious means, believing that it was essential to national security that America enter the war in Europe and defeat Germany. He would wage an undeclared naval war and look for incidents that would unify the country behind a war in Europe.

Having committed the country to undeclared naval war by the fall of 1941, President Roosevelt then asked Congress to repeal the remaining neutrality legislation in order to permit the arming of American merchant ships and allow them to sail into war zones. On October 17, a U-boat torpedoed a U.S. destroyer, the USS *Kearny*, inflicting severe damage and killing eleven crewmen. Two weeks after the attack on the Kearny, a submarine sank an American destroyer, the USS *Reuben James*, killing 115 sailors. These two incidents strengthened public opinion supporting Roosevelt's request. Public opinion polls taken in October showed that a large majority favored repeal of the neutrality laws. Congress repealed the Neutrality Acts on November 13, 1941, although the votes in both houses were close. Isolationists were still a powerful minority. American merchant ships were armed and permitted to sail through war zones to British and Soviet ports. Repeal of the Neutrality Acts had removed the last remaining restrictions on American actions.

While Roosevelt was taking these fateful measures in November 1941, his foreign policy of pro-Allied nonbelligerency, with its drift toward military intervention, continued to draw fire from various isolationist groups and individuals. The All-American hero Charles Lindbergh, who did not see Fascism as a threat to American interests, believed that Roosevelt "could make a deal with Hitler" if he had to. An odd coalition of ethnic isolationists, religious pacifists, liberal intellectuals, Socialists, Communists, and Fascists opposed Roosevelt's foreign policies. The most prominent isolationist organization called itself the America First Committee. America First spokesmen kept their views constantly before the public, and their agents formed a powerful lobby in Washington. Committee spokesmen denied that Germany posed any significant threat to American or Western Hemispheric security. They claimed that America had sufficient military strength to defend itself, regardless of who controlled Europe.

At the same time that isolationists accused Roosevelt of secretly plotting to take the country to war, interventionists believed that Roosevelt was moving too slowly and too cautiously in extending aid to the Allies and preparing for possible military intervention. Interventionists were recruited from the ranks of Eastern Anglophiles, moderate New Dealers, and liberal Republicans like Thomas Dewey and Wendell Willkie. The most influential interventionist organization was the Committee to Defend America by Aiding the Allies, chaired by a prominent Progressive journalist from Kansas, William Allen White. White and his organization worked to increase the amount of military aid going to the Allies. They also tried to move

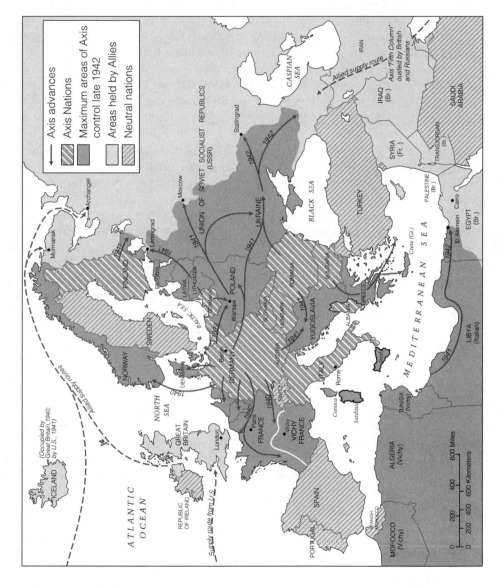

Figure 7.5   The European Theater, 1939–1942.   *Source: Moss, Rise of Modern America,* p. 304.

the American people in the direction of supporting Roosevelt's foreign policy. Above all, interventionists rejected the isolationist premise that an aggressive Germany posed no threat to the security of the United States.

Neither the America First Committee nor the Committee to Defend America by Aiding the Allies had much influence on public opinion. It was the events themselves, the rapidly deteriorating military situations in Europe and the Far East, that swayed growing numbers of Americans to support Roosevelt's foreign policy, even though most Americans clung to the hope of avoiding war.

As November 1941 ended, the United States was at war unofficially with Germany. But Roosevelt could only wait upon events, hoping that German submarines would provide him with incidents that would allow a declaration of war and full-scale involvement against the Fascist powers. The initiative lay with Hitler and his submarine forces. Ironically, with all eyes upon the European conflict, Japanese military actions on the other side of the world rescued Roosevelt from the uncertain drift of his European foreign policy. American entry into World War II came first in the Pacific following the surprise Japanese attack on Pearl Harbor on December 7, 1941.

Many Americans have found it difficult to understand why the Japanese attackers caught the Americans in Hawaii by complete surprise. Revisionist historians have resorted to conspiracy theories to solve the riddle: President Roosevelt, wanting badly to get into war in Europe, but unable to generate popular support for a formal declaration of war, put economic pressure on the Japanese and forced them to fight. He then lured them to Pearl Harbor by exposing the American fleet and let the raid come without alerting American commanders in Hawaii. The surprise attack angered and united Americans in support of war. Revisionists, in effect, have accused Roosevelt of forcing America into the European war through the "back door" of Asia.

The case for conspiracy at Pearl Harbor is flimsy. It rests entirely on circumstantial evidence, a kind of simplistic plausibility, and on Roosevelt's accusers' willingness to believe that he was a Machiavellian monster capable of sacrificing the American Pacific fleet and thousands of lives to get the United States into the war in Europe. No documentary proof of conspiracy has ever been found. No professional historian of World War II takes this devil theory seriously. It is easily refuted by knowledgeable scholars who can explain Japanese success at Pearl Harbor in nonconspiratorial terms.

IMPASSE OVER CHINA

War in the Pacific between the United States and Japan occurred fundamentally because of an impasse over China. Since 1937, Japan had been extending its control over China. But the Japanese, although able to conquer the populous coastal areas of China, had been unable to defeat Jiang Jieshi's Nationalist forces, who had retreated into China's vast interior regions. America supported the Chinese Nationalists and condemned Japanese aggression. The German defeat of the Netherlands and France in 1940 left these two nations' colonial possessions in Southeast Asia defenseless. Japan set out to incorporate these territories, which were rich in rubber, oil, tin, tea, spices, and rice, into their imperial orbit. President Roosevelt tried to use American economic pressure to pry the Japanese out of China and prevent its expansion into Southeast Asia.

Knowing that the Japanese were heavily dependent upon the United States for shipments of petroleum as well as scrap iron and steel, on July 26, 1939, Roosevelt renounced the major commercial treaty between Japan and the United States as of January 1, 1940. This action would allow the United States to curb or halt Japan's access to American iron, oil, and other strategic goods. The president hoped that Japan would ease its pressure on China instead of risking an American embargo of essential raw materials. The threatened embargo did not deter the Japanese; they were determined to conquer China and forge an empire they called the Greater East Asia Co-prosperity Sphere. But they did not want a rupture of relations with the United States that would dry up sources of needed commodities. Roosevelt also cautiously applied economic pressure on the Japanese. His first priority was the European war, where he perceived the threat to American interests to be much greater than Japanese imperialism in Asia. He also had to be careful, lest economic sanctions provoke the Japanese to war, for which the United States was completely unprepared.

Japanese-American relations deteriorated further during the summer and fall of 1940. A more militant government came to power in Japan, headed by Prince Konoye. A key official in his new government was the war minister, General Hideki Tojo. Konoye and Tojo were determined to defeat China and end the drain on Japanese men and materiel. The Japanese also intended to ally with the European Fascist powers and expand into Southeast Asia. They planned to take advantage of German victories in Europe by seizing the lightly protected European Southeast Asian colonies.

In July 1940, the Japanese moved into northern Indochina, a lightly defended French colony in Southeast Asia. In September, Japan concluded a Tripartite Pact with Germany and Italy, creating the Rome-Berlin-Tokyo Axis. The treaty bound the three nations to help one another if attacked by a power not currently involved in fighting in Europe or Asia. The treaty clearly aimed to prevent the United States from joining either the British against the Germans or from directly opposing Japan's efforts to carve out an empire in China and Southeast Asia.

America responded to Japan's signing the Tripartite Pact by embargoing all shipments of scrap metal to Japan. Roosevelt also began coordinating U.S. Far Eastern policy with the British and increasing U.S. aid to China. He sent the Chinese fifty fighter planes and arranged for American volunteers to go to China to fly them. These volunteers formed the nucleus of the famed "Flying Tigers," commanded by Claire Chennault. Roosevelt believed that aiding China was the most effective way of restraining Japanese expansion, because keeping China in the war would keep the Japanese tied down in that vast country. He also sent additional forces to Guam, the Philippines, and other American territories in the Pacific.

THE STRATEGY OF STALL

In February 1941, Japan sent a new ambassador to the United States, Admiral Kichisaburo Nomura. He and Secretary of State Cordell Hull held a series of talks that continued off and on until the Japanese attack on Pearl Harbor. Nomura urged America to restore trade with Japan and to stop supporting Jiang Jieshi. His proposals were unacceptable to the United States, but Roosevelt told Hull to avoid outright rejection of Nomura's suggestions and to leave open the possibility of American concessions. Roosevelt hoped to encourage moderate elements within the Japanese government who might restrain the militant expansionists. He also was following a strategy of stalling the Japanese. He wanted to restrain Japan yet avoid a showdown with them because of the increasing danger of American entry into the European war. Roosevelt and Hull hoped that a combination of limited economic sanctions, the threat of additional sanctions, and aid to the Chinese might eventually force Japan to withdraw from China and refrain from further aggression in Southeast Asia.

These negotiations between American and Japanese officials did not have a realistic possibility of success; the two sides were too far apart, and neither was willing to compromise. The Japanese wanted a free hand to continue their war of conquest against China and an end to U.S. economic sanctions. The United States demanded that the Japanese withdraw from China and not attack the Southeast Asian territories belonging to European colonial powers that had been defeated by the Germans.

Relations between America and Japan worsened in July 1941, when the Japanese forced the French to let them take over eight air and two naval bases in southern Indochina. Roosevelt, interpreting the action as the opening move in a campaign of conquest in Southeast Asia, froze all Japanese assets in the United States. The freeze order was a major step down the road to war. It became the American instrument for ending trade between the United States and Japan. A few days after the freeze went into effect, America embargoed all oil and steel shipments to Japan. The trade cutoff pushed the Japanese into a corner. Without these crucial commodities, their industrial economy and war machine would grind to a halt within a few months. Either a way had to be found quickly to restore trade with America, or Japan would have to get these essential commodities elsewhere.

Since all but the most extreme Japanese leaders opposed war with the American colossus at this date, Japanese diplomats sought to negotiate an arrangement with Washington that would restore the lost strategic trade. Nomura met several more times with Hull. He also met with the president. Roosevelt told him that the United States wanted improved relations with Japan. FDR indicated that he was interested in meeting with Prince Konoye if Japan was ready "to suspend its expansionist activities" and the two countries could resolve their "fundamental differences." Even as he made these statements, Roosevelt was skeptical that a meaningful rapprochement was possible; he basically continued to stall the Japanese in order to allow the American military buildup more time and to avoid a war in Asia when preparing to enter one in Europe.

High-level Japanese meetings held in early September proved that American-Japanese differences were irreconcilable. Convinced that they must move before American economic sanctions hindered their ability to fight, army militants insisted that Konoye settle differences with the Americans by mid-October. If no agreement was made, Japan would prepare for war with the United States. The conditions for a settlement agreed to on September 6 by an Imperial Conference set Japan firmly on the road to war: the United States would not interfere with Japanese efforts in China, would not increase its forces in the Pacific, and would restore trade with Japan. In return, Japan pledged no further moves into Southeast Asia and guaranteed the neutrality of the Philippines. In late September, Nomura conveyed these terms to Roosevelt.

Roosevelt found them unacceptable, confirming his sense that irreconcilable differences separated the two nations, especially regarding China, and that a meeting with Konoye would be pointless. He also read public opinion polls showing that Americans were firmly opposed to any appeasement of Japanese aggression in China. He and Hull continued negotiations, but they made no concessions on China or agreements to restore trade. They continued the strategy of stalling, of trying to buy time in the Pacific to allow the United States to build up its air forces in the Philippines, hoping that the added striking power might deter Japanese expansion into Southeast Asia. Roosevelts's top military advisers, General George Marshall and Admiral Harold Stark, cautioned the president against taking any actions that might provoke the Japanese to war, since the American forces in the Pacific were not ready and the United States could soon be at war in Europe.

In early October 1941, when it became evident that Prince Konoye could not achieve a diplomatic agreement with the United States, he and his cabinet resigned. General Tojo headed the new government, a military dictatorship committed to ending what Tojo called the "deadlock of indecision." On November 5, Japanese leaders, meeting in the presence of Emperor Hirohito, reached a crucial decision: they would continue diplomacy for three more weeks, but if no agreement were reached by November 26, Japan would go to war. The date for the attack was set for December 8, Tokyo time (December 7, Washington time).

Japan's final proposals offered no prospect of avoiding war. The proposals were divided into Plan A and Plan B, with Plan B to be offered only if Plan A were rejected by the Americans. Admiral Nomura presented Plan A to Roosevelt on November 10. Plan A made clear Japan's continuing refusal to get out of China and its refusal to leave the Tripartite Pact. Roosevelt rejected these terms. Tokyo sent another envoy to join Nomura in Washington, Saburo Kurusu, and together they presented Plan B to Secretary of State Hull on November 20. It was a more complex proposal, but it still left Japan a free hand in China and called for a full restoration of American trade with Japan. The United States rejected Plan B on November 26 and told Japan to "withdraw all military, naval, air, and police forces" from China and Indochina. The Japanese prepared to assault the Dutch East Indies, Malaya, and the American territory of the Philippines. They also planned a surprise attack on Pearl Harbor to destroy the American Pacific fleet, the only military force that posed a serious threat to their imperial ambitions in Asia.

PEARL HARBOR ATTACKED!

Because a brilliant U.S. Army cryptanalyst, Colonel Lawrence Friedman, had cracked the principal Japanese diplomatic code, which the analysts called code "Purple," President Roosevelt knew that the Tojo government had set a November 26 deadline for a diplomatic solution, and that now war would soon follow. The decoding machines enabling Americans to read the coded Japanese messages were named "Magic." But "Magic" intercepts never contained specific information pinpointing where and when any attacks would occur.

On November 27, the day after the Tojo government's deadline for diplomacy, Washington sent a final alert to American military commanders in the Pacific. The message sent to Admiral Kimmel at Pearl Harbor read in part:

> This dispatch is to be considered a war warning . . . an aggressive move by Japan is expected within the next few days.[3]

On November 29, Tokyo learned that the European Axis powers promised to declare war on the United States if new Japanese actions in the Pacific provoked war. The Japanese now knew that they would not be fighting America alone. On that same day, Emperor Hirohito assented to war.

In Washington, American leaders waited grimly for the Japanese blow, wherever it might come. "Why not attack first?" Roosevelt's top aide, Harry Hopkins, asked the president. "No," said Roosevelt, "we would have to wait until it came." Secretary of War Stimson, concerned about divisions of public opinion within the country, explained that the United States had to let Japan fire the first shot "so there should remain no doubt in anyone's mind as to who were the aggressors." Where would the Japanese strike? Roosevelt's guess, based on his analysis of information available from "Magic" intercepts and many other intelligence sources, was that Japan would strike somewhere in Southeast Asia. Neither Roosevelt nor any of his senior advisors anticipated an attack on U.S. military installations in Hawaii.

On the evening of December 6, "Magic" began decoding a long message from Tokyo to Nomura. Its final section announced that there was no chance of reaching a diplomatic settlement with the United States. Reading the intercept, Roosevelt

[3]Quoted in John E. Wiltz, *From Isolationism to War, 1931–1941* (New York: Thomas Y. Crowell, 1968), pp. 126–27.

said: "This means war." Another intercept received early Sunday morning, on December 7, indicated that an attack could occur at any time. Another alert was sent to the commanders at Pearl Harbor; tragically, that message did not reach them until after the Japanese attack had begun.

The Japanese naval task force that was assigned to attack Pearl Harbor had set sail from its home port in the Kurile Islands on November 26. To avoid detection, all ships, sailing across more than 3,000 miles of ocean, observed radio silence and sailed in lanes unused by commercial vessels. On December 2, the task force received final clearance to attack from imperial headquarters. In the early morning on December 7, the task force reached the point from which it would launch air strikes. Shortly after 6:00 A.M. local time, the planes began taking off from four carriers; they were launched in two waves, 360 planes in all. Pearl Harbor lay 275 miles southwest, or 105 minutes flying time.

Conditions for the attack were ideal, and visibility was perfect. The Americans were caught by complete surprise. The attackers encountered no antiaircraft fire, and no interceptors rose to challenge them. Spread out before them in neat

Figure 7.6   December 7, 1941, a date which will live in infamy. . . . After the Japanese attackers have flown back toward their carriers, battered U.S. warships burn at their moorings. Left to right: the U.S.S Arizona, U.S.S Tennessee, and U.S.S West Virginia. The U.S.S Arizona later capsized and sunk, carrying 1,100 sailors to a watery grave.   *Source:* National Archives.

alignment was the American Pacific fleet. At 7:55 A.M., Hawaiian time, the first wave of dive bombers screamed to the attack. Their primary targets were the American battleships and airfields. The assaults lasted about two hours. At 9:45 A.M., the planes withdrew and headed back to their carriers.

Although caught off guard, the Americans recovered quickly and fought courageously. But the odds were hopeless, and American losses were severe. The Japanese sank or crippled eighteen warships, destroyed or damaged 204 planes on the ground, extensively damaged five airfields, and killed 2,403 Americans—over 1,000 of whom were entombed in the USS *Arizona* when it exploded and sank. Japanese losses were light: twenty-nine planes, forty-five pilots and air crewmen, one regular submarine, and five midget subs.

The Japanese attackers exceeded even their most optimistic expectations. Their carrier task force escaped detection and returned to its home waters undamaged and with no casualties. On the same day, other Japanese forces attacked U.S. bases on Guam and Midway Island. Japanese planes also destroyed the American air forces in the Philippines, catching the planes on the ground. December 7, 1941, was the worst day in American military history.

American military blunders contributed to the smashing Japanese successes at Pearl Harbor and elsewhere in the Pacific. Intelligence analysts seriously underestimated Japanese military capabilities. The costliest error was the failure of the American commanders, Admiral Kimmel and General Short, in Hawaii to respond properly to the war alert from Washington, which they had received on November 27. Expecting the Japanese attack to come elsewhere, they had taken precautions only against sabotage.

The Japanese made serious errors carrying out their attacks on Pearl Harbor. They failed to destroy oil storage and ship repair facilities, which the Americans soon put to good use. Most of the eighteen ships left battered and helpless that day were restored, and they later entered into the battles that would destroy Japanese sea power. The attackers also failed to seek out and destroy the two American aircraft carriers that were, as luck would have it, operating at sea on that fateful December morning. One carrier was at sea on a training exercise; the other had been sent to Midway Island to ferry some aircraft back to Pearl Harbor. The war in the Pacific was principally a naval war, and naval aviation played a far more important role than battleships in determining the eventual American victory.

Put in a larger context, although achieving a decisive tactical victory, the Japanese committed a colossal strategic blunder by attacking Pearl Harbor. Had they attacked European colonial possessions in Southeast Asia, as expected, Roosevelt would have had difficulty bringing America promptly into the war. A sizeable number of Americans would have strongly opposed a declaration of war against Japan following an attack on Borneo or Malaya. Roosevelt later told Churchill that if "it had not been for the Japanese attack, he would have had great difficulty in getting the American people into the war."

The Japanese solved Roosevelt's dilemma. Eager to destroy the American fleet at Pearl Harbor, the only military force in the Pacific capable of blocking their planned Pacific conquests, they directly attacked American soil and shed American blood. The surprise attack, and the death and destruction that it caused, enraged and united nearly all Americans in support of an immediate declaration of war against Japan. Admiral Isoruku Yamamoto, the brilliant strategist who conceived the Pearl Harbor attack, upon learning that it had been a great success, felt no joy. Instead, he somberly told his colleagues: "I fear all we have done is to awaken a sleeping giant and fill him with a terrible resolve."

The next day, President Roosevelt, calling December 7, 1941, "a date which will live in infamy," asked a joint session of Congress to declare war on Japan effective from the moment the first bomb struck Pearl Harbor. Within hours, Congress complied, with only one dissenting vote. Three days later, Germany and Italy declared war on the United States, honoring their commitments under the terms of the Tripartite Pact. America replied in kind on the same day. In four days, Americans had gone from peace to war in both Europe and the Pacific.

IMPORTANT EVENTS

1921	The Washington Naval Conference takes place
1924	The Dawes Plan is enacted
1928	The Kellogg-Briand Pact is negotiated
1929	President Hoover proclaims the Good Neighbor policy
1930	The Smoot-Hawley Tariff is enacted
1931	Japan invades Manchuria
	President Hoover declares a one-year moratorium on debt payments
1933	Cuba cancels the Platt Amendment
1934	The Nye Committee hearings begin
1935	The first Neutrality Act is passed
	Italy attacks Ethiopia
1936	Germany reoccupies the Rhineland
	The Spanish Civil War begins
1937	Japan invades northern China; World War II in Asia begins
	President Roosevelt delivers his "quarantine the aggressors" speech
1938	The Munich Conference is held
1939	Germany occupies Czechoslovakia
	The Nazi-Soviet Pact is signed
	Germany invades Poland; World War II in Europe begins
1940	The fall of France occurs
	America and Great Britain complete a destroyers-for-bases deal
	The Battle of Britain takes place
1941	Roosevelt and Churchill sign the Atlantic Charter
	Pearl Harbor is attacked; the United States enters World War II

BIBLIOGRAPHY

The two best general studies of American foreign policy during the 1920s are L. Ethan Ellis's *Republican Foreign Policy, 1921–1933* and Joan Hoff Wilson's *American Business and Foreign Policy, 1920–1933.* Dana Munro's *United States and the Caribbean Republics, 1921–1933* and Irwin F. Gellman's *Good Neighbor Diplomacy: United States Policies in Latin America, 1933–1945* are good accounts of the United States' Latin American policies between the wars. Walter LaFeber, in *Inevitable Revolutions: The United States in Central America,* offers a fine recent study of American foreign policy in Central America and its consequences. Charles DeBenedetti's *The Peace Reform Movement in American History* accurately chronicles American peace activities during the 1920s and 1930s. Robert Dallek, in *Franklin D. Roosevelt and American Foreign Policy, 1932–1945,* presents the best, most comprehensive treatment of Roosevelt's foreign policy available. Robert A. Divine's *The Illusion of Neutrality* is a good study of 1930s' isolationism. Arnold Offner's *The Origins of the Second World War* is an excellent work. John Wiltz, in *From Isolation to War, 1931–1941,* offers a good short account of United States' entry into World War II. Waldo Heinrichs' *Threshold of War: Franklin D. Roosevelt and American Entry into World War II* is an excellent recent study. William L. Langer's and S.E. Gleason's *The Undeclared War, 1940–1941* is a detailed account of the deteriorating relations between the United States and Germany. The best study of the isolationists who were attacking Roosevelt's foreign policy in 1940 and 1941 is Wayne S. Cole's *America First: The Battle Against Intervention, 1940–1941.* Warren F. Kimball, in *The Most Unsordid Act: Lend-Lease, 1939–1941,* presents a good study. The attack on Pearl Harbor is the subject of many books. By far the best of these is Gordon W. Prange's *At Dawn We Slept,* an excellent account of the Japanese surprise attack on U.S. military installations in Hawaii that plunged America into the vortex of war. Roberta Wohlstetter's *Pearl Harbor: Warning and Decision* is a brilliant study of American intelligence gathering and includes the most powerful refutation of the Pearl Harbor conspiracy theories.

8

World War II

W HEN the United States entered World War II immediately following the Japanese surprise attack on U.S. military installations in Hawaii, the vast conflict became history's first global war. The struggle consisted of two wars waged simultaneously. In Europe, North Africa, and the Middle East, the United States, Great Britain, and the Soviet Union battled Germany and Italy, with both sides aided by minor allies. In the Pacific basin and along the East Asian perimeter, America, with help from the British, Dutch, Australians, New Zealanders, Indians, and Chinese, fought the Japanese, who had no allies in Asia. World War II was also history's largest, costliest, and bloodiest war. About 50,000,000 people perished between 1939 and 1945, half of them civilians. The war also claimed about $2 trillion of the world's wealth.

From its entry into World War II, American armed forces played crucial roles in winning both the European and Pacific conflicts. In addition to supporting its own far-flung forces fighting around the world, the United States furnished its major allies with substantial amounts of food, equipment, ammunition, and weapons. The war revitalized the American economy. Lingering vestiges of the Great Depression were quickly swept away, and a sustained economic boom that was to last for thirty years began in 1942. World War II ended in the summer of 1945 in total victory for the Allied cause. America emerged from the ashes of war as the richest, freest, and most powerful nation in the history of the planet.

WAR IN EUROPE

American industry undergirded the Allied war effort, producing millions of planes, tanks, trucks, rifles, howitzers, and ships. American military production more than doubled the Axis output, enabling the United States and its allies to win a grueling war of attrition.

American and British leaders agreed on a "beat Hitler first" strategy for three compelling reasons: Germany posed a potential threat to the Western Hemisphere; their military technology was more likely than Japanese technology to achieve a breakthrough weapon that might enable them to win the war; and Germany, in late 1941, was putting tremendous pressure on the Soviet Union.

Determined to engage the Germans in decisive battle, American war planners proposed an invasion of France scheduled for the fall of 1942. The embattled Soviets, fighting for their lives against the best German armies, pleaded with their allies to open a "second front" in the west as soon as possible to ease the pressure on their forces. The British rejected the American invasion proposal. They preferred to strike initially at the periphery of Axis power, and to delay a frontal assault until after German resistance had weakened. The British proposed an alternative campaign, a joint Anglo-American invasion of North Africa. President Roosevelt accepted the British offer with the understanding that the North African assault would soon be followed by an invasion of France.

On November 8, 1942, Anglo-American forces, under the command of General Dwight Eisenhower, stormed ashore at points along the coast of the French North African colonies of Morocco and Algeria. The operation succeeded tactically, but political complications soon developed. The invaded territories were controlled by the collaborationist French regime at Vichy, and its forces resisted the Allied invaders. General Eisenhower negotiated an armistice agreement with Admiral Darlan, the Vichy leader in North Africa, in exchange for Allied recognition of Darlan's authority. The arrangement outraged Charles De Gaulle's Free French government, backed by the British, which claimed authority in North Africa.

Hitler, surprised by the Allied thrust into French North Africa, rushed German troops to neighboring Tunisia. Eisenhower responded by sending his forces into Tunisia from the west. British forces from Egypt, under the command of General Bernard Montgomery, invaded Tunisia from the east, catching the German and Italian forces in a giant pincers. Tunisia proved to be a hard campaign. Its terrain was rugged and arid; vast deserts were punctured by sheer cliffs. The Allies also came up against one of Hitler's best generals, Field Marshall Erwin Rommel. His veteran Afrika Korps defeated inexperienced American forces in early encounters. One of America's ablest generals made his debut as a field commander during the Tunisian campaign—General George S. Patton, Jr., whose flamboyant attire and severe discipline earned him his nickname "Old Blood and Guts." After months of heavy fighting, the Axis forces surrendered. Although the North African diversion delayed opening a second front in France, it proved to be a significant victory. The Mediterranean was reopened to Allied shipping, the British lifeline through Suez was secured, and the Middle Eastern oil fields were saved.

As fighting raged in North Africa, President Roosevelt met with the British prime minister at Casablanca to plot the next campaign. Roosevelt wanted to attack France; the absent Soviets, with the German wolf still at their throats, strongly

Figure 8.1 General George S. Patton, Jr. *Source:* National Archives.

endorsed his proposal. Churchill proposed instead a move into Sicily and southern Italy to maintain the Mediterranean initiative. Roosevelt reluctantly accepted Churchill's suggestion, and the French invasion was put off until after 1943.

Anglo-American forces invaded Sicily in July 1943, and southern Italy in September. These attacks toppled the shaky Mussolini government. General Eisenhower recognized a new Italian government formed by Field Marshall Pietro Badoglio, who promptly surrendered to the Allies. The invasions had knocked Italy out of the war, but German forces fighting in Italy formidably resisted Allied invaders. Fighting continued in Italy almost to the end of the war.

As the Allies were winning the North African campaign, Soviet forces began driving the Germans back from the gates of Moscow. Soviet armies also surrounded a large German force at Stalingrad, a city in the south of Russia. Both armies fought ferociously in the depths of winter. In January 1943, the Germans, having lost 300,000 men, surrendered. The Battle of Stalingrad was a turning point in the European war. Bolstered by Lend-Lease aid from the United States, by 1943 the Soviets had forged the largest army in the world. In summer offensives across a thousand-mile front, Soviet armies drove the Germans back.

At sea, Allied naval forces were winning the Battle of the Atlantic. By the end of 1943, Allied convoy tactics, teamed with antisubmarine forces, contained German submarines. Huge quantities of Lend-Lease supplies reached England and the Soviet Union, and hundreds of American troop ships arrived in Europe.

The air war also turned in favor of the Allies. By 1943, Allied strategic bombers flew both day and night over Germany and its Central European allies. U.S. Eighth Air Force planes flying from English bases pounded Germany's great industrial web. By year's end, Allied planes controlled the air over Germany. American and British bombs destroyed German factories, railroads, and military installations. Air raids also severely damaged many German cities, including Hamburg, Berlin, and Dresden, killing thousands of civilians.

In the summer of 1944, the Allies, under the supreme command of General Eisenhower, launched the long-delayed second front. The invasion occurred early in the morning on June 6, 1944, "D-Day," with landings along the Normandy coast of France. The most dramatic moment of the European war had arrived. Historian Stephen Ambrose wrote, "June 6, 1944, was the pivot of the twentieth century." At stake was the future of democracy, Fascism, and Communism, all locked in a death struggle that meant certain doom for one if not two of the competing ideologies. D-Day was the largest amphibious operation in history—an armada of landing craft spilling 150,000 American, British, Canadian, French, and Polish soldiers onto the French beaches. Thousands of fighter planes and bombers raced in over the French coast to take control of the air. Hundreds of warships stood offshore in the English Channel, pounding German fortifications. By the end of the day, the Allies had secured their beachhead, but success had come at a terrible price in lives and materiel. The successful landings and buildups on the beaches were only possible because the bulk of the German army and its best divisions were committed to the war against the Soviet Union.

Figure 8.2   D-Day, June 6, 1944. American troops wade ashore at Omaha Beach in the face of fierce resistance from German gunners.   *Source:* U.S. Army Photo.

Even so, the depleted German defenders kept the invaders pinned to the coast until July 26, when General Patton's Third Army broke through to Brittany. Racing through holes torn in the German lines, Patton's forces led a lightning advance across western France. The German army began reeling backward. Allied forces liberated Paris on August 25. To the south, Allied forces captured Rome. The invaders reached German soil in September.

WAR IN THE PACIFIC

Victory at Pearl Harbor had marked the beginning of a period of rapid Japanese expansion in the Far East. One after another, the bastions of Western imperialism fell to their advancing forces: Hong Kong, Singapore, Java, and the Philippine archipelago. For six months after Pearl Harbor, the Japanese ruled the Pacific. The Japanese navy was the most powerful fleet in the world. American forces trying to stem the Japanese tide were hampered by the damage done at Pearl Harbor, and by the priorities of war planners in Washington, who gave the European war preference in men and weapons.

But the naval war in the Pacific suddenly turned against Japan in mid-1942. In two hard-fought battles, American fleets halted the Japanese expansionist thrusts south and east. From May 5 to May 8, in the Battle of the Coral Sea northeast of Australia, American and Japanese aircraft carrier task forces fought a series of engagements. It was history's first sea battle in which surface ships did not fire a shot at each other, the battle being fought entirely with aircraft from carriers. U.S. forces prevented Japanese control of the Coral Sea region and ended any possibility of Japanese attacks on northern Australia.

The most important naval battle of the Pacific war, the Battle of Midway, occurred a month after the Coral Sea one. The Japanese objective was to capture Midway Island, located 1,000 miles west of Hawaii, and to take islands in the Aleutian chain, southwest of Alaska. These islands would then serve the Japanese navy as anchor points for an expanded defense perimeter for their island empire in the Pacific basin. Japanese control of Midway also would allow them to launch further attacks on Hawaii. The Japanese also intended to force American forces to defend Midway in order to finish what the attack at Pearl Harbor had begun, the temporary destruction of U.S. sea power in the Pacific.

For the Midway campaign, the Japanese assigned four aircraft carriers; the Americans had three, one of which had sustained severe damage during the Battle of the Coral Sea. Japanese naval aircraft were superior to U.S. planes. The Japanese had hundreds of the finest navy pilots in the world. American naval aviators were mostly young and inexperienced.

American code breakers scored an intelligence coup when they intercepted and analyzed a Japanese message that enabled them to learn the exact time and place of the Japanese attack, and the composition of their forces. Using this valuable information, Admiral Chester Nimitz, commander of the Pacific Fleet, prepared a battle plan to surprise the Japanese attackers by assaulting them early.

The crucial encounters during the Battle of Midway occurred on June 4, 1942, the most important single day's fighting of the entire Pacific war. Admiral Richard Spruance, commander of Task Force 16, boldly executed the American battle plan. His planes caught the Japanese carriers before they could launch their aircraft. American dive bombers sank all four Japanese aircraft carriers, destroying the heart of their mighty task force. American losses included a carrier, a destroyer, and dozens of planes and pilots, but the Americans scored a critical victory at Midway.

Following the victory in the Coral Sea and the miracle at Midway, American Marines and Army infantry invaded Japanese strongholds in the South Pacific. Guadalcanal, an island in the Solomon chain, was one of the most important campaigns of the Pacific war. Both sides waged a savage war of attrition that went on for months. The turning point came during the November 13–15 period, when the Americans won a decisive naval victory. In February 1943, after seven months of air and sea battles, and grueling combat in steamy jungles and rugged, mountainous terrain, the Japanese abandoned the island. Guadalcanal was a decisive victory for the Americans and a crushing defeat for the Japanese.

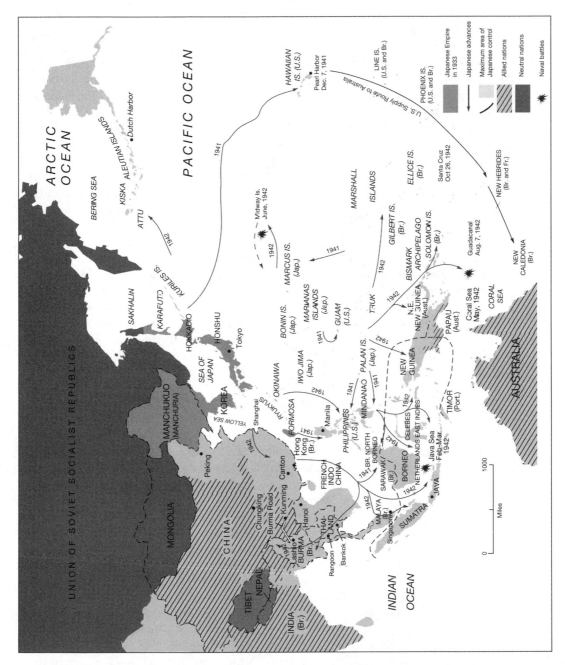

Figure 8.3   World War II: Japanese advances, 1941–1942.   *Source:* George D. Moss, *Rise of Modern America*, p. 335.

By mid-1943, American war planners had developed a strategy that would bring victory in the Pacific. It comprised two parallel offensives. Forces commanded by General Douglas MacArthur would advance from the South Pacific through New Guinea to the Philippines, and then to Japan. Other forces, commanded by Admiral Nimitz, would advance through the Central Pacific via the Marianas Islands to Formosa (Taiwan), along the China coast, and then to Japan. As these two forces battled toward Japan, Army Air Corps planes bombed and strafed Japanese shipping and their island garrisons. Battles at sea continued as carrier task forces encountered Japanese fleets. Under the sea, American submarines attacked both Japanese merchant ships and naval warships. As the U.S. campaigns progressed, strategists discovered that they could bypass heavily fortified Japanese-held islands because American air and sea power could prevent the enemy from reinforcing them. Isolated and impotent, these bases posed no threat to American forces. This bypass technique, called "leapfrogging," saved thousands of American lives and accelerated the war effort across the Pacific toward Japan.

During 1944, the Pacific war turned decisively against Japan. Admiral Nimitz's forces advanced into the Marianas, an island chain located within 1,500 miles of Tokyo. During the Battle of the Philippine Sea, on June 19, 1944, waves of Japanese planes attacked the American task force off the coast of Saipan. U.S. Navy pilots massacred the Japanese aviators. At day's end, fewer than 100 of the 373 Japanese planes returned to their carriers. America lost twenty nine planes. Saipan fell after a bloody struggle on July 9; U.S. forces liberated Guam on August 10.

Conquest of the Marianas provided forward bases for American submarines, which cut off Japanese shipping to and from the home islands and the South Pacific. The Army Air Corps got bases from which its powerful new bomber, the B-29 "Superfortress," could strike Japan directly. On November 24, 1944, 144 Superfortresses left Saipan for a raid on Tokyo. The size and frequency of air raids steadily increased through the remaining months of war, devastating most of Japan's cities.

Following the occupation of the Marianas, President Roosevelt approved a campaign to liberate the Philippines, which had been seized by the Japanese in 1942. A gigantic combined force of air, sea, and land units assembled. The Japanese gathered their still formidable forces for an all-out defense of the vital archipelago linking Japan to Malaya and the East Indies.

Leyte, one of the central islands, would be the point of attack by the most powerful strike force in military history. The Battle of Leyte Gulf, the largest naval battle in all of history between the two mightiest fleets ever assembled, preceded the invasion. It was a series of engagements between various units of both navies that took place over several days. During one of these battles, the Japanese first used a suicide attack unit known as the *Kamikaze.* This unorthodox military tactic inflicted heavy losses on American naval forces before war's end. But *Kamikazes* could not prevent a crushing Japanese defeat in the battle for Leyte Gulf. In the end, U.S. naval air power proved decisive. On October 20, 1944, General MacArthur waded ashore on a Leyte Beach proclaiming, "People of the Philippines: I have returned!" Between October 25 and 27, the American fleets completed their destruction of the world's once-mightiest navy. American sea power now controlled the Pacific. Leyte was liberated on Christmas Day, 1944.

The invasion of Luzon, the largest Philippine island, began on January 9, 1945. Japanese defenders numbered 250,000. The battle for Luzon proved to be a long, fierce, and very bloody campaign. Japanese troops occupying Manila refused to surrender, and much of that beautiful city was destroyed by weeks of vicious fighting in the streets. It took six months to pacify Luzon. Brave Filipino guerrillas furnished valuable help to the American forces during that long, hard campaign.

President Roosevelt had hoped that China could play a major role in the war against Japan. But Jiang Jieshi's Nationalist regime, exhausted from years of warfare, could not take effective action against the Japanese, even with extensive American aid and support. In 1941 and 1942, American pilots, flying from India "over the hump" of the Himalayas, ferried supplies to the Chinese government. In 1943, Allied forces, under General Joseph "Vinegar Joe" Stilwell, constructed the Burma Road across northern Burma to the Chinese city of Kungming. Roosevelt then assigned Stilwell to Jiang's government, with orders to maximize the Chinese war effort against Japan. But Stilwell discovered that Jiang was more concerned about fighting an enemy within China, the spreading Communist movement led by Mao Zedong. Frustrated, Stilwell fired off a report to Washington accusing Jiang of preventing the fulfillment of his mission to China. A furious Jiang then demanded that Roosevelt recall General Stilwell. Roosevelt complied with Jiang's request. China's military potential went down the drain of internal political conflict.

WARTIME DIPLOMACY

During the war, the Axis powers failed to coordinate their military and diplomatic strategies. The Allies, despite much tension and disagreement, maintained a wartime harmony of interests. The Americans and British forged a partnership even before the United States entered the war. In December 1941, the two nations created a Combined Chiefs of Staff to coordinate grand strategy in both Europe and Asia. Although they agreed on war aims, American and British leaders disagreed on the timing and location of a second front in Europe. Churchill also refused to apply the principle of self-determination, embodied in the Atlantic Charter, to the British empire. The Soviet Union, the third member of the Allied coalition, endorsed the Charter with reservations about its applicability to eastern Europe. Generally, the Soviets were willing to mute their political and ideological differences with Western powers as long as military necessity bound them together. But Stalin protested bitterly the continual delays by the Western nations in opening a second front in France. The Grand Alliance remained a shotgun wedding; only the need to defeat Germany kept the unnatural marriage together. The origins of the Cold War lay in the wartime tensions and conflicts of the Allies.

Wartime coalition required periodic meetings among the Allied leaders. Early in 1943, Roosevelt and Churchill met at Casablanca to plot strategy following the successful North African landings. There they adopted the doctrine of "unconditional surrender," meaning that they would press the war until the Axis leaders gave up without any assurances that they would remain in power.

The Big Three (Roosevelt, Churchill, and Stalin) met for the first time at Teheran in November 1943. A meeting in Cairo among Roosevelt, Churchill, and Jiang Jieshi preceded the Teheran conference, where the leaders discussed the Asian war in which the Soviets were not engaged at the time. The three allies agreed that Manchuria and Formosa would be returned to China after the war. The Teheran conference focused primarily on military strategy. Stalin received his long-sought commitment from the Western powers that a second front would be opened in France within six months. The three leaders also discussed postwar political questions involving Germany and eastern European countries. Roosevelt, during his meetings with Stalin, used his talents at personal diplomacy to try to win the trust and cooperation of the Soviet leader.

Another year of war occurred before the Big Three met again. As the end of 1944 approached, the Allies were winning both the European and Asian wars, although much bloody fighting remained. In December, the Germans mounted a counteroffensive in the Ardennes Forest region of southern Belgium. For three weeks, Nazi Panzers drove the Allies back, but the Germans could not sustain their momentum. This "Battle of the Bulge," named for the big bulge created in the Allied lines at Bastogne, ended on Christmas. Approaching victory generated a host of related strategic and political questions that required the personal attention of the Big Three; they had to chart the final drives of the European war, discuss the Pacific war, talk about the postwar political status of eastern European countries, plan for occupying Germany, and arrange for the creation of a proposed United Nations. The three leaders met at Yalta, a Crimean resort on the Black Sea coast, from February 4 to February 11, 1945.

The first important matter discussed at Yalta involved the occupation policy for postwar Germany. Roosevelt and Churchill rejected a Soviet request to strip Germany of $20 billion worth of reparations. To prevent this dispute from dividing the conference, all parties accepted the principle of reparations and referred the matter to an appointed commission to determine specific amounts. The Big Three agreed to divide Germany into four occupation zones, with France assigned the fourth zone. They also agreed to a joint occupation of Berlin, which lay deep within the Soviet zone in eastern Germany, an arrangement both sides deeply regretted after the rise of the Cold War.

Roosevelt initiated discussions at Yalta on the pending formation of the United Nations. Vigorous U.S. participation in an international organization armed with power to maintain peace by using economic sanctions or military force was FDR's chief concern at Yalta. He wanted Stalin, without whose cooperation it could not succeed, to commit himself to full support for the new agency to be created at San Francisco in April 1945. To encourage Soviet cooperation, he accepted Stalin's demand for three votes in the General Assembly; he also accepted a veto designed to protect great power prerogatives within the United Nations (UN).

The postwar political status of Poland caused the most controversy at the conference, particularly the composition of its new government. There were, at the time, two governments claiming to represent all Poles, one headquartered in London and championed by the British, and one in Lublin, backed by the Soviets. Stalin, who made it clear that Poland was a vital Soviet interest, proposed that the Communist-controlled government at Lublin become the government of a new Poland. Roosevelt proposed a government comprising representatives of Poland's five major political parties. The Soviets rejected it, but Stalin agreed to add "democratic elements" to the Lublin regime. To avoid letting differences over Poland undermine conference harmony, the Allies worked out an agreement that papered over significant differences with vague, elastic language. Stalin agreed to "free and unfettered elections" at an unspecified time in the future.

Roosevelt understood that the presence of Soviet troops in Poland, and elsewhere in eastern Europe, gave them controlling influence in determining the political future for these countries. He did not expect to achieve genuine democracy for Poland, but he hoped to convince American public opinion that he had succeeded in doing so. Roosevelt also got Churchill and Stalin to sign a Declaration of Liberated Europe, which committed the Big Three to help the liberated people of eastern Europe to form democratic governments through free elections.

Roosevelt also wanted to commit the Soviets to entering the Asian war against Japan as soon as possible. On February 10, Stalin and Roosevelt signed a secret treaty in which the Soviet Union agreed to enter the war within three months following Germany's surrender. In return, the Soviets were given many concessions: they got a Soviet-controlled satellite in Outer Mongolia; they were guaranteed the return of the southern portion of Sakhalin Island; the port of Darien would be internationalized; a lease would be given to the Soviets for the use of Port Authur as a naval base; a joint Chinese-Soviet consortium would be established to operate the Manchurian railways; and the Japanese would cede the Kurile Islands to the Soviets.

Roosevelt and his advisers considered the price of Soviet entry into the Asian war reasonable at the time. The expectation that an atomic bomb would be ready in August did not alter Roosevelt's goal of getting the Soviets into the war. His military advisers told him that Soviet participation at the earliest possible moment would ensure the defeat of Japanese forces in Manchuria, and that Soviet air raids on Japan flown from Siberia would ensure the disruption of Japanese shipping from the Asian mainland. Most important, Soviet intervention would shorten the war and save American lives. Roosevelt did not consult with Jiang Jieshi before granting the Soviets the concessions affecting China.

The atmosphere at Yalta was cordial, as befitted members of a wartime coalition who still needed one another to achieve victory over their enemies. Both sides

Figure 8.4   The Big Three—Prime Minister Winston Churchill of Great Britain, President Franklin Roosevelt of the United States, and Premier Joseph Stalin of the Soviet Union—held several wartime conferences. At Yalta, a Black Sea resort in the Crimea, they met for the last time in February 1945.   *Source:* U.S. Army Photo.

made compromises and concessions. Roosevelt left the conference believing that he had attained Soviet cooperation in winning the war and building a postwar structure of peace. But the Soviets achieved important diplomatic victories at Yalta. Stalin used the military situation favoring the Soviet Union at the time to achieve his objectives. The role of the Allied military in the ultimate defeat of the Germans was minor compared to the Soviet effort. As Red forces overran eastern and southern Europe, Stalin used military occupation to gain political control of countries within these strategic regions. Stalin also used the American desire for Soviet entry into the war against Japan to exact major diplomatic concessions in the Far East. Roosevelt did not "sell out" China to the Soviets at Yalta as Republican critics later charged, but the Yalta agreements amounted to a significant diplomatic victory for the Soviet Union.

VICTORY IN EUROPE

Shortly after Yalta, advancing American forces reached the Rhine River. With the Nazi regime approaching extinction, the Soviets installed the Lublin Communists in power in Poland, violating the Yalta agreement. Roosevelt warned Stalin that his actions jeopardized "future world cooperation." He also warned Churchill on April 6 that they would have to be firm in their dealings with the Soviets about Poland's political future. But on April 12, Roosevelt died of a cerebral hemorrhage at his vacation retreat in Warm Springs, Georgia.

Harry Truman, an unknown professional politician with an undistinguished record, succeeded Roosevelt. Truman initially doubted if he could handle the responsibilities of the world's most demanding job. After taking the oath of office, a shaken Truman told reporters that he felt as if "the moon, the stars, and all the planets had suddenly fallen on me." Fate had thrust Truman into the presidency, an office he had never sought and one for which he was ill prepared. The new president assumed office at a time when momentous strategic and political decisions had to be made.

As Truman struggled to take hold of the reins of office, the European war ground toward its inevitable conclusion. Churchill, reacting to Soviet political moves in Poland, advised Roosevelt just before his death that Anglo-American forces should "beat the Russians to Berlin" to stretch Western postwar political leverage as far east as possible. Roosevelt died before he could make a decision, and he was replaced by the inexperienced Truman. The Supreme Allied Commander in Europe, General Eisenhower, rejected Churchill's proposal and permitted the Soviets to capture Berlin. He ordered American advance forces to halt at the Elbe River, fifty miles from the German capital. The Joint Chiefs and President Truman both accepted Eisenhower's decision, which he made for strategic reasons.

Eisenhower made his decision to stop at the Elbe because all of his efforts were aimed at defeating Germany and ending the war as quickly as possible. He feared that a Berlin campaign would enable remaining German forces in southern Germany to regroup into guerrilla units that could prolong the war and increase American casualties. Further, he knew that a U.S. drive on Berlin could result in military conflicts with the Soviets. American public opinion would have exploded at the prospect of substituting Soviets for Germans as enemies. His most important consideration was that America still had another war to win in the Pacific. Washington wanted to end the European war as soon as possible so that troops fighting in Europe could be sent to Asia.

It is unlikely that American forces could have beaten the Soviets to Berlin if they had tried. On April 11, General William Simpson had 50,000 troops within fifty miles of the city. A weak Germany army and some water barriers stood between them and the capital. On that date, the Soviets were fifteen miles closer, had 1,250,000 men, and faced two weak German armies. The terrain was flat, dry land. It cost the Soviets over 100,000 casualties to take Berlin, more than America had suffered in fighting on German soil during the final months of war. After war's end, the Soviets had to give up half of the city they had captured at a fearsome price. The Allies got their Berlin sectors without losing a single man. As the Soviets took Berlin, Eisenhower's forces crushed the remaining pockets of German resistance. Fighting ended on May 5, and Germany surrendered on May 7.

As Allied armies liberated Poland and conquered Germany, they discovered the death camps that revealed the radical evil at the heart of the Nazi regime. Battle-hardened soldiers stared in disbelief at open, mass graves filled with skeletons, and still-living, emaciated victims of Nazi savagery. Early in the war, Hitler had approved a plan prepared for "a final solution to the Jewish question": their systematic destruction. The Nazis built five extermination centers, the most infamous located near the Polish village of Auschwitz. For three years, trains of cattle cars from all of the German-occupied areas of Europe hauled doomed human cargoes to their final destinations. Jews were not the only Holocaust victims. Slavs, gypsies, criminals, homosexuals, the mentally retarded, resistance fighters, and German political prisoners were all liquidated, all victims of Germany's ferocious racism and technical efficiency.

But Jews remained the primary targets, and before the victorious Allies halted the horrid process, an estimated 5 to 6 million of the 7 million European Jews were

Figure 8.5   The Supreme Allied Commander General Dwight D. Eisenhower, flanked by General Omar Bradley (right) and British General Bernard Montgomery.   *Source:* National Archives.

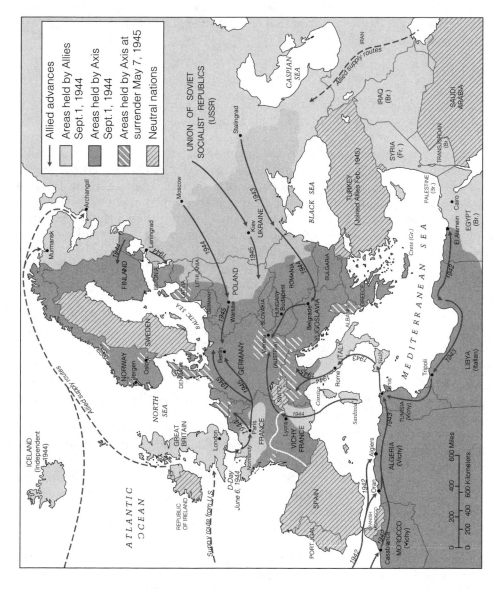

Figure 8.6 The European Theater, 1942–1945. *Source: Moss, Rise of Modern America*, p. 322.

murdered, or they died from starvation, disease, abuse, and overwork. Besides the Jews, the other victims together numbered about 6 million. As many as 12 million human beings were killed by a self-styled master race that had decreed whole races of people unfit to live. In a brutal war that featured many barbaric acts by both sides, the enormity of Nazi genocide overwhelmed all others. The Holocaust was the ultimate atrocity, an atrocity that has defeated all subsequent efforts at explanation and understanding.

VICTORY IN THE PACIFIC

As war ended in Europe, Japanese resistance in the Pacific stiffened. They made last-ditch stands at Iwo Jima and Okinawa. Iwo Jima was a tiny volcanic atoll situated midway between the Marianas and Japan. American strategists determined that Iwo Jima had to be taken because Japanese interceptors based on the island attacked B-29 bombers flying to and from Japan. U.S. pilots needed the atoll as a haven for crippled planes that were unable to reach their bases at Tinian and Saipan. During March 1945, over 6,000 U.S. Marines died in one of the most bitter battles of the Pacific war. The most famous photograph of the Pacific war came out of the Battle for Iwo Jima—it depicts four marines and a sailor proudly raising the American flag atop Mount Suribachi in the midst of battle.

Control of Okinawa, a large island located 325 miles from southern Japan, would give American forces a staging area from which to launch amphibious attacks against the China coast and the Japanese home islands. The largest amphibious assault of the Asian war occurred at Okinawa; over 180,000 troops hit its beaches at various landing sites. The Japanese made extensive use of *Kamikazes* who inflicted severe damage on the American Fifth Fleet supporting the invasions. U.S. casualties exceeded 50,000 during a three-month war of annihilation, ending on June 22. The Battle of Okinawa was the bloodiest campaign of the Pacific war. The capture of Okinawa secured the final stepping-stone for the invasion of Japan, scheduled to begin in November 1945.

But an extraordinary new weapon radically altered the course of the Pacific war. In 1939, noted scientist Dr. Albert Einstein had informed President Roosevelt that it might be possible to build "extremely powerful [atomic] bombs." Einstein also warned him that German scientists might already be developing a nuclear bomb. Roosevelt, after conferences with scientific advisers, ordered work to begin to develop nuclear weapons, mainly to beat the Germans to the bomb.

Between 1941 and 1945, U.S. and British scientists labored intensively to build atomic bombs. General Leslie Groves headed the secret program, code-named the "Manhattan District Project." A brilliant scientific team gathered under the leadership of Dr. J. Robert Oppenheimer, and working at Los Alamos, New Mexico, eventually solved the complex theoretical and technical problems involved in creating the immensely powerful new weapons.

The Manhattan District Project was so secret that congressmen who appropriated the vast sums of money for the bomb had no idea what the money was for.

Harry Truman came to the presidency ignorant of the project. He was astonished to learn in April 1945, from Secretary of War Stimson, that the United States would soon have "the most terrible weapon ever known in human history, one bomb of which could destroy a whole city." In July, the world's first atomic device, nicknamed "the Gadget," was exploded in the desert near Los Alamos at a site called Trinity.

Before the weapon was completed, Stimson convened an Interim Committee that recommended unanimously to the president that the atomic bomb, when ready, be used without warning against Japan. Truman concurred. Some scientists who had worked on the project opposed this recommendation at committee hearings and proposed instead that the Americans invite Japanese observers to witness a harmless demonstration of the bomb's power, perhaps inducing their surrender. Committee members unanimously rejected their recommendation. Other officials also urged holding back and trying to get Japan to surrender without having to use atomic weapons. Truman consistently rejected such advice.

Meanwhile, a new government took power in Japan. Its moderate faction sought a way to end the hopeless war. Unaware of the secret Yalta agreements that would soon bring the Soviet Union into the war against Japan, a member of the peace faction sought Soviet mediation to get a modification of the unconditional surrender terms that would permit the Japanese to keep their emperor. The Soviets rebuffed the Japanese approach and informed Washington.

After discussions with his advisers, Truman issued a final warning to Japan before dropping the bombs. The message urged Japan to surrender unconditionally or else face "the utter devastation of the Japanese homeland," but it made no mention of atomic weapons. The divided Japanese government ignored the ultimatum.

Interpreting their silence as rejection, Truman saw no need to rescind an order given on July 30 to proceed with the atomic bomb attack. Early on the morning of August 6, 1945, three B-29s lifted off the runway at Tinian, bound for Hiroshima. The lead aircraft, the *Enola Gay*, carried a five-ton atomic bomb in its specially configured bomb bay. The other two planes were escorts, carrying cameras and assemblages of scientific recording instruments.

At 8:45 A.M. local time, the sky exploded over Hiroshima: the world's first atomic bomb struck with the force of 12,000 tons of TNT. It killed some 80,000 people instantly, many of them vaporized by the intense heat. By the end of the year, 60,000 more people had died from burns, wounds, and radiation poisoning. A city of 320,000 inhabitants was reduced to instant rubble. A few hours after the bombing, Truman announced to the world the existence and first use of the bomb. He also warned the Japanese that unless they surrendered unconditionally, immediately, "they may expect a rain of ruin from the air, the like of which has never before been seen on earth." The Japanese did not surrender. Military leaders in Japan urged death over defeat.

Bad weather delayed the dropping of the second bomb for a few days. On August 8, Red Army units invaded Manchuria and Korea. The next day, an atomic bomb was dropped on Nagasaki. The bomb that devastated it was a Plutonium one that yielded about 20,000 tons of TNT. It destroyed large sections of the city and killed 26,000 people. It would have killed far more people and done far greater damage if it had not fallen off target. Even after the second atomic bombing and the Soviet entry into the war, Japanese military leaders wanted to fight on. Only the personal intercession of Emperor Hirohito induced them to surrender. On August 10, the Japanese offered to surrender if they could keep their emperor. Truman accepted surrender unconditionally on August 14, although he did offer veiled assurances that the Japanese could retain their emperor, providing that he was stripped of his status as a divinity. Surrender ceremonies occurred on September 2 aboard the battleship USS *Missouri,* anchored in Tokyo Bay, with General Douglas MacArthur presiding.

Most Americans have accepted President Truman's justification for using the atomic bomb: "We have used it in order to shorten the agony of war, in order to save the lives of thousands and thousands of young Americans." But since the 1960s, radical critics have contended that the Japanese, perceiving their cause as hopeless, would have surrendered soon without the atomic bombings. They argue that Truman had other motives for using nuclear weapons besides ending the war. He wanted to enhance American postwar diplomatic leverage against the Soviet Union. Critics also accuse him of using the bombs on the already beaten Japanese to hasten their surrender in order to keep the Soviets from sharing in the postwar occupation of Japan and to make them more manageable.

The atomic bomb project, started by Roosevelt years earlier, was nearing completion at the time Truman became president. Roosevelt had understood that the bomb, when available, would be used on the Germans and the Japanese if the wars were still raging. Since Germany surrendered on May 8, 1945, Truman assumed that atomic bombs would be used on Japan as soon as they became available.

Truman and his advisers discussed where, when, and how to use atomic weapons; they did not debate whether or not to use them. Truman himself later said, "I regarded the bomb as a military weapon and never had any doubt that it should be used." There were additional considerations. Political leaders feared *post hoc* criticism if they did not use the weapons. Suppose it came out after the war that they had wasted $2 billion on a giant atomic boondoggle that was developed and never used? Suppose it came out that they had developed a powerful weapon that might have shortened the war and saved thousands of U.S. soldiers' lives and they failed to use it?

It appears that Truman's primary concern was to shorten the war and to save American soldiers' lives, just as he always claimed. He wished to avoid a protracted and bloody campaign to conquer the Japanese home islands. Truman hoped that American use of the powerful new weapon would make the Soviets more cooperative, that it would give the United States additional bargaining leverage with them. He also hoped that use of the bombs might induce the Japanese to surrender before the Soviet Union entered the war, but the Soviets intervened between the dropping of the bombs. Truman also was disappointed to discover that U.S. possession and use of atomic bombs did not soften Soviet diplomacy.

American willingness to use the atomic bombs in war, coupled with Washington's failure to keep Stalin informed of the progress of the Manhattan project,

Figure 8.7   **The Atomic Age began on August 6, 1945, when a lone American bomber dropped the world's first atomic bomb on Hiroshima, a city of 320,000 people in southern Japan. Tens of thousands of people died, and most of the city was turned into instant rubble.**   *Source:* U.S. Army Photo.

and the American refusal to share any broad scientific information about nuclear weaponry with the Soviets, contributed to the development of the Cold War. At a garden party held one afternoon following a Potsdam conference session, Truman told Stalin that the United States had recently tested an extremely powerful new weapon. He did not tell the Soviet dictator that it was a nuclear device. Stalin merely smiled and said that that was fine and that he hoped that it would soon be used on Japan. Truman did not have to tell Stalin that the United States had developed an atomic bomb; the Soviet leader understood instantly what Truman was talking about. As soon as Truman walked away, Stalin hastily conferred with his top aides and decided on the spot to speed up a Soviet atomic weapons project that had been curtailed during wartime. The USSR–USA nuclear arms race began at that moment.

FBI files, subsequently made public, revealed that a spy ring working for the Soviet Union, whose most prominent members included an English physicist, Klaus Fuchs, and Americans David Greenglass, Harry Gold, and Julius Rosenberg, had penetrated the Manhattan District Project. By the time Americans had atomic bombed the two Japanese cities, the spy ring had already delivered about 10,000 pages of classified government documents to their Soviet masters. These secret data significantly shaped the Soviet atomic bomb project. Experts have estimated that espionage accelerated the Soviet bomb project by as much as two years.

Perhaps the Japanese should have been forewarned. Perhaps a demonstration explosion should have been made. Perhaps the unconditional surrender terms should have been modified before the bombs were used in order to strengthen the peace party within the Japanese government. Any or all of these measures might have induced Japanese surrender before the bombs were used, although no one can know for sure how the Japanese would have responded to any of these initiatives, or when they might have surrendered.

It also is important to remember that even if Japan could have been induced to surrender without having to endure the horrors of two atomic bombings, the conceivable alternative scenarios would have in all probability been worse. Had the war gone on even for a few weeks more, the continuing fire bomb raids over Japanese cities would have killed more people and destroyed more property than did the two atomic bombs. And had invasions by U.S. forces been necessary, there would have been devastating losses on both sides. While fighting went on in Japan between the Americans and Japanese, Soviet soldiers would have annihilated the Japanese armies in Korea, Manchuria, and northern China.

So victory came to America and its allies. They had prevailed in the costliest, most destructive war in the planet's history. The war cost Americans about $350 billion, claiming over 1 million American casualties, including 292,000 battle deaths. That summer of 1945, Americans could gaze into a future bright with hope, because the Axis menace had been destroyed and democracy appeared to have no significant enemies in the world. They also gazed at a world darkened by the nuclear shadow that they had allowed to be cast over its future.

HOME FRONT USA

Americans in the late fall of 1941 drifted into history's largest war. As they faced and eventually defeated dangerous threats to the American way of life and democratic values, they got caught up in the greatest collective experience of their lives. Sharing a sense of common purpose under the inspired leadership of Franklin D. Roosevelt, Americans enjoyed greater national unity than any other time in their history. Citizens who remained behind on the home front contributed in many ways large and small to the war effort. They gave blood, bought war bonds, planted victory gardens, and collected scrap metal. They worked as volunteers on civil defense, as school aides, in hospitals, in first aid programs, as volunteer firemen and police, and as airplane spotters.

The war effort involved many home front sacrifices. Between the attack on Pearl Harbor and V-J Day (December 7, 1941, and August 14, 1945), about 300,000 workers died in industrial accidents, and 1,000,000 workers were permanently disabled. More workers were killed or crippled in home front accidents than soldiers were killed or crippled in battle! Consumers had to do without many of the civilian goods and services normally churned out by the American economy. Major consumer items were rationed. People traveled less, dressed more informally, entertained more at home, and went to bed earlier.

DEMOGRAPHIC CHANGES

The war experience set in motion demographic trends that would persist for the next half-century. Military bases and war industries transformed cities and

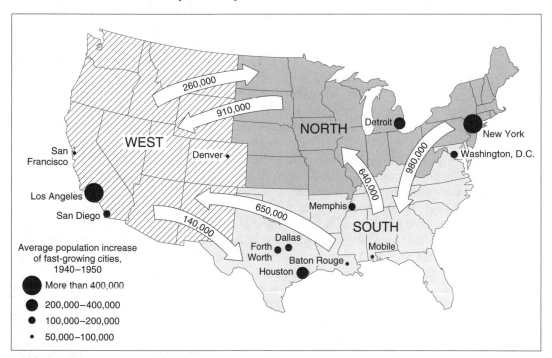

Figure 8.8   Internal migration in the United States during World War II.   *Source: Statistical Abstract of the United States, 1974 ed.*

revitalized entire regions of the country. The West Coast, especially California, which had been a relatively isolated, underdeveloped area of the nation, became the most dynamic region in the country. The Western coastal states, with 10 percent of the nation's population, accounted for 20 percent of total wartime production. Economists estimated that the coastal states' economies did about fifty years of growing in less than four years.

Between 1941 and 1945, approximately 16 million men, 95 percent of whom were drafted, and 250,000 women served in the armed forces. About half of those who went into the military during the war never left the continental United States. But many of those servicemen who never left the states were assigned to bases in different parts of the country that they had never before seen. After the war had ended and they had been discharged, they returned with their families to become permanent residents of the locales were they had done military service. In addition to service personnel, millions of civilian war workers moved from rural areas to the cities where jobs in war industries could be found. In many cases, those transplanted civilian war workers did not go home after the war. They and their families joined the burgeoning postwar urban and suburban populations.

Several important population shifts occurred in wartime that would shape the demographic contours of postwar America for decades. Population flowed from the rural interior of the country outward toward the cities along the Pacific, Atlantic, and Gulf coasts. People also left inland farms and villages for the cities of the Upper Midwest, because it was in the coastal and Midwestern cities that the major military installations, shipyards, aircraft assembly plants, and other war industries were located. Population also made a major shift westward. California's population increased by 40 percent from 1940 to 1945. Millions of the military personnel and war workers who came to California during wartime remained or returned after the war to become permanent residents of the Golden State. The Sunbelt, that Southern rim of states stretching from South Carolina to California, also began to grow rapidly during the war years. The Sunbelt states, especially Florida, Texas, and Southern California, would become the nation's most dynamic centers of economic expansion during the postwar decades.

Good-paying jobs in war industries also lured over a million African Americans out of the Old South and on to New York, Chicago, Philadelphia, Detroit, and the rapidly growing cities along the West Coast. Many African Americans and their families also remained in these new locales after the war. The geographic mobility induced by the war resulted in permanent relocations for millions of American families. The oldest demographic trend in American history, the depopulation of the countryside, accelerated dramatically during the years of the nation's involvement in World War II. The demographic foundations for the postwar surge of urban and suburban communities were lain.

Despite the mobilization of America's vast human and economic resources for the war effort, there occurred more social reform affecting the quality of American lives during the war than had previously occurred during the New Deal era. Prepaid health insurance became available for the first time for working people. Millions of young men from disadvantaged backgrounds drafted into the armed forces enjoyed a nutritious diet and adequate medical and dental care for the first time in their lives. Even with the nation at war and with the dangers of war work, the overall health of the American people improved dramatically during the war years. Birth rates rose rapidly; death rates sharply diminished. Median life expectancy increased by five years.

A huge increase in the the size of the American middle classes was the most significant demographic transformation of the war years. The United States became, for the first time in its history, a middle-class nation in the sense that more than half of the nation's families enjoyed middle-class incomes and lifestyles. Personal income more than doubled during the war, and national income was more equitably distributed than ever before. It was during the early 1940s that prosperity levels that had been reached in the late 1920s, before the Great Crash, were finally eclipsed.

Figure 8.9   American industry made a major contribution to eventual military victory. This ship was completed in ten days, a remarkable feat that brought FDR (in the foreground, left) to the Portland, Oregon, shipyard where it was accomplished.   *Source:* Franklin D. Roosevelt Library.

ECONOMIC TRANSFORMATION

In addition to raising a vast military force, the United States had to gear its economy for global war. Its factories had to produce arms for its armed forces and for its major allies, the British and the Soviets. During the first half of 1942, the federal government placed orders for over $100 billion in war contracts, more commodities than the economy had ever produced in a year. Converting the economy to a war footing challenged American industrialists and government bureaucrats. Initial government efforts to organize the war economy proved ineffective. But by 1943, the Office of Economic Stabilization, headed by James F. Byrnes, brought order to the gigantic wartime industrial effort. Byrnes used the immense powers granted his office to weave together the various strands of America's domestic war effort into a relatively efficient system.

Fueled by federal expenditures that dwarfed all spending for New Deal era programs, the gross domestic product more than doubled during the war years. It grew from $95 billion in 1940 to more than $211 billion by 1946. During those years, economic expansion added 10 million new jobs. The federal government during World War II spent more than twice as much money than all previous governments combined had spent since the creation of the federal state in 1789.

To help pay for these prodigious wartime expenditures, Congress broadened and deepened the tax structure. The Revenue Acts of 1942 and 1943 created the modern federal income tax system. Most Americans had never filed an income tax return before World War II, because the income tax, on the books since 1913, had been a tax imposed on upper-income families. Starting in 1942, anyone earning $600 or more annually had to file an income tax return. A withholding tax went into effect in 1943. Income tax revenues rose from $5 billion in 1940 to $44 billion in 1945. Even with the nine fold increase in federal income taxes, the largest federal tax increase in U.S. history, tax revenues paid only 41 percent of the cost of the war. Government paid the majority of war costs by borrowing. War bonds, peddled by movie stars, war heros, and professional athletes, added $100 billion. By war's end, the national debt had climbed to $280 billion, seven times its prewar level of $40 billion.

Vast federal spending for war quickly ended the lingering depression that had afflicted Americans for a decade. The New Deal had failed to find a cure for economic depression. On the eve of war, over 7 million Americans were out of work, or 14 percent of the labor force. A year after U.S. entry into the war, unemployment in America had vanished. Wartime economic expansion, fueled by unprecedented levels of government spending, combined with mass conscription to create severe labor shortages.

The discovery that government spending could banish the specter of depression confirmed the claims of the world's foremost economist, England's John Maynard Keynes. Keynes contended that government spending could cure economic depression. He insisted that if private sector investment proved inadequate, government could cut taxes and begin large-scale spending programs to stimulate demand and restore the business cycle. During the New Deal of the mid-1930s, government spending was not large enough and taxes were generally regressive, so Keynes' theories could not be confirmed until the war years. Their wartime success at eliminating the depression also gave American political leaders a confidence that they could regulate the economy. They believed they now possessed the fiscal tools to monitor spending levels in order to maintain prosperity, keep unemployment low, and prevent the recurrence of recession, the entire time controlling inflation.

Farmers and industrial workers, two classes devastated by depression, prospered during the war years. Farm output rose 20 percent, even though the farm population declined by more than 50 percent, and farmers struggled with chronic labor and fuel shortages and worn-out equipment. Congress created the War Labor Board in 1942, which set guidelines for wages, hours, and collective bargaining. Employers, unions, and government officials generally cooperated during the war. Unions added over 6 million new members between 1940 and 1945; real wages for workers employed in manufacturing rose 50 percent from 1941 to 1945.

There were some labor problems that the War Labor Board could not resolve. The American Federation of Labor and the Congress of Industrial Organizations engaged in bitter, sometimes violent, jurisdictional disputes. Although organized labor had given a no-strike pledge for the duration of the war, it could not be enforced. In 1943, over 3 million workers went on strike, although most work stoppages lasted only a few days. These wartime strikes never caused serious production delays in the industries that cranked out the huge amounts of war materials required by the armed forces.

Increased federal spending also unleashed powerful inflationary forces. The shift from peacetime to wartime production sharply reduced the amount of consumer goods available to buy, just when people had more money than ever to spend. A giant inflationary gap generated by too much money chasing too few commodities threatened to drive prices up and rob Americans of their wartime economic gains. To clamp a lid on inflation, the government imposed price controls and joined them to a rationing system that used coupon allotments to consumers for scarce items such as sugar, butter, coffee, beef, tires, and gasoline.

Roosevelt created the Office of Price Administration (OPA) to administer the control apparatus nationally. The OPA had a daunting task. Business lobbyists, farm bloc politicians, and union leaders waged unceasing battles against the OPA for the duration of the war. Consumers chafed under rationing restrictions, particularly those on beef and gasoline. A ban on all "pleasure driving" and a 35 mph speed limit accompanied gasoline rationing. The average motorist got three gallons of gas a week. Most people walked to work or took public transportation. Black markets in gasoline flourished; racketeers had not had it so good since Prohibition. At times, motorists could not get any gas, legal or illegal. Service stations often closed, stranding motorists and truckers. When a station could get gas, customers lined up their cars for miles waiting to buy it. Beef rationing also caused serious problems. Butcher display cases frequently emptied. Frustrated shoppers often abused butchers and occasionally rioted. Despite grievances and injustices, the universally unpopular OPA maintained a semblance of price stability and distributed scarce goods reasonably fairly. Most people complied with the system of controls, considering it both a wartime necessity and to their economic advantage.

Despite annoying shortages and rationing, people in wartime with money to spend found ways to spend and enjoy it. Wartime prosperity strengthened materialistic values and revived consumerism, largely suspended during the depression decade. Americans spent money going to bars and nightclubs, going to movies, and going out to dinner. People resorted to black markets when rationed goods could not be found. Many saved their money for new cars, homes, appliances, radios, and clothes they knew they would buy after the war. Advertisers promised consumers new and better products when civilian production patterns were restored following victory over the Axis powers. Consumerism, reborn during World War II, would become a powerful engine driving the postwar economy.

For millions of American families, hardship, danger, and social upheaval were integral parts of their wartime experience. The sudden influx of hordes of war workers swamped the coastal cities. Trailer parks and shanty towns sprang up on the outskirts of towns and cities. Housing, schools, hospitals, maintenance services, and fire and police protection often could not meet the needs of war workers and their families.

WOMEN IN WARTIME

Between 1941 and 1945, over 6 million women entered the labor force, about half of whom worked in the manufacturing sector. Women also joined the branches of military service that were open to them. They served in the WACS (Women's Auxiliary Army Corps) and the WAVES (Women Accepted for Voluntary Emergency Service). They also served in women's units in the Coast Guard and Marine Corps, and over 1,000 women became noncombat military pilots.

Married women, many with children, made up three-quarters of working women during wartime. By 1945, more than half of working women had married, and their median age was thirty-seven. Before the war, women had been excluded from most manufacturing jobs. Employers considered them unsuitable for heavy labor amidst the masculine atmosphere prevailing in factories. Acute wartime labor shortages quickly changed those attitudes. Women learned skilled trades, joined unions, and earned high wages. They performed certain jobs better than men, such as those requiring close attention to detail and good manual dexterity. Women worked in munitions factories. They also became riveters, welders, crane operators, tool and die makers, iron workers, and train engineers. Women increased their geographic and occupational mobility tremendously in wartime. Black women quit work as domestics to join the factory labor force. Millions of women moved from the rural South and Midwest to coastal cities where the war-generated jobs were located. In southern California and elsewhere, hundreds of thousands of women went to work in aircraft assembly plants.

Figure 8.10   Three Native American Marine Corps Woman Reservists at Camp Lejeune, North Carolina, October 1943. They are (from lift to right) Minnie Spotted Wolf (Blackfoot), Celia Mix (Potawatomi), and Viola Eastman (Chippewa).   *Source:* National Archives.

Government-sponsored media campaigns portrayed women's work in shops and factories as being both necessary and noble. "Rosie the Riveter" became a popular symbol, celebrated in a hit tune of the era. "Do the job HE left behind," exhorted the billboards.

But women's wartime factory work was considered only a temporary response to a national emergency. Once victory was achieved and the soldiers returned, women were expected to surrender their jobs to a returning GI. But surveys showed that most women wanted to continue working after the war. After the war, when their war contracts were canceled or phased out, employers fired their women employees. Others were pressured by their husbands to quit and return to the kitchen. Many single working women after the war could often find only low-paying jobs in domestic service, restaurants, and department stores.

Traditional patterns of gender discrimination persisted during wartime. Women in manufacturing earned about 60 percent of what men earned for comparable work. Factories offered limited promotional opportunities for women. Even though the war emergency opened up hitherto closed occupations to women,

Figure 8.11   Over 6 million women entered the labor force during World War II. Many of them worked in industries, such as these two "Rosie the Riveters," helping to build military aircraft.   *Source:* National Archives.

most jobs in the sex-segregated labor market remained classified as "male" or "female" work. Where women worked in factories, they often worked on all-female shop floors, under male supervisors and managers.

The most serious problem faced by working mothers in wartime was the almost complete absence of child care centers. During the war, juvenile delinquency, venereal disease, and teenage pregnancies rose sharply. "Latchkey children," children left home alone while their mothers worked their shifts at a factory, became a national scandal. Children roamed the streets or were locked in cars. Police arrested many teenage girls for prostitution and apprehended boys for theft and vandalism.

Marriage rates rose sharply in 1942, as increased numbers of women got married at the same time they went to work in war industries. Many young couples got married to spend time together before the man got shipped overseas. The birthrate climbed sharply. Many births enabled men to qualify for military deferments. Returning prosperity provided the main reason for the increase in marriages and rising birthrates. The population, which had only grown by 3 million people during the entire decade of the 1930s, added 6.5 million people during the war years. The baby boom had begun before war's end.

AFRICAN AMERICANS AT WAR

World War II proved to be a mixed blessing for African Americans, providing both unprecedented economic opportunities and continuing encounters with the hardships and humiliations of racism. About 1 million black men and women served in the armed forces during the war, entering all branches of military service. Even though the American military was still segregated during World War II, African Americans attained far more opportunities than had been available during World War I. The Army Air Corps trained black pilots who flew in all-black squadrons. African American Marines, fighting in all-black units, fought heroically in savage island battles in the Pacific.

Black-white race relations within the military reflected the racist society it served. Many race riots occurred on military bases. White civilians often attacked African American soldiers stationed in the South. The morale and motivation of black soldiers often suffered from encounters with racist whites. African American soldiers sometimes found that enemy prisoners of war were treated better than they were. But most black soldiers found reasons to fight the Axis powers, even though at times they could see little difference between German racism and the homegrown kind. They planned to trade their wartime military service for improved educational and job opportunities after the war. African Americans fought for a double victory: over the Axis powers abroad and racism at home.

The war also opened many new employment opportunities for African Americans. In January 1941, A. Philip Randolph, angered because employers with war contracts refused to hire African American workers, threatened to stage a march on Washington to protest both employer discrimination and segregation in the armed forces. President Roosevelt, wanting to avoid the embarrassment of a protest march and possible ensuing violence, persuaded Randolph to call off the proposed march in return for an executive order establishing a Fair Employment Practices Committee (FEPC). It ordered employers in defense industries to make jobs available "without discrimination because of race, creed, color, or national origin." The FEPC was understaffed and underfunded, and it proved to be of limited effectiveness during the war. Acute labor shortages much more than government policy opened up war employment opportunities for African Americans.

Over 2 million African American men and women left the South to find work in the industrial cities of the North and West. Many joined CIO unions. Black voters in Northern cities became an important constituency in local and state elections. Most African American families who left the South during the war remained a permanent part of the growing Northern urban population in the postwar era. Southern black migrants often encountered racist hostility as they struggled to adapt to their new lives in Northern cities. They discovered that there was little difference between Northern and Southern white racial attitudes. Many whites hated competing with African Americans for housing, jobs, and schools for their children. They resented coming into contact with African Americans at parks, beaches, and other public facilities.

Figure 8.12   African Americans made a major contribution to American victories during World War II. Here the Army Air Force's all-black 99th Fighter Group assembles at the beachhead of Anzio, Italy, in 1944.   *Source:* National Archives.

These racial antagonisms flared violently during the summer of 1943. About 250 race riots occurred in nearly fifty Northern cities. The largest riots were in Detroit and Harlem—the worst violence in Detroit—which had been building for years. The immediate provocation had been an angry struggle for access to public housing demanded by both African American and white workers during a time of acute housing shortages for everyone. One hot night in June, things got out of control. A full-scale race riot exploded, lasting several days. When the violence ended, twenty-five African Americans and nine whites lay dead.

Despite these outbreaks of home front racial violence, World War II proved to be a watershed for African Americans; the war experience aided the black struggle for full citizenship. Military service gave most African American veterans greater self-esteem and a sense of empowerment and raised their expectations. Many black veterans took advantage of the GI Bill to attend college or learn a skilled trade after the war. These educated black professionals and technicians formed a new and much larger African American middle class. The National Association for the Advancement of Colored People (NAACP) increased its membership from 50,000 members at the time of the Pearl Harbor attack to ten times that number at war's end. A combination of vastly improved economic opportunities and continuing encounters with racism generated a new militancy among black people. They were determined to not accept second-class citizenship after the war. These African American veterans and their children took the lead in challenging segregation in postwar America. The roots of the modern civil rights movement can be found in the black experiences of World War II.

HISPANIC AMERICANS IN WARTIME

According to the 1940 census, about 2.7 million Hispanic people lived within the United States. Most were of Mexican descent, living mainly in California, Texas, and the Southwest. Much of this predominantly rural population endured poverty, discrimination, and segregation. They lacked decent jobs, housing, and educational opportunities, and they had no political influence. However, the war created opportunities for Hispanic Americans. Thousands of families moved to urban areas to find work in war industries. About 350,000 Hispanic Americans served in the armed forces, nearly all of them draftees. Mexican American warriors joined elite units such as the airborne rangers, and they often volunteered for dangerous missions. Eleven Mexican Americans won the nation's highest military award, the Congressional Medal of Honor.

Because so many Hispanic Americans moved to the cities or went into the armed forces, farmers faced acute shortages of workers. American growers persuaded the government to make arrangements with Mexico to import farm workers from Mexico. Under a program established in 1942, nearly 2 million Mexican *braceros* entered the United States. Because of lax government supervision, employers often ruthlessly exploited these imported contract laborers.

Hispanics in the war labor force often suffered discriminations similar to those encountered by African Americans and women. They sometimes got paid less than "Anglo" employees for doing the same work. They found that their problems were most acute in the crowded cities. Many young Mexican Americans belonged to neighborhood gangs. They called themselves *pachucos* and favored a distinctive style of dress, called a "zoot suit". The zoot suit consisted of baggy trousers flared at the knees and fitted tightly around the ankles, complemented by a wide-brimmed felt hat. These costumes represented an assertion of a distinct cultural identity and a defiance of Anglo styles.

In June 1943, at a time when black-white racial tensions were erupting in violent encounters, ethnic relations in Los Angeles also were strained. Hundreds of sailors and Marines on leave from bases in southern California assaulted Mexican Americans on the streets of Los Angeles and tore off their zoot suits. Police either looked the other way or arrested only Mexican American youths during these encounters. The local media supported the violent attacks on the *pachucos*. Only after the president of Mexico threatened to cancel the *bracero* program did President Roosevelt intervene to stop the violence.

Despite the zoot suit incidents, Hispanic American wartime experiences brought many advances. As was the case for African Americans, military service gave thousands of Mexican Americans an enhanced sense of self-worth. They returned from the war with greater expectations and enlarged views of life's possibilities. Many Hispanic veterans took advantage of the GI Bill. In the postwar years, Mexican American veterans led the fight against discrimination in Southwestern states.

NATIVE AMERICANS IN WARTIME

In addition to the 25,000 Native Americans who served in the armed forces during World War II, thousands more left their reservations to work in war industries in various cities around the country. Most of these mobile people did not return to reservations after the war, remaining within the cities after the war industries had shut down and becoming part of the nation's rapidly growing postwar urban and suburban population. Some Native Americans did return to the reservations after the war and brought with them new ideas and technologies.

In 1944, in California, lawyers who were representing a group of Native Americans filed suit in federal court for $100 million. The group was seeking compensation for lands taken illegally from their ancestors during the 1850s. Congress enacted legislation to pay them for their lands, but President Franklin Roosevelt vetoed the bill. Litigation on this matter continued off and on for the next thirty five years. Finally, both parties reached a compromise. The Native Americans accepted a settlement that brought them about 47 cents per acre.

ASIAN AMERICANS IN WARTIME

In some areas, civil liberties violations during World War II were not as severe as during World War I. Most conscientious objectors were permitted to serve in non-combatant roles in the military or else perform essential civilian work. Of the more than 5,500 conscientious objectors jailed for refusing to serve in the military, most belonged to the Jehovah's Witnesses, who refused to cooperate with the Selective Service authorities. German Americans were not harassed or persecuted, as in World War I, nor were Italian American citizens. Congress never enacted repressive measures like the Espionage Act or the Sedition Act.

But during the spring and summer of 1942, 120,000 Japanese Americans, two-thirds of them native-born American citizens, were uprooted from their homes along the Pacific Coast and taken to internment centers located in remote interior regions of the country. There they lived in tar paper barracks behind barbed wire for three years. The internment of Japanese Americans for the duration of World War II represented the worst violation of civil liberties during wartime in American history.

The initiative was taken by the military commander in charge of security along the West Coast, General John Dewitt. Dewitt and other officials claimed that relocation of Japanese Americans was necessary to guarantee military security along the West Coast. They argued that if the Japanese Americans were not relocated, some of them would aid the enemy in case of attack. Their accusations were false. FBI agents admitted that they never discovered a single proven act of disloyalty committed by any Japanese American. The real reasons for their removal included anti-Japanese race prejudice, wartime hysteria, and greed. The claim of military necessity was based on unfounded suspicion, not on evidence. The relocation of Japanese Americans during wartime also was the culminating act of a half-century of anti-Japanese agitation and assaults in California, Oregon, and Washington.

Japanese American spokesmen asserted their loyalty to no avail. Earl Warren, California's attorney general in 1942, strongly advocated removal. The removal order, Executive Order No. 9066, came from President Roosevelt and could not be challenged. In 1944, the Supreme Court sustained the relocation of Japanese Americans. In the case of *Fred Korematsu v. the United States*, the Court accepted the claim of Army lawyers that the relocation was a wartime military necessity. A five to three majority ruled that in time of war, individual rights could be sacrificed to military necessity. Associate Justice Frank Murphy filed a powerful dissenting opinion, stating that the relocation of Japanese Americans fell "into the ugly abyss of racism."

Virtually the entire Japanese American population complied with the relocation order without resistance or protest. They submitted in accordance with the spirit of *Shikata Ga Nai* (realistic resignation). Because they were given little time to gather at assembly centers and allowed to take only what they could carry to the camps, families lost homes, businesses, farms, and personal property worth an

Figure 8.13   U.S. soldiers uprooted about 120,000 Japanese Americans, most of them U.S. citizens, from their homes in early 1942 and imprisoned them in various internment centers. The move, spawned by panic and prejudice, was both unnecessary and wrong. Here a family awaits a bus to haul them away.   *Source:* National Archives.

estimated $400 million. They arrived at the camps to find hastily built tar paper barracks amidst bleak, desert landscapes that would be their homes for three years. The internment centers were de facto prisons. The camps were under continuous surveillance by armed guards, and they were enclosed by barbed wire fencing. During the course of the war, some internees were allowed to leave the camps, provided that they agreed to settle in Eastern states. By war's end, all were allowed to leave. A fortunate few families had friends who had saved their homes or businesses for them while they were incarcerated. But many internees had no homes or businesses to return to. They discovered that interlopers now resided in their former residences and owned their former businesses.

Even though their families were imprisoned in camps, thousands of young men volunteered for military service. They were determined to prove their loyalty to a government that had betrayed them. Japanese American soldiers contributed much to the war effort. They fought in the European theater, and many served in the Pacific war as translators, interpreters, and intelligence officers. One Japanese American unit, the 442nd Regimental Combat Engineers, remains the most decorated unit in American military history.

Ironically, the government refused to relocate Japanese Americans living in Hawaii. Thousands of them continued to work for the U.S. military at Pearl Harbor and other installations following the Japanese attacks. They were not removed because of military necessity. They made up one-fifth of the Hawaiian population, their labor was essential, and there was no place to put them, nor ships to transport them.

Loyal Americans were the victims of an egregious injustice. Congress authorized token restitution for Japanese Americans in 1948, and a total of about $38 million was paid to claimants during the 1950s. These payments amounted to about 10 cents for each dollar of loss. Years later, after much litigation and quiet political pressure, Japanese Americans belatedly received vindication and additional restitution. In 1983, U.S. District Court Judge Marilyn Hall Patel vacated Fred Korematsu's conviction. Judge Patel's action came after Korematsu's attorneys discovered secret documents proving that government officials knew that Japanese Americans posed no dangers to national security during wartime and withheld this evidence from the Supreme Court. On August 10, 1988, President Ronald Reagan signed legislation authorizing $20,000 in reparations to each of the estimated 60,000 survivors of wartime relocation. As he signed the historic legislation, President Reagan, speaking for all Americans, apologized to the Japanese American community: "We admit a wrong. Here we reaffirm our commitment as a nation to equal justice under the law."

After the war, Japanese Americans chose to not protest the gross injustices they were forced to endure in wartime. They internalized the anger and shame associated with their relocation experience. They rarely talked about those experiences, even among close friends and family. Instead, Japanese Americans vowed to put their wartime experiences behind them and to move forward—to prove emphatically to the government and to the people who had abused them that they were good citizens and productive members of society.

Their postwar record of achievement has been astonishing. Japanese Americans, by any measure, are among the most successful and prosperous groups in the country. They have integrated themselves into the larger society, achieved distinction in the sciences, the arts, medicine, the law, engineering, academic life, business, finance, athletics, and politics, and are among the leaders in the amount of education attained and annual per capita income.

In contrast to the persecution of Japanese Americans during wartime, Chinese Americans fared comparatively well. They enjoyed the goodwill of most Americans, because China was a wartime ally of the United States. Americans also felt much sympathy for the Chinese people who were suffering terribly at the hands of the Japanese soldiers during the war years. Because of acute labor shortages in war industries, unprecedented opportunities for Chinese workers suddenly opened up. By the thousands, Chinese families streamed out of the

Chinatown ghettos into the mainstream of American life. Most of these mobile Chinese families never returned to the Chinatowns, and after the war they headed for the suburbs.

In 1943, Congress at long last repealed the Chinese Exclusion Act that had been in place since 1882. For the first time in over sixty years, it was now possible for people to emigrate from China to the United States. In addition, the government extended citizenship to thousands of Chinese, many of whom were quite elderly, who were long-time residents of the United States but had hitherto been ineligible for citizenship.

THE POLITICS OF WAR

War moved the country toward the Right. Resurgent Republicans gained seventy seven seats in the House and ten seats in the Senate in the 1942 midterm elections. A conservative coalition of Northern Republicans and Southern Democrats, which had emerged following the 1938 elections, consolidated its control of Congress. Roosevelt, sensing the political drift and preoccupied with the vast tasks of running the war, put social reform on the back burner. Conservatives snuffed out many New Deal agencies in 1942 and 1943 on the grounds that wartime economic revival had rendered them obsolete. Among their most prominent victims were the WPA and the CCC.

Antitrust activity ceased. Businessmen poured into Washington to run new wartime bureaucracies. They regained much of the popularity and prestige that they had lost during the depression years. Popular resentment of business greed and social irresponsibility gave way to a popular image of businessmen as patriotic partners providing the tools needed to win the war. Roosevelt, needing business cooperation for the war effort, cultivated a cordial relationship among his former adversaries. Populistic, antibusiness rhetoric vanished from the public dialogue. Secretary of War Henry Stimson observed: "If you are going to go to war . . . in a capitalist country, you have got to let business make money out of the process or business won't work." Businessmen switched their political strategy from one of trying to dismantle big government to using it to their advantage.

The war effort further centralized the corporate economy, because 90 percent of the billions of dollars the government spent on war contracts went to about 100 large corporations. Big business got bigger in wartime, and most companies enjoyed historic high profits. Wartime politics showed that the positive state, erected by liberals to fight the Great Depression and promote social reform, could be manned by conservatives who would use its power to promote business interests, curtail reform, and attack trade unions—while winning a war.

During the 1944 election, President Roosevelt faced the challenge of Republican New York Governor Thomas E. Dewey. Roosevelt, to keep his party unified in wartime, dumped his vice president, Henry Wallace, a fervent New Dealer who had alienated powerful big city bosses and conservative Southerners. Political insiders knew that Roosevelt's health was failing and that he probably would not serve a full four years if reelected. They understood that they were not just picking a vice president, but the probable successor to FDR. But because Roosevelt was very much a candidate for reelection, despite his growing infirmities, the stakes involved in the battle for the vice presidency could not be discussed openly.

Roosevelt replaced Wallace with a candidate acceptable to all factions within the Party, Missouri Senator Harry Truman. Truman had rendered valuable service to the country in wartime, heading a watchdog committee that had investigated government war contracts. Senator Truman's energetic, scrupulous efforts saved taxpayers billions of dollars and expedited the delivery of crucial war materials. Despite his wartime service, though, Truman was still a relative unknown in 1944, an undistinguished journeyman politician but acceptable to all of the power brokers within Democratic Party ranks.

The contest between Roosevelt and Dewey was a rather dull and one-sided affair. To many observers, Dewey did not appear presidential. He was a neat little man who came across as rather aloof, cold and stiff. He hurt his chances of winning by failing to cultivate good relations with the working press covering the campaign.

Newly empowered, organized labor played a major role in the 1944 campaign. The CIO, through its Political Action Committee (PAC), circumvented laws restricting union activities. The PAC funneled millions of dollars into the campaign for the Roosevelt ticket and many liberal congressional candidates. It also registered voters, circulated campaign literature, and got out the vote on election day.

Dewey's campaign strategy differed from previous Republican efforts. He accepted the New Deal welfare state but accused New Dealers of waste and inefficiency. He also refused to make Roosevelt's foreign policy a campaign issue, not wishing to revive isolationist issues amidst the war. By embracing the welfare state and internationalism, Dewey placed both the New Deal and the war beyond partisan debate.

Roosevelt exploited his prestige as wartime commander in chief of a vast military effort that was winning everywhere. He called attention to legislation benefiting veterans, including the pending "G.I. Bill of Rights." During the campaign, friends, political associates, and perceptive journalists all noticed that Roosevelt had grown thin and frail. His doctors knew that he was suffering from heart disease and hypertension. Most Americans, however, were not informed of his medical conditions and took no notice of his failing health. In accordance with the journalistic practices of the era, reporters, even those hostile to Roosevelt, made no public mention of his rapidly deteriorating health.

Roosevelt easily won his fourth presidential election victory in November. His electoral vote count was 432 to 99, but his popular vote tally was only 25.6 million to 22 million for Dewey, his narrowest margin of victory ever. The 1944 vote revealed that the Democratic Party was becoming more urban as a result of the wartime migration that had lured millions of workers from rural regions into the cities. The Democrats regained twenty two of the seats in the House that they had lost in 1942, but they lost another Senate seat. The conservative coalition retained its control of Congress.

The huge increase in the size and scope of the federal government, particularly the executive branch, represented the most important wartime political development. As government spent more money, it became more centralized. Federal bureaucracies assumed many economic functions previously performed by the private sector. The number of federal employees nearly quadrupled in wartime—from 1 million in 1940 to 3.8 million in 1945. Wartime agencies proliferated, generating an alphabetical avalanche that dwarfed the New Deal. Roosevelt issued more executive orders during the war than all previous presidents had during the entire history of the nation. The most powerful politicians, after Roosevelt, were men he appointed to run the war agencies, most of whom he recruited from the ranks of business. During the war, politicians forged the permanent welfare and regulatory state by providing it with a permanent bureaucratic base and an ample source of tax dollars.

As the executive branch made a quantum leap in size and power, Congress suffered a relative decline in power and prestige. Through his active participation in foreign conferences and various domestic agencies coordinating the gigantic war effort, Roosevelt significantly enhanced the powers of the presidency and set an example followed by all postwar presidents. The "imperial" presidency had its origins in World War II.

The Supreme Court, dominated by Roosevelt's liberal appointees, refused to review any cases involving wartime extensions of federal power into economic affairs, an arena in which it had been especially active during the New Deal years. The Court also refused to intervene in cases involving wartime violations of civil liberties, except to affirm the relocation of Japanese Americans from the Pacific Coast. The FBI's force of special agents increased fivefold, from 785 in 1939 to 4,370 at war's end. The FBI in wartime also obtained enhanced authority to spy on Americans and to tap telephones in national security cases.

The war multiplied the points of contact between the federal government and its citizens. Millions were added to the Social Security rolls, and everyone who worked paid federal income taxes. War experiences strengthened the tendency to look to Washington for solutions to problems. This trend weakened social bonds and undermined local governments. During the years of war, the American people traded some of their personal freedom for greater governmental control and an enhanced sense of social security.

Washington became the biggest of all war boomtowns. In 1942, the Pentagon, the world's largest office building, opened. Lobbyists stalked the corridors of political power seeking ever-larger shares of the vast expenditures flowing out of Washington into corporate coffers. The Pentagon also developed generous tax write-offs to motivate business participation in the war effort. It developed the cost-plus contract, whereby the federal government underwrote all developmental and production costs and guaranteed a percentage profit to contractors providing needed war material. The government also subsidized the creation of new industries required by the necessities of war. With supplies of natural rubber from Southeast Asia cut, Washington spent nearly a billion dollars to create a synthetic rubber industry to provide substitute products.

Much basic research for new weaponry and war industries came from universities and colleges, which became committed to meeting the needs of military research. Most colleges and universities suffered no loss of enrollment during the war, despite the draft, because the government utilized their campuses for training enlisted men and officers. After the war, the GI Bill, which paid for millions of veterans' college educations, ensured continuing growth and expansion of higher education.

World War II created a wartime partnership among business, universities, Congress, and the Pentagon, engaged in the procurement of war contracts. This "military-industrial complex," as President Eisenhower would later call it, nurtured during the war, came of age during the Cold War. It became a powerful lobby for creating the permanent war economy. The military-industrial complex guaranteed that the vastly enhanced authority of government in American economic and scientific affairs would continue after the war.

CULTURE AND WAR

Popular culture flourished in vigorous variety during the war. Sales of books, both fiction and nonfiction, increased sharply. Many war novels and journalistic accounts of the war made the best-seller charts. The most popular war correspondent was Ernie Pyle, who wrote with great insight about ordinary soldiers in combat. His *Brave Men*, published in 1945, after he had been killed covering the Okinawa campaign, remains the finest account of GI life ever written. Bill Mauldin, a cartoonist whose panels portrayed two weary, dirty, unshaven GIs named Willie and Joe, also realistically recorded battlefield conditions.

Not everyone remained home at night reading about the war. Ballroom dancing flourished during wartime. The popularity of jitterbugging, a carryover from the late 1930s, continued unabated, especially among young people for whom it offered a distinctive world with its own clothes, language, and ritualistic behaviors. Energetic, athletic youngsters spun, whirled, and tossed their partners to the pulsing rhythms of hot jazz. Older couples enjoyed the more sedate pleasures of fox trots and waltzes. Nightlife, particularly New York nightlife, sparkled. Patrons at the Copacabana or the Latin Quarter could spend $100 on an evening of drinking, dancing, and enjoying the singing of young crooners like Frank Sinatra or the sounds of Tommy Dorsey's Big Band. Spectator sports drew large crowds in wartime, despite the loss of most skilled athletes to the war. Major league baseball continued its pennant races and annual World Series, using mostly teenagers, castoffs, and overaged players.

Hollywood was still king during wartime. Movies remained the most popular mass entertainment medium, although the film industry had to adapt to wartime conditions. Most top male stars either got drafted or they enlisted, and thousands of technicians and production personnel went off to war. Jimmy Stewart flew bombing missions over Germany. Clark Gable, "The King," joined the Army Air Corps. A lesser star, Ronald Reagan, was assigned to an Army motion picture unit in Hollywood that made training films. Many actors not in the armed forces and top women stars like Dorothy Lamour, Rita Hayworth, and Betty Grable entertained the troops both in the states and around the world.

Wartime Hollywood mostly made war movies. The studios churned out a flood of war and spy stories. Many Chinese actors obtained work in Hollywood films for the first time, playing Japanese villains in war movies. John Wayne starred in a series of war epics that glorified various branches of the military service— *Flying Tigers, Fighting Seabees*, and *The Sands of Iwo Jima*, the last about the Marine Corps. The best war film was *The Story of GI Joe*, adapted from Ernie Pyle's reporting. It contained no preaching, no propaganda, no hateful enemy stereotypes, and no heroes. It depicted American soldiers as skilled professionals doing a dirty job, mainly trying to survive and return home after the war. Hollywood also made several excellent war documentaries; the best was a series produced by Frank Capra and John Huston. "Canteen films" represented another Hollywood wartime film genre. They were celluloid USO shows, hosted by a big name star featuring celebrity guests who sang, danced, and told jokes—all promoting the war effort.

African American soldiers occasionally appeared in war films, usually as stereotypical "happy Negroes," jiving, dancing, and laughing. Jewish soldiers usually were stereotypically portrayed as guys named "Brooklyn" who looked forward to returning to Ebbets Field after the war and jeering at the Giants. American allies were shown as being heroic in war films. Wartime movie Russians were hearty, simple people and gallant fighters.

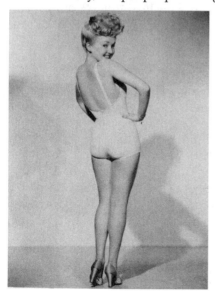

Figure 8.14   Hollywood does its bit for the war effort . . . Pin-up photos of Betty Grable, famed for her "million dollar legs," adorned thousands of soldiers' footlockers around the world.   *Source:* National Archives.

One World War II film has become a classic. In 1942, Warner Brothers brought out a melodrama set in Morocco. It told a tale of an American nightclub owner, Rick Blaine, who hides patriotic idealism beneath a hard-boiled surface. In the end, Rick sacrifices both his business and the woman he loves to rescue an anti-Nazi resistance fighter. Humphrey Bogart played Rick Blaine in *Casablanca,* becoming a cult hero to millions of moviegoers.

Radio, more popular than ever, became a prime source of news about the war. World War II was the first war given live media coverage. War correspondent Edward R. Murrow described the Battle of Britain for American radio audiences in the summer of 1940. He brought the European war into American living rooms. Foreign correspondents in Europe and Asia went everywhere the soldiers went to transmit firsthand accounts of battles to the folks back home. Never had war journalism been so direct or authentic. But censors often edited the news. Broadcasters often sacrificed factual accuracy for dramatic effect. War news had entertainment as well as informational value. Wartime radio remained essentially an entertainment medium. Programming continued as usual: soap operas by day and variety shows, sitcoms, and melodrama by night—and always, incessant commercial messages urging listeners to buy soap, cigarettes, and chewing gum.

WORLD WAR AND ITS CONSEQUENCES

World War II was an intense, transforming experience for most Americans. The war fundamentally changed American society in many ways. These war-induced changes were more profound and permanent than any occurring in this country since the industrial revolution. On the eve of war, Americans suffered from the lingering effects of the Great Depression—high unemployment, low productivity, and massive poverty, accompanied by lurking doubts about the vitality of American institutions and the purpose of national life. They looked out at a threatening world engulfed in war, a world in which their nation played only a peripheral role. Within the nation, Americans quarreled bitterly among themselves over President Roosevelt's conduct of foreign policy, until the bombing of Pearl Harbor abruptly ended all arguments.

Four years later, a unified, proud, and powerful nation emerged victoriously from war. Its armed forces and industrial might had played decisive roles in destroying Fascism, militarism, and imperialism around the globe. America had won the largest war in human history. War revitalized the American economy. It emerged from the war far more productive than it had ever been, and most Americans were more prosperous than they ever had been. American faith in capitalism and democratic institutions also had been restored. Compared to other nations, American war casualties had been light, and Americans had been spared the devastations and terrors of a war fought outside of its continental boundaries.

At war's end, the United States strode the world as an international colossus; its armed forces, linked to its nuclear monopoly, made it the most powerful nation-state in the history of the planet. Its statesmen took the lead in creating a new international agency to preserve peace and build a prosperous postwar world. Fittingly, the United Nation's permanent home would be New York, the greatest metropolis of the new imperium.

World War II ushered in a new age for the United States. The war was a watershed from which emerged the dominant patterns of postwar life. The war forced Americans to accept involvement with the world beyond national boundaries; there could be no reversion to isolationism after 1945. Americans' war experiences gave them a new confidence that they could solve all serious problems, both internal and external. They had proved that they had the savvy, the will, and the technologies to lick depression at home and aggression abroad.

The major contours of post–1945 American history originated in the war experience. The Cold War with the Soviet Union stemmed from the tensions and conflicts that strained the Grand Alliance. Postwar economic policies derived from the awareness that federal spending in wartime had finally ended economic depression. Political leaders during the postwar era assumed that similar fiscal practices could stabilize the business cycle and promote economic growth. A new understanding of the role of consumerism in sustaining economic growth meant that government would promote spending instead of saving after the war. The struggles and achievements of women and minorities in wartime planted the seeds of their postwar drives for equal access to the American dream.

The war restored America's philosophic birthright, an optimistic sense of individual and national potential that would shape the national experience for the next three decades. The Axis powers were destroyed, the Soviet Union was exhausted, and western Europe was depleted. But America was strong, prosperous, and free. Its people felt ready for the "American Century" that they knew lay ahead. America's economy was powerful, its resources were abundant, and it had the scientific and technological talent to use them. Success in wartime gave Americans confidence and great expectations for an unbounded future.

Americans also soberly confronted a future that they feared could bring a recurrence of the Great Depression. Could prosperity, growth, and full employment be sustained in a postwar era without the stimulus of the war economy? Could jobs be found for the millions of returning veterans and displaced war workers? Americans also worried about threats to their peace and security posed by the Soviet Union. Perhaps the war had not made the world safe for democracy. Perhaps there was not going to be an "American Century" after all, or at least not an uncontested one. Most of all, Americans were alarmed by the nuclear shadow that they had cast over the postwar era.

And so, Americans in the summer of 1945 faced the future with mixed feelings—of pride, confidence, and hope. They also faced the future with feelings of fear—of the return of depression, expanding Soviet power, and a nuclear Armageddon.

IMPORTANT EVENTS

1942	Japanese Americans are interned
	The Battle of the Coral Sea occurs
	The Battle of Midway takes place
	Allied troops invade North Africa
	The Manhattan District Project begins
1943	Soviets win the Battle for Stalingrad
	FDR and Churchill announce unconditional surrender at Casablanca
	Allied forces invade Italy; Italy surrenders
	A race riot breaks out in Detroit
	The Big Three meet at Teheran
1944	D-Day: Allied invasion at Normandy
	Paris is liberated
	The Battle of Philippine Sea occurs
	The Battle of the Bulge takes place
1945	The conference at Yalta is held
	The Battle of Iwo Jima occurs
	Roosevelt dies; Truman becomes president
	Germany surrenders
	The Battle of Okinawa takes place
	The Potsdam conference is held
	Japanese cities are atomic-bombed
	Japan surrenders; World War II ends

BIBLIOGRAPHY

There is a vast literature on all facets of American involvement in World War II. The following books are recommended for those who want to know more about the war experience in general or want to explore a particular aspect of it. Two good short surveys of World War II are Martha Byrd Hoyle's *A World in Flames: A History of World War II* and Mark Arnold-Forster's *The World At War*. Basil Collier, in *The Second World War: A Military History*, offers a good short account of the U.S. military role in World War II. A longer general history is A. Russell Buchanan's *The United States and World War II* (2 vols.). A recent book on the Pacific war is Ronald H. Spector's *Eagle Against the Sun*. Samuel Eliot Morison, in *The Two Ocean War* (2 vols.), presents a naval history of World War II. A recent study that highlights the racial antagonisms that undergirded the war between the United States and Japan is John Dower's *War without Mercy: Race and Power in the Pacific War*. An outstanding recent addition to the historical literature on World War II is Stephen E. Ambrose's *Citizen Soldiers: The U.S. Army From the Normandy Beaches to the Bulge to the Surrender of Germany*. Ambrose's book, which made the best-seller lists, might be the finest book ever written about U.S. fighting men. The best war journalism can be found in Ernie Pyle's classic, *Brave Men*. The best short study of U.S. wartime diplomacy is Gaddis Smith's *American Diplomacy during World War II*. For the best study of President Roosevelt's conduct of diplomacy during the war, read Robert Dallek's *Franklin Roosevelt and American Foreign Policy, 1932–1945* (pp.

171–538). The best account of the decision to build and use atomic bombs on Japan is Martin J. Sherwin's *A World Destroyed*. John Hersey, in *Hiroshima*, offers an eyewitness account of the tragedy that launched the atomic age. The horrors of the Jewish Holocaust have been recorded by Arthur D. Morse in *Six Million Died*. The best studies about the home front are Richard Polenberg's *War and Society: The United States, 1941–1945* and John Morton Blum's *"V" Was for Victory: Politics and American Culture during World War II*. The best social history of the United States at war is Geoffrey Perrett's *Days of Sadness, Years of Triumph: The American People, 1939–1945*. Susan M. Hartmann, in *The Homefront and Beyond: American Women in the 1940s*, features an account of women and the war. Neil A. Wynn, in *The Afro-American and the Second World War*, has recorded the experiences of black people during wartime. The best account of the wartime relocation of Japanese Americans is Edward Spencer's *Impounded People: Japanese Americans and World War II*. Jeanne Wakatsuki Houston and James D. Houston, in *Farewell to Manzanar*, offer a compelling story of a Japanese family interned for the duration of the war. Richard R. Lingeman's *Don't You Know There's a War On?* is a general account of popular culture in wartime. Joel Greenberg's *Hollywood in the Forties* is an account of wartime movies and their effects on the populace. John Brooks, in *The Great Leap: The Past Twenty-Five Years in America*, presents an important book highlighting the immense changes brought about in this country by World War II that shaped the postwar era. Of the many World War II era novels, the best include Harriet Arnow's *The Dollmaker*, which movingly describes the disruptions and dislocations of war; James Jones' *From Here to Eternity*, which chronicles enlisted life in the Army on the eve of Pearl Harbor; Norman Mailer's *The Naked and the Dead*, a powerful novel that uses a platoon of infantrymen to symbolize American society, its class structure, and social values; and Herman Wouk's *The Caine Mutiny*, the dramatic story of a ship's officers rebelling against a mentally ill, tyrannical ship commander.

9

The Rise of the Cold War

ORLD War II had left a large part of Europe and many nations of Asia and elsewhere in ruins, and it had shattered the old balance of power. Even most of the victors had fared badly. The Soviets had lost more than 30 million people, and much of their economy had been ruined by war. The British, depleted economically and militarily, faced the imminent loss of much of their vast empire. After 1945, Britain's ability to play a major role in world affairs would depend mainly on American friendship and support. France had been humiliated by defeat and occupation during the war. The French economy was weak, its government was unstable, and the French Communist Party was a rising force.

The war had so weakened the British, French, and Dutch nations that they could no longer control many of their rebellious colonies in Asia, Africa, and the Middle East. Throughout the postwar era, the decolonization process begun during World War II accelerated, presenting challenges to the United States in what became known as the Third World. In the Far East, China was sinking into the chaos of civil war, dashing any hopes that it would be a major factor in postwar Asian diplomacy. Only America emerged from the awful devastation of global war with its wealth and power enhanced, and with most of its citizens better off than they had ever been.

Postwar American celebrations of victory and expectations of a peaceful and prosperous world order dominated by the United States quickly gave way to conflicts between America and its erstwhile ally, the Soviet Union. A multitude of difficult postwar political problems generated decades of tension, ideological warfare, and a thermonuclear arms race that historians have called the Cold War. The Cold War would remain the dominant international reality shaping the conduct of U.S. foreign policy for over forty years. Cold War preoccupations also exerted a powerful influence on American domestic politics during this era.

THE UNITED NATIONS

It was a grim world into which the United Nations (UN) was born. President Roosevelt had made the creation of a postwar international organization to prevent aggression in the world his major diplomatic objective. Most influential Americans shared his goal, determined to not repeat the mistake they believed Americans had made after World War I, when they had refused to join the League of Nations. These leaders believed that America's failure to join the League had helped undermine international order during the 1930s, which had led to World War II.

The UN experienced significant birthing pains. Soviet and American delegates quarreled frequently over many features of the new organization. Delegates from many of the gathered nations all played politics as usual. Eventually they wrote and signed a charter. Despite some concessions to the Soviets to ensure their participation, the UN was largely an American creation. It was Woodrow Wilson's League of Nations Covenant reborn, and slightly revised.

The UN Charter created an "upper house," the Security Council, and a "lower house," the General Assembly. It also fashioned a permanent administrative structure, called the Secretariat, and many allied agencies, including the International Court of Justice, the International Monetary Fund, the Export-Import Bank, and the United Nations Relief and Rehabilitation Agency (UNRRA). The Security Council consisted of five major powers—the United States, the Soviet Union, Great Britain, France, and China—and six associate members, elected from the General Assembly to serve for two years on a rotating basis. Action on all important matters required unanimous approval from the five permanent Security Council members, giving each an absolute veto of any UN action it found contrary to its interests. In the General Assembly, every nation was represented, but only for debate, not for decision. The UN was a federation of sovereign states. It had only the power the major nations permitted it to have. It had no tax powers, could not raise its own military force, and depended on member contributions for funds.

U.S. officials were mainly responsible for creating an international agency with only contingent powers. Roosevelt had insisted on devising an organization that would not impair national sovereignty and allowed the major powers to police their regional spheres of influence. There was a core of realpolitik underlying Roosevelt's commitment to Wilsonian internationalism. Neither the United States nor the Soviet Union would have joined any postwar international agency that did not permit them to retain an absolute veto over its actions.

Immediately after the war, the UN provided relief to the war-ravaged populations of Europe and Asia. The United States funneled billions of dollars through the UNRRA for food, clothing, and medicines for needy people in Germany, Japan, China, and eastern Europe. The British borrowed $3.75 billion from the United States in 1946, much of which was used to pay for food imports. Postwar Germany faced economic disaster. German industrial and agricultural production had shrunk to pitiful fractions of prewar levels. Germany's population had swelled from the addition of 10 million "displaced persons," German refugees who had either been expelled or had fled from various eastern European countries.

The United States shared occupation responsibilities in Germany with the Soviets, the British, and the French, but it had sole authority in Japan. In Germany, U.S. officials tried to eliminate all traces of Naziism. Special courts punished over 1,500 major Nazi offenders and over 600,000 minor Nazi officials. The most famous trial occurred at Nuremberg, the former site of huge Nazi party rallies held during the 1930s. An international tribunal put twenty-two former high Nazi officials on trial. Nineteen were convicted, of whom twelve were hanged for "war crimes and atrocities." In Japan, U.S. officials under the command of General Douglas MacArthur staged a Tokyo equivalent of Nuremberg. Twenty-eight former high Japanese officials were tried, and all were convicted of war crimes; seven were hanged.

Americans also completely remade Japanese society. They broke up industrial monopolies, abolished feudal estates, and implemented land reform. They introduced political democracy and established independent trade unions. And they forced the Japanese to destroy all military weapons and to renounce war as an instrument of national policy. The Japanese have depended on America's nuclear shield to protect their national security ever since. Most important for the future of Japan, U.S. engineers modernized Japanese industry, introducing new management and quality control techniques. From the ashes of war, with help from their conquerors, the Japanese fashioned a working democratic and capitalistic system.

ORIGINS OF COLD WAR

During 1945 and 1946, American and Soviet leaders clashed over many issues. Their wartime alliance deteriorated rapidly. Even before war's end, the Allies had quarreled over the opening of a second front in western Europe and the future political status of eastern European countries. The immediate origins of Cold War conflict lay in these wartime strains within the Grand Alliance. Historians have traced the roots of Cold War to the American response to the 1917 Bolshevik revolution and Lenin's profound hatred of Western liberal capitalist culture. From 1917 until 1933, a succession of American presidents refused to recognize the Soviet state. Even after the normalization of U.S.–USSR relations in 1933, friendly relations between the two nations did not evolve. When Stalin concluded his cynical nonaggression pact with Hitler in August 1939, most Americans equated the Soviet Union with Nazi Germany. It was the wartime alliance between the Americans and the Soviets, born of strategic necessity, that represented a departure from the historic norm of mutual distrust and ideological hostility.

In March 1945, President Roosevelt perceived Soviet efforts to impose a Communist regime on Poland to be a violation of the Yalta accords and protested to Stalin. Roosevelt's successor, Harry Truman, inexperienced in the craft of diplomacy and lacking FDR's poise and style, rebuked the Soviet foreign minister, V. M. Molotov, over Yalta violations. But military force gave the Soviet Union control of Poland's and eastern Europe's political destinies. Between 1945 and 1948, the Soviet Union imposed Communist-controlled regimes on these nations. Stalin, determined to protect his empire and its Communist system from future security threats, and from Western cultural influences and U.S. investment, erected a ring of submissive client states along the Soviet Union's vulnerable western periphery.

American political leaders and prominent journalists strongly condemned Soviet domination of Poland and other east European countries. American statesmen would not concede, at least for the record, that the new Soviet empire in eastern Europe constituted a legitimate "sphere of influence," for several reasons: besides the sense of betrayal felt over Yalta, there were domestic political considerations. Millions of Americans of east European background were enraged at the Soviet Union's brutal domination of their ancestral homelands. Americans also anticipated having economic relations with eastern European countries in the postwar era until Communist control sealed them off. In addition, American leaders felt a sense of righteous, missionary power: that they could move eastern Europe toward democratic capitalism. Soviet intrusions frustrated America's good intentions and imposed an abhorrent system of political economy on the region that many Americans equated with Fascism.

At a time when American-Soviet relations were strained because of Stalin's intrusions into eastern Europe, the Soviets applied for a $6 billion loan from the United States to rebuild their wrecked economy. The State Department refused to consider the loan unless, as U.S. Ambassador to the Soviet Union Averill Harriman put it, the Soviets "work cooperatively with us on international problems in accordance with our standards." The Soviets refused U.S. terms, and Americans rejected the loan request. The Soviets rebuilt their economy using their own resources, plus what they could extract from Germany and eastern Europe. U.S. efforts to extract Soviet concessions in exchange for credits angered Stalin, reinforcing his distrust of Western capitalist powers. Stalin also resented America's refusal to accept Soviet domination of eastern Europe, while excluding the Soviets from Italian and Japanese occupations.

But there were clear limits as to what actions the Truman administration would take to prevent Soviet domination of eastern Europe. It could denounce Soviet actions; it could apply economic and diplomatic pressures; it could even use its temporary atomic monopoly as a veiled threat. But the United States never directly threatened the Soviets with military action. When Stalin forcibly incorporated the eastern half of Europe into the Soviet empire between 1945 and 1948, the United States, in effect, grudgingly accepted the creation of a Soviet sphere of influence while waging rhetorical warfare.

The Potsdam conference, held in late July 1945, the final wartime meeting of the Big Three, revealed the strains within the Grand Alliance. They often quarreled—over German boundaries and reparations, over the composition of the new Polish government, and over when the Soviet Union would enter the Pacific war against Japan. At Potsdam, the Soviets pressed their demand, made at Yalta, for $20 billion of reparations to be taken from the German occupation zones. The Americans and the British refused to affix a dollar amount for reparations but permitted the Soviets to remove some industry from their zones. But in May 1946, the U.S. military governor suddenly halted all reparations shipments from the American zone. Continual conflicts between the Soviets and the Western powers over occupation policy in Germany were the core causes of the Cold War, which originated in the heart of Europe.

At war's end, America was the world's preeminent power. With about 5 percent of the world's population, the United States produced over 60 percent of the world's manufactured goods and controlled over half of the world's wealth. Its $14 billion in gold reserves stored at Fort Knox represented about 75 percent of the world's gold supply in 1945. Despite its great wealth and power, the United States could not prevent the growing division of Europe nor bring stability to the Far East. When American, British, and Soviet foreign ministers met in London in September 1945, they quarreled bitterly over who threatened whom. Mutual suspicion and hostility rendered traditional diplomacy impossible. The Western powers demanded that the Soviets ease their control of eastern Europe. In response, the Soviet leaders accused the West of capitalist encirclement and atomic blackmail.

The former allies appeared to be on collision courses: the Soviets were determined to dominate the lesser states of eastern Europe to erect a security sphere around their nation. The United States was determined to break down international trade barriers and rebuild Germany. Further, American leaders shared a vision of a national mission. In the postwar era, America intended to build a prosperous new world order, a world order based on free governments and free trade. America, having launched itself on a mission to build a brave new world in its own image, with an atomic holster hanging on its hip, enraged and frightened the Soviet leaders.

From the American perspective, neither its great wealth nor its atomic monopoly guaranteed U.S. security in the postwar era. The destruction of German and Japanese power had removed historic barriers to Soviet expansion in Europe and northeastern Asia. Anticolonial rebellions against lingering Western imperialism also gave the Soviet Union opportunities to expand its influence. From the Soviet perspective, expanding American influence in Europe and Asia alarmed the Soviet leaders. They were fearful of the vastly superior American wealth and military power. Stalin tried to isolate the Soviet Union and its newly acquired empire in eastern Europe from contact with the Western powers.

In early 1946, both sides escalated their rhetoric. On March 5, 1946, former Prime Minister Winston Churchill, visiting in the United States, declared "From Stettin in the Baltic to Trieste in the Adriatic, an iron curtain has descended across the continent." He called for an Anglo-American effort to roll back the Soviet iron curtain. Stalin accused Churchill of calling for war against the Soviet Union. U.S. public opinion polls showed widespread disapproval for Soviet actions in Germany and eastern Europe. Stalin also had given a speech in February in which he reasserted the Leninist doctrine of the incompatibility of capitalism and socialism, and the necessity of revolutionary conflict in the world. Following Stalin's belligerent speech, the Soviets rejected an American offer to join the World Bank and International Monetary Fund, the two principal agencies for promoting free trade and stable currencies in the postwar world.

In an atmosphere of growing hostility and suspicion, Truman and his advisers tried to work out a plan for the international control of nuclear weapons through the United Nations. Bernard Baruch, the American delegate, proposed a plan calling for international control of atomic weapons to be achieved in stages, during which the United States would retain its nuclear monopoly. His plan called for inspections within the Soviet Union by a UN commission to ensure compliance. The Soviets, working feverishly to develop their own nuclear weapons, rejected on-site inspections within their territory, proposing an alternative plan calling for the destruction of American nuclear weapons before any control system would be devised. The Americans rejected the Soviet plan. The United States then opted for its own internal control mechanisms. Congress enacted the Atomic Energy Act in 1946, which empowered the newly created Atomic Energy Commission (AEC) to control all atomic energy research and development in the nation under tight security restrictions.

Thus vanished the world's only chance, admittedly a slim one, to eliminate the nuclear arms race before it became a central feature of the Cold War. It was the nuclear arms race that added a terrifying dimension to the U.S.–USSR rivalry, making it unlike any previous great power conflict in history. Since about 1955, both sides have possessed the technical capability to destroy the other. Ironically, nuclear weapons also functioned to keep the Cold War cold. Had it not been for nuclear weapons, the Americans and the Soviets would probably have had a war, for there has been enough provocation on both sides. But neither side dared attack, because it knew the other would resort to nuclear weapons before it would accept defeat. Mutual terror deterred both nations from combat for the duration of the Cold War.

The failure of Washington and the Kremlin to find a mutually acceptable formula for controlling atomic weapons technology highlighted the dawn of the atomic age. At about the same time the UN was debating the weapons issue, the United States conducted a series of atomic bomb tests in the South Pacific at Bikini atoll. Radio accounts and dramatic photos of the tests forced Americans to the horrific realization that humankind had produced weapons of mass destruction that could destroy cities in an instant. Some jaunty folks tried to make light of the matter, to laugh it off. Later that year, a French designer brought out a new type of women's bathing suit, which he named the "bikini." It had an explosive impact on women's fashion, because the new-style swimsuits exposed much more of the female body than had any previous model. Despite these brave efforts to laugh it away, fear of a nuclear holocaust had taken root in the American psyche. American imaginations in the postwar era were haunted by twin symbols of catastrophe—the mushroom cloud and nuclear missiles striking America's great cities. According to historian Paul Boyer, "A primal fear of extinction pervaded all society." The atomic age ushered in the age of anxiety that continuously undercut celebrations of the affluent society.

There were many other conflicts, misperceptions, and misunderstandings arising during the period 1945–1946 that poisoned the postwar U.S.–USSR diplomatic atmosphere. The major conflicts—over the postwar political status of eastern Europe, over occupation policy in Germany, and over international control of atomic weapons—drove America and the Soviet Union apart. They were the major causes of the Cold War.

These disputes between America and the Soviet Union grew out of the power vacuum created by the smashing of German power, a vacuum into which rushed the two expansionist powers: the United States, a global power, its leaders motivated by a sense of righteous power based on America's prosperous economy and atomic monopoly, by strong ideological convictions, and by important economic interests; and the USSR, a strong regional power, its leaders motivated by ideology, an urgent desire to protect vital security interests, and a pressing need to rebuild its shattered economy. The United States and the Soviet Union collided at many points in central and eastern Europe. Emotions flared as leaders on both sides struggled to solve challenging and frustrating problems. Given their fundamental differences, the intrinsic difficulties of their many problems, the pressures and antagonisms inherent in their many disputes, and their clashing goals and ambitions, in retrospect, it appears that conflicts between the Americans and Soviets were inevitable.

The Cold War was apparently inevitable. It occurred because of the tragic failure of the two most powerful nations emerging from World War II to resolve their conflicts of interest through the traditional processes of diplomacy. Instead, the leaders of the two nations, quick to read the worst intentions into the actions of

Figure 9.1   Atomic Age begins. The mushroom cloud became one of the haunting symbols of catastrophe, proving that the age of affluence was also the age of anxiety.
Source: U.S. Navy, The Pentagon.

Figure 9.2   Division of Europe, 1945–1955.   *Source:* George D. Moss, *Moving On* (Englewood Cliffs, NJ: Prentice Hall, 1994), p. 38.

their rivals and to habitually anticipate worst-case scenarios, believed themselves compelled to resort to over four decades of ideological warfare. They also felt compelled, "like two apes on a treadmill," in analyst Paul Warnke's phrase, to engage in a costly and dangerous thermonuclear arms race without precedent in human history. The Cold War became an interlocking, reciprocal process, involving gen-

uine differences of principle, clashes of interest, and a wide range of misperceptions and misunderstandings.

THE TRUMAN DOCTRINE

To Washington in early 1947, the world appeared to be sinking into chaos. A nearly
bankrupt Great Britain prepared to abandon India, Palestine, and Greece. The Vietnamese refused to accept the return of French colonialism, and Indochina was engulfed in war. Likewise, the Indonesians refused to accept the return of the Dutch
and ignited a war. In China, a civil war raged between the Nationalists and Communists. Amidst rubble-strewn cities and ruined economies, the Japanese and Germans struggled to avoid famine. American leaders feared that the Soviet Union
would try to exploit the severe political and economic problems of Europe and Asia.

In 1947, crises arose in the Balkan region involving Greece and Turkey. Greece
was engulfed in a civil war that pitted Communist insurgents against a Rightist
government backed by the British. Simultaneously, the Soviets were pressuring the
Turkish government to grant them joint control of the Dardanelles, a vital link between the Black Sea and the Mediterranean. The Turks rebuffed the Soviets and
Stalin threatened to take action against them. The British also were backing the
Turks in their dispute with the Soviets over control of the waterway. On February
21, 1947, citing economic problems, the British government informed Washington
that it could no longer provide support to the Greek and Turkish governments.

President Truman wanted the United States to replace the British in the
Mediterranean and to help the Greeks and Turks. But he had to convince the Republican-controlled and economy-minded 80th Congress that his initiative served
the national interest. The principal architect of the American aid program to Greece
and Turkey was Undersecretary of State, Dean Acheson. Acheson evoked an early
version of the "domino theory" to stress the need for American aid to the two countries. He stated that if Greece fell to the Communists and the Soviets gained control of the Dardanelles, North Africa and the Middle East would be endangered.
Morale would sink in Italy, France, and western Germany; all would become vulnerable to a Communist takeover. Three continents would be opened to Soviet penetration. Acheson's alarmist presentation persuaded Senator Arthur Vandenberg,
Chairman of the Senate Foreign Relations Committee, to support Truman's proposed aid bill for Greece and Turkey. George Kennan, a brilliant State Department
Soviet expert, also furnished arguments supporting Truman's interventionist policy. Kennan wrote of the need to develop

> a policy of firm containment, designed to confront the Russians with unalterable
> counter-force at every point where they show signs of encroaching upon the interests
> of a peaceful and stable world.[1]

[1]George Kennan, *American Diplomacy* (New York: New American Library, 1952), p. 104.
(Reprinted with permission of the editor from *Foreign Affairs*, XXV, No. 4 (July 1947), pp. 566–82.

His analysis coincided with Truman's views of Soviet behavior; his recommendations accorded with the president's desire to get tough with the Soviets. Containment, stopping the spread of Communist influence in the world, became the chief operating principle of American foreign policy in the postwar era. It remained the cornerstone of U.S. foreign policy for forty years.

Truman also actively promoted the aid bill. In a speech given at Baylor University on March 6, 1947, he said that the American system of free enterprise could survive only if it were part of a free world economic system. He contended that American aid to Greece and Turkey was part of his strategy for preserving economic freedom in the world. Only a peaceful and prosperous world ensured American security in the Cold War era.

Truman's Baylor University speech preceded his major address before a joint session of Congress on March 12 to ask Congress to appropriate $400 million for Greek and Turkish aid. In the most important foreign policy speech of his presidency, Truman told the American people that the Communist threat to Greece and Turkey represented Hitler and World War II all over again. Truman then spoke the famed words that became known as the Truman Doctrine. The Truman Doctrine became, in the words of historian Thomas G. Paterson, "the commanding guide to American foreign policy in the Cold War."

> At the present moment in world history, nearly every nation must choose between alternative ways of life.
> One way of life is based upon the will of the majority, and is distinguished by free institutions . . . and freedom from political oppression. The second way of life is based upon the will of a minority forcibly imposed on the majority . . . and the suppression of personal freedom.
> I believe that it must be the policy of the United States to support free peoples who are resisting attempted subjugation by armed minorities or by outside pressures . . . If we falter in our leadership, we may endanger the peace of the world—we shall surely endanger the welfare of our own nation.[2]

Truman's speech amounted to a declaration of ideological warfare against the Soviet Union. He depicted a world engaged in a struggle between the forces of freedom and the forces of tyranny. The political fate of mankind hung on the outcome. In this mortal struggle, American aid to Greece and Turkey would serve the American mission of preserving freedom in the world and preventing World War III. Polls, which had been negative before his speech, soon showed a large majority favoring the U.S. aid program.

Not everyone accepted Truman's fervent invitation to join the anti-Communist crusade. Liberal and conservative critics both opposed aid to Greece and Turkey. Henry Wallace denounced it as a waste of money and provocative to the Soviets. Walter Lippmann, the nation's premier political journalist, also opposed it, observing that the United States could not police the world. But after a brief debate,

---

[2]Taken from a printed copy of Truman's speech found in Armin Rappaport, ed., *Sources in American Diplomacy* (New York: Macmillan, 1966), pp. 329–30.

large bipartisan majorities in both houses of Congress supported the aid bill. Truman's powerful rhetoric had carried his cause.

The Truman Doctrine defined a new U.S. foreign policy direction. Isolationism had been abandoned and the United Nations bypassed. Truman had committed America to actively resist Soviet expansionism in southern Europe. The Truman Doctrine proclaimed that the era of the containment of Communism had begun. Although the first application of the new containment policy was limited, the doctrine justifying it was unlimited. During the early 1950s, U.S. foreign policy based on the containment of Communism would expand to become a global commitment to contain Communism everywhere.

Congress fashioned several new governmental agencies to implement the containment policy more effectively. The National Security Act (1947) created the Department of Defense and established the Joint Chiefs of Staff. The act also made the Air Force a separate branch of military service and put the administration of the Army, Navy, and Air Force under a single department. The National Security Act also created the National Security Council (NSC), a cabinet-level advisory body to coordinate military and foreign policy for the president. Creation of the NSC indicated the growing influence of military considerations in the conduct of American foreign policy. The National Security Act also created the Central Intelligence Agency (CIA) as an agency directly under the authority of the National Security Council. The CIA, a child of the Cold War, became a covert arm of American foreign policy during the late 1940s. The National Security Act institutionalized the Cold War.

THE MARSHALL PLAN

In 1947, European recovery from the devastation of war was flagging. Washington feared that continuing hardships could force cold and hungry Europeans to turn to Communism, particularly in France and Italy, which had popular Communist parties. A prostrate Europe also endangered American prosperity because of a huge "dollar gap" that had emerged. The dollar gap, totaling about $8 billion in 1947, represented the difference between the value of U.S. exports and the amount of dollars European customers had on hand to pay for them. The dollar gap threatened to undermine overseas trade and erode U.S. postwar economic growth and prosperity.

Europeans could not buy U.S. products unless they received dollars from the United States. To offset the lure of Communism and to pump dollars into the impoverished European economies, American officials drafted a comprehensive European aid program. On June 5, 1947, Secretary of State George Marshall announced the plan directed against "hunger, poverty, desperation, and chaos," which came to bear his name. Truman urged Congress to back the proposed Marshall Plan with a $27 billion appropriation.

The Marshall Plan called for a cooperative approach in which Europeans would plan their recovery needs collectively and the United States would underwrite a long-term recovery program. All European nations were invited to participate in the Marshall Plan, including the Soviet Union and the east European nations. With the British and French leading the way, Europeans responded enthusiastically. A general planning conference convened in Paris on June 26, 1947, to formulate a European reply. But the Soviets walked out of the conference, denouncing the Marshall Plan as an American scheme to dominate Europe. Stalin may also have feared that U.S. economic aid would undermine his control of eastern Europe, so he forced these nations to abstain from the recovery program. On July 16, Europeans established a Committee on European Economic Cooperation, which drew up plans for a four-year recovery effort.

Within the United States, Senator Vandenberg led a bipartisan effort to obtain congressional approval for the plan. Support for the aid program increased when Americans learned of a Communist takeover in Czechoslovakia, which occurred as Congress debated the bill. Stalin ordered the Czech coup as a response to the increasing integration of the West German economy into the liberal capitalist order. Congress enacted a slimmed-down version of the aid plan. The legislators appropriated $5.3 billion to implement the Marshall Plan in the summer of 1948. When the Marshall Plan ended in 1952, the United States had provided over $13 billion for European economic recovery.

The Marshall Plan worked. European industrial production increased 200 percent from 1948 to 1952. The foundations for the West's later affluence were firmly laid. The appeal of Communism in the West diminished. The program worked because of its planned, long-term, cooperative approach. It succeeded also because Europe possessed the industrial base and skilled manpower needed to use the aid funds effectively. European economic recovery restored a region of crucial importance to the United States. It also proved to be a major stimulus to American economic activity, and it accorded with Cold War ideological goals. George Marshall expected American economic aid to permit the "emergence of political and social conditions in which free institutions can exist." The Marshall Plan gave the U.S. policy of containment of Communism in Europe a sound economic foundation.

NATO

While furnishing the means for Europe's economic reconstruction, America also concerned itself with rebuilding western Germany. With the rise of Soviet power in eastern Europe, there was a power vacuum in central Europe that America wanted to fill with a democratic and capitalistic Germany. Near the end of 1946, the Americans and British merged their German occupation zones and began to assign administrative responsibilities to German officials. By mid-1947, the effort to rebuild Germany's industrial economy had begun.

The Soviets reacted to Western efforts to rebuild the German economy and incorporate it into the European recovery plan by tightening their control of eastern Europe. Perceiving that he had failed to prevent the restoration of the West German state, Stalin also tried to squeeze the Western powers out of Berlin. In June 1948, the Soviets suddenly shut down all Western access routes to their Berlin sector that lay deep inside the Soviet zone. The Berlin Blockade confronted Washington with a serious crisis. Truman ordered U.S. strategic bombers with the capability of hauling nuclear weapons to targets within the Soviet Union to fly to bases in England. The Western powers also devised an Anglo-American airlift that flew food and fuel to 2.5 million West Berliners. The Soviets, not wanting war, did not interfere with the airlift. After 324 days, the Soviets canceled the blockade. It had failed to dislodge the Allies, and it had failed to prevent the integration of the West German economy into the European recovery program.

In American eyes, the Berlin airlift symbolized Western resolve to maintain an outpost of freedom in the heart of Soviet tyranny. Truman had outmaneuvered the Soviets and forced them to rescind the blockade. The airlift also appeared to confirm George Kennan's contention that only force could contain Communist expansionism. The Western powers created the Federal Republic of Germany (West Germany) soon after the blockade ended. In retaliation, the Soviets erected the Democratic Socialist Republic of Germany (East Germany). The Berlin Blockade represented the first major American-Soviet conflict of the Cold War. It also was the paradigmatic conflict that established the pattern of U.S.–USSR confrontations that would periodically recur until the Cold War ended.

The Czech coup, the Berlin Blockade, and other Soviet actions hostile to Western interests convinced Washington officials that containment required military as well as economic measures. The germ of the North Atlantic Treaty Organization (NATO) appeared in a Senate resolution passed in 1948, expressing America's resolve to defend itself through collective security if necessary. The Truman administration began planning for the defense of western Europe.

NATO came to life on April 4, 1949; ten European nations, Canada, and the United States signed the treaty. The heart of the mutual security pact could be found in the language of Article 5: "an armed attack against one or more members . . . shall be considered an attack against them all." Attack any NATO member and you have to fight them all. With the creation of NATO, Soviet aggression against any western European nation would mean World War III. The Senate ratified the treaty, 82 to 13, on July 21, 1949, with little debate.

Congress followed its approval of American membership in NATO by voting to grant military aid to its allies and to contribute American troops to NATO defense forces. By early 1950, a NATO command structure had been created. U.S. forces stationed in Europe would function as a "tripwire" in case of Soviet aggression, guaranteeing that American strategic bombers would attack the Soviet Union if western Europe were invaded. The Soviets responded to the creation of NATO by creating the Warsaw Pact among eastern European countries.

Because U.S. forces were not sent to Europe until 1952, the creation of NATO did not immediately alter the strategic balance of power in that critical region. At the time of NATO's creation, there was no imminent threat of war in Europe. America appeared to be winning the Cold War in western Europe and Japan. The Marshall Plan nations and the Japanese were both well on the road to economic recovery. The new state of West Germany, under the leadership of Konrad Adenauer, had been firmly established. Soviet efforts to keep Japan and Europe weak and divided, and isolated from the United States, obviously had failed. By 1949, Stalin was clearly on the defensive.

Given the geopolitical realities in Europe, it is evident that NATO had other uses besides giving containment of Communism in Europe military muscle. NATO gave these nations the confidence to combat internal subversion and the will to resist Communist pressure. NATO conveyed a sense of security that encouraged western European economic recovery under the Marshall Plan. It also served as a means to bind western Europeans more tightly into an American sphere of influence and to discourage any separatist tendencies to make deals with the Soviets. Ironically, NATO later proved useful in providing a way to rearm West Germany. By integrating the new West German military forces into NATO, the United States could allay French alarm at a rearmed Germany.

From 1947 to 1949, American leaders made many crucial decisions that shaped American Cold War policy for decades. First came the formulation of containment ideology, the declaration of principles embodied in the Truman Doctrine. Then the Marshall Plan offered economic aid enabling western Europeans to stay clear of the iron curtain and rebuild their war-shattered economies. NATO added a strategic component. It also represented a historic departure for the United States: America joined its first binding military alliance in modern history. Ironically, in the nuclear age, foreign entanglements now appeared necessary to ensure U.S. security.

Soon after Senate ratification of NATO came the alarming news that the Soviets had developed an atomic bomb. The American nuclear monopoly, which had functioned as a security blanket to dampen Cold War anxieties, had vanished. Soviet possession of nuclear weapons prompted President Truman to consider ordering the development of a hydrogen fusion weapon, a "superbomb" many times more powerful than atomic fission weapons. In January 1950, an intense secret debate occurred between scientific supporters of the H-bomb, led by Edward Teller, and its opponents, led by J. Robert Oppenheimer, the leader of the scientific team that had created nuclear weapons in 1945. Teller carried the debate with his argument that if the United States failed to develop the weapon and the Soviets did, they could blackmail the United States. Truman ordered the hydrogen bomb to be built.

After obtaining permission to build the new weapon, U.S. scientists exploded a hydrogen bomb in November 1952. But the American technological edge in the arms race against the Soviet Union proved to be short-lived. The Soviets tested their own hydrogen bomb in August 1953. These thermonuclear weapons were a thousand times more powerful than the bombs that had destroyed Hiroshima and

Nagasaki in August 1945. With the advent of the hydrogen bomb, the potential thermonuclear threat to world survival had taken a quantum leap.

THE CHINESE REVOLUTION

Since the Cold War began, the Truman administration had pursued a Europe-oriented foreign policy. But the collapse of the Chinese Nationalist government in 1949, after years of civil war between its forces and Communist troops, brought American Asian policy to the fore. As the Communist leader Mao Zedong established the People's Republic of China, the American people were disheartened at the loss of a favored ally. Conservative critics of the Truman administration's China policy went on the warpath.

America's China policy had been in disarray since the end of World War II. The long civil war between the Nationalists and the Communists, suspended during the war with Japan, resumed soon after the Japanese surrendered. Between 1945 and 1949, the United States had provided the Nationalist government with $2 billion in economic and military aid. In 1946, Truman had sent General George Marshall to China on a futile mission to arrange a political compromise with the warring parties. Both sides, each believing that it could win a military victory over the other, refused to share power.

In 1947, Nationalist leader Jiang Jieshi, aided by American logistical support, launched a major offensive designed to destroy his Communist foes. His armies captured the major cities of China, but in doing so, Jiang's forces spread themselves thin. The Communists controlled the countryside, which contained over 85 percent of the vast Chinese population and provided food for the cities. The Maoist armies besieged the Nationalist troops in the cities. By the summer of 1949, Nationalist forces had lost their will to fight and surrendered en masse. As 1949 ended, Jiang, with a remnant of his government, fled to the island of Formosa (Taiwan).

Washington cut itself loose from the failing Nationalist government in August 1949, a few months before Jiang fled China. A State Department White Paper insisted that the United States had done all it could for the Nationalists. The Nationalists had lost the civil war because they had not used U.S. assistance properly.

The Communist victory in China triggered an intense debate within the United States over foreign policy in general and Asian policy in particular. Bipartisanship, which had prevailed during the years of containing Communism in Europe, disintegrated as Republican leaders attacked Truman's Far Eastern policy. The Asia-first wing of the Republican Party and the China Lobby, led by Senator Styles Bridges and Congressman Walter Judd, charged the Democratic-controlled Congress and the Truman administration with responsibility for Jiang's fall. They insisted that U.S. military involvement in the Chinese civil war could have saved Jiang's government.

In reality, China was not America's to lose. If anyone could be saddled with the responsibility for losing China, it would be Jiang and his corrupt, inept government. The U.S. failure in China was not due to insufficient aid or lack of concern. American leaders never understood the dynamic force of a peasant society ripe for change and the strong appeal of the Maoist land reform program among the Chinese peasants. The mistake the Truman administration made was to continue to cling to Jiang until it was much too late.

But millions of Americans believed the charges brought by the Asia-firsters and the China Lobby. Such beliefs stemmed from a false assumption that many Americans made about U.S. foreign policy during the early Cold War era—that the rich and mighty United States could control political events around the globe if only the right leaders took the right actions. They could see no limits to American power. China had fallen to Communism, only because U.S. leaders had blundered, or worse, as McCarthy and others charged, because disloyal American officials, secretly favoring the Communist forces, had subverted America's China policy.

If the Chinese revolution could have been thwarted, it would have taken a massive and sustained U.S. military intervention. In 1949, the United States lacked the ground troops to intervene in China. Had Truman confronted Congress with the hard choices of either large-scale military intervention or Communist victory in China, it would most likely have opposed direct American involvement in an Asian civil war. But Truman tried to hide the declining status of the Nationalist regime until near the end, hence its collapse came as a sudden shock. His own actions left him vulnerable to Republican accusations that he had lost China. Containment of Communism had worked in Europe; it had failed in China. The Maoist victory in China was a devastating diplomatic defeat for the United States and a political disaster for the Truman administration.

After the Maoist victory, the United States implemented a policy of nonrecognition and clamped a trade boycott on the world's most populous nation. American officials insisted that Jiang's government, now ensconced in Formosa, constituted the legitimate government of China. Nonrecognition of mainland China would be the official U.S. policy for the next twenty years, until Richard Nixon made his famous journey to Beijing in February 1972.

VIETNAM: THE BEGINNINGS

The success of the Chinese Communist revolution also influenced U.S. foreign policy in Southeast Asia. Since 1946, the French had been trying to reimpose colonialism on the Vietnamese people. The Vietnamese refused to accept the return of their former imperial masters and waged a guerrilla war that the French could not suppress. U.S. views toward the war in Indochina had been ambivalent. Publicly, the United States took a neutral stance; the Americans did not wish to align themselves with European colonialism in Southeast Asia, and they were skeptical that the French could defeat the Vietnamese Nationalists. But since most of the Vietnamese leaders were Communists, Americans strongly opposed the idea of another country joining the Communist world. Hence Americans covertly supported the French effort in Vietnam. America also supported the French war in Vietnam, because Washington feared that a French defeat in Indochina might weaken Paris's resolve to resist Soviet expansionism in Europe. In 1949, the French made their cause in Southeast Asia more palatable to the Americans when they set up a puppet government in Saigon under the nominal leadership of Bao Dai, a descendant of the last Vietnamese royal family. Now the French could claim that they were fighting to preserve Vietnamese national independence from the threat of Communism.

The Communist victory in China had a major impact on the Indo-Chinese war. Hitherto the Vietnamese had been fighting alone against the French. Now they had a powerful friend and ally in the Chinese Communists, with whom they shared a common border. Soon Chinese economic and military aid flowed to the Viet Minh, and the war began to go badly for the French. In February 1950, China and the Soviet Union formally recognized the Vietnamese revolutionary government. Alarmed, the French appealed to the United States for help. Dean Acheson, who had become Secretary of State in 1949, succeeding Marshall, responded by formally recognizing Bao Dai's pseudo-government. In May 1950, the United States began to send economic and military aid to the French forces fighting in Vietnam. On a modest scale, the Truman administration began an American involvement in Vietnam during the summer of 1950 that would last for twenty-five years, and ultimately end in disaster for the United States and the people in Southeast Asia, whom it tried to help.

NSC-68

Truman's response to the news that the Soviets had developed atomic weapons and the fall of China directed Secretary of State Acheson to conduct a full-dress review of American foreign and military policy. Under Acheson's guidance, the review was carried out by the State and Defense Departments and coordinated by the National Security Council. Six months later, analysts produced National Security Council Document Number 68 (NSC-68), an important top-secret paper that influenced American foreign policy for the next twenty years.

Truman received NSC-68 in April 1950. It assumed continual conflict in the world between the United States and the Soviet Union. It depicted this struggle in stark terms—what was at issue was no less than the survival of America, its free institutions, and its ideals. It assumed that the Soviets would achieve the nuclear capability to destroy the United States within a few years. Hence, NSC-68 called for a massive buildup of American military force to resist the Soviet menace anywhere in the world that it might arise. It recommended defense budgets of $50 billion a year, a fourfold increase over the $13 billion appropriated for 1950. The outbreak of the Korean War would give President Truman the opportunity to implement many of the recommendations contained in NSC-68, which militarized containment and transformed it from a regional to a global policy.

WAR IN KOREA

After the fall of China, the Truman administration forged a new Asian policy. Secretary of State Acheson delineated a new defense perimeter in the Far East, incorporating Japan, Okinawa, and the Philippines. It excluded Formosa, Korea, and Southeast Asia. The new line suggested that nations located within the excluded regions would have to defend themselves against Chinese aggression, or they would have to seek help from the United Nations. Republican leaders vigorously attacked Truman's Asian policy. Senator McCarthy said it proved that the State Department was riddled with Communists and their fellow travelers.

As partisan political controversy over American Asian policy continued, the Truman administration confronted another Far Eastern crisis—North Korea's invasion of South Korea. The invasion was rooted in divisions within the country stemming from World War II. As the war ended, Soviet and American troops had occupied Korea. The two nations arranged for Soviet soldiers to accept the surrender of Japanese troops north of the thirty-eighth parallel of north latitude and for American soldiers to accept the surrender of Japanese forces south of that line. Efforts to unify Korea failed, and the nation remain divided at the thirty-eighth parallel. North of the boundary, the Soviets helped Kim Il-Sung create a Communist state and trained an army to defend it. South of the border, the United States supervised the creation of a government headed by Syngman Rhee. The Soviet Union and America removed their troops from the divided land in the late 1940s. Both Rhee and Kim Il-Sung sought to unify Korea—one under capitalism and the other under Communism.

Kim moved first. With direct assistance from the Soviets, North Korean forces invaded the South on June 25, 1950, in an effort to unify Korea under Communist control. Kim expected to win an easy victory, having calculated that the United States would not intervene. Kim had received Stalin's permission to invade South Korea, and Mao Zedong concurred. Stalin and Mao anticipated a quick victory for the North Koreans and saw the move as one that advanced their national interests.

President Truman, surprised by the invasion, hastily conferred with his advisers. He understood that if the United States did not intervene quickly, North Korea would overrun the South. He decided to send American troops to try to save South Korea from Communism. He compared Communist aggression in Korea with Fascist aggression during the 1930s, and said that if the United States let aggression go unchallenged, as the democracies had done in the 1930s, "it would mean a third world war." Truman viewed the conflict in global terms. He assumed that the Soviets had masterminded the attack, and he believed that U.S. national security and world peace were threatened. Truman also believed that the Soviets might be using the invasion as a feint to suck American troops into Korea, leaving western Europe vulnerable to Soviet attack, just at the time that NATO was being implemented. He further shared a concern about Japanese security. Conquest of South Korea would give the Communists airfields within thirty minutes flying time of Japanese cities. Finally, Truman dared not serve up the loss of Korea to the Republicans in an election year that followed so soon after the "loss" of China.

When Truman committed U.S. troops to the Korean War, he failed to seek a declaration of war from Congress. He claimed that he lacked time, and he relied on what he called his "inherent war-making powers" as commander in chief of the armed forces. But the United States did obtain UN endorsement for its Korean intervention. The Security Council approved U.S. military intervention, because the Soviet delegate was absent from its sessions. Officially, the Korean War was a United Nations' "police action" to repel aggression against South Korea. In reality, UN sanction furnished a cover for what was mainly an American effort. The United States provided 90 percent of the ground forces, and all of the sea and air power aiding the South Koreans. All battlefield commanders came from the United States. General MacArthur, whom Truman appointed to head the Korean campaign, took orders from the American Joint Chiefs of Staff.

North Korean troops overran most of South Korea, except for a small area around Pusan, a seaport at the southern tip of the peninsula. For a time, Washington feared that the defenders would be pushed into the sea. But American and South Korean forces finally halted the invaders at Pusan in August 1950. General MacArthur then dramatically turned the war around with a brilliantly executed amphibious landing at Inchon, 150 miles north of Pusan. American forces moved south from Inchon as other forces broke out at Pusan and headed north. They caught the North Koreans in a giant pincers and a rout was on. By the end of September, the UN forces had pushed the retreating North Koreans back across the thirty-eighth parallel.

Within three months, the UN mission had been accomplished. The aggressors had been cleared from South Korea. But with the North Korean army in disarray, and the USSR and China apparently not inclined to intervene, Truman decided to go north across the thirty-eighth parallel. General MacArthur enthusiastically approved. Truman's decision to cross the border transformed the Korean War. Containment became rollback, an effort to liberate North Korea from Communism. The UN forces set out to destroy a Communist satellite and to unify Korea under a pro-Western government. The Security Council obediently endorsed Truman's decision.

The UN forces drove their foes north. Meanwhile, the general U.S. military buildup, in accordance with NSC-68, continued. The draft had been reinstated. Congress doubled the Pentagon's budget, from $13 billion to $26 billion. Additional troops were earmarked for NATO. The Seventh Fleet was stationed between the Chinese mainland and Formosa to shield Jiang's forces from a possible Communist attack. The war effort enjoyed broad popular approval. The UN forces appeared headed for victory.

As the UN forces advanced northward, the Chinese issued a series of warnings. When General MacArthur ignored their warnings, the Chinese stated publicly that if UN forces continued to advance, they would intervene. On October 15, 1950, President Truman flew to Wake Island in the mid-Pacific to confer with

General MacArthur. MacArthur assured the president that the Chinese would not intervene, and if they did, they would be slaughtered. He also told Truman that he would win the Korean War and "have the boys home by Christmas." Truman accepted MacArthur's assessment and discounted the Chinese warnings. MacArthur launched what he intended to be the final Korean offensive on November 24. The UN forces advanced along two widely separated routes toward the Yalu River border with China and toward Pyongyang, the North Korean capital. Two days later, the Chinese sent more than 300,000 troops swarming across the frozen Yalu. The Chinese armies split the UN forces and sent them reeling backwards. They drove MacArthur's forces back across the thirty-eighth parallel and down the Korean peninsula.

U.S. officials, who had walked into disaster together, were now divided over how to respond to it. MacArthur wanted to expand the war and strike at China. He was supported by many Republicans and some Democrats. He believed the Chinese made the decision to invade Korea on their own. Truman and Acheson assumed the Chinese were carrying out Soviet policies. If they were correct, going to war with China meant going to war with the Soviet Union in Asia. President Truman opted for a return to the original limited UN mission of restoring the prewar status quo in Korea and for continuing the U.S. military buildup in accordance with NSC-68.

In December, the U.S. field commander in Korea, General Matthew Ridgway, brought in reinforcements and rallied the American forces. Heavy artillery slaughtered the Chinese forces, advancing in massed formations. American naval and air forces helped blunt the Chinese drive. Ridgway's Eighth Army fought its way back to a point near the thirty-eighth parallel and held that line for the rest of the war. Truce negotiations began on July 10, 1951, but they were unproductive for a long time. A seesaw war of trenches and fortified hills would continue for two more years.

During the first months of 1951, as Ridgway's troops held the line in Korea, Truman continued his implementation of NSC-68. Annual military spending reached $50 billion. America committed additional forces to NATO and obtained additional overseas bases. The Army expanded to 3.6 million men, six times its size when the Korean War began. Military aid was sent to Jiang's Nationalist forces on Formosa. The United States also began to supply military aid to French forces fighting to reimpose colonialism in Southeast Asia. Washington signed a peace treaty with Japan that ended the occupation and restored Japanese sovereignty. However, the treaty permitted the United States to maintain military bases in Japan. The Truman administration embraced the general strategy of ringing China and the Soviet Union with U.S. military might. Containment had become a global commitment and now packed potent military muscle.

The vast and rapid American military buildup did not satisfy Republican critics supporting General MacArthur's proposal to take the war to China. He did not want to hold the line at the thirty-eighth parallel and negotiate; MacArthur wanted a military victory over China and a unified, pro-Western Korea. Ordered by Tru-

Figure 9.3   **The war in Korea was the first war in U.S. history in which soldiers fought in racially integrated units. SFC Major L. Cleveland (left), of Fort Valley, Ga., weapons squad leader, points out Red positions to his machine gun crew. Gunner is Cpl. Freddie L. Howard of Los Angeles, Calif. Others are Assistant Gunner PFC George W. Marsh (right), of Covington, KY, and Ammunition Bearer PFC Herbert Blount of Marianna, Fla.** Photographer: Dept. of Defense/Acme/UPI, Corbis-Bettmann, neg. #W957493.

man to make no public statements, he defied his commander in chief. On April 5, House Republican leader Joseph Martin read a letter from MacArthur to Congress, calling for an alternative foreign policy. If victory in Asia required bombing Manchurian bases, blockading Chinese ports, and using Nationalist forces from Taiwan, so be it: "In war there is no substitute for victory." MacArthur's letter also stated: "Here in Asia is where the Communist conspirators have elected to make their play for global conquest." MacArthur rejected Truman's Europe-first orientation, his effort to achieve limited political goals in Korea, and his containment policy. He had issued a fundamental challenge to the administration's foreign policy. Truman dismissed MacArthur from his command and ordered him home. Truman's actions provoked one of the great emotional events of modern American history. The White House was swamped with letters and phone calls, mostly supporting MacArthur; polls showed that 75 percent of the people supported him.

MacArthur's Republican supporters heaped abuse upon the embattled Truman. Many newspaper and magazine editors called for his impeachment.

Much of the uproar over Truman's firing of MacArthur reflected popular disenchantment with the war. Many Americans neither understood nor accepted the concept of limited war for particular political objectives. After all, when an easy military victory appeared possible, Truman himself had tried to take all of Korea, only to revert to the original, limited objective following Chinese intervention. The president wanted to avoid a major war that he feared could escalate into World War III. But MacArthur's contempt for half measures and his stirring call for victory appealed to a nation of impatient idealists. The United States had the power to destroy North Korea and China. Why not use it?

MacArthur returned to America to a hero's welcome. About 500,000 people turned out to greet him when he arrived in San Francisco on April 16, 1951. Three days later, he addressed a joint session of Congress. His moving speech was interrupted thirty times by applause.

As MacArthur basked in public acclaim, Congress investigated the circumstances of his removal. Hearings were held before the combined Senate Armed Services Committee and Foreign Relations Committee. At first, the senators favored MacArthur, but the testimony of the Joint Chiefs, particularly of General Omar Bradley, made the case for containment in Korea forcibly and clearly: the Soviet Union, not China, was America's main enemy; Europe, not Asia, was the most important region of American interest. General Bradley stated that fighting China in Asia "would be the wrong war in the wrong place at the wrong time against the wrong enemy." There also was MacArthur's refusal to follow orders and his efforts to make foreign policy over the President's head. The constitutional principle of civilian control of foreign policy and military strategy was at stake. Truman had fired an insubordinate general. Gradually the tumult subsided, and MacArthur faded into quiet retirement.

Meanwhile, in Korea, the truce talks between the Americans on one side and the North Koreans and Chinese on the other side dragged on inconclusively, and the fighting continued. The fighting and talking would occur for two more years, and thousands more American soldiers would die. The main reason for the impasse at the talks was the Chinese insistence that captured North Korean and Chinese soldiers be returned to them, even though these soldiers wanted to remain in South Korea. The United States refused to return them against their will. An armistice was finally reached on July 27, 1953, when President Eisenhower threatened the Chinese with an expansion of the war. The Chinese yielded, and the prisoners remained in the South. The thirty-eighth parallel was restored as the boundary between North and South Korea. To appease Syngman Rhee, who was unhappy with the settlement, the United States furnished his government with military aid and kept 50,000 American troops in South Korea.

Although it has been forgotten by many Americans, Korea was a major land war in Asia. It lasted three years and involved over 3 million U.S. military personnel. Its costs exceeded $100 billion. About 54,000 Americans died in Korea, and an-

Figure 9.4   The Korean War, 1950–1953.   *Source:* Moss, *Moving On*, p. 50.

other 150,000 were wounded. Millions of Koreans and Chinese perished during the war. Korea proved to be an unpopular, frustrating, and confusing war, which ended in a draw. No celebrations greeted its end. Returning Korean veterans melted into society to became part of the 1950s "silent generation."

The Korean conflict significantly influenced U.S. foreign policy. Containment was transformed from a regional policy to a general global stance. U.S. foreign policy shifted from its Eurocentric focus toward increasing concern about the Far East. War with the People's Republic of China ensured that the United States and China would remain bitter, Cold War adversaries for decades. The image of an aggressive Soviet Union commanding a centralized, worldwide Communist movement fastened itself on the American mind. China was seen as an extension of Soviet power. Truman incorporated the defense of Formosa and French interests

Figure 9.5   General Douglas MacArthur. MacArthur (1880–1964) secured the Philippines from the Japanese in July of 1945 and accepted the Japanese surrender in September. He later commanded United Nations forces during the Korean War until his public disagreements with U.S. war policies led President Harry Truman to relieve him of his command in 1951.   *Source:* National Archives.

in Southeast Asia into the larger framework of American containment of Communism in the Far East.

The Korean War transformed the Cold War from a political and an ideological conflict into a military struggle. Prior to the war in Korea, containment primarily represented an effort to eliminate the political and economic conditions that spawned Communism. After Korea, containment consisted of setting up military frontiers behind which free societies could develop. America committed itself to maintaining a huge permanent military force in peacetime, although given the crisis atmosphere that prevailed during much of the Cold War, the traditional distinction between peace and war was blurred. The military-industrial complex expanded rapidly as a major component of the permanent war economy. Foreign aid was militarized, and the power of the presidency expanded. Although it failed to imprint itself indelibly on the national memory, the Korean War transformed the Cold War and influenced U.S. foreign policy for decades.

THE COLD WAR CONSENSUS

From war's end to the spring of 1947, the emergent Cold War between the United States and the Soviet Union shaped America's foreign policy in the postwar world. Containment of Communism evolved as the major American foreign policy response to the rise of the Cold War. Beginning as a response to perceived Soviet threats to the security of small nations in southern Europe, containment expanded to include the periphery of East and Southeast Asia in 1950, following the Maoist triumph in China, the U.S. decision to support the French in Indochina, and the outbreak of the Korean War.

As the world split between the former allies widened, most Americans came to support President Truman's "get tough" approach to the Soviet Union. Influenced by the media, Americans increasingly viewed the Soviet Union as the aggressive successor of the destroyed Third Reich. Communism was equated with

Fascism, and Stalin was seen as a Red Hitler, a despotic ruler with megalomaniacal ambitions to dominate the new postwar world order. Soviet leaders were depicted as Marxist-Leninist zealots in the service of a master plan for imposing Communism on the world. The great lesson of World War II appeared to be that aggressors could not be appeased. As the Soviet leaders came to be seen as the New Nazis in the world, American leaders vowed to contain them, to prevent aggression, and to ensure that there would be no World War III.

Some Americans dissented from Truman's new foreign policy approach. They opposed the enormous costs of rearmament and foreign aid. They disliked the new internal security controls clamped onto American life, the complexities and tensions of great power rivalries, and the domination of public life by foreign policy issues. Some idealistic Americans did not relish having to support reactionary governments just because they appeared to be threatened by Communism.

But the dramatic events of the early Cold War years—the Soviet takeover of eastern Europe, Soviet pressures on Turkey, the civil war in Greece, the Communist coup in Czechoslovakia, the Berlin Blockade, Soviet acquisition of nuclear weapons, the "Fall" of China, and the Korean War worked on the American public consciousness to create a consensus supporting the Truman administration's policy of containment of Communism. During World War II, cooperation with the Soviets had been a strategic necessity. By 1947, the world had changed dramatically. A revolution in world affairs brought about by World War II necessitated a revolution in U.S. attitudes and approaches to foreign policy. Containing the expansionist tendencies of the Soviet Union had become the new American strategic imperative.

Despite continuing criticism from both the Left and the Right, a bipartisan consensus in support of the main direction of U.S. foreign policy had emerged in this country by 1947. There was broad agreement spanning all but the fringes of the political spectrum that the major objective of American foreign policy would be the containment of Communism. The American bipartisan foreign policy consensus in support of the containment of Communism would remain intact until the Vietnam War cracked it during the late 1960s and provoked the first major debates over American foreign policy goals in nearly twenty years.

COLD WAR AT HOME

As a result of the growing hostility between the United States and the Soviet Union, frustrations, tensions, and anxieties gripped American society. The Cold War hit home in early 1950, when millions of Americans were alarmed by charges that the Communists had infiltrated their government and many other institutions. Fears of internal threats posed by the Communists long preceded the Cold War era. Following World War I, jittery Americans worried lest a Bolshevik-style uprising occur in America. The Red Scare of 1919 and 1920 had culminated in the Palmer raids and in the mass deportations of radical aliens. In 1938, Southern opponents of New

Deal agricultural policies established the House Committee on Un-American Activities (HUAC), chaired by Martin Dies. Dies and his colleagues accused New Deal farm officials of marching to Moscow's beat. In 1940, Congress enacted the Smith Act, which made it a federal crime for anyone to advocate the overthrow of the government.

Neither the Palmer raids nor HUAC's accusations of the late 1930s were justified, but fears of Communist subversion arising after 1945 had a basis in reality. During the late 1930s and early 1940s, U.S. government security procedures had been lax. Communists had infiltrated government agencies, some of whom spied for the Soviets. Unfortunately, during the Second Red Scare, opportunistic politicians exploited the popular fear of Communism to enhance their power. They vastly exaggerated the menace, harmed innocent people, divided and confused Americans, and undermined basic political freedoms.

The drive to root Communists out of government agencies began in 1945. The Office of Strategic Services (OSS), a wartime intelligence agency, discovered that some of its classified documents had been delivered to Soviet agents. The next year, a Canadian investigating commission exposed the operation of Soviet spy rings within Canada and the United States and documented subversion that had occurred during the war. These spy revelations, coming at a time when United States–Soviet relations were deteriorating, energized Washington. President Truman established a loyalty program for federal employees in March 1947. Truman also directed the attorney general to publish a list of ninety organizations that were considered disloyal to the United States. Truman's efforts resulted in 2,900 resignations and 300 dismissals from various federal agencies. Although federal investigators found no Communists and no spies, the Truman loyalty program heightened public fears of subversion.

Congress also was active. In October 1947, HUAC, with rookie Congressman Richard Nixon as its junior member, launched a sensational two-week-long investigation of Hollywood to see if the film industry had been subverted by Reds. Actor Ronald Reagan, president of the Screen Actors Guild (SAG), appeared before the committee to defend the loyalty of his industry. HUAC found little evidence of "celluloid" Communism. But in the aftermath of its investigation, the major studios blacklisted ten writers, directors, and actors who had been uncooperative witnesses during committee hearings. The studios later added others to the blacklist for alleged Communist affiliations. The blacklist spread to radio and television and eventually affected hundreds of people.

As the Cold War escalated into a tense, unrelenting, occasionally terrifying struggle, a great fear of anyone who was thought to be disloyal spread across the land. Teachers and professors were fired for expressing dissenting views. Books were removed from library shelves. Parent-Teacher Association (PTA) leaders were attacked as subversives. Liberal ministers were harassed. Ironically, those who waged the domestic Cold War in the name of national security often undermined the democratic rights and intellectual freedoms for whose sake the United States waged the Cold War against the Soviet Union. The idea that a free and an open society, tolerant of wide-ranging discussions and rigorous criticism of American institutions, might be the best defense against the spread of Communism in the United States, appeared to be an alien notion to those engaged in the quest for internal security.

The domestic Cold War also engulfed the American trade union movement. Within the ranks of the CIO, Communist Party members or individuals supportive of the Communist Party program held leadership positions in many of the affiliated unions. Often these Communist labor leaders had been skilled organizers who had helped build the CIO unions. The Communists had risen to positions of power within the ranks of labor because they were committed trade unionists, not because they belonged to the Communist Party. Most of the rank-and-file members of these Communist-led unions were either indifferent or hostile to Communism. In 1948, Philip Murray, head of the CIO, fearing his organization's vulnerability to attack by powerful anti-union forces for having Communist leaders, began to purge the CIO of its Communist influences. Within a year, eleven unions had been expelled from the CIO, and its membership fell from 5.2 million to about 3.7 million.

In 1949, the Truman administration went after the leadership of the American Communist Party. The Justice Department put the top leaders of the Party on trial for violating the Smith Act. They were convicted, and the Supreme Court upheld the verdicts. After the Court had sustained the convictions of the top leaders, the Justice Department prosecuted dozens of lesser figures within the Communist movement over the next several years.

Truman's loyalty program did not quiet popular fears of Communist subversion, nor did it prevent Republicans from exploiting the Communists-in-government issue. One event severely damaged the reputation of the Truman administration. In 1949, after the most famous political trial in American history, Alger Hiss was ostensibly convicted of perjury, but in reality, he was convicted for having been a Communist spy. Hiss, a participant in a Soviet espionage ring during the late 1930s, had risen to become an assistant secretary of state. He had been an adviser at Yalta and had chaired the founding sessions of the United Nations in San Francisco. He left the State Department in 1947 to become president of the Carnegie Endowment for International Peace. Outwardly, Hiss's public career had been that of a brilliant bureaucrat and model New Dealer.

Hiss's downfall came in 1948, when Whittaker Chambers, a confessed former courrier in the same spy ring to which Hiss had belonged, appeared before the HUAC in a closed session to accuse Hiss of having been a Communist spy while working for the State Department in 1937 and 1938. He offered no evidence to substantiate his charges. In a later HUAC session, Hiss confronted Chambers and threatened him with a libel suit if he dared to make his accusations public. Chambers appeared on the television show *Face the Nation* and repeated his charge that Hiss was a former Communist spy. Hiss denied the charge and filed his libel suit. Many prominent public figures backed Hiss and dismissed the charges against him. Among HUAC members, only Richard Nixon, who believed that Hiss was lying, initially backed Chambers's unsubstantiated charges.

To defend himself against Hiss's libel suit, Chambers produced evidence: microfilm copies of sixty-five classified State Department documents, which Chambers claimed Hiss had passed to him in 1937 and 1938 to give to Soviet agents. A federal grand jury could only indict Hiss for perjury because the statute of limitations on espionage had expired. Hiss was tried twice, his first trial having ended with a hung jury. During the second trial, the prosecution established that many of the documents had been copied in Hiss's handwriting and others had been typed on a typewriter that had belonged to Hiss at the time. Hiss was convicted and sentenced to five years in prison.

Hiss was HUAC's greatest catch and vaulted Richard Nixon into national prominence. Many liberals believed that Hiss was innocent; they believed that he had been framed by a conspiracy of vindictive conservative political forces. But the Hiss conviction, more than any other event of the domestic Cold War, convinced millions of Americans that there was truth to the oft-made Republican charges that Roosevelt and Truman had not been sufficiently alert to the dangers of Communist infiltration, subversion, and espionage. Americans worried about other undetected Communist agents who might still be working at the State Department and other government agencies.

Other events shook the Truman administration. The FBI caught Judith Coplon, a Justice Department employee, passing information to a Soviet agent. In 1949, the Soviets exploded an atomic device, ending the American nuclear monopoly. Soon after this shock came the Communist victory in China. The stage was set for the emergence of a demagogue: widespread fear of a hidden enemy thought to be everywhere, and frustration that victory in the Second World War had brought not eternal peace but Cold War and the possibility of nuclear holocaust.

Enter Senator Joseph McCarthy. In 1950, casting about for an issue that might get him reelected, decided to see if he could get any political mileage out of the Communists-in-government issue. McCarthy was by no means the only politician who practiced the politics of anti-Communism, in fact, he was something of a latecomer to the issue. But McCarthy quickly became the political star of the domestic Cold War, and he retained his top billing until his Senate colleagues destroyed him in late 1954.

McCarthy opened his anti-Communist campaign on February 9, 1950, in Wheeling, West Virginia. He told the Ladies' Republican Club of Wheeling that the United States found itself in a weak position in the Cold War because of the actions of disloyal officials in the State Department. Holding up a piece of paper in his right hand, he apparently told his fascinated audience, "I have in my hand" a list of 205 names of Communists working at the State Department. Further, he charged that some of them were in policy-making positions and their names were known to the secretary of state. A Senate committee, convened to investigate McCarthy's sensational charges, quickly demonstrated that McCarthy not only did not have 205 names, he did not have even one name. It dismissed his charges as a "fraud and a hoax." Undaunted, McCarthy then accused Owen Lattimore, a prominent expert on Far Eastern affairs, of being the leader of "the espionage ring in the State Department." McCarthy's charges against Lattimore also collapsed.

Such setbacks at the outset of his campaign might have discouraged a less nervy politician, but McCarthy persisted. He sensed that he had a vast following among a public primed by the Hiss case and frustrated by the Korean War. He kept on the offensive. He kept making unsubstantiated charges and naming names. He implied guilt by association, and he told outright lies. It was impossible to keep up with his accusations or to pin him down. He called Secretary of State Acheson the "Red Dean of the State Department." He denounced George Marshall, a man with a distinguished record of public service, as a liar and a traitor. His smear tactics and his use of the "big lie" technique added a new word to the American political lexicon—"McCarthyism."

Several factors accounted for McCarthy's spectacular success. The ground had been prepared by years of Cold War conflict with the Soviet Union, and by politicians who had dramatized the issue, frightening Americans with their accounts of the enemy within. Alarms raised by politicians were seconded by prominent media editorials. McCarthy's sense of timing, his ruthless tactics, and his ability to voice the fears of many ordinary American citizens all strengthened his cause. He made skillful use of the news media. Radio and television newscasts carried his charges. Newspapers headlined his accusations. Millions of Americans, frightened by revelations of real espionage, found McCarthy's lies plausible. McCarthy's appeal also came from his being the man with the simple explanation for America's Cold War setbacks: Traitors working within the State Department bureaucracy and other government agencies were responsible for Soviet and Chinese Cold War triumphs. When McCarthy showed popular support during the 1950 elections, his Republican colleagues encouraged him to go after the Democrats.

Events also played into McCarthy's hands. Two weeks after his Wheeling speech, British intelligence agents discovered the Anglo-American spy ring that had penetrated the atomic bomb project at New Mexico during the period 1944–1945. The key man in the ring had been a nuclear physicist, Dr. Klaus Fuchs, a German-born, naturalized British citizen assigned to the bomb project. He was arrested and confessed everything. He told the British that he had succeeded in

Figure 9.6   The preeminent practitioner of the politics of anti-Communism, Senator Joseph McCarthy of Wisconsin. For a few years during the early 1950s, this ruthless and clever demagogue was the second most powerful politician in Washington. McCarthy continued his campaigns after formal condemnation by the Senate.   *Source:* National Archives.

delivering complete information on the bomb to Soviet agents. Using information from Fuchs's confession, FBI agents arrested his American accomplices, Harry Gold and David Greenglass. They in turn implicated Julius and Ethel Rosenberg. The Rosenbergs were tried for espionage, convicted, and executed in 1953. The stalemated Korean War also aided McCarthy significantly. As American morale sagged, he attacked those whom he called "the traitors and bunglers in the State Department who were losing the Cold War to the Communists."

POSTWAR POLITICS

Harry S. Truman assumed the presidency in April 1945, ill prepared and nearly un-known. He had difficulties early in his presidency because of his inexperience and because he had inherited an administration, many of whose members viewed him as being an inferior successor to Roosevelt. They lacked confidence in him, and he did not trust them. Prominent New Dealers departed, and Truman replaced them with more conservative, sometimes mediocre, or even corrupt men. Honest and able himself, Truman tolerated cronies belonging to the "Missouri gang," led by an obese politician named Harry Vaughn.

When the war ended, Truman's first major domestic issues involved demo-bilizing the armed forces and reconverting the war economy to peacetime produc-tion. The rush to disarm after the war was irresistible. The armed forces were quickly dismantled. A force that had numbered 12 million at its peak quickly shrank to 1.5 million, and the draft was canceled.

As it demobilized its military forces, the nation also confronted the tasks of economic reconversion. Most Americans in 1945 shared a persistent fear that the American economy, no longer stimulated by war spending, would regress to mas-sive unemployment and depression. They feared that millions of suddenly re-leased war workers and veterans could not be absorbed by a peacetime economy. Worried about the economic future, New Dealers called for the federal government to assume responsibility for full employment by enhancing purchasing power and spending for public works. Congress enacted a measure in 1946 called the Em-ployment Act, which established the government's responsibility for maintaining prosperity without prescribing the means to achieve it.

The economy shrank during the first year after the war, mainly because the government abruptly canceled $35 billion in war contracts. The GDP for 1946 was slightly smaller than for 1945, the last year of the war. Unemployment, which had vanished during wartime, rose to 4.5 percent in 1946. But the widely feared rever-sion to depression never happened; most war workers and veterans were absorbed into the postwar economy. Many factors accounted for the economy's unexpected resiliency. The GI Bill provided low-interest loans to help veterans buy homes, farms, and businesses. It granted billions of dollars of educational benefits, per-mitting millions of veterans, many with families, to attend college. Tax cuts strengthened consumer purchasing power and stimulated business activity. Gov-

Figure 9.7   Harry Truman takes the oath of office on the evening of April 12, 1945, in the Cabinet Room at the White House. Swearing him into office is Chief Justice Harlan Fiske Stone. Standing between them is the new First Lady, Elizabeth "Bess" Wallace Truman. Standing behind Chief Justice Stone are, from left to right: Speaker of the House Sam Rayburn, Office of War Mobilization Director Fred Vinson, and House Minority Leader Joseph Martin.   *Source:* National Archives.

ernment also aided the business sector by transferring over $15 billion worth of government-owned plants to the private sector, adding some 20 percent to industrial capacity. Further, government spending, although much reduced from wartime levels, remained far higher than prewar levels. But the most important reason for the economy's transition from war to peacetime production without depression lay in an unforeseen powerful force. American consumers came out of the war with billions of dollars in savings and with long-frustrated desires to buy new homes, cars, and appliances. Consumer power kept factories humming and people working after the war had ended.

But unleashed consumer demand, which voided the danger of depression, ignited runaway inflation as the economy was decontrolled. By early 1946, the Office of Price Administration had removed most rationing restrictions but had kept wage, price, and rent controls. Inflation soared. Desired goods such as new cars and refrigerators remained scarce. Businessmen, farmers, and trade unionists demanded the removal of all remaining restrictions on their economic activity. A rash of strikes broke out in the auto, meat packing, electrical, and steel industries, idling productive capacity and delaying fulfillment of consumer demands. Truman tried and failed to ensure a gradual, orderly phaseout of controls by restraining all interest groups.

In the spring of 1946, the bipartisan conservative coalition controlling Congress battled the president over extending the life of the OPA. Congress enacted a weak control measure that Truman vetoed, causing all controls to expire on July 1. There followed the worst surge of inflation since 1919. Congress, deluged with angry complaints, hastily passed another, even weaker bill, which Truman signed. Prices continued to soar. Thereafter, the OPA lifted all remaining controls and faded away. The cost of living rose 20 percent in 1946 and shortages persisted.

Strikes threatened in the two primary industries—railroads and coal. Walkouts in both of these industries might have paralyzed the economy. The railroad strike was averted, but not before the president had asked Congress to grant him authority to draft striking railroad workers into the Army. John L. Lewis took his coal miners off the job in April 1946 over wage and pension fund disputes with mine owners. Industrial production dropped. Efforts to settle the strike failed. On May 21, with the nation's supplies of coal nearly exhausted, President Truman ordered the government to seize the mines. The coal mines were administered by Julius Krug, the Secretary of the Interior, who promptly began negotiations with Lewis. They reached an agreement within two weeks, and the coal strike ended. The mines were returned to their owners. Truman's bold efforts to prevent the strikes hurt him politically; he and his party lost support among resentful workers which affected the upcoming elections.

As the 1946 elections approached, Truman and his party faced serious political trouble. The Democrats split into their Northern and Southern wings, with Southern conservative Democrats often joining Northern Republicans to block liberal measures. Many liberal Democrats still yearned for Roosevelt, dismissing Truman as an inept successor. Truman and his party were damned both for shortages and skyrocketing prices. Organized labor, sullen over Truman's threat to draft strikers, made only token efforts to support the Democrats.

Republican congressional candidates attacked the failures of the price control program. When beef disappeared from meat markets, housewives rioted. When it was back on the shelves a week later, they were shocked to discover that prices had doubled. On the eve of the elections, polls showed that Truman's popularity had dropped to 32 percent. The election results mirrored the popular mood. Republicans won majorities in both houses of Congress for the first time since before the Great Depression. Many working-class voters deserted the Democrats, shattering the labor bloc that had been solidly Democratic since 1932.

THE 80TH CONGRESS

Many new faces appeared in Washington as members of the 80th Congress. They were young war veterans, representing a new generation of politicians who had come of age. One congressional rookie, Republican Richard Nixon, hailed from southern California. Another, Democrat John F. Kennedy, represented a working-class district of the south side of Boston. To the Senate came a conservative Republican from Wisconsin, Joseph McCarthy.

The Republicans took charge of the new Congress. So long out of power, the GOP set out to reassert the authority of Congress and to trim the executive branch. They proposed the Twenty-second Amendment, which limited future presidents to two elected terms. They wanted to ensure that there would be no more presidential reigns such as Franklin Roosevelt's. The 80th Congress tore to shreds Truman's liberal domestic program to extend the welfare state. It rejected all of his important proposals. Although it did not abolish basic New Deal programs, the 80th Congress certainly trimmed its edges.

Senator Robert Taft of Ohio, son of a former president, spearheaded the Republican assault on the New Deal. Taft, who had been in the Senate since 1938, hoped to create a record that would vault him into the White House one day. He believed that the voters had given the Republicans a mandate to eradicate the New Deal. He said that most Americans wanted lower taxes, less governmental interference in business, and especially curbs on the power of organized labor. Twice in 1947 Congress enacted tax cuts. Truman vetoed both measures. A third tax cut was passed over his veto in 1948.

Figure 9.8   Class of 1946: A group of freshman Congressmen introduce themselves in January 1947. Standing to the right rear of this gathering of rookies are two future presidents, John F. Kennedy and Richard M. Nixon. *Source:* National Archives.

In 1947, Taft led the fight to enact a measure, passed over Truman's veto, modifying the National Labor Relations Act (Wagner Act), the nation's basic labor law and centerpiece of the Second New Deal. The new law, the Labor Management Relations Act, popularly called the Taft-Hartley Act, made many changes in the Wagner Act. It extended the concept of "unfair labor practices," previously confined to management, to unions. Among forbidden union practices were the closed shop, which mandated that a worker join a union before working. The act required unions to file annual financial statements with the Department of Labor. Cold war concerns could be seen in the requirement that all union officials file affidavits, showing that they were not members of the Communist Party or any other subversive organization. The act also prohibited union contributions to national political campaigns, and it forbade strikes by federal employees. In cases of strikes that "affected the national welfare," the Taft-Hartley Act empowered the attorney general to seek a court injunction ordering an eighty-day delay in the strike. During this eighty-day "cooling-off period," federal mediators would try to settle the conflict. If, after eighty days, union members rejected the mediator's final offer, the strike could occur. One section of the new law, Section 14(b), permitted states to legalize the open shop, making union membership voluntary.

Organized labor vigorously attacked the Taft-Hartley Act. William Green, head of the AFL, charged that the bill was forged "in a spirit of vindictiveness against unions." President Truman claimed that it was both unworkable and unfair. In addition to general denunciations, labor leaders attacked particular provisions of the new law, such as the mandatory eighty-day strike delay feature. Repeal of the new law became the major political goal for organized labor.

The Taft-Hartley Act was the most important social legislation enacted during Truman's presidency. It did not undermine the basic strength of American trade unions, which conservatives hoped and liberals feared might happen. The Communist registration requirement was nullified by the Supreme Court. Union membership increased from 14 million at the time of passage to 16 million five years later. During the 1950s, collective bargaining between teams of labor and management representatives generated wage increases and improved fringe benefits that made American industrial workers members of the most affluent working class in history.

THE ELECTION OF 1948

As the 1948 election approached, Truman appeared to have no chance. At times he was discouraged by his inability to lead the country as well as his low ratings in the polls. In the fall of 1947, he even sent a member of his staff to talk to General Eisenhower, then Army Chief of Staff, to see if Ike might be interested in the Democratic nomination for 1948. Eisenhower was not. Truman then decided to seek reelection. At the Democratic Convention, held in Philadelphia in July, delegates, convinced that Truman could not win, tried to promote a boom for Eisenhower—it fizzled.

To add to his woes, Truman's party was fragmenting. Splinter groups formed on the Left and on the Right. At the Convention, Northern liberals forced the adoption of a strong civil rights plank over the furious objections of Southern leaders. When it was adopted by a floor vote after a raucous debate, delegates from Mississippi and Alabama marched out in protest. These renegade Southerners later formed their own party, the States' Rights, or "Dixiecrat" party. At their convention, delegates from thirteen states nominated South Carolina Governor J. Strom Thurmond, as their candidate for president. These Southern defections appeared to remove any remaining Democratic hopes for success. The Solid South, a Democratic stronghold since the end of Reconstruction, had vanished.

The liberal wing of the Democratic Party also threatened to split off. Back in 1946, Truman had fired his Secretary of Commerce Henry Wallace for publicly criticizing his "get tough" foreign policy toward the Soviet Union. In 1948, Wallace became the presidential candidate of a Leftist third party, the Progressive Party. Many New Dealers considered Wallace, whom Truman had replaced as Roosevelt's vice president in 1944, the true heir to the Roosevelt legacy, and they supported his candidacy. Polls taken that summer showed that Wallace could cost Truman several Northern industrial states. It appeared that the remnants of his party had given Truman a worthless nomination. But the gutsy leader told the assembled Democrats, "I will win this election and make those Republicans like it—don't you forget that." Few believed him at the time.

The confident Republicans, eager to regain the White House after a sixteen-year Democratic hold on the presidency, again nominated New York Governor Thomas E. Dewey and adopted a moderate program. Dewey, soundly beaten by Roosevelt in 1944, was determined to avenge that defeat this time around. All polls showed him running far ahead of Truman. Dewey opted for a safe, restrained strategy to carry him to the executive office. He raised no controversial issues, and he never mentioned his opponent by name.

Truman devised an electoral strategy he believed could win. He would stress his adherence to the New Deal tradition by advocating an advanced program of liberal reform. As soon as he got the nomination, he called the 80th Congress into a special session and reintroduced all of his reform programs that Congress had failed to pass in regular sessions. Again, Congress rejected them. This bold move set the tone for the campaign.

Truman took off on a transcontinental train tour in search of an electorate. He traveled over 32,000 miles and made hundreds of speeches, talking directly to about 12 million people. He repeatedly blasted what he called the "do nothing, good for nothing" 80th Congress, blaming all of the ills of the nation on the Republican-controlled legislature. He called the Republicans "gluttons of privilege" who would destroy the New Deal if elected. He evoked dire images from the Great Depression and depicted Dewey as Hoover reborn. He insisted that a Republican administration would bring back the grim days of depression. Speaking in an aggressive, choppy style, he delighted his crowds. "Give 'em hell, Harry!" they would yell. "I'm doin' it!" Truman would yell back. Despite his strenuous campaign, he apparently faced certain defeat. Two weeks before the election, fifty political experts unanimously predicted that Dewey would win. Pollsters stopped interviewing a week before the election, assuming that Dewey already had it wrapped up.

On election day, Truman scored the biggest upset in American political history. He beat Dewey in the popular vote, 24.2 million to 22 million, and 303 to 189 in the electoral college. His party also regained control of Congress with a 54 to 42 margin in the Senate and a whopping 263 to 171 margin in the House. Wallace's campaign fizzled. Most liberals ended up voting for Truman. The Dixiecrats carried only four Deep South states. In reality, a trend toward Truman had surfaced in the final week of the campaign, but the pollsters missed it since they had already quit taking opinion samples.

How could Truman score such a surprising victory and confound all of the experts? Republican overconfidence helped. Many Republicans, assuming victory, did not bother to vote. Truman's spirited, grassroots campaign effort was a factor. But he mainly won because he was able to hold together enough of the old New Deal coalition of labor, Northern liberals, blacks, and farmers to win. Truman successfully pinned an anti-New Deal label on the Republicans and identified them with depression memories. The splits within his party worked to his advantage. It sheared off the Democratic Left and Right, and it allowed Truman to concentrate on the political center, where most of the votes were.

Figure 9.9   How sweet it was! A jubilant Harry Truman holds up a Republican paper whose prediction of victory for Thomas Dewey was, to say the least, a bit premature.   *Source:* St. Louis Mercantile Library. Used with permission.

THE FAIR DEAL

Now president in his own right, Truman moved to expand the New Deal as he had promised during his campaign. In the fall of 1945, Truman had sent an ambitious package of legislative proposals to Congress, only to see them shunted aside during the political scrambling over decontrol and inflation. His January 1949 program began, ". . . every individual has the right to expect from our government a fair deal." The Fair Deal included controlling prices, improving civil rights, expanding public housing, raising the minimum wage, expanding Social Security, repealing the Taft-Hartley law, supporting farm prices, providing federal aid to education, and implementing national health insurance.

The 81st Congress enacted only a small portion of the Fair Deal. It raised the minimum wage and extended Social Security to 10 million additional workers, increasing benefits by 77 percent. The most important Fair Deal measure to pass in 1949 was the National Housing Act. It provided funds for slum clearance and for the construction of 810,000 units of low-income housing over a period of six years. Most of the Fair Deal never cleared Congress. Truman's civil rights proposals were thwarted by the threat of a Southern filibuster. Federal aid to education was opposed by the Catholic Church for not including funds for parochial schools. Truman's controversial proposal for compulsory health insurance provoked opposition from the American Medical Association (AMA), a powerful doctors' lobby that blocked what it called "socialized medicine."

Most of the measures that passed only extended existing programs. Truman's efforts to expand the boundaries of the welfare state were defeated by a combination of lobbyists, the congressional conservative coalition, and public opinion, which had drifted toward the center. By 1950, the Fair Deal had lost momentum, submerged by Cold War concerns and growing complacency about domestic institutions. Truman, after an initial push for his program, retreated. He spent the rest of his presidency on foreign policy and on defending his administration against mounting Republican attacks.

CIVIL RIGHTS

After the war, Americans wanted to recreate the prosperity of the Roaring Twenties, the prosperity they remembered before the long interludes of depression and war. But postwar economic dislocations, particularly rampant inflation and shortages of consumer goods, delayed achieving the goal of affluence. By the late 1940s, middle-class Americans enjoyed the benefits of the most productive economy the world had ever seen. Disadvantaged groups had begun their long, slow struggle to achieve their fair share of the American dream as well.

African Americans continued their struggle against discrimination, which had gained momentum during the war. The NAACP pushed court cases that chipped away at the judicial foundations of segregation. Starting in 1947, the Justice Department began to submit friends-of-the-court briefs on behalf of civil rights cases involving public schools and housing. A dramatic breakthrough occurred in 1947, when Branch Rickey, the general manager of the Brooklyn Dodgers, broke the color line of major league baseball by adding a gifted black athlete, Jackie Robinson, to his team's roster. Robinson quickly became an all-star player and future Hall-of-Famer on a team that won six National League pennants in the next ten years. His success paved the way for other gifted African American athletes, who were previously confined to segregated black leagues, to play major league baseball.

The Cold War brought additional pressure for integrating African Americans and other nonwhite minorities into the mainstream of American life. The United States was now seeking the support of African and Asian nations whose leaders resented American mistreatment of its racial minorities. Jim Crow laws also made the United States vulnerable to Soviet propaganda that sought to highlight the inequities of American democracy and win influence among Afro-Asian peoples.

Truman was the first modern president to promote civil rights causes. His involvement came from both moral and political considerations. He felt a strong need for justice for African Americans. He also was aware of the growing importance of the black vote in Northern cities, and he wanted to offset efforts by Republicans to regain African American support that they had enjoyed before the Great Depression. Truman had supported the creation of the Fair Employment Practices Commission (FEPC) in 1941, and he wanted to extend it after the war, but Congress refused to renew it. In December 1946, President Truman established a Committee on Civil Rights to draft a program. In February 1948, Truman sent Congress the first civil rights message since Reconstruction, calling for the enactment of a federal anti-lynching law, the creation of a permanent FEPC, the abolition of segregation in interstate commerce, and federal protection of voting rights. Congress rejected all of Truman's civil rights proposals.

Truman acted where he had the power to do so. He issued an executive order in February 1948, barring discrimination in government bureaucracies. He also began the desegregation of the armed forces. Progress was slow at first in desegregating the military. Segregation persisted in the Army until the Korean War. Integration of the Army occurred during that conflict. Army officers discovered that African American soldiers fought more effectively in integrated units than in segregated ones. It was Truman's most important civil rights victory. Within a few years, the U.S. Army became the most integrated American institution, and many African Americans found opportunities in the military during the 1950s and 1960s that were not available to them in civilian life. Truman played a major role in bringing civil rights issues to the center of the American political stage. It was his greatest domestic political achievement.

IMPORTANT EVENTS

1945	Harry Truman becomes president
	The United Nations is founded in San Francisco
	Two atomic bombs are dropped on Japanese cities
	World War II ends
1946	The Nuremburg war crimes trials begin
	The Atomic Energy Commission is created
1947	The Truman Doctrine is announced
	Major League baseball is desegregated
	The HUAC investigates Hollywood
	The Marshall Plan for European recovery is inaugurated
	The National Security Act is enacted
	The Taft-Hartley Act is enacted
1948	The Berlin Blockade is established
	Truman orders the armed services desegregated
	Truman is elected
1949	NATO is created
	The Soviets explode an atomic device
	The Chinese revolution succeeds
	Alger Hiss is convicted of perjury
1950	Truman orders work to begin on the hydrogen bomb
	Senator Joseph McCarthy launches his anti-Communist campaign
	The Korean War begins
	NSC-68 is implemented
1951	Truman dismisses General MacArthur from his command

BIBLIOGRAPHY

Dean Acheson's *Present at the Creation* is a superb account of the origins of the Cold War by a former high official in the State Department who was one of the principal architects of U.S. Cold War foreign policy. Stephen Ambrose, in *Rise to Globalism: American Foreign Policy, 1938–1980,* offers an excellent account of the origins of the Cold War. Another good study is by John L. Gaddis, *The United States and the Origins of the Cold War.* Gaddis, America's most imminent diplomatic historian, has recently written an important new study of the origins of the Cold War, *Now We Know: Rethinking Cold War History.* The book, based on materials recently found in Soviet archives, makes a convincing case that Stalin is primarily responsible for provoking the Cold War. Walter LaFeber's *America, Russia, and the Cold War* is a classic account of the Cold War conflict between the United States and the Soviet Union. A fine recent interpretive study of the Cold War is by Thomas J. McCormick, *America's Half-Century: United States Foreign Policy in the Cold War.* Thomas Parrish, in *Berlin in the Balance, 1945–1949: The Blockade, the Airlift, the First Major Battle of the Cold War* presents an excellent recent study of the first major confrontation of the Cold War. John Gimbel's *The Origins of the Marshall Plan* and R. E. Osgood's *NATO, Entangling Alliance* are two important studies of major American postwar foreign policy initiatives in Europe. Akira Iriye's *The Cold War in Asia* is the best account of this important dimension of the Cold War. The best short history of the Korean War is Burton I. Kaufman's *The Korean War*. Robert H. Ferrell, in *Harry S. Truman and the Modern Presidency,* offers a recent short biography of the American leader who presided over the rise of the Cold War. Alonzo L. Hamby's *Beyond the New Deal: Harry S. Truman and American Liberalism* is an account of Truman's Fair Deal programs and their underlying political philosophy. Two good studies of Senator Joseph McCarthy are by Richard Rovere, *Senator Joe McCarthy,* and Robert Griffith, *The Politics of Fear*. Allen Weinstein's *Perjury: The Hiss-Chambers Case* is a brilliant study that argues persuasively that Hiss was a secret member of the Communist Party and a spy. Stephen J. Whitfield's *The Culture of the Cold War* recreates the atmosphere of the 1950s, when the fear of Communism pervaded American culture.

10

The Age of Consensus

D URING the middle of the twentieth century, a majority of American families enthusiastically participated in a culture of abundance and leisure. The world's most productive economy generated a cornucopia of consumer goods that crowded the shelves and display racks of supermarkets and department stores everywhere. Millions of working-class families owned these twin symbols of American affluence—a home in the suburbs and a gleaming new automobile.

In the larger world, the Cold War conflict between the United States and the Soviet Union raged unrelentingly throughout the 1950s. During this decade, the focus of the U.S.–Soviet rivalry shifted to the Third World, those nations of Africa and Asia emerging from long periods of colonial domination by fading European imperial powers. At home, a bipartisan consensus spanning the American political spectrum supported the American global commitment to contain Communism. The domestic Cold War climaxed in 1954 when the Eisenhower administration combined with the Senate leadership to destroy the power of the preeminent Red-hunter in Washington, Senator Joseph McCarthy.

At home, critics took a closer look at the affluent society and discovered base metal beneath the glittering surface. Millions of American families were mired in poverty amidst plenty. Many young people were growing up alienated and rebellious. Millions of middle-class Americans, many with all of the outward trappings of affluence, found achieving their versions of the American dream insufficient. Some of these anxious souls sought comfort and meaning in religion; some sought escape in popular music, sports, alcohol, and a frenetic social life. Others continued to live lives of quiet desperation. For many Americans in the 1950s, the age of affluence also was an age of anxiety.

DEMOGRAPHIC PATTERNS

The postwar "baby boom" caused a tremendous surge in population as returning veterans and their wives made up for lost time. The American population grew from 153 million in 1950 to 179 million in 1960, the largest decennial increase ever. In 1957, 4.3 million births were recorded, the highest one-year total in American history. That year, demographers discovered that over 50,000,000 Americans were age fourteen or younger. These young baby boomers created powerful demands for new houses, station wagons, appliances, toys, and diapers. During the decade of the 1950s, the number of youngsters enrolled in schools from grades K–12 increased from 28 million to 42 million. More new schools were constructed during the 1950s, mostly in the burgeoning suburban communities surrounding central cities, than had been built during the first fifty years of the twentieth century. As the U.S. birthrate shot up, the death rate fell. Americans added five years to their life expectancy during the 1950s. Death rates among young people declined dramatically during this decade, and new "miracle drugs" such as penicillin and cortisone took much of the misery out of life. In addition, polio vaccines tamed a cruel childhood disease that often had left its victims crippled and helpless for life.

Suburban growth exploded during the 1950s. Millions of families moved from metropolitan centers to outlying communities. By the end of the decade, the suburban population of 60,000,000 equaled that of the rest of urban America. During the 1950s, most large cities within the United States lost population.

Americans in the 1950s were not only the richest and healthiest generation ever, they were also the most mobile. The American population continued its shift west and south. By the millions, people poured into the South, the Southwest, and the West. California, Florida, and Texas added millions of new residents. Americans moved in search of better jobs and business opportunities and the more spacious lifestyles that were possible in Sunbelt suburbs. The economic foundations of the Sunbelt's spectacular population boom included agribusiness, aerospace, electronics, oil, real estate, and a large infusion of military spending. Low taxes and right-to-work laws also attracted industry to the Southern rim. While the culture of mobility flourished during the decade, rural America continued to lose population.

AN ECONOMY OF ABUNDANCE

War spending restored American prosperity in the early 1940s, ending a decade of depression and beginning an era of sustained economic expansion and rising living standards that reached into the 1970s. Between 1945 and 1960, the Gross Domestic Product (GDP) doubled. During the 1950s, the American economy grew at an average rate of 4 percent per year. Between 1946 and 1960, the American workforce grew from 54 million to 68 million jobholders. Median wages in manufacturing industries rose 60 percent, and median family income rose from $3,000 to $5,700 during that same period. Since the rate of inflation remained low, wage increases translated into significant gains in purchasing power and rising standards of living. Unemployment rates remained low, averaging around 4 percent in the 1950s. During the 1950s, the United States, with about 5 percent of the world's population, consumed over one-third of its goods and services.

Credit significantly enhanced consumer purchasing power. Short-term installment credit, mainly for new cars, increased fivefold from 1946 to 1960. A revolution in spending patterns got underway in 1950 when the Diners' Club introduced the general credit card, followed soon by the American Express card. During the decade, oil companies and department stores issued millions of revolving credit cards. Private debt within the affluent society climbed from $73 billion to $200 billion in the 1950s. Consumer demand stimulated huge private sector investment in new plant capacity and new technology, an average of $10 billion a year.

Big business grew bigger during the postwar era. Another wave of mergers swept the industrial economy. By 1960, America's 200 largest industrial corporations owned over half of the nation's industrial assets. But unlike the merger waves of the 1890s and 1920s, which joined businesses within the same economic sectors, the 1950s' mergers brought together businesses in unrelated fields. Conglomerates like International Telephone and Telegraph (ITT) combined a car rental company, a home construction company, a retail food outlet, a hotel chain, and an insurance company under the same corporate roof.

THE CAR CULTURE

The manufacture of automobiles remained the most important American industry during the 1950s. New car and truck sales averaged 7,000,000 units annually during the decade. By 1960, there were 70,000,000 vehicles on the nation's roads and highways. Two-thirds of the nation's employees commuted to work by car. The number of service stations, garages, and motels all increased.

The growth of suburbia and the automobile boom occurred together. Suburbia required automobiles. Mothers driving station wagons piled full of kids on their way to school, to shopping centers, or to team practice became the reigning symbol of the 1950s' suburban lifestyle. In the late 1950s, the federal government undertook a project to build an interstate highway system funded mainly by gasoline taxes. Summer traveling vacations became the great American pastime. The huge highway building project also included the construction of thousands of miles of freeways, which connected the new suburbs to the central cities. Government road-building amounted to a subsidy for the American car culture that promoted suburban growth and urban decay.

As the number of cars on the road multiplied, cars became longer, wider, more powerful, and gaudier. Detroit reached its pinnacle in the late 1950s. Automakers outdid themselves creating chromium ornaments, two- and three-tone color combinations, soaring tail fins, and gas-guzzling V-8 engines. The buying public was delighted with Detroit's offerings, which also included wrap-around

Figure 10.1   A big gleaming new car was one of the supreme status symbols of the affluent society. Here a 1954 Buick Super Riviera shines in all of its glory.   *Source:* National Archives.

windshields, power steering, automatic transmissions, air conditioning, and hi-fi radios. Advertisers stressed the power, the flashiness, and even the sex appeal of these elaborate machines. Popular entertainers such as Dinah Shore appeared on television to sing, "See the U.S.A. in your Chevrolet." Advertisers linked owning a new car with participating in the very essence of what it meant to be a successful American: What was more American than apple pie, mom, and your new Ford or Chevrolet? Domestic automakers had the American market all to themselves; imports accounted for less than 1 percent of sales in 1955. Gas was cheap and plentiful at 25 cents to 30 cents a gallon. A big gleaming new car was the preeminent status symbol of the affluent society, a shining testament to America's technological world supremacy.

GROWTH INDUSTRIES AND OTHERS

The chemical industry grew even faster than the auto business during the 1950s. Du Pont's slogan, "Better things for better living through chemistry," became known to every television viewer. Du Pont, Dow, and other corporate giants spewed forth a never-ending feast of new synthetic products—aerosol spray cans, dacron, and new plastics like vinyl and teflon.

Electricity and electronics also grew rapidly in the postwar era. A horde of new electric appliances sprang forth—air conditioners, electric blankets, automatic clothes washers, clothes dryers, and hair dryers. The electronics industry expanded mainly because of the advent of television. By the early 1950s, dealers were selling 6 million new TV sets each year. Other popular electronics products enjoyed wide sales during the 1950s. Most of the nearly 60 million new cars sold in the decade had a radio. Transistors made possible the development of new computer technologies. International Business Machines (IBM) marketed its first mainframe computers, inaugurating the postindustrial age. In 1960, the Xerox Corporation marketed its 914 copier, thereby inaugurating a revolution in document copying. The aerospace industry kept pace with other growth industries, stimulated by multibillion dollar contracts to supply the Pentagon with sophisticated military hardware. Air travel increased rapidly after 1945 and took a quantum leap forward in 1958 with the introduction of regularly scheduled commercial jet travel.

Although postwar growth industries flourished, some traditional heavy industries and manufacturing declined, such as railroads, coal mining, and textiles. Long-haul trucking and air travel cut heavily into the railroad freight and passenger business. Coal could no longer compete with oil, natural gas, and electricity. Cotton and woolen manufacturers succumbed to synthetic fibers spun out by the chemical companies. Americans increasingly wore clothes made of nylon, orlon, and polyester. Industrial decline brought permanent depression to New England mill towns and Appalachia, creating pockets of poverty amidst general affluence.

Agriculture changed drastically in the postwar years. Farmers produced more foodstuffs than consumers could buy; commodity prices dropped. Profits could be made in farming only by reducing the unit costs of production through intensive use of fertilizers, pesticides, expensive farm machinery, and sophisticated managerial techniques. Larger farms prospered from a combination of greater efficiency and government subsidies. Small farmers got squeezed out and joined the rural exodus to the cities. The nation's farm population dropped from 25 million at the end of the war to 14 million in 1960. The number of agricultural workers dropped to just 6 percent of the workforce. In regions of Arizona, Florida, and California, huge corporate farms dominated many agricultural sectors. "Agribusiness" replaced the family farm.

THE MIXED ECONOMY

The federal government stimulated economic growth during the 1950s in many ways. Washington dispensed billions of dollars annually as welfare payments, Social Security checks, and farm subsidies. Congress funded over half of the nation's industrial research and development, and over half of all university scientific research. The Federal Reserve Board regulated the money supply and interest rates. Other government bureaucracies regulated the securities industry, interstate transportation, aviation, and communications. During the 1950s, military spending pumped $40 billion to $50 billion a year into the economy. During the 1950s, government spending as a percentage of the GDP increased steadily. The number of Americans working for government at all levels increased by 50 percent during the decade. The prosperity of many locales became dependent on government purchases or government payrolls.

Americans at mid-century celebrated what they were fond of calling the American free enterprise system. But economic reality was more complex and ambiguous than their simplistic rhetorical labels implied. Out of their efforts to battle the Great Depression and produce the materials needed to win World War II, Americans had fashioned a mixed economy that blended public and private enterprise. Government spending and regulatory activities had become integral elements of the mixed economy. The mixed economy conformed to no economic model or theory. Most Americans did not understand how it worked, but they were delighted with its prime creation—the culture of abundance.

LABOR AT MID-CENTURY

Organized labor prospered during the 1950s as trade unions won wage increases and new fringe benefits from corporate employers. The United Auto Workers and General Motors agreed to a clause in their contracts calling for automatic annual cost-of-living adjustments in wages. That agreement set a pattern soon copied in other industries and occupations. Corporate managers discovered that it was more profitable to negotiate wage increases with union representatives and then pass their increased labor costs on to consumers in the form of higher product prices than to engage in lengthy strikes with strong unions. Organized labor remained a powerful force within the Democratic Party, which normally controlled Congress during the 1950s. Labor's major achievement during the decade came with the merger of the AFL and the CIO in 1955. The creation of the AFL–CIO brought 90 percent of America's 18 million unionists into a single national labor federation, headed by George Meany.

Labor also faced serious problems during the era. Corruption riddled several unions. Senator John McClellan of Arkansas chaired a Senate committee that investigated union racketeering in 1957. The McClellan committee exposed widespread corruption in the Teamster's Union. Robert "Bobby" Kennedy served as chief counsel for the committee and his brother, Senator John F. "Jack" Kennedy, also served on the committee. The committee found that Teamster officials had involved themselves in a wide range of crooked activities, including the misappropriation of union funds, rigged elections, extortion, and association with members of organized crime. Committee investigations led to the enactment of the Landrum-Griffin Act in 1959. This mild labor reform measure expanded the list of union unfair labor practices. It also contained anticorruption provisions to safeguard democratic election procedures within unions and to make the misuse of union funds a federal crime.

Trade unions also confronted a more fundamental problem than racketeering during the late 1950s. Union membership peaked in 1956 at 18.6 million and declined thereafter. The American economy continued to grow and prosper after 1958, but organized labor could not keep pace. Many industries moved to the South to take advantage of lower wage levels and nonunion workers. But even where unions remained strong, workers were less inclined to join unions than before, primarily because, without joining, they received the higher wages and benefits that union negotiators had obtained. Most important, the economy was shifting from a production-oriented to a service-oriented one, which meant a shift from blue-collar occupations to white-collar jobs. White-collar workers generally resisted the efforts of union organizers in the 1950s. As white-collar jobs multiplied in the growth sectors of the economy, technological innovations eliminated jobs in mining, manufacturing, and transportation.

POVERTY AMIDST PLENTY

During the 1950s, millions of American families lived outside of the boundaries of abundance. In 1960, according to the Bureau of Labor Statistics, about 40 million Americans, representing 25 percent of the population, were poor. The elderly, people over age sixty-five, made up one-fourth of the poor. One-fifth were nonwhite, including 45 percent of the black population. Two-thirds of the poor inhabited households headed by a person with an eighth-grade education or less. One-fourth of poor people lived in a household headed by a single woman. The poor congregated in the inner cities, as middle-class people moved to suburbia. Between 1945 and 1960, over 3 million black people, most of them unskilled and many of them illiterate, moved to Northern and Western cities from the rural South. Poor whites from Appalachia joined blacks in this migration from the country to the cities. Many poor people also inhabited rural America in the 1950s. White and black tenant farmers and sharecroppers were mired in a life cycle of poverty and hard work.

Some of the poverty in mid-century America could be attributed to the failure of the welfare state forged during the New Deal era to provide for poor people. Its benefits had gone to groups that were organized to pressure Congress. The Wagner Act did nothing for nonunion workers. Minimum wage laws and Social Security benefits did not extend to the millions of low-income workers who were employed in dozens of occupations.

Women comprised a large percentage of poor Americans at mid-century. Few well-paying jobs were open to them in the 1950s. A greater portion of women's than men's jobs was not covered by minimum wage or Social Security protection. Also, divorced women usually were saddled with major child-rearing responsibilities. Ex-husbands often failed to make child support payments, and many divorced women with children slipped into poverty.

Few officials showed any interest in the plight of poor Americans during the 1950s. Publicists focused on celebrating the achievements of the affluent majority. The poor themselves were silent. They lacked the organization and the leaders to call attention to their problems. They inhabited another America, neglected and suffering in silence, beyond the boundaries of affluence.

THE RISE OF SUBURBIA

America experienced the greatest internal population movement in its history in the fifteen years following World War II, when 40 million Americans fled the cities for the suburbs. Young, well-educated, white, middle-class people led the flight to the suburbs. Families fled traffic jams, high taxes, contact with racial minorities, overcrowded schools, high real estate prices, and high crime rates. Suburbia beckoned for many reasons: the obvious attraction of open country, where spacious houses could be built for a fraction of what big-city construction would cost; the lure of homes with yards where, as one father put it, a kid could "grow up with grass stains on his pants." Suburban homes also promised the privacy and quietness not found in crowded city apartments. Many suburbanites sought a community of like-minded people and accessible local government.

The rapid rise of suburbia in the postwar era occurred because of an alliance between the central government and the private sector. Low-interest mortgages requiring little or no down payment and tax subsidies produced a postwar housing boom. A burst of federally funded highway construction connected the central cities to surrounding bedroom communities.

During the 1950s, contractors built an average of 2 million new homes a year. Across the country, developers busily tossed up new housing tracts, replacing forests, bean fields, fruit orchards, and grazing lands. By 1960, over 60 percent of American families owned their homes, the most significant accomplishment of the affluent society. Businesses also moved to the suburbs in response to the growing demands of suburbanites. Suburban shopping centers multiplied; by 1960, there were 3,840 such centers sprawled across the nation, transforming shopping patterns throughout the nation.

Some suburban developments sprung up virtually overnight. Using mass-production and merchandising techniques, William Levitt built Levittown on Long Island, thirty miles east of New York. Between 1947 and 1951, Levitt built 17,000 homes, along with seven village greens and shopping centers, fourteen playgrounds, nine swimming pools, two bowling alleys, and a town hall—on land where farmers had only recently grown potatoes. Other Levittowns soon appeared in Bucks County, Pennsylvania, and Willingboro, New Jersey.

The Levittowns were immediate successes; tens of thousands of young families, many of them headed by veterans, left their urban neighborhoods and joined the rush to the suburbs. But social critics made Levittown stand as a metaphor for the postwar failings of American suburban society. They condemned Levittown for its uniform houses lined up on uniform roads in a treeless communal waste. According to critic Lewis Mumford, Levittown homes represented a culture of ticky-tacky. They were inhabited by people of the same class, the same income, and the same age group, watching the same fare on television and eating the same tasteless, prefabricated foods from the same home freezers. Both inwardly and outwardly, in every aspect of their lives, the denizens of Levittown conformed to a common mold.

Figure 10.2   Levittown, Long Island, New York, U.S.A., during the 1950s.
Source: National Archives.

Mumford's elitist indictment was not so much incorrect as beside the point. Levittown appealed to the mass of ordinary American families precisely because it was safe and reassuring as well as affordable. Although suburbs tended to be internally homogeneous, they were typically differentiated along social and economic lines. Suburbs were identified as working class, middle class, or enclaves of upper-middle-class families. Analysts of suburban culture observed that ethnic identities attenuated in suburbia; in that sense, suburbs tended to make people more homogeneous. Suburban community identities were based more on shared styles of consumerism than on ethnic ancestry or culture.

While ethnicity declined in mid-century America, suburbanization separated Americans racially. Most African American and Hispanic families were left behind in big cities as white families headed for the suburbs. The developer of the famed Levittown initially put a whites-only clause in both his lease and his sales contracts. The national metropolitan pattern became one of predominantly black cities encircled within white suburbs. The 1960 census showed suburbia to be 98 percent white; it also showed that some of the nation's larger cities—Washington, D.C., Newark, Richmond, and Atlanta—had black majorities. As the white middle classes moved out, the central cities declined. Urban tax bases shrank, social services shriveled, and crime rates soared.

THE CULTURE OF AFFLUENCE

A vast increase in the size of the middle classes was the most important character-istic of the affluent society. The postwar class structure resembled a diamond in-stead of a pyramid, with the bulge of the diamond representing the 60 percent of the population that had joined the middle classes. A large increase in college en-rollments accompanied the growth in the number of middle-class households. As the 1950s ended, nearly 4 million young people were enrolled at more than 2,000 colleges and universities across the land. College campuses were quiet, business-like places during the 1950s. Most students shunned politics, radicalism of any kind, and intellectual adventure.

American teenagers often set popular cultural trends during the 1950s. A teen culture flourished that had money to spend and clear consumer preferences. Mer-chandisers responded synergistically to these teenaged consumers. Ray Kroc, a traveling salesman from Chicago, observed a small drive-in restaurant in San Bernardino, California, that was doing a thriving business. It sold only hamburgers, french fries, and milk shakes, and it sold them fast. Its owners, Dick and Mac McDonald, had applied assembly-line, mass-production technology to the prepa-ration of food, and in the process had invented the fast food restaurant. With bor-rowed money, Kroc concluded a business arrangement with the McDonalds that permitted him to establish a chain of fast food restaurants using their name and modeled on their format. The first McDonald's, complete with twin golden arches, sprang out of the prairie soil of Des Plaines, Illinois, a suburb of Chicago, on April 15, 1955. By the end of the decade, there were hundreds of McDonald's spreading across the country, selling hamburgers for 15 cents, french fries for ten cents, and milk shakes for 20 cents.

In the same year that Ray Kroc opened the first McDonald's fast food restau-rant in the Midwestern heartland, Walt Disney offered Disneyland, the first theme park, to American consumers. Disneyland, located in Anaheim, California, a sub-urb that lay thirty miles southeast of Los Angeles, immediately attracted hordes of visitors, mostly families with children. It featured combinations of fairy tale images derived from Disney's earlier animated masterpieces and sanitized historical im-ages from his live-action films.

Some areas of the park—Main Street, Frontierland, and Adventureland—featured a vast display of the icons of Americana. Young people also could take the Jungle Cruise and conquer the "dark continent." They could take a cruise on the steamboat *Mark Twain* down a man-made river. They could enter the Enchanted Tiki Room, where mostly white visitors mingled with friendly ethnic stereotypes. They could be inspired by a larger-than-life robotic Abraham Lincoln who, in a deep, rumbling voice, declaimed the virtues of constitutional democratic governance.

Much of what 1950's culture was about can only be explained by recapitulat-ing the American historical trajectory since the Great Depression of the 1930s. As Franklin Roosevelt famously observed, the dominant reaction to the financial col-lapse and severe economic downturn of the early 1930s was fear, "stark unreason-

Figure 10.3   Elvis Presley with fans.
Source: St. Louis Mercantile Library.
Used with permission.

ing terror." Add to that the disruptions of the 1940s—the horrors of World War II, the Holocaust, and the rise of the Cold War. Americans had to endure nearly twenty years of frightening historical experiences before they could enjoy the widespread prosperity and popular culture of the 1950s. Finally, Americans could once again believe that the conventional order of things could be relied upon, and they could believe that American institutions and core values were fundamentally sound. Americans could once again feel safe and secure. The awful fears caused by economic collapse, global war, and the rise of the Soviet menace could be banished as Americans took refuge in a culture of conformity and mass consumerism. Disneyland epitomized this popular culture of reassurance.

Much teenage spending centered around fads and pop music. The most popular musical style to emerge in the 1950s was rock'n'roll, an amalgam of black rhythm-and-blues and country-and-western idioms. Elvis Presley, the first rock'n'roll superstar, shot to the top of the hit parade in 1956 with a series of megahits, including "Heartbreak Hotel," "Blue Suede Shoes," and "Hound Dog." Crowds of teenage girls screamed hysterically over Presley's highly suggestive stage performances, particularly his gyrating hips keeping time with the frenetic chords he banged out on his electric guitar. Presley's performing style became a symbol of youthful rebellion. His concerts provoked criticisms from parents, teachers, and ministers. The Presley rebellion was implicit in his music and rhythms, which excited youngsters and provoked sexual fantasies. Presley himself was anything but a rebel. He was an artist and a showman, a champion of traditional values. Student radicalism and drug use during the 1960s outraged him.

Controversy over the moral threat to young people posed by rock'n'roll music in the late 1950s was closely linked to a taboo subject, sexual behavior. An Indiana biology professor, Dr. Alfred Kinsey, had published *Sexual Behavior in the Human Male* (1948) and its sequel, *Sexual Behavior in the Human Female* (1955). Kinsey interviewed thousands of subjects and used statistical analyses to produce the first scientific study of American sexual behavior. Among his most important findings, Kinsey discovered that premarital sexual relations, adultery, and homosexuality were more widespread than previously thought. Subsequently, investigators would discredit many of Kinsey's findings, particularly his use of statistical data that significantly exaggerated the number of homosexuals inhabiting American society.

WOMEN: FAMILY LIFE AND WORK

The immediate postwar years were a time of transition, frustration, and confusion for millions of American women. *Life* ran a feature in 1947 entitled "The American Woman's Dilemma." Its author found that many women were torn between the traditional expectations that they stay at home and their desire to work outside of the realm of domesticity. Millions of women continued to work outside of the home, mostly because they had to. Whether they wanted to work or not, more and more women married and gave birth to children in the postwar era. During the late 1940s and the decade of the 1950s, the family was the most rapidly growing social institution. It was these new families, which held down well-paying jobs, purchased suburban homes, reared children, and made the consumer purchases, that kept the mighty U.S. economy growing and prospering.

America became more child oriented after the war. Dr. Benjamin Spock published the first edition of his *Baby and Child Care* in 1946, which strongly influenced child-rearing practices in the postwar era. Dr. Spock advised women to make child rearing their most important task, to put their children's needs first. Early editions of his book also advised women to stay at home and not work outside of the home so that they would be available to meet their babies' needs. Some psychiatrists, influenced by Sigmund Freud's writings, criticized working women. They claimed that women could only be fulfilled and happy through domesticity. They considered women who held jobs outside of the home to be neurotic feminists trying to be "imitation men." They argued that a women's gender determined her role in life. Anatomy was destiny.

In 1956, *Life* published a special issue on American women. It profiled housewife Marjorie Sutton as a successful woman who fulfilled her feminine potential. She was a mother, wife, home manager, and hostess. She was active in the

PTA, the Campfire Girls, and charity work. Married at age sixteen, Sutton had four children, and she did all of the cooking, cleaning, and sewing for her family. She also helped her husband's career by entertaining his business clients.

Mid-century women were caught in a dilemma. According to the prevalent ideologies, the ideal role for women was found in the home. Her fulfillment lay in creating an island of love and security for her children and husband, with scant regard for her own needs. But millions of women, continuing the wartime trend, worked outside of their homes during the 1950s. The female labor force expanded from 17 million in 1946 to 22 million by 1958. By 1960, 40 percent of women were employed full time or part time. Millions of working women had to work, being their family's only source of income. Other women worked to supplement their family's income. Despite the burgeoning cult of motherhood, most new entrants into the female job market after the war were married women with children. The feminine mystique collided with the economic reality and caused confusion and stress.

Social history strongly influenced family life and the roles of women. Millions of American families during the 1950s were headed by men and women who had grown up amidst the economic deprivations of the Great Depression of the 1930s. They had been young adults during World War II, experiencing the loneliness and physical separation from friends and family inherent in military service during wartime. After experiencing fifteen years of economic and emotional insecurity, they were determined to enjoy the material security of the affluent society, and they were equally determined to have the emotional security found in cohesive family life. These men and women made the baby boom and championed "togetherness." The term *togetherness* first appeared in a 1954 *McCalls* article. It meant a happy family melded into a team, specifically the woman fusing herself with her husband and children. Family life was oriented around shared activities—television watching, backyard barbecues, outings to parks and beaches, and vacation trips.

THE ADVENT OF TELEVISION

The new electronic medium of television fit neatly into suburban lifestyles. It provided an ideal way to entertain families at home as well as sell them consumer goods. Television became a mass medium remarkably fast. In 1949, Americans owned fewer than a million sets. They were expensive, poor in quality, and the programming available was distinctly inferior to popular radio programs and Hollywood movies. Pundits were skeptical that "radio with pictures" would ever amount to more than a passing fad. By 1953, two-thirds of American households owned television sets. Radio had lost much of its audience, and most of the established radio stars quickly transitioned to the tube. Thousands of neighborhood movie theaters were forced to close. Television entered politics in 1948 when it provided coverage of both the Democratic and Republican conventions. It became an all-encompassing cultural force.

Mostly television brought popular entertainment and commercials. Prime-time television entertainment included situation comedies, action-suspense thrillers, family drama, variety shows, and Westerns. Tuesday night belonged to the king of comedy, "Uncle Miltie," Milton Berle. Other comedic stars included Phil Silvers as *Sergeant Bilko,* Lucille Ball in *I Love Lucy,* and Sid Caesar and Imogeen Coca in *The Show of Shows. Dragnet,* a detective series starring Jack Webb, was popular year after year. Family togetherness was the theme of *Father Knows Best,* starring Robert Young. The most popular television shows during the fifties proved to be Westerns. At one time there were thirty-nine Western shows on each week. CBS showed most of the top Westerns, including *Have Gun Will Travel,* which starred Richard Boone as "Palladin," a hired gunman from San Francisco who killed wicked men in the Old West. The most durable of the 1950s television Westerns turned out to be *Gunsmoke,* starring James Arness as Marshall Matt Dillon enforcing the law in Dodge City, Kansas.

But television functioned mostly as a commercial instrument, an advertising conduit, the most intrusive yet invented. Television quickly became the vital center of the consumer culture, an omnipresent educational enterprise teaching American consumers about the latest styles of mass consumption and creating wants and needs for the multitudinous products of the consumerist civilization.

RELIGION REVIVED

Religion enjoyed a revival during the 1950s. President Eisenhower tied religion to patriotism when he stated that recognition of God was "the most basic expression of Americanism." With America locked in Cold War with godless Communists, religious worship became one of the crucial demarcators of Americanism. Religion also bound family members together in worship: "The family that prays together stays together." Congress inserted the words "under God" in the Pledge of Allegiance to the American flag, recited in classrooms.

From 1945 until 1960, church attendance in this country increased 50 percent. A Baptist evangelist, Billy Graham, emerged as the major leader of a mass movement back to Bible fundamentalism. Roman Catholic Bishop Fulton Sheen developed a popular television ministry extolling traditional values and attacking Communism. A minister with training in psychology, Norman Vincent Peale was the most popular preacher of the 1950s. His book *The Power of Positive Thinking* sold millions of copies. Peale preached a gospel of reassurance. He told anxious listeners that God watched over Americans, ensuring individual success in careers and victory over Communism in the Cold War. A public opinion poll taken in 1955 showed that 97 percent of Americans believed in God, and two-thirds said they attended church regularly. Religion played a serious role in the lives of millions of American families. For others, religious beliefs were intermixed with patriotism, family togetherness, and Thursday night bingo.

SOCIAL CRITICS

Suburban society, mass culture, and the consumer economy generated a new American social character. William Whyte, author of the best-selling *Organization Man*, claimed that Americans no longer followed the traditional individual success ethic. They embraced what Whyte termed an *organizational ethic* that stressed belonging to a group and being a team player. Corporations employed more and more Americans. Within these large companies, bureaucratic management styles prevailed. Businesses encouraged their employees to look, dress, and act alike. Each appeared to be *The Man in the Gray Flannel Suit,* the title of an important 1950s novel by Sloan Wilson.

The urge to conform spread to the general society. A classic study of the postwar social character, found in sociologist David Riesman's *Lonely Crowd,* highlighted the lonely individual lost within mass society. Riesman observed that mobility had uprooted people from their traditional moorings. Old values no longer offered guidance or meaning. Young people adapted to the new social environment by embracing peer group norms and turning to television for guidance. They consumed their values as they did their breakfast cereals. Unpopularity with peers was more to be feared than violations of personal standards, which often were confused. People valued success in the personality market more than retaining their integrity.

Riesman called this new American character type "other-directed" in contrast to the traditional "inner-directed" American who internalized individualistic success values early in life from his or her parents and thereafter followed his or her destiny. Other-directed men or women preferred to join the lonely crowd, not to lead it. Other-directed workers were better adapted to fill the niches of the consumer economy. The American workforce at mid-century was predominantly white collar. New jobs were mostly generated in service sectors. Organization men, whose tickets to employment were high school diplomas or college degrees instead of union cards, proliferated.

REBELS

Not everyone was caught up in the culture of conformity during the 1950s; rebels, especially young people, rejected the manners and mores of the affluent society. Juvenile delinquency increased, and violent gangs of brawling teenagers staged gang fights in the streets of New York City and Chicago. Bands of motorcyclists roamed the streets and highways. Some middle-class youngsters dropped out of the college-career "rat race." They joined Bohemian enclaves in New York City's Greenwich Village and San Francisco's North Beach district. Herb Caen, a San Francisco columnist, dubbed these dropouts "beatniks"; they preferred to call themselves the "beat generation." "Beats" confronted the apathy and conformity of American society. They abandoned materialistic values to embrace poverty.

They lived in cheap flats, did not work or study, listened to jazz, explored Asian mystical religions and philosophy, smoked marijuana, and indulged in casual sex. The beats were harbingers of the hippie rebellion of the 1960s.

Beats also produced a serious literary movement. Beat writers authored poems and novels espousing the values of their rebellious generation. Jack Kerouac wrote the best beat novel, *On the Road* (1958), a tale of two young men without any money, Sal Paradise and Dean Moriarty, who traveled across America and into Mexico in a frantic search of emotionally engaging adventures, what Kerouac and his buddies called "kicks." Poet Allen Ginsberg wrote the most famous beat poem, *Howl*. It scathingly indicted a conformist, materialistic age that destroyed sensitive souls:

> I saw the best minds of my generation destroyed by madness, . . . burned alive in their innocent flannel suits on Madison Avenue.[1]

In addition to the beat writers, there were individual authors who powerfully expressed alienation from the conformist culture. Novelist J. D. Salinger expressed the theme of personal alienation in one of the finest 1950s' novels, *Catcher in the Rye*. Salinger's hero, Holden Caulfield, is a schoolboy trapped in a world populated by adults with whom he cannot communicate and who do not understand him. Holden rebels, runs away, and has a weekend fling in New York, desperately trying to find an island of integrity amidst a sea of conformity. His efforts fail, and in the end, the system triumphs. He returns to home and school. Salinger's novel was especially popular among 1950s' college students, for he expressed their discontent with a culture that masked a painful reality—not everyone fitted easily into the culture of conformity.

THE ELECTION OF 1952

President Dwight D. "Ike" Eisenhower was an appropriate political symbol for the 1950s. He was the reigning hero, not only for his great accomplishments but because he had established himself as the embodiment of the cardinal values of American culture. He had risen from humble farm folk, a self-made man whose extraordinary personal success affirmed the chief myth of America, that talented folks can rise from the depths to the pinnacles of power, wealth, and fame.

Shaped by the late nineteenth century into which he had been born, Eisenhower accepted its values without question; in the words of historian Alonzo Hamby, "He merely layered the requirements of the present century over them, and thus combined the reassurance of old tradition with the needs of the contemporary world." He projected an image of confidence and optimism. He shared the

[1]From Allen Ginsberg, *Howl* (New York: Harper & Row, 1956), p. 12.

views and values of the executive elite, who dominated the corporate world with which he identified. He admired efficiency and organization, had a contempt for politicians and politics, and generally distrusted mass democracy. Eisenhower was the consummate organization man.

At heart, Ike also was a determined anti-Communist, committed to maintaining American strength during continuing Cold War conflicts with the Soviets. British writer Godfrey Hodgson wrote that Americans in the 1950s were "confident to the verge of complacency about the perfectibility of American society, anxious to the point of paranoia about the threat of communism." Americans embraced a consensus in the 1950s, that America was the greatest nation in the world, and they also agreed that the American dream required thermonuclear defenses in the Cold War era.

Eisenhower and the Republicans had swept to power in 1952. The Korean War had boosted their chances. The Republicans also capitalized on many scandals unearthed within Truman's administration. As the Republican presidential race shaped up in 1952, Senator Robert Taft, leader of the conservative heartland, appeared to have the inside track to the nomination. But the powerful Eastern, internationalist wing of the party promoted the candidacy of the war hero, General Eisenhower, currently commanding NATO forces in Europe. At the Republican Convention held in Chicago in July, Eisenhower won a close first ballot nomination. He chose Richard Nixon, a fast-rising political star who had nailed Alger Hiss to be his running mate. When Truman chose to not seek reelection, the Democrats chose Illinois governor Adlai Stevenson to challenge Eisenhower.

Eisenhower launched the Republican drive for the White House by announcing a "great crusade" for honest, efficient government at home and for freedom abroad. Nixon and Senator Joseph McCarthy turned their rhetorical siege guns on the Democrats. They convinced millions of voters that Communist infiltration of government agencies posed a serious threat to internal security, for which the Democrats were mainly responsible. Eisenhower's genial smile caused crowds to shout, "We like Ike!" He proved an adroit campaigner. His most dramatic move came when he took up the Korean War, the chief issue of the campaign. In a speech given in Detroit, he declared that "an early and honorable" peace required a personal effort, and he pledged, "I shall go to Korea."

In September, a hitch developed that threatened briefly to derail the Republican campaign. Reporters discovered that Richard Nixon had benefited from a secret fund raised by wealthy southern California businessmen to pay his political expenses. The party that had been scoring points from its moral crusade against its scandal-plagued opposition suddenly had a scandal of its own. A wave of anti-Nixon sentiment swept the land. Stevenson had a glimmer of hope. Eisenhower appeared to be considering dumping Nixon from the GOP ticket.

But the Republican National Committee purchased airtime, and Nixon went on television and radio to defend himself successfully before the bar of public opinion. He convinced most of his huge television audience that he had not broken the law or done anything wrong. The emotional highpoint of his speech came when he referred to a cocker spaniel puppy a supporter had sent the family, which one of his daughters had named "Checkers":

> And you know the kids, like all kids, love the dog, and I just want to say this right now, that regardless of what they say about it, we're going to keep it.[2]

The "Checkers" speech outmaneuvered the Democrats and turned a potential disaster for his party to political advantage. He stayed on the ticket, and the Republican campaign rolled on.

On election day, Eisenhower score a landslide victory. Victory was in large measure a personal triumph for the popular general. But, in defeat, the Democratic Party showed considerable strength. The Republicans managed only a narrow majority in the House and broke even in the Senate. Eisenhower ran far ahead of his party. Issue differences between the parties appeared to be slight. The politics of consensus prevailed.

DYNAMIC CONSERVATISM

President Eisenhower projected an image of bland, moderate nonpartisanship. He came across as the amateur in politics, a disinterested leader serving the nation. He appeared happy to leave the details of government to energetic subordinates. But in reality, Ike embraced a strong conservative philosophy. He believed in fiscal restraint, balanced budgets, and devout anti-Communism. Beneath the mask was an able, effective politician who controlled his administration and its policies. Eisenhower also was a skilled, precise writer. His writing stands in sharp contrast to the rambling, incoherent utterances characteristic of his press conference responses to reporters' questions. Liberal pundits made fun of Eisenhower's apparent muddleheadedness and ignorance without realizing that they had fallen for one of his ploys. Eisenhower often feigned ignorance or resorted to gobbledygook to avoid premature disclosures of information or policy decisions.

Eisenhower began his presidency proclaiming a new "dynamic conservatism," which he said meant "conservative when it comes to money, liberal when it comes to human beings." Most of Ike's leading advisers came from the ranks of big business. Charles E. Wilson, the president of General Motors, became Secretary of Defense. The Treasury Department went to George Humphrey, a wealthy industrialist. Secretary of State John Foster Dulles was a corporation lawyer.

The new administration tried to implement conservative policies in several important policy areas. Humphrey put conservative fiscal policies in place. Income taxes and federal spending were both cut by 10 percent. Interest rates were raised and credit tightened to reduce inflation, which had averaged 10 percent between

---

[2]Quoted in Stephen Ambrose, *Nixon, The Education of a Politician, 1913–1962* (New York: Simon & Schuster, 1987), p. 289.

1950 and 1953. Republicans tried hard to balance the budget but usually failed. Republican efforts to reduce the role of the federal government and strengthen local and state governments also failed. For agriculture, the administration pushed for more flexible and lower price supports for farmers. Crop production increased, farm income dropped, and farmers protested the new policies.

But it soon became evident that "dynamic conservatism" was not an effort to repeal the New Deal. Although he was a fiscal conservative, Eisenhower accepted the expansion of several New Deal programs. Congress expanded Social Security coverage, raised the minimum wage, and extended unemployment insurance. It also created a new Department of Health, Education, and Welfare to coordinate government social programs. The federal government continued to expand during the Eisenhower years.

Eisenhower proposed the largest domestic spending program in American history in 1955, a federal-state highway construction program. Congress enacted the Interstate Highway Act in 1956, setting in motion the largest public works project in U.S. history. The federal government provided 90 percent of the costs through the Highway Trust Fund, financed by user taxes on cars, trucks, buses, gasoline, tires, lubricants, and auto parts. It projected a 42,000-mile network of freeways, linking all major urban areas. Construction of mammoth freeway systems continued into the 1970s, and the government spent billions of dollars annually on them. The mammoth road-building projects had an enormous impact on American life. Annual driving increased fourfold. Shopping centers, linked by the new roads, sprang up to serve the rapidly growing suburban communities. Every suburb had a highway strip, replete with drive-in movies, bowling alleys, gas stations, and fast food restaurants.

Eisenhower's moderation accorded with the public mood of the 1950s. Most Americans felt smugly complacent about their society. They believed that economic growth would solve all social problems, gradually enlarging the economic pie until poverty vanished. There was no need for higher taxes, special programs, or sacrifices by anyone. The 1950s were a time for holding the line against inflation, recession, and social disorder—of balancing liberty and security within a moderate framework acceptable to nearly everyone.

The New Deal was legitimated during Ike's reign. It became the status quo undergirding consensus politics. The pragmatic accommodation that the conservative Eisenhower made by protecting and expanding the welfare state signaled the breakdown of traditional political categories. Politicians no longer battled one another over fundamental issues; they merely quarreled over which interest group got how much. Previously, big government had been linked to liberalism, and limited government tied to conservatism. In the 1950s, except for a few traditional ideologues on the Left and the Right, the real issue was no longer whether government was large or small but whose interests it served. Conservatives often voted for huge spending programs like defense budgets, highway programs, and Social Security extensions. Liberals often voted for huge defense budgets in the name of Cold War bipartisanship and to protect national security in the nuclear age.

MCCARTHY: ZENITH AND RUIN

National alarm over Communist infiltration of government agencies persisted well into Eisenhower's presidency. Joseph McCarthy continued his investigations of alleged subversion in various government agencies. For eighteen months, he was the second most powerful politician in Washington, dominating the news with his spectacular accusations. A 1954 poll showed that 50 percent of Americans approved of his activities and only 29 percent opposed them. Many of his Senate colleagues, knowing that he was a fraud, despised him. But they feared him even more, and refused to challenge him openly, having seen what McCarthy could do to an opponent at election time. Eisenhower also refused to confront him because he did not want a party rupture over the controversial demagogue.

The State Department continued to be McCarthy's favorite hunting ground, even though it was now controlled by Republicans. In 1953, McCarthy went after the State Department's overseas information service. Secretary of State John Foster Dulles ordered Department personnel to cooperate fully with McCarthy's investigation. Supposedly, subversive books were dutifully removed from the shelves by State Department functionaries, some of which were burned.

In 1954, McCarthy took after the U.S. Army. His subcommittee investigated alleged Communist subversion at Fort Monmouth, New Jersey, the site of sensitive communications technology. During the inquiry, McCarthy discovered that the Army had promoted a dentist, Irving Peress, to the rank of major and then gave him an honorable discharge when it learned that he had once invoked the Fifth Amendment when asked about Communist affiliations. An angry McCarthy bullied General Ralph Zwicker, Peress's commanding officer, when he refused to give him Peress's file.

The Army mounted a counterattack against McCarthy, accusing him of trying to blackmail the Army into giving preferential treatment to a former McCarthy staffer who had been assigned to Fort Monmouth. McCarthy retorted that the Army was holding his former staffer hostage to keep his committee from investigating the Army. McCarthy's subcommittee voted to hold hearings on the charges made by the two adversaries, with Senator Karl Mundt of South Dakota temporarily assuming the chairmanship. On April 22, 1954, the famed Army–McCarthy hearings began. For six weeks they were telecast daily to 15 million viewers.

McCarthy starred in the televised political drama, interrupting the proceedings frequently. The hearings also made a star out of Joseph Welch, a soft-spoken trial lawyer who was the Army's chief counsel. At one point, Welch left McCarthy temporarily speechless by asking rhetorically, "At long last, sir, at long last, have you left no sense of decency?" Although the hearings made for great political melodrama, they ended inconclusively. It is not true that television exposure or Welch's dramatic remark undermined McCarthy's popularity. Polls taken shortly after the hearings showed that McCarthy still retained his 50 percent approval ratings.

McCarthy's methods and his unruly behavior provoked his downfall. He went too far when he attacked the Army. In August 1954, the Senate established a committee to study a set of censure charges brought against McCarthy by Republican Ralph Flanders of Vermont. Chairing the committee was conservative Republican Arthur Watkins of Utah. The committee recommended that the Senate censure McCarthy. After noisy hearings, the full Senate voted to "condemn" McCarthy for contempt of the Senate and for abuse of Watkins committee members. The vote was 67 to 22.

Senate condemnation destroyed McCarthy. He still made accusations, but his attacks no longer made headlines. His health failed, and he did not live out his Senate term. He died in May 1957 of infectious hepatitis, aggravated by heavy drinking. McCarthy could perform only as long as his colleagues were willing to tolerate his unruly behavior.

THE POLITICS OF CONSENSUS

1954 was the last election year in which the Communist-in-government issue had any force. Anticommunism as a major issue in American domestic politics died with McCarthy. But anticommunism remained a staple of American political culture, far outliving its foremost practitioner. Most Americans regarded as axiomatic the notion that the Soviet Union headed an international conspiracy unrelentingly hostile to the United States. The Cold War bipartisan consensus on the conduct of American foreign policy remained intact.

Political alignments during the 1950s remained unstable. Eisenhower's 1952 victory signaled the breakup of the Roosevelt coalition of labor, farmers, ethnics, and Southerners forged during the 1930s, but the Republicans could not form a majority coalition to replace it. As traditional political allegiances declined during the 1950s, a large independent "swing" vote emerged, varying in size with each election. Millions of citizens voted a split ticket, supporting a man or an issue instead of a party, and shifted sides in response to particular situations. The two major parties attained a rough equality for the first time since the early 1890s. An unstable equilibrium prevailed.

National elections held during the 1950s reflected the unstable balance of political forces. Except for 1952, the Democrats won all of the congressional elections and the Republicans all of the presidential elections. The 1956 election was a dull replay of 1952. Ike was at the peak of his popularity and almost immune to criticism. Stevenson campaigned tentatively, groping for an issue and never finding one. He tried to make issues of Ike's age and health. Eisenhower had suffered a serious heart attack in September 1955 and had been incapacitated for weeks. But he recovered, and in 1956 he enjoyed good health. In 1956, the Democrats had nothing to match the Republican slogan of "four more years of peace and prosperity." Eisenhower won reelection by a larger margin than his 1952 landslide victory. But the Democrats carried both houses of Congress. The year 1956 was the first time in American political history that a party won both Houses while losing the presidency.

But the nominal Democratic congressional majorities were undercut by the bipartisan coalition of Southern Democrats and Northern Republicans who could gut or block most liberal legislation. During the 1950s, moderate Texas politicians led the Democrats in Congress. Speaker Sam Rayburn led the House, and his protégé, Lyndon Johnson, led the Senate. Both leaders pursued a strategy of compromise and cooperation with the Republican White House.

CIVIL RIGHTS

Soon after taking office, President Eisenhower appointed Governor Earl Warren of California Chief Justice of the Supreme Court. The Court had been chipping away at the constitutional foundations of racial discrimination since the 1940s in two areas—denial of voting rights and school segregation. It was in the realm of education that the Court chose to nullify the "separate but equal" principle that had provided the constitutional basis for segregation.

Several cases challenging school segregation were before the Court. The justices decided a representative case, *Brown v. the Board of Education of Topeka,* on May 17, 1954. A unanimous Court ruled that public school segregation was unconstitutional under the Fourteenth Amendment, reversing the "separate but equal" doctrine established in *Plessy v. Ferguson* (1896). The Court's decision incorporated much of the legal brief filed by Thurgood Marshall, chief counsel for the NAACP:

> In the field of public education, the doctrine of "separate but equal" has no place. Separate educational facilities are inherently unequal.[3]

A year later, the Supreme Court instructed federal district courts to order school desegregation to begin in their areas and to require "good faith compliance with all deliberate speed." Having destroyed the legal basis of school segregation, the courts proceeded to undermine Jim Crow everywhere. Federal court decisions nullified segregation in public housing, recreational facilities, and interstate commerce. The *Brown* decision was the most important Supreme Court decision of modern times.

The white South defied the *Brown* decision. In 1956, a group of 101 congressmen and senators from eleven Southern states that had composed the Confederacy almost a century before signed the Southern Manifesto. It pledged to "use all law-

---

[3]Quoted in Anthony Lewis, *Portrait of a Decade: The Second American Revolution* (New York: Bantam Books, 1965), p. 26.

ful means to bring about a reversal of this decision which is contrary to the Constitution." The Southern Manifesto also encouraged Southern officials to try to prevent implementing desegregation. The crucial confrontation between federal and state authority over school desegregation came at Little Rock, Arkansas, where Eisenhower faced the most serious domestic crisis of his presidency.

In September 1957, Central High in Little Rock planned to enroll nine African American students under court order. But Arkansas Governor Orville Faubus prevented integration by ordering National Guardsmen to block the school entrance. A federal court ordered the troops to leave, and the African American students enrolled. But white students threatened them, and they were removed from the school. Faced with clear defiance of the law, Eisenhower acted. For the first time since Reconstruction, a president sent federal troops into the South to protect the rights of African Americans. Paratroopers entered Central High, and the National Guardsmen were placed under federal command. Guarded by soldiers, the nine teenagers enrolled.

There is a close interrelationship between the Supreme Court decision outlawing segregation and the Southern civil rights campaigns of the mid-1950s. Civil rights activists were tremendously encouraged by the Court's ruling. They responded by escalating their attacks on racial injustice. When state and local jurisdictions refused to obey the *Brown* decision, activists took to the streets in an effort to pressure white Southerners into compliance with the law or else provoke federal interventions to enforce it. Civil rights activists used radical tactics such as civil disobedience and boycotts to bring about enforcement of federal law. The civil rights revolution was a very conservative type of revolution.

Eighteen months after the *Brown* decision, in Montgomery, Alabama, Rosa Parks refused to surrender her seat at the front of a bus to a white man and ignited the modern civil rights movement. A charming myth has risen about Ms. Parks as the seamstress who was simply too tired to move to the back of the bus and whose arrest set off a spontaneous demonstration that ended happily with integrated bus service. Such an account misrepresents a carefully planned and well-organized movement for social change. It also omits Parks's long prior career as a community leader and social activist. Her action brought to prominence a young Baptist minister who, for the rest of his tragically short life, would be the foremost leader of the civil rights revolution. He was Dr. Martin Luther King, Jr., and he declared:

> Integration is the great issue of our age, the great issue of our nation, and the great issue of our community. We are in the midst of a great struggle, the consequences of which will be world-shaking.[4]

Under Dr. King's leadership, Montgomery African Americans organized a boycott of the city's bus lines. Helped by a Supreme Court decision declaring bus segregation unconstitutional, and after an arduous campaign lasting 381 days, they

[4]Quoted in *Ibid.*, p. 62.

Figure 10.4   An African-American drinking at "colored" water cooler in streetcar terminal, Oklahoma City. Photographer: Russell Lee.   *Source:* Library of Congress, neg.# AH 1930-1939.

eventually forced the city to integrate its bus service and to hire African American drivers and mechanics.

At the same time, the NAACP mounted an intensive legal campaign against segregation. Victorious in forty-two of forty-six appeals to the Supreme Court, the NAACP advanced voting rights and integrated housing, transportation, public accommodations, and schools in many parts of the South. While Thurgood Marshall and the NAACP fought their civil rights battles in the federal courts, Dr. King and his followers fought theirs in the streets of Southern towns and cities.

A drive to guarantee African American voting rights also started. The Civil Rights Act of 1957, the first since Reconstruction, created a Civil Rights Commission and gave the attorney general the power to take local officials to court in cases in which they denied African Americans the right to vote. Congress enacted a stronger civil rights law in 1960; it provided legal penalties against anyone interfering with the right to vote. The civil rights movement made a powerful start during the 1950s. Most progress came from efforts by African Americans themselves, however, they were aided considerably by Supreme Court decisions that nullified the legal foundations of segregation.

THE NEW LOOK

During the 1952 campaign, Republicans charged that the Truman–Acheson policy of containing Communism had failed, especially in Asia, with the loss of China and the stalemated war in Korea. John Foster Dulles insisted that the United States, instead of pursuing containment, should make it "publicly known that it wants and expects liberation to occur." But in office, Eisenhower and Dulles continued the containment policies that they had condemned during the 1952 campaign. They had no choice. The logic of liberation led inescapably to one conclusion—Americans would have to fight to free the captive nations, because the Communists would never voluntarily set them free. Freedom for eastern Europe meant war with the Soviet Union. Further, Eisenhower had committed himself to cutting military expenditures. Liberation, far costlier than containment, could never be carried out by fiscal conservatives. Republicans hid their failure to liberate anyone from Communism behind tough talk.

Republicans called their foreign policy the New Look. It relied on strategic air power to destroy the Soviet Union with nuclear bombs if Communist aggression occurred anywhere in the world. Dulles believed that the threat to obliterate the Soviets would "deter" them from hostile actions. The New Look strategy allowed the administration to reduce outlays for conventional forces. Dulles described their approach as "massive retaliation." Secretary of Defense Wilson observed that the New Look provided "more bang for the buck." President Eisenhower insisted that cuts in defense spending were necessary to preserve the American way of life.

Critics of the New Look strategy charged that "massive retaliation" locked America into an all-or-nothing response to Communist aggression. A Communist-led uprising in a small country would not warrant an attack on the Soviet Union, hence the revolution would probably succeed. The Soviets also could see the limitations of massive retaliation and would not be deterred from helping small insurrections. Freedom would be nibbled away at the periphery.

Ike defended his foreign policy by contending that the United States could not afford to police the entire world; it must concentrate on defending its vital interests. If NATO nations or Japan were attacked, the United States' response would be swift and overwhelming. Dulles also tried to compensate for the limitations of the New Look strategy by forging regional security pacts with allies in which the United States would furnish the military hardware and its allies would furnish the troops if the Communists attacked. By 1960, the United States had committed itself to defend forty-three countries.

VIETNAM: GETTING IN DEEPER

Dulles described his diplomatic method as the willingness to go to the brink of war to achieve peace. "Brinkmanship" was more threatening as rhetoric than as action.

Dulles never used brinkmanship on the Soviets, nor did the United States become embroiled in any major wars during the Eisenhower–Dulles tenure. Brinkmanship was tried mainly in Asia, with mixed results. It worked in Korea. The president told Dulles to warn the Chinese that if they did not accept a settlement, the United States might use nuclear weapons in the war. That threat broke a two-year-old deadlock and ended the conflict on American terms.

Dulles then applied brinkmanship to Southeast Asia where, since 1946, the French, trying to reimpose colonialism in Indochina, had been fighting Vietnamese guerrillas. In 1950, the Truman administration began sending economic and military aid to support the French efforts to contain Communism in Asia following the Maoist triumph in China. Eisenhower expanded American aid to the French; by 1954, the United States was paying 78 percent of the cost of the war. Eisenhower, like Truman before him, applied Cold War ideology to this struggle between Asian nationalists and European imperialists. Washington viewed the Indochina War as part of the global conflict between Free World forces and Communism.

Despite U.S. help, the French were losing the war. By 1954, Viet Minh forces held most of Vietnam. French generals tried to retrieve the military initiative, putting 11,000 of their best troops in a remote fortress deep within guerrilla-held territory at Dien Bien Phu and daring them to fight an open battle. The French believed that Asians could not defeat European forces in a conventional battle. Vietnamese forces besieged the garrison. Within weeks, it was on the verge of surrender. With war weariness strong in France after eight years of war, the fall of Dien Bien Phu would mean victory for the Vietnamese and the end of French Indochina.

Facing imminent ruin in Southeast Asia, the French made an eleventh-hour appeal to the Americans to save them. President Eisenhower considered air strikes to relieve the siege around Dien Bien Phu, but he insisted that America's allies join the effort and that Congress support it. Prime Minister Winston Churchill rebuffed Dulles's efforts to enlist British support. Senate leaders told the president that without British involvement the Senate would not approve U.S. military intervention. Lacking support from allies or Congress, Eisenhower rejected the French request. On May 7, 1954, Dien Bien Phu fell to the Communists.

Meanwhile, an international conference had convened in Geneva to find a political solution to the Indochina War. Conferees worked out a settlement in July 1954. By its terms, the French and Viet Minh agreed to a cease-fire and a temporary partition of Vietnam at the seventeenth parallel of north latitude, with French forces withdrawing south of that line and Viet Minh forces withdrawing to the north. Free elections were to be held within two years to unify the country. During the interim, the French were to help prepare southern Vietnam for independence and then leave.

The United States opposed the Geneva accords but could not prevent them from being adopted by the conferees. The American delegate refused to sign them, but he agreed to accept them and pledged not to use force to upset the arrangements. But at the time, President Eisenhower announced that the United States "has not been party to nor is bound by the decisions taken by the conference." Ho Chi Minh, whose forces verged on taking all of Vietnam, settled for just the northern half of the country at Geneva because he was confident of winning the forthcoming elections over the French-backed regime in the south.

After Geneva, Dulles salvaged what he could from what Washington regarded as a major Communist victory that threatened all of Southeast Asia. In September 1954, Dulles arranged for Great Britain, France, Australia, New Zealand, Thailand, Pakistan, and the Philippines to create the Southeast Asia Treaty Organization (SEATO). Members agreed to "meet and confer" if one of them were attacked. A separate agreement covered Laos, Cambodia, and "South Vietnam," that is, Vietnam south of the seventeenth parallel.

The United States also supported a new government emerging in southern Vietnam, headed by Ngo Dinh Diem. Americans trained and equipped Diem's army and security forces. The Eisenhower administration promoted the diplomatic fiction that the seventeenth parallel had become a permanent national boundary separating two states, "South Vietnam" and "North Vietnam." America also backed Diem when he refused to allow the scheduled elections to unify the country to take place in 1956.

Eisenhower believed that if southern Vietnam fell to the Communists, all of Southeast Asia would be imperiled. He compared the nations of Southeast Asia to a row of dominoes: knock one over and the rest would fall quickly. After Geneva, America committed its resources and prestige to creating a new nation in southern Vietnam that would "serve as a proving ground for democracy in Asia." The survival of the new South Vietnam would sabotage the Geneva settlement that assumed the emergence of a unified, Communist-controlled Vietnam within two years.

With U.S. backing during the late 1950s, Diem attempted to suppress all opposition to his regime. His repressive actions provoked violent opposition. Local officials and Diem informers were assassinated by Communist and non-Communist opponents, all of whom Diem called the "Viet Cong," meaning Vietnamese who are Communists. The Viet Minh infiltrated men and supplies south of the seventeenth parallel to take control of the anti-Diem insurgency. Small-scale civil war had begun. By 1959, the second Indochina War was underway.

THE CHINA CRISIS

While Americans were trying to build a nation in Southeast Asia, they faced a crisis with mainland China over Formosa. Nationalist Chinese pilots, flying from Formosan bases in U.S. planes, had bombed mainland shipping and ports since 1953. The U.S. Seventh Fleet patrolled the waters between China and Formosa, protecting the Nationalists from Communist reprisals. In September 1954, Communist Chinese artillery began shelling Quemoy and Matsu, two small islands situated in

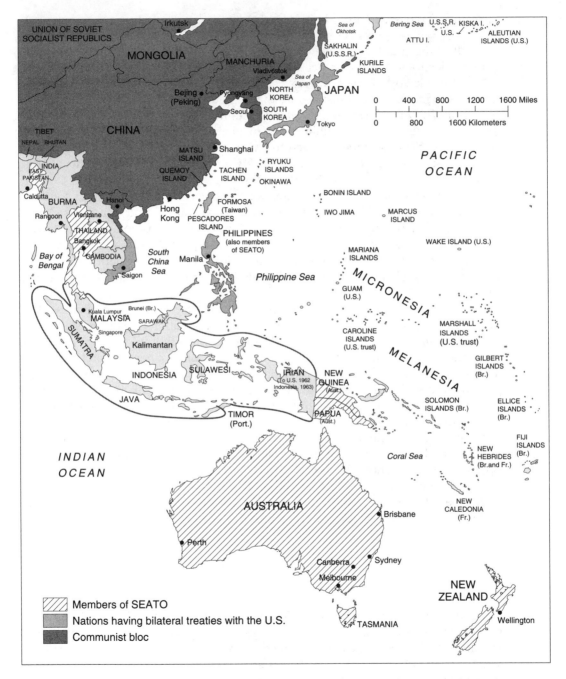

Figure 10.5   The Alliance System in the Far East.   *Source:* George D. Moss, *Moving On*, p. 119.

the mouths of two mainland ports about 100 miles from Formosa. These islands were held by Nationalist forces. Eisenhower was determined to hold these islands because he believed that they were essential to the defense of Formosa.

Washington reacted to the shelling by increasing the American military presence in the Taiwan Strait, strengthening Nationalist defenses, and issuing stern warnings to Beijing. In December 1954, Washington and Taiwan signed a mutual defense treaty. The following year, Congress gave President Eisenhower the authority to use military force if necessary to defend Taiwan and the offshore islands. The Chinese, lacking nuclear weapons and receiving no help from the Soviets, reduced the shelling and offered to negotiate "a relaxation of tensions." The United States, which did not recognize the legitimacy of the mainland Chinese government, refused to negotiate with Beijing, but it stopped its war preparations and the situation calmed. Beginning quietly at Geneva in the summer of 1955, Chinese and U.S. officials held talks about Taiwan, trade, and other topics.

American problems in Asia highlighted the emergence of Third World nations as a major force in world affairs during the 1950s. These nations, many of them recently independent former European colonies, increasingly became the focus of the Cold War conflict between the Soviet Union and the United States. Third World nations were sources of raw materials, attracted foreign investment, and provided markets, particularly for American exports. Many Third World nations wanted to remain neutral in the Cold War. But to U.S. Secretary of State Dulles, neutralism in a bipolar world dominated by two superpowers, one of which was "immoral," was wrong. He opposed a conference of twenty-nine African and Asian nations held at Bandung, Indonesia, in April 1955, during the height of the Quemoy-Matsu crisis. Leaders of these Afro-Asian nations wanted to form an alternative to the two superpowers and their alliance systems. Chinese Premier Jou En-lai played a prominent role at Bandung; China assumed leadership of the emerging Third World nations.

AT THE SUMMIT

When the U.S. considered using nuclear weapons during the Formosan crisis, it highlighted a frightening world reality. Thermonuclear weapons of the mid-1950s were a thousand times more powerful than the two bombs that had devastated Hiroshima and Nagasaki in 1945. Both the Soviets and Americans possessed hydrogen bombs, and both were developing intercontinental missiles. Both sides had to face the possibility of a nuclear exchange if they went to war. They agreed to hold a "summit conference" to try to reduce the possibility of nuclear catastrophe.

The conference convened at Geneva on July 18, 1955. President Eisenhower, Premier Nikolai Bulganin of the Soviet Union, Prime Minister Anthony Eden of England, and Premier Edgar Faure of France attended. Geneva signaled a turning point in the Cold War. Both sides conceded in effect that the Cold War could not be won militarily. The atmosphere at the summit was cordial. A "spirit of Geneva" emerged, symbolized by a photograph of Eisenhower shaking hands with Bulganin. President Eisenhower also scored a propaganda victory when he offered, and the Soviets rejected, his "Open Skies" proposal to the Soviets that would permit aerial surveillance of both countries' nuclear development and testing facilities. The conference yielded no substantive agreements, and the arms race continued after the summit ended. But a thermonuclear stalemate had forced a relaxation of tensions. Both sides agreed to start arms control negotiations, and they later suspended atmospheric testing of nuclear weapons.

THE CIA AT WORK

In 1953, Ike appointed Allen Dulles, younger brother of the secretary of state, as director of the Central Intelligence Agency (CIA). Allen Dulles recruited Cold Warriors eager to fight Communism, many of whom were liberal intellectuals from elite Ivy League universities. Under his leadership, paramilitary covert operations became a secret arm of U.S. foreign policy. The CIA's first major triumph came in Iran in 1953. A nationalist government led by Mohammed Mossadegh had nationalized oil fields controlled by the British and had forced the young Shah of Iran into exile. The United States, fearing that Mossadegh might sell oil to the Soviets and align himself with Iranian Communists, sent CIA operatives to Iran. Working with British and Iranian army officials, they helped overthrow Mossadegh and restored the Shah to power. Iran then made a deal that gave U.S. oil companies 40 percent of Iranian oil production, gave the British 40 percent, and gave the Dutch 20 percent. The CIA helped subvert a popular government, and the United States now controlled a major share of Iranian oil production.

The CIA also helped overthrow a leftist government in Central America. Jacob Arbenz Guzman had been elected president of Guatemala in 1951. Arbenz was not a Communist, but Communists supported his government and held offices within it. In 1953, the government expropriated 234,000 acres of land belonging to an American corporation, the United Fruit Company, Guatemala's largest landowner, for a land reform program. The company claimed that Latin America was being threatened with Communism.

The United States cut off economic aid and sent CIA forces to Guatemala to overthrow Arbenz. They recruited an army of exiles in neighboring Honduras led by Colonel Carlos Castillo Armas. When Armas's forces were ready for attack, CIA pilots airlifted their supplies and bombed the Guatemalan capital. Arbenz, facing military defeat, fled into exile. Armas established a military dictatorship and returned the expropriated lands to the United Fruit Company. Buoyed by their success in toppling a leftist government perceived to be hostile to U.S. economic and strategic interests in Guatemala, CIA officials would try to replicate their efforts in Cuba in 1961 with disastrous results.

TROUBLE IN SUEZ

The Cold War spread to the Middle East after World War II, deeply involving the United States in a region that had previously been only of peripheral interest. The Middle East is a compound of many parts: Arab nationalism, political instability, regional rivalries, religious fanaticism, superpower penetration, and most of all, the intractable Arab–Israeli conflict. It is the presence of a Jewish state of Israel on land that was formerly Palestine that lies at the core of many Middle East conflicts.

The modern Arab–Israeli conflict dates from the end of World War II. Most of the European Jews who survived the Holocaust wanted to go to Palestine where a sizeable Jewish population had been built up since 1900. Palestine was administered by the British who tried to prevent Zionist refugees from entering Palestine in order to safeguard their Anglo-Arabian oil interests. But the British, weakened by losses in World War II, withdrew from Palestine in 1947, turning it over to the United Nations. At that time, the United States and the Soviet Union united to carve an Israeli homeland out of the western portion of Palestine. The UN partitioned Palestine to create a Jewish state, Israel, along the Mediterranean coast. On May 14, 1948, Israel proclaimed its independence. America recognized Israel immediately and the Soviet Union soon afterward.

Instantly, Arab armies attacked, determined to drive the Jews into the Mediterranean Sea, to destroy the new Jewish state, and to preserve all of Palestine for the Palestinian Arabs. At first, the outnumbered Israelis were driven back. Their cause appeared to be lost. They asked for a truce, and the Soviets and Americans imposed one. During the cease-fire, the Soviets flew in quantities of heavy arms, violating the truce. Soviet military aid at that critical juncture saved the fledgling Israeli state. When fighting resumed, the well-armed Israelis routed the Arab forces. Israeli forces also advanced far beyond the original boundaries assigned by the UN partition. The beaten Arabs sued for peace in 1949.

An African American diplomat, Ralph Bunche, arranged an armistice ending the first Arab–Israeli war. Israel survived because of Soviet arms and American diplomatic support. Its inflated borders included thousands of Palestinians. Another 700,000 Palestinians fled or were driven from their homes by the advancing Israeli forces, creating a Palestinian refugee problem that has never been solved. The Soviets supported Israel until 1955, when they switched to the Arab side. The United States continues to be Israel's major supporter, while trying to maintain friendly relations with moderate Arab nations.

With U.S. assistance, Gamal Abdul Nasser came to power in Egypt in 1952, the first of a new generation of Arab Nationalists. America offered him $270 million to build a huge dam on the Upper Nile to control flooding and generate hydroelectric power. The aid money for the Aswan Dam represented an American effort to tilt its Middle East policy in an increasingly pro-Arab direction. In 1955, Dulles arranged the signing of the Baghdad Pact, linking Britain, Turkey, Iran, Iraq, and Pakistan in an agreement to strengthen the Middle East against Soviet penetration. The pact angered Nasser, who viewed it as an effort to bring the Cold War to the Middle East and to strengthen Iraq, Egypt's rival for Arab leadership. The Soviet Union reacted to the signing of the Baghdad Pact by becoming more active in Arab affairs, particularly in Egypt and Syria.

Egyptian and Israeli forces clashed along the Gaza Strip, territory that both nations claimed, inhabited mainly by Palestinian refugees. The Israelis suddenly attacked in force in 1955, inflicting a major defeat on the Egyptians. Nasser, angry and humiliated, asked the United States for arms. Washington refused him. Nasser then turned to the Soviet bloc and concluded an arms deal with the Communists. Dulles, fearing that Egypt was becoming a Soviet client, withdrew U.S. aid for the Aswan Dam. Nasser responded by nationalizing the Suez Canal. He used its $30 million annual revenues to finance the Aswan Dam. He also closed the canal to Israeli shipping. The Soviets supported Nasser's actions.

Britain and France, dependent on Persian Gulf oil shipped through the Suez Canal, proposed overthrowing Nasser and returning the canal to its former owners. The United States, afraid such actions would involve the Soviets and lead to war, rejected the Anglo-French proposal. The British and French decided to overthrow Nasser and incorporated the Israelis into their plans. On October 29, 1956, Israeli forces invaded Egypt. A week later, the French and British landed troops in Egypt to seize the canal. The United States condemned the Anglo-French–Israeli actions before the United Nations. America also cut off oil shipments to France and Britain and threatened to wage financial war against the British pound sterling. The French and British, reeling from a combination of U.S. and UN opposition, Soviet threats to intervene, and an Arab oil boycott, withdrew without occupying the canal. The Soviets used the occasion to provide funds for the Aswan project; in return, the Egyptians granted the Soviets use of a former British military base at Suez.

U.S. efforts to avoid war in the Middle East yielded mostly negative consequences for American foreign policy interests. Administration efforts weakened NATO, humiliated America's major European allies, alienated Nasser, angered the Israelis, helped the Soviets get a military base in Egypt, and failed to improve relations with other Arab countries. But Nasser eventually paid the French and British $81 million for the Suez Canal, and Middle Eastern oil supplies remained in Western hands.

While the Suez crisis raged, crises erupted in eastern Europe. Early in 1956, the new Soviet leader, Nikita Khruschchev, promised to ease Soviet restrictions in satellite countries. Ferment spread quickly throughout eastern Europe. Riots in Poland forced the Soviets to grant the Poles substantial concessions. Hungarian students and workers overthrew a Stalinist puppet. He was replaced by Imre Nagy. Nagy demanded removal of Red Army forces and implementation of democracy; the Soviets conceded to both of these demands. Dulles promised the Hungarians economic aid if they broke with the Soviets. On October 31, Hungary announced that it was leaving the Warsaw Pact. Liberation appeared at hand; a captive nation was freeing itself from Communist tyranny.

The Soviet Union, unwilling to let the Warsaw Pact disintegrate, invaded Hungary. Soviet tanks crushed the Hungarian revolution and killed 30,000 Hungarians. Radio Budapest pleaded for help, but none came from America or elsewhere. Eisenhower had never considered sending troops, nor would he have, had there been no Suez crisis. Neither he nor any other U.S. president would ever risk World War III to help liberate an eastern European country from Soviet clutches. American talk of liberation for eastern Europe had always been a sham. American forces were not strong enough to defeat the Red Army in Hungary, except with the use of nuclear weapons that would have ruined the country and killed millions of people.

After the Suez crisis, America announced the Eisenhower Doctrine to try to offset Soviet influence and militant Arab nationalism in the Middle East. It offered military aid to any country requesting it to resist Communist threats. The Eisenhower Doctrine extended containment to the region. It was implemented twice. In 1957, U.S. troops were sent into Jordan to protect its government from Egyptian threats. In 1958, about 14,000 Marines landed in Lebanon to protect its government from an insurgency supported by Nasser.

As the 1950s ended, America enjoyed good relations with traditional Arab states like Saudi Arabia, the region's major oil producer, which had become a U.S. client through economic aid and arms sales. Middle Eastern oil continued its flow through the Suez Canal. But U.S. influence in the Middle East was declining. Arab nationalism and Soviet influence were growing. Arab hostility toward Israel, combined with the U.S. commitment to the survival of the Jewish state, allowed the Soviets to champion Arab nationalism. American efforts to balance Arab and Israeli interests largely failed during the1950s.

SPUTNIK

After the Suez crisis, the strategic balance appeared to shift toward the Soviet Union. In September 1957, the Soviets test-fired an intercontinental ballistics missile (ICBM), over a year ahead of the United States. A month later, they launched the first space satellite, which they called "Sputnik." Sputnik's strategic implications were ominous, proving that the Soviets had powerful booster rockets and had solved guidance problems essential to delivering a thermonuclear warhead to its target. America appeared to face both a missile "gap" and a space "lag" with the Soviets.

At first President Eisenhower played down the Soviets' achievements, trying to reassure anxious Americans. But he was not convincing. He offered no new programs to catch the Soviets in either the arms or the space race. For the first time, Ike was vigorously attacked in Congress and in the media. The attacks were reinforced by the sluggish performance of the economy, which slipped into recession, and the revelation of a scandal in the administration. Eisenhower's special assistant, Sherman Adams, was forced to resign for accepting favors from a business man who needed help from the federal government. The Soviets had scored a tremendous ideological victory over their rivals. American technological superiority over the supposedly backward Soviets, a source of security during the Cold War, had been wiped away. Senator Lyndon Johnson conducted a thorough investigation of the nation's missile and space programs, thereby establishing the Democrats as favoring stronger national defense and space efforts than the Republican administration.

Critics faulted American public schools for not demanding excellence from students and for stinting on math and science training. There had been persistent criticisms of public schools preceding Sputnik. Dr. Rudolf Flesch, in his best-selling *Why Johnny Can't Read* (1955), had attacked overcrowded schools that used obsolete teaching methods and offered diverse, aimless curricula to bored students. After Sputnik, educational shortcomings became a national security issue. Educators insisted that Americans must put greater emphasis on mathematics, foreign language study, and science to regain its technological edge over the Soviets. Eisenhower and Congress responded in 1958 by enacting the National Defense Education Act (NDEA), which funded high school math, language, and science programs and offered fellowships and loans to college students entering those fields.

Initial American efforts to match Soviet rocketry embarrassed the nation. Two months after Sputnik's launching, an American rocket blew up on its launch pad; a U.S. journalist promptly dubbed it "kaputnik." Not until January 1958 did an Army rocket team manage to get a small American satellite into orbit. But the Russians then hurled aloft a 3,000 pound satellite. Khrushchev claimed that Soviet leadership in rocketry demonstrated the superiority of socialism over capitalism and told alarmed Americans that their grandchildren would sleep under a Communist moon.

CUBA AND CASTRO

Eisenhower, preoccupied with the arms race with the Soviets and with conducting Cold War diplomacy in Europe, Asia, and the Middle East, usually gave relations with Latin America a low priority. Latin American politics during the 1950s swung between the extremes of leftist democracies and rightist military dictatorships. Washington, while paying lip service to democracy, preferred military regimes that maintained order, protected private property, supported U.S. foreign policy, and suppressed Communists.

In the 1950s, U.S. economic interests dominated the Cuban economy, a result of the neocolonial relationship between the countries that had evolved in the aftermath of the Spanish–American War. American companies owned Cuba's oil industry, 90 percent of its mines, 80 percent of its utilities, 50 percent of its railroads, 40 percent of its sugar plantations, and 40 percent of its cattle ranches. Most of Cuba's major export crop, sugar, was sold on U.S. markets, and two-thirds of Cuban imports came from the United States.

At the end of 1958, Fidel Castro overthrew Fulgencio Batista, a corrupt dictator who had protected U.S. economic interests in Cuba. Castro quickly implemented a social revolution. He broke up the large cattle ranches and sugar plantations and distributed the land to peasants. He established summary courts that condemned former Batista supporters, thousands of whom were shot or imprisoned. Communists took over Cuban trade unions and infiltrated Castro's army.

Although alarmed by Castro's radical actions, the United States quickly recognized his government. Castro had considerable support within the United States; he was viewed as a liberal reformer who would restore Cuban democracy. He visited the United States in April 1959. In meetings with American officials, he spoke reassuringly about future relations with the United States. He promised that any future expropriations of American property would be legal and the owners compensated, but these were pledges he failed to keep. He tried to borrow money from U.S. bankers but rejected their terms because they conflicted with his plans for Cuban economic development. He then returned to Cuba and began nationalizing more U.S. property.

Relations between the United States and Cuba continued to deteriorate as Castro's revolution continued its left-wing tack. Cuban liberals, many of whom were former Castro supporters, fled Cuba for Florida. Castro, who had come to power with only vague notions about implementing an economic program once in power, joined the Communists in mid-1959. By the end of the year, his government had confiscated about $1 billion in U.S. properties. In February 1960, Castro signed an agreement with the Soviet Union in which the Soviets traded oil and machinery for sugar and also loaned Cuba $100 million. Washington responded by sharply cutting the import quota on Cuba's sugar.

Eisenhower decided by mid-1960 that Castro would have to be removed from power by whatever means necessary. The president preferred to work through the Organization of American States (OAS), but that route proved to be ineffective. Castro had supporters among OAS members; they admired him as a nationalist who had defied the United States. Others were afraid to oppose Castro, lest he foment unrest among their people. Frustrated by OAS inaction, Ike approved a CIA project to train Cuban exiles for an invasion of Cuba to overthrow Castro. The CIA established a training camp on an abandoned coffee plantation at a remote site in Guatemala and began preparations. The United States then embargoed all trade with Cuba and severed diplomatic relations.

Cuban agents meanwhile spread Castroism elsewhere in Latin America, and Washington tried to blunt Castro's appeal by promoting social reform. Administration officials, working through the OAS, promoted a reform agenda including tax reform, improved housing and schools, land reform, and economic development. Congress appropriated $500 million to launch the ambitious program.

CONTROVERSY IN EUROPE

During the late 1950s, the Cold War in Europe intensified, erasing any lingering "spirit of Geneva." The Soviets used the psychological advantage gained by their space exploits to put pressure on the United States. In November 1958,

Khrushchev, unhappy with the integration of West Germany into NATO, and with the unresolved German question, announced that within six months he would sign a separate peace treaty with East Germany, thereby ending Western occupation rights in West Berlin. Another Cold War crisis was at hand.

Ike stood firm. He refused to abandon West Berlin, but he also used diplomacy to avoid a confrontation with the Soviets. Khrushchev extended the Berlin deadline following Eisenhower's invitation to him to visit the United States. Khrushchev spent two weeks in the United States in the summer of 1959; he was the first Soviet leader ever to set foot in America. Following meetings with Eisenhower at Camp David, an ebullient Khrushchev announced the cancellation of his Berlin ultimatum. At the same time, Ike suggested that the troubling question of West Berlin ought to be speedily resolved. Once again, a Cold War crisis over Berlin receded. A month after Khrushchev's American tour, Eisenhower announced that there would be another summit meeting in Paris scheduled for May 1960, and he invited the Soviet leader to attend. Khrushchev accepted and invited the president to visit the Soviet Union following the summit. Ike accepted Khrushchev's invitation. The Cold War appeared to be thawing once again.

But the Paris summit never occurred. Two weeks before its scheduled date, the Soviets shot down an American U-2 spy plane over Soviet soil. Initially Eisenhower lied; he stated that a weather reconnaissance plane had flown off course and had inadvertently violated Soviet air space. An angry Khrushchev then revealed that the aircraft had been shot down 1,200 miles into the Soviet Union and that the Soviets had captured the pilot who admitted that he had been on a spy mission. When President Eisenhower took full responsibility for the flight and refused to re-

Figure 10.6   On July 7, 1959, Vice President Richard Nixon, accompanied by Soviet leader Nikita Khrushchev, made an official visit to the American pavilion at an exhibit in Moscow. Moments later, the two leaders staged their famous "kitchen debate," arguing over the merits of their respective systems of government. The debate was one of the dramatic moments of the Cold War. *Source:* National Archives.

pudiate it, Khrushchev angrily denounced him, canceled the summit, and withdrew Ike's invitation to visit the Soviet Union. Eisenhower deeply regretted the breakup of the summit, seeing all of his efforts for peace dashed because of the U-2 incident.

END OF AN ERA

The U-2 incident, the launching of Sputnik, and the seemingly endless crises of the Cold War all took their toll on the American people in the late 1950s. A sense of declining power to control events in the world spurred a rising debate in this country over national purpose. Social critics wondered if Americans retained the same drive to achieve goals that had motivated previous generations. Did they have the will to face future Soviet challenges? Adlai Stevenson said the nation suffered from a "paralysis of will." Americans appeared committed only to pleasure and profit and the pursuit of ease.

In the spring of 1960, both *Life* magazine and the *New York Times* published a series of commentaries on the national purpose, written by prominent authors. All agreed that something was lacking in the national spirit. President Eisenhower established a National Goals Commission to develop national objectives. The commission produced a book, *Goals for Americans*, in which it recommended an increase in military spending to meet the Soviet challenge, a government commitment to an expanding economy, a college education to be made available to all, the promotion of scientific research and the arts, and a guaranteed right to vote for all citizens. The commission's suggested goals expressed a need felt by many Americans—to restate the meaning of national existence; to reaffirm the American identity in a dangerous world; and to point to the direction in which American society should be heading.

As Eisenhower prepared to leave office, the United States faced crises in Cuba, Berlin, and Southeast Asia. All were bequeathed to his young successor. On January 17, 1961, Ike spoke to the American people for the last time as president. His Farewell Address consisted of a series of warnings, as had George Washington's famed address of 1797. Eisenhower warned of the Communist menace, of squandering the nation's resources, and of spending too much on either welfare or warfare. The most famous part of his valedictory warned of the power of the military establishment and its corporate clients:

> We must guard against the acquisition of unwarranted influence, whether sought or unsought, by the military-industrial complex.[5]

Ike asserted that the military-industrial complex could endanger basic liberties and democratic processes. In light of Vietnam and Watergate, the old general's

[5]Quoted in Charles C. Alexander, *Holding The Line: The Eisenhower Era, 1952–1961* (Bloomington: Indiana Univ. Press, 1975), p. 289.

warnings proved to be prophetic. He understood more clearly than any other modern president the potential dangers that the Cold War posed to his people's wealth and freedom.

Eisenhower presided over a peaceful, prosperous interlude in American history. But as he exited public life, the nation faced many foreign crises and unsolved domestic problems: The civil rights movement was gathering momentum, and other disadvantaged groups would soon challenge the status quo. Although the United States remained the world's wealthiest, most powerful nation, its prosperity and power had suffered relative decline in the late 1950s. The Soviet Union's military power and diplomatic influence were expanding. Anti-Western nationalism intensified among Third World countries. Eisenhower's successors in the 1960s would increase American military power and intensify the Cold War. They also would propose a broad range of social reforms. Troublesome times lay ahead.

IMPORTANT EVENTS

1950	*The Lonely Crowd* is published by David Riesman and others.
	J.D. Salinger's, *Catcher in the Rye* is published
1952	Dwight D. Eisenhower is elected president
1953	Eisenhower appoints Earl Warren as Chief Justice of the Supreme Court
1954	The Supreme Court rules on *Brown v. Board of Education of Topeka Kansas*
	The Geneva conference partitions Vietnam at the seventeenth parallel
	The Army–McCarthy hearings results in Senate condemnation of McCarthy
1955	The Montgomery, Alabama, bus boycott ignites the modern civil rights movement
	The AFL and the CIO merge
	The "Summit" conference is held at Geneva
1956	Elvis Presley's first superhit, "Heartbreak Hotel" is sold
	The Interstate Highway Act is passed
	The Suez crisis erupts
	Soviet tanks crush the Hungarian revolution
1957	School desegregation crisis occurs in Little Rock, Arkansas
	The first modern Civil Rights Act is enacted
	Jack Kerouac's *On the Road* is published
	The Soviets launch "Sputnik"
1958	NASA is established
	U.S. Marines hit the beaches in Lebanon
	The Berlin crisis occurs
	Congress enacts the National Defense Education Act
1959	Castro comes into power in Cuba
1960	U-2 incident causes impending summit meeting to be cancelled
1961	Eisenhower delivers his Farewell Address

BIBLIOGRAPHY

Many fine books have been written about American economic, social, and cultural history during the period 1945–1960. David Halberstam's *The Fifties* is a recent, well-written general history. William L. O'Neill, in *American High*, offers a recent lively account of the suburban decade. John Kenneth Galbraith's *The Affluent Society* is a good analysis of the postwar prosperity. John B. Rae, in *The American Automobile*, writes about the car culture of the 1950s. Landon Y. Jones's *Great Expectations: America and the Baby Boom Generation* is the best study of the most important demographic development of postwar America. One of the finest accounts of suburbia is John Keats's *The Crack in the Picture Window*. Will Herberg, in *Catholic–Protestant–Jew* writes about the important role of religion in mid-century American society. C. Wright Mills's *White Collar: The American Middle Class* is a radical critique of the affluent society. Two classic studies of the social and cultural history of the 1950s are David Riesman's and others *The Lonely Crowd: A Study of the Changing American Character* and William H. Whyte, Jr.'s *The Organization Man*. Myron Matlaw, in *American Popular Entertainment*, writes sections about television, pop music, and films of the 1950s. Erik Barnouw's *Tube of Plenty* is a fine study of television during its "golden age." Bruce Cook, in *The Beat Generation*, writes about the beat writers who flourished in the late 1950s. Juan Williams's *Eyes on the Prize: America's Civil Rights Years, 1954–1965* is a stirring account of the civil rights movement. The political history of the 1950s is generally well covered in Charles C. Alexander's *Holding the Line: the Eisenhower Era, 1952–1961*. Stephen E. Ambrose, in *Eisenhower the President*, offers the best account of the Eisenhower presidency. Robert A. Divine's *Eisenhower and the Cold War* is the best diplomatic history of the Eisenhower years. Michael A. Guhin, in *John Foster Dulles: A Statesman and His Times*, provides the fullest treatment of Eisenhower's energetic secretary of state. Using recently released documents and records, Keith Kyle, author of *Suez*, has written a good account of that crucial episode in U.S.–Middle Eastern diplomatic history.

11

New Frontiers

IN the early 1960s, Americans regained the confidence in their national destiny that had faltered in the late 1950s, when the economy went slack and the Soviets appeared to have gained an ideological and a strategic advantage in the Cold War. The economy revived. Most middle-class American families enjoyed unprecedented affluence, and their children's prospects never looked better. An energetic, articulate young president kindled this resurgent optimism. John Fitzgerald Kennedy voiced national goals in language that Americans, particularly young Americans, could understand and accept. He told them that they could face the challenges of mid-century life, hold their own in world affairs, and solve nagging social problems at home. A new activist spirit surged across the land. For a few years, a spirit of "Camelot" reigned, a belief that anything was possible, that nothing was beyond the grasp of Americans.

A PATH TO THE PRESIDENCY

John F. "Jack" Kennedy inherited a rich political legacy. Both of his grandfathers, second-generation Irish immigrants, had been prominent ethnic politicians in Boston. His father, Joseph P. "Joe" Kennedy, a Harvard graduate, made a fortune estimated at $150 million in banking, real estate, the film industry, and other enterprises. Joe Kennedy, a conservative Democratic supporter of Franklin Roosevelt, served as the Security and Exchange Commission's first chairman and later as ambassador to Great Britain. Jack's political career began successfully when he won election to Congress in 1946, representing a working-class district of Boston. His father played a major behind-the-scenes role, providing both money and influence to help his son win.

While in Congress, Kennedy introduced no important legislation nor identified himself with any major issue. He usually took liberal positions on domestic issues. He worked to purge Communists from union ranks, and he opposed the Taft-Hartley Act. On foreign policy, he sometimes aligned himself with conservative Republican critics of Truman's Far Eastern policy. He supported General MacArthur's call for war against China in 1951, and Truman's firing of the old general outraged him. He formed political friendships with two rising Republican stars, Congressman Richard Nixon and Senator Joseph McCarthy.

Jack sought to move up to the Senate in 1952, even though it was clearly a Republican year. The GOP ran the popular war hero, General Dwight Eisenhower, for president. Jack Kennedy faced a formidable challenge and began his campaign against the incumbent, Henry Cabot Lodge, Jr., as a decided underdog. He ran as a moderate Democrat and dissociated himself from the Democratic national ticket, which was obviously losing that year. In a close race, his father's money and Kennedy's superb campaign organization, led by his younger brother Robert, proved to be the decisive factors. His election to the Senate in November 1952 signaled the arrival of a new-style Democratic politician. Kennedy was the leader of an emergent generation of postwar Democrats who were less ideological and less partisan than the traditional New Deal–Fair Dealers.

The young senator-elect began his career as a national leader that would carry him to the presidency. In the Senate, Kennedy could devote more attention to foreign affairs, always his major interest. He consistently advocated a strong Cold War policy and called for increased defense spending. He became a critic of the Eisenhower–Dulles New Look foreign policy. He opposed giving aid to the French in Southeast Asia unless the administration prodded them to grant the people of Indochina independence.

At the 1956 Democratic Convention, Kennedy made a strong bid for the vice presidential nomination. He lost narrowly to Senator Estes Kefauver of Tennessee. Many voters got their first look at Kennedy during his fight for the vice presidency, and they liked what they saw. As it turned out, it was to his political advantage to be defeated at the convention. Had he received the vice presidential nomination and run with Adlai Stevenson, he would have shared the humiliation of another lopsided electoral defeat at the hands of the popular incumbents, Eisenhower and Nixon. Such an outcome could have derailed his future presidential bid.

THE ELECTION OF 1960

A Democratic resurgence began with the 1958 midterm elections. A series of events had shaken public confidence in the Eisenhower administration: Sputnik and the apparent missile and space race gaps; crises in the Middle East; and a sharp recession at home that had driven unemployment above 7 percent, the highest since 1941. The Sherman Adams scandal also tarnished the clean image the Republicans had enjoyed since coming to office. The Democrats increased their majorities to 64 to 32 in the Senate and 283 to 153 in the House, their largest margins since the New Deal heyday of 1936. In Massachusetts, John Kennedy won a lopsided reelection victory. His impressive performance made him the Democratic front-runner in 1960.

Many Democratic leaders entered the race for their party's 1960 presidential nomination. With the popular Eisenhower forced to resign because of the Twenty-second Amendment, prospects for a Democratic victory looked better than any time since the glory days of FDR. Other candidates included Senator Hubert Humphrey, Senator Stuart Symington, and Senate majority leader Lyndon Johnson. Adlai Stevenson was still a contender, even though he had lost twice to Eisenhower.

Two obstacles blocked Kennedy's path to the nomination. First he would have to dispel the myth that a Catholic could never be elected president. The second obstacle was the candidacies of his powerful rivals, all of whom had longer, more distinguished political careers than he. Kennedy was an upstart among seasoned veterans of the political wars. Many informed observers believed that Kennedy lacked the experience, maturity, and stature necessary to run the country in the 1960s.

Victories in the early primaries gave him the momentum that carried him to the nomination. Only Humphrey challenged him in these popularity contests. Symington and Johnson took the organizational route to the nomination, seeking delegates from the thirty-four states that did not hold primaries. Stevenson did not campaign, relying on his liberal followers to orchestrate his nomination at the convention if Kennedy's bid fell short. Jack eliminated Humphrey early. He beat him decisively in New Hampshire, Wisconsin, and West Virginia. Kennedy demonstrated that he could win and put the Catholic issue to rest. His organization contained a Stevenson boom that developed at the convention, and Kennedy won a close first ballot nomination. Kennedy chose Lyndon Johnson, who had come in second to Jack in the balloting for president, as his vice presidential running mate. He needed Johnson to win Texas and to hold the South if he was to have any chance of winning the presidency in November.

In his acceptance speech, Kennedy attacked the Eisenhower administration's handling of Cold War issues; he claimed that the Republicans had been too soft in responding to Communist threats, and he pledged a stronger approach. He set forth an agenda of unfinished business facing the nation in the 1960s:

> We stand today at the edge of a New Frontier—the frontier of the 1960s—a frontier of unknown opportunities and perils—a frontier of unfulfilled hopes and threats.[1]

When the Republicans gathered in Chicago a week later, Richard Nixon had the nomination sewn up. The nearest thing to a challenge came from Nelson Rockefeller, governor of New York. He had no chance and withdrew long before the convention. But Rockefeller influenced the party platform. Two days before the convention opened, Nixon accepted Rockefeller's proposals calling for stronger

[1] Quoted in Herbert Parmet, *JFK: The Presidency of John F. Kennedy* (New York: Penguin Books, 1984), p. 31.

defense programs, faster buildup of missiles, stronger civil rights measures, and government stimulation of the economy to promote economic growth. Conservative Republicans reacted angrily to the Rockefeller-influenced platform. Arizona Senator Barry Goldwater called it "The Munich of the Republican Party." Nixon had to use all of his considerable powers of persuasion to keep the unhappy conservatives in the party fold.

The 1960 presidential campaign broke all records for money spent and miles traveled by candidates. Nixon campaigned in all fifty states. Kennedy traveled over 100,000 miles in a jet leased by his family for the campaign. It was the toughest, closest presidential election in modern American political history.

Despite the candidates' dramatically different backgrounds—Nixon, the poor boy from rural southern California who had fought his way up the political ladder—and Kennedy, the privileged aristocrat whose political career depended largely on his father's wealth and influence—they shared similar political views. Nixon was a moderate conservative with liberal tendencies. Kennedy was a moderate liberal with conservative tendencies. Both were Cold Warriors. Both accepted the basic structure of the New Deal welfare state. Both advocated civil rights and believed in a strong presidency. Both were young men, Nixon, forty-seven, and Kennedy, forty-three. Because they shared similar political views, the campaign featured few substantial debates over the issues. Each challenged the other's capacity to govern, and each insisted that he was the better man. Because the electorate perceived their views to be so similar, the outcome of the election turned on personal image and the voter's feel for one or the other, not on the issues.

Nixon began the campaign with some liabilities. The sagging economy was the most serious. Also, Eisenhower gave him only lukewarm support. Even so, the early advantage clearly lay with Nixon. He was far better known to the American people because of his active role in Eisenhower's administration, and he used this role to make his point that he was better qualified for presidential leadership than Kennedy. As the campaign got underway, public opinion polls gave Nixon the lead. The election appeared to be Nixon's to lose.

Kennedy's religious affiliation was an important campaign issue, and he met his detractors forthrightly. He clearly stated his views: there was nothing in his religion that would prevent him from obeying his constitutional oath and governing the nation; he supported the First Amendment's separation of church and state; he opposed federal aid to parochial schools; and he favored birth control. He appeared before a gathering of prominent Protestant leaders in Houston and he told the ministers, "I am not the Catholic candidate for president, I am the Democratic Party's candidate for president, who also happens to be a Catholic." As he neared the end of his short speech, he told the assembled divines:

> If this election is decided on the basis that 40 million Americans lost their chance of being President on the day they were baptized, then it is the whole nation that will be the loser in the eyes of history, and in the eyes of our own people.[2]

[2]Quoted in *Ibid.*, p. 43.

When he finished, the ministers gave him a warm, standing ovation. His performance could not remove anti-Catholicism from the campaign, but it defused the religious issue and freed Kennedy to concentrate on attacking Nixon and the Republicans.

The highlight of the campaign occurred when the candidates staged four nationally televised debates between September 26 and October 21, the first televised debates between presidential candidates. The debates reflected the growing influence that television was now playing in the nation's political life. The first debate was decisive and Kennedy won it. On camera, under hot lights, Nixon's makeup powder streaked as he noticeably sweated. He faltered when answering some of the questions. Kennedy, in contrast, exuded cool, cheerful confidence. He displayed a sure grasp of the issues, an agile intelligence, and a sharp wit. He dispelled any lingering doubts about his maturity or ability to be president. Nixon did much better in the three subsequent debates and had a slight advantage overall, but he could not completely overcome the disadvantage of his appearance and performance during that first debate.

In none of the debates did the candidates explore issues in depth, and no clear issue distinctions between them surfaced. The debates were essentially popularity contests, whose outcomes depended on the cosmetic factors of personality and appearance. Kennedy won the one that counted most. October polls showed Kennedy taking the lead for the first time. In the final month of campaigning, Kennedy attracted large, excited crowds. He had momentum, and the Democrats sensed victory.

But in the final week of the campaign, the Republicans almost pulled it out. Nixon strongly defended the Eisenhower record and hammered away at Kennedy's inexperience in international affairs. Republicans staged a media blitz across the nation. Eisenhower campaigned energetically for Nixon in those final days and the old lion nearly eliminated Jack's lead.

Kennedy's 303–219 edge in electoral votes masked the closest presidential election in American history. In some states the outcome was in doubt for days. Kennedy, by narrowly winning populous states such as New York, Pennsylvania, Michigan, and Texas, squeezed out victory. Out of a record 68 million votes cast, Kennedy's margin of victory was about 118,000. Kennedy received 49.7 percent of the popular vote to Nixon's 49.5 percent. Republicans picked up twenty-two seats in the House and two seats in the Senate, leaving the Democrats with large majorities in both. Most Democratic candidates ran better than Kennedy. His party was more popular than he.

It is impossible to say precisely what factor determined Kennedy's hairline victory. In such a close election many variables could have determined the outcome, and there are too many imponderables involved. Suppose Eisenhower had entered the campaign a week earlier? Kennedy's religion cut both ways: in rural, Protestant areas of the South, Southwest, and West, it cost him votes; however, in Northeastern, Midwestern, and Western urban states it gained him votes. On balance, he may have gained more votes than he lost from his religion, for the states

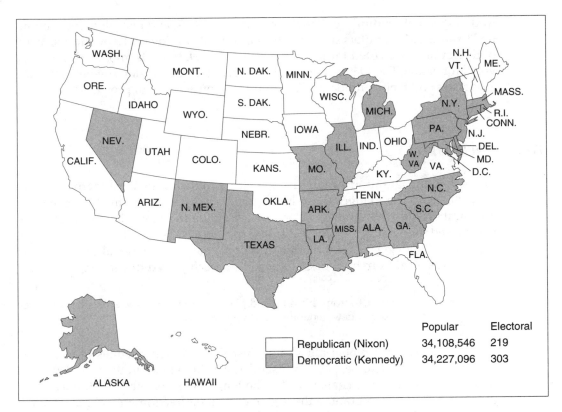

Figure 11.1   The election of 1960.   *Source:* George D. Moss, *Moving On*, p. 138.

where people voted for him because of his religious affiliation contained the largest clusters of electoral votes. Kennedy benefited from the televised debates, particularly the first one. A poll showed that 57 percent of voters felt that the debates had affected their choice, and of these, 75 percent voted for Kennedy. The winner also ran well among black voters, getting more of them than Stevenson had in 1956. Kennedy had followed a bold strategy during the campaign of relying on Johnson to hold white Southerners while he appealed for black voters. He responded to an appeal to help Dr. Martin Luther King, Jr. gain release from a Georgia jail, where his wife feared he would be killed. Kennedy promised to sign an executive order forbidding segregation in federally subsidized housing. Black votes provided his winning margin in Texas and North Carolina, and he got most of the Northern black inner-city vote.

The 1960 election signaled the end of the Solid South. Nixon got about half of the Southern vote in 1960. After the race, he noted that had he concentrated his efforts on the South in the final week, he might have won the election. He would put that knowledge about the changing South to good use in the 1968 presidential election. Kennedy did well in traditional Republican strongholds in New England, the

Midwest, and the suburbs everywhere. Sectional, class, and party loyalties continued to erode. Many voters split their tickets in 1960. Millions of Republicans, many of them Catholics, voted for Kennedy. Millions of Democrats, mostly Protestants, voted for Nixon. The 1960 election further blurred the distinctions between the major parties and their candidates. The politics of consensus still prevailed.

THE KENNEDY STYLE

Kennedy's inauguration occurred on a clear, cold day in Washington on January 20, 1961. The inaugural ceremony vividly expressed the fresh start his administration intended to make. Consciously emulating Franklin Roosevelt, who had roused the country from depression torpor in 1933, Kennedy intended to "get the country moving again." Marion Anderson sang the national anthem. Poet Robert Frost read from his works. Kennedy's speech stirred the nation:

> Let the word go forth from this time and place, to friend and foe alike, that the torch has been passed to a new generation of Americans. . . . [3]

He called for a global alliance against the common enemies of mankind, "tyranny, poverty, disease, and war itself." It was high noon in the Cold War, and Kennedy welcomed the challenge: "In the long history of the world, only a few generations have been granted the role of defending freedom in its hour of maximum danger. I do not shrink from this responsibility, I welcome it." He sent a warning to the Kremlin: "Let every nation know, whether it wishes us well or ill, that we shall pay any price, bear any burden, meet any hardship, support any friend, oppose any foe to assure the survival and the success of liberty. . . . " As he approached the end of his splendid speech, he spoke his most famous line. He appealed to his countrymen, especially to young Americans, to

> ask not what your country can do for you—
> ask what you can do for your country.[4]

Kennedy and his beautiful young wife Jacqueline exuded stylish charm. Kennedy hosted a dinner for Nobel Prize winners. Distinguished classical musicians performed there. The Kennedys and their friends played touch football on the White House lawn, conveying the youthful energy and exuberance characterizing the new government. White House parties attended by many show biz celebrities sometimes lasted all night.

[3]Quoted in Arthur M. Schlesinger, Jr., *A Thousand Days* (Greenwich, CT: Fawcett Publications, 1965), p. 13.
[4]Quoted in *Ibid.*, p. 14.

Figure 11.2   **A new generation comes to power. . . . John F. Kennedy chats with outgoing President Dwight D. Eisenhower on the way to the inauguration ceremony on January 20, 1961.** *Source:* National Archives.

Kennedy believed in a strong, centralized presidency that operated free of the restraints of Congress, public opinion, and the media. Kennedy was determined to energize the presidency. He would be at the center of action.

He selected able advisers to assist him. Secretary of State Dean Rusk came from the Rockefeller Foundation. For secretary of defense, he chose Robert S. McNamara, the president of Ford Motor Company. McGeorge Bundy, a brilliant professor and administrator from Harvard, was appointed national security adviser. Bundy managed foreign policy. Kennedy's talented young staffer who had served with him in the Senate, Theodore Sorensen, took charge of domestic issues and wrote many of his speeches. Kennedy's younger brother Robert became attorney general. He appointed several Republicans to try to reassure the business community that his administration would not be antibusiness.

THE COLD WARRIOR

Kennedy gave top priority to the conduct of American foreign and military policy that centered on America's global rivalry with the Soviet Union. Cold War

Figure 11.3   John F. Kennedy (President, 1961–1963) projected a vision of national renewal. He encouraged Americans, especially young people, to "ask not what your country can do for you—ask what you can do for your country."   *Source:* Library of Congress.

ideology shaped his view of the world. He viewed the Communist system itself as the Free World's main enemy:

> . . . implacable, insatiable, unceasing in its drive for world domination. For this is not a struggle for supremacy of arms alone—it is also a struggle for supremacy between two conflicting ideologies: Freedom under God versus ruthless, godless tyranny.[5]

Kennedy and his advisers made the restoration of American primacy in world affairs their major goal. They viewed the Third World as the key to winning the Cold War. It was among the underdeveloped countries of Asia, Africa, and Latin America where the battle against Communism would be joined and won. Kennedy told an audience at the University of California in Berkeley that "freedom and diversity," the essence of the American way, would prevail in the "lands of the rising people" over the Communist monolith. He had a bold vision, rooted in a deep faith in the American system, confident that American technology and expertise could prevail in the long, twilight struggle with the Soviet menace.

[5]Quoted in Herbert Parmet, *Jack: The Struggles of John F. Kennedy* (New York: Dial Press, 1980), p. 328.

THE BAY OF PIGS

The new administration encountered its first Cold War crisis in Cuba. The CIA project to overthrow Castro, begun by Eisenhower six months earlier, readied for action. Anti-Castro Cuban exiles, many of whom were former liberal supporters of the Cuban dictator, had been trained for an amphibious assault on Cuba at a secret camp set up in the Guatemalan mountains. CIA officials believed that an invasion of Cuba would activate a general uprising within Cuba that would overthrow Castro. Kennedy, after consultations with his senior advisers, gave the operation the green light. The invasion would be risky, but Kennedy and his New Frontiersmen were eager to strike the Communists.

About 1,450 invaders, debarking from a Nicaraguan port in ships provided by the CIA, landed before dawn at the Bay of Pigs, a remote area on the southern Cuba coast. Castro quickly deployed his forces to meet them. The invaders, lacking adequate artillery support and air cover, were pinned on the beach and overwhelmed. All but about 100 of them were killed or captured within three days. The invaders never made contact with Cuban underground elements, and the expected anti-Castro uprising never occurred.

The Bay of Pigs disaster humiliated the Kennedy administration. America's European allies criticized its actions, and Third World spokesmen took turns condemning the United States at the United Nations. Within the United States, liberals attacked Kennedy for undertaking the invasion, and conservatives condemned him for failing to overthrow Castro. America stood exposed as both imperialistic and inept, a pathetic combination of wickedness and weakness.

The U.S.-backed invasion had violated the Organization of American States (OAS) charter that prohibited any Western Hemispheric nation from intervening in another's affairs. Latin American nations, resenting the thinly disguised American reversion to gunboat diplomacy, refused the United States' request to quarantine Cuba from inter-American affairs. Castro emerged from the affair stronger than ever. Both Soviet aid to Cuba and the pace of Cuban socialization of private properties accelerated in the aftermath of the failed invasion.

The invasion project had been ill conceived and mismanaged from the start. The CIA victimized itself with faulty intelligence data and wishful thinking. It underestimated Castro's military strength and exaggerated the extent of anti-Castro sentiment in Cuba. Kennedy ensured the mission's failure when he curtailed CIA air strikes preceding the landings and then refused all requests for naval air support that might have salvaged the failing operation. Kennedy had concluded that the invasion had failed and that air cover could not save it, so he decided to cut his losses. He also did not want a war with Cuba, and he wanted to preserve the fiction that the invasion was a Cuban affair.

Kennedy got a rough baptism of fire and his first serious criticism as president. He assumed full responsibility for the fiasco, but afterwards he ordered an investigation of the CIA. He forced its aged director, Allen Dulles, into retirement and replaced him with John McCone, a conservative California oilman. Kennedy

Figure 11.4   Cuban director Fidel Castro reviews Cuban troops with his brother, Raul, the commander of the Cuban armed forces. Looming behind them is a statue of Jose Marti, Cuba's first president.   *Source:* National Archives.

also made an aggressive speech before a convention of newspaper editors in which he reaffirmed his determination to be rid of Castro.

According to the findings of a special Senate investigating committee that later examined CIA covert operations, Kennedy ordered the CIA to eliminate Castro following the failure of the Bay of Pigs invasion. Robert Kennedy took charge of Operation Mongoose, which included efforts to disrupt the Cuban economy and support anti-Castro elements. During 1961 and 1962, CIA operatives tried various bizarre schemes to kill the Cuban dictator. These efforts included cigars laced with explosives and deadly poison, and an attempt to spear him with a harpoon while he was snorkling at a Caribbean resort. CIA agents also plotted with Mafia elements to get rid of Castro, but they had to abandon the project because of opposition from FBI director J. Edgar Hoover. Castro knew about Operation Mongoose, and he was aware of some of the CIA plots to assassinate him. He appealed to his allies in Moscow for help. The Soviets responded by sending troops to Cuba.

THE THIRD WORLD

During his campaign for the presidency, Kennedy had repeatedly criticized the Eisenhower administration for failing to promote economic development and the growth of political democracy among the nations of Latin America, Asia, and Africa.

Kennedy insisted that such neglect had given the Soviet Union opportunities to get ahead of the United States in the race for influence among the strategically important developing nations of the Third World. Kennedy pledged to help these nations modernize their societies and to restore American influence among them.

For Latin America, the Kennedy administration developed a multifaceted assistance program called the Alliance for Progress. Kennedy proposed the Alliance in a dramatic speech given in Mexico City in May 1961. The Alliance expanded Eisenhower's previously announced aid program for Latin America. Congress appropriated $500 million to start the program, designed to eradicate poverty and social injustice in the Western Hemisphere. Over the life of the program, billions of dollars in loans and grants from both public and private sources were fed into the Alliance for Progress.

In most Latin American countries, the results were disappointing. Conservative governments refused to reform their tax systems, to grant land reform, or to democratize their politics. Economic growth was sluggish throughout the 1960s in the region. Unemployment rates, mortality rates, and literacy rates did not improve in most Latin American countries. The elite classes that held power in these lands feared Castroism as much as Kennedy, but they preferred to rely on repression rather than to take their chances with social reform.

In the summer of 1961, the Kennedy administration launched the Peace Corps, a much more successful initiative to help people in Third World countries. The Peace Corps derived from the same Cold War concern to involve the United States more directly in Third World countries and to give idealistic young Americans an opportunity for public service. Over the next two years, about 7,500 Peace Corps volunteers were sent to forty-four nations in Asia, Africa, and Latin America. Most of them worked as teachers; others found jobs in health care, agricultural reform, and community development. For many of the young people who served in the Peace Corps, they not only found an opportunity to help poor people but also returned to America with a greater appreciation of the diversity of the world's cultures. Most recipients of Peace Corps assistance were grateful and admired the young Americans that they got to know.

Although Africa remained a relatively low priority with the Kennedy administration, the United States did intervene in Zaire, formerly the Belgian Congo, in 1961, to support an anti-Communist leader as head of the government. The CIA maneuvered to block more radical candidates, whom Washington feared might have the backing of the Soviet Union, from coming to power. Amidst chaotic conditions, civil war broke out, and the United States pulled out. Washington then backed ultimately successful United Nations' efforts to end the civil war and to prevent Zaire from disintegrating.

BERLIN

At the beginning of his presidency, Kennedy and Secretary of Defense McNamara began a crash program to expand and diversify America's military forces. They believed that Eisenhower's reliance on massive retaliation and his refusal to engage the Soviets in a missile race had set dangerous limits on the American ability to counter Soviet-backed insurgencies in Third World countries. The United States rapidly increased its strategic nuclear forces that included ICBMs, missile-launching Polaris submarines, and long-range bombers. They also built up conventional war capabilities, adding a Kennedy favorite, counterinsurgency forces. The president sought strategic versatility, which he termed *flexible response*—the ability to intervene anywhere in the world with flexible force levels in response to Soviet or Soviet-backed initiatives.

The Kennedy military buildup had broad bipartisan congressional and popular support. At the same time the United States expanded its military capacities, Kennedy repeatedly urged the Soviets to join in arms limitation talks aimed at reducing the arms race. But Khrushchev responded by increasing Soviet military spending for more ICBMs, the backbone of the Soviet strategic system. The American arms buildup triggered another upward spiral in the nuclear arms race.

Having been badly burned by the Bay of Pigs fiasco, Kennedy was more determined than ever to respond strongly to Communist threats. He worried lest his administration appear weak willed and lose prestige in the eyes of the world and its own people. Three months after the invasion, he met for a series of private talks with Khrushchev in Vienna in June 1961. The two leaders exchanged views on a wide range of issues. Kennedy was calm, rational, and polite in these conversations. Khrushchev's moods varied. At times he talked warmly of peaceful coexistence between Communism and capitalism. At other times he got angry, even threatening. He turned ideologue, asserting the inevitable triumph of socialism in the world. He bullied the young president, coming away from those meetings with the mistaken impression that Kennedy could be pressured. Khrushchev misread the young aristocrat's civility as weakness. His misjudgment would later contribute to the most dangerous moment in modern history.

The major issue discussed at Vienna was the long-standing problem of Berlin. The German question had never been formally settled after World War II because of Cold War conflicts. At war's end, Germany had been divided into occupation zones by the victorious nations. In 1948 and 1949, the Western zones were merged into one zone, which became the Federal Republic of Germany (West Germany), a Western liberal state. The Soviet zone in eastern Germany became the Socialist Democratic Republic of Germany (East Germany) on which the Soviets imposed a Communist system. By 1950, there existed two de facto German states. Neither state accepted the other as legitimate, but most Germans clung to the hope that one day Germany would again be a unified nation.

Berlin, lying deep within East Germany, also remained divided between East and West, causing periodic crises during the Cold War. Tensions had flared in 1948, when the Soviets had tried to drive the Western nations out of Berlin and Truman thwarted them with the Berlin airlift. Khrushchev pressured Eisenhower over Berlin in 1958 and then backed off when Ike stood firm. Now, with Kennedy in office, the Soviet leader pressed for a peace treaty between the two German states that would legitimate the de facto division of the country, remove the possibility of reunion, and deprive the West of any legal basis for its occupation of West Berlin. Khrushchev told Kennedy that he wanted the Berlin issue settled by year's end and that if it were not settled, he may conclude a separate peace treaty with East Germany, forcing the West to negotiate with a government that none of the Western states recognized. Khrushchev and the East German rulers also wanted to stop the flow of East Germans into West Berlin.

Kennedy rebuffed Khrushchev's proposals and reaffirmed the Western presence in West Berlin. He also asked Congress to increase military appropriations by $3 billion, and he tripled draft calls, called up reserves, and extended enlistments of all military personnel on active duty. Kennedy also asked for $207 million from Congress to increase significantly the number of civil defense fallout shelters, dramatizing the implications of the Berlin crisis.

The Soviet response came on August 13, when workers suddenly erected a wall across Berlin imprisoning East Germans in their own country and staunching the flow of refugees. Before the Berlin Wall, nearly 3 million East Germans had escaped to the West since 1945. During the first twelve days of August 1961, about 46,000 had fled Communism. The Soviet action caught the Americans by surprise. Some of Kennedy's hawkish advisers urged him to tear down the Wall. Kennedy

Figure 11.5   President Kennedy goes to the Berlin Wall in June 1963 on a visit to West Berlin. The Wall, erected in August 1961, quickly became a stark Cold War symbol of the impasse between the Communist World and the Free World, and it perpetuated the division of Germany in the heart of Europe.   *Source:* National Archives.

never considered doing that, because he did not want to risk war. To reassure West Berliners that accepting the Wall did not presage eventual Allied withdrawal from the divided city, Kennedy sent an additional 1,500 combat troops to West Berlin. In June 1963, he visited West Berlin and told a huge crowd, "Ich bin ein Berliner" (I am a Berliner) to dramatize the American determination to stay.

East Germans who tried to escape over the barrier were shot by military police. The Berlin Wall quickly became a potent Cold War symbol of the impasse between East and West, and of the division of Germany and its major city. It also was a stark admission of Communism's failure to win the hearts and minds of East Germans. But the Wall also provided a practical solution to the conflict over Berlin. It stopped the flow of refugees, which was Khrushchev's immediate goal, and it allowed West Berlin to remain in the Western orbit, which was Kennedy's main goal. German reunification was deferred to the indefinite future. Khrushchev announced in October that he would no longer insist on Western withdrawal from West Berlin. The crisis ended, and Berlin was never again a major source of Cold War conflict. But the Wall endured for nearly thirty years as the most vivid symbol of European Cold War divisions—until the people of East Germany themselves tore the Wall down in November 1989 as they began the process of dismantling the Communist system imposed on them after World War II.

THE MISSILE CRISIS

Following the Bay of Pigs, the Soviets sent technicians and weapons to Cuba to protect that Communist satellite from American hostility. By the summer of 1962, American intelligence sources estimated that there were from 10,000 to 40,000 Soviet troops stationed in Cuba. Castro also supported guerrilla actions and subversion in other Latin American countries. Republicans, looking for election year issues, attacked the Kennedy administration for allowing the Soviet arms buildup in Cuba. Kennedy opposed attacking or invading Cuba as long as the Soviets placed only defensive weapons in Cuba that posed no threat to the United States or any other hemispheric nation. But Khrushchev and Castro decided on a daring move to deter any further U.S. action against Cuba and to score a Cold War coup. The Soviets secretly tried to install medium-range and intermediate-range nuclear missiles and bombers in Cuba. These missiles and bombers were offensive weapons, capable of carrying nuclear payloads to American cities and military installations.

On October 14, 1962, a U-2 reconnaissance plane photographed a launching site for an intermediate-range missile nearing completion in western Cuba. Kennedy immediately determined that the missiles must be removed from the island. His sense of strategic and political reality told him that they had to go. But how to get the missiles out of Cuba? And how without triggering a nuclear war? The most dangerous crisis of the Cold War had begun.

Kennedy convened a special executive committee of thirteen senior advisers to find a way to remove the missiles and planes. The committee met secretly for the next twelve days. Their duty was to propose tactics that would force the Soviets to remove the missiles from Cuba without igniting World War III. The president's brother and closest adviser, Robert, chaired the committee sessions.

Beginning with their initial session, all members of the committee agreed that the missiles had to be removed, but they disagreed on the tactics. Some members, led by Chairman of the Joint Chiefs of Staff, Army General Maxwell Taylor, wanted to take the missile sites out with surprise air strikes that would likely kill both Soviet technicians and Cuban soldiers. Robert Kennedy, who proved to be the most influential member of the executive committee, rejected that idea, saying that he wanted "no Pearl Harbors on his brother's record." The Taylor-led faction then proposed an invasion to get rid of both the offensive weapons and the Castro regime. The president rejected this suggestion as being too risky; it could involve a prolonged war with Cuba, provoke a Soviet attack on West Berlin, or even bring nuclear war. Secretary of Defense McNamara proposed a naval blockade to prevent further shipments of weapons to Cuba. The blockade would allow both sides some freedom of maneuver. The United States could decide to attack or negotiate later, depending on the Soviet response to the blockade. A majority of the

Figure 11.6   Medium-range ballistic missile base in Cuba. The United States detected Soviet efforts to install missiles in Cuba when reconnaissance aircraft photographed missile bases under construction on the island. This photograph is an example of the evidence shown to President Kennedy in October 1962.   *Source:* U.S. Air Force, neg.# USAF167183.

committee member's endorsed McNamara's proposal. The president accepted the blockade tactic.

President Kennedy attended few of the committee sessions, and when he did attend, he said little, to allow free deliberations by the committee members. With the 1962 midterm elections only three weeks away, he was on the campaign trail, acting as though everything were normal. On his campaign trips, he talked mostly about domestic issues, trying to build support for his New Frontier reform programs that were stalled in Congress. Neither the media nor the public had any inkling of the serious crisis that was building. The Soviets did not know that the missile sites had been detected, nor that Kennedy was planning the U.S. response.

On Monday morning, October 22, the blockade began. That evening, Kennedy went on television to inform the nation and the Soviets about the missile crisis. He bluntly told his audience around the world: "Unmistakable evidence has established the fact that a series of offensive missile sites is now in preparation on that imprisoned island." He spoke of the naval blockade, which he called a "quarantine," that was in place around Cuba. He demanded that the Soviets dismantle and remove all missile bases and bombers from Cuba immediately, and he stated that the quarantine would remain in place until all offensive weapons had been removed. Then he spoke these chilling words:

> It shall be the policy of this nation to regard any nuclear missile launched from Cuba against any nation in the Western Hemisphere as an attack by the Soviet Union on the United States, requiring a full retaliatory response upon the Soviet Union.[6]

Kennedy confronted Khrushchev with the risk of nuclear war if he did not remove the missiles. For the next five days, the world hovered on the brink of catastrophe. Khrushchev denounced the United States and denied that the Soviets were installing offensive weapons in Cuba. Meanwhile, work on the missile sites continued. The first sites would be operational in a few days. The U.S. Air Force prepared strikes to take them out before they would be capable of launching missiles at targets in the United States. Soviet merchant ships hauling more weapons continued to steam toward Cuba. The U.S. Navy positioned its blockade fleet to intercept them. American invasion forces gathered in Florida. The B-52 strategic bombers took to the air with nuclear bombs on board. U.S. strategic missiles went to maximum alert. The moment of supreme danger would come if a Soviet ship tried to run the blockade, for American ship commanders had orders to stop them.

The first break came on October 24. Soviet ships hauling offensive weapons turned back. Two other Soviet freighters, hauling no offensive weapons, submitted to searches and were permitted to steam on to Cuba. Two days later, Khrushchev sent a letter to President Kennedy offering to remove all offensive weapons from Cuba in exchange for a U.S. pledge to not invade Cuba. Kennedy accepted the offer, but before he could send his reply, Khrushchev sent a second letter raising the stakes: America would have to give a no-invasion-of-Cuba pledge, plus remove its

---

[6]Quoted in Elie Abel, *The Missile Crisis* (New York: Bantam Books, 1966), p. 106.

Jupiter missiles stationed in Turkey, which were targeted at the Soviet Union. Kennedy refused to bargain. It was his view that Khrushchev's reckless initiative had threatened world peace, and it was the Soviet leader's responsibility to remove the missiles from Cuba quickly.

Kennedy, heeding the advice of his brother, made one last try to avoid the looming cataclysm. The president sent a cable to Khrushchev accepting the offer in the first letter and ignoring the second letter. The next night, on October 27, Robert Kennedy told the Soviet ambassador to the United States, Anatoly Dobrynin, that this was the Soviets' last chance to avoid war: if the Soviets "did not remove those bases, we would remove them." He also indicated to Dobrynin that the American missiles in Turkey, although not part of any quid pro quo, would be removed soon after the Cuban missiles were removed.

While these tense negotiations were in progress, a U-2 spy plane was shot down over Cuba, and the pilot was killed. Angry hawks on the executive committee wanted to launch airstrikes and to invade Cuba, not only to destroy the missile sites but to overthrow Castro's regime and send the Soviet troops back home. Robert Kennedy, McNamara, and others restrained them, pleading that a few more days were needed to allow the president to work out a diplomatic solution to the crisis.

The next morning, on October 28, Khrushchev agreed to remove the missiles and bombers in return for the president's promise to not invade Cuba. He claimed that he had achieved his goal of protecting Cuba from American attacks. The United States suspended its blockade. The United Nations supervised the dismantling and removal of the Cuban bases. American missiles were removed from Turkey a few weeks later. The missile crisis had been resolved without war. Kennedy received high praise for his actions. The Democrats gained in the fall elections. Kennedy's standing in the polls soared to new heights. America had stood up to the Soviets and had forced them to back down.

Although Kennedy was showered with praise for his handling of the missile crisis, it proved humiliating to Khrushchev. The Soviet leader fell from power within a year, and his actions during the crisis contributed to his demise. The missile crisis had exposed the Soviets as strategic inferiors to the Americans. An angry Soviet official told his American counterpart, "Never will we be caught like this again." The Soviets embarked on a crash program to expand their navy and to bring their missile forces up to parity with the United States.

Why had Khrushchev tried to put the missiles in Cuba? Had he really believed that Washington would acquiesce in the stationing of nuclear missiles ninety miles from U.S. territory? Surely Khrushchev and his colleagues on the Politburo would not expose the Soviet Union to nuclear obliteration just to protect Castro's regime. Historians who have examined documents found in Soviet archives, recently made accessible to scholars, believe that what Khrushchev hoped to accomplish by placing the missiles in Cuba was to use them as bargaining chips. He would offer to withdraw them in exchange for U.S. concessions on Berlin. He hoped to extract a German peace treaty from the West and possibly an Allied withdrawal from West Berlin.

This ploy was blocked by the discovery of the missile sites on October 14 and Kennedy's proclamation of a "quarantine" on Cuba, effective on October 22. Khrushchev did not expect Kennedy's strong response, having sized him up as being weak under pressure. Kennedy's behavior in previous crises had fed Khrushchev's suspicions that he lacked courage. During the Bay of Pigs invasion, Kennedy had backed off from a war with Cuba, let the invasion fail, and allowed Castro to consolidate a Communist revolution right in America's backyard. He had let the Berlin Wall stand. These acts of restraint sent the wrong signals to the adventurous Soviet ideologue. Khrushchev was not looking for a confrontation with the United States over Cuba, and he certainly did not want a war.

The missile crisis forced both sides to tone down their Cold War rivalry. Khrushchev shifted back to emphasizing peaceful coexistence. Kennedy stressed the need for arms reductions. Direct communication, a "hot line," was established between Moscow and Washington so the two leaders could talk to each other in time of crisis to reduce the chances of miscalculation and war. A mutual desire to control nuclear testing gave the two leaders an opportunity to improve relations.

President Kennedy, hoping to move arms negotiations forward, spoke at American University on June 10, 1963. He called peace between the superpowers "the necessary end of rational men." He spoke of "making the world safe for diversity," conceding that every world problem did not require an American solution. Following the speech, he sent Undersecretary of State Averill Harriman to Moscow to negotiate an agreement. The Soviets proved eager to conclude a treaty. The agreement, signed on July 25, banned all atmospheric and underwater testing of nuclear weapons. The Senate promptly ratified the treaty. The Nuclear Test Ban Treaty was the first agreement that imposed a measure of control on the nuclear arms race. Soon after signing the treaty, the United States and the Soviet Union concluded an agreement for Soviet purchases of U.S. wheat. A year after the showdown in Cuba, Americans and Soviets enjoyed relations that were friendlier than any other time since World War II.

VIETNAM: RAISING THE STAKES

During Kennedy's presidency, the United States increased its involvement in Indochina. The president first turned his attention in that region to Laos, which had been the scene of conflict for years. Neutral under the terms of the 1954 Geneva accords, Laos was engulfed in a three-way civil war among pro-Western, pro-Communist, and neutralist forces. Kennedy, inheriting the conflict from Eisenhower, sought a political solution involving the Soviets that guaranteed a "neutral and independent Laos." Another Geneva conference worked out a settlement. On June 12, 1961, the leaders of the three Laotian factions formed a neutralist coalition government. But in southern Vietnam, Kennedy significantly escalated U.S. involvement in response to the Communists' stepped-up efforts to topple the American-backed government of Ngo Dinh Diem.

Kennedy viewed the civil war in southern Vietnam as a crucial part of the global cold war struggle between the United States and the Soviet Union. Ironically, Kennedy, when he had been a senator, often criticized the Eisenhower administration's Third World foreign policy for failing to understand the powerful appeal of nationalism in countries emerging from long periods of colonial domination by Western imperial powers. Kennedy had criticized American backing of French efforts to reimpose colonialism in Indochina by suppressing a nationalist revolution. But as president, Kennedy failed to understand that Ho Chi Minh's government embodied the nationalistic aspirations of millions of his compatriots, and that many Vietnamese viewed the American presence in Vietnam as a continuation of Western imperialism. Kennedy also applied the domino theory to Vietnam:

> Vietnam represents the cornerstone of the Free World in Southeast Asia, . . . Burma, Thailand, India, Japan, the Philippines, and obviously, Laos and Cambodia are among those whose security would be threatened if the red tide of Communism overflowed into Vietnam.[7]

Kennedy and his senior foreign policy advisers all shared the ideological fundaments of the Cold War with Eisenhower and Truman. They believed that it was imperative to contain Communist expansionism in Southeast Asia. The legacy of McCarthyism also stalked the Democrats in power. Since the early 1950s, they had been politically vulnerable to charges that they were "soft on Communism" at home and abroad. Kennedy dared not appear to be irresolute in Southeast Asia, lest his administration suffer political reprisals at the hands of Republicans in subsequent elections. Further, the Kennedy team shared a faith in American power, technical expertise, and national goals. They believed that the Americans would succeed in southern Vietnam where the French had failed. To them, Vietnam furnished a bright opportunity for nation building. They believed that aid programs, military support, and the use of America's counterinsurgency forces would show the world that Moscow-backed wars of national liberation could not succeed. Kennedy also deployed the Army Special Forces, the Green Berets, in Southeast Asia. They represented a key component of the flexible response capability to counter Communist insurgencies in peripheral regions without risking confrontations with China or the Soviet Union. Kennedy believed that the Army Special Forces, using counterinsurgency techniques, would win the hearts and minds of the Vietnamese people for Ngo Dinh Diem.

When Kennedy assumed office in January 1961, there were about 600 U.S. military advisers in South Vietnam assisting Diem's forces. Kennedy sent Vice President Lyndon Johnson to Saigon to emphasize the American commitment to Diem and to assess his needs. Upon his return, Johnson advised Kennedy to increase American aid to South Vietnam. During the next eighteen months, Kennedy sent some 16,000 American troops to South Vietnam. Even though the soldiers went officially as advisers, some units occasionally engaged Viet Cong forces in combat.

[7]Quoted in George C. Herring, *America's Longest War,* 2d ed. (New York: Knopf, 1986), p. 43.

Despite the huge increase in American support, Diemist forces were losing the civil war to the Viet Cong insurgents and their North Vietnamese backers. U.S. officials tried to persuade Diem to implement social reforms, including land reform, and to curb his repressive police forces. Diem refused to do either. Diem's decline stemmed mainly from the inability of his military forces to fight effectively and his failure to win the loyalty of the peasants who comprised 85 percent of the South Vietnamese population.

Diem provoked a political crisis in June 1963 that led to his downfall when he ordered Buddhists to obey Catholic religious laws. When they refused and took to the streets to protest, Diem's police, led by his brother Nhu, brutally crushed their rebellion. In response to this repression, an elderly Buddhist monk immolated himself by fire at a busy intersection in downtown Saigon. Other monks followed suit, as opposition to Diem's government escalated. Observing that Diem's political base had been reduced to family members and a few loyal generals and bureaucrats, and fearing that his army would lose the civil war, the Kennedy administration decided that Diem had to go. On November 1, an army coup, acting with the foreknowledge and support of the CIA, overthrew Diem. American officials backed a directorate of generals who formed a new government and continued the war. Three weeks later, Kennedy was assassinated.

At the time of Kennedy's death, U.S. Vietnam policy was in disarray and his advisers divided over what to do. Although he had significantly increased the U.S. stake in Indochina, Kennedy hinted that he might reappraise his commitment to South Vietnam because of Diem's political failures. In September 1963, Kennedy had attempted to warn Diem:

> I don't think that unless a greater effort is made to win popular support the war can be won out there. In the final analysis it is their war. They are the ones who have to win it or lose it. . . . For us to withdraw from that effort would mean a collapse not only of South Vietnam, but Southeast Asia, . . . so we are going to stay there.[8]

Kennedy had inherited a deteriorating situation in Southeast Asia; his actions ensured that the United States would remain there a long time. Had Kennedy lived and been reelected in 1964, he probably would have reacted as Lyndon Johnson did in 1965 and committed the United States to a major war in Vietnam.

The pattern of Kennedy's foreign policy was akin to that of an orthodox Cold Warrior striving to fulfill the extravagant rhetorical claims of his inaugural address. Undeniably, Kennedy had the intelligence and insight to see that the world was changing, that Third World independence movements were redrawing the map of the world. He also understood that the old bipolar world was being replaced with a more polycentric one. He knew that the American–Soviet rivalry had to be replaced by detente. But the main thrust of his foreign policies was to escalate the arms race, sustain a tense relation with the Soviet Union for most of his presidency, and, at one terrifying point, in tandem with the reckless Soviet leader Nikita

[8]From the transcript of a televised interview with Walter Cronkite, broadcast on CBS news, on September 2, 1963.

Khrushchev, push the world perilously close to nuclear disaster. He significantly increased the U.S. commitment in Vietnam, ensuring the debacle that followed.

THE SPACE RACE

In mid-April 1961, at the time that the United States was being humiliated at the Bay of Pigs, a Soviet cosmonaut, Yuri Gagarin, became the first human to orbit the earth. Once again, the Soviets boasted of their accomplishments in space technology. Even though NASA scientists assured the president that American space science was superior to Soviet efforts, it had been the popular perception in this country since Sputnik that the United States trailed the Soviets.

President Kennedy was determined to rally the American people to face a Cold War challenge he believed America could win. He put Vice President Lyndon Johnson in charge of the Space Council and told him to do whatever had to be done to defeat the Soviets. Kennedy also persuaded Congress to vote for a large increase in NASA's budget to develop a space program "to put a man on the moon in ten years." He went before Congress in May 1961 to push the moon project:

> No single space project in this period will be more impressive to mankind or more important for the long-range exploration of space . . . than putting a man on the moon.[9]

To fulfill Kennedy's vision, NASA created the APOLLO program. Soon complexes of aerospace facilities mushroomed from southern California to Texas to Florida. NASA employed thousands of technicians, engineers, and scientists. Private-sector subcontractors hired thousands more. Within five years, upwards of a half-million people were employed on the vast and costly APOLLO project.

As scientists worked toward the goal of putting a man on the moon, they also tried to match the Soviet Union's space achievements. Seven military test pilots were recruited for Project MERCURY, and they became the nation's first astronauts. After months of rigorous training, the astronauts readied for their flights. On May 5, 1961, Navy Commander, Alan B. Shepard, Jr., strapped in a space capsule fastened to the nose of an Army Redstone rocket, was fired from a launch pad at Cape Canaveral, Florida, into a fifteen-minute suborbital flight 116 miles aloft. On February 20, 1962, nearly a year after the Soviets had put a man in space, Marine Colonel John H. Glenn, Jr. was blasted into orbit aboard his space capsule, Friendship 7. During his five-hour flight, Glenn orbited the earth three times.

Americans were delighted by Glenn's achievement. He made an attractive hero. He was a much-decorated jet fighter pilot from the Korean War, an All-American boy grown up to become the first American to reach outer space. After his epic flight, President Kennedy invited Glenn to the White House. Glenn also addressed a joint session of Congress, and he later received a frenzied ticker tape parade down Manhattan's famed Broadway. Following Glenn's flight, other

---

[9]Quoted in Tom Wolfe, *The Right Stuff* (New York: Bantam Books, 1979), pp. 228–29.

Figure 11.7   Three American heroes. The three Project Mercury Astronauts training for the nation's first manned space flight area: John H. Glenn Jr., (left), Virgil L. (Gus) Grissom (center), and Alan B. Shepard, Jr. (right), shown during their training for manned space flights. The forthcoming sub-orbital launch will be in a Mercury-Redstone rocket to give the astronaut realistic space flight experience and to obtain additional test data on operational Mercury spacecraft systems in the space environment. A Mercury-Redstone rocket is shown in the background on a launching pad at Cape Canaveral, Florida.   *Source:* NASA Headquarters, neg.# 61-MR3-52.

astronauts rocketed into space and orbited the earth. At the time of Kennedy's death, the American space program was gaining momentum, the seven MERCURY astronauts had all become national heroes, and Project APOLLO was ahead of schedule.

SOCIAL REFORM

President Kennedy had more successes in the diplomatic arena than in the realm of domestic reform legislation. Although espousing liberal goals, he failed to get enacted most of his ambitious New Frontier program of medical care for the elderly, tax reform, federal aid to education, housing reform, aid to cities, and immigration reform. His New Frontier faced many political obstacles. In Congress, the bipartisan conservative coalition could block any effort to expand the welfare state and could often dilute measures designed to broaden existing programs. Kennedy's thin electoral victory in 1960 carried with it no mandate whatsoever for social reform.

Two years later, Kennedy tried to focus the 1962 midterm elections on New Frontier issues, but the dangerous Cuban missile crisis forced him to curtail his campaign efforts. The new Congress of 1962 was similar to its predecessor. Public opinion in the early 1960s reflected the complacency toward unsolved social problems that had been characteristic of the 1950s. Kennedy's efforts to make most Americans share his sense of urgency for social reform through televised speeches and remarks at press conferences failed. Most New Frontier proposals never made it out of committee. These few that did were either defeated on the floor of the House or cleared Congress in diluted form.

Kennedy also failed to assert effective legislative leadership. Congress questioned the depth of his commitment to social reform, understanding that he gave higher priority to foreign policy, military matters, world trade, and strengthening the economy. In addition, Kennedy wanted to maintain bipartisan support for American foreign policy initiatives and was reluctant to strain the unity of Congress with battles over divisive reform measures. Kennedy disliked using political muscle, and he disliked losing. He could see that the votes simply were not there for many New Frontier measures, and he thought it was unreasonable to battle for a losing cause.

A major defeat came early when Congress rejected Kennedy's $2.3 billion education bill. It foundered over the issue of federal aid to parochial schools. A Catholic himself, Kennedy knew that he would be accused of showing favoritism toward his coreligionists if he supported federal aid to Catholic schools. His bill excluded federal aid for private schools with a religious affiliation that he claimed would violate the First Amendment principle of separation of church and state. Opposition to the bill from the Catholic lobby was intense. The education bill never got out of the House Rules Committee. Members of Congress, observing that Kennedy had little leverage with its members, understood that they could go their own political ways on important White House measures without fear of reprisal. The failure of the education bill foreshadowed the defeat of the rest of the New Frontier agendum.

Although Kennedy failed to achieve his broad program of reform, he scored a few small victories. Congress enacted an Area Redevelopment Act in 1961 to provide funds for economically depressed areas. The Manpower Retraining Act of 1962 provided $435 million over three years to train unemployed workers in new job skills. Congress raised the minimum wage from $1.00 to $1.25 an hour and extended coverage under the minimum wage law to 3.6 million more workers.

THE ECONOMY

When Kennedy took office, the American economy was suffering from lingering recession. The new president tried to work with the business community to restore prosperity. He consulted with several of his cabinet advisers recruited from the business world. He held meetings with corporate leaders to get their policy suggestions. He tried to reassure them that he was not a reckless spender nor a liberal ideologue, and that he was committed to a stable price structure. He told them that the age of ideology had ended and the time had come for government, business, labor, and academic leaders to combine their expertise in seeking solutions to complex technical problems that afflicted the economy. Corporate leaders refused their cooperation, angering the president. They insisted on blaming the Kennedy administration for all of their problems, and they rejected his technocratic approach to problem solving.

A major confrontation with business came in the spring of 1962. Earlier in the year, a strike in the steel industry had been averted when Secretary of Labor Arthur Goldberg had persuaded the steel workers to accept a modest pay increase that eliminated the need for a steel price rise. At the time, the president had praised both labor and management for their "industrial statesmanship." Ten days later, Roger Blough, the head of United States Steel, announced that his company was raising the price of steel $6 a ton. Other major steel producers promptly announced identical increases.

Kennedy, feeling betrayed, denounced the steel companies. At a press conference, he said that he was shocked that "a tiny handful of steel executives can show such utter contempt for the interests of 185 million Americans." He promptly mobilized all of the considerable powers of the federal government to force the steel companies to rescind their price hikes. The Federal Trade Commission announced that it would investigate the steel industry for possible price-fixing. Robert Kennedy hinted that he might open antitrust proceedings against the steel industry. Secretary of Defense McNamara announced that the military would buy steel only from companies that had not raised their prices. Under an all-out assault from the White House, the steel companies quickly surrendered. U.S. Steel and the other companies canceled their price increases. Kennedy had won, but he paid a political price for winning: the business community remained intensely hostile toward his administration.

Kennedy proposed innovative economic policies to end the business slump of the early 1960s. Aware that huge budget deficits during World War II had promoted prosperity, he reasoned that deficit financing also would work during peacetime. In June 1962, he proposed a deliberately unbalanced budget to promote economic growth. Six months later, he asked Congress to enact a $13.5 billion cut in corporate and personal income taxes over the next three years. The tax cuts, coupled with increases in spending for military and space programs already in place, would guarantee budget deficits. Kennedy insisted that these applied Keynesian economic strategies would generate capital spending that would stimulate economic growth, create new jobs, and provide increased tax revenues—all without rampant inflation. But Kennedy's tax bill never cleared Congress.

Even though Kennedy failed to get his new economic policy enacted, the economy recovered from recession in 1962 and 1963 and began an extended period of growth that would last for a decade. Recovery mainly occurred because the Kennedy administration sharply increased military and space spending. Kennedy's first defense budget called for spending $48 billion, a 20 percent increase over Eisenhower's final budget. Kennedy's economic foreign policies also contributed to the economic rebound of 1962 and 1963. Most of his foreign aid requests were approved, including increased spending for technical assistance and economic development for Third World countries. The Senate ratified a treaty in 1961, making the United States a member of the newly created Organization of Economic Cooperation and Development (OECD), comprising the United States, Canada, and eighteen European nations. Congress also enacted Kennedy's proposed Trade Expansion Act in 1962, his most important legislative victory, which established closer ties with European Common Market countries, America's most important trading partners. The Trade Expansion Act allowed the president to reduce tariffs on commodities which accounted for most of the trade between the United States and European nations. American overseas trade increased significantly during the years of Kennedy's presidency.

LET FREEDOM RING

During the 1960 presidential campaign, Kennedy had spoken out strongly for civil rights to prevent Nixon's siphoning off of African American voters, but at the same time he also had sought the votes of Southern whites. His campaign rhetoric was bold: "If the President himself does not wage the struggle for equal rights, then the battle will inevitably be lost." He promised to issue an executive order ending racial segregation in federally funded housing. During the campaign, he helped release Dr. Martin Luther King, Jr. from jail. African Americans appreciated these gestures from the candidate and gave Kennedy a large black majority in 1960, which helped him win his narrow victory.

But Kennedy in office proved to be a cautious leader on civil rights for much of his presidency. He delayed introducing civil rights legislation, fearing that it would fail and also that it would alienate Southern Democrats, whose votes he needed on other measures. He appointed African Americans to some federal offices, the first president to do so. Robert Weaver became head of the Housing and Home Finance Agency, and Thurgood Marshall became a Circuit Court judge. But Kennedy also appointed many segregationist judges to Southern courts, and he delayed issuing his promised housing desegregation order for nearly two years.

At the beginning of his administration, the official lead in civil rights was taken by the president's brother, Attorney General Robert Kennedy. The Justice Department worked to end discrimination in interstate transportation and supported the voting rights of African Americans in the South. President Kennedy believed that the best civil rights policy would be a gradual achievement of integration over the years without disruption and violence.

But from the outset of his presidency, Kennedy had to respond to pressures created by violent confrontations between civil rights activists and their segregationist foes. In the spring of 1961, the Congress of Racial Equality (CORE) sponsored "freedom rides." Groups of black and white travelers rode through the South deliberately entering segregated bus terminals and restaurants. Local mobs often attacked the "freedom riders." In Anniston, Alabama, the Greyhound bus in which one group had been riding was burned. Responding to the freedom riders and their violent encounters, the Interstate Commerce Commission (ICC) ordered bus companies to desegregate all of their interstate routes and facilities. The companies complied, and black passengers began entering previously "whites-only" restaurants, waiting rooms, and restrooms. The Justice Department persuaded thirteen of the nation's fifteen segregated airports to desegregate and filed suits against the two holdouts.

The following year, Mississippi became a civil rights battleground. In September 1962, an African American Air Force veteran, James Meredith, attempted to enroll at the all-white University of Mississippi. Although he met the university's entrance requirements, university officials refused to admit him. Meredith then obtained a court order from Supreme Court Justice Hugo Black enjoining the university to admit him, whereupon Governor Ross Barnett personally intervened to prevent his enrolling. President Kennedy responded to Barnett's defiance of federal authority by sending federal marshals and troops to the university. They were met by a mob, who treated them as though they were foreign invaders. Violence ensued, in which vehicles were burned and destroyed. Tear gas covered the campus, and it took several thousand troops to restore order. During the mayhem, two men were killed and hundreds were injured.

Another violent confrontation occurred on April 12, 1963, Good Friday, when Martin Luther King, Jr. led a demonstration in Birmingham, Alabama. King and his followers sought to end discrimination against African American customers in shops and restaurants, and in employment and hiring policies. Their protests were nonviolent; the city's response was not. During the next month, Birmingham police arrested over 2,000 African American demonstrators, many of them schoolchildren. The police commissioner ordered his police force to use high-pressure fire hoses, electric cattle prods, and police dogs to break up the demonstrations. Newspapers and television news broadcasts conveyed to the nation the brutal police assaults on African Americans. King was jailed. During his stay in jail, he composed his famed *Letter from Birmingham Jail*, an eloquent defense of the tactic of nonviolent civil disobedience.

The Justice Department intervened during the Birmingham demonstrations. Government officials and city leaders worked out an agreement, calling for the desegregation of municipal facilities, the hiring of African Americans, and the creation of a biracial committee to keep the channels of communication open between the races.

A few months after the Birmingham encounter, two young African Americans, Vivian Malone and James Hood, tried to enroll at the University of Alabama. Governor George Wallace stood at the entrance to Carmichael Hall on the campus of the university. With television cameras rolling and over 200 reporters looking on, Wallace raised his hand and refused to allow the two black students to enter the school. Two hours later, the crisis was over. President Kennedy, hoping to avoid a replay of the Mississippi violence, federalized the Alabama National Guard. He confronted Wallace with an overwhelming show of force, using native Alabama white and black soldiers. Wallace had stood in the doorway only long enough to have his picture taken for the papers and to ensure that his actions made the nightly news. He then stepped aside. Malone and Hood enrolled at the university, peacefully.

That night, on June 11, 1963, President Kennedy gave the first civil rights speech ever delivered by a president. Part of his speech was extemporaneous, and he conveyed a sense of moral urgency, an emotional concern for civil rights:

> If an American, because his skin is black, cannot eat lunch in a restaurant open to the public; if he cannot send his children to the best public school available; if he cannot vote for the public officials who represent him; if, in short, he cannot enjoy the full and free life which all of us want, then who among us would be content to have the color of his skin changed and stand in his place?
>
> One hundred years of delay have passed since President Lincoln freed the slaves, yet their heirs, their grandsons, are not fully free. They are not yet free from the bonds of injustice; they are not yet freed from social and economic oppression. And this nation will not be fully free until all its citizens are free.[10]

A week later, the president, stating that "the time has come for this nation to fulfill its promise," proposed the most comprehensive civil rights bill in American history, calling for the desegregation of all public accommodations, the protection of voting rights for African Americans, and the end of job discrimination. Congress gave no indication that it would enact the measure any time soon.

To show support for the pending legislation, civil rights leaders organized a march on Washington. Over 200,000 people gathered in front of the Washington monument on August 28. Black and white people joined in a peaceful, festive occasion.

The highlight of the gathering came when Dr. King, the leader of the growing civil rights movement, passionately affirmed his faith in the decency of humanity and in victory for his cause:

> I have a dream that one day this nation will rise up and live out the true meaning of its creed: We hold these truths to be self-evident; that all men are created equal. I have a dream that one day on the red hills of Georgia, the sons of former slaves and the sons of former slaveowners will be able to sit together at the table of brotherhood."[11]

The crowd was caught up in the power of his fervent rhetoric. Each time he shouted, "I have a dream," the massive crowd roared its support. Dr. King concluded his stirring speech with a magnificent peroration:

> When we let freedom ring, when we let it ring from every village and every hamlet, from every state and every city, we will be able to speed up that day when all of God's children, black men and white men, Jews and Gentiles, Protestants and Catholics, will be able to join hands and sing in the words of the old Negro spiritual, "Free at last! Free at last! Thank God almighty, we are free at last!"[12]

[10]From the transcript of Kennedy's televised speech over the three major television networks, June 11, 1963.

[11]Quoted in Lewis, *Portrait of a Decade*, pp. 218–19.

[12]Quoted in *Ibid*.

Figure 11.8   On August 28, 1963, supporters of the pending civil rights bill staged a march on Washington to show their support. Over 200,000 people rallied in front of the stately Washington Monument to sing songs and to hear speeches.   *Source:* National Archives.

Immediately following the demonstration, King and other civil rights leaders met with President Kennedy. But Congress continued to stall; southern Senators threatened to filibuster any civil rights bill to death. Three weeks after the march on Washington, Ku Klux Klan terrorists bombed a Sunday school in Birmingham, killing four little girls. Two months later, President Kennedy was assassinated, his civil rights legislation still pending.

TRAGEDY IN DALLAS

In the fall of 1963, President Kennedy was giving much thought to next year's election. He traveled to Texas in late November to mend some political fences. With the help of Vice President Johnson, who accompanied him on that fateful rendezvous, he came to unify warring factions of Texas Democrats who had feuded over policies and patronage. Texas was a populous state with a large bloc of electoral votes that Kennedy and Johnson had carried narrowly in 1960 and hoped to win again in 1964. Kennedy arrived at the Dallas airport on the morning of November 22. The presidential motorcade proceeded from the airport into downtown Dallas. Thou-

Figure 11.9   Dr. Martin Luther King, Jr., preparing to deliver his most famous speech in front of the Washington Monument on August 28, 1963. He inspired the huge crowd with his vision of a color-blind America: "I have a dream. . . ." *Source:* National Archives.

sands of people lined the motorcade route, most of them smiling, waving, and cheering the president as he passed by. Kennedy responded warmly to their enthusiasm, waving, frequently flashing his million-dollar smile, and stopping the motorcade twice to shake hands with well-wishers.

At 12:30 P.M., the motorcade turned onto Elm Street and drove by the Texas Book Depository Building. At 12:33 P.M., three shots rang out. The president clutched his neck with both hands and slumped downward. The first bullet, deflected by a tree limb in the line of fire, had missed. The second bullet had passed through his throat, and the third bullet had struck the back of his head, blowing off part of his skull. Texas governor John Connally, sitting beside the president, also had been hit by the second bullet after it had passed through Kennedy's throat. The president's limousine quickly pulled out of the motorcade and raced the mortally wounded leader to the nearby Parkland Hospital, where in its emergency room he was pronounced dead at 1:00 P.M.

Within two hours of the shooting, police captured the apparent assassin, twenty-four-year-old Lee Harvey Oswald, who worked in the Texas Book Depository Building. Oswald was a loner, a drifter with a troubled past, who had recently moved to Dallas after spending two years in the Soviet Union. He had a wife, Marina, whom he had met and married in the Soviet Union. He had previously served in the Marine Corps. He was a Marxist sympathizer. Earlier in the year, he had tried to go to Cuba, but the Cuban embassy in Mexico City refused to grant him a visa.

Aboard the presidential plane, still on the ground at the Dallas airport, ninety-nine minutes after Kennedy's death, Lyndon B. Johnson was sworn in as the thirty-sixth president of the United States. The former president's widow, Jacqueline, stood at Johnson's side. Two days later, a Dallas nightclub owner, Jack Ruby, shot and killed Oswald at point-blank range in the basement of the Dallas police station, in full view of a national television audience. Ruby's murder of Oswald eliminated the possibility of ever knowing for sure Oswald's political beliefs, his motives for killing the president, and whether he was part of a conspiracy.

From the moment of Kennedy's death, many people doubted that Lee Harvey Oswald had acted alone. A public opinion poll, taken within a week of the president's murder, showed that only 29 percent of Americans believed that Oswald was a lone killer. Within two weeks of Kennedy's murder, President Johnson appointed a special commission, headed by Chief Justice Earl Warren, to investigate the assassination and to report its findings to the American people. Ten months later, the commission published its conclusion: "The Commission has found no evidence that anyone assisted Oswald in planning or carrying out the assassination."

The commission's findings failed to satisfy those who felt others had to be involved in a plot to murder the president. Critics undermined the credibility of the Warren Commission's analysis of evidence and its findings, which were seriously flawed and limited. Many people have proposed conspiracy theories to account for Kennedy's death, and millions of people have found them credible. These theories have implicated both pro- and anti-Castro Cubans, leftists, rightists, Texas oil men, segregationists, Vietnamese, rogue elements within the Pentagon, the FBI and the CIA, the Mafia, the KGB, and even Lyndon Johnson. Most historians of the assassination do not believe that a conspiracy was involved in the murder of the president, and they accept the Warren Commission's finding. The few responsible journalists and scholars who believe that it is at least possible that a conspiracy killed Kennedy think that Cubans and elements within organized crime were involved.

The most important critique of the Warren Commission came in 1979, when a special congressional investigating committee released the results of a two-and-one-half-year examination of the deaths of both President Kennedy and Dr. Martin Luther King, Jr. Its key finding was: "The scientific evidence available to the committee indicated that it is probable that more than one person was involved in the president's murder." But FBI experts demonstrated that the committee's evidence was flawed.

In all of the time that has passed since Kennedy's murder, no tangible evidence has been found that proves that the Warren Commission's conclusion was incorrect, despite its flawed investigation of the murder; nor has any evidence turned up that links any particular group to the assassination. If a group of conspirators killed the president, which is doubtful, their identities remain unknown and probably will never be known.

The persistence of the belief, especially among young people, that a conspiracy killed Kennedy mainly represents an effort to make sense out of a horrific act that frightened Americans and shook their faith in the decency and viability of American political institutions. The notion that a sociopath, an utterly insignificant wretch acting alone, could bring down a great leader and wreak such havoc made the crime seem senseless and devoid of political meaning. Novelist Norman Mailer has suggested that many Americans cling to conspiracies to explain the president's death because they refuse to recognize the irrationality, the absurdity, of historical events. The belief that a great man had been destroyed by powerful evil forces lurking in the dark underside of American politics made sense in a bleak sort of way to many people.

In the years following Kennedy's death, Americans watched other leaders die at the hands of assassins—Malcolm X, Martin Luther King, Jr., and Robert Kennedy. These assassinations reinforced a growing sense among American in the 1960s that they inhabited a violent, dangerous country where criminal conspirators thought nothing of snuffing out the lives of idealistic leaders. For them, the age of innocence ended on November 22, 1963, and they have found it difficult to trust and support government leaders ever since.

Kennedy's murder gouged a deep wound in the nation's psyche. People around the world wept openly at the horrid news. A weeping woman on a Moscow street grabbed an American reporter by the arm and shouted, "How could you let it happen? He was so young, so beautiful!" A stricken nation numbly watched the solemn aftermath of the absurd tragedy. The president's body lay in state on the rotunda of the Capitol on the same catafalque that had held the body of Lincoln. Kennedy's funeral was held on November 25, a clear, cold day in Washington. At St. Matthews Cathedral, Kennedy's friend, Richard Cardinal Cushing, Archbishop of Boston, said a funeral mass. The funeral train slowly wound its way past national monuments to Arlington Cemetery. There, on a knoll overlooking the capital of the nation, John Fitzgerald Kennedy was buried. Adlai Stevenson, in a moving eulogy, observed that

> Today we mourn him, tomorrow we shall miss him. . . . No one will ever know what this blazing political talent might have accomplished had he been permitted to live and labor long in the cause of freedom.[13]

THE LEGACY OF CAMELOT

Kennedy's violent death instantly transformed the man into a myth. After conversations with Kennedy's widow, journalist Theodore White wrote an essay in which he compared Kennedy's presidency to Camelot. Camelot had recently been popularized in this country by the successful Broadway run of a musical of that same name. Kennedy had seen *Camelot,* and he loved to listen to the recorded sound track. Camelot referred to the Arthurian legend, to the mythical kingdom of Arthur and the Knights of the Round Table. Because the country, soon after Kennedy's death, became caught up in a full-scale war in Southeast Asia and in violent domestic rebellions, followed a few years later by the sordid Watergate scandals, people viewed the Kennedy years as a brief golden age. Those who came of age during Kennedy's reign felt an especially painful loss. For them, the Kennedy years had been a glorious interlude between the dull days of Eisenhower and the dark days of Johnson and Nixon.

For those who believed in Camelot, Kennedy had been the democratic prince whose achievements symbolized the American dream of success. His family

---

[13]Taken from the documentary film, *The Age of Kennedy,* part 4.

history had been a saga of upward mobility from humble immigrant origins to the upper reaches of wealth, power, and fame. Then, in a few seconds, a loser's bullets had turned spectacular achievement into tragic loss.

The historical record belies the myth. Kennedy's record of accomplishment is mixed. Much of his New Frontier agenda failed to be enacted in his lifetime. He usually was a cautious leader on civil rights issues. He only belatedly sensed the moral passion that motivated civil rights activists like Martin Luther King, Jr. He got only a portion of his economic program enacted. Posthumous revelations about his many extramarital affairs, drug use, serious health problems, and other Kennedy family scandals tarnished his moral stature and diminished his reputation.

His foreign policy achievements were more significant. America's putting a man on the moon in 1969 was a belated triumph. The Peace Corps and the Trade Expansion Act succeeded. But the Alliance for Progress flopped, neither undercutting the appeal of Castro nor promoting democracy and economic growth in most Latin American countries. Kennedy's crisis managing in Cuba was a disaster at the Bay of Pigs, and he risked nuclear war to pry Soviet missiles out of Cuba. The Berlin issue was defused after years of tension, but its resolution owed more to Khrushchev's Berlin Wall than to any initiatives taken by Kennedy. The test ban treaty and detente with the Soviets in 1963 decreased the danger of nuclear war, but Kennedy had previously ordered major increases in American military spending, particularly for strategic thermonuclear weapons, which had escalated the arms race. Kennedy also significantly expanded American involvement in Vietnam, putting the country on course for war in Southeast Asia.

Kennedy's best speeches proved that he had the imagination and courage to see beyond the confines of the Cold War. But he spent his presidency fighting it. The man who could see the need for developing new relations with Third World people nevertheless applied counterrevolutionary Cold War ideologies to all nationalistic insurgencies. He remained until the end a Cold Warrior at heart.

Any account of his leadership must include intangible dimensions. Kennedy was a superb politician. His intelligence, wit, and immense personal charm set a high tone for his presidency. Many of his countrymen felt great admiration and affection for him, viewing him as a fine symbol of the nation that he had been elected to lead. Kennedy was devoted to the ideal of national service. His administration cultivated the arts. He paid high tribute to science and scholarship. And he sought always to bring out the best in Americans, to challenge them to seek excellence in all things, especially young people, with whom he felt a special bond. Whatever the failings of the private man, the public image that Kennedy cultivated was positive, energetic, and effective. Always there must be the rueful speculation, what if he had lived? Any fair historical judgment must take into account the brutal fact of his abruptly abbreviated career, a young man in his prime, cut down before he could make his full mark on his times. The Kennedy presidency was not a great one; historians rate him "above average" during his thousand days in office. But given a second term, it is possible that he would have attained distinction.

IMPORTANT DATES

1960	The Kennedy–Nixon televised debates occur
	John F. Kennedy is elected president
1961	The Bay of Pigs fiasco takes place
	CORE "freedom rides" to the South occur
	The Berlin Wall is built
	The Peace Corps is created
	The Alliance for Progress is implemented
1962	James Meredith desegregates the University of Mississippi
	The Cuban Missile Crisis takes place
1963	Martin Luther King, Jr. leads demonstrations in Birmingham, Alabama
	The Nuclear Test Ban Treaty is signed
	The March on Washington to support the civil rights bill occurs
	Ngo Dinh Diem is assassinated in Saigon
	John F. Kennedy is assassinated in Dallas

BIBLIOGRAPHY

A large and growing literature exists on John Fitzgerald Kennedy, his family, and all facets of his political career. The best and most balanced biography is Herbert Parmet's two-volume study *Jack: The Struggles of John F. Kennedy* and *JFK: The Presidency of John F. Kennedy*. The best recent scholarly history of the Kennedy presidency is James N. Giglio's *The Presidency of John F. Kennedy*. Two highly favorable insider accounts of his presidency are by Arthur M. Schlesinger, Jr., in *A Thousand Days* and by Theodore C. Sorensen, in *Kennedy*. Kenneth P. O'Donnel and David F. Powers, two political associates of Kennedy, have left an affectionate account in *Johnny, We Hardly Knew Ye*. Bruce Miroff's *Pragmatic Illusions: The Presidential Politics of John Kennedy* and Garry Wills's *The Kennedy Imprisonment* are both negative assessments of his presidency. A controversial recent work by investigative reporter Seymour M. Hersh, *The Dark Side of Camelot*, amounts to a lengthy catalogue of the sins of a president. By far the best account of the exciting and significant election of 1960 is found in Theodore H. White's *The Making of the President, 1960*. The best account of Kennedy's World War II career is Robert J. Donovan's *PT 109: John F. Kennedy in World War II*. Carl M. Brauer, in *John F. Kennedy and the Second Reconstruction*, offers a favorable assessment of the president as a civil rights leader. See also Peter Wyden's *Bay of Pigs: The Untold Story*, for the best account of Kennedy's most embarrassing foreign policy venture. The best short account of the missile crisis is Elie Abel's *The Missile Crisis*. Two critical accounts of Kennedy's conduct of foreign policy include Richard J. Walton's *Cold War and Counterrevolution* and David Halberstam's *The Best and the Brightest*. A fine recent study of Kennedy's foreign policy can be found in Ernest R. May and Philip D. Zelikow, eds., *The Kennedy Tapes: Inside the White House during the Cuban Missile Crisis*, which makes available for the first time the conversations of the Executive Committee as members discussed how to respond to the Soviet challenge. A fine recent critical account of Kennedy's foreign policy is Michael R. Beschloss's *The Crisis Years: Kennedy and Khrushchev, 1960–1963*. Anyone who cares to know about Kennedy's assassination must start by reading the *Report of the Warren Commission on the Assassination of John F. Kennedy*. Readers also might want to read one of the responsible accounts of the assassination as found in Michael L. Kurtz's *Crime of the Century: The Kennedy Assassination from a Historian's Perspective*. Gerald Posner, in *Case Closed: Lee Harvey Oswald and the Assassination of JFK,* does an effective job of demolishing the leading conspiracy theories and providing plausible answers to the lingering questions about the assassination.

12

Reform, Rebellion, and War

T HE consensus that had united most Americans in support of domestic reform at home and containment of Communism abroad fragmented following Kennedy's assassination. But for a time, under Kennedy' successor Lyndon Johnson, the cracks in the American system remained below the surface. Johnson was able to score a decisive electoral victory in 1964 over the ineffective challenge of Senator Barry Goldwater. Following his victory, Johnson pushed through Congress a broad range of social legislation labeled the "Great Society." By 1967 the escalating Vietnam War combined with militant domestic insurgencies to collapse the American consensus. The late 1960s witnessed the most violence and disorder within the United States since the early 1890s.

THE TALL TEXAN

Lyndon Johnson's political career began in 1932 when he joined the staff of his district's congressman. In 1935, the young politician became state director of the National Youth Administration (NYA), an important New Deal agency whose prime mission was to help young people finish high school and attend college during hard times. In 1937, he was elected to Congress where he quickly made a name for himself as an ardent Populist and New Dealer. The young, ambitious politician impressed President Roosevelt as being an avid fund-raiser and future leader of the Democratic Party. In 1948, Johnson moved up to the Senate.

Johnson's rise in the Senate was meteoric. He quickly made himself indispensable to senior Democratic leaders like Richard Russell of Georgia. Russell and his colleagues saw to it that Johnson became Senate minority leader in 1953. When the Democrats regained control of the Senate in 1955, Johnson became majority leader. From 1955 to 1960, as Senate majority leader, Johnson was the second most powerful politician in Washington. The key to his power was his mastery of the Senate legislative process. He did his best work behind the scenes; he was a skilled negotiator and deal maker. He always seemed to know just the right mix of carrots and sticks required to put together winning coalitions of diverse interest groups in support of important legislation.

Johnson was in his element in the Senate. He was the consummate professional politician. Although a Southerner, he transcended his regional roots by identifying with the West. As he became more powerful, he increasingly took national positions on important issues. In 1960 he made a bid for the presidency, finishing second to Kennedy in the balloting at Los Angeles. During his vice presidency, he had an active, visible role in governance. When Kennedy was gunned down in Dallas, Johnson was ready to take his place.

JOHNSON TAKES COMMAND

The new president assumed office under horrendous circumstances. The nation's newspapers all carried the photo of a somber Lyndon Johnson being sworn into office by a federal judge on board Air Force One, less than two hours after the president's murder. Also on board was Kennedy's body, awaiting its mournful flight back to Washington.

Johnson's immediate task was to preside over an orderly transition of power that ensured continuity in government and restored the people's shattered confidence in the political order. He handled this delicate task with consummate skill and remarkable sensitivity. He persuaded almost all of Kennedy's key White House staff and cabinet officials to remain at their jobs. His first speech to Congress and to the American people, given five days after the assassination, demonstrated that a sure hand was at the helm. Johnson pledged to continue what Kennedy had started. He made it clear that stalled New Frontier legislation would be the top priority on his domestic agenda. He called specifically for Congress to swiftly enact the stalled civil rights and tax reduction bills.

During his first six months in office, President Johnson used a successful strategy for getting Congress to enact much previously blocked New Frontier legislation. He evoked memories of the deceased Kennedy as a moral lever to pry bills out of congressional committees. He also sought to overcome conservative resistance to social reform by insisting on balanced budgets and reducing government expenditures. He obtained congressional passage of Kennedy's long-stalled tax cuts, which reduced personal and corporate income taxes about 5 percent across the board. Enactment of these tax cuts represented the first deliberate use of Keynesian fiscal policy to stimulate demand and promote investment to keep the economy prosperous and growing, thereby generating the tax revenues to pay for

Figure 12.1   Less than two hours after President Kennedy's murder, a somber Lyndon Johnson was sworn into office aboard Air Force One, still parked on the ground at the Dallas airport. He is flanked on the left by Kennedy's widow, Jacqueline Bouvier Kennedy, and on the right by his wife, and new First Lady, Clarisa "Lady Bird" Johnson. Federal Judge Sarah T. Hughes (foreground) officiated. *Source:* National Archives.

proposed reforms. His underlying fiscal conservatism made many of his social reform measures palatable to conservatives in Congress.

Johnson also persuaded Congress to enact the most comprehensive civil rights bill in American history. It passed in the House in February 1964, but it ran into a Southern filibuster in the Senate that delayed its passage until June 1964, when a bipartisan effort broke the filibuster and passed the measure by a vote of 77 to 18. The Civil Rights Act of 1964 went well beyond Kennedy's initial proposal. It was the most sweeping affirmation of equal rights and the strongest commitment to their enforcement ever made by the federal government. Its key provision guaranteed equal access to all public accommodations such as restaurants, bars, hotels, and theaters. Other provisions strengthened federal machinery for combating discrimination in hiring and promotions. The bill also empowered the federal government to file school desegregation suits, and it strengthened voting rights. It further required corporations and trade unions to ensure equal employment opportunities to all applicants.

In addition to promoting tax cuts and civil rights, Kennedy was considering an antipoverty program at the time of his death. He had ordered his chief economic advisor, Walter Heller, to draft a plan for an assault on poverty. Heller informed Johnson of the plan, and the new president eagerly adopted it. In his first State of the Union address, delivered in January 1964, Johnson declared "unconditional war on poverty in America." Congress, a few months later, enacted the Economic Opportunity Act, authorizing the spending of $1 billion over three years, beginning in 1965. The act created an umbrella agency, the Office of Economic Opportunity (OEO), to administer antipoverty programs. The most radical feature of the new antipoverty law created "community action programs" (CAP) that involved poor people in devising the kinds of programs they wanted. CAP quickly generated controversy as poverty advocates fought with local politicians for control of OEO funds and programs.

THE ELECTION OF 1964

As Lyndon Johnson took control of the reins of power during the first six months of 1964, the Republicans sought a candidate to run against him. Within Republican ranks, angry conservatives, unhappy with their party's tendency since the New Deal to nominate nonideological centrists for the presidency, were determined this time to nominate one of their own. Conservatives represented diverse groups: Midwesterners, Southerners, Westerners, and far-right groups such as the John Birch Society, and New Right newcomers to the GOP such as former screen actor Ronald Reagan and an activist attorney from Illinois, Phyllis Schlafly. These aggressive conservatives supported the candidacy of Arizona Senator Barry Goldwater. Goldwater's political philosophy blended traditional conservatism with New Right ideological discontent, and with the restraints imposed on the American system by the welfare state and the Cold War. Goldwater, a product of Sunbelt politics, called for free enterprise at home and unilateral military action against the Communists abroad.

Moderate Eastern Republicans mounted an all-out effort to stop Goldwater's drive for their party's nomination in the California primary in June. Nelson Rockefeller challenged Goldwater in a bruising battle that split the California Republican Party. Goldwater scored a narrow victory, and with it he secured his presidential candidate nomination.

At the Republican nominating convention, moderates hoped to persuade the party to adopt a moderate platform. But Goldwater's acceptance speech was a New Right manifesto. He denounced government, especially the federal government. In memorable words, he read the moderates out of the GOP:

> Those who do not care for our cause, we don't expect to enter our ranks. . . . Extremism in the defense of liberty is no vice! Moderation in the pursuit of justice is no virtue![1]

In the election campaign, Goldwater never had a chance. Early in the campaign, Goldwater urged that NATO field commanders be given control of tactical nuclear weapons. His proposal frightened most Americans, who thought it made nuclear war more likely. Goldwater often did not need Democratic help to drive away voters, as he insisted on waging an ideological rather than a pragmatic campaign. He told an audience of elderly people in Florida that he favored making Social Security voluntary. He chose Memphis, Tennessee, the cotton capital, to attack farm subsidy programs. He then journeyed to Knoxville, located in the center of a region made prosperous by the Tennessee Valley Authority, to tell voters that the TVA must be sold to private power companies. In Charleston, West Virginia, located at the edge of Appalachia, one of the poorest regions in the nation, he announced that the impending war on poverty was unnecessary.

---

[1]Quoted in Michael Schaller, Virginia Scharff, and Robert D. Schulzinger, *Present Tense: The United States Since 1945* (Boston: Houghton Mifflin, 1992), p. 250.

Johnson refused to debate Goldwater on television. Because all of the polls showed him holding a large lead, Johnson did not bother to campaign until the final month. When he did enter the fray in October, he campaigned as a unifier and peacemaker. He forged a broad electoral consensus, including much of the business community, trade unions, farmers, most middle-class voters, liberals, intellectuals, the elderly, the poor, blacks, and other minorities. A sizeable part of Johnson's support came from Republican voters who were fleeing Goldwater's extremist campaign. Goldwater showed strength among white Southerners and hard-core Republicans.

On election day, Johnson won his predicted landslide. In the popular vote, he received 43 million votes to Goldwater's 27 million, and 486 electoral votes to Goldwater's 52. Johnson carried forty-four states and received 60.7 percent of the popular vote. Democrats added thirty-seven House seats and two more in the Senate. The new House of Representatives would have 295 Democrats to 140 Republicans. The new Senate would have sixty-eight Democrats to only thirty-two Republicans.

In the aftermath of the Goldwater debacle, some analysts spoke of the impending demise of the Republican Party as a major political force. Such epitaphs proved to be premature; it turned out that Goldwater was merely ahead of his time. Ronald Reagan, inheriting Goldwater's cause, would ride it to the White House in 1980. While celebrating their landslide victories, some Democratic Party leaders nervously noted that five out of the six states carried by Goldwater were Southern. The Solid South was disintegrating as white voters, perceiving the Democratic Party to be increasingly identified with the drive by African Americans for full participation in public life, abandoned their historical allegiances and voted Republican.

GREAT SOCIETY

Soon after his overwhelming victory, Johnson, backed by the most liberal Congress since 1936, set out to create the New Jerusalem. He organized task forces made up of his staffers, social scientists, bureaucrats, and activists to draft legislative proposals to send to Congress. Johnson and his liaison people also worked closely with Congress during all stages of the legislative process to get passage of the programs, which became known as Great Society. Among the most important measures enacted during 1965 was the Appalachian Regional Development Act. Appalachia, a mountainous region extending from Pennsylvania to northern Alabama, which contained 17 million people, was a vast pocket of poverty. The act provided over $1 billion in subsidies for a variety of projects, stressing the economic development of the region.

Congress also attacked the problem of America's decaying central cities. The Housing and Urban Development Act of 1965 provided funding for 240,000 units of low-rent housing. It also authorized the spending of $2.9 billion over four years for urban renewal projects. Federal rent supplements for low-income families were added in 1966. Congress also created a new cabinet-level Department of Housing and Urban Development (HUD). President Johnson appointed Robert Weaver to head the new agency, the first African American Cabinet member.

In addition to attacking urban problems, Congress enacted both the Medicare and the Medicaid programs in 1965. Medicare provided health care for people age sixty-five and over, while Medicaid provided health care for low-income people not eligible for Medicare. Both programs would be funded through Social Security. At the time of the passage of these programs, the United States was the only industrial democracy in the world without some form of national health insurance. Organized physicians, working through their powerful lobby, the American Medical Association (AMA), had blocked all efforts to enact national health insurance since Truman first proposed it in 1945. President Johnson overcame the opposition of the AMA and conservative legislators by limiting the insurance program to the elderly and the poor, and by funding it through the Social Security system. Funding Medicare and Medicaid through the extant Social Security system was another example of Johnson's fiscal conservatism that won conservative support for social reform.

One of the most important achievements of Great Society was the enactment of federal aid to education. The Elementary and Secondary Education Act of 1965 ended a long debate in Congress over the use of federal funds to support public schools. President Kennedy had made federal aid to public schools a top New Frontier priority and had suffered a serious defeat because of Catholic opposition to his bill, which did not fund parochial schools. On the other hand, Protestant and Jewish leaders strongly opposed funding parochial schools. Kennedy could never resolve the impasse. Johnson, believing that supporting education was the primary way the federal government could promote equality of opportunity in America, overcame the religious roadblock. He persuaded religious leaders to accept an aid program that provided federal funds for states based on the number of low-income students enrolled in their schools. The funds would be distributed to both private and public schools to benefit all children in need.

Johnson rescued another stalled New Frontier reform when he secured congressional passage of the Immigration Act of 1965, the first comprehensive overhaul of U.S. immigration policy in forty years. The new law abolished the discriminatory national origins quota system implemented during the 1920s, which had restricted immigration to this country on the basis of ethnic and racial background. Under the new legislation, each country would have an annual quota of about 20,000 slots. Eligibility would be based upon the skills and education of the individual immigrant, plus close family ties to people already here.

Additional civil rights legislation joined the Great Society agenda in 1965. Many African Americans could not yet vote in the Deep South states, despite the enactment of three previous civil rights bills and voter registration drives by civil rights groups. Hundreds of student volunteers working in Mississippi in the summer of 1964 to register African American voters encountered stubborn, sometimes violent, opposition from white segregationists. In the spring of 1965, Martin Luther King, Jr. prepared to lead a march of demonstrators from Selma, Alabama, to the state capitol in Montgomery to publicize the continuing denial of African American voting rights. A few days before the march was scheduled to begin, Johnson made a nationally televised speech to a joint session of Congress, calling for a voting rights bill that would close all remaining loopholes in civil rights laws. Near the end of his speech, Johnson raised his arms in the style of a country preacher and recited the words from an old black spiritual that had become the anthem of the civil rights movement: "And we shall overcome!" The demonstrators in Selma, poised to begin their march, listened to his speech through tears of joy.

As they began their march for the right to vote, they were attacked by Alabama state troopers, mounted on horseback, who gassed, clubbed, and whipped them. These vicious attacks on nonviolent protesters marching on behalf of a fundamental democratic right were televised nationally to a shocked nation. An angry president, viewing the attacks, federalized the Alabama National Guard and ordered it to provide protection for the marchers all the way to Montgomery. Johnson then maneuvered the Voting Rights Bill through Congress. The Voting Rights Act of 1965 gave the attorney general the power to appoint federal registrars to register voters in districts where historical patterns of disfranchisement prevailed. Empowered by the new law, federal officials registered hundreds of thousands of African American and Hispanic voters in six Southern states during the next three years. The 1966 election was the first one held in this country in which most adult Southern African Americans could vote.

THE IMPACT OF THE VOTING RIGHTS ACT IS SHOWN IN THE PERCENTAGE OF ADULT WHITE AND BLACK REGISTRATIONS IN THE SOUTH IN 1964 AND 1969.

	1964		1969	
	WHITE	BLACK	WHITE	BLACK
Alabama	69.2	19.3	94.6	61.3
Arkansas	65.6	40.4	81.6	77.9
Florida	74.8	51.2	94.2	67.0
Georgia	62.6	27.4	88.5	60.4
Louisiana	80.5	31.6	87.1	60.8
Mississippi	69.9	6.7	89.8	66.5
North Carolina	96.8	46.8	78.4	53.7
South Carolina	75.7	37.3	71.5	54.6
Tennessee	72.9	69.5	92.0	92.1
Texas			61.8	73.1
Virginia	61.1	38.3	78.7	59.8
Total	73.4	35.5	83.5	64.8

Source: U.S. Department of Commerce, *Statistical Abstract of the United States, 1970* (Washington, D.C., 1970), p. 369; and Steven Lawson, *Black Ballots, 1944–1969* (New York: Columbia University Press, 1976), p. 331.

Congress enacted many more Great Society measures. The first session of the 89th Congress approved ninety administration-sponsored reform bills. The legislative pace slowed the following year, but more measures continued to flow from Congress. Two important pieces of consumer protection legislation passed in 1966, a "Truth-in-Packaging" act and a "Truth-in-Lending" act. The former required sellers to accurately label the contents of packages sold for household use. The latter required detailed information about the true rate of interest charged on bank loans and credit purchases. Conservation and wildlife preservation laws were enacted. Congress added a new cabinet-level Department of Transportation in 1966 and enacted a series of highway safety laws. Consumer advocate Ralph Nader did more than anyone to secure the passage of these new safety laws. His book, *Unsafe At Any Speed* (1966), documented the hazardous design defects in Detroit-made automobiles, promoting public awareness of these problems.

Great Society measures enacted between 1964 and 1966 represented the most far-reaching assault ever mounted on a vast array of social problems by the federal government. Reform measures left over from the New Deal and Fair Deal eras were enacted during the mid-1960s. Most of the social problems that the Great Society tried to solve had been around for years, but they were challenged during the mid-1960s because of a confluence of circumstances that gave reformers opportunities normally unavailable within the American political system. The nation was prosperous, and there existed a widespread sense that Americans could afford the costs of social reform. Large liberal majorities prevailed in both houses of Congress, breaking the bipartisan conservative bloc's control. Johnson's smashing victory in the 1964 election had given the activist reform leader a mandate for social change. Most of all, his special political skills made the Great Society a reality. He formed broad-based coalitions incorporating conservative forces in support of social reform, and he used his remarkable abilities to steer complex legislation through congressional minefields of special interest groups.

For a time, many of the Great Society programs worked. In part stimulated by tax cuts, the economy grew rapidly. The GDP increased by 25 percent from 1964 to 1966, providing billions of dollars of additional tax revenues to fund the new programs without incurring budget deficits, raising interest rates, or igniting inflation. Unemployment dropped below 4 percent in 1965, the lowest rate since World World II. The number of poor people declined by millions; this reduction came from both antipoverty programs and new jobs generated by the strong economy. Medicare and Medicaid improved the quality of health care available to the elderly and the poor. Students at all educational levels benefited from federal programs, and African Americans in the South at long last had the vote.

But the Great Society immediately incurred a flurry of criticism from both the Left and the Right. Conservatives assailed its high costs, its centralization of government authority, and its proliferation of new federal bureaucracies. They insisted that social problems could not be solved by creating new federal agencies and throwing money at them. A few leftist radicals charged that most of the Great Society programs were woefully inadequate.

Johnson's war on poverty, which was launched in 1965 with much fanfare, came under heavy fire. Some of its programs worked well, particularly those that helped prepare poor minority youngsters for school and those that furnished job training for disadvantaged young men and women. But radical critics insisted that if government officials were serious about eradicating poverty in America, then a few billion dollars could not begin to meet the needs of the nation's 40 million poor people. In their view, the poverty program was both oversold and underfunded. It generated unrealistic expectations among poor African Americans and fierce resentments among working-class whites who perceived antipoverty programs as favoring militant protesters over hardworking people. Michael Harrington, whose book *The Other America* (1962) had helped President Kennedy discover poverty in America, observed: "What was supposed to be a social war turned out to be a skirmish, and in any case, poverty won."

After 1966, Congress, concerned about rising crime rates and inflation, was reluctant to vote for more funds for reform and welfare programs. Johnson had expected to finance Great Society from increased tax revenues derived from an expanding economy. He believed that Great Society would enable the one-fourth of Americans who were disadvantaged to join the affluent three-fourths without requiring any tax increases or redistribution of wealth. He promised much more than the Great Society could deliver. He both exaggerated American wealth and underestimated the profound structural barriers to achieving affluence for all within the framework of a liberal capitalist order. He believed that America could fight a major war in Vietnam and continue to build the Great Society at home. Ironically, the leader who wanted to achieve his place in history as the man who fulfilled the social vision of the New Deal escalated the war in Vietnam and strangled his beloved Great Society. The man who most wanted to extend and complete the New Deal presided over its collapse and prepared the way for a profound rightward shift of American politics over the next twenty years.

Liberal reformers lamented the fact that by 1967, except for token gestures, the Great Society was dead. The fight for civil rights, the struggle to save the cities,

Figure 12.2　Poverty, 1969.　*Source:* Bureau of the Census, *Current Population Reports*, Series P-60, No. 194, and unpublished data.

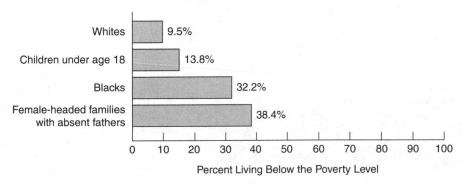

Percent Living Below the Poverty Level

Category	Percent
Whites	9.5%
Children under age 18	13.8%
Blacks	32.2%
Female-headed families with absent fathers	38.4%

the efforts to improve the public schools, and the efforts to clean up the environment—all were starved for the sake of the escalating war.

THE WARREN COURT

Led by its energetic Chief Justice Earl Warren, the activist liberal majority that controlled the Supreme Court during the 1960s rendered a series of landmark decisions that struck down the last remnants of the segregation system. The Court also protected the right of dissent, expanded the freedom of the press, regulated obscene materials, and restricted the role of religion in public schools. It further altered criminal legal procedures, expanded the right to privacy, and made the American political system more inclusive.

In *Bond v. Floyd* (1966), the Court ordered the Georgia House of Representatives to admit an elected representative, civil rights activist Julian Bond, who had been denied his seat because of his opposition to the Vietnam War and the conscription system that sustained it.

In *New York Times v. Sullivan* (1964), the Court ruled that people in the public eye—elected officials and celebrities—could not win a libel suit against a publication solely because its editors had published untrue statements. Under the Court's reading of libel laws, plaintiffs had to prove that the statements were "recklessly false" and made with "malice aforethought." Since motivation was extremely difficult to establish within a court of law, the practical effect of *New York Times v. Sullivan* was to make it unlikely that a public figure could win a libel suit against a newspaper or magazine publisher.

In *Roth v. United States* (1957), the Court defined obscenity as material "without any redeeming social importance." The Court also defined as obscene material as what "the average person, applying community standards, regarded as appealing to prurient interests." However, the Court found it impossible to come

Figure 12.3   The Warren Court. Photo taken on November 22, 1965. Standing (left to right) are: Byron White, William Brennan, Potter Stewart, and Abe Fortas; seated are Tom Clark, Hugo Black, Earl Warren, William Douglas, and John Marshall Harlan. *Source:* National Archives.

up with objective criteria to determine what materials were obscene under its definitions. The problems were twofold: community standards varied, and any definition of obscenity involved inherently subjective judgments.

The Court also broadened the First Amendment's ban on the establishment of religion. In *Engel v. Vitale* (1962), the Court banned prayer in public schools. In a later decision, the Court banned Bible readings from public school classrooms. The Court also nullified an Arkansas law that mandated the teaching of "creation science" as an alternative to Darwinian evolutionary theory. The cumulative effect over the years of these decisions was to remove religious observances from public schools.

In two controversial five-to-four decisions, the Supreme Court also enhanced the procedural rights of citizens accused of crimes. In the first case, *Gideon v. Wainwright* (1963), the Court ruled that Clarence Gideon, a career criminal, had never gotten a fair trial because he had never had an attorney to defend him in court. The Court, in effect, ruled that the right to a fair trial included the right to be represented in court by a lawyer. As a consequence of the Court's rulings in *Gideon v. Wainwright*, all cases in the country where defendants had been convicted of felonies without the benefit of attorneys to represent them had to be retried. If the defendant could not afford an attorney, the state, at the expense of taxpayers, had to furnish one. In the second case, *Miranda v. Arizona* (1966), the Court enhanced citizens' Fifth Amendment rights against self-incrimination. In this case, the Court ruled that Ernesto Miranda, a suspect charged with burglary, had been coerced by the Phoenix police into confessing. The police questioning Miranda had told him that if he did not confess, the judge would give him a longer sentence. According to the new rules implemented in *Miranda v. Arizona*, police were required to inform a suspect of his or her rights at the time of arrest: the suspect's right to remain silent, that anything said could and would be used in a court of law to convict him or her, the right to have an attorney represent him or her in court, and in the event that he or she could not afford a lawyer, that the state would provide one free.

In 1965, the Warren Court struck down a Connecticut law that forbade the sale or use of contraceptives. In *Griswald v. Connecticut*, Associate Justice William O. Douglas, writing for the majority, found the Connecticut law to be an unwarranted invasion of privacy. Nowhere in the Bill of Rights is there delineated a specific right to privacy; Douglas apparently inferred a right of privacy.

Warren Court rulings also affected political practices in this country. In *Baker v. Carr* (1962), the Court declared that it could determine whether state legislative districts had been fairly drawn. The principle that the courts used during the 1960s to determine this was "one person, one vote," derived from the equal protections clause of the Fourteenth Amendment. During the 1960s, as a consequence of *Baker v. Carr*, several states, in which rural voters were overrepresented in state legislatures at the expense of urban residents, had to redraw the boundaries of their legislative districts to make them equal in population.

The cumulative effects of these landmark court decisions were to enhance significantly the rights of individuals, curtail the arbitrary powers of government, and make the political system more democratic. Ironically, the least democratic branch

of the federal government, and the only one beyond the reach of the voting majority, had done much to strengthen American democracy and validate the growing
pluralism of the political culture. In doing so, the Warren Court provoked many
powerful enemies. Conservatives were enraged by what they considered judicial
usurpations of the lawmaking process. Law enforcement officials complained that
Court decisions made their jobs more difficult, allowed obviously guilty people to
avoid punishment, and seemed to place the law on the side of criminals rather than
on their law-abiding victims. Devoutly religious people often were offended by the
Court's proscriptions of religious observances in the public schools. As the conservative revolt gathered momentum in this country during the 1970s, one of its
salient issues was curtailing the judicial activism of the Supreme Court.

LYNDON JOHNSON AND THE WORLD

Johnson's early ventures in world affairs met with mixed results. In time, his efforts to achieve an American military victory in Vietnam would destroy his presidency and bring his nation and those whom he had tried to help in Southeast Asia
to disaster.

In Europe, Johnson could not prevent relations with NATO allies from deteriorating. His chief difficulties came with French leader Charles de Gaulle, who
wanted France and western Europe to rid themselves of U.S. domination. The
French leader spurned Johnson's offer to create a multilateral nuclear force and directed France to accelerate development of its own nuclear forces. In early 1966,
France withdrew its forces from NATO and ordered the United States to remove
all of its military installations and personnel from France. France's dramatic actions
signaled that de Gaulle believed that the Cold War in Europe was waning. European countries no longer feared Soviet aggression, hence they no longer felt dependent on U.S. support.

As de Gaulle challenged American influence in Europe, tensions in the
Middle East caused Johnson persistent problems. The president perceived Egyptian leader Gamal Abdul Nasser's efforts to promote Arab nationalism as the chief
threat to American Middle Eastern interests. The Soviet Union, backing Nasser,
was gaining influence in the region. Then came another Arab–Israeli war. It occurred in June 1967, following border clashes between Israelis and Syrians in the
Golan Heights area. Nasser, backing Syria, mobilized his forces and blockaded Israel's Red Sea port of Elath. Egypt also worked out an agreement with Jordan that
placed its forces under Egyptian command. The Israelis, concluding that an Arab
attack was imminent, launched an offensive on June 5. Israeli forces quickly destroyed the Egyptian air force, decimated Jordan's army, and defeated Syrian
forces. Israeli tanks routed the Egyptian army. Israel won the war in six days. When
a UN-proposed cease-fire went into effect, Israel occupied the Sinai and that part
of Jordan west of the River Jordan (the West Bank). Israeli forces also held Syrian

territory in the Golan Heights. Egyptian military power was shattered, Nasser was humiliated, and Soviet interests suffered a setback. Israel, now a major power in the region, kept all occupied territories, determined to use them to enhance its territory and security. Israeli imperialism intensified already powerful Arab anti-Zionist animosities.

Nasser remained popular with the Egyptian people. The Soviets quickly rebuilt his military forces. The Soviets also expanded their naval forces in the eastern Mediterranean to challenge the U.S. Sixth Fleet. America remained Israel's chief supporter. As LBJ's presidency ended, the danger of another Arab–Israeli war remained great. It now carried with it the ominous potential of a U.S.–USSR confrontation.

Johnson also had to face crises in the Caribbean, where he made preventing further Castro-like insurgencies his top priority. His first crisis came in Panama, long a U.S. protectorate. Violent conflicts erupted between Panamanians and American citizens living in the Canal Zone in January 1964. The violence began when Panamanian students demanded that their national flag be flown alongside the American flag at a high school located in the Canal Zone. American authorities rejected the students' demand. American soldiers killed twenty-one Panamanians, and three Americans died in riots. Panama severed diplomatic relations with the United States. The Organization of American States (OAS) mediated the dispute. Normal relations between the two countries were quickly restored. American and Panamanian negotiators then produced a series of agreements, allowing Panamanian participation in the management of the Panama Canal and granting Panama a share of canal revenues.

Another crisis occurred in the Dominican Republic, which also had a long history of American domination. A right-wing dictator, Rafael Trujillo, was overthrown in 1961 by a military coup, ushering in years of political instability in that island country. President Kennedy, delighted to see Trujillo go, sought free elections in the country. The elections brought Juan Bosch to power in 1962. Bosch, a social Democrat, was overthrown by another military coup seven months later. In early 1965, a coalition of liberals, radicals, and young army officers launched a revolution to restore Bosch to power.

President Johnson, fearful that pro-Castro elements might come to power and turn the country into another Cuba, sent troops to suppress the insurgency. U.S. Marines and Army infantrymen prevented Bosch's return to power. American spokesmen announced that U.S. intervention had prevented a Communist takeover of the Dominican Republic. An occupation force was set up to maintain order. Elections were held in 1966, and Joaquin Balaguer defeated Bosch. Balaguer was able to establish an effective government that protected U.S. interests, and Johnson withdrew the American forces. But the Bosch movement was an independent, nationalistic movement, not a Communist conspiracy. American intervention violated the OAS charter and canceled the U.S. pledge to not intervene militarily in the affairs of other Western Hemisphere countries. American public opinion supported Johnson's intervention. Liberals and foreign critics attacked his actions, but he ignored them. The campaign was limited in duration, and few American lives were lost. Johnson achieved his objectives, and his success silenced his critics. Success in the Dominican operation encouraged Johnson to try more of the same in Vietnam, expecting U.S. military success there to also silence any detractors who might emerge.

VIETNAM: GOING TO WAR

The roots of U.S. intervention in Southeast Asia could be traced back to Truman's presidency, but it was not until the Kennedy years that the United States became inextricably involved in a war in Vietnam. At the time Johnson replaced Kennedy, the political situation in South Vietnam was deteriorating. A succession of inept military governments had followed Diem, none of which governed or fought effectively. National Liberation Front forces, the "Vietcong," supported by supplies and troops from North Vietnam, extended their control in southern Vietnam.

Johnson did not concern himself greatly with Vietnam during his first year in office; he continued Kennedy's policy of supporting the South Vietnamese government. He retained Kennedy's top advisers, sharing their commitment to contain the spread of Chinese Communism into Southeast Asia. LBJ, just as Truman, Eisenhower, and Kennedy had before him, embraced the Cold War ideology. His primary foreign policy objectives were to contain the two Communist powers, the Soviet Union and the People's Republic of China, and to prevent revolutionary change in the Third World. Johnson dismissed any possibility of an American withdrawal from Vietnam or any political solution that did not guarantee the survival of an independent, non-Communist state in southern Vietnam. He increased both the number of American advisers in South Vietnam and the level of economic aid. He also approved a series of covert operations against North Vietnam, including commando raids along the North Vietnamese coast and infiltration of CIA operatives into the North. This subtle shift toward the North opened the way to a wider war.

In the summer of 1964, as the presidential campaign was getting underway in the United States, there occurred a relatively minor event in the war that was developing in Vietnam that had major consequences. On August 1, while engaged in electronic espionage off the coast of North Vietnam, the American destroyer USS *Maddox* was attacked by North Vietnamese torpedo boats. The *Maddox* returned the fire and repulsed the attackers with the aid of U.S. naval aircraft, resuming its spy operations. It was joined by another destroyer, the *Turner Joy*. On the night of August 4, as they operated in heavy seas about fifty miles off the coast of North Vietnam in the Gulf of Tonkin, both ships reported that they were under attack. No one on either ship sighted any attackers; their initial reports were based on radar and sonar contacts. Later, the *Maddox*'s captain reported that weather effects and a misreading of sonar data may have been responsible for the reported attacks.

Even though evidence of a second attack was not certain, Johnson authorized retaliatory air strikes against North Vietnamese naval bases. He also asked Congress to approve a resolution, authorizing him to take "all necessary measures to repel any armed attack against the forces of the United States and to prevent further aggression." Johnson's use of force, coupled with his appeal for public support, silenced his Republican challenger, Barry Goldwater, who earlier had called for the bombing of North Vietnam. In presenting their case for the resolution, administration officials misled the Congress. Congressmen and senators were not told that the *Maddox* was on a spy mission when it was attacked, nor that the second attack may not have occurred. Secretary of Defense McNamara characterized both incidents as mindless acts of aggression against American ships on routine patrol in international waters. Congress quickly gave the president what he wanted, without serious debate. The House passed the resolution unanimously, and the Senate enacted it by a vote of 88 to 2.

During the final month of the 1964 presidential campaign, Johnson said little about the war in Vietnam. Goldwater did not make an issue out of it, and most Americans did not concern themselves with a dirty little war in a faraway place. But at times Johnson did appear to be telling the American people that Americans would not be sent to fight there. In Akron, Ohio, on October 21, he stated, "We are not about to send American boys nine or ten thousand miles away from home to do what Asian boys ought to be doing for themselves."

At the time he made those remarks, Johnson had not yet committed himself to the further bombing of North Vietnam, nor had he decided to send U.S. combat troops there. But he knew the situation in southern Vietnam was deteriorating, despite his own public assurances to the contrary. He also was involved with advisers who had developed contingency plans that could be implemented in the future, including bombing the North and sending American combat troops to South Vietnam. During his reelection campaign, he deliberately misled the American people, conveying the impression that he would limit American efforts in Vietnam to helping one side in a civil war. He offered himself as a peace candidate who did not seek a wider war in contrast to the hawkish Goldwater, who called for an unlimited American military effort in Vietnam.

As the new year began, the South Vietnamese government was on the verge of defeat, and Johnson was confronting a dilemma largely of his own making. Since he had ruled out American withdrawal from Southeast Asia, there remained only the options of negotiation or escalation. But negotiations with Hanoi in early 1965, given the military realities in southern Vietnam, could only mean having to accept a neutral coalition government for South Vietnam, with National Liberation Front (NLF) participation. Johnson knew that such a government would soon be dominated by the NLF, since the Saigon regime could only survive with strong American support. He therefore ruled out negotiations until the military situation was more favorable, and he made his decision to escalate the war.

Johnson authorized a sustained, gradually expanding bombing campaign against North Vietnam beginning on February 13, called Operation Rolling

Thunder, and he significantly expanded the much larger air war in southern Vietnam. There was a direct connection between the air war against North Vietnam and Johnson's decision to send combat forces to South Vietnam. Within two weeks, General William Westmoreland, the U.S. commander in Vietnam, requested Marine combat units to defend a large U.S. Air Force base at Danang because he could not rely on South Vietnamese security forces. Johnson quickly approved his request. On March 8, two Marine battalions in full battle gear waded ashore at beaches south of Danang.

In July 1965, Johnson and his advisers made a series of fateful decisions that set the United States on a course in Vietnam, from which it did not deviate for nearly three years and from which also began seven years of war. They approved General Westmoreland's requests for saturation bombing in southern Vietnam and for expanding the air war against North Vietnam. They also authorized sending an additional 100,000 combat troops to South Vietnam. Most important, President Johnson gave General Westmoreland a free hand to assume the major burden of fighting in the South. These decisions, made during the last week of July, represented a conscious decision to conduct an American war in Vietnam.

When he committed the United States to war in Southeast Asia, LBJ refused to tell the American people what he had done, and he refused to seek a formal declaration of war against North Vietnam. He claimed that the Gulf of Tonkin resolution granted him the authority to wage war. Since the Supreme Court never ruled on the matter, it remains a moot question whether the resolution amounted to a declaration of war against North Vietnam. Senator Fulbright, along with other legislators who later turned against the war, believed that Johnson had tricked them into supporting a war. At the time, Johnson felt confident that he could win the war in a few years and persuade Congress and most Americans to support it.

Washington's decisions for war were based on two fundamental errors in judgment. The United States seriously underestimated the capacity of the NLF and the North Vietnamese to resist large-scale applications of U.S. military power over a long period of time. Johnson and his advisers assumed that within a year or two, North Vietnam would "break" from the ever-increasing punishment inflicted by American bombers, and that they would accept U.S. terms for settlement. Johnson could not conceive of a poor Asian country about the size of New Mexico standing up to the military power of the United States. The second error was to underestimate drastically the cost of the war, in both lives and dollars, and to overestimate the willingness of Americans to go on passively paying those costs year after year.

THE AMERICAN WAY OF WAR

The United States relied heavily on air power to win the war. U.S. Air Force and Navy pilots had two primary missions—to check infiltration of men, equipment, and supplies coming south from North Vietnam along the "Ho Chi Minh Trail," and to punish the North Vietnamese from the air until they abandoned the insurgency in the South and came to the bargaining table on American terms. Bombing failed to achieve either objective, even though the Americans waged the largest aerial war in history. The bombing slowed the rate of infiltration down the Ho Chi Minh Trail, although never enough to seriously hamper the NLF war effort. Bombing disrupted North Vietnam's agriculture, destroyed its industry, and severely damaged some of its cities. Thousands of civilians were killed or wounded. But bombing never appreciably reduced North Vietnam's war-making ability, nor broke its morale.

American ground combat operations also escalated drastically between July 1965 and the end of 1967, when the United States had deployed nearly 500,000 troops. General Westmoreland used a strategy of attrition against the enemy. He believed that "search and destroy" operations would eradicate the enemy and force them to the negotiating table. U.S. troops used their technological superiority to counter the enemy's guerrilla warfare tactics. Herbicides were used on a wide scale to deprive the Vietcong of forest cover and food crops. These chemicals caused widespread ecological devastation and posed health hazards within southern Vietnam. Americans also relied on artillery, helicopter gunships, and bombing to destroy enemy bases and to drive the guerrillas into open country. Since all of South Vietnam became a combat zone, American soldiers found themselves

Figure 12.4   Vietnam was primarily a small unit war in which squads of American troops engaged the NLF forces in jungles, swamps, and rice paddies. Here soldiers carry a wounded comrade through a swampy area. Photographer: SSG Paul Halverson. *Source:* U.S. Army Photo, neg.# SG651408.

fighting an unconventional war without fronts or territorial objectives. The only measure of progress toward victory in a war of attrition was the number of enemy supplies captured or destroyed, the number of enemy weapons and ammunition captured or destroyed, and most of all, the number of enemy soldiers captured, wounded, or killed.

The American takeover of the war in early 1965 had prevented certain South Vietnamese defeat. But the United States could only achieve a stalemate, not a victory. The attrition strategy was based on the assumption that U.S. forces, using their superior firepower, could inflict irreplaceable losses on the enemy while keeping their own casualties low. Even though the Americans inflicted heavy casualties, both the NLF and the North Vietnamese replaced their losses and matched each American escalation with one of their own during the period 1965–1967. They retained the strategic initiative, and the NLF political structure in the South remained intact.

American artillery and bombing campaigns below the seventeenth parallel disrupted the southern Vietnamese economy. Large numbers of civilians were killed, and millions more were driven into the arms of the Vietcong, or became refugees. The violent American assault undermined the social fabric of a fragile nation and alienated villagers from the South Vietnamese regime that had never enjoyed much support from the rural population. The American takeover of the war further weakened the resolve of the South Vietnamese forces, who became more dependent than ever on American combat forces.

In 1967, with firm prodding from Washington, the South Vietnamese government, headed by General Nguyen Van Thieu, attempted to build popular support among the rural population. It focused on pacification and rural development. Government cadres moved into villages, providing medical supplies and social services. They tried to insulate the villagers from both Vietcong appeals and reprisals, and they sought to promote a national rebirth while American forces tried to defeat the Communists militarily. These pacification efforts sometimes succeeded, but they more often failed. Americans occasionally bombed or shelled pacified villages by mistake. Vietcong terrorists assassinated many rural development leaders. Often the cadres were inept or corrupt. The inability of the South Vietnamese military government to win mass allegiance or to solve its country's massive social problems were major reasons for the eventual failure of the American effort in Vietnam.

The Thieu government survived not because it was strong, because it was popular with most South Vietnamese or its soldiers fought well, but because it was backed by massive American firepower. But relations between American advisers and their Vietnamese clients often were ambivalent. The Vietnamese resented the Americans' arrogance and inability to understand them. The Americans were frustrated by pervasive Vietnamese corruption and inefficiency. American soldiers, fighting in the steamy jungles and swamps of an alien land, and not always able to tell a friendly Vietnamese from a deadly enemy, often expressed hostility and mistrust toward the people they were defending.

The steady escalation of the war between 1965 and 1967 generated both international and domestic pressures for a negotiated settlement. But the continuing stalemate on the battlefields ensured that neither side wanted negotiations. For political reasons, both sides had to appear responsive to peace initiatives, but neither side would make concessions necessary to get serious negotiations started. Hanoi's strategy was to get maximum propaganda value out of peace initiatives, while matching U.S. escalations until the Americans tired of the war and pulled out. President Johnson believed that the steadily expanding American military effort would eventually break Hanoi.

Hanoi maintained that the American military presence in South Vietnam violated the 1954 Geneva accords and that the bombing of North Vietnam was criminal aggression. The North Vietnamese refused to negotiate until the United States ceased all acts of war against their country and withdrew its forces. Hanoi also insisted that the government in Saigon would have to be replaced by a coalition government dominated by the NLF. The United States refused to withdraw its forces until a political solution could be reached in the South, which excluded the Vietcong. It also refused to stop the bombing, which Washington insisted was necessary to keep the Communists from overrunning the South. The United States remained committed to achieving a non-Communist South Vietnam. So the war went on, and numerous peace initiatives from various sources failed in 1966 and 1967.

WAR AT HOME

While the expanding military stalemate continued, within the United States, supporters and opponents of the war engaged in debates of rising intensity. On one side were the Hawks, mostly conservative Republicans and Democrats, strongly supportive of the war, who wanted to increase the U.S. war effort. On the other side were the Doves, challenging both the effectiveness and morality of the war. The Doves represented a more diverse group: old-line pacifists, student radicals, civil rights leaders, some college professors, and liberal politicians. The most prominent Dove was Senator Fulbright. Initially a supporter, Fulbright had turned against the war by 1966.

Opposition to the war took many forms. Senator Fulbright held hearings on the conduct of the war before his Senate Foreign Relations Committee, providing a forum for war critics and helping legitimate opposition to the war. The Doves staged many rallies and protest demonstrations during 1967, the first year of extensive antiwar activity. On October 21, about 50,000 opponents of war demonstrated in front of the Pentagon. Thousands of young men resisted or evaded the draft. Some fled America and its war for Canada or Sweden.

Most Americans in 1967 were neither Hawks nor Doves. Nearly all citizens had supported the initial escalations that Americanized the Vietnam War. Confident of quick victory, they had rallied around the flag. But after two years of rising costs and casualties, popular frustration with the Vietnam War had mounted. Polls taken in August showed for the first time that a majority of Americans believed that sending American combat troops to Vietnam had been a mistake. But opponents of Johnson's war policy in 1967 formed no consensus on Vietnam. They were divided over whether to escalate the war drastically and win it, or to negotiate an American withdrawal. But the growing divisiveness, combined with declining confidence in the integrity and competence of government officials, strained the social fabric.

The president, trying to dampen growing criticism within the Congress of his war policy, brought General Westmoreland to Washington in November. Speaking before the National Press Club on November 21, Westmoreland gave an optimistic appraisal of the war. He said that pacification was going so well that the Vietcong could no longer mount a major offensive anywhere in South Vietnam. He stated, "We have reached an important point where the end begins to come into view." Popular support for the war increased as the year ended.

TET-68 AND ITS CONSEQUENCES

Then came Tet. On January 30, 1968, choosing the Lunar New Year, the most important Vietnamese holiday, as a time to strike in order to catch their opponents by surprise, about 80,000 NLF and North Vietnamese troops suddenly brought the war to the cities and towns of South Vietnam. They simultaneously attacked provincial capitals, district towns, and a dozen major U.S. military bases all over the country. At most attack sites, the Vietcong were beaten back within a few hours or a few days and sustained heavy losses. Within a month, they had lost all of the cities they had originally taken.

Hanoi had planned the Tet Offensive carefully; it was designed to give them a smashing victory over the Americans, demoralize the Army of the Republic of Vietnam (ARVN) forces, and bring the urban population of South Vietnam over to their side. They would show the urban populations of the South that neither the American nor the South Vietnamese forces could protect them. The Communists hoped that their assaults would provoke popular uprisings against the South Vietnamese government, forcing Americans to leave and hastening the end of the war. But Tet turned out to be a major tactical defeat for the Communists; they failed to achieve most of their goals and suffered heavy losses.

Within the United States, the Tet Offensive had a tremendous impact. It turned out to be a crucial political victory for the Communists. It had caught the South Vietnamese and Americans by surprise, although they had responded quickly to counteract it.

Although General Westmoreland spoke confidently about having anticipated and suppressed the Tet offensive, while inflicting heavy losses on the enemy. He soon requested an additional 206,000 troops to be able to follow up and win the

Figure 12.5   Members of Rifle Company "D", 2nd Battalion, 28th Infantry, provide security for a minesweeping team from the 1st Engineering, in Co Trach, located approximately 27 miles west of Lai Khe. (Mekong Delta, December, 1969) Photographer: SP5 Dennis L. Viets. *Source:* U.S. Army Photo, neg.# SC653104.

war. The Chairman of the Joint Chiefs, General Earle Wheeler, gave the president the first pessimistic appraisal of the war that he had ever heard from a military adviser. Wheeler hinted that the Americans could lose the war unless the requested reinforcements were sent. Johnson, confused by events and conflicting military opinions, asked his new Secretary of Defense Clark Clifford to conduct a thorough review of the troop request before the president responded to the military's request for more troops.

Clifford formed a committee whose investigations ranged far beyond the troop request issue; it conducted the first full review of the American war effort in Vietnam. Clifford demanded precise answers to fundamental questions: What were the ultimate objectives of the United States in Vietnam? How would additional forces contribute to attaining these goals? What would be the impact of a major escalation of the war on the public and on the economy? Was there a definable limit to the American commitment to Vietnam? Was there a point at which the price became too high? How would General Westmoreland deploy these troops, and exactly what results could be expected from this additional manpower?

The answers he received from both military and civilian officials in the Pentagon discouraged him. To provide 206,000 more troops for Vietnam required further reductions of U.S. military commitments elsewhere, which already were stretched dangerously thin. Meeting these troop requests would necessitate calling up reserves, increasing draft calls, and raising taxes. Casualties would rise, and domestic opposition would intensify. Civilian analysts in the Pentagon told Clifford that the current war strategy could not bring victory, even with the proposed escalation; they recommended that the United States start phasing back its military involvement and trying to achieve a negotiated settlement. They also proposed turning over more of the fighting to the South Vietnamese forces. Clifford subsequently recommended to the president that he reject Westmoreland's request for additional troops, assign the ARVN a greater fighting role, and seek a negotiated settlement rather than continue his futile efforts to win the war.

The Tet Offensive also influenced the way the media, particularly television news, covered the Vietnam War. Previously, television had usually presented a well-ordered vision of the war—on-the-scene reports of combat operations that usually were reported as American victories, along with periodic analytical reports of the war's progress and of pacification programs. With Tet, viewers for the first time saw the results of a major Communist offensive striking all over South Vietnam. A rush of violent and confusing images flooded television—fighting in the streets of Saigon and Hue. The chaos in Vietnam viewed on television appeared to contradict all of the official reports and media coverage of the past three years, which had conveyed the idea of steady progress toward military victory. The fact that the enemy could stage surprise attacks all over South Vietnam caused a growing number of Americans to wonder if all that was achieved after three years of escalating war in Vietnam was an unending stalemate.

Congressional opposition to the war also escalated after Tet. Antiwar sentiment on Capitol Hill boosted the candidacy of an obscure Minnesota Senator, Eugene McCarthy, who had announced in December 1967 that he would challenge Lyndon Johnson for the presidency as an antiwar candidate. In the New Hampshire primary, held on March 12, 1968, McCarthy received 42 percent of the vote, almost as many votes as Johnson, indicating more widespread opposition to Johnson's war policy than previously thought. Johnson appeared to be politically vulnerable. Four days after the New Hampshire primary, a more formidable antiwar candidate, Robert Kennedy, announced that he too would seek the Democratic nomination.

At the White House, Johnson convened a panel of distinguished civilian and military advisers who had previously endorsed his war policy. But in March these "wise men" told the president that the Vietnam War could not be won, "save at unacceptable risk" to national interests at home and abroad. Their advice influenced Johnson. He accepted Clark Clifford's recommendations to scale back the war. On March 31, 1968, Johnson told the American people that he would reduce the bombing of North Vietnam in an effort to get negotiations underway. As he neared the end of his speech, he stunned the nation by stating, "I shall not seek, nor will I accept, the nomination of my party for another term as your president." To restore unity to America, he would remove himself from politics and seek peace in Vietnam. To end the war at home that was tearing the nation apart, he would abandon the strategy of gradual escalation in Vietnam that he had begun three years earlier.

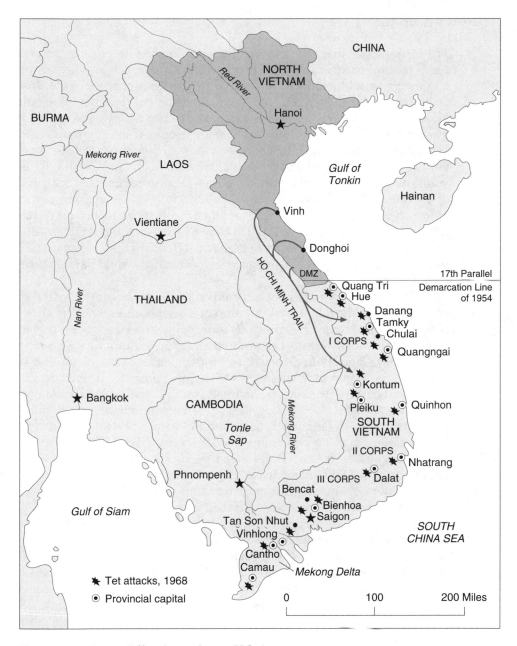

Figure 12.6   Tet-68 Offensive.   *Source:* U.S. Army.

YOUNG RADICALS

The insurgencies that characterized the middle and late 1960s began on the campuses of some of America's leading universities, the prestigious Ivy League schools and the great public universities such as the Berkeley campus of the University of California and the University of Michigan at Ann Arbor. A new generation of politically committed young people had already became involved in the civil rights movement and also tried to organize poor people at the community level. After 1965, many of these youthful insurgents, most of them from affluent, middle-class families, became involved in protests against the Vietnam War. In 1960, a group of young activists organized the Students for a Democratic Society (SDS). In 1962, one of its leaders, Tom Hayden, wrote a manifesto for the new organization, "The Port Huron Statement." He criticized apathetic college students and attacked the military-industrial complex. Hayden called for an end to poverty in America and for the creation of "a democracy of individual participation," in which all members subject to the authority of a governmental institution would participate in its decision-making processes.

The first student uprising occurred on the Berkeley campus of the University of California in the fall of 1964. A group of students, many of them civil rights activists who had spent the previous summer registering voters in Mississippi, protested university efforts to prevent their using a campus area for rallying support for off-campus political activities. Student leaders Mario Savio and Jack Weinberg, both veterans of the Mississippi "Freedom Summer," formed the Free Speech Movement (FSM) to lead the resistance. When university officials attempted to discipline leaders of the FSM, about 600 students and nonstudents occupied Sproul Hall, the university administration building. After university efforts to persuade the protesters to leave peacefully failed, Governor Edmund G. "Pat" Brown ordered state police to remove and arrest them. The forced removal of the demonstrators provoked a student strike that was supported by a large majority of the faculty. After two months of turmoil on campus, university officials rescinded the order and permitted "free speech" on campus.

Leaders of the Free Speech Movement aimed their attacks at the university itself. They saw it as a willing servant of a corporate order that controlled society and maintained an economic system that oppressed blacks and poor people. In their view, Berkeley had become an "impersonal machine," serving the established power structure and preparing students for careers as corporate functionaries. Cards designed by IBM and used to classify and identify students became for young radicals symbols of an educational system that had lost sight of its primary goals of making people better and improving society.

The rebellion that began at Berkeley soon spread to other campuses around the country. Insurgents attacked university complicity with racial injustice and the Vietnam War. They also attacked the universities themselves. Curricula and methods of instruction came under fire. Students objected to taking "irrelevant" courses, mostly the required science and language classes. Other protesters demanded the elimination of college parietal rules that set curfews and visiting hours for university housing.

By the mid-1960s, the stalemated Vietnam War had become the main student protest issue. Since the military draft was the prime way in which the war could reach young people, opposition to the draft brought thousands of new recruits into protest politics. When the SDS launched a national draft resistance program, new chapters proliferated, as thousands of recruits rushed to join. The SDS organized a "Stop the Draft Week" for October 16 to 21, 1967. It staged sit-ins at army induction centers, held meetings for draft card burnings, opposed campus ROTC programs, demonstrated against corporations known to be prime Defense Department contractors, and harassed military recruiters. Thousands of protesters besieged the Oakland, California, Army Induction Center, blocking busses hauling in draftees. Between 1965 and 1968, the SDS led or joined hundreds of demonstrations at over 100 colleges and universities involving about 50,000 students.

SDS also joined a violent student uprising, which occurred at Columbia University during the first six months of 1968. The issues that sparked the conflict were two potent catalysts of student militancy, civil rights and Vietnam. Antiwar radicals and civil rights activists joined forces to attack one of the nation's leading universities. The SDS sought an end to university ties with a military research institute on campus. The Black Student Union opposed university plans to construct a gymnasium on land adjacent to Harlem. Both groups occupied campus buildings to force the university to sever its ties with the military and to abandon the gym project. When negotiations between administration officials and radicals failed, police stormed the buildings to remove the protesters. Hundreds of students were injured, and about 700 were arrested. Following the arrests, the SDS organized a campus strike that forced the university to close early that spring.

American student protests in 1968 were part of a larger web of student and worker militant actions around the world. While students barricaded buildings at Columbia, 10 million workers went on strike in France, and students battled police in the streets of Paris. Mass demonstrations occurred in Sao Paulo, Brazil; the most violent street fighting in decades occurred in Italy. In London, 25,000 people protested the Vietnam War. Radical political movements of every kind convulsed the planet during one of the most transformative years of the twentieth century.

At its 1969 annual meeting, the New Left split into warring factions. Its left wing, calling itself the "Weathermen," went off on its own. In October, hundreds of Weathermen staged "the days of rage" in Chicago, which they intended to be the opening campaign of a new American revolution. They broke windows in buildings and smashed automobile windshields. Police arrested and jailed most of them. About 100 Weathermen went underground, forming terrorist bands that carried out sporadic bombings of public buildings and corporate headquarters during the early 1970s.

The New Left radicalized only a small portion of the millions of young people attending college during the 1960s. Most students attended class, pursued their social lives, worked part time, and sought conventional goals, never participating in radical protests on or off campus. Student rebels were mostly clustered on major metropolitan university campuses such as Berkeley and Columbia. Because they were a highly visible, articulate group that received extensive media coverage, especially television news coverage, the public's perception was that student radicalism was much more extensive than the demographic data confirmed. Most of the nation's 2,300 community colleges, state universities, private liberal arts colleges, and campuses with religious affiliations, which educated the vast majority of the nation's collegians, remained quiet, orderly, businesslike places during the 1960s. The young radicals of the 1960s were mostly the children of college-educated, liberal, affluent, and often influential parents. They formed a radical elite who rebelled against some of the institutions and practices of the affluent society. But these comparatively few privileged insurgents provoked a rebellion that spread beyond politics to challenge the entire culture. This cultural rebellion posed a more fundamental challenge to the values and mores of the consumerist culture than did the New Left, and it had far greater appeal to the young people of the 1960s.

THE GREENING OF AMERICA

Far more young people who felt alienated and frustrated by the affluent liberal society of the 1960s fled from it rather than radically confronted it. These "hippies" took a path previously traveled by Bohemians during the Roaring Twenties and the Beats during the 1950s. In fact, the best of the Beat poets, Allen Ginsberg, was a prominent member of the 1960s counterculture. The hippies embraced a new youth culture that ran counter to much that was cherished by middle-class Americans—affluence, economic growth, high technology, and, according to historian William Leuchtenburg,

> the institutions and value systems associated with the Protestant ethic of self-denial and sexual repression and more modern premises of the consumer culture and the meritocracy.[2]

The discipline of parents, schools, and jobs was abandoned for a free-flowing existence expressed by the hippie motto: "Do your own thing."

Hippies grew long hair and donned jeans, tank tops, and sandals. These refugees from the "uptight, straight" world of parents, schools, and nine-to-five jobs flocked to havens in the Haight-Ashbury section of San Francisco, the Sunset Strip in Hollywood, and New York City's East Village. They joined communes that cropped up in both urban neighborhoods and rural retreats. The appeal of the commune movement lay in a romantic urge to return to the land: to adopt a simpler life, to regain physical and mental health, and to perhaps seek spiritual renewal.

The counterculture repudiated science, systematic knowledge, and rationalism. It embraced a notion of organic, mystical consciousness in which the Self

---

[2]William E. Leuchtenburg, *A Troubled Feast*, rev. ed. (Boston: Little, Brown, 1983), p. 179.

merged seamlessly with Community and Nature. Infinite "being" supplanted the linear boundaries of time and space. Feeling and intuition replaced thought and knowing. Hippies explored ancient Asian and African mystical religions. Saffron-robed skinheads on San Francisco street corners chanted the "Hare Krishna." Others found the Age of Aquarius in astrology. Some hippies turned to witchcraft and demonology. Nature was valued as being superior to society and technology. A wide array of synthetic consumer products was rejected as being artificial—"plastic." Hippies prized being natural, using nature's products, and eating natural foods. The hippie ideal was personal authenticity: to live a life free of conflict, exploitation, and alienation, a life in harmony with society, nature, and one's true self.

Hippies also repudiated the restrictive sexual practices of "Puritan" America. Although sexual behavior in this country had become more liberal, hippies moved far beyond middle-class proprieties and inhibitions. The freer sexuality of the hippie lifestyle became one of its main attractions and also provoked the wrath of elders. Casual sex was often tied to countercultural music, as flocks of teenage "groupies" sought out rock musicians. English groups, especially the Beatles and the Rolling Stones, expressed the central themes and ideals of the hippie worldview. Bob Dylan was the main American countercultural bard. He composed and sang "The Times They Are A-Changing" and "Blowing in the Wind." In San Francisco, "acid rock" appeared. Promoter Bill Graham staged concerts at the Fillmore West, featuring the psychedelic sounds of San Francisco's homegrown bands, the Grateful Dead and the Jefferson Airplane. A young white blues singer from Port Arthur, Texas, Janis Joplin, became the queen of San Francisco's psychedelic music scene. Drugs and music formed the vital center of the counterculture. "Tune in, turn on, and drop out" urged the high priest of LSD, Timothy Leary, a former Harvard psychologist who had been fired for conducting psychedelic drug experiments on his students. Steppenwolf sang "Magic Carpet Ride," celebrating drug tripping.

Drugs reached into the countercultural literary scene, continuing a beat generation tradition. A gifted young writer, Ken Kesey, wrote part of his best-selling first novel, *One Flew Over the Cuckoo's Nest,* under the influence of LSD. With money from the book's sales, Kesey purchased a bus and named it "Further." He painted it in psychedelic Day-Glo colors, wired it for stereo, and he and his friends, who called themselves the Merry Pranksters, toured up and down the West Coast. Everywhere they went, they conducted "acid tests," wild parties featuring LSD-spiked Kool-Aid, loud rock music, and light shows.

Marijuana use was far more widespread than LSD. "Pot" became the common currency of the counterculture and spread into mainstream society. Marijuana turned up at high school and college parties during the 1960s. Hippies experimented with other drugs as well, including mescaline and methedrine. Countercultural drug use provoked a pathetic debate over whether smoking marijuana was less harmful than smoking cigarettes or drinking alcoholic beverages. All of these substances could be harmful if used excessively, but that fact was beside the point because the debate really was about values and lifestyles, not the pharmacological properties of marijuana, tobacco, and alcohol.

Figure 12.7   The Beatles. . . . (left to right): John Lennon, Paul McCartney, George Harrison, and Ringo Starr.   *Source:* St. Louis, Mercantile Library. Used with permission.

One of the major events in the life of the counterculture occurred in the summer of 1967 in San Francisco's Haight-Ashbury district,—"the summer of love." Hippies sought a cultural counterpart to the SDS's proclaimed summer of protest against the Vietnam War. Just as radical politics was transforming American political life, the summer of love would transform society by creating a community of young dropouts uninhibitedly enjoying the pleasures of the flesh. The reality of what occurred was dismal. Thousands of youngsters showed up, most of them runaways from troubled homes, utterly unprepared to support themselves. Often they were reduced to panhandling, drug dealing, and prostitution to survive. Sexual promiscuity and rampant drug use led to epidemics of venereal disease and drug overdoses. Far from fleeing the social problems of the larger society, the runaways brought them with them. Writer Joan Didion, who visited the Haight-Ashbury district during the summer of 1967, in a famous essay entitled "Slouching Toward Bethlehem," depicted the squalor and aimlessness of hippie existence.

The hippie triad of "drugs, sex, and rock music" came together at rock festivals, the most important ritual of the countercultural community. The greatest of these "happenings" occurred at Woodstock in August 1969. At a site in New York's Hudson River Valley, between 300,000 and 400,000 young people gathered to hear music, enjoy drugs, and engage in casual sex.

Intellectuals fashioned ideologies for the counterculture. Charles Reich wrote in *Greening of America* about a new consciousness that would renew America, forming the basis of another American revolution, one without tears or violence. The new order would just happen. But the counterculture's expected new utopia never arrived. Instead it turned sour and disintegrated. Hard drugs replaced marijuana. Violence, most of it connected with illegal drug traffic, destroyed much of what had been attractive in the hippie culture.

Greed and selfishness also pervaded the counterculture, contradicting its presumptions of innocence. Another rock festival, promoted by the Rolling Stones and held at the Altamont Raceway in northern California, revealed the crass commercialism of the rock music business. The Altamont concert ended in violence when the Hell's Angels, an outlaw motorcycle gang, hired by promoters to provide security, savagely beat people and even killed a person.

The counterculture lasted half a decade, then it simply evaporated, quickly becoming only an exotic memory. It had sprung to life because of some special circumstances prevailing during the 1960s. The postwar baby boom had created a large population cluster of young people between the ages of fourteen and twenty-five. Such a huge youth population created, for a moment, a consciousness of a separate culture. Permissive child-rearing practices also contributed to the formation of the counterculture. These children of abundance confronted a complex world of protracted education, large-scale corporate and government bureaucracies, an intricate, powerful technology, severe social conflicts and inequities, and most of all, the military draft and a controversial war in Vietnam. Young people recoiled in fear and loathing over a world that they had never made, and they became "flower children," urging others "to make love, not war."

But only a minority of young people joined the counterculture. Most went about the difficult enterprise of growing up and entering the adult world without visible alienation or protest. The greatest gap in the 1960's social fabric was not a generational one between children and parents, but between different segments of the youth population. The more significant gap was intragenerational, not intergenerational. Value conflicts between middle-class and working-class young people were profound and occasionally violent. Upper-middle-class campus radicals scoffed at bourgeois sensibilities and burned their draft cards. Young workers, for whom middle-class respectability remained a cherished ambition, defended their way of life and patriotically supported the Vietnam War. Long-haired hippies and antiwar demonstrators infuriated working-class youth who regarded them as privileged cowards and traitors. One of the most violent riots of the era occurred in New York City, where hard-hat construction workers attacked a crowd of antiwar demonstrators.

Although short-lived and engaging only a fraction of young people during the 1960s, both the New Left and the counterculture left their marks. They heightened consciousness of war and racial injustice; they called attention to the negative ecological and human consequences of technology; and they forced some people to confront the disparities between their professed ideals and the lives they lived. But the most enduring impact of the counterculture came in lifestyle realms—in diet, dress, decorative art, music, and sexual practices. People became more concerned with developing their inner selves, with achieving their "human potential," than with seeking the external trappings of success.

THE FIRE THIS TIME

The civil rights movement crested in 1965 when Martin Luther King, Jr. led the Selma march and Congress passed the Voting Rights Act. Five days after President Johnson signed that historic measure, the Watts section of Los Angeles went up in flames, ushering in the first of several successive "long, hot summers." The Watts riot, a week-long orgy of burning and looting, claimed thirty-four lives, injured 1,100 people, and destroyed $40 million worth of property. The Watts explosion dismayed civil rights reformers, because the residents of Watts generally lived much better than most African American slum dwellers in America. Watts was not physically a ghetto, since families did not live in crowded, dilapidated tenements, but in single, detached houses with lawns located along palm-lined boulevards. Three African Americans sat on the Los Angeles City Council; Watts was represented by a black congressman and two black state assemblymen. Economically, African Americans living in Watts were better off than blacks in any other large American city.

Watts revealed a depth of antiwhite bitterness and alienation that few civil rights workers of either race even knew existed. African American progress in recent years and the promise of more to come had raised expectations and intensified the rage of many Watts residents. A special commission investigating the Watts upheaval warned that if the breach between the races was not healed, the riot might be a curtain raiser for future racial blowups. The commission's warning proved to be prophetic. Between 1965 and 1968, hundreds of inner cities exploded into major riots. The worst violence occurred in Newark and Detroit within a week of each other, in July 1967. In Newark, twenty-six people died and 1,200 were injured. In Detroit, forty-three people died and another 2,000 were hurt. Fires burned out the center of the nation's fifth largest city. For two weeks that summer, Detroit was a war zone with tanks rolling through the streets and the sounds of machine-gun fire piercing the air.

Detroit's riot was the most alarming, not only because of the extensive destruction of life and property but also because it occurred in a city governed by a coalition that included extensive African American participation. Great Society reformers had lavished extensive antipoverty and urban renewal programs on the Motor City. One-fourth of all workers employed in the automobile industry, Detroit's major business, were black; the UAW was a progressive, integrated union. Forty-five percent of Detroit's African American families owned their own homes.

Analysts of the Detroit riot drew a portrait of the typical rioter—a young adult black male, a high school graduate, employed, often an auto worker and a union member, a veteran, married, with an annual income slightly below the national median for his age group. These data suggest that the typical Detroit rioters were neither juveniles out on a spree nor despairing members of a black underclass. The rioting did not occur in the worst neighborhoods but in the black working-class neighborhoods containing a high percentage of owner-occupied homes and intact families. Black rage and violence in Detroit were apparently provoked more by insensitive police tactics than by deprivation and despair.

Nearly all major race riots started from minor episodes, often from incidents stemming from white police arresting African Americans. Watts blew up when a crowd gathered to protest the arrest of a drunken motorist. Newark exploded after police arrested an African American taxicab driver for following a police car too closely. Detroit erupted when police raided an after-hours bar hosting a party for two Vietnam veterans.

Studies revealed a general pattern prevailing in the urban riots. Most rioting occurred within ghetto confines. Most of the destruction was inflicted upon ghetto homes and businesses; most of the violence occurred between rioters and law enforcement personnel. Over 80 percent of the fatalities were rioters, shot either by the police or by soldiers. Studies of all major riots also suggested that the underlying cause of the uprisings was chronic slum conditions, aggravated by rough police tactics and hot weather. The National Advisory Commission on Civil Disorders called attention to a crucial reality about the black ghetto: "White institutions created it, white institutions maintain it, and white society condones it."

BLACK POWER

Urban riots were the most dramatic, destructive display of black militancy. The slogan "black power" made its appearance in 1966 when James Meredith attempted to march from Memphis, Tennessee, to Jackson, Mississippi, to inspire African Americans of his native state to assert their rights. He got only ten miles into Mississippi when a sniper severely wounded him. Dr. King and other civil rights leaders quickly arrived to complete his march. Two of the marchers, young leaders of the Student Non-Violent Coordinating Committee (SNCC), began chanting "black power." Soon, most of the marchers were chanting the same. Initially, "black power" was a cry of outrage and defiance. It later became political doctrine, although remaining diffuse, meaning different things to different people. For SNCC leader Stokely Carmichael, "black power" meant that African Americans should take control of the civil rights movement and develop their own institutions and instruments of power. Implicit in these actions were the rejection of integration, scorning white allies, and the approval of violence. At the extreme, "black power" became an expression of African American separatism. Separatist doctrine traced its roots to a long tradition of black nationalism in this country.

The Black Muslims articulated the most important expression of 1960s' black nationalism. Founded during the 1930s in Detroit by Elijah Poole, who called himself the Prophet, Elijah Muhammad, it remained a small, obscure religious sect with about 100,000 members until the 1960s. Black Muslims had recruited many of their followers from the bottom ranks of ghetto society—street hustlers, drug addicts, and ex-cons. Their most famous recruit was world heavyweight boxing champion Cassius Clay, who changed his name to Muhammad Ali following his conversion to the Black Muslim sect in 1965.

The sect's most articulate spokesman was Malcolm Little, an ex-con who took the name of Malcolm X. During the early 1960s, he offered a nationalistic alternative to civil rights. He jeered at Dr. King's tactics of nonviolent Christian love. He both angered and frightened whites with his tirades against integration with "white devils." In 1964, he was expelled from the Black Muslim organization after a dispute with Elijah Muhammad. He moved to New York and founded his own movement. His political ideas were still evolving in the spring of 1965. He appeared to be groping for an integrationist strategy when he was murdered. His assassination had been ordered by Elijah Muhammad, or by members of his inner circle. Malcolm X's book, written with Alex Haley, *The Autobiography of Malcolm X*, became a posthumous best-seller. Actor Ossie Davis said of the fallen leader: "Malcolm expressed what was in all our hearts; he redeemed our manhood."

"Black power" also expressed African American pride; it became a celebration of African American history and culture, of "blackness itself." African American students in high schools and colleges demanded that courses be added to established curricula in African American history, literature, and languages. Black hair and dress styles appeared. "Black power" encouraged young blacks to seek success and to remain "black," to avoid emulating white role models. The popular soul singer James Brown sang, "Say it loud, I'm black and I'm proud."

During the late 1960s, as the civil rights movement became radicalized and fragmented, Dr. King, who remained committed to the tactic of nonviolence and to the goal of an integrated, color-blind society, remained the foremost black leader. But he found that his methods did not work in the North. He tried and failed to desegregate Chicago. Tactics that had been effective against the de jure segregation of Southern towns could not overcome the de facto segregation of Northern cities. Dr. King also became increasingly involved in protesting the Vietnam War because it drained away funds for civil rights and Great Society reforms. His attacks on the war alienated President Johnson and cost him the support of the NAACP. The civil rights movement, politically successful in the South but an economic failure in the North, was faltering by 1967. In the spring of 1968, trying to regain momentum, Dr. King prepared to lead a poor people's march on Washington. He also took time to go to Memphis to support a garbage workers' strike. While standing on a Memphis motel balcony, he was shot by James Earl Ray, a white drifter and ex-con. News of King's murder provoked race riots across the land. The worst occurred in the nation's capital. Buildings burned within a few blocks of the White House, and soldiers mounted machine guns on the Capitol steps.

RED AND BROWN POWER

Other minorities, spurred by the example of African American insurgents, rebelled during the 1960s. Puerto Rican students in New York demanded that courses in Puerto Rican studies be added to high school and college curricula. Native Americans demanded respect for their cultural traditions and called attention to their economic needs, particularly repayment for their ancestral lands that had been illegally taken from them by white men. "Red power" militant, Vine Deloria, Jr.,

Figure 12.8   Cesar Chavez (plaid shirt, right) leads striking grape pickers. Most of the pickers working the grape fields of California in the 1960s and 1970s were of Mexican origin.   *Source:* National Archives.

wrote *Custer Died for Your Sins,* emphasizing the historical injustices that European settlers in the New World had committed against Native Americans.

Mexican American militants also waged campaigns for recognition and self-assertion. "Brown power" militants took to calling themselves "Chicanos," turning a term of opprobrium into a badge of pride and an assertion of ethnic identity that did not depend on a relationship with the "Anglo" world. The most prominent Chicano militant of the 1960s was labor leader Cesar Chavez. Chavez founded the National Farm Workers Association (NFWA) in 1963. The NFWA joined other farm worker unions to form the United Farm Workers Organizing Committee (UFWOC), affiliated with the AFL–CIO. Chavez organized lettuce workers and grape pickers using techniques developed by civil rights organizers, including marches, rallies, songs, and symbols that stressed the Chicano cultural heritage. He led successful strikes in California's San Joaquin Valley in the 1960s. His movement obtained crucial assistance from urban, liberal, middle-class support groups who raised funds for the strikers and staged consumer boycotts, making table grapes picked by "scab" (nonunion) labor forbidden fruit.

GAY–LESBIAN LIBERATION

Another expression of the 1960s' insurgent spirit was the open avowal of homosexuality by former deeply closeted gays and lesbians. If people could mobilize for political action around the issues of race, ethnicity, and gender, they also could fight for their rights on the basis of their sexual identities and preferences. A dramatic event created the gay liberation movement: on June 29, 1969, police raided the Stonewall Inn, a gay bar in Greenwich Village. Instead of meekly submitting to arrest, patrons defiantly hurled bottles at the police. They sent the message that there was a new militancy and pride growing among members of the gay community; they were no longer willing to passively accept police abuse and society's condemnations.

Gay and lesbian intellectuals developed ideologies that defined homosexuality as a legitimate sexual preference; they insisted that it was not abnormal, that it was not sick, and that it was not perverse. Gay and lesbian theorists attacked the psychoanalytic establishment for diagnosing homosexuality as a form of mental illness. Within gay–lesbian communities, a debate occurred over whether homosexuality was innate or constructed, that is, a consequence of socialization. Although gays and lesbians could not resolve the debate over essentialism versus constructivism, the gay liberation movement enabled millions of homosexuals to make their claim for acceptance into the larger society. Militant homosexuals marched in gay liberation parades, chanting, "Say it loud, gay is proud." Gay and lesbian activists organized for political action, seeking an end to job discrimination against homosexuals and a diminution of massive homophobic prejudices.

THE REBIRTH OF FEMINISM

The social and cultural ground was being prepared during the 1950s for a rebirth of feminism. By 1960 it had become the norm for middle-class white married women to perform paid work outside of the home. By 1962, married women accounted for nearly two-thirds of the female workforce. At the same time that they were entering the paid workforce in ever-greater numbers, more and more women were going to college and earning degrees. In 1961, women received over 40 percent of all baccalaureate degrees awarded.

Despite such progress, women still entered a sex-segregated job market. They took mostly "women's jobs" such as nursing, clerical work, teaching, and domestic service, jobs that paid less than men's and offered few prospects for promotion. In 1960, the median compensation for women working in full-time, year-round employment was 61 percent of men's earnings. Traditional assumptions about the proper societal roles for men and women remained deeply ingrained. There was no organized feminist alternative to challenge the established hierarchy or male hegemony. The wife who worked was perceived to be helping her family achieve a middle-class status and lifestyle, not pursuing a career of her own. As the 1960s began, there existed an ideological lag; feminine consciousness lagged behind social reality. Even though cultural norms remained unquestioned, there was increasing evidence that many college-educated, middle-class women were unfulfilled by lives that increasingly diverged from prescribed roles.

Because women, as women, did not share a common social experience, they tended to view their problems as being individually rather than socially derived. It was left to the founder of the modern women's movement, Betty Friedan, author of the best-selling *Feminine Mystique* (1963), to show women that what they had previously understood to be their individual problems were in fact women's problems. They were caused not by personal inadequacies but by deeply rooted attitudes that would have to be changed before women could achieve equality and fulfillment. Friedan, giving eloquent voice to the discontent of middle-class women, called the suburban, split-level home "a comfortable concentration camp." She called attention to the "problem which has no name": feelings of emptiness, of being incomplete, of wondering, "Who am I?" She asked: "What is the cause of the identity problems which bothers so many women who have ostensibly fulfilled the American dream?" She urged women to listen to that still-small voice within that demands "something more than my husband and my children and my home."[3]

The civil rights movement of the early 1960s catalyzed a sense of grievance among women. Women often joined, civil rights demonstrations. The civil rights movement also offered a model for political activity. Women made connections between black demands for freedom, equality, and dignity and their own lives; they saw possibilities for acting for themselves, of mobilizing for group political action. Women perceived that the same society that oppressed blacks also oppressed women; both groups had been assigned separate and unequal spheres and told to stay in their respective places. Any efforts at self-assertion or challenges to the status quo were considered deviant and were suppressed. Women reasoned that if it was wrong to deny an opportunity to one group because of skin color, it was wrong to deny it to another group because of gender.

Great Society inadvertently helped the cause of women's rights. When the bill that eventually became the Civil Rights Act of 1964 was being drafted in committee, conservatives tried to kill it. Title VII contained a provision banning discrimination in hiring and promotion on the basis of race. Howard Smith introduced an amendment to Title VII, banning job discrimination on the basis of sex. Smith believed that his amendment would defeat the proposed Title VII by reducing the whole matter of civil rights to an absurdity. He was mistaken. Supporters of Title VII pushed it through, along with Smith's amendment, and it became the law of the land.

Initially, the Equal Opportunity Employment Commission (EEOC), which had responsibility for enforcing Title VII of the Civil Rights Act, did not enforce the provision against sex discrimination. In response to the EEOC's failure to enforce Title VII on behalf of women workers, Betty Friedan and other women activists formed the National Organization For Women (NOW) in 1966 to pressure the commission to take sex discrimination in hiring seriously. Other groups soon mobilized, and the women rights movement was reborn. These women's organizations were political pressure groups that sought to mobilize public opinion and obtain litigation on behalf of their cause. They sought change from within the existing structure. In part, the new feminism was a species of liberal reform. It called for equal pay for equal work and demanded that women have equal access to all pro fessional schools and occupations. To allow women to compete equally in the job market with men, feminists demanded publicly funded child care centers for

---

[3]Betty Friedan, *The Feminine Mystique* (New York: Dell, 1963), *passim.*

women with pre-school-aged children, and they sought legislation ending all forms of gender discrimination.

WOMEN'S LIBERATION

There also was a radical dimension to the emerging feminism of the 1960s that grew out of the experiences of young women in the New Left. Mary King and Casey Hayden, both civil rights activists within SNCC, had come to resent the arrogance of male activists who expected the women to work hard, take responsibilities and risks, and leave leadership and policy making to the men. When they raised these issues at a SNCC convention, the male leaders responded by laughing at them. The SNCC chairman, Stokely Carmichael, quipped, "The position of women in our movement is prone."

These radical women gradually evolved a language to express their grievances. They defined the problem as "sexism," or "male chauvinism." Having diagnosed the illness, they proposed a cure—"women's liberation." While liberal feminist reformers in NOW fought for equal pay for equal work, radical feminists like King and Hayden demanded control over their own bodies. They called for wider distribution of birth control literature, tougher enforcement of rape laws, the sharing of housework and child-rearing duties with husbands, and the right to abortion on demand. They met in small groups for intense "consciousness-raising" sessions. These sessions also allowed women to understand that their personal problems were connected to the larger realms of social power, of "sexual politics." Feminist writer Robin Morgan contributed the defining slogan of the women's liberation movement: "The personal is political."

The reborn feminist movement encountered a formidable array of obstacles from the beginning. Many women as well as men rejected feminist demands. A 1970 Gallup poll showed that 70 percent of American women believed that they were treated fairly by men. Feminist leader Gloria Steinem acknowledged that she spoke for only a minority of women, but she attributed that reality to cultural conditioning. She asserted that women had been brainwashed to accept their oppression; they required "consciousness-raising" sessions to ignite a sense of grievance. Many men worried about the loss of male prerogatives that had long been "givens" in the culture. Fundamentalist Christians were incensed because feminist demands violated Biblically ordained roles for women.

The most serious obstacle faced by feminists trying to build a movement based on women's common problems and concerns was the diversity of the women the movement was trying to organize. Women were differentiated on the basis of race, ethnicity, class, age, education, occupation, and sexuality. Feminists quickly discovered that they had sharp differences among themselves on many matters. There were disagreements over priorities, long- and short-term goals, and methods and tactics. Was the most pressing problem economic—an economic system that oppressed women? Or was it cultural—male chauvinism? Because of the diversity prevailing among women activists, the reborn feminist movement of the 1960s spawned a proliferation of organizations, tactics, ideologies, and goals.

BACKLASH

By 1967, it seemed as though some unspoken signal had been sent coursing through the culture; the message had been received by SDS radicals, by black, brown, and red militants, and by activist women. Those who perceived themselves as oppressed, disadvantaged, and denied their full measure of freedom, equality, opportunity, and dignity, rose in rebellion. Perhaps they sensed their time had come: that the system was more responsive to their claims of justice and inclusion in the American dream; that it would not, perhaps could not, repress them or deny them their due. These militants were no longer willing to play the game by the old rules. Never in the history of the Republic had so many groups mounted such a radical assault on cherished national values, mores, and institutions.

The radical insurgencies of the late 1960s provoked a furious response from the middle-class majority of Americans determined to uphold traditional American ways. The media dubbed their response the "backlash." Millions of citizens had worked hard all of their lives and played the game by the rules. They had raised their families, attended church, worked on community projects, voted, paid taxes, obeyed the law, accumulated a modest estate, and sent their sons to fight the Vietnam War. The militant minority of blacks who rioted in the cities, students who opposed the Vietnam War and carried Vietcong flags, and long-haired hippies who openly flaunted their sexuality infuriated the middle-class majority.

White, working-class ethnics felt especially threatened by African American militants and were galvanized into action. These people had worked hard to achieve a modest piece of the American dream: a decent home, a secure job, and perhaps to see a bright son or daughter graduate from college. To them it appeared that ghetto blacks were demanding that the government give them these same things; that they were entitled to them now—without working and without a struggle. White, working-class ethnics especially resented the antipoverty programs that appeared to reward black militants, while law-abiding whites got nothing except higher tax bills. Middle Americans, those earning between $8,000 and $15,000 a year, who constituted the rank-and-file blue-collar and white-collar workforces of the country, generally opposed and resented the challenges posed by the insurgents.

A mix of forces drove the backlashers. In part, it was simply residual antiblack racism. Many Northern white ethnics and Southern white, working-class people had been taught to hate and fear black people and consider them inferior. They did not want to associate with them, they did not want their children attending school with them, and they surely did not want to have to compete with them in the workplace. Economic insecurities also drove the backlash. By the late 1960s, many middle-class Americans were feeling the effects of inflation, heavy indebtedness, and declining real income. A lot of them, while not poor, had obtained a marginal prosperity. Black demands for employment, rising taxes, and expensive governmental programs appeared to be direct threats to the economic well-being of hard-pressed, middle-class Americans.

Most of all it was a sense of cultural crisis that activated the backlash response. The demands of the militants—antiwar protesters, "black power" advocates, and feminist radicals, all magnified by extensive media coverage and commentary, represented an attack on the traditional American way of life and its most cherished values and institutions: patriotism, the work ethic, mobility, family, and religion. While the sons of Middle America were fighting and dying in Vietnam, the sons of upper-middle-class families were opposing the war from the safe havens of prestigious university campuses and denouncing American society. To many parents of soldiers, and to the soldiers themselves, these antiwar protesters appeared to be a privileged corps of impudent cowards and traitors.

The rise of the backlash was another important indicator of the conservative drift that was underway in the American political culture. By the late 1960s, many working-class white families had come to distrust what they had held in high regard since the 1930s: centralized governmental power. During the 1930s, New Dealers had used the power of the federal government to establish a lifeline for millions of Americans who were left impoverished and bewildered by the Great Depression. By the 1960s, prosperity had created a new middle class that included millions of working-class families that opposed higher taxes and many of the social programs they funded. These Middle Americans also embraced traditional values and were unhappy when liberal Democratic leaders did not denounce immorality and social disorder. It also appeared to them that liberals were much too attentive to the needs of the dispossessed—the poor, minorities, and radicals—and were neglecting the needs of the hard-working, patriotic, and God-fearing folks like themselves. The backlash was the most visible issue feeding the growing antigovernment mood, but it was only part of a larger revolt, a much deeper disillusionment with liberal government and those politicians and pundits who championed it.

IMPORTANT EVENTS

1963	Lyndon Johnson accedes to the presidency
1964	The Civil Rights Act is enacted
	The Beatles hold their first American concert
	Johnson announces the beginning of a "war on poverty"
	The Gulf of Tonkin incidents occur
	Johnson is elected president
	The Free Speech Movement at the Berkeley campus of the University of California inaugurates an era of student protest

IMPORTANT EVENTS *(continued)*

1965	Malcolm X is assassinated
	The Voting Rights Act is enacted
	The United States intervenes in the Dominican Republic
	A race riot occurs in Watts
	The United States goes to war in Vietnam
	Federal aid to public education is enacted
	Medicare and Medicaid are enacted
	The Immigration Act is enacted
1967	Major race riots occur in Newark and Detroit
1968	The Communists launch the Tet Offensive
	Johnson announces that he will not seek reelection
	Martin Luther King, Jr. is assassinated
	Robert Kennedy is assassinated
	Richard Nixon is elected president
1969	The Woodstock festival takes place

BIBLIOGRAPHY

Robert Caro has completed two volumes of his massive biographical study of Lyndon Johnson in *The Path to Power* and *Means of Ascent*. Caro's research has given him encyclopedic knowledge of the details of Johnson's life, and he writes well. His books are marked by his remorseless hostility to his subject. Robert Dallek has written a substantial two-volume biography of Johnson, *Lone Star Rising: Lyndon Johnson and His Times, 1908–1960* and *Flawed Giant: Lyndon Johnson and His Times, 1961–1973*. Dallek's work is balanced and more sophisticated than Caro's. Doris Kearns, in *Lyndon Johnson and the American Dream*, offers an insightful study of Johnson's political career. Eric Goldman's *The Tragedy of Lyndon Johnson* is a sympathetic account of his presidency. Michael Harrington's analysis of poverty in the United States, *The Other America*, helped start the war on poverty. James C. Harvey's *Black Civil Rights during the Johnson Administration* is a good account of this important issue. Johnson's foreign policy is studied by Philip L. Geyelin in *Lyndon B. Johnson and the World*. The best general military and diplomatic history of U.S. involvement in Vietnam is George Donelson Moss's *Vietnam: An American Ordeal*. For student radicalism during the 1960s, see Irwin Unger's *The Movement: A History of the American New Left, 1959–1972*. The best-written biography of Dr. Martin Luther King, Jr. is Stephen Oates's *Let the Trumpet Sound: The Life of Martin Luther King, Jr.* Reading *The Autobiography of Malcolm X* will provide an understanding of the sources of black militancy during the 1960s. Alfredo Mirande, in *The Chicano Experience*, documents militancy in the Mexican American world. Vine Deloria, Jr., in *Custer Died for Your Sins* records centuries of white mistreatment of Native Americans. Barbara Deckard's *The Women's Movement* is a fine account of the revived feminist movement. Theodore Roszak, in *The Making of a Counter Culture*, features a nicely written, sympathetic account of the hippie movement. Julian Messner's *The Superstars of Rock: Their Lives and Their Music* offers insight into the pop music of the 1960s. Richard Krickus's *Pursuing the American Dream: White Ethnics and the New Populism* is a fascinating study of blue-collar culture and why these workers resented liberal welfarism, student radicals, hippies, and black militants.

13

The Nixon Era

IN November 1968, Richard M. Nixon was elected president by a narrow margin amidst the worst domestic violence and disorder in nearly 100 years. He made his top priorities restoring national unity and phasing out the American war in Vietnam. He partially succeeded in calming the country, although the American Vietnam War continued for four more years. Nixon's greatest accomplishments came in the realm of foreign policy, particularly the opening to China and reaching détente with the Soviet Union. He was greatly aided in these foreign policy achievements by his chief adviser and special envoy, Henry Kissinger. Reelected by a landslide margin in November 1972, President Nixon never exercised the full powers of the presidency and achieved all of his political goals because of the developing Watergate scandals. Watergate became a public issue early in 1973; thereafter, Nixon was increasingly preoccupied with his efforts to contain and survive Watergate. Ultimately, the president and his men were overwhelmed by media investigations, federal grand jury probes, the Congress, the courts, and public opinion. Richard Nixon resigned from the presidency on August 9, 1974, mainly to avoid impeachment for "high crimes and misdemeanors" committed while he was president.

THE ELECTION OF 1968

The 1968 election occurred against a backdrop of the worst conflict and violence within American society since the Civil War. The Democratic Party, closer to the social pulse than the Republicans, was splintered by divisions seething within the deeply troubled nation. The antiwar candidacies of Senators Eugene McCarthy and Robert Kennedy gained momentum in the spring primaries. Party regulars backed Vice President Hubert Humphrey, a Cold War liberal supporting Johnson's Vietnam policy. It was a wide-open race, with public opinion polls giving Kennedy an edge over Humphrey and McCarthy.

Although Robert Kennedy focused his presidential bid on opposing Johnson's Vietnam War policy, he appears to have been searching for a new political vision for his troubled nation. Sensing that the old liberal vision of social reform at home and containing Communism abroad was losing its appeal, he groped for alternatives. He visited Native Americans on reservations, and he broke bread with Cesar Chavez. He was the only established white political leader that had any credibility among black people after the assassination of Martin Luther King, Jr. He also reached out to white, working-class "backlashers," stressing the importance of self-government, of citizen participation in the political life of the nation. He sought a new community, more inclusive and more involved in the process of self-government. For the most part, he sought to revitalize and reshape liberalism, but he also sensed the growing conservatism of Middle Americans and sounded some of its themes. He criticized welfare programs because they rendered millions of American citizens dependent on government handouts. He proposed jobs programs and community development programs involving local people and the private sector. His was a lonely voice, trying to refashion a vision of the American community that could include everyone, to soothe the agony and breach the divisions that set Americans against one another during that terrible year.

In the California primary, Kennedy and McCarthy waged a decisive showdown battle. Kennedy, cashing in on his remarkable ability to attract black, Hispanic, and white voters, narrowly defeated McCarthy. With his California victory, Robert Kennedy appeared to have the Democratic nomination within his grasp. But on victory night, he was shot and killed in Los Angeles. His assassin was Sirhan Sirhan, an Arab nationalist who hated Kennedy for his strong support of Israel. Robert Kennedy's murder destroyed any chance that antiwar forces could win at the Democratic Party's Chicago convention. Humphrey won an easy first-ballot nomination. Convention delegates, after a lengthy emotional debate, adopted a pro-administration plank on the Vietnam War. The rest of the platform focused on domestic issues, such as providing consumer protection, increasing farmers' incomes, and strengthening trade unions. Humphrey chose Senator Edmund Muskie of Maine as his running mate.

As the Democratic delegates gathered in Chicago to nominate a presidential candidate, antiwar radicals gathered in the Windy City to protest the war. Most came to support the efforts of antiwar Democratic politicians. More militant groups came to disrupt the convention and provoke confrontations with the police. The antiwar demonstrators came up against Chicago Mayor Richard Daley, the convention host, who had vowed that there would be no disruptions. Police cordoned off the convention site and staked out the parks of Chicago where protesters had gathered. Daley also had thousands of National Guardsmen and federal troops available to back up the police if he needed them.

The night Hubert Humphrey was nominated, violence reigned in the streets of Chicago. Protesters, attempting to march on the convention, were blocked by police. They sat down in the street, blocking traffic. Police then moved in to remove them by force. They indiscriminately clubbed and gassed demonstrators, newsmen, and bystanders. Television cameramen brought the violence into millions of living rooms. Many liberal Democrats were everlastingly horrified by the actions of the Chicago police. But millions of other Democrats in white-collar suburbs and blue-collar neighborhoods cheered the police, seeing in the radical politics and countercultural lifestyles of the youthful protesters an intolerable threat to order and morality. The different reactions to the televised violence reflected the profound divisions seething within the American political culture created by Vietnam, race riots, and other domestic insurgencies. Hubert Humphrey emerged from the political ruins as the candidate of a profoundly divided party.

The divisive Democratic Convention helped the Republicans who were meeting in Miami. They nominated Richard Nixon, who had made a remarkable comeback. Nixon had retired from politics following a disastrous defeat in the 1962 California gubernatorial election, but he had worked hard for Republican candidates in 1964 and 1966, building support among party regulars. He came to Miami the front-runner and easily repelled his only serious challenger, California Governor Ronald Reagan, who was making the first of his several runs at the presidency. Nixon chose Spiro T. Agnew, the governor of Maryland, to be his running mate. The Republican platform resembled the Democratic slate. On the war issue, Republicans called for peace, but not peace at any price.

Behind the Republican platform rhetoric and the choice of Agnew for vice president lay a shrewd political strategy. Nixon perceived that Southerners had become a power within his party and that Americans had become more conservative since 1964. He cut his ties with declining Northeastern liberal Republicans to forge an alliance with conservative Southerners led by South Carolina Senator Strom Thurmond. Nixon promised Thurmond that he would never abandon the South Vietnamese government and that he would slow the pace of school desegregation. He also promised to crack down hard on demonstrators who broke the law. This "Southern strategy" stopped Reagan's bid for the presidency. The only reason it did not give Nixon the entire South was because a strong third-party candidate who had a Southern base entered the campaign.

George Wallace, governor of Alabama and leader of the American Independence Party, mounted a presidential campaign with popular appeal in all sections of the nation. He articulated the frustrations and resentments of his followers, who were upset by radical disruptions in the country and by liberal politicians who appeared to sanction them. Wallace attacked liberal intellectuals, black militants, antiwar protesters, and hippies. His main issue was playing to white antipathy toward civil rights measures and antipoverty programs. He was the first important political leader to exploit the changes in attitudes that pundits labeled the "backlash."

Wallace had a remarkable talent for voicing the fears and resentments of working-class whites, especially young men. Although his message was never a purely racist one, most of his strength derived from white anxieties about integration and black progress. Opposition to race-related federal initiatives was always the vital core of the Wallace message. But he learned to soften his language; he replaced the crass, racist venom spewed by extremists with a set of coded phrases such as "law and order" and "welfare chiselers" that ignited the raw racial anger without making his supporters appear or feel racist.

Wallace championed free enterprise, traditional moral values, and was a Hawk on Vietnam. He was a political force to be reckoned with. A mid-September survey gave him 21 percent of the vote, almost as many as supported Humphrey. Had he held that 21 percent to November, he would have denied any candidate an electoral college majority and thrown the election into the House of Representatives. He hoped to play the role of "spoiler" and to force Nixon and Humphrey to bargain for his support to win the presidency.

Figure 13.1   The election of 1968.   *Source:* George D. Moss, *Moving On,* p. 215.

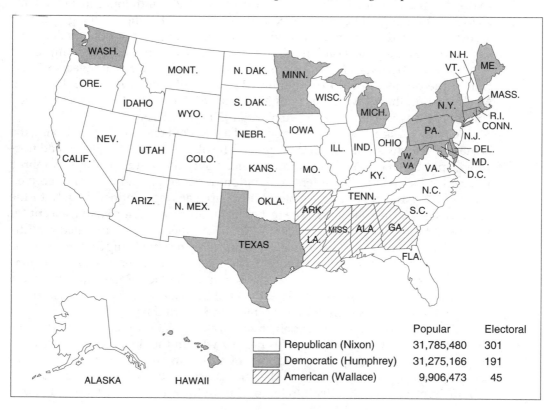

Meanwhile, Nixon's campaign was running smoothly. His acceptance speech had sounded his principal theme, a promise to heed the voice of " the great, quiet forgotten majority—the non-shouters and the non-demonstrators." He called for peace, unity, and a lowering of voices. His appeal reached millions of voters who were yearning for an end to years of discord. Nixon projected an image of maturity and inner tranquility; commentators spoke of a "new Nixon" who had replaced the fiery Red-baiter of the 1950s. His campaign featured slick television commercials and short speeches filled will patriotic generalities. His vice presidential running mate, Spiro Agnew, took the offensive. Agnew attacked the media for promoting radicalism, and he took a hard law-and-order line. Journalists dubbed him "Nixon's Nixon." Polls taken in early October showed that Nixon was well ahead of both Humphrey and Wallace.

Humphrey's campaign floundered along, disorganized, short of both money and campaign workers. McCarthy's followers initially refused to support Humphrey. He was hurt badly by his identification with an unpopular administration and its unpopular war. Millions of nominally Democratic voters were turning to Nixon and Wallace. But in October, Humphrey's campaign came to life. He distanced himself from Johnson's war policy by calling for a bombing halt. Union leaders campaigned hard for Humphrey, and antiwar liberals drifted back into his fold. McCarthy endorsed Humphrey on October 29, and Johnson helped his chances by halting all bombing of North Vietnam and talking as though the war were about to end. Humphrey cut into Nixon's lead. Wallace's popularity declined. On election eve, pollsters said the election "was too close to call." But Humphrey's late surge fell just short. Nixon held on for a narrow victory. He received 43.4 percent of the popular vote to Humphrey's 42.7 percent and Wallace's 13.4 percent. Nixon carried thirty-two states with 301 electoral votes. The Democrats retained control of Congress, with sizeable majorities in both houses.

On the surface, the electorate appeared to speak in many voices, reflecting the acute political divisions within the country. The old Democratic coalition had fractured, split by civil rights issues and divisions over the Vietnam War. Humphrey retained urban and union voters, although in reduced strength, and he received most of the African American vote. But his appeal was confined largely to the Northeastern industrial states. The rest of the country voted for Nixon, except for five Deep South states that went for Wallace. The 1968 election revealed that the Democratic "Solid South" had vanished. Humphrey received only 31 percent of the Deep South vote, mostly from newly enfranchised African Americans. Ninety percent of Southern whites voted either for Nixon or Wallace. Racial attitudes were significant vote determiners in 1968, the year of the backlash. The election also signaled that the American electorate was moving toward the Right.

Although they cannot be certain in such a close election, most analysts believe that the Vietnam War gave Nixon his narrow win. In the final weeks of the campaign, he attracted support with his talk of a plan to end the war, the details of which he refused to divulge because he said its prospects for success depended on its remaining secret until after the election. Humphrey might have won had he disavowed Johnson's war policy sooner. Nixon won, and radicalism was contained because the large "silent majority" of American voters, as political analyst Richard Scammon observed, constituted "the unyoung, the unblack, and the unpoor."

THE POLITICIAN

Nixon's political career was characterized by relentless ambition and sustained effort to achieve his personal goals. He combined incisive intelligence with hard work to master the art of politics. But Nixon was in many ways ill suited for the public career he chose. Shy, introverted, and a loner, he lacked the easy charm and affability characteristic of most American politicians. He armored himself for politics by imposing a tight discipline on his behavior and emotions. Many people intuitively regarded Nixon's public personality as a fabrication; they wondered who the "real Nixon" was.

The real Nixon inhabited a complex, conflicted personality. He prized hard work, tenacity, self-reliance, and seriousness of purpose. But Nixon also had used smear tactics to identify his political opponents with Communism in order to win elections. His ruthless tactics appeared to serve no larger political cause than his own advancement. He held a cynical view of politics as a process in which all politicians advocated principles and ideals as a cover for self-interest. For Richard Nixon, politics was never a friendly game. His opponents were not rivals to be defeated but enemies to be destroyed. Nixon's blend of moral self-righteousness, coupled with dirty campaign tactics, accounts for his most singular quality—his ability to inspire strong loyalty among Republican supporters and intense loathing among Democratic opponents. He was a complete partisan who divided everyone into two political groups—"us against them," the foremost modern practitioner of the politics of division. Nixon combined in one complex personality an unusual mix of admirable and despicable traits. His tragedy was rooted in a paradox—the qualities that enabled him to win the presidency and made him a world statesman also rendered him arrogant, insensitive to the American preoccupation with political means, and susceptible to the corruptions of power. These character flaws ultimately destroyed his presidency and deprived him of an honored place in national history.

PRAGMATIC CENTRISM

Nixon came to office determined to restore the consensus politics that had prevailed in this country during the 1950s and early 1960s before being shattered by the Vietnam War, civil rights, and other domestic insurgencies. To achieve his goal, he moved in different policy directions simultaneously. His general thrust was toward the center, but he also struck out in conservative directions in pursuit of his

Southern strategy, and he proposed far-reaching reforms to co-opt liberal causes. He failed to restore the lost consensus during his first term because he could not end the American war in Vietnam. His pursuit of his Southern strategy perpetuated the divisions he hoped to end. Various activists and reformers continued to press their causes, despite his efforts to co-opt or suppress them.

Like Kennedy, Nixon always considered domestic affairs secondary to foreign policy concerns. His own lack of enthusiasm, the fact that 57 percent of the voters in 1968 preferred another candidate to him for president, and Democratic control of Congress, all diminished his influence over domestic affairs. Liberal Democrats in control of Congress extended the Voting Rights Act of 1965, increased spending for food stamps, increased Social Security benefits, and increased federal aid to education. Congress also proposed the Twenty-sixth Amendment, which was ratified in 1971, enfranchising eighteen-year-olds. The new amendment added 12 million potential voters to the rolls. Nixon was not enthusiastic about any of these measures, but he did not oppose them.

Nixon proposed policies reflecting the growing conservatism of voters who were opposed to solving social problems by expanding the powers of the federal government and spending more money on them. A major target was the welfare system. He proposed a work-incentive program to replace the costly Aid to Dependent Children Program. Called the Family Assistance Plan, it guaranteed a family of four with no income $1,600 a year plus food stamps and Medicaid. It further required that all heads of households on welfare, except for single mothers with pre-school-age children, register for job training. Congress passed only the "Workfare" feature, requiring heads of households to register for job training. Nixon's other innovative proposal, revenue sharing, was part of what he called the "New Federalism," designed to reduce the power of the federal government and to strengthen state and local agencies. Congress enacted a revenue-sharing program to begin in 1972, when $30 billion in federal funds would be split over five years, two-thirds to local governments and one-third to the state.

NIXONOMICS

Nixon had to spend much of the time that he devoted to domestic affairs trying to manage an increasingly erratic American economy. The economic difficulties stemmed mainly from the Vietnam War and former President Johnson's fiscal irresponsibility. Johnson had drastically increased spending for the war in the midst of a booming economy, without raising taxes. Prices rose 5 percent in 1968, the highest inflation rate since the Korean War. Nixon initially applied the monetarist theories of economist Milton Friedman, who claimed that prices could be lowered by reducing the money supply. The results were disastrous. The stock market suffered its worst crash since 1929. Unemployment doubled, from 3 percent to 6 percent, and prices continued to rise. Monetarism generated both inflation and recession, creating "stagflation."

Appalled by its results, Nixon abandoned monetarism for a new economic approach, "jawboning," which amounted to pressuring both business and trade unions to keep down prices and wages. Jawboning produced only continuing stagflation. Nixon then decided that economic decline was a greater evil than inflation. Reverting to Keynesian practices, he deliberately unbalanced the budget to stimulate demand and increase employment. These efforts also failed. Stagflation stubbornly persisted as unemployment and inflation both remained high. The economy also ran its first trade deficit since 1893.

Still searching for an effective policy, Nixon again revamped his economic policies. On August 15, 1971, he froze wages, prices, and rents for ninety days, asked Congress for tax cuts to promote business expansion, devalued the dollar, and clamped a 10 percent tax on imports. At the end of ninety days, he replaced the freeze with more flexible guidelines, allowing annual price increases of 2.5 percent and wage increases of up to 5.5 percent. These drastic measures worked for a time. The trade deficit vanished, and inflation was halved. The economy snapped out of recession, and the GDP rose sharply. But within a few months, pressures from business and labor undermined the controls, and the inflation rate soared.

THE SOUTHERN STRATEGY

Despite his appeals for unity and peace, Nixon only partially succeeded in reuniting and quieting the American people. Discords inherited from the Johnson years continued and, at times, intensified. A rash of terrorist bombings damaged government and corporate buildings in various cities. Nixon's most divisive actions occurred when he implemented his Southern strategy, which aimed to outflank George Wallace and secure the Middle American vote consisting of Southern whites, Northern ethnics, and suburbanites. He also sought to attract voters from the Sunbelt, the most dynamic region of the country. The Southern strategy involved stressing "law and order," phasing out most antipoverty programs, and slowing the rate of school desegregation in the South.

Nixon's efforts to slow the pace of school desegregation involved his administration in a controversy over bussing to achieve school integration. The Justice Department filed suits prohibiting transporting children to desegregate public schools. The bussing issue had risen in 1971 when the Supreme Court had ordered the Charlotte-Mecklenburg school system in North Carolina to use bussing to achieve school integration after its efforts at voluntary desegregation had failed. Soon, many other Southern school districts were under court orders to bus children to achieve school integration. It was effective, and within a few years the Southern public school system was largely desegregated.

Court-ordered bussing spread to the North, where resistance was fierce and occasionally violent. The worst incidents occurred in Boston in 1974, when a federal judge ordered bussing to integrate its public school system. Over half of the public schools in Boston had student bodies that were 90 percent black. White pupils boycotted South Boston High School rather than accept integration. Buses hauling in African American students were stoned, and several youngsters were injured. Racial conflict in South Boston and other Northern cities led to a flight of white students from the public school system.

Administration efforts to thwart bussing in order to slow the pace of school integration infuriated civil rights leaders. But the Supreme Court upheld bussing, which infuriated Nixon. Despite Nixon's efforts, many Northern and Southern cities used bussing to achieve desegregation. Far more schools achieved integrated student bodies during Nixon's presidency than during the administrations of Johnson and Kennedy. African Americans progressed in other areas as well. The size of the African American middle class increased rapidly. Black college enrollment nearly doubled between 1968 and 1972. Thirteen black congressmen and eighty-one black mayors held office in 1971. Nixon tried to steer a middle course between what he called "instant integration and segregation forever." He also wanted to please his growing middle American and white Southern supporters.

Nixon's Southern strategy also influenced his choices to fill Supreme Court vacancies, four of which opened up during his first term. He tried to appoint a Deep South conservative, but the Senate rejected both of his choices. His four appointees, including the new Chief Justice Warren Burger, who replaced the retired Earl Warren in 1969, were all strict constructionist conservatives. But the more conservative "Nixon Court" did not overturn any of the controversial decisions of its activist predecessor, and many of its decisions went against the Nixon administration grain. It upheld bussing, the right of women to have an abortion on demand, and the publication of the *Pentagon Papers*. It struck down death penalty laws and limited Justice Department efforts at electronic surveillance. It did sustain laws banning pornography, where those statutes reflected "community standards." The Nixon court proved to be an unpredictable, politically independent agency, whose decisions often angered conservatives.

Nixon used Vice President Agnew to implement part of the Southern strategy. Agnew campaigned extensively during the 1970 midterm elections on behalf of Republican congressional candidates. During the elections, he tried to link his Democratic opponents to campus upheavals, race riots, bombings, rising crime rates, drug use, and pornography. Agnew's verbal onslaughts had little noticeable impact on the elections. Republicans gained two Senate seats, but lost nine seats in the House.

As part of its law-and-order campaign, the Justice Department prosecuted antiwar activists. The most important trial occurred in Chicago in 1971, involving a group of radicals known as the "Chicago Seven." The trial turned into a farce because of the disruptive antics of the defendants and the extreme bias against them of the judge, Julius Hoffmann. Six of the seven activists were convicted of various charges stemming from their roles in organizing demonstrations at the 1968 Democratic Convention in Chicago. But all of the convictions were overturned on appeal because of Judge Hoffmann's procedural errors and bias.

DÉTENTE

Nixon applied most of his considerable political talents to the conduct of U.S. foreign policy, where he often proved to be an able diplomatist. Nixon, who had built his political reputation as a hardline cold warrior, with help from Henry Kissinger, launched a new era of détente with the Soviet Union, built on a relaxation of tensions and realistic diplomacy. The development of new relations with the Soviets reversed the direction American foreign policy had taken since 1945. A glimmer of détente had surfaced in 1963 in the aftermath of the missile crisis with the signing of the Nuclear Test Ban Treaty, but Lyndon Johnson had been unable to sustain it. Relations between the United States and the Soviet Union were strained at the time of Nixon's accession to office, and ongoing efforts at arms control negotiations were unproductive.

Since the beginning of the Cold War, U.S. foreign policy had been premised on the necessity of responding to threats to American interests posed by expansionist Communist states. Both Nixon and Kissinger knew that the model of a world dominated by a bipolar struggle between Communism and the Free World had been rendered obsolete by the late 1960s. They understood that power now flowed along a pentagonal axis representing the United States, western Europe, the Soviet Empire, China, and Japan.

Nixon and Kissinger also understood that U.S. power had suffered relative decline since the late 1950s. America no longer dominated its major allies. They also understood that the unity of the Communist world had been fatally sundered. In early 1969, the most serious international conflict pitted the two major Communist states, the Soviet Union and the People's Republic of China, against each other. Kissinger and Nixon perceived that, in the case of the quarreling Communist giants, questions of conflicting national interests overrode their ideological kinship. Nixon and Kissinger set out to use this rift between the two Communist powers to improve U.S. relations with both, and to enhance American power in the world.

Nixon and Kissinger had many reasons for seeking détente with the Soviets. They hoped to persuade them to help them achieve a satisfactory peace in Indochina by linking Soviet willingness to persuade the North Vietnamese to accept U.S. terms with improved relations between the two superpowers. They also expected détente to enable America to maintain influence over its NATO allies, who had recently shown a distressing tendency to make deals of their own with the Soviets and with the Eastern bloc countries. Prosperous and no longer fearful of Soviet aggression, the French and West Germans had been pursuing their own détentes with the Communists. Another powerful motive for détente was the desire of American industrial and financial interests to move into Soviet and eastern European markets. Powerful U.S. agricultural interests saw the Soviets as major customers for their wheat and other commodities. Most important, Nixon and Kissinger had to be concerned by the ever-present danger of nuclear war arising from the spiraling arms race. Both sides strongly desired to bring a measure of control to the arms race that would significantly reduce the threat of nuclear catastrophe.

In 1969, Nixon signed a Nuclear Nonproliferation Treaty with the Soviets. At Nixon's initiative, U.S. and Soviet delegates began strategic arms limitation talks (SALT) in April 1970 at Helsinki and Vienna. At the same time, Kissinger began talks with the Soviet ambassador to the United States, Anatoly Dobrynin. Nixon wanted nuclear weapons agreements with the Soviets to be the key to détente and to an expanding network of agreements with the Soviets. As he pushed for SALT to begin, Nixon expanded America's nuclear arsenal, believing that the United States must always negotiate from a position of strength with the Soviets. At the time, both nations possessed roughly equal nuclear arsenals, and both were refining and expanding their nuclear weapons systems. Nixon wanted to add two new weapons systems to the U.S. arsenal, an antiballistics missile (ABM), which would protect U.S. missiles from a possible first strike, and a multiple, independently targeted reentry vehicle (MIRV), which would make it possible for multiple nuclear warheads to be fired from a single missile in flight at several targets simultaneously. The Soviets also had begun work on ABMs and MIRV missiles.

Nixon also began a phased reduction of U.S. conventional military forces. These military cutbacks coincided with a general scaling back of American global commitments. In August 1969, the president proclaimed a new Asian policy, the Nixon Doctrine. According to this new doctrine, America would no longer provide direct military protection in the Far East. Asian nations must henceforth assume greater responsibility for their strategic security. The United States could furnish economic and technical assistance and logistic support, but not troops. There would be no more Vietnams or Koreas. The Nixon Doctrine also had applications for other regions and other conflicts outside of Southeast Asia. The new doctrine also signaled that a new dynamic U.S. policy of negotiation and maneuver was supplanting the essentially static policy based on military containment of Communism.

While SALT negotiators representing both sides grappled with the intricate technical questions involved in controlling the asymmetric nuclear weapons systems of the United States and the Soviet Union, other negotiators concluded a series of important economic agreements. In November 1971, representatives of both governments signed agreements whereby the United States would sell the Soviets $136 million worth of wheat and $125 million worth of oil drilling equipment. Arrangements also were concluded on a joint venture, the building of a large truck factory within the Soviet Union. These and many other smaller deals led to a threefold increase in U.S.–Soviet trade over the next three years.

In March 1972, Nixon sent Kissinger to Moscow to make preparations for a summit meeting between the American president and Leonid Brezhnev, general secretary of the Soviet Communist Party. Nixon later journeyed to Moscow where he and Brezhnev met for a series of talks. Three major agreements, signed by both leaders in May 1972, came from these talks. The first agreement limited each country to two ABM sites and also set a ceiling on the number of ABMs per site. The second agreement, an interim one called SALT I, froze the number of strategic missiles in both arsenals at the 1972 levels for five years, but it put no limit on MIRVs, which both sides continued to build. Neither the ABM treaty nor SALT I ended the thermonuclear arms race, but the arms agreement did bring a measure of stability and control welcomed by both powers. The third agreement, "Basic Principles of U.S.–Soviet Relations," committed both sides to accept strategic equality as the basic premise for future arms control negotiations. Americans no longer sought nuclear superiority over the Soviets; they had accepted sufficiency. Congress subsequently approved all three agreements. These breakthrough agreements fundamentally altered American–Soviet relations in the world and constituted the bedrock of the new superpower relationship founded on détente, a relaxation of tensions.

Other significant diplomatic agreements between the United States and the Soviet Union were concluded. The Berlin question, a recurring flash point in the Cold War, was resolved. Both sides signed the Berlin Agreement of 1971, which clearly defined the political status of Berlin and created mechanisms for the peaceful resolution of any conflicts that might arise. The next year, the two German states normalized relations, and America recognized East Germany as a legitimate state. The United States and the Soviet Union even settled the long-standing question of the Soviet Lend-Lease debt left over from World War II. The Soviets agreed to pay a portion of a scaled-down debt annually for the next twenty years.

All of these agreements forged during the most productive era in U.S.–USSR relations since World War II did not make the two superpowers allies. But détente had created the opportunity for realistic agreements between the two countries, which stabilized the arms race, reduced the risk of nuclear war, and resolved several long-standing political problems that had divided them. Competition and rivalry between the superpowers would continue, especially in the Third World, but "peaceful coexistence" had become a reality.

The Nixon and Kissinger policy of détente with the Soviet Union came under attack from Democratic Cold Warriors who controlled Congress. Senator Henry "Scoop" Jackson, from the state of Washington, emerged as the leader of the Democratic opposition to détente. Jackson attacked SALT I as giving the Soviets a dangerous advantage over the United States, because it allowed them to keep more land-based ICBMs. Jackson ignored the fact that the United States relied for strategic deterrence on a triad of land-based missiles, submarine-launched missiles, and strategic bombers. The Soviets, lacking equivalent submarine and bomber forces, required additional ICBMs to offset the American advantage. Jackson also criticized the Nixon administration for its tolerance of Soviet human rights violations, particularly Moscow's refusal to let Soviet Jews emigrate.

Jackson's criticism was valid, although the Soviets liberalized their emigration policy and permitted 30,000 Jews to leave the country during 1973, the largest number ever. Jackson, who harbored presidential ambitions, helped push the Jackson–Vanik Amendment through Congress, which denied the Soviet Union "most favored nation" trading status with the United States, until they stopped human rights abuses and allowed unlimited emigration. The Jackson–Vanik

Amendment effectively prevented Washington from granting equal trading rights to the Soviet Union, hindered the developing commerce between the two nations, weakened détente, angered President Nixon, and disappointed Brezhnev.

THE CHINA OPENING

Nixon's most dramatic foreign policy achievement was the famed opening to China. Since the Chinese revolution in 1949, the United States had insisted that Jiang Jieshi's regime on Taiwan was the true government of China and had refused to recognize the government in Beijing. For over twenty years, America and China had had no commercial, diplomatic, or cultural relations, and the United States had successfully prevented China from joining the United Nations. Americans were forbidden to travel to China. The United States also maintained a trade boycott and loan ban against China, and it attempted to prevent other nations from trading with the Chinese. When Nixon took office in 1969, China was emerging from years of upheaval caused by Mao Zedong's "Cultural Revolution." Chinese leaders, worried about threats to China's security posed by conflicts with the Soviets, sought contacts in the West. Mao was hopeful that friendly relations could be developed with the United States, a country he had long admired.

Beijing sent friendly signals to Western nations. Nixon, sensing possibilities for rapprochement with the People's Republic, responded positively. Trade and travel restrictions between the two countries were eased. In April 1971, the Chinese invited an American table tennis team to visit China to play against Chinese athletes. This "ping pong gambit" preceded the major breakthrough that came in July when Henry Kissinger secretly visited China. Nixon then stunned the American people when he suddenly announced on July 15 that Kissinger had made arrangements for him to visit China in early 1972.

Nixon sought improved relations with China for several reasons. Most of America's European allies had long since normalized relations with China, and he knew that the American policy of nonrecognition no longer worked. China was an established major power in world affairs. Nixon also knew pressures were mounting within the United Nations to evict Taiwan and seat China in its stead. Further, Nixon expected to use friendly relations with China as a diplomatic weapon against the Soviets; he wanted to be able to play the "China card" to incline the Soviets to conclude arms control and other agreements with the Americans. Improved relations with China also were part of Nixon's and Kissinger's strategy for freeing America from its Vietnam entanglement. They hoped that Chinese leaders would be helpful in persuading Hanoi to negotiate a settlement of the war that Washington could accept. Normal relations with China also would help America reassert its power in Southeast Asia and develop a wider network of interests in that important region. Nixon knew that his impeccable anti-Communist credentials protected him from right-wing attacks about his being soft on Communism.

He also knew that media coverage of the China trip would boost his political stock at home during an election year.

The announcement that Nixon was going to China was greeted with tremendous enthusiasm by almost all Americans, regardless of their political leanings. Many Democratic political leaders put aside their usual criticisms of Nixon's and Kissinger's diplomacy to praise both men effusively. Kissinger returned to China in November 1971 to finalize the arrangements. While he was in Beijing, the United Nations expelled Taiwan and awarded its seat on the Security Council to China. Some critical voices, mostly on the Republican Right, were raised in protest over Washington's quick abandonment of its longtime ally and friend.

President Nixon arrived in China on February 22, 1972, accompanied by advisers and a host of U.S. journalists. Back in America, millions of fascinated viewers watched spectacular live television coverage of Nixon's arrival at the Beijing airport, his journey into the Forbidden City, and many other highlights of his five-day visit. Nixon's party were the first Americans to officially go to China in over twenty years. The video images beamed back to America through a communications satellite were the first live U.S. television coverage ever shot in China. Nixon met with Premier Jou En-lai several times for hours of discussion. Nixon and Kissinger also had a lengthy meeting with the legendary Mao ZeDong. The American delegation was the guest of honor at a lavish banquet hosted by the Chinese leaders inside of the Great Hall of the People.

Figure 13.2   Nixon's greatest achievement was the opening to China, achieved when he journeyed to that great country in February 1972. Here he is greeted by the legendary Mao Zedong at the latter's apartment in Beijing.   *Source:* National Archives.

Figure 13.3   During their historic visit to China, President Nixon and First Lady Catherine "Pat" Ryan Nixon posed for a picture at the famed Great Wall.   *Source:* National Archives.

At the conclusion of the historic visit, Nixon and Jou En-lai issued a joint statement, the Shanghai Communique, which defined the terms of the new U.S.–Chinese relationship. Each country agreed to open a legation in the other's capital. America removed its restrictions on trade and travel to China and it acknowledged that Taiwan was part of China. Both sides criticized the Soviet Union.

There was no agreement on the Vietnam War. Both China and the United States reaffirmed support for their respective sides in that ongoing war. But the joint communique itself, the fact that it was being jointly promulgated by former adversaries, signaled that the United States was moving beyond Vietnam, beyond the war, toward a larger role in Southeast Asia. U.S.–Chinese relations would go forward, regardless of the Indochina War. Within a year of Nixon's visit, American travelers flocked to China. Trade between the two nations increased dramatically. Both countries exchanged diplomatic missions. The China opening was the high point of Nixon's presidency and the most significant diplomatic achievement of any modern American president.

VIETNAM: A WAR TO END A WAR

The most urgent problem confronting Nixon was extricating America from Vietnam. He tried new approaches to end the war, including implementing the plan announced during his presidential campaign. But his policies suffered from the same flaw as Johnson's. Nixon still sought to achieve an independent non-Communist South Vietnamese state, which the North Vietnamese refused to accept, thus the war went on.

Even though Hanoi had consistently rejected any settlement that would leave a non-Communist government in the South, Nixon and Kissinger believed that they could compel Hanoi to accept one. They planned to use the improved relationship between the United States and the USSR by linking increased trade and arms agreements with the Soviets to their willingness to pressure Hanoi into accepting U.S. terms in Vietnam. Nixon also escalated the war by removing the limits Johnson had placed on the use of military force in Southeast Asia. In the spring of 1969, Nixon ordered a bombing campaign to begin against Vietcong and North Vietnamese sanctuaries in Cambodia. Because Cambodia was a neutral nation, the bombing was illegal. It was kept secret from Congress and from the American people. In addition, Nixon, through Soviet intermediaries, offered the North Vietnamese more realistic peace terms. He proposed withdrawing both American and North Vietnamese troops from the South and reinstituting the demilitarized zone as the boundary between North and South Vietnam. At the same time, to please American public opinion that had turned against the war, Nixon announced a phased withdrawal of American combat troops from Vietnam.

But Hanoi was neither intimidated by threats nor lured by concessions into changing its terms. The Paris talks remained deadlocked. Hanoi continued to demand the unilateral withdrawal of all U.S. forces from South Vietnam and the installation of a coalition government in the South, excluding General Thieu. Nor did the Soviets cooperate. The linkage strategy proved to be a failure in 1969. Nixon faced a dilemma; unable to extract the slightest concession from Hanoi, he had to choose between a major escalation of the war or a humiliating withdrawal. Unwilling to make concessions and unable to use greater force because he did not want to arouse domestic opponents of the war and because of doubts about its effectiveness, Nixon offered what Secretary of Defense Melvin Laird called "Vietnamization"—the United States would gradually continue to withdraw its troops while building up South Vietnamese forces in order to enable them to prevent a Communist takeover following the U.S. pullout. At the time Nixon announced his Vietnamization plan, it had already been in place for a year. He had inherited it from Johnson and given it a new label. While U.S. forces battled the North Vietnamese and the Vietcong, American advisers built up the South Vietnamese armed forces. Pacification and rural development programs accelerated. In March 1970, President Nixon announced that 150,000 U.S. combat troops would be withdrawn that year.

In neighboring Cambodia, neutralist leader Prince Sihanouk was suddenly overthrown by his pro-American Prime Minister, Lon Nol. Nixon, fearing that the North Vietnamese might take over Cambodia following the coup, and responding to a U.S. Army request to attack North Vietnamese sanctuaries in that country, ordered American troops into an area of Cambodia about fifty miles northwest of Saigon. The Cambodian incursion produced mixed results. It relieved pressure on Saigon and bought more time for Vietnamization. It also widened the war and provoked Hanoi into a full-scale support of Cambodian insurgents fighting Lon Nol's forces. America now had two fragile client states in Southeast Asia to defend against insurgents backed by North Vietnam and China. The Vietnam War had been widened; it had become an Indochina war. The Cambodian campaign proved to be the last major campaign of the Indochina War involving U.S. ground combat forces.

Nixon did not anticipate the furious domestic reaction to the Cambodian invasion. College campuses across the land exploded at the news of an unexpected widening of a war that he had promised to phase out. At Kent State University, tragedy occurred when Ohio National Guardsmen opened fire into a crowd of student protesters, killing four of them and wounding nine others. Following these shootings, hundreds of student strikes forced many colleges to shut down. More than 100,000 demonstrators gathered in Washington to protest the Cambodian invasion and the "Kent State Massacre." The Cambodian initiative also caused the most serious congressional challenge to presidential authority to conduct the war. The Senate repealed the Gulf of Tonkin resolution and voted to cut off all funds for Cambodia. But the fund cutoff failed to clear the House. Both the North Vietnamese and the Vietcong broke off negotiations in protest, confident that domestic and international pressures would eventually force U.S. withdrawal from both Cambodia and South Vietnam.

To appease Dovish critics at home, the president accelerated the timetable for troop withdrawals in 1971. He expanded the air war by ordering more bombing missions into Cambodia and along the Laotian panhandle. He also authorized an ARVN raid into Laos to disrupt enemy supply routes and staging, but the raid failed to achieve most of its objectives. Within the United States, Doves attacked another widening of the Indochina War.

During the spring and summer of 1971, two events at home shocked the war-weary nation. On March 29, a military court convicted Lieutenant William Calley of multiple murders and sentenced him to life imprisonment for ordering his infantry platoon to kill hundreds of Vietnamese civilians at a hamlet called My Lai. Calley's men had been brought in to destroy the hamlet suspected of harboring Vietcong. But instead of evacuating the population beforehand or eliminating the village with long-range artillery and bombs, Calley's men had massacred the villagers at close range with pistol, machine gun, and automatic rifle fire.

Calley claimed that he only followed orders. U.S. Army attorneys insisted that Calley had misunderstood his orders. No one else was convicted of war crimes. Many Americans felt sympathy for Calley and his men; a public opinion poll showed that a majority of Americans blamed the media for reporting the incident, which had exposed the army's efforts to cover up the affair. Responding to the angry outcry over Calley's conviction, President Nixon intervened to reduce Calley's sentence. Some Americans wondered how many other My Lai-type massacres had gone undetected. Others found cold comfort in the fact that Vietcong and South Vietnamese army forces had murdered thousands of civilians. There also was the troubling inconsistency of convicting one young junior officer for mass murder in a war where long-range artillery fire and aerial bombing had killed thousands of villagers since the Americanization of the war in 1965.

No sooner had the uproar over Calley's conviction subsided than the *New York Times* began publishing excerpts from the *Pentagon Papers,* secret government documents pertaining to the Vietnam War stolen from files of the RAND Corporation by a former employee, Daniel Ellsberg. The papers revealed that American leaders had deliberately escalated the war, had ignored peace offers, and had often lied to the public about their actions. These revelations further undermined the credibility of government officials and weakened support for the war.

An increasingly frustrated president fought back against the mounting opposition to his war policy. He ordered that wiretaps be placed on National Security Council staffers and journalists suspected of leaking secret information to the media. He ordered the illegal surveillance of antiwar groups by both the FBI and the CIA. He accused congressional Doves of encouraging the enemy and prolonging the war. Nixon administration lawyers tried to prevent the *New York Times* from publishing the *Pentagon Papers* by securing a court injunction against their publication on the grounds that their release compromised national security. An appellate judge quashed the injunction and the Supreme Court sustained his ruling. Blocked by the U.S. Supreme Court, the president approved the creation of a special White House undercover unit, the "Plumbers," to prevent leaks from within the government and to discredit Ellsberg. Under extreme pressure, Nixon developed a siege mentality, feeling beset by enemies in Congress, the media, the bureaucracies, and the streets, all of whom, he believed, were working to undermine his authority to govern. These paranoid attitudes, which drove him to order his men to commit illegal acts, were one of the prime causes of the Watergate scandals.

By the summer of 1971, polls showed that public support for Nixon's war policies had dropped to 31 percent. Another survey revealed that two-thirds of Americans approved of the withdrawal of all American troops from Vietnam by the end of the year, even if that meant a Communist takeover in the South. Twice the Senate passed resolutions setting a deadline for withdrawal of all troops as soon as North Vietnam released U.S. prisoners of war (POW). Nixon responded to those signs of war-weariness by making new, secret peace proposals to Hanoi: in exchange for the release of American prisoners, the United States would withdraw all of its troops within six months and would no longer insist that Hanoi withdraw its troops. These new U.S. concessions started the first serious negotiations since talks had begun in 1968, but deadlock continued because Washington insisted that Thieu remain in power in the South, whereas Hanoi insisted that his removal was a precondition of any settlement.

The war entered its final phase in 1972. Knowing that there were only 6,000 American combat troops remaining in the South, North Vietnam launched its largest offensive of the war—120,000 North Vietnamese regulars struck directly at ARVN forces across several fronts. Simultaneously, Vietcong guerrillas resumed their attacks in rural areas to disrupt pacification efforts. The United States retaliated with massive B-52 bombing raids against targets in the Hanoi-Haiphong area. Tactical bombers pounded the North Vietnamese invaders and their supply lines.

The North Vietnamese and Vietcong continued to press their attacks. Nixon then carried out his boldest escalation of the war. He ordered a naval blockade of North Vietnam and the mining of Haiphong Harbor, and he escalated the bombing campaigns. In addition to his military responses, Nixon also approached the Soviets again about persuading Hanoi to accept a diplomatic settlement of the war.

Nixon's decisive response to the North Vietnamese assault received strong support at home. The bombing and blockade sufficiently disrupted North Vietnamese supply lines to enable the hard-pressed ARVN forces to stabilize their lines around Hue and Saigon. The North Vietnamese offensive had stalled by summer. South Vietnam managed to survive the assaults, due to the strong response by the United States. Both the Soviets and the Chinese, while loudly condemning the U.S. response publicly, privately exerted pressure on Hanoi to end its war with the United States. Détente with the two Communist powers at last bore fruit and helped Nixon bring the U.S. war in Southeast Asia to a belated end.

With the onset of the summer rains in 1972, the war stalemated once more. The North Vietnamese had expected its spring offensive, combined with the approaching American election, to force Nixon to accept their terms and remove Thieu. But the president's powerful response had neutralized their assault and inflicted heavy losses. Soviet and Chinese pressures on Hanoi pushed the North Vietnamese toward a diplomatic settlement. George McGovern, the Democratic challenger for the presidency in 1972, proved to be a weak candidate who posed no threat to Nixon or his war policy. A combination of military losses, economic strains, and diplomatic isolation forced Hanoi to seek a settlement with the United States, as long as it did not conflict with their long-range goal of achieving a unified Vietnam under Communist control.

Secret negotiations resumed in Paris. Hanoi dropped its demand that Thieu must go before any settlement could be reached. Kissinger and the North Vietnamese emissary, Le Duc Tho, bargained intensively. By October 11, 1972, they had forged an agreement: within sixty days, after a cease-fire, America would remove all of its remaining troops, and North Vietnam would release the U.S. POWs. The Thieu government would remain in power, pending a political settlement in the South. North Vietnamese troops would remain in the South, and the National Liberation Front, now known as the People's Revolutionary Government (PRG), would be accorded political status in southern Vietnam.

But General Thieu, who had the most to lose from these arrangements, refused to accept them. Nixon supported Thieu. The North Vietnamese, believing themselves betrayed, angrily broke off negotiations. The October agreement was placed on hold, and the war went on. Nixon, reelected by a landslide, tried to secure peace terms that were more favorable to the South Vietnamese government that could ensure its survival. He ordered unlimited air attacks on North Vietnamese targets in the vicinity of Hanoi and Haiphong. There ensued the most powerful attack in the history of aerial warfare. This "Christmas bombing" lasted from December 18 to December 29. Nixon was determined to pound Hanoi into resuming negotiations. At the same time he turned the U.S. Air Force loose on the

North, Nixon significantly increased U.S. aid to South Vietnam and bluntly told General Thieu to accept U.S. peace terms or the United States would settle without him.

The Christmas bombing provoked worldwide criticism and a storm of protest at home. Congress moved to cut off all funding for the war. With time running out on his options, Nixon told the North Vietnamese that if they agreed to resume negotiations, he would halt the bombing. The battered North Vietnamese accepted his offer, and the talks resumed. Kissinger and Tho reached an agreement signed by all parties on January 27. The January agreement was similar in all of its major provisions to the suspended agreement of October 11. This time Nixon imposed the agreement on Thieu, who signed reluctantly. In order to make the treaty more palatable to Thieu, Nixon pledged in writing that the United States "would respond in full force" if North Vietnam violated the agreement.

Although Nixon insisted that the peace agreement had brought "peace with honor" to Indochina, the January accords represented a disguised defeat for the United States, which permitted the Americans to extricate themselves from a war that they no longer believed in and to retrieve their POWs. It also permitted North Vietnamese forces to remain in the South, and it granted the PRG political legitimacy. It allowed the Thieu regime to survive in the South for a time. The major question over which the war had been fought for nearly a decade, who would govern in the South, was deferred, to be resolved by political means in the future. But the political provisions of the treaty proved unworkable in practice, so that question would finally be settled by force of arms in two years.

THE END OF THE TUNNEL

The war went on, even as Kissinger and Tho signed the agreements; there never was an effective cease-fire because neither side made a sincere effort to stop fighting or to resolve their differences through negotiations. Nixon continued to support the Thieu government after the U.S. withdrawal, but his efforts were limited, by the terms of the Paris accords, by a lack of public and congressional support, and by his own deepening involvement in Watergate. Between 1973 and 1975, Congress restricted the president's power to involve America in the ongoing Indochina War and significantly reduced the amount of aid going to Saigon. When North Vietnam mounted a spring offensive in 1975, South Vietnam suddenly collapsed. The invaders overran its territory. President Ford wanted to honor U.S. commitments to intervene, but lacking congressional support, he did nothing. Saigon fell to the Communists on April 30.

The twenty-five-year-long American effort to prevent a Communist takeover in southern Vietnam had ended in disaster for the United States and for the people it tried to help. It had been the longest, least popular war in U.S. history. It had divided Americans worse than any other conflict since their own civil war. It was the first major war that Americans had lost. Its aftermath refuted every Cold War assumption upon which American involvement had been based. American security was not threatened. American alliances elsewhere were not weakened, nor were American allies disheartened by the outcome. American power and prestige in the world community was not significantly diminished. There was no unified Communist takeover of Southeast Asia, because the victorious Communist states fell to warring among themselves. A vicious Marxist regime, which overthrew Lon Nol in Cambodia about the time the North Vietnamese conquered Saigon, was responsible for the death of at least a million of its own people. Communist Vietnam invaded Cambodia, now called Kampuchea. China, supporting the Kampuchean regime, attacked Vietnam. The Soviets backed Vietnam in these intramural Communist wars. America, which had gone to war in Southeast Asia to stop the spread of Chinese Communism, found itself quietly backing Chinese efforts to contain Vietnamese expansionism. Southeast Asian national interests turned out to be a stronger force than Marxist ideology in determining the behavior of nations. There was no bitter "who lost Vietnam?" debate in the United States or a resurgence of McCarthyite Red-baiting. Instead, amnesia set in; no one wanted to talk about Vietnam for years.

The harm done to the United States and Vietnam by the war was severe and lasting. The war killed perhaps 2 million Vietnamese and turned a fourth of its population into refugees. It left 58,000 Americans dead and another 300,000 wounded. There were few parades for returning Vietnam veterans. Except for the POWs, they were not welcomed home. A people who had carelessly sent them off to fight in Vietnam for a cause they no longer believed in were embarrassed by their presence and sought to ignore them, or worse, to denounce them.

The war experience for many veterans had been an ordeal. In addition to facing the ravages of war, many soldiers returned home disillusioned by their combat experiences. To these veterans, the war appeared futile, pointless, and wrong. The rejection of the war by the civilian population made it more difficult for many soldiers to justify their efforts or to derive any meaning from them. The large majority of returning veterans were neither war criminals or victims. They did not suffer from drug addiction or have acute psychological or physical disabilities. But most had to struggle to come to terms with their war experiences, readjust to civilian routines, and reintegrate into American society. The Vietnam War cost more than any other war in U.S. history except World War II—$167 billion. President Johnson's efforts to finance both the Great Society and the war ignited inflation. His refusal to trim domestic spending, to raise taxes, or to apply economic controls, because he was trying to hide the costs of war, brought economic decline to the nation.

There were other costs of war. A bitter controversy erupted over whether draft evaders and deserters should be granted amnesty or severely punished. This nasty debate perpetuated the war-sown divisions between the Doves and the Hawks. The war also undermined public faith in the competence and honesty of elected officials. Military service was discredited for years. The war shattered the bipartisan ideological consensus that had guided U.S. foreign policy since the late 1940s. Americans discovered that there were limits to U.S. power and limits to the burdens Americans were willing to bear in pursuit of foreign policy objectives. The ordeal of Vietnam also marred the American spirit. The ultimate domino was America's vision of itself as a benevolent nation whose great mission in the world was to defend and extend democracy. That lofty self-image perished in the jungles, swamps, and rice paddies of southern Vietnam.

ACTIVISTS AND REFORMERS

Many of the insurgencies that had risen during the 1960s continued into the 1970s. The women's movement gained momentum as more women changed their perceptions about themselves and their roles in society. The number of American women in medical schools, law schools, and graduate business programs doubled between 1970 and 1974. New magazines devoted to women's issues emerged. The most successful of these publications was *Ms.*, edited by Gloria Steinem, which gave feminists a forum of their own. The women's movement of the 1970s continued to be divided between reformers in the National Organization for Women (NOW), who sought equality before the law, no-fault divorces, equal pay for equal work, childcare centers, and abortion rights and radical feminists, who wanted fundamental changes in the structure of society and changes in sexual identity.

Political opposition to feminism in the 1970s came from a conservative leader, Phyllis Schlafly, head of the Eagle Forum. Schlafly led an effort to defeat the Equal Rights Amendment (ERA). She insisted that its passage would not help women and would take away the rights they already enjoyed, such as the right to be supported by a husband, the right to be exempted from conscription, and the right to special job protections. Schlafly and her cause succeeded when ERA fell three states short of the thirty-eight needed for ratification.

While feminists organized for action, so did Native Americans. In 1973, a militant Native American group, the American Indian Movement (AIM), seized the South Dakota town of Wounded Knee, the site of an 1890 massacre of Lakota Indians by the U.S. Seventh Cavalry. The AIM activists wanted to call attention to the misery of the impoverished Indian inhabitants of Wounded Knee and to the hundreds of treaties with Native Americans that had been broken by the federal government. Armed federal agents reclaimed the town, killing an AIM member in the process. In the negotiations that followed, government officials agreed to examine conditions among the Indians and their treaty rights. The Second Battle of Wounded Knee signaled a new era of Indian activism.

Hispanic organizations also were active in the early 1970s. Young Chicanos formed a militant organization, the Brown Berets, who were active in the Midwest and Southwest. The Brown Berets also joined the antiwar movement. Aware of the growing political involvement of Mexican Americans, President Nixon set out to win their support, offering them political appointments and programs. The effort paid off; in the 1972 election, Nixon received 31 percent of the Chicano vote, which helped him carry California and Texas. In 1974, the Supreme Court responded to another Chicano concern when it ruled that public schools had to meet the learning requirements of youngsters who had limited English language skills. That decision led to the federal funding of bilingual educational programs in several states that had large Mexican American populations.

ECOLOGY AND CONSUMERISM

Environmentalism was one of the many movements that emerged during the 1960s and grew rapidly during the early 1970s. Congress enacted the Water Quality Improvement Act in 1970, which tightened existing safeguards against threats to water quality. The National Air Quality Standards Act required automakers to significantly reduce exhaust emission pollutants by 1975 and required the federal government to set air quality standards. The Resource Recovery Act provided $453 million for resource recovery and recycling systems. In 1971, Congress created the Environmental Protection Agency (EPA), which combined federal agencies concerned with pesticides, radiation, auto exhaust emissions, air and water quality, and waste disposal under a single cabinet-level department. Nixon appointed former Assistant Attorney General William Ruckelshaus to head the new agency. The EPA quickly initiated action on several fronts, provoking a reaction from Detroit automakers, who insisted that EPA emission and safety standards were too expensive and beyond their technological capabilities. Nixon's Secretary of the Interior Walter Hickel, a conservative, self-made oil millionaire, also turned out to be an energetic environmentalist who protected the public domain.

Ecology was not a major Nixon priority, and at times he opposed the environmentalists. He pushed hard for funds to construct a supersonic jet transport in 1970, only to have the Senate kill the project because the design of the plane was too noisy and expensive. Nixon also vetoed a mammoth $24.7 billion measure to clean up America's polluted rivers and lakes, but Congress enacted the law over his veto. Environmentalism was a political issue that cut across party, class, and ideological lines. Most everyone endorsed, in principle, the need for clean air and water and the protection of scenic landscapes and wilderness areas. But not everyone was willing to pay its high costs. At times, economic interests collided with environmentalist causes, provoking ideological warfare.

A strong consumer movement developed during the early 1970s that concerned itself with protecting consumers from unsafe, shoddy products. It also sought to make business more responsive to consumers. Ralph Nader headed the consumer movement of the 1970s. From an office in the nation's capital, he organized task forces of volunteers called "Nader's Raiders," who examined many industries and governmental agencies. They followed up these investigations with critical reports about their operations and proposals for reform.

Nader's Raiders attacked governmental regulatory agencies for being more protective of the businesses they were supposed to regulate than of the consumers. These latter-day Muckrakers also attacked the multibillion-dollar processed food industry, accusing it of serving American consumers a "chemical feast" of harmful food additives. And they attacked agribusiness for its use of chemical fertilizers and pesticides, which harmed the environment and put toxic substances into the nation's food supplies.

THE ELECTION OF 1972

The president and his men carefully prepared for his 1972 reelection campaign. Attorney General John Mitchell resigned from his office to devote all of his time to directing the newly formed Committee to Reelect the President (CREEP). The CREEP fund-raisers accumulated a $60 million war chest to finance his campaign, making it the most costly presidential campaign in American history. CREEP also recruited men who were fiercely loyal to the president and shared his siege mentality of "us against them." They appeared ready to do anything to ensure the president's reelection, including breaking laws and violating the ethical norms of democratic electoral practices. Nixon had always campaigned with fierce determination to win. He remembered his narrow loss to John Kennedy in 1960 and that he had barely beaten Humphrey in 1968. The 1970 midterm election results had shown strong continuing support for congressional Democrats. In 1972, Mr. Nixon was determined to leave nothing to chance to secure his reelection.

The Democratic Party was still in disarray from the upheavals of 1968, and its members remained deeply divided over emotional issues such as the war, bussing, and "law and order." Nevertheless, many Democrats sought their party's nomination at the outset of the 1972 campaign. They included Senators Edmund Muskie, who was impressive as the vice presidential candidate in 1968; Hubert Humphrey, who was around for another go; and George McGovern, who was an outspoken critic of the Vietnam War. After these contenders came two formidable possibilities,

Figure 13.4 George McGovern on the campaign trail in 1972.
Source: National Archives.

Senator Edward "Ted" Kennedy and George Wallace. Kennedy's appeal had been tarnished by his behavior following an auto accident in which a young women had been killed; but he still retained the vote-getting magic of the Kennedy name. George Wallace, returned to the Democratic fold, also remained a major player.

Muskie flamed out early, in part the victim of Watergate "dirty tricks," as the nation would discover a year later. A would-be assassin eliminated Wallace by wounding him severely and forcing him out of the campaign in May. With Muskie and Wallace eliminated, McGovern moved strongly ahead. He won a series of primary victories, including California, where he beat Humphrey, and he rolled on to a first-ballot nomination. State delegations at the Democratic Convention in Miami contained high proportions of women, blacks, and young antiwar activists. These insurgent practitioners of a "new politics" took control of the convention and forged McGovern's victory.

McGovern's victory was largely a triumph of organization. He had borrowed savvy political professionals from the Kennedy organization, and his aides had enlisted young enthusiasts who rallied to McGovern's call for ending the war in Vietnam. He chose Thomas Eagleton, a young liberal senator from Missouri, as his running mate. His supporters drafted a platform calling for an "immediate total withdrawal of all American forces in Southeast Asia." It also supported bussing to achieve school integration, full employment, tax reform, and various social reforms.

Meeting in Miami after the Democrats, the Republicans unanimously chose Nixon and Agnew to run again. The Republican platform staked out a clear strategy. It called for a "new American majority" to repudiate the "far-out goals of the Far Left," meaning McGovern's program. It also called for arms limitations with the Soviets, full employment, and tax reform. It opposed bussing. On the crucial war issue, Republicans insisted that America could not withdraw from Vietnam until all of the prisoners of war had been returned.

The presidential campaign turned out to be boring and one-sided. McGovern never had a chance, and most Americans quickly lost interest in the contest. The Democrats remained divided. Most Wallace supporters and about half of Humphrey's followers voted for Nixon. Organized labor, the strongest power bloc within the party, refused to support McGovern. McGovern's campaign suffered serious damage at the outset when the public learned that Senator Eagleton had undergone psychiatric care in the past. At first, McGovern stood behind Eagleton, but after a week's adverse publicity, he panicked and forced Eagleton off the ticket. McGovern then began a search for a substitute and suffered six embarrassing turndowns before finally persuading Sargent Shriver, former director of the Peace Corps and the War on Poverty, to accept. McGovern's inept, expediential handling of the Eagleton affair managed to alienate both young idealists and party regulars. To many of the new politics enthusiasts, McGovern appeared to be just another opportunistic politician; to the regulars, he appeared to be an incompetent bumbler.

The qualities that brought McGovern the nomination proved to be political liabilities in the contest against Nixon. His left-of-center appeal to the new politics cost him the political center inhabited by most voters. Republicans put McGovern on the defensive early in the campaign by depicting him as a radical, even though he was a mild-mannered preacher's son, a decorated World War II hero, and a former college professor. McGovern was an old-fashioned Midwestern liberal, in the New Deal–Fair Deal–Great Society mold, with perhaps a whiff of 1930s Prairie Populism thrown in the ideological mix. But in the conservative political atmosphere of 1972, McGovern's advocacy of traditional liberal reforms sounded radical to many voters. He alienated far more voters than he attracted with his stands on emotion-laden issues such as his calls for amnesty for Vietnam draft resisters and liberalizing abortion and marijuana laws.

Nixon campaigned very little. He stayed in Washington and concentrated on appearing "presidential," while the hapless McGovern struggled. Nixon possessed formidable political assets that made him practically unbeatable. The president had achieved impressive diplomatic victories, capped by détente with the Soviets and the opening to China. The American war in Vietnam was winding down, and most U.S. troops had been withdrawn. At home, the economy was reasonably strong and the society had calmed. Nixon also stood foursquare against all of those features of American life that so upset Middle Americans and had given liberalism a bad name during the late 1960s and early 1970s—bussing, hippies, the coddling of criminals and welfare chiselers, antiwar activists, drug use, and sexual permissiveness. He also employed, it was later revealed, an undercover army of political hirelings, using their arsenal of "dirty tricks" to sabotage the Democratic campaign.

Figure 13.5   President Nixon confers with his top aides in the Oval Office. Standing in front of Nixon is Henry Kissinger, National Security Adviser. Sitting to Kissinger's right is Harry R. "Bob" Haldeman, Chief of Staff. To Kissinger's left is John Erlichman, Chief Adviser for Domestic Affairs.   *Source:* National Archives.

There was a potential chink in Nixon's political armor—corruption. McGovern called Nixon's administration "the most morally corrupt in history." He cited several seamy deals where corporations and trade associations had given the GOP large campaign donations in exchange for political favors. The most blatant case of corruption involved a break-in at Democratic Party national headquarters at Watergate Towers in Washington on June 17, 1972. Seven men, including two former White House aides and a member of CREEP, had been caught trying to photograph and steal documents and install electronic bugging equipment. It appeared that members of the Republican campaign organization and even members of the president's staff had engaged in espionage against their opponents. But news of the burglary produced little public concern at the time, and the prominent mass media exhibited little sustained interest in the bizarre event after a day or two of sensational headlines. Republicans denied all of McGovern's charges and dismissed the Watergate break-in. Even though he tried, McGovern failed to generate much voter interest in Watergate or in the corruption issue. Within less than a year, it would turn out that McGovern had touched only the tip of the corruption iceberg.

In November, Nixon scored his predicted landslide victory, carrying forty-nine of fifty states and rolling up an electoral vote of 521 to 17. He swept the South and even got a majority of the urban vote. The "silent majority," whom the president had courted—middle- and lower-middle-class whites, blue-collar voters, ethnics, Sunbelt inhabitants, and Westerners—all voted for him. The 1972 election was the first in which newly enfranchised eighteen-to-twenty-one-year-olds could vote. McGovern spent much of his time campaigning for their vote, considering the youth vote his secret weapon. Only one-third of them voted, and half of these opted for Nixon.

Despite Nixon's sweep, Democrats retained control of Congress, even gaining two seats in the Senate while losing twelve seats in the House. Such ticket-splitting suggested that millions of voters had cast their ballots for Nixon because they could not abide McGovern. Voter turnouts were lower than for any election since 1948. Clearly the political environment had become more conservative by 1972; however, except for the South, the results gave no indication that political realignment was occurring, or that a new Republican majority was emerging. American voters mainly repudiated a candidate who they saw as lacking in leadership qualities, and they chose to keep the incumbent, whom they perceived as a successful leader.

WATERGATE

President Nixon began his second term in January 1973, convinced that his landslide victory was a mandate for conservative policies. His new budget cut spending for welfare and education. He removed all remaining controls from the economy and impounded billions of dollars appropriated by Congress for purposes he opposed. Nixon also began reorganizing the federal government to make the bureaucracies more efficient and subject to his control. He believed that the great mass of Americans supported him, that the tides of history were flowing in the direction he wanted to take the country. Richard Nixon was riding high that spring of 1973, but then his administration began to self-destruct.

Watergate, latent since the break-in, suddenly erupted with a rash of disclosures and confessions that made it one of the most serious political scandals in American history. Watergate activities fell into two categories—those occurring before the June 17, 1972, break-in, and those following. The break-in turned out to be only one event in an extensive dirty-tricks campaign developed by CREEP and White House staffers to prevent news leaks, to spy on radicals, and to ensure Mr. Nixon's reelection. Investigators eventually unearthed an astonishing web of illegal activities and abuses of power that had begun early in Nixon's presidency. These activities included illegal wiretaps placed on government bureaucrats and journalists suspected of leaking embarrassing information about administration policies to the press, using the Internal Revenue Service to harass political opponents, raising millions of dollars in illegal campaign funds, and ordering a break-in of Daniel Ellsberg's psychiatrist's office.

The burglars caught inside of the Democratic Party national headquarters had previously tried, unsuccessfully, to break into McGovern's campaign headquarters. Other dirty tricksters circulated literature slandering Democratic candidates and disrupting their meetings. All dirty tricks were cleared with the president's top advisers. Nixon's defenders argued that many of the dirty tricks had been used by previous administrations and were part of the political process. That was true, up to a point, but the extent of Nixonian dirty tricks vastly exceeded any previous administration's efforts. More seriously, these practices flowed from a mind-set that was contemptuous of law and fair play, viewed politics as war, and saw political opponents as enemies to be destroyed.

Dirty tricks proved to be only the beginning. The Watergate burglars had been caught red-handed. CREEP officials and White House staffers who sent them in could have confessed and resigned. Such actions would have embarrassed the Nixon administration, but the president still would have been easily reelected. However, White House officials instead chose to cover up their and CREEP's complicity. They moved to destroy all evidentiary links between the burglary, themselves, and CREEP, and to concoct denials and alibis. An FBI investigation of the break-in and testimony before a grand jury were carefully limited so that they could not uncover any tracks leading to CREEP or the White House. The cover-up began immediately after White House officials learned that the burglars had been caught and President Nixon was directly involved in the cover-up activities from the start. He put White House Counsel John Dean in charge, and at times Nixon himself directed the cover-up activities. From the moment the cover-up efforts began, a process was set in motion that would strain the American constitutional system of government, cause many Americans great anguish, provide some of the most bizarre political theater in American history, and eventually destroy Nixon's presidency.

The cover-up orchestrated by Nixon, Dean, and other top White House aides succeeded, for a time. In September 1972, a federal grand jury indicted only the seven men directly involved in the burglary. The cover-up also held through the November election. It was still holding as the trial of the seven burglars began in March 1973. Meanwhile, it was business as usual for the president and his men, who believed that they had contained the incident and remained in the clear.

But too many people were involved in the cover-up. Too many connections among the burglars, CREEP, and the White House survived. Too many investigators were looking for answers to puzzling questions. The *Washington Post* had assigned two young reporters, Carl Bernstein and Bob Woodward, to find answers. They were able to trace some of the illegal campaign funds to CREEP. The Senate created a Select Committee on Presidential Campaign Activities, soon to be known as the Watergate Committee, chaired by Senator Sam J. Ervin, to investigate the burglary and other dirty tricks that may have influenced the outcome of the 1972 election. Federal prosecutors, continuing the federal grand jury probe, continuously investigated the burglary, other "dirty tricks," violations of campaign spending laws, and the cover-up. Watergate trial judge John J. Sirica, who did not believe the burglars when they told him that they alone had planned the break-in, pressured them to tell the truth.

The cover-up began to come unglued when one of the convicted burglars, James McCord, hoping to avoid a long prison term, wrote a letter to Judge Sirica implicating CREEP and prominent White House officials in the planning of the Watergate burglary. After McCord cracked, the whole cover-up edifice crumbled. The accused officials hired lawyers and promptly implicated other noteworthy officials in hopes of getting immunity from prosecution or a lighter sentence. Federal prosecutors often entered into plea bargaining arrangements with accused lesser officials to gather evidence against the ringleaders, including President Nixon.

In April, President Nixon was forced to fire several key advisers who were implicated in the cover-up—L. Patrick Gray III, acting director of the FBI, and John Erlichman, H.R. Haldeman, and John Mitchell. Nixon fired John Dean, the White House counselor, for telling the Watergate Committee that the president had been involved in the cover-up from the beginning. Nixon maintained publicly that he had only learned about the cover-up from Dean in March, and since then had done everything he could to cooperate with investigators, to get out the truth about Watergate, and to punish wrongdoers. Nixon also tried to discredit Dean's testimony by suggesting that he had directed the cover-up without the president's knowledge. To reinforce the image of a president concerned with getting to the bottom of the scandal, Nixon requested that Attorney General Elliot Richardson appoint a special prosecutor to investigate the cover-up. Richardson appointed a friend, Archibald Cox, a Harvard Law School professor, to head the investigation.

On May 17, 1973, public interest in the scandal picked up when the Senate Watergate Committee began holding televised hearings. The committee started with low-level hirelings, who did the dirty work and delivered illegal payments. Gradually they worked their way up the chain of command in CREEP and the Nixon White House. On the way up, the millions of viewers who watched the proceedings on a daily basis got a fascinating tour through the dark underside of American politics. They learned about political dirty tricks and the details of the cover-up. They learned about shredding documents, blackmail, bribery, forgery, perjury, and "laundered money." They also learned about the misuse of government agencies, including the FBI and the IRS. In addition, they learned about fund-raising techniques that violated election laws and often amounted to blackmail. The televised hearings made a folk hero out of the committee's chairman, seventy-nine-year-old Sam Irvin. Irvin's folksy manner and good humor cloaked a keen intellect and a fierce moral outrage over the steady stream of criminals and unethical politicians who appeared before his committee.

By mid-June, the key question was whether President Nixon had been involved in the Watergate cover-up. In the words of Senate Committee member Howard Baker, "What did the President know and when did he know it?" On June 25, John Dean appeared before the committee. For two days he read a lengthy 250-page statement describing the details of the cover-up: Nixon knew all about it, had approved it, and indeed had played a central role in it from the outset. Despite efforts by the White House to discredit Dean, the fired counselor came across as credible to members of the committee and to the large television audience. He displayed a phenomenal memory, he knew too much, and he had too many details at his command. The testimony of Nixon loyalists before the committee further damaged the president's position. Men like Haldeman, Erlichman, and Mitchell often gave evasive answers to direct questions.

But Dean's testimony, while sounding authentic, was legally inconclusive. It depended entirely on his ability to recall the events and conversations that he described before the committee. He had no corrobative evidence or documents to back it up. Only John Dean had implicated Nixon. The president had denied all charges and fired Dean. Dean himself was a suspect source, deeply involved in the cover-up. To a man, all of the Nixon loyalists insisted on the president's innocence and accused Dean of being the evil mastermind of the cover-up, trying to pin the blame on Nixon in order to save himself.

THE DECLINE AND FALL OF RICHARD NIXON

Then, on July 13, there came a sensational discovery. The chief counsel for the Watergate committee, Sam Dash, discovered that President Nixon had recorded White House conversations and phone calls on a secret tape recording system installed in the Oval Office in 1970. If the disputed conversations between Dean and Nixon were on tape, it would be possible to find out which one of them was telling the truth and if the president had been involved in the cover-up. From that date on, the Watergate drama focused on the tapes and the prosecution's efforts to get them from the president, who was determined to not surrender them.

Immediately, both the Watergate Committee and the special prosecutor subpoenaed the tapes of the Nixon–Dean conversations. Nixon rejected both subpoenas. Both investigators then asked Judge Sirica to force Nixon to honor their subpoenas. Nixon's attorneys defended his right to refuse to surrender the tapes on the grounds of "executive privilege." Judge Sirica rejected the argument and ordered Nixon to release the tapes. Nixon's attorneys appealed his ruling. The appeals court upheld the ruling, saying that, "The President is not above the law's commands."

While the battle for control of the tapes was raging, another White House scandal surfaced, unrelated to Watergate, involving Vice President Agnew. Justice Department investigators learned that Agnew, when governor of Maryland during the 1960s, had taken bribes from construction companies in return for favorable rulings on their bids. In August 1973, federal prosecutors charged Agnew with bribery, extortion, conspiracy, and income tax evasion. Nixon, upon examining some of the evidence against Agnew, and convinced of his guilt, pressured Agnew to resign. To get rid of him, Nixon offered him a deal: resign and plead "no contest" to a single count of tax evasion, and the other charges would be dropped. The other charges and evidence sustaining them would be published so people would know why Agnew resigned. Knowing that the federal prosecutors had hard evidence against him, Agnew accepted the offer, otherwise he knew that he would go to prison. He resigned, was fined $10,000, and was given three years' unsupervised probation. The evidence released to the public showed that the case against Agnew amounted to fifty indictable offenses.

Shortly after Agnew's forced resignation, President Nixon chose House minority leader Gerald R. Ford of Michigan to succeed the fallen vice president. Ford was a conservative, a Nixon loyalist, and popular with his colleagues. Further, there were no political or personal scandals in his life. This last factor was crucial, because many senators who voted to confirm Ford knew that if the tapes substantiated Dean's charges, Mr. Nixon was not only selecting a vice president, he was choosing his successor.

Meanwhile, Archibald Cox was pressing the Nixon administration for more tapes. The release of these tapes posed a mortal danger to the president, which he knew better than anyone. Nixon decided on a bold move to avoid surrendering the tapes: unless a compromise was arranged, permitting him to retain custody of the tapes, Nixon would dismiss Cox and prepare his own summaries of the tapes for Judge Sirica. Efforts to forge a compromise failed. On Saturday evening, October 20, Nixon ordered Attorney General Richardson, the man who had hired Cox, to fire him. Richardson refused and resigned. Nixon then directed Deputy Attorney General William Ruckelshaus to fire him. Ruckleshaus also refused, and

Nixon fired him. Finally, the third-ranking officer at the Justice Department, Robert Bork, dismissed Cox. Nixon also abolished the special prosecutor's office and ordered the FBI to seal all of the office files.

Journalists dubbed these actions taken by Nixon the "Saturday Night Massacre." The firings provoked a dramatic outpouring of public protest. During the next forty-eight hours, over a million letters, telegrams, and phone calls poured into the Senate and congressional offices, nearly all of them denouncing the "Saturday Night Massacre." Eight resolutions of impeachment were introduced into the House of Representatives. Nixon's approval rating in the polls dropped to 27 percent. The polls also revealed that most Americans suspected that the president was trying to hide his involvement in criminal activities. In addition to his Watergate activities, Nixon also came under attack for his questionable financial dealings involving his real estate holdings in California and Florida. The IRS also investigated him for tax evasion.

Nixon tried hard to repair the largely self-inflicted damage with a public relations campaign. He agreed to release the original tapes ordered by Judge Sirica. He replaced Cox with another special prosecutor, Leon Jaworski, a Houston corporation lawyer. Nixon met with congressmen and senators to reassure them of his innocence. He released a detailed financial statement to dispel doubts about his personal finances. And he went on a national speaking tour to reclaim his lost reputation. In a speech delivered to an audience of newspaper publishers, Nixon insisted that he was "not a crook." His efforts failed. Except for hard-core loyalists, the public, the media, and Congress remained skeptical of Nixon's efforts at reassurance. The president's lingering credibility was further undermined when White House officials admitted that two of the nine subpoenaed tapes, covering important conversations with Dean, did not exist. Even worse, an eighteen-and-a-half-minute segment of a crucial conversation between Nixon and Haldeman, which occurred three days after the break-in, had been mysteriously erased. The calls for Nixon's impeachment grew louder.

With the failure of his public relations campaign, Nixon became defiant, refusing Jaworski's requests for more tapes. On March 1, 1974, the grand jury indicted several key players in the cover-up, including Erlichman, Haldeman, and Mitchell. It would have indicted Nixon as well if Jaworski had not told them that a sitting president was not indictable under the U.S. Constitution. At about the same time the grand jury issued its indictments, the House Judiciary Committee began impeachment proceedings against the president. When its staff sought tapes and documents from the White House, Nixon refused its requests as well. Both Jaworski and the House Judiciary Committee then issued subpoenas to obtain the desired evidence and to overcome the president's "stonewalling" tactics.

Nixon was caught in a serious bind. He knew that his refusal to comply with subpoenas would not work; he also knew that conversations on several of the requested tapes would ruin him if they were released. He tried to escape the trap. He decided to release edited transcripts of the requested tapes. In a speech to the

American people, delivered on April 29, 1974, he made a final effort to retrieve his failing political reputation. He told his audience about his intent to release the transcripts. "These materials will tell all," he said. The next day, the transcripts were published.

The public response to Nixon's ploy was again emphatically negative. House Judiciary Committee members, comparing the edited versions with tapes already released, discovered many discrepancies. The content of the edited tapes was even more damning to the president's cause because of the impression they conveyed of Nixon's conduct of the presidency: crude, vulgar language; the use of racial and ethnic stereotypes; wheeling and dealing; and a complete lack of scruples or morality. Nixon failed to understand that the inner workings of his government could not stand public exposure. Republicans, as well as Democrats, were appalled by Nixon's way of governing. Senate Republican leader Hugh Scott called the transcripts, "deplorable, disgusting, shabby, and immoral." House Republican leader John Rhodes of Ohio called upon Nixon to resign. Both the House Judiciary Committee and Jaworski continued their demands for more tapes from the White House. Nixon refused all of their requests. Jaworski subpoenaed sixty-four additional tapes. Nixon tried to quash the subpoena, but Judge Sirica upheld it and ordered Nixon to release the tapes.

When the White House announced that it would appeal the ruling, Jaworski asked the Supreme Court to decide the matter. It agreed to do so. The question before the Court was clear: Who had the final authority to decide whether a president had to obey a subpoena, himself or the courts? In July, the Court heard arguments from both sides. Nixon's attorneys argued that the president had the right to decide; the only way the law could be applied to the president was through the impeachment process. Jaworski countered with the argument that if the president decides what the Constitution means, and "if he is wrong, who is there to tell him so?"

In the case of *The United States of America v. Richard M. Nixon*, the Supreme Court ruled unanimously that Nixon had to surrender the subpoenaed tapes to Judge Sirica. On the same day the Court announced its verdict, the House Judiciary Committee began voting on articles of impeachment against the president. Within a week, it voted to send three articles of impeachment to the full House. Article I accused the president of obstructing justice. Article II accused him of abusing power. And Article III accused him of refusing to honor the committee's subpoenas. Two other proposed impeachment articles were defeated. If the full House of Representatives adopted at least one of the three approved articles, Nixon would become the second president in U.S. history to be impeached. (Andrew Johnson had been the first, in 1868.) Nixon would then go on trial before the Senate, who would sit as a jury of 100 members and decide whether the evidence warranted conviction and removal from office.

The evidence that destroyed Nixon's presidency was a taped conversation between Nixon and Haldeman, held on July 23, 1972, six weeks after the Watergate burglars had been caught: Nixon can be heard ordering Haldeman to tell the CIA to fabricate a national security operation to keep the FBI from pursuing its investigation of the burglary. Here was the "smoking gun," proof of criminal acts, conspiring to obstruct justice and abuse of power. Both were felonies. The taped conversation also proved that Nixon had been lying about his Watergate involvement. He had known of the cover-up, and he had been involved with it from the beginning.

For several days, Nixon wavered between resigning and fighting the impeachment process. On August 7, Republican congressional leaders told Nixon that he faced certain impeachment, conviction, and removal from office. Some of the president's advisers worried about Nixon's mental health; they believed that he had been broken by the stresses of the long Watergate ordeal. Both Secretary of Defense James Schlesinger and White House Chief of Staff Alexander Haig informed all U.S. military commanders around the world to check with them before carrying out any unusual orders that might come from President Nixon. That evening, he decided to resign.

On the evening of August 8, he spoke to the American people for the last time. He told the nation that everything he had done he believed had been done with the best interests of the country in mind. He expressed regret for any harm that he might have done to others. He admitted to making "errors in judgment." But he could not bring himself to admit to breaking the law or to any wrongdoing. He claimed that he was resigning only because he had lost his political base and could no longer govern effectively. His resignation became effective at 12:00 noon, on August 9, 1974. At that point in time, Mr. Nixon was aboard the Spirit of 76, flying over Middle America en route to "exile" in southern California. At 12:00 noon, Gerald R. Ford took the oath of office as the thirty-eighth president of the United States. The new president began his short acceptance speech by saying "our long national nightmare is over."

Ford was right; Watergate had been a long national nightmare, its impact accentuated by extensive media coverage for over a year. Americans reacted differently to the Watergate scandals. For well-educated, well-informed citizens who understood that the integrity of the American system of governance was at issue, the events of Watergate were the stuff of high drama. For less well-informed people, the revelations of Watergate appeared confusing and perhaps much ado about not very much. For millions of Middle Americans who had voted for Nixon in 1972 in good faith, Watergate was a series of painful disillusionments. For young people especially, Watergate was traumatic. Many of these youngsters sought refuge in a pathetic cynicism, shrilly insisting that Watergate was what all politicians did; Nixon and his minions merely got nailed. And even to the bitter end, Nixon retained many defenders. These sturdy souls insisted that the only mistake Nixon made was to not burn the tapes. It was the tapes that ruined him because they made him vulnerable. They gave his enemies among the liberal political and media establishments the opportunity to destroy him. Many liberals rejoiced in his humiliation and his fall from power. For them, his disgrace was richly deserved and was poetic justice.

Thoughtful analysts searched out the multiple causes of the Watergate scandals. Some found the springs of Watergate within the personality and approach to politics of Richard M. Nixon. Relentlessly ambitious, intensely partisan, insecure, and perhaps even paranoid, Nixon was willing to use ruthless, even illegal, means to advance his career or to achieve his policy goals. Some analysts located Watergate in the institution of the presidency itself, in the rise of an "imperial presidency" since the 1940s. The presidency dominated the federal government, particularly in the realms of national security and foreign policy. All modern presidents wielded awesome powers and came to be regarded as special people, as a kind of royalty, above the restraints of the Constitution and the claims of morality. Other analysts saw the rise of a Cold War mentality as contributing to the Watergate syndrome. In a struggle for survival against ruthless and powerful adversaries, it is sometimes necessary to employ the same ruthless methods that the Communists used, and to employ them more extensively than they. It was necessary to enter an Orwellian world where undemocratic methods were required to preserve democracy. Still others saw the Watergate scandals deriving from an ethic that held that winning was so important that there were no limits on what could be done to achieve victory. This do-whatever-it-takes-to-win attitude also reflected the political ethics of the many nouveau-riche Sunbelt politicians who rode to power on Nixon's coattails. Nixon was the leader of this dangerous new class of "cowboy" politicians who did not play the game of politics by traditional establishmentarian rules, therefore, they had to be destroyed.

George McGovern was right when he labeled Nixon's administration the most corrupt in history. But the corruption of the Nixon White House, Agnew excepted, was not the commonplace corruption of crooks, thieves, bribers, grafters, chiselers, and influence peddlers who had infested past presidencies; it was a more dangerous kind of corruption that threatened the integrity of the American system of government; it threatened to replace a government based on constitutional law with the rule of a powerful leader who headed a staff of fanatical loyalists, whose highest calling was to do his bidding and vanquish his enemies. His enemies list included Democratic Party leaders, prominent journalists, bureaucrats, antiwar protesters, black militants, and hippies who posed threats to the leader's personal authority, which he equated with national security. Their threat would be contained by any means necessary, including wiretapping, surveillance, burglary, blackmail, political sabotage, and intimidation. President Nixon and his men for a time posed the most serious threat to constitutional governance, democratic political processes, and civil liberties in American history.

But they failed. Arbitrary power was thwarted. Eventually, due process ran its course. Three hundred seventy-eight officials, including three former cabinet members and several top-level White House aides, either pleaded guilty or were convicted of Watergate-related offenses. Thirty-one went to prison. Only President Ford's pardon probably kept Nixon from prison. The system met the challenge. A free press sounded alarm bells. Various investigations exposed the culprits. The Supreme Court firmly established the principle that no one, including the president, is above the law. Congress, spearheaded by the Senate Watergate Committee and the House Judiciary Committee, overrode efforts at executive usurpation. The forces of democracy united to drive a would-be tyrant and his lackeys from office.

Watergate left a mixed legacy. Paradoxically, it revealed both the terrible vulnerability and the underlying strength and resiliency of American political democracy. The abuses of power by the president and the president's men were finally checked, but it took an agonizingly long time for the mainstream media to get involved, for the public to become aroused, and for Congress to take action. Suppose the tapes had not been discovered? Or suppose that Nixon had ordered them destroyed? Watergate's outcome provides no guarantee that the system would be able to contain a subsequent president's abuse of power. Watergate, along with the Vietnam War, made Americans skeptical, even cynical, about politics and politicians. It reminded Americans of what the Founding Fathers knew to be the chief threat to republican government, that power can corrupt fallible leaders. Within the psyches of political leaders, the grubby demons of greed and a lust for power compete with desires to serve and to do good. And sometimes the demons prevail. Above all, Watergate reaffirmed the oldest lesson of our political heritage: Eternal vigilance is the price of liberty.

POSTMORTEM

It is exceedingly difficult to render a balanced judgment of Richard Nixon's presidency. This complex, divided man rendered both great service and did great harm to his nation. His was a long and distinguished public career. His presidency was perhaps the most significant since the great Franklin Roosevelt's. He was a bold and an innovative diplomatist with major achievements: the historic opening to China, stabilizing relations with the Soviet Union and reducing the threat of nuclear war, eventually ending the disastrous war in Southeast Asia, and placing U.S. foreign policy worldwide on a sound, realistic basis. He ensured that the United States would continue to occupy the central role in world affairs. In the process of bringing about these historic accomplishments, Nixon achieved the stature of world statesman. His accomplishments in domestic policy are less impressive, but he restored a measure of social peace, wrestled energetically with economic problems, and supported some ecological causes. He proposed innovative solutions to welfare problems and arrested the decline of local government.

But, in the ultimate crisis of his political career, he strained the American system of constitutional government that he had sworn to defend, damaged the presidency, harmed the Republican Party, destroyed his public career, and ruined his historical reputation. He was forced to resign in disgrace and fled into "exile" within his own country.

By the 1980s and 1990s, the American people's anger at Nixon had diminished. He achieved a partial rehabilitation, acquiring the stature of an elder statesman. Presidents occasionally sought his advice on matters of foreign policy. Nixon achieved respect and became rich by authoring several substantial books about politics and foreign policy. His memoir is the best and most revealing of any president's. Upon his death in June 1994, he was honored with a splendid state funeral in front of the magnificent Nixon Presidential Library, located in his hometown of Yorba Linda, California. Nearby stood the modest frame house in which he had been born in 1913. Everyone could see how high in the world the shy Quaker boy had risen. Thousands of citizens braved the driving rains to pay their final respects. All of the prominent people who spoke at Nixon's funeral praised his patriotic service to his nation, especially his foreign policy achievements. No one mentioned Watergate, or the fact that his presidency had ended in humiliation and disgrace.

IMPORTANT DATES

1968	Nixon is elected president
1969	Secret bombing of Cambodia begins
	Warren Burger is appointed Chief Justice of the Supreme Court
	Vietnamization is announced
1970	Cambodia is invaded
1971	Lieutenant William Calley is convicted of war crimes
	The *Pentagon Papers* are published
1972	Nixon visits China
	Nixon visits the Soviet Union and signs SALT 1
	The Watergate break-in occurs
	Nixon is reelected by a landslide
1973	American involvement in the Indochina War ends
	The existence of Nixon's secret White House taping system is discovered
	The U.S. Supreme Court decides *Roe v. Wade*
	The Yom Kippur war takes place
	The first energy crisis occurs
	Agnew resigns from the vice presidency
1974	Nixon resigns from the presidency
	Gerald Ford assumes the presidency
1975	South Vietnam falls
	The Khmer Rouge seize power in Cambodia

BIBLIOGRAPHY

James T. Patterson's, *Grand Expectations: The United States, 1945–1974* is a comprehensive survey of the first three decades of post–World War II U.S. history that includes virtually every major development that marked American life during those years. There have been several major studies of Richard Nixon undertaken in recent years. The best of these is *Nixon,* Stephen E. Ambrose's masterful three-volume political biography: Volume 1 is subtitled *The Education of a Politician, 1913–1962*; Volume 2 is *The Triumph of a Politician, 1962–1972*; and Volume 3 is *Ruin and Recovery*. Roger Morris, a scholar who also worked for the National Security Council staff under both Johnson and Nixon, has written a major study of Nixon covering the years of his life and his political career up until 1952, entitled *Richard Milhous Nixon: The Rise of an American Politician*. Another fine study is Garry Wills's *Nixon Agonistes*. The former president is himself the author of several books, the best of which is his autobiography *RN: The Memoirs of Richard Nixon,* the finest presidential memoir ever done. The Nixon administration's foreign policy is analyzed by Henry Brandon in *The Retreat of American Power*. A critical view can be found in Tad Szulc's *The Illusion of Peace: Foreign Policy in the Nixon Years*. Henry Kissinger, Nixon's brilliant foreign policy adviser, has analyzed their policies in *Years of Upheaval*. For Nixon's Vietnam policies, see the relevant chapters of George Donelson Moss's *Vietnam: An American Ordeal*. The best historical study of Watergate is Stanley I. Kutler's *The Wars of Watergate*. Kutler sees Watergate as a reflection of the essence of Nixon's political career and presidency. Kutler also has edited *Abuse of Power: The New Nixon Tapes*. These newly released tapes fill in some of the remaining gaps in the Watergate story. See also the two books by *Washington Post* reporters Carl Bernstein and Bob Woodward, *All the President's Men* and *The Final Days*. The best of many books written by the men involved in the scandal is Harry R. Haldeman's *The Ends of Power*. Theodore H. White, in *Breach of Faith: The Fall of Richard Nixon,* attempts to explain the causes of the Watergate scandal.

14

An Era of Limits

VIETNAM and Watergate ushered in a time of trouble for Americans. They experienced ineffective presidential leadership, partisan squabbling, continuing social divisions, severe economic dislocations, energy crises, and international disorders. All of these problems were compounded by a massive loss of faith in politics, especially among young people. They feared that the American system would not be able to maintain affluence at home, and they worried about declining American influence in the world. Americans experienced a crisis of confidence, fearful that their leaders and institutions could not find solutions to their many complex, often interrelated, problems.

The decade of the 1970s was characterized by a series of significant social and cultural transformations that confirmed both the pluralism and volatility of American life. These changes often paralleled underlying technological, economic, and demographic developments that rapidly altered the contours of American society and altered the ways most Americans lived and worked. New attitudes toward sex, family, and work altered the nature of many important institutions. Many members of two significant groups, African Americans and women, maintaining the momentum generated by the movements of the 1960s, made dramatic gains during the 1970s in education and income. But at the same time thousands of women and African Americans were taking advantage of new opportunities to achieve middle-class status, many other women and blacks remained locked into low-paying, low-status jobs, or slipped even further into the ranks of welfare dependency and poverty.

The most important development of the 1970s represented a historic shift in the direction of the American economy. The longest boom cycle in American history that had ignited during World War II and had continued, with occasional recessions, for thirty years, halted during the early 1970s. The seemingly perpetual prosperity, caused by a high growth rate, the creation of jobs, federal spending, innovative technology, and most of all, credit-fueled consumerism, stalled. It was replaced by "stagflation," which eroded purchasing power and lowered living standards for millions of American families. The apparent end of economic progress frustrated and bewildered Americans. Stagflation robbed them of their sense of control over their destinies. For the first time since the depression decade of the 1930s, millions of Americans regarded their economic future with fear and pessimism.

A FORD NOT A LINCOLN

The new president stood in dramatic contrast to his deposed predecessor. Gerald Ford was warm, open, and outgoing. A nation that was weary of war and political scandal appreciated his personal charm, modesty, and integrity as he reminded his fellow citizens that, "I am a Ford, not a Lincoln." Ford had represented Michigan's fifth district for thirteen consecutive terms until he was appointed vice president in 1973. He had risen through the ranks of the seniority system to become House Minority Leader in 1965. As president, Ford retained many of Nixon's advisers and vowed to continue his policies.

Sensing the malaise of the nation in the wake of war and Watergate, Ford made "binding up the nation's wounds" and restoring national confidence his top priorities. But a month after he took office, Ford granted former President Nixon a "full, free, and absolute" pardon for any crimes he may have committed while in office. He did this to spare the nation the divisive spectacle of putting a former president on trial. He insisted that there was no advance understanding between himself and Nixon. Whatever his intent, Ford's decision to pardon Nixon backfired, ruining his chances for receiving bipartisan support for his policies from the Democratic-controlled Congress. Despite his denials, many Americans suspected that Ford and Nixon had made a deal—Nixon had chosen Ford to replace Agnew, with the understanding that if Nixon resigned or was removed from office, Ford would pardon him. Further, it was patently unfair to send underlings to jail for their parts in Watergate while the leader whose directives they followed went free. Most Americans believed that if Nixon had broken the law, he should have to face trial like any other citizen. Ford's pardon of Nixon perpetuated the suspicions and resentments of Watergate that the new leader was trying to dispel, tied his presidency to that of his despised predecessor's, hurt his party in the 1974 elections, and may have cost him the 1976 presidential election.

Ford generated further controversy when he established an amnesty program for the thousands of young men who had violated draft laws or deserted from the military during the Vietnam era. According to its terms, if they agreed to perform public service for one to two years, their prison terms were waived or reduced. Hawks condemned the plan as being too lenient; Doves denounced it as punitive. Another of Ford's efforts to bind up national wounds had had the opposite effect of reopening them.

The president also provoked another uproar when he selected Nelson Rockefeller as his vice president. During Rockefeller's Senate confirmation hearings, it was learned that he had given some of his vast personal wealth to officials prominent in Ford's administration, including Secretary of State Henry Kissinger, formerly a Rockefeller aide. These gifts and loans gave the appearance that a rich man was trying to buy the vice presidency. Rockefeller's confirmation was delayed and the credibility of the new administration harmed.

The 1974 midterm elections took place amidst an atmosphere of continuing political controversy and public mistrust, much of which had been inadvertently perpetuated by Ford's own actions. The Democrats gained forty-three seats in the House and four seats in the Senate, increasing their margins to 291 to 144 in the House and to 61 to 38 in the Senate. More voters than ever before called themselves "Independents" and only 38 percent of those eligible to vote went to the polls.

Shortly after the midterm elections, a Senate committee investigating CIA operations discovered that over the years it had been involved in numerous assassinations or attempted murders of foreign leaders, including Fidel Castro. A commission headed by Vice President Rockefeller found that the CIA had routinely kept citizens under surveillance and had conducted drug experiments on unwitting victims. The CIA also had engaged in illegal domestic espionage and compiled files on dissenters. Other investigations revealed that the FBI also had engaged in a variety of lawless actions, including wiretapping, spying, burglary, blackmail, and sabotage. Former FBI director J. Edgar Hoover had conducted a personal vendetta against civil rights leader Martin Luther King, Jr. FBI agents spied on King and his associates, read his mail, tapped his phones, bugged his hotel rooms, and blackmailed him.

These discoveries of official lawlessness, most occurring during Nixon's presidency, confirmed that the CIA and the FBI, in their obsessive pursuit of internal security, had repeatedly violated the constitutional rights of American citizens. In response, President Ford issued new directives providing for greater congres-

Figure 14.1   President Gerald R. Ford. Gerald Rudolph Ford (1913–) was the 38th President of the U.S. (1974–1977). He is the only President to come into office under the 25th Amendment to the Constitution, assuming the office when Nixon resigned. *Source:* National Archives.

sional oversight of CIA activities and restricting its covert operations. The Justice Department issued new guidelines for the FBI. The new FBI director, Clarence Kelly, publicly apologized to the American people for the past sins of the Bureau and pledged that they would never recur.

ECONOMIC AND ENERGY WOES

While Americans learned more about official wrongdoing in Washington, their economy deteriorated. The inflation rate soared beyond 10 percent in 1974, spurred by wage hikes, increased consumer demand, budget deficits, and competition from the surging Japanese and western European economies. The Ford administration, resorting to traditional conservative economic policy, attacked inflation by slowing down the economy with tight money. Tight money brought the worst downturn since the Great Depression of the 1930s. Some traditional U.S. mass-production industries with inefficient methods of production, poor quality control, and high payroll costs struggled to compete with manufacturers in Europe and the Pacific Rim. American multinational corporations relocated their manufacturing facilities overseas to take advantage of lower costs, tax breaks, and cheap labor. The primary manufacturing industry of the U.S. economy, automobiles, lost a sizeable portion of its domestic market to Japanese and German imports. Unemployment climbed to 7 percent by year's end and reached 9 percent in 1975, the highest since before World War II.

In October 1973, an alarming new factor disrupted American economic life—the energy crisis. It appeared suddenly when the Organization of Oil Exporting Countries (OPEC) embargoed oil shipments to the United States. The oil cutoff was initiated by Saudi Arabia and other Arab members of OPEC to protest U.S. support of Israel in its recent war with Egypt and Syria and to force a settlement of the war favoring the Arabs. Americans experienced shortages of heating oil and power "brownouts." Impatient motorists formed long lines at the gas pumps.

The energy crisis had been building for years; the OPEC embargo triggered it. American postwar growth and prosperity had been founded on cheap energy. U.S. domestic oil production began declining in 1969, while demand continued to rise. By 1970, America, with only 6 percent of the world's population, used over one-third of the world's energy. To meet the ever-increasing demand for oil, U.S. oil companies bought more and more imported oil. Daily consumption of imported oil rose from 12 percent in 1968 to 36 percent by 1973. An increasing proportion of imported oil came from OPEC nations, and two-thirds of OPEC oil came from the Middle East. U.S. oil companies became the mechanisms for maintaining the OPEC cartel, since they refined the oil for U.S. markets. When OPEC shut off oil in October 1973, these companies made huge profits from the rapid rise in oil prices.

The OPEC embargo was short-lived. Arab countries removed it after a few months, and oil supplies returned to normal. But gasoline prices rose from 30 cents to 70 cents a gallon during that period, and they stayed there. Much higher energy prices became a permanent fact of U.S. economic life. Higher oil prices sent a large inflationary jolt coursing through all facets of the American economy, because oil had seeped into the fabric of American life. Oil heated homes; it was synthesized into fibers and plastics; farmers used it for fertilizer, pesticides, and fuel; and it was crucial to all forms of transportation. Rising energy prices struck hardest at the older industrial centers of the Northeast and the Great Lakes region, because they had to import most of their energy. Factories constructed during the days of cheap energy proved to be wasteful and inefficient. Cutbacks in federal spending fell hardest on cities in these regions, given their shrinking tax bases, declining industries, and expensive social services.

Before he was forced to resign, Nixon had battled the energy crisis. He created the Federal Energy Office to formulate a national energy policy and to promote conservation. He proposed a plan called "Project Independence" to make America energy-independent by 1980. The plan called for increasing domestic oil production by tapping Alaskan oil fields and accelerating offshore drilling; producing more natural gas, coal, and nuclear energy, extracting oil from shale deposits; and developing renewable energy sources. Project Independence made little progress. With the lifting of the embargo and the return of normal supplies of oil, most people forgot about the energy crisis, although motorists complained about the high price of gasoline. As Ford took office, America continued to import one-third of its daily oil requirements.

Ford tried to continue Nixon's energy program, but he encountered much opposition. Environmentalists opposed many of its features. Antinuclear groups opposed building additional nuclear power plants. Ford tried to deregulate domestic oil and natural gas prices, only to be blocked by the Democratic majority in Congress, who believed that deregulation would hurt low-income families and aggravate inflation. Congress enacted legislation in 1975, giving the president standby authority to ration gasoline, to create a strategic petroleum reserve, and to set

Figure 14.2   Energy Crisis U.S.A. . . . Motorists line up to get gas at a service station in Los Angeles.   *Source:* National Archives.

mandatory fuel economy standards for new cars. Three years later, the United States imported 40 percent of its daily oil requirements.

Partisan conflicts between the Republican president and the Democratic-controlled Congress hampered government effectiveness during Ford's tenure. He vetoed sixty-six bills enacted by Congress, including federal aid for education, a heath care measure, a housing measure, and a bill to control strip mining. During Ford's presidency, Congress enacted a few important measures; among them was the extension of the Voting Rights Act of 1965 and an increase in Social Security benefits.

FORD, KISSINGER, AND THE WORLD

Henry Kissinger, whom Ford had inherited from former President Nixon, doubled as secretary of state and head of the National Security Council. He played a major part in shaping foreign policy. As a political realist, Kissinger understood that U.S. economic and military power had suffered a relative decline in the world since the late 1960s, and that America could no longer expect to dominate its allies in Europe, Latin America, and the Middle East. Kissinger had a major part in implementing U.S. Middle Eastern policy following a fourth Arab–Israeli war that began on October 6, 1973. It started when Syria and Egypt, re-equipped with massive Soviet aid, suddenly attacked Israel, catching the Israelis off guard because they were observing Yom Kippur, the holiest Jewish holiday. Both sides sustained heavy losses, but America provided Israel with military support, while the Soviets replenished Arab armies.

The United Nations tried to work out a cease-fire formula. Before it became effective, Israeli armies crossed the Suez, enveloped large numbers of Egyptian troops, and placed troops on Egyptian soil. With Egypt threatened, its leader, Anwar Sadat, invited both the United States and the Soviet Union to send troops to police a cease-fire. The Soviets accepted Sadat's proposal, but Washington, which did not want Soviet troops in the Middle East, refused it. The Soviets then announced their intention to send troops unilaterally. These actions brought the two superpowers to a point of direct confrontation. As the Soviets prepared to airlift troops to Egypt, the United States placed its armed forces on worldwide alert. These actions provoked the most dangerous U.S.–USSR conflict since the Cuban missile crisis.

The UN, backed by both the United States and the Soviet Union, defused the tense situation by creating a peacekeeping force, excluding both American and Soviet forces. Kissinger, shuttling between Cairo and Jerusalem, persuaded the Egyptians and Israelis to accept a cease-fire. The cease-fire was the first of a series of Middle Eastern agreements facilitated by Kissinger's "shuttle diplomacy." The Suez Canal was reopened. The Arabs lifted their oil embargo. Egypt and Syria resumed diplomatic relations with the United States. Kissinger capped his Middle Eastern efforts in 1975 by arranging an important new Sinai agreement between

Egypt and Israel. According to its terms, UN peacekeeping forces would remain, and an early warning system would be set up in the Sinai to prevent future surprise attacks by either side. These Sinai accords made possible the subsequent achievement of the Camp David agreements.

Ford and Kissinger tried to improve relations with China and the Soviet Union, without much success. Ford visited China in 1975, but American support of Taiwan prevented him from forging closer ties with Beijing. At the time, China's leadership was changing. Rival factions of pragmatists and radicals vied for power as China's aged revolutionary leaders, Jou En-lai and Mao Zedong, passed from the scene. Any new diplomatic initiatives had to wait until a new leadership established control. Efforts to extend détente and to forge a second SALT agreement with the Soviets failed. Negotiators became bogged down in technical details as advances in nuclear weapon technologies outstripped efforts to impose political controls. Another effort to extend détente brought together Ford and Soviet leader Leonid Brezhnev with European leaders at Helsinki in August 1975. Both sides agreed to recognize the political boundaries dividing eastern and western Europe since the end of World War II. For the first time, the United States recognized the legitimacy of East Germany. For his part, Brezhnev agreed to ease restrictions of the right of Soviet Jews to emigrate. Kissinger's overtures to the Communists outraged conservatives within the Republican Party, such as presidential hopeful Ronald Reagan, who denounced both détente and Kissinger for trafficking with the Reds.

The Vietnam War ended in April 1975, when North Vietnamese forces overran the South and captured Saigon, two years after all U.S. forces had been with-

Figure 14.3   An American soldier assisting a family fleeing Vietnam as the Communists take over on April 30, 1975. *Source:* U.S. Army Photograph.

drawn. President Ford tried to help the dying South Vietnamese regime, but Congress refused to enact his request for additional aid. About a month after the Communist conquest, Khmer Rouge forces in Cambodia seized an American merchant ship, the *Mayaguez,* cruising near the Cambodian coast. Ford sent in a detachment of 350 U.S. Marines, who rescued the ship and crew. Most Americans applauded the president's show of force at a time when Americans were feeling pushed around in Southeast Asia. During the final years of the U.S. involvement in Southeast Asia, Congress sought a greater role in the conduct of foreign policy and sought to reduce the power of the president to make war. The War Powers Act, passed over president Nixon's veto in 1973, ordered the president to consult with Congress before sending U.S. forces into war.

THE ELECTION OF 1976

As the 1976 election approached, Ford appeared to be politically vulnerable. Having achieved the office of president only through the grace of Nixon's appointment, Ford had proven to be an ineffective caretaker during his two years of office. He faced a powerful challenge from within Republican ranks by Ronald Reagan, the leader of a growing conservative movement. A large field of Democratic contenders sought their party's nomination. Candidates included Senators Henry Jackson and Frank Church, Governors George Wallace and Jerry Brown, and Morris Udall, an Arizona congressman. The surprise of the 1976 Democratic race proved to be the sudden emergence of James Earl Carter, Jr., who called himself "Jimmy." Carter beat them all to capture the Democratic nomination. He was unknown outside of his native Georgia, where he had served one term as governor.

Carter won a series of primary victories, in both the North and the South. His major pitch was the need for a leader untainted by the corruptions of Washington, an outsider who could restore integrity to government. People responded positively to the man and to his message. When the Democratic Convention opened in New York, Carter had more than enough votes to ensure a first-ballot nomination. He chose a Midwestern liberal for his running mate, Senator Walter Mondale, from Minnesota, and they ran on a platform attacking Ford's "government by veto" and Kissinger's "manipulative" foreign policy. Carter's capturing of the Democratic Party nomination in 1976 was one of the most remarkable achievements in modern American political history. His victory could only have happened within the context of post–Vietnam, post–Watergate massive disillusionment with politics as usual in this country.

Ford, meanwhile, was locked in a fierce struggle for the Republican nomination with Ronald Reagan, leader of the resurgent Republic Right. Ford adopted a centrist stance, projecting an image of a moderate leader healing the nation's wounds, promoting economic recovery, and keeping the nation at peace. His strategy worked initially. He beat Reagan decisively in the early primaries. But when the Sunbelt primaries came up in the spring, Reagan ran off a string of victories, surging ahead of Ford in the delegate count. Ford rallied with victories in several Northern industrial states. Reagan countered with a big win in California. When the Republican Convention assembled in Kansas City, the two candidates were so close that the winner would be the one who captured a majority of the few uncommitted delegates. Ford managed to win a close first-ballot nomination, but the Reaganites forced Ford to move to the Right in order to survive, and they influenced the drafting of a conservative platform. Ford chose a sharp-tongued conservative, Kansas Senator Robert Dole, to replace Rockefeller, who chose not to run. Although Reagan endorsed Ford, many of his supporters did not. Ford led a divided party into battle against a Democratic Party united behind the candidacy of Jimmy Carter.

The presidential campaign turned out to be rather dull and unenlightening. Neither man made much impact on a wary electorate. Neither candidate stood out in a series of three televised debates. Carter appeared especially fuzzy on the issues. Ford ran on his record, which was unimpressive. Carter conducted a vaguely liberal, populistic, and moralistic campaign. He promised to tame Washington's bureaucracy and he pledged to craft a government that was "as good and honest as are the American people."

When the contest started, the polls gave Carter a large early lead. Within six weeks, his waffling and Ford's attacks had eliminated it. On election eve, pollsters labeled it too close to call. Carter managed to score a narrow victory, receiving 41 million votes to Ford's 39 million. His winning margin in the electoral vote was 297 to 241. Carter carried the South, several border states, and some Northern industrial states. He lost most of the Midwest and carried no state west of the Mississippi River. Black votes provided his margin of victory in the South. He also did well among traditional Democratic voters—labor, urban, Jewish, liberals, and intellectuals. Carter's party ran much better than he did. Democrats retained their large majorities in both houses of Congress.

Carter's victory suggested that a majority of voters shared his revulsion over abuses of power by Washington-based professional politicians. They were willing to entrust the reins of government to an inexperienced outsider from a Southern village. Given a choice between "fear of the known and fear of the unknown," the citizenry opted for a fresh, new face who promised to tell the truth.

Carter's winning the Democratic nomination before the convention signaled an important new political reality; most states were now holding presidential primaries. The primary process opened up the nominating process to the mass of voters and reduced the importance of political parties. It also lengthened the campaigns, greatly increased their costs, and enhanced the role of television. Ford and Carter both accepted $22 million of federal funds to finance their fall campaigns, and both renounced private fund-raising. They were the first presidential candidates to use new federal spending laws that were enacted following the Watergate disclosures of fund-raising abuses.

PRESIDENT "JIMMY"

The thirty-ninth president grew up on a farm in the Southwest Georgia village of Plains. His first career choice was the U.S. Navy. He graduated from the U.S. Naval Academy in 1946 and spent seven years in the nuclear submarine program. When his father died in 1953, Carter gave up his naval career and returned to Plains to take over the family business. Carter, elected governor of Georgia in 1970, proved to be an able administrator and a moderate reformer. His chief accomplishment was to announce the end of racial discrimination in Georgia. He brought about a marked increase in the number of black state employees.

One of Carter's most valuable political assets proved to be his wife Rosalyn, who was attractive, strong, and politically shrewd. She made a dynamic First Lady, going well beyond the usual roles of hostess, ornament, and goodwill ambassador. She was her husband's principal adviser on many issues, a member of his inner circle. Not since Eleanor Roosevelt had a First Lady played such an important political role or achieved such power in her own right.

MR. CARTER GOES TO WASHINGTON

Carter came to office knowing that millions of Americans were still deeply suspicious of the political system. He strove from the outset to "deimperialize" the White House and to restore popular faith in national politics. He also brought many previously excluded groups into the higher levels of the federal government. Out of his 1,195 full-time federal appointments, 12 percent were women, 12 percent were black, and 4 percent were Hispanic, far more coming from these historically disadvantaged backgrounds than any previous president's appointees. But Carter's populistic campaign style contradicted his managerial and technocratic approach to governing. Carter was the most conservative Democratic president since Grover Cleveland. His top priority became slashing the size and the cost of government.

Carter's policies also reflected the conservative mood that increasingly gripped the country by the late 1970s. More and more Americans repudiated 1960s-style liberalism, which they associated with foreign policy failures, inflationary domestic policies, oversized government, high taxes, and a generalized permissiveness and moral decay. The antigovernment, antispending inclinations of voters were expressed dramatically in California's 1978 election. An elderly real estate lobbyist, Howard Jarvis, led a successful taxpayer's revolt that slashed property taxes by two-thirds. A 1978 poll revealed that conservatives outnumbered liberals by a ratio of more than two to one.

When Carter took office, the inflation rate stood at 6 percent and the unemployment rate at 8 percent. Carter had gotten political mileage during his campaign against Ford by attacking the incumbent's failure to solve these serious economic problems, labeling the combined total of inflation and unemployment rates the "misery index." He called the "misery index" of 14 intolerable and promised to reduce it drastically. Carter first tried stimulating the economy to reduce unemployment by implementing Keynesian "pump priming" programs. Congress enacted a $6 billion local public works bill, an $8 billion public service jobs bill, tax cuts, and an increase in the minimum wage. Unemployment declined to 6 percent in two years.

But the inflation rate rose rapidly, back to 7 percent in 1977 and 10 percent in 1978. It zoomed to 12 percent in 1979 and 13 percent in 1980, the worst two years since World War I. Confronted with runaway inflation, Carter radically shifted his economic focus. He concentrated on attacking inflation, adopting fiscal restraints similar to Ford's. In 1979, Carter appointed Paul Volcker as chairman of the Federal Reserve Board. Volcker immediately imposed severe monetary restrictions on the economy that drove interest rates to historic highs, pulling the economy into a recession without immediately curbing inflation. The ensuing "stagflation" of 1979 and 1980 was far worse than it had ever been under either Nixon or Ford. In 1980, the "misery index" had reached 21, a figure that Carter's Republican opponent, Ronald Reagan, would use against him with devastating effectiveness.

Declining productivity signaled another kind of economic rot that beset Americans. Productivity had increased an average of 3 percent a year between 1945 and 1965. During the 1970s, productivity only rose at an annual rate of 1 percent. As late as 1968, the American economy had been the most productive in the world; by 1980, it had slipped to twentieth place. Energy problems added to America's

Figure 14.4   Inflation was the most serious economic problem afflicting the American people during the 1970s. Note that the cost of living, as measured by the consumer price index, nearly doubled between 1967 and 1979.   *Source:* George D. Moss, *Moving On,* p. 282.

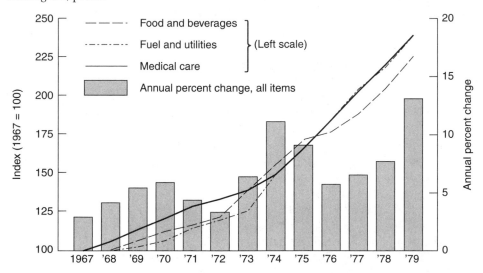

economic difficulties. Despite the 1973 energy crisis, Americans continued to use more oil and to import a high proportion of their daily requirements throughout the 1970s. Domestic oil production continued to decline. In April 1977, Carter developed a comprehensive energy plan that he called "the moral equivalent of war (MEOW)." Congress rejected the plan, and MEOW quickly faded from view, but not before humorists had a field day with Carter's acronym.

In 1979, a second oil crisis hit the deteriorating American economy when the new Islamic revolutionary government of Iran cut off its oil exports after toppling the Shah. Gasoline shortages again forced angry motorists to line up at the pumps. Carter responded to this second crisis by implementing a phased deregulation of domestic oil prices to spur production. Oil deregulation immediately raised gasoline prices by 50 percent (from 70 cents to over $1 a gallon) and increased oil company profits, some of which the government siphoned off as excise taxes.

President Carter, baffled by the failures of Americans to solve their serious economic and energy problems, invited 130 leaders from all walks of life to Camp David for ten days of meetings to determine what was wrong with the nation. From these intensive discussions, the president concluded that the nation was facing "a crisis of the spirit." In what proved to be his finest speech, he told Americans that they faced a crisis of confidence that posed a fundamental threat to American democracy—they had lost faith in themselves and in their institutions; they had lost faith in the future. Where was the old American optimism and "can-do" spirit?

Critics of the Carter administration suggested that the nation faced a different problem than a loss of national spirit—the failure of presidential leadership. Carter never firmly grasped the reins of government, never asserted control over executive bureaucracies, and never established an effective liaison with Congress. He failed to develop a consistent approach to public policy. He mastered the details of problems, but he could never project a broad national vision or a sense of direction. His presidency was a perpetually floundering, rudderless government that ultimately lost the trust and respect of many citizens. He never learned to

Figure 14.5   Jimmy Carter. James (Jimmy) Earl Carter Jr. (1924–) was the 39th President of the U.S. (1977–1981). *Source:* National Archives.

communicate effectively with the press or with the American people. His speaking style often took on a whiny quality. At the time he made his "malaise" speech, his approval rating in the polls stood at 26 percent. Liberal journalist Tom Wicker called Carter's administration the greatest failure since Herbert Hoover's performance during the Great Depression.

CARTER AND THE WORLD

Carter came to office with almost no background in foreign affairs. His only previous international experience came from his having served on the Trilateral Commission, an association of businessmen, bankers, politicians, and intellectuals gathered from the United States, Japan, and European countries committed to strengthening economic ties among major free-world nations. Carter recruited his two top foreign policy advisers from the commission, his Secretary of State, Cyrus Vance, a Wall Street lawyer, and his National Security Adviser, Zbigniew Brzezinski, a professor of international relations at Columbia University.

Carter announced at the outset of his administration that he would make human rights the distinctive theme of his foreign policy. The new president's emphasis on human rights expressed both his streak of Wilsonian idealism and his desire to move beyond the realm of Nixon–Kissinger realism. He wanted to reclaim the ideological high ground in the ongoing Cold War competition with the Soviet Union. While human rights espoused traditional American ideals, it proved in practice to be a difficult slogan to implement.

Carter's greatest diplomatic triumph occurred in the Middle East, where he played a major role in achieving peace between Egypt and Israel. He built upon a foundation laid by Kissinger's shuttle diplomacy and the extraordinary actions taken by Egyptian leader Anwar Sadat. Sadat, perceiving that the Egyptians could never dislodge the Israelis from the Sinai by force, offered them peace in exchange for the return of Egyptian lands. Sadat electrified the world when he went to Jerusalem in the fall of 1977. He told Israelis that any permanent agreement between Egypt and Israel must include Israeli withdrawal from the West Bank and the Golan Heights, a homeland for Palestinian Arabs, and recognition of the Palestine Liberation Organization (PLO) as their government.

Israeli Prime Minister Menachem Begin was willing to strike a bargain with Egypt on the Sinai, but he balked at the Palestinian issues. Negotiations between the two countries reached an impasse after six months. Carter then invited both leaders to Camp David for conferences. After two weeks of intense negotiations in which Carter was fully engaged, they achieved a framework of peace for the Middle East. Egypt agreed to a separate peace with Israel, and the Israelis agreed to return the Sinai region to Egypt. The Palestine issue was left vague. Both sides agreed to "self-governing" authority for the people inhabiting the West Bank, with their specific political status to be worked out in subsequent negotiations. Sadat and Begin signed the historic peace agreement, which ended more than thirty years of war between their countries, on March 26, 1979, in Washington. Egypt and Israel then proceeded to normalize their relations.

President Carter hoped that these Camp David accords would launch a new era of peace in the Middle East, but insurmountable obstacles persisted. No other Arab nation followed Egypt's lead. Negotiations on the Palestine question went nowhere. Israel refused to recognize the PLO or any other Palestinian political organization, and these groups all refused to recognize the results of any negotiations excluding them. The Palestine issue was further complicated by the outbreak of civil war in Lebanon between Muslim and Christian factions over PLO camps in southern Lebanon.

Carter also had some diplomatic successes in Latin America. In April 1978, he persuaded the Senate to ratify two treaties turning the Panama Canal over to Panama by 2000. These treaties permitted the gradual phasing out of the last vestiges of U.S. colonialism in Central America. The United States reserved the right to intervene to keep the canal open and also retained priority of passage in the event of a foreign crisis. The treaties protected U.S. interests and removed a source of resentment for Panamanians and other Central American nationalists.

Elsewhere in Latin America, Carter changed U.S. policies. He withdrew support for a tyrannical rightist dictatorship in Chile that Ford and Kissinger had

Figure 14.6   The signing of the Camp David Accords. . . . President Carter looks on as Israeli Prime Minister Menachem Begin (to Carter's left) and Egyptian President Anwar Sadat (to Carter's right) sign the historic pact on March 26, 1979 at a formal ceremony held on the north Lawn of the White House.   *Source:* National Archives.

backed. In February 1978, he cut off military and economic aid to the Nicaraguan dictator, Anastasio Somoza. Deprived of aid, Somoza was soon overthrown by revolutionaries who called themselves Sandinistas. The United States promptly extended a $75 million aid package to the new government. In El Salvador, Marxist guerrillas, assisted by the Sandinistas, began a civil war against the government. The rightist government fought back brutally. The United States suspended aid to the Salvadoran government following the murder of three American nuns by government troops.

In the Far East, Carter completed the process Nixon had begun with his historic opening to China in 1972. The two nations established normal relations with an exchange of ambassadors in 1979. Carter wanted to use good relations with China as a lever to pry cooperation out of the Soviet Union. American businessmen eagerly anticipated tapping into China's consumer economy of 1 billion people.

U.S. relations with black Africa improved during Carter's tenure. He appointed Andrew Young, a black minister and former civil rights activist, as the U.S. ambassador to the UN. President Carter made a successful trip to Liberia and Nigeria in 1978. Good relations with Nigeria were especially important, as it was the richest, most populous black African nation and the second largest foreign supplier of oil to the United States.

THE DECLINE OF DÉTENTE

Détente had already begun to decline under Ford and Kissinger, and it continued to decline during Carter's presidency. Carter's diplomatic efforts toward the Soviet Union were hindered by his inexperience. Carter sent what he intended to be a friendly signal to the Soviets: he announced his intention to withdraw U.S. troops from Korea. Far from responding in kind, the Soviets took Carter's friendly words and gestures as signs of weakness. They responded to these conciliatory acts by becoming more aggressive. Escalating their arms buildup, they extended their influence in Africa, using Cuban soldiers as proxies, and they increased their military forces stationed in Cuba. The president had hoped to achieve quick ratification of SALT II, but he angered the Soviet leaders by proposing additional cuts in the two nations' strategic arsenals. His granting of full diplomatic recognition to China further annoyed the Soviets. It took years before SALT II negotiators could complete their work. The treaty limited both sides to 2,400 nuclear launchers and 1,320 MIRVs, and it was intended to further stabilize the arms race.

SALT II also encountered strong opposition within the Senate. The chief senatorial critic was Henry "Scoop" Jackson, who insisted that the proposed agreement allowed the Soviets to retain strategic superiority in several weapons categories. Other critics of SALT II were uncomfortable with the fact that the treaty acknowledged that the Soviets had achieved nuclear parity with the United States, a reality that they interpreted as symbolizing the relative decline of U.S. strategic power. Some liberal senators were unhappy with SALT II because it did not eliminate key weapons systems such as the huge Soviet land-based ICBMs and the new American cruise missiles. Carter himself lost faith in SALT II and did not press the Senate for ratification. Instead, he persuaded NATO allies to agree to install new Pershing II missiles in western Europe to counter the SS-20 intermediate-range missiles that the Soviets were installing in eastern Europe. Installing these weapons in Europe represented a major escalation of the nuclear arms race.

While the Senate was debating the merits of SALT II, in December 1979, 85,000 Soviet troops invaded Afghanistan to suppress a Muslim rebellion against a faltering Marxist regime. Alarmed, President Carter called the Soviet invasion "the most serious threat to world peace since the Second World War." Carter canceled grain shipments to the USSR, suspended high technology sales to the Soviets, and ordered U.S. athletes to boycott the Olympics that were to be held in Moscow the following summer. He also increased military spending and removed restrictions on CIA covert operations. He withdrew SALT II from Senate consideration and proclaimed the Carter Doctrine for Southwest Asia. Calling the Persian Gulf a vital U.S. interest, he declared that the United States would repel "by any means necessary" an attack in that region by outside forces. Carter's hard line toward Moscow reversed U.S. policies toward the Soviet Union that went back to the Kennedy years. Ironically, the man who began his presidency espousing kind words for the Soviets killed détente and resuscitated the Cold War.

DEBACLE IN IRAN

It was in the Persian Gulf region that the United States suffered a major foreign policy disaster that humiliated President Carter and contributed to his political downfall. Iran was America's major ally in the Persian Gulf area. It played a key role in containing the Soviet Union. It was a major supplier of top-grade oil, and Iranians annually purchased billions of dollars worth of American arms. The Shah, whom a CIA covert operation had helped restore to power in 1953, permitted the intelligence agency to station electronic surveillance equipment along Iran's border with the Soviet Union. American oil companies supplied the state-owned Iranian oil industry with equipment and technicians; they also shared in its profits. Iran was a vital U.S. interest, much more important than Korea or Vietnam had ever been.

Iran in the late 1970s seethed with anti-Shah and anti-American fervor. Only the Shah and a ruling elite were genuinely pro-American. Carter, in contradiction of his human rights policy and unaware of the tensions in Iran, traveled to Iran in late 1977 to pay tribute to the Shah. At a state banquet held in his honor, President Carter toasted the Shah for "the admiration and love your people give to you." He called Iran "an island of stability in one of the most troubled areas of the world." The CIA station chief in Teheran issued a report in 1978, stating that Iran was not even near a revolutionary situation.

The assault on the Shah was led by Islamic clergy who were intent on replacing Iran's modern, Westernized state with an Islamic republic. Their leader was

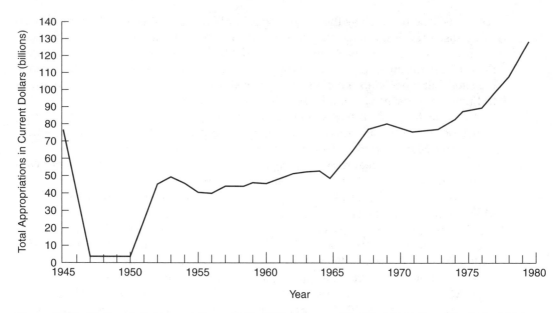

Figure 14.7   National defense outlays, 1945–1980.   *Source: Historical Statistics of the United States. Colonial Times to 1970,* and *Statistical Abstract of the United States,* 1980.

Ayatollah Ruholla Khomeini. From his exile in France in 1978, Khomeini ordered his legions to demonstrate, to disrupt the economy, to do anything to create chaos in order to force the Shah to abdicate. Carter initially dismissed Khomeini's revolution, assuming that the Shah would suppress it. Carter watched in disbelief as Iran's oil production stopped and its economy ground to a halt. The Iranian army, forbidden by the Shah to fire upon the rioters for fear it would ruin the chances of his son succeeding him, was demoralized. On January 16, 1979, the Shah fled his country. Khomeini returned to Iran to a frenzied hero's welcome from revolutionary crowds. One of the most bizarre events of modern times had occurred; a virtually unarmed people led by clergymen had overthrown one of the world's most powerful rulers.

U.S. leaders, thinking in customary Cold War terms, did not know how to deal with a man who denounced both the United States and the Soviet Union with equal vehemence. Fearing Soviet intrusion into Iran and the loss of a crucial source of Western oil, Carter tried to establish normal relations with the new Iranian government, which proved to be impossible. Khomeini, who called the United States the "Great Satan," refused all American overtures.

Meanwhile, President Carter allowed the Shah, who was suffering from terminal cancer, to enter the United States for medical treatment. In retaliation, on November 4, 1979, Iranian militants overran the U.S. embassy in Teheran and took fifty-three Americans hostage. Carter retaliated by freezing all Iranian assets in the United States, suspending arms sales, and clamping a boycott on all U.S. trade with Iran.

Carter made the return of the hostages his number one priority, which it remained for the rest of his presidency. The hostage crisis dominated U.S. foreign policy for the next fourteen months. It also dominated American television screens. Each night, when the most popular television news program, the *CBS Evening News with Walter Cronkite,* would sign off, the viewing public would be reminded of just how many days of captivity the hostages had endured. The popular late-night news show *Nightline* originated as a series of special reports on the hostage crisis. For months, American officials negotiated futilely for release of the hostages with a series of Iranian governments, but no Iranian leader could acquire the necessary stable authority to make a deal with the Americans.

Six months after the hostages were taken, Carter severed diplomatic relations with Iran and authorized a military operation to attempt a rescue. On the night of April 24, 1980, three helicopters transporting the rescue team suffered mechanical failures. At a staging area in the Iranian desert, a fourth chopper crashed into a C-130 transport plane, killing eight soldiers and severely burning five more. For days afterwards, the news media bombarded Americans with pictures of the wreckage and charred American corpses. Each photo and television image reinforced the sense that America was not what it used to be. The failed rescue attempt also symbolized the impotence of the United States and its inability to protect its citizens against terrorism.

Prospects for resolving the hostage crisis improved in late 1980. The ailing Shah died in July. On September 22, Iraq suddenly invaded Iran and provoked a war between the two nations. In October, Carter offered to release frozen Iranian assets and to resume normal relations and trade with Iran in exchange for release of the hostages. On November 4, Ronald Reagan was elected president. Khomeini was responsive to the U.S. offer. He needed money for the war with Iraq, and he also feared that the new president might take stronger action. On January 21, 1981, Carter's last day in office, Iran agreed to release the hostages in exchange for the return of $8 billion of Iranian assets. The hostages came home 444 days after their capture.

THE ELECTION OF 1980

As the 1980 election approached, Carter was clearly in deep political trouble. His "misery index," the sum of the rate of inflation plus the unemployment rate, was much higher than when he had run against Ford in 1976. And, there was the daily embarrassment of the hostages. Carter also had to fight off a primary challenge from Senator Edward "Ted" Kennedy. Kennedy's old-fashioned liberal philosophy was out of sync with the times and Carter easily deflected his challenge. Carter was renominated on the first ballot.

The Republicans entered the 1980 presidential race brimming with confidence. Many candidates entered the race for the Republican nomination, but from the outset, the clear choice of most of the party faithful was the old right-wing war horse Ronald Reagan. Of the others, only George Bush showed any strength in the primaries. Reaganites controlled the Republican Convention and pushed through a conservative platform, calling for deep tax cuts, a balanced budget, large increases in defense spending, constitutional amendments banning abortions and restoring prayer in public schools, and opposition to the Equal Rights Amendment. Reagan chose Bush for the vice presidential slot after failing to get former President Ford for the position.

A third party candidate joined the race, John Anderson, running as an Independent. He had no organization, constituency, or particular issues that set him apart from the major candidates. He offered the electorate his self-proclaimed integrity and competence. He qualified for federal election funds, and his campaign received extensive media coverage. Anderson attracted mainly Democratic voters who were turned off by Carter's performance, although his candidacy had no bearing on the outcome of the election.

Reagan was favored to win when the presidential campaign began in August. But he made several incorrect statements concerning important issues, which conveyed the impression that the old campaigner might be dangerously out of touch with the times. Within a month, Carter had caught up. Sensing an advantage, Carter attacked Reagan personally. He accused him of racism and warmongering, and he raised the question of his age. At sixty-nine, Reagan was the oldest major party candidate to ever seek the presidency. But Carter's attacks backfired, because voters resented them. Polls taken at the end of September showed Reagan back in the lead.

Reagan attacked Carter's handling of the economy at a time of historically high "stagflation." He attacked his handling of foreign policy at a time when the world was especially unstable and when the hostages were in Iranian hands. Carter, hoping to salvage his failing campaign, challenged Reagan to debate him on television. Carter was confident that his detailed knowledge of the issues would expose Reagan as a windy fraud. Reagan agreed to one debate, which took place at Cleveland's Convention Center on October 28.

It was the best of the televised presidential debates. The panelists chose excellent questions about major issues. The candidates were evenly matched through the early rounds of questioning. Then Carter, responding to a question about nuclear arms control, said that he had consulted with his thirteen-year-old daughter Amy about the important issues of the campaign. His answer unintentionally suggested to the vast television audience that the president of the United States relied on the advice of a child when considering important policy matters. Reagan scored impressively when he responded to Carter's attacks on his record on Medicare. Using his actor's skills, Reagan shook his head ruefully, saying, "There you go again"; then, in the manner of a parent correcting an erring child, he firmly set the record straight.

In terms of content, the debate was a draw. On image and personality, Reagan won decisively. In ninety minutes, he had erased the image of himself that Carter had been projecting throughout the campaign, the image of Reagan as a combination scrooge and mad bomber. During the debate, Reagan came across as a firm, genial leader who would never push the nuclear button in panic or anger.

He sealed Carter's fate when he closed the debate by asking the huge television audience a series of rhetorical questions: Are you better off than you were four years ago? Is America as respected throughout the world as it was four years ago? Are we as strong as we were four years ago?

A close contest had been turned into a rout for Reagan. He received 44 million votes to Carter's 35 million and Anderson's 5.7 million. Reagan swept the election with 489 electoral votes to Carter's 49, with zero for Anderson. The Republicans gained thirty-three seats in the House. The most surprising outcome of the 1980 election was the Republican reconquest of the Senate for the first time since 1954. Republicans gained twelve senatorial seats, giving them fifty-three, the largest Republican total since 1928. Reagan received nearly half of the labor vote. He carried blue-collar voters, middle-income voters, the Catholic vote, the ethnic vote, and the Southern vote. He carried all of the populous Northern industrial states. He brought an important new class of voters into the Republican fold, "Reagan Democrats." He got a third of the Hispanic vote. Only African American voters remained faithful to Carter.

The vote revealed two cleavages among voters. African Americans voted 90 percent for Carter; whites voted 56 percent for Reagan. There was another division among voters. For the first time in the sixty years since women had achieved the vote, a gender gap appeared in the electoral results. Whereas 56 percent of men voted for Reagan and only 36 percent for Carter, only 47 percent of women voted for Reagan and 45 percent for Carter. Reagan's opposition to abortion and the ERA, plus his aggressive foreign policy rhetoric and initiatives, alienated women voters. Many working women, struggling to cope with precarious economic circumstances, perceived that Reagan did not represent their interests, and they feared that he might call for Congress to eliminate governmental programs upon which they and their families depended.

Some analysts read the 1980 election as a harbinger of a new conservative Republican majority coalition. More saw it as the rejection of an ineffective leader who could not control inflation or retrieve the hostages. The main issue apparently was Reagan himself. Could he be a safe replacement for the discredited incumbent? Many people thought Reagan too old, too conservative, and too dangerous—until the debate. Reagan's adept performance in that forum turned a close election into a landslide.

Jimmy Carter was not a particularly successful or popular president, and he suffered a humiliating reelection defeat at the hands of Ronald Reagan in November 1980. However, since the end of his presidency, after nearly two decades of tireless work as a practicing Christian and elder statesmen, Jimmy Carter achieved a stature and respect from his fellow citizens that he never attained while he was in the White House. He established the Carter Center near his presidential library in Atlanta as a place where the parties to the world's most stubborn political conflicts could come together and try to find solutions. He also set himself up as a crusader for world peace. He supervised elections and guaranteed their legitimacy in Panama and Nicaragua. He inserted himself into dangerous confrontations in Haiti and North Korea to head off conflict. Carter was not a great president, but he has been a great ex-president.

A DEMOGRAPHIC PROFILE

There were 205 million Americans in 1970, 215 million in 1975, and 227 million by 1980. Regionally, Southern and Western states accounted for 90 percent of that population increase. Many Northeastern and Midwestern states showed little or no growth, and several lost population. Population trends that had first appeared in this country soon after World War II continued. The Sunbelt regions, stretching from South Carolina to southern California, contained the dynamic centers of the nation's technological innovation, economic growth, and population increase.

Two additional demographic shifts with profound social implications occurred during the 1970s—the birthrate fell, and human longevity increased. Twentieth-century birthrates peaked in 1947, at 26.6 live births per thousand, and tumbled to 18.1 per thousand in 1975. Low birthrates meant that adults were not bearing enough children to replace themselves, and that only expanded immigration prevented long-term U.S. population decline. Increasing longevity derived from advances in medicine and nutrition. Doctors perfected cures for some forms of degenerative diseases such as heart disease and cancer. But the most important causes of rising longevity were reductions in the infant mortality rate and the childhood death rate. By 1975, average longevity in America had reached 73.1 years. The fastest-growing age group consisted of people age seventy-five and older. The median age of the U.S. population reached thirty years on April 1, 1980, making America one of the older societies in the world.

Census data also showed that the traditional American household comprising a nuclear family of four declined sharply during the 1970s. Nearly half of the households added in the 1970s consisted of persons living alone or with nonrelatives. Declining birthrates, declining marriage rates, high divorce rates, households occupied by unmarried couples, households occupied by single-parent families, and the existence of millions of men and women living alone all suggested that household arrangements in America increasingly reflected the sociological diversity that had become America's most salient characteristic.

By the late 1970s, one of the most rapidly growing population segments comprised the thirty-somethings, the advance wave of baby boomers. This group received much media attention, particularly the better-educated "yuppies" among them. Yuppies were upwardly mobile, affluent young Americans earning $40,000 or more a year. Having few or no children, yuppie couples often held two high-paying jobs. Merchants and advertisers catered to their large disposable incomes and lifestyle preferences based on buying upscale homes, cars, and clothes, dining in expensive restaurants, and taking costly vacations.

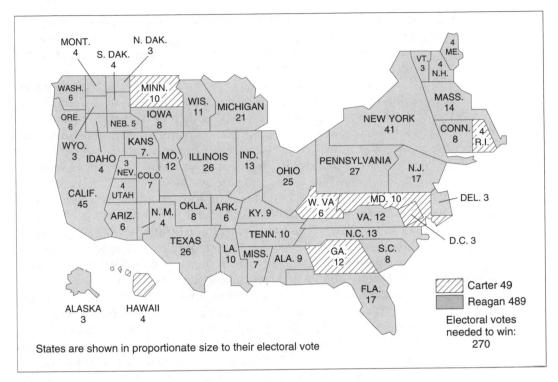

Figure 14.8   The electoral vote, 1980.   *Source:* Moss, *Moving On*, p. 292.

But yuppies did not represent the norm. According to Census data, of the 78 million baby boomers, only 5 percent had incomes of $40,000 or more in the late 1970s. The median income for baby boomers in 1977 was $16,000, below the national average. The fundamental problem baby boomers faced was one of demographics: too many people chasing too few economic opportunities. Opportunities for baby boomers also were curtailed by the energy crisis and the high inflation of the late 1970s and early 1980s. Further, the annual growth rate of the American economy averaged a sluggish 1.6 percent per annum during the 1970s, and long-term unemployment rates were the highest since the 1930s. Baby boomers as a whole were less upwardly mobile than their parents, the first such group in America since the generation that came of age during the Great Depression of the 1930s.

ECONOMIC STASIS

During the thirty-year boom cycle lasting from the early 1940s to the early 1970s, most Americans families had enjoyed unprecedented prosperity. Real per capita family income doubled, and the GDP more than doubled during those three decades of strong economic growth. The steadily expanding economy and rising living standards over a long period of time convinced most Americans that prosperity was perpetual. But during the early 1970s, stagflation replaced perpetual growth and created a set of economic circumstances that eroded the prosperity that middle class Americans took for granted.

During the early 1970s, the declining U.S. economy also was showing the effects of strong foreign competition. Rebuilt after having been destroyed during World War II, the industrial economies of West Germany and Japan were more productive than the older U.S. industries. U.S. shares of many world markets declined. Within America, many industries lost large shares of the domestic market to their foreign competitors. In 1970, about 10 percent of new cars sold in America were imported; by 1980, that figure had reached 30 percent.

Inflation, deficits, and loss of both domestic and export markets combined to create a serious balance of payment problem by 1972, which threatened to undermine the value of the dollar. When the Nixon administration devalued the dollar by severing it from gold, this action unleashed an orgy of gold speculation in the world that drove the price of gold from $35 an ounce to over $800 an ounce and added to the inflationary burden of American consumers.

In geopolitical terms, the U.S. defeat in Vietnam signaled that U.S. hegemony in the world had ended. In economic and financial terms, the declining U.S. position in the world economy likewise signaled that the era of American dominance had ended. The OPEC embargo that kicked in during October 1973 compounded American economic difficulties, added to the inflation rate, and highlighted the dangers of continued dependency on foreign sources of oil. Yet during the 1970s, America became more dependent on foreign sources of oil. The bill for oil imports in 1970 was $5 billion. By 1980, it was in excess of $90 billion. The huge rise in the cost of imported oil was another dramatic sign of American economic decline in the world. It also served as a potent reminder that America no longer controlled its own economic destiny. The American economy had become increasingly connected to the emerging global economy.

The struggles of millions of American families for economic survival during the 1970s were exacerbated by structural trends that weakened the economic foundations of American middle-class society. As the economy became increasingly based on high-tech service and information-oriented industries, the number of jobs that provided middle-class incomes declined. A service economy employs millions of clerical workers, salesclerks, waiters, bartenders, cashiers, and messengers. Wages for these jobs are comparatively low. While millions of new service-sector jobs were created during the 1970s, the number of higher-paying manufacturing jobs decreased.

During the 1970s, millions of factory jobs disappeared because of declining productivity and cutbacks in capital spending, and because production work became increasingly automated. Trade unions lost hundreds of thousands of members to automation and to declines caused by foreign competition in the steel, rubber, auto, and other manufacturing industries. The manufacturing jobs that disappeared during the 1970s tended to be skilled jobs from middle-income spectra. These displaced workers usually could not find alternative employment that offered comparable pay and fringe benefits. Their options were early retirement, if they could afford it, or they could take jobs in the rapidly expanding service sectors of the economy. But many of these service jobs were low-paying ones with minimal opportunities for advancement or for a career. Most of these new service sector jobs went to women, minorities, and youngsters. The fastest-growing sector of the service economy in the 1970s, which carried into the 1980s, was the fast food industry. McDonald's became the nation's largest employer. During the 1970s, the fast food industry added workers faster than manufacturing lost them, at wages that averaged one-third as much and with far fewer fringe benefits.

There were other signs of economic decline during the 1970s. Real income declined by 15 percent from 1973 to 1980 in this country. By 1980, working-class family purchasing power had fallen back to 1960 levels. Meanwhile, the inflation engine drove housing and new car prices upward. The median price of new homes doubled during the decade. The 1970s appeared to reverse the social and economic trends of the 1950s and 1960s. There was a wholesale loss of faith in economic progress; during the 1970s, millions of families faced what they had been led to believe could never recur—economic retrogression, the first since the 1930s.

For generations, Americans had been sustained by their belief in economic individualism: talent, initiative, and hard work generated upward mobility and economic security, enabling men (and women) to provide for their families and ensuring that their children would have a better life than they. But during the era of limits, faith in the Protestant ethic was eroded. Old men evoked the promise of American life, while young people had to struggle harder than ever to achieve it. Millions of Americans could not find steady work in the 1970s. Millions who worked found not affluence but subsistence. For millions of young people, the struggle was to not reach the top, but to not fall any lower. Millions of middle-class youngsters could not realistically expect to earn as much, to own as much, and to be as successful as their parents. Ironically, at a time when racist and sexist barriers to advancement were shrinking and the American dream was open to all Americans for the first time, declining economic opportunity shrunk the dream.

CARS AND COMPUTERS

The car culture was alive and well in America during the era of limits. Automobile registrations reached 90 million in 1970 and 118 million in 1980. Millions of Americans purchased automobiles manufactured in Europe and Japan during the 1970s. High-performance small sports cars, pickups, and vans became more popular. Consumers became more value-conscious and safety-conscious; manufacturers responded by offering their customers far greater choices in vehicles than had previously been available. The application of new technologies meant that 1970s automobiles were more aerodynamically designed, fuel-efficient, safer, and much easier to handle than the cars of the 1950s and 1960s. The 1970s automobiles also were much more expensive and, especially the American-made cars, much more prone to breakdown.

Automobiles continued to be the primary means of intercity travel in the United States during the 1970s, although commercial airlines did increase their share of the travelers' market, from about 5 percent to 10 percent. Despite sizeable increases in their business, most domestic airlines found themselves in serious financial difficulties during the late 1970s, primarily derived from the deregulation of the airline industry implemented during the Carter administration. Several well-known airlines went out of business, including Eastern and Braniff.

Deregulation of the airline industry probably created more problems than it solved. Passengers obviously benefited from the far greater variety of flights offered at lower prices, generated by the new era of cutthroat competition. In the long run, deregulation created conditions reminiscent of the era of cutthroat competition in the railroad industry of 100 years ago: weaker competitors were driven to bankruptcy and were either forced to shut down or be absorbed by the stronger airlines. Serious questions of reliability and safety also arose.

The most dramatic technological innovations of the 1970s were all connected with the computer revolution. The computerization of America began during the 1970s. There were approximately 6,000 computers in use in this country in 1972; by 1980, there were tens of thousands, and the number was expanding exponentially every year. The agent of revolution was the microcomputer. Use of microcomputers enhanced the abilities of individuals working in a wide variety of fields to calculate, sift through, and retrieve information. They also could build statistical models and process words. The key invention that brought forth the microcomputer was Ted Hoff's perfection of the microprocessor, or computer chip, in 1972. Hoff was a young engineer on the staff of Intel Corporation when he designed the world's first microprocessor that revolutionized electronic technology. The computer revolution made possible the information revolution of the 1970s and 1980s that transformed the way America worked.

The first personal computers were marketed in the mid-1970s. In California's Silicon Valley, a suburban area located about fifty miles south of San Francisco, dozens of small computer companies found themselves on the cutting edge of revolution. In 1976, two young men, Steven Wozniak, a computer genius, and Steve Jobs, an entrepreneurial visionary, opened a small business in a garage they rented for $50 a month. Wozniak designed and Jobs sold small, inexpensive personal computers (PC). They called their fledgling company "Apple." Sales were slow at first. No one appeared to be very interested in a small personal computer; however, sales picked up in the late 1970s and in 1985 Americans bought 6 million PCs. By the mid-1980s, Apple had become a multibillion dollar business, and Wozniak and Jobs had become fabulously rich.

NEW IMMIGRANTS

Because the Immigration Act of 1965 abolished the discriminatory national origins system dating back to the 1920s, there occurred both a large increase in immigration and a significant shift in the sources of immigrants. Most of the millions of immigrants who came to the United States in the 1970s and 1980s were Asians and Latin Americans. Mexico furnished the most immigrants. Along with Mexicans came Cubans, Puerto Ricans, and Central Americans, particularly people from El Salvador and Nicaragua. Some of these new arrivals were fleeing religious and political oppression, but most came for the same reasons that have always attracted newcomers to America—opportunities for a good job and a better life for their families.

The United States, true to its ancient heritage, remained one of the few countries in the world to freely welcome these millions of newcomers from foreign lands. But many native-born Americans were alarmed by the flood of poor immigrants arriving annually, especially the "illegals" who came mostly from Mexico through a porous membrane called the United States–Mexico border. They feared that these people would take jobs from American workers, lower wages and living standards, overload the welfare and school systems, and become an underclass of poor people amidst an affluent society.

Their fears were exaggerated, based upon dubious assumptions and misperceptions. Studies have shown that most immigrants take jobs at pay levels that most native-born Americans scorn, and they pay more in taxes than they ever collect in government services. Many of these immigrants also strive to become law-abiding, hard-working, and productive citizens.

Another problem posed by elements in the Hispanic American population, fueled by large-scale immigration from Mexico and other Hispanic countries, is the ancient question of assimilation. By 2000, if present growth rates continue, Hispanic Americans will compose the largest minority population group within the United States. This demographic trend worries some native-born Americans, who focus on the fact that Hispanics often have formed their own communities, or *barrios*, where they can get along quite well without having to speak or write English. Some Hispanics also insist that their children be taught in bilingual schools. The Supreme Court has authorized bilingual instruction in public schools.

Spokesmen for the native-born population have argued that the existence of large, Spanish-speaking populations clustered in southern California, southern Florida, the Southwest, and sections of New York and Chicago pose a threat to national unity and to the political cohesiveness of the American system. Hispanic spokesmen insist on their rights to have their children educated as they see fit. They also insist on retaining their language and identity as a distinct ethnic group within a pluralistic society.

A Mexican American journalist, Richard Rodriquez, has written about the need for Mexican Americans and all other Spanish-speaking citizens of the United States to learn English in order to realize their full opportunities, and he accepts, as a painful necessity, the loss of some parts of the traditional Hispanic culture and the comfort it provided. It is the price exacted for full participation in American life, a price he believes individuals from all immigrant groups have paid historically and must continue to pay.

After Hispanics, Asians have furnished the largest supply of newcomers. They have come mainly from Hong Kong, Taiwan, China, Vietnam, Korea, and Japan. Their numbers boosted by large-scale immigration, the Asian American population has doubled in the past decade, from 2 million people to more than 4 million. Asians are among the most upwardly mobile population groups within American society. Seventy-five percent of Asian Americans have graduated from high school. One-third of Asian American adults have four or more years of college, twice the rate for Americans of European descent. In the economic sphere, data from the 1980 Census show that the Asian American median annual income was more than $2,000 above the national median annual income.

Success has not come easy for Asian Americans. Historically, they have been the victims of exclusion, prejudice, discrimination in various forms, and violence. And not all Asians have achieved success in America. Many recent Asian immigrants remain mired in poverty, alienated from the mainstream of American life, and tempted by vice and crime. Many struggle to fathom a mysterious language and culture that is neither open nor friendly to them. Incidents of violence against Asian immigrants abound. Many recent arrivals from Vietnam, Cambodia, and Laos, the "boat people," refugees from oppression in their homelands, have encountered only grief and failure in this country. But there also is the saga of Jean Nguyen. Nguyen, at age eleven, escaped from Vietnam with her family by boat when Saigon fell to the Communists in 1975. She spoke no English upon her arrival in America that same year. In 1981, she graduated number one in her high school class, and in May 1985, she graduated from West Point, receiving a commission as

Figure 14.9   Mr. And Mrs. Van Ngo Vu stocking shelves in their family grocery store. Vu's Market opened in 1987.   *Source:* National Archives.

a second lieutenant in the U.S. Army. President Reagan paid tribute to Nguyen in his 1985 State of the Union Address, calling her "an American hero."

AFRICAN AMERICANS: A DUAL SOCIETY

For millions of African American families, the 1970s was a decade of significant progress. Institutionalized racism and other obstacles to black achievement diminished. Affirmative action programs spawned by the civil rights movements of the 1960s paid off for middle-class African Americans in the 1970s and 1980s. The greatest progress for African Americans came in education. By 1980, more than 1 million black people had enrolled in colleges, and thousands attended the finest universities and professional schools in the country. Thousands of young African American men and women became doctors, lawyers, college professors, government bureaucrats, and business executives. The size of the black middle class increased rapidly, and black per capita income rose appreciably. African American couples married, had children, and bought homes in the suburbs, their lifestyles much like that of their white counterparts in similar circumstances. Many young black professionals, reared and educated in the North, flocked to the Sunbelt cities to live and work.

Despite significant gains for many, millions of African Americans have not made it in white America; in fact, they have lost ground. Affirmative action admissions programs were challenged by the *Bakke* case. Allen Bakke, a white applicant to the University of California at Davis Medical School, sued the university when his application was rejected. He showed that his qualifications were superior to several minority candidates who were admitted as "disadvantaged students" under a special quota reserved for them. The state supreme court ruled in his favor, as did the Supreme Court, in a 1978 five-to-four decision. The Supreme Court held that Bakke's rights to equal protection under the Fourteenth Amendment had been violated, and it nullified the school's affirmative action program based on racial quotas. But by a similar five-to-four decision, the Court upheld the right of the university to use race as "one element" in its effort to recruit medical students. The Court appeared to be saying that affirmative action programs were legitimate, as long as strict quotas were not established.

But the plight of poor African Americans trapped in urban ghettos worsened in the 1970s and 1980s. Unemployment among African Americans remained high, about twice the national average, averaging 14 percent to 15 percent for the past decade. Unemployment among African American teenagers skyrocketed to the 40 percent to 50 percent range by 1980. Black median family income was $13,500 in 1985, only half of that for whites.

Among poor urban African Americans, statistics revealed an appalling pattern of intertwined social pathologies—rising drug usage, delinquency, vice, and crime; rising school dropout rates and unemployment rates; and rising numbers of illegitimate births and households headed by an unmarried female parent. Many social analysts fear that a permanent underclass has been forged within black America, without the possibility of integration into the mainstream, or of achieving personally fulfilling lives.

According to sociologist William J. Wilson, the fundamental cause of the social misery and disorganization afflicting the black inner city was economic. Factories and businesses offering good jobs at good wages have disappeared. Most black working-class and middle-class families have moved out of once-thriving neighborhoods. Without the prospect of good jobs and without positive role models to set examples, many of the inner-city dwellers have been deprived of opportunies to seek happy, productive, and meaningful lives. Wilson believed that without the economic and moral anchor of respectable employment, there is little chance to solve the serious, interrelated social problems of the black inner cities.

Within America, African Americans have forged a dual society—on the one hand, a thriving middle class that has achieved a place for itself in recent years that is roughly equal to white America—and on the other hand, a declining underclass rotting on the mean streets of urban ghettos.

WOMEN: CHANGING ATTITUDES AND ROLES

Women continued many of the trends established in the late 1960s and early 1970s. Female enrollments in colleges, graduate schools, and professional schools continued to expand. By 1980, women college enrollment surpassed male enrollment. Middle-class women continued to enter the professional and corporate worlds in ever-increasing numbers. Working-class women continued to join unions, enter the skilled trades, and increase their numbers in previously all-male economic occupations. Both federal and state laws were enacted that helped women obtain credit, start their own businesses, and buy homes. Other women made their way in politics.

But despite their many successes, women continued to encounter barriers in their struggle to overcome historical disadvantages and to achieve genuine equality in contemporary American society. Women antifeminists like Phyllis Schlafly and Anita Bryant successfully campaigned against the Equal Rights Amendment. They also fought to repeal the right of women to have an abortion on demand, as sanctioned by the Supreme Court. Antifeminists won a partial victory in 1980, when the Supreme Court upheld the constitutionality of a congressional law prohibiting the federal funding of abortions for poor women. Antifeminists have charged the women's movement with being responsible for the spiraling divorce rate and the breakdown of family life in America. "No-fault divorces," initially hailed as a great victory for women, proved to be a two-edged sword, because equality before the law did not bring equality in the marketplace. Compounding their economic difficulties, divorced women, who usually have custody of their children, found that former husbands defaulted on child support payments and the courts often did not force them to pay.

Many men responded negatively to women's liberation and abandoned their traditional roles as financial providers and authority figures for the family. Post-feminist analysts faulted the liberal leaders of the women's movement for being too concerned with achieving legal and political equality, thereby neglecting the fundamental economic pressures that women faced in a society where male economic domination remained a continuing reality. They also criticized feminists who were obsessed with getting middle-class women into previously all-male professions and occupations, while neglecting the interests of the more numerous working-class women mired in low-paying occupations traditionally reserved for women.

Harsh economic realities continued to limit opportunities for women. For every glittering career success scored by ambitious, capable, upwardly mobile women, many more women only found work in low-paying jobs, which offered few opportunities for promotion or substantial pay increases. Occupational segregation, in which women remained concentrated in low-paying positions while men earned much higher incomes for their work, was a persistent problem for women. Most of the new jobs created in the service sectors of the economy were taken by women, and they invariably paid less than manufacturing or professional jobs.

In 1980, women earned only 60 cents for every dollar earned by men. The 60 cents represented an improvement over previous decades, but it fell far short of economic parity with men. Women also have been the victims of the "superwoman syndrome." Early feminist leaders proffered an idealized image of the woman who could have it all—career, home, husband, and family—a life of perfect equality and fulfillment. In practice, having it all often meant women worked full time outside of the home, then came home to continue working without pay, doing all of the cleaning, cooking, and caring for children, while men watched television, drank beer, and played with their dogs.

Most women have worked to support themselves or to head a single-parent household. Millions of married women have felt it necessary to work to enable their family to enjoy a middle-class lifestyle that, because of inflation, was no longer affordable with a single income. Many women have slipped into the ranks of the working poor in recent years as a result of divorce and of being saddled with child-rearing duties. The feminization of poverty and the fact that millions of American children were being reared in poverty have been two ominous socio-economic realities directly affecting the status of women.

EDUCATION

Most American colleges and universities continued to thrive in the 1970s and 1980s. In 1980, an estimated 11 million students were enrolled full time or part time in the nation's 2,500 institutions of higher learning. Americans continued to spend far more on post–high-school education than any other people, and America possessed more than 100 of the world's finest universities. More students than ever before were getting the best undergraduate educations available in the world. Distinguished university faculty members continued to perform important research and publish their findings. America scholars led the world in many disciplines, especially in the sciences. American universities remained the vital centers of the nation's flourishing intellectual life.

In contrast to the turbulent 1960s, college campuses were mostly tranquil places in the 1970s and early 1980s. Surveys revealed that college students of the 1980s often embraced conservative social and political views. Students were much more interested in preparing for well-paying careers than they were in protesting public issues. College students in recent years have been much less interested in the humanities and social sciences than they were a generation earlier. Students of the 1970s and early 1980s flocked to majors in math, economics, finance, business, engineering, and computer science. Many students, including bright ones, demonstrated deficiencies in verbal skills and a general decline in cultural literacy.

While colleges flourished, American public schools deteriorated. Scholastic aptitude scores were 50 points lower in 1980 than they were in 1963. The high school dropout rate in 1980 was over 20 percent, the highest since the 1950s. About one in three eighteen-year-olds in this country were declared functionally illiterate in 1980. At a time when competition for jobs and all of the accoutrements of the American-style good life were intensifying, when the economic and social life of the nation was becoming more complex and demanding, and when employers were demanding brighter and better-educated employees, the public school system increasingly failed to meet individual and national needs.

Many culprits have been blamed for the dismal performance of the public schools. Television has been cited for keeping youngsters from reading books and for fostering boredom in the classroom. Indifferent and incompetent parents, who neither set a good example nor encourage their children to do well in school, have been part of the problem. Popular entertainers and professional athletes whose riches and fame have derived from talent rather than study in schools have been indicted for setting bad examples and leading youngsters astray. In addition, the best and brightest college graduates rarely went into teaching. Entry-level salaries were low, and teaching commanded little prestige as a profession. Americans once believed that education could solve all social problems; now they viewed the schools as a social problem.

There were signs in the 1980s that educators were trying to turn their public schools in the direction of excellence. Polls showed that people were willing to pay more taxes to improve their schools. California and other states implemented legislation lengthening the school day and year, strengthening the curriculum, raising teachers' salaries, and requiring new teachers to pass competency tests. The fundamental question raised by the public school issue was one of cultural value: How highly did the nation prize learning? How highly did parents prize learning, and how much were they willing to pay for good schools? Did most students really care about becoming educated, or were they only interested in an active social life, a career, and money?

RELIGION IN AMERICA

The United States remained the most religious nation in the Western world. Nearly all Americans espoused a belief in God, and 60 percent of the population claimed membership in a church in 1980. Members of the more liberal Protestant churches as well as Reformed Jews became more accepting of divorce, homosexuality, birth control, and women clergy. The ministers and rabbis of these groups often urged their congregants to work for a more humane and just social order.

American Catholics in the 1970s and 1980s were concerned about the continuing consequences of Vatican II, the Church Council that had met in the early 1960s to bring the Church more into accord with modern life. The liturgy was given in English and the laity sang hymns during services. Priests were allowed more latitude in their interpretations of the Bible, and they sought ecumenical dialogues with ministers and rabbis. Catholics recognized non-Catholic and non-Christian faiths, and they condemned anti-Semitism.

Roman Catholic Church leaders spoke out on issues. In 1983, American bishops condemned nuclear war and urged the superpowers to disarm. In 1985, the bishops criticized the American capitalist economy for not meeting the needs of the millions of disadvantaged Americans. Many educated, liberal, middle-class Catholics welcomed the changes induced by Vatican II. But many traditionalists felt betrayed and were disturbed by these changes. They continued to adhere to the Church's traditional teachings about matters of sex, birth control, and abortion.

THE RISE OF THE RELIGIOUS RIGHT

Evangelical Christians formed one of the most powerful elements within the ranks of the growing conservative movement of the late 1970s and early 1980s. These fervent souls emphasized the personal responsibility of each individual believer. A sinner could be redeemed only by being "born again," that is, by confessing his or her sins, accepting Jesus Christ as a personal savior, and thereafter leading a righteous life. Books by evangelical authors became best-sellers. "Christian Yellow Pages" appeared in many large cities. Millions of schoolchildren attended Christian elementary, middle, and high schools, where subjects were taught from an evangelical perspective. By the late 1970s, over 1,500 radio stations were owned by evangelical Christians.

Television quickly became the chief conduit for spreading the evangical message and promoting its conservative social and political agenda. Pat Robertson started the "700 Club," aired over his Christian Broadcasting Network. One of the regulars on his show, Jim Bakker, went off to create his own program, the Praise the

Lord (PTL) Club. Bakker's show combined sermons, faith healing, inspirational stories, and entertainment. The PTL Club quickly became the most viewed daily television program on the planet. By 1980, Bakker's organization was receiving $25 million a year in contributions.

Born-again Christians attacked what they called "secular humanism," the view that all truths were relative, all moral values were situational, and all ethical judgments were necessarily tentative. They supported the "right to life" movement, denounced *Roe v. Wade,* and condemned abortion. They opposed most feminist demands and the Equal Rights Amendment. They initiated a war on pornography and insisted that homosexuality was a sin. Evangelicals sought to reintroduce school prayer, and they campaigned to have "creation science" offered as an alternative to the theory of evolution in public schools.

An evangelical leader became a prominent conservative political activist. Jerry Falwell, for many years the pastor of the Thomas Road Baptist Church in Lynchburg, Virginia, had attracted a constituency of thousands. He also had his own television show, *The Old Time Gospel Hour.* In July 1979, Falwell formed the Moral Majority. Combining old-time religion with the latest computer technology, his organization targeted potential contributors and kept scorecards on how politicians voted on key issues such as the ERA, school prayer, and funding for abortions.

For the 1980 election, Falwell's Moral Majority activists developed a "hit list" of liberal senators and congressmen, then mailed out more than 1 billion pieces of campaign literature to selected voters, gleaned from their computerized mailing lists. The Moral Majority played a major role in bringing about the Republican takeover of the Senate in January 1981. The Moral Majority also threw all of its considerable political resources into campaigning for Ronald Reagan. Reagan also incorporated the Moral Majority's social and political agenda into his successful campaign for the presidency.

THE "ME" DECADE

While some Americans carried the activist reform spirit of the 1960s into the 1970s and 1980s, many more turned inward. They wanted to reform their inner selves, not the outer world of politics and culture. They incorporated many of the elements from the hippie countercultural rebellion into their lifestyles—drug use, permissive sexuality, and above all the "consciousness revolution." Participants included mostly young, middle-class professionals who prized affluence but defined success primarily in psychological rather than material terms. It was more important to them to fulfill their "human potential" and to cultivate "relationships" than to accumulate as much wealth as possible.

The cutting edge of the consciousness revolution could be found in California, the home of the new lifestyles based on developing one's inner resources. Facilities such as the Esalen Institute at Big Sur offered weekend encounter sessions for seekers wanting to "get in touch with themselves." Another entrepreneur of the human potential movement offered Erhard Seminars Training (est), built around marathon encounter sessions in which participants were encouraged to confront their most powerful feelings. Journalist Tom Wolfe labeled these "psychonauts of inner space" the "Me Generation" and compared their movement to a religious revival.

As millions of Americans joined the consciousness revolution, others sought refuge from the stresses of secular society by joining religious cults. Some of these religious orders embraced Asian mystical religious practices, such as transcendental meditation or Zen Buddhism. One cult, led by East Indian holy man Bhagwan Shree Rajneesh Mahareshi Yogi, established a flourishing colony near the small town of Antelope, Oregon. Thousands of people, attracted by the Bhagwan's message of spiritual rebirth and free sex, lived and worked in apparently joyous harmony for a time. But the cult disintegrated in 1986 because of internal dissension among its leaders. The most prominent of these cults was the Unification Church, founded by a Korean businessman and preacher, Sun Myung Moon, who relocated in the United States. Moon, trained as a Presbyterian minister, developed his own religion. He claimed to be the son of God and to receive divine revelations. His movement was controversial. Some of his disciples were accused of kidnapping and brainwashing some of their teenage recruits. Reverend Moon also ran afoul of the law and was convicted of income tax evasion.

POPULAR CULTURE

America calmed in the early 1970s; the era of limits also was an era of comparative civic and social tranquility. In the words of historian John Wiltz, in America during the 1970s, "the national society became more mellow." No more fiery urban riots or militant campus protests convulsed the nation. Gone was the strident rhetoric of youthful radicals denouncing government policies at home and abroad and challenging traditional American values, mores, and institutions.

Several factors accounted for the calming down of America during the 1970s. The end of the Vietnam War removed the single most powerful source of dissidence. The decline of the economy, stagflation, and energy crises shifted the attention from political troubles to more fundamental economic and financial dysfunctions. The successes, or at least the partial victories, of many of the 1960s movements led some of their participants to cease their activism in the 1970s with a sense of having accomplished their missions. Some radicals, suffering from moral and political exhaustion, abandoned their futile efforts to refashion American politics and society, retreating into a sullen personalism and quietism. Some joined the "me generation," redirecting their reformist energies away from the world and toward their own personalities. Others, reaching adulthood, prepared to make an accommodation for the system they had previously spurned. Many hippies and campus radicals abandoned their countercultural ways, discarded their tie-dyed tank tops and sandals, shaved their beards, trimmed their hair, donned three-piece suits, and became yuppies.

As the society calmed down in the 1970s, Americans, retreating into private realms, embraced a variety of fads and activities. Disco dancing appealed to youths mainly because of its strong, rhythmic beat, accompanied by simple, repetitive lyrics. Couples danced the night away beneath pulsating lights in one of the hundreds of nightclubs that sprung up across America in the mid-1970s. An attractive African American soul singer, Donna Summer, became the "Queen of Discoland"; her records sold millions of copies during the years of the disco craze. Many, mostly young people, came to discos just to listen to Summer's sound and other disco artists. Many more learned to dance the "hustle," the "bus stop," or the myriad of other new disco dances.

During the 1970s, millions of Americans became more diet-conscious than ever before. People reduced their salt and cholesterol intake. Others stopped drinking alcoholic beverages and caffeinated drinks. Closely related to dieting and part of the new health consciousness, millions of people embraced the so-called fitness revolution. They became avid weight lifters as well as weight watchers. They swam, jogged, and rode bicycles; they joined health clubs, played racquetball, and performed aerobic exercises. And another indicator of the growing health consciousness during the 1970s—millions of people abandoned smoking cigarettes. By the end of the 1970s—approximately 30 percent of the adult population smoked, the lowest percentage since the 1920s.

If Americans were smoking fewer cigarettes during the 1970s, they were drinking more alcoholic beverages, especially beer. The per capita alcoholic consumption increased from 22 gallons in 1970 to 27 gallons in 1980. Televised sporting events invariably featured numerous beer commercials associating good times with their products, directing their ads mainly toward single young men; breweries strove to link beer drinking with male fantasies about sexy young women.

During the late 1970s, alcohol abuse among teenagers and college students became a serious national issue. Studies found that thousands of high school students were teenaged alcoholics. In 1975, out of the approximately 45,000 Americans killed in traffic accidents, more than half died in accidents in which at least one of the drivers had been drinking. Fatal auto accidents were one of the leading killers of young people between the ages of fifteen and twenty-five. Another survey found that at least 10 million Americans were alcohol abusers.

Americans used other drugs besides ethanol in increasing amounts during the 1970s. The use of marijuana ("pot"), which had become a potent symbol of the youth revolt during the turbulent 1960s, expanded in the 1970s. Pot farming became a major underground industry in many parts of the country. Surveys showed that nearly half of the nation's college students during the 1970s used marijuana. Because most experts believed that the effects of the drug were comparatively mild if used in moderation, the federal government and most states reduced the legal penalties for possession of small amounts of pot from felonies to misdemeanors. A far more serious drug problem arose in the early 1970s when there occurred a surge in heroin addiction. The nation discovered that it had nearly a million heroin addicts on its hands by 1975.

Americans during the 1970s discovered the microwave oven, and they consumed a record number of TV dinners annually. American families also dined out much more often than ever before, especially at fast food establishments. Probably the single most important reason for the 1970s' eating-out phenomenon was the fact that more than 50 percent of married women with children now worked full time outside of the home. The new dining-out patterns attested to a major cultural change that had occurred: the great American dinner was being redefined for families with children. Dinner was no longer a private familial activity; it had increasingly become a public activity.

The movie industry flourished during the 1970s. Hollywood turned out many fine films, some of which set box-office records. In 1972, the brilliant young director, Francis Ford Coppola, made the *The Godfather,* starring Al Pacino, Marlon Brando, and Diane Keaton. Based on a novel by Mario Puzo, the film was an epic about a powerful Mafia family making it in America. Then in 1973 there came the occult classic *The Exorcist,* starring a talented child actress, Linda Blair. Based on a novel by William Blatty, the film dealt in dramatic fashion with demonic possession and the valiant efforts of a Roman Catholic priest to exorcise the devil from the body of the child. The techno-thriller *Jaws,* was released in 1975, by a brilliant young filmmaker, Stephen Spielberg. It was a terrifying account of a killer great white shark attacking swimmers. The star of the film turned out to be jaws himself, the technological monster that terrorized a New England town: it was shown devouring swimmers in gruesome detail. *Jaws* had the largest box-office gross of any film ever made.

Jaws' record take at the box office was broken in 1977 by *Star Wars,* the first of a brilliant series of science-fiction films by George Lucas, another major filmmaking talent that burst on the Hollywood scene in the 1970s. Set in the far distant past, *Star Wars* was essentially a child's fantasy, a fairy tale about high-tech adventures in space, starring Mark Hamill as Luke Skywalker, Harrison Ford as Hans Solo, and Carrie Fisher as Princess Leia. They were supported by a charming cast of bizarre-looking but gentle aliens and humanlike machines called androids. The plot is a simple morality tale, of the good guys triumphing over the bad guys, who control the evil Galactic Empire. Lucas reasserted the pleasures of straightforward, unironic storytelling, along with accessible, two-dimensional characters whose adventures ended happily. Much of the appeal of *Star Wars* lay in the fact that it had no message, no sex, and only mild violence. It could be enjoyed by "kids" of all ages. It relied on a dazzling array of special effects and technological wizardry to mesmerize its audience. One critic called it a Wild West adventure in outer space. Another analyst, pondering the deeper meanings of *Star Wars,* suggested that it pointed the way toward a new American mythology in the wake of the disillusionment with the Vietnam War, which destroyed the American frontier myth. *Star Wars* represented a creative effort to reclaim lost American innocence. Lucas himself has suggested that "Star Wars" tapped into the latent religiosity of young people who felt spiritually unfulfilled in an increasingly hedonistic and secular age.

Surveys revealed that Americans watched more television shows than ever before during the 1970s. New technologies significantly enhanced the range and capabilities of the electronic medium. Communication satellites in geosynchronous orbits hundreds of miles in space enabled television news to provide live, instantaneous coverage of news events from anywhere on the planet. The 1970s also featured the beginning of cable television. Viewers were freed from having to rely on the three major networks that controlled prime time programming and the few shows appearing on local independent stations that were worth watching. By the late 1970s, due to the advent of cable utilizing the VHF channels, viewers who signed on for their services had a choice of twenty to thirty stations to watch. During the 1980s, cable television grew exponentially, and viewers could receive up to eighty channels. The most important new television technology of the 1970s was the introduction in 1975 of the videocassette recorder, or VCR. Early versions of VCRs were difficult to use and rather expensive; they were slow to catch on. Sales boomed in the 1980s and wrought another revolution in the nation's television and movie-viewing habits.

Because so many sporting events were televised during the 1970s, commercial spectator sports became a more important part of popular culture than ever before. Major professional spectator sports flourished, especially the National Football League (NFL), the National Basketball Association (NBA), and Major League baseball. Due in large part to television, professional football became the most popular national sport. Pro football is a fast-paced, complex, fiercely competitive, violent game played by tough, highly skilled athletes. Some analysts have linked its powerful hold on fans to the fact that pro football was a microcosm of the corporatist economy that America had become in the 1970s.

College sports, particularly football and basketball, grew rapidly in popularity, due in large part to television. The growth of these major college sports was tinged with scandals. Some schools recruited athletes who were simply not equipped to succeed academically. Unless they were among the very few elite athletes who went on to successful careers as professional athletes, most left school after their athletic eligibility was expended without degrees and without the prospect of professional careers of any kind.

Other scandals that plagued college football and basketball programs included illegal payments to "amateur" athletes by alumni boosters and drug use and criminal behavior among some athletes. The National Collegiate Athletic Association (NCAA) exercised a rather ineffectual policing function over intercollegiate athletics. From time to time, they would investigate collegiate athletic programs, find illegalities, and impose penalties. One had a sense that the NCAA sporadically discovered the tip of a scandalous iceberg. Amidst the commercialism and scandals of collegiate sports there was one positive innovation. Women athletes demanded parity with men at the nation's colleges and universities. Although most schools fell far short of achieving gender equality in their sports programs, scholarship support for female athletes significantly increased. Several college women's sports flourished, including basketball, volleyball, swimming, and softball; these breakthroughs for women athletes represented another victory for the powerful women's movement of the 1970s.

A DISMAL DECADE

The 1970s appear to have been a dismal decade for many Americans. The economic growth cycle that had sustained the affluent society for thirty years stalled. American power and prestige in the world declined. Politicians failed to provide effective leadership at home or abroad. The failure of the American war in Vietnam filled most Americans with shame. The revelations of the Watergate scandals filled most Americans with disgust. Revelations of wrongdoing by the CIA and the FBI infuriated most Americans. The Iranian hostage crisis humiliated most Americans.

For many citizens, 1970s' America no longer worked in accordance with traditional ideals and expectations. Young people coming of age during the 1970s enjoyed fewer opportunities and less mobility than their parents. Double-digit inflation undermined real per capita income. For the first time in over 100 years, the average workweek lengthened, reversing a long-running historic trend. Millions of Americans had to work harder for less money during the 1970s. With more and more married women with children having to work or choosing to work, family life often deteriorated. People had less leisure time and fewer satisfying or fulfilling ways of using it. Those with disposable incomes threw themselves into a mindless, frantic consumerism. They often bought trendy, new technologies, only to discard them after a short period of time. Many a personal computer sat idle, or perhaps found use as an expensive planter.

Americans of the 1970s had to face a plethora of troubling, divisive problems, many of which proved to be interrelated and intractable. Abortion, legalized by the Supreme Court in 1973, generated enormous strife and anguish. The country's growing dependence on expensive foreign oil remained a worrisome issue. The decline of America's manufacturing industries in the face of fierce foreign competition, and the decisions of American-based multinational corporations to export manufacturing operations presaged a bleak economic future for millions of American workers. Rising deficits in international trade balances and the federal budget made America the world's leading debtor nation. The failing public school system suggested that young people would be poorly prepared for good jobs that were becoming scarce. Social problems abounded: medical care was too expensive for the millions of working-class families who did not have health insurance coverage. There were serious shortcomings in the care available for the handicapped, the very elderly, and the terminally ill. An epidemic of drug use swept the nation in the 1970s. There was a rising tide of crime, especially serious and violent crime. Massive poverty continued, as did discrimination against racial minorities, women, and gay and lesbian people, despite the gains that these groups had made during the 1960s. Continuing serious ecological problems fouled the air and poisoned the environment.

It is little wonder that the American people turned to an aging former film actor in 1980 who promised to restore American primacy in world affairs and revitalize the American economy. Even more important, Ronald Reagan promised to restore the American dream and make Americans feel good about themselves once again.

IMPORTANT EVENTS

1974	Gerald Ford assumes the presidency
	President Ford pardons Nixon
1975	Saigon falls to the Communists
1976	Jimmy Carter is elected president
1977	Panama Canal treaties are signed
1978	The U.S. Supreme Court delivers the *Bakke* decision
	The Revolution in Iran occurs
1979	The Camp David accords are signed
	U.S. hostages are taken in Teheran
	The United States and China resume normal diplomatic relations
	The USSR invades Afghanistan
	The Carter Doctrine is announced
	The Sandinistas triumph in Nicaragua
1980	Ronald Reagan is elected president

BIBLIOGRAPHY

One of the most important general studies of American history from 1945 to the mid-1970s has been done by Godfrey Hodgson, in *America in Our Time*. Peter N. Carroll's *It Seemed Like Nothing Happened* is a general political and social history of the 1970s. Both President Ford and President Carter have written their memoirs. Ford's is called *A Time to Heal;* Carter's is entitled *Keeping Faith: Memoirs of a President*. John Osborne has written the best account of the Ford presidency in *White House Watch: The Ford Years*. A. James Reichley's *Conservatives in an Age of Change* is an interesting account of the rising conservative cause throughout the 1970s. Peter Steinfels, in *The Neo-Conservatives*, offers a critical account of the emergence of a neoconservative intelligentsia in the late 1970s. A lively account of the rise of the Sunbelt region to political prominence is Kirkpatrick Sale's *Power Shift: The Rise of the Southern Rim and Its Challenge to the Eastern Establishment*. Stanley Hoffmann, in *Primacy and World Order*, features a critical assessment of the Ford administration's foreign policy. A critical study of the Carter presidency has been done by Clark Mollenkoff, in *The President Who Failed: Carter Out of Control*. Barry Rubin's *Paved with Good Intentions: The American Experience in Iran* is the best study of the Iranian fiasco. A good study of the energy crises of the 1970s is Richard Victor's *Energy Policy in America Since 1945*. CIA abuses of power are portrayed in Victor Marchetti's and John D. Marks's *The CIA and the Cult of Intelligence*. David Halberstam, in *The Reckoning*, accounts for the decline of the American auto industry during the 1970s. The implications of recent demographic shifts are discussed in Joseph J. Spengler's *Population and America's Future*. Several economists have written important books on the 1970s' economic crises. See Robert L. Heilbroner's *An Inquiry into the Human Prospect*; Lester Thurow's *The Zero Sum Game*; and Robert Reich's *The New American Frontier*. American economic decline during the 1970s is charted in Barry Bluestone's and Bennett Harrison's *The Deindustrialization of America*. A fine recent study, edited by Michael A. Bernstein and David E. Adler, *Understanding American Economic Decline*, is the best analysis of the causes of the economic downturn that began in the early 1970s. A good study of the impact of computer technology on American society and culture is Tracy Kidder's *The Soul of a New Machine*. For information about African Americans during the 1970s, read Ken Auletta's *The*

Underclass and William J. Wilson's *The Declining Significance of Race*. Wilson, one of the nation's most imminent sociologists, has recently completed another important study, *When Work Disappears: The World of the New Urban Poor*. *Today's Immigrants: Their Stories* is a recent study by Thomas Kessner and Betty Caroli. There is an extensive and generally excellent literature on women during the 1970s and 1980s. See Winifred D. Wandersee's *On the Move: American Women in the 1970s*. Mary Ann Mason's *The Equality Trap* is a perceptive study of the limitations of liberal feminism and its failure to cope with the economic plight of divorced working women. Christopher Lasch, in *The Culture of Narcissism: American Life in the Age of Diminishing Expectations*, captures many of the anxieties and the discontent of the American people during the era of limits. Gillian Peele's *Revival and Reaction: The Right in Contemporary America* is a study of current religious and political conservatism. Current education trends are analyzed in Sanford W. Reitman's *Education, Society, and Change*.

15

America in the Eighties

W
HEN President Ronald Wilson Reagan addressed the nation on inauguration day on January 20, 1981, it marked the coming to power
of a resurgent conservatism. Left for dead in the wake of the Goldwater debacle of 1964, conservatism had revived, gathered momentum during the
1970s, and captured the White House and the Senate in 1980, when Reagan easily
defeated the discredited Democratic incumbent Jimmy Carter. Resurgent conservatives did not form a monolithic political movement; rather, they represented a
diverse collection of people, unhappy with the results of what they saw as nearly
fifty years of liberal mismanagement of government. There was no essential conservative philosophy accepted by all politicians who called themselves conservatives. They formed no consensus and often bickered among themselves over issues
and priorities. Libertarians and the religious rightists often locked horns over fundamental principles and the use of governmental power. In reality, a miscellany of
ideas, policy proposals, and critiques were melded together under the marketing
label "conservative."

In the early 1970s, conservatives of various stripes voiced their vehement opposition to many liberal public policies that they believed were bringing about too
much social change too quickly. Many conservative whites, in both the North and
the South, attacked what they called "forced bussing" to integrate the public
schools. They also denounced affirmative action programs that guaranteed minorities, particularly African Americans, equal opportunity in their quest for
schooling and employment. Antifeminist conservatives opposed the Equal Rights
Amendment and helped defeat it. They also opposed efforts to protect the rights
of gays and lesbians. Most conservatives opposed all gun control measures and favored the restoration of capital punishment. They were outraged when the
Supreme Court issued its controversial *Roe v. Wade* (1973), which granted women

the right to an abortion on demand during the first trimester of a pregnancy. Conservatives also attacked other Supreme Court rulings made during the 1970s that outlawed prayer in the public schools and appeared to strengthen the rights of criminals at the expense of law enforcement personnel. Evangelical Christians stressed the cruciality of tradition, religion, and family values. Most conservatives attacked welfare programs and high taxes, and they deplored the erosion of wave-the-flag patriotism. Traditional business conservatives championed free-enterprise capitalism, criticized government regulation of economic activity, and attacked trade unions.

New Right conservatives, whose chief national leaders were Barry Goldwater and Ronald Reagan, believed that Soviet leaders were the personification of evil and responsible for all that had gone wrong in the world since 1945. They insisted that America must maintain an arsenal of thermonuclear and conventional weapons to contain the aggressive tendencies of the Kremlin and its clients. These conservatives lamented the decline of U.S. power and prestige in the world, symbolized by the Vietnam debacle and the Iranian hostage crisis.

The varied groups that called themselves conservative, led by Ronald Reagan, brought about a remarkable transformation in the way the American people viewed conservatism. Since the New Deal era of the 1930s, the term *conservative* had been a political epithet; conservativism connoted selfishness, antiintellectualism, and most of all, an irrational clinging to traditional ways in the face of novel, unprecedented challenges. But since the 1970s, with the Democratic Party and especially its liberal wing under siege as the icons of discredited and dysfunctional policies, conservatives have stepped forward as dynamic agents of change. Carter appeared to be the inept defender of the status quo in the face of Reagan's dynamism and calls for renewal. It may have been hard for liberal Democrats to understand, but in the election of 1980, to a large majority of voters, the conservative Republican agenda of evangelical Christianity, family values, supply-side economics, and a hard-line, anti-Soviet foreign policy looked quite like a much-needed reform program to revitalize and redeem America.

THE MEDIA MAN

Reagan emerged nationally in 1964 when he made a televised fund-raising speech on behalf of Barry Goldwater's conservative crusade. "The Speech," as it came to be called, had a powerful impact on his audience and launched Reagan's political career. In his first try for public office in 1966, the voters elected Ronald Reagan governor of California. Quickly the former television host, screen actor, and radio sportscaster assumed national leadership of the rising conservative cause. He made his first bid for the presidency in 1968, but he was stymied by Nixon's Southern strategy in Miami. Reagan tried again in 1976, narrowly losing to Ford, and at age sixty-nine, he won the office in 1980 on his third try.

Reagan had been an evangelical Christian since childhood, and his religious beliefs strongly influenced his life and thought. A large, handsome man with a sunny disposition, Reagan's essential traits included a kind of "aw shucks" modesty that voters found irresistible. He also had a sense of himself as destiny's child, a blessed man fated for distinction. Reagan possessed a lively sense of humor and a limitless fund of stories and anecdotes, which he used with great political skill. The private man differed from the affable public persona that Reagan consistently projected. He was a shy man, emotionally reticent. He was never close to his children, none of whom could ever remember having an intimate conversation with their famous father. No one, except possibly his second wife Nancy, ever got close to him or really knew him.

He mastered the art of media politics. Reagan's ability to deliver prepared remarks rivaled that of Franklin Roosevelt's, the new president's idol and role model. Nicknamed the "Great Communicator," Reagan showed great political skill by appealing to all varieties of conservatives and keeping these disparate constituencies united as well as attracting a broad spectrum of Independent and Democratic voters. The outcome of the 1980 election and the subsequent popularity that he sustained for most of his presidency convinced Reagan that most Americans shared his conservative vision and rejected what he called the "liberal special interest groups."

THE ADVENT OF REAGANOMICS

When Reagan took office in January 1981, runaway inflation had ravaged the American economy for years. The average family's purchasing power was about $1,000 less than it had been a decade earlier. The new president called upon his fellow Americans to join him "in a new beginning" to clean up "the worst economic mess since the Great Depression." He blamed "the mess" on high levels of government spending and taxation. He said, "Government is not the solution to our problems; government is the problem."

Influenced by an economist on the faculty of the University of Southern California, Arthur Laffer, Reagan grounded his program for economic recovery in "supply-side" economic theory. Contradicting the long-prevailing Keynesian theory, which relied on government spending and tax cuts to boost consumer demand, supply-siders favored cutting both federal spending and taxes at the same time. According to supply-siders, high taxes siphoned capital that otherwise would be invested in productive enterprises. They believed that the private sector, freed from shackles imposed by government regulation and high taxes, would increase its investment in productive enterprises, thereby generating economic growth and creating millions of new, well-paying jobs. Economic growth also would cut inflation and generate increased tax revenues, despite the lower tax rates. Government expenditures would be trimmed by shrinking government benefits. Spending cuts, combined with the projected economic expansion, would bring in a balanced budget. To many skeptics, "Reaganomics" sounded almost too good to be true. When George Bush had campaigned for the presidential nomination in the 1980 Republican primaries, he had ridiculed Reagan's economic notions, calling them "voodoo economics."

The president brought a mixed group of senior advisers to Washington. He appointed James A. Baker as his chief of staff. Baker urged Reagan to move quickly on his key issues—tax cuts and the military buildup. At the Treasury Department, he installed Donald Regan, a securities broker and conservative Republican. David Stockman became director of the Office of Management and Budget. Stockman, who was a supply-side zealot, carried to Congress Reagan's program of cutting spending and reducing taxes. Stockman mastered the intricacies of the congressional budgetary process. While Stockman overhauled the federal budgetary process, Paul Volcker, a Carter holdover and chairman of the Federal Reserve Board, kept a tight rein on the money supply with high interest rates.

Stockman made cutting federal spending the Reagan administration's top priority. He slashed $41 billion in social spending for food stamps, public service jobs, student loans, school lunches, urban mass transit, and welfare payments. Middle-class entitlements, such as Social Security, were exempted, and Reagan also

Figure 15.1   President Ronald Reagan taking the oath of office from Supreme Court Justice Warren Earl Burger. At the new president's side stands the new First Lady, Nancy Davis Reagan. Photographer: Bill Fitz-Patrick. *Source:* The White House Photo Office, neg.# 2681717A.

left what he called a "safety net for the truly needy." At the same time he was cutting back social spending, Reagan increased military spending sharply.

Reagan persuaded many Sunbelt Democratic congressmen to support his programs. These "boll weevils," led by Representative Phil Gramm of Texas, were crucial in getting his program through the Democratic-controlled House. Reagan made a dramatic personal appearance before a joint session of Congress to plead for his budget only a few weeks after being seriously wounded during an attempt on his life. His performance was dazzling; even Democrats who opposed his budget and could not abide Reagan's conservative political philosophy were on their feet applauding the gallant old actor. He had built up a strong bipartisan coalition in the House and won a commanding 253-to-176 victory. His winning margin in the Senate was even more impressive, 78 to 20. Many liberal Democrats were skeptical that supply-side economics could work, but they lacked an alternative program that commanded public support.

Congress enacted the key element of Reagan's economic policy—tax cuts. The Economic Recovery Tax Act of 1981 was the most significant legislation of the Reagan era. Based on a proposal by Senator William Roth and Congressman Jack Kemp, the across-the-board tax cuts reduced basic personal income tax rates by 25 percent over three years. It also indexed tax brackets, which kept tax rates constant when incomes rose solely because of inflation. Congress wrote additional tax concessions into an omnibus bill. Taxes on capital gains, inheritance taxes, and gift taxes also were reduced. Business tax write-offs were enhanced. The Reagan tax cuts, with congressional sanction, were the most generous tax reductions in the nation's history.

Reagan also sought to achieve his goal of reducing federal regulation of the economy. He appointed men and women to federal regulatory agencies who shared his views that markets, not governmental agencies, ought to direct the national economy. He appointed Anne Gorsuch Burford, who opposed air quality and toxic waste regulations, to head the Environmental Protection Agency (EPA). During her tenure, the EPA budget was slashed, and all of its enforcement efforts were weakened. Reagan's most controversial appointment was James Watt, to head the Department of the Interior. Watt had directed an antienvironmentalist legal action group before his appointment to the Interior Department. He supported stripmining and favored opening up public lands to private developers, including offshore oil-drilling sites. Reagan tried to eliminate the Department of Energy; failing to do that, he settled for severe cuts in its budget and operations. He persuaded Congress to cut federal spending for elementary and secondary education. Much of the responsibility, and the costs, of regulatory activity was shifted to the states.

Drew Lewis, Reagan's secretary of transportation, removed many of the regulations to reduce pollution and increase driver safety that had been imposed on the U.S. auto industry during the 1970s. He also persuaded the Japanese to voluntarily restrict automobile imports to the United States. Lewis opposed an illegal strike by an air traffic controller's union (PATCO) in the summer of 1981. President Reagan fired the 11,500 striking workers, decertified the union, and ordered Lewis to train and hire thousands of new air controllers to replace them. The destruction of the air traffic controller's union was the most devastating defeat for organized labor in modern times. It demoralized a labor movement already reeling from the decline of American manufacturing and loss of political clout.

By the end of the summer of 1981, "Reaganomics" was in place. The new leader had wielded executive power with great skill and effectiveness. Reagan had asserted a popular mandate, seized the political initiative, redefined the public agenda, and got most of his program implemented. *Time* magazine observed that, "No President since FDR had done so much of such magnitude so quickly to change the economic direction of the country." Reaganomics amounted to nothing less than a radical assault on the liberal welfare state erected during the previous fifty years.

Aware that few African Americans had voted Republican, the Reagan administration was unresponsive to black concerns. Federal support for civil rights weakened. Reagan opposed affirmative action hiring programs, which he believed amounted to reverse discrimination. His Attorney General, Edwin Meese, opposed bussing to achieve school desegregation. The number of African American officials appointed to major government positions declined. The budgets for federal agencies responsible for enforcing civil rights programs were curtailed. Both the staff and budget of the Civil Rights Division of the Justice Department were cut. The Justice Department filed few school desegregation and fair housing suits during Reagan's first term as president.

Reagan's record for appointments of women was better than his record for African Americans. He appointed a few highly visible women to top government positions. He fulfilled a campaign pledge and made a major symbolic gesture to women when he appointed Sandra Day O'Connor to the Supreme Court, the first women jurist ever chosen. He appointed Jeane Kirkpatrick as the U.S. Ambassador to the United Nations. Several women served in his cabinet. Reagan opposed the Equal Rights Amendment, and he was an outspoken foe of abortion, denouncing *Roe v. Wade*.

RECESSION AND RECOVERY

After a year, it was evident that Reaganomics had not brought about an economic revival but instead had produced a recession. Unemployment exceeded 9 percent, the highest rate since 1941. Business bankruptcies rose to depression levels. Steep interest rates priced homes and cars beyond the reach of millions of families and plunged those two major industries into depression. The nation was mired in its worst slump since the Great Depression. Manufacturing output declined, and the construction industry slumped. Big cities fared the worst. In Detroit, unemployment reached 20 percent. Bewildered and angry workers, many of them "Reagan Democrats," lined up to receive their unemployment checks. A class of "new poor," not seen since the 1930s, appeared on the streets: homeless, unemployed workers and their families.

Figure 15.2   Sandra Day O'Connor, the first woman to be appointed to the U.S. Supreme Court. O'Connor (1930–) was the first female justice of the U.S. Supreme Court.   *Source:* Supreme Court Historical Society.

Supply-side economics did not work as advertised, and the promised increased tax revenues from economic growth never materialized. Instead, a combination of deep tax cuts, steep hikes in military spending, and drastic economic shrinkage drove the federal budget deficit to over $100 billion, the highest ever. The one bright spot in an otherwise dark economic picture was declining inflation. It dropped from 13 percent in 1980 to 9 percent in 1981, and fell to 5 percent in 1982. The short-term failure of Reaganomics derived from two fiscal realities: the failure of the tax cuts to stimulate increased business investment and continuing high interest rates that put a crimp in both business spending and consumer purchases. Reagan, confronting a declining economy and a rising storm of criticism, pleaded for time. He insisted that Reaganomics did not cause the downturn, that it came from the accumulated mismanagement and mistaken policies of his Democratic predecessors. Reagan promised that prosperity would come but that it would have protracted birthing pains. The recession worsened throughout 1982. Toward the end of the year, unemployment reached 10 percent; over 11 million Americans were out of work.

The 1982 midterm elections took place amidst the worst economic conditions this country had seen in over forty years. Undaunted, Reagan campaigned hard for his program and for Republican candidates. The election amounted to a referendum on Reaganomics. The Democrats picked up twenty-five House seats, but the Republicans held on to the Senate. When the new Congress convened in January 1983, Reagan lost his bipartisan majority coalition that had pushed through Reaganomics. House Speaker Thomas "Tip" O'Neill, the leader of the opposition to Reaganomics, forced the president to accept budget compromises in 1983. Cuts in social spending were lessened, and increases in military spending were reduced.

The economy recovered strongly in 1983, and the surge continued in 1984. The gross domestic product rose by 6.8 percent in 1984, the largest one-year gain since the Korean War. Unemployment and interest rates declined. Housing starts and new car sales picked up; domestic automakers reported strong sales and record profits in mid-1984. The rate of inflation dropped to 4 percent for both years, the lowest since the early 1970s. Personal income rose, and consumer and business confidence soared. Abundant world oil supplies were an important cause of the drop in the rate of inflation. By the end of 1984, OPEC was in disarray and world oil prices were plummeting. The economic expansion that began in 1983 continued into the early 1990s. It was the longest sustained period of prosperity in modern American history. Economic growth generated 18 million new jobs and tripled the price of stocks by 1990.

Despite the strong rebound in 1983, serious problems continued to plague the American economy. Tax cuts combined with large increases in military spending to generate record federal deficits. The nation's international trade deficit reached a record $108 billion in 1984. The main causes of the soaring international debt were the nation's continuing thirst for foreign oil and imported manufactures, such as autos, VCRs, cameras, and stereos. By the end of his first term, Reagan had managed to double the national debt. All talk of balanced budgets had been replaced by a frenzied concern to staunch the flow of red ink. Amidst the economic boom, over 7.5 million Americans remained out of work. The Census Bureau reported that the nation's poverty rate reached 15.2 percent in 1983, the highest since 1965, when Lyndon Johnson had begun his war on poverty. There were 35 million poor people in America, 6 million more than when Reagan assumed office.

THE COLD WAR REVIVED

Because of his lack of experience and because he made reviving the economy his top priority, from the outset Reagan relied heavily on advisers both for forging and implementing U.S. foreign policy. For the new president, the traditional verities of the Cold War still prevailed: America and its allies were locked in a life-or-death struggle for survival with a ruthless, expansionist Soviet empire. Reagan repudiated previous efforts at détente and announced his intention to challenge the Soviets around the globe. He launched a rapid buildup of military power to give the United States the muscle it needed to prevail in the long, twilight struggle with its global rival. He also announced what came to be known as the "Reagan Doctrine"—that the United States would help anti-Communist resistance movements wherever they cropped up in the world.

Reagan also made clear that he intended to make major use of the CIA as an instrument of American foreign policy, especially its covert paramilitary operations. He freed U.S. arms sales from the restrictions imposed by the Carter administration and scrapped Carter's human rights policies. Reagan appointed his campaign manager and good friend William Casey to head the restored CIA. Reagan viewed the Cold War between the United States and the Soviet Union as fundamentally a moral conflict. Perhaps borrowing from his Hollywood days as an action hero, he saw himself as the leader of the "good guys" against the "bad guys" in the Kremlin. He denounced the Soviet Union in a speech before the United Nations in 1982, charging that Soviet agents were working everywhere in the world, "violating human rights and unnerving the world with violence." Addressing a convention of evangelical Christians in Orlando, Florida, in May 1983, he called the Soviet Union "an evil empire" and declared that the Soviet leaders were "the focus of evil in the modern world."

Secretary of Defense Caspar Weinberger proposed a $1.2 trillion defense buildup, which Regan strongly supported. It called for doubling U.S. military spending over five years, from $171 billion in 1981 to over $360 billion in 1986. This huge increase fulfilled Reagan's campaign pledge to "make America Number One again." Weinberger insisted that during Carter's presidency the Soviets had achieved strategic superiority over the United States. A "window of vulnerability" existed for American land-based missiles that could tempt the Soviets to try a "first strike" nuclear attack. Weinberger ordered building a new strategic bomber, a new strategic missile, and an expanded Navy, with 450 to 600 ships. Reagan strongly supported all of Weinberger's proposals for the military buildup. Reagan and other top officials spoke of being able "to prevail" in the event of a nuclear war with the Soviets. Such rhetoric, yoked to the gigantic increases in military spending, frightened millions of Americans, who feared that Reagan was preparing for a nuclear war with the Soviets.

Despite his tough anti-Communist rhetoric and expensive military buildup, Reagan initially found it difficult to assert pressure on Communist states. In late 1981, the Soviet Union forced Poland to impose martial law in order to crush a trade union movement that was pushing Poland toward democratic socialism. Reagan, outraged, found his options limited. He could not risk nuclear war with the Soviet Union. He could not persuade NATO allies to impose economic blockades on the USSR or Poland. He imposed an American boycott on the nearly bankrupt Polish economy, which only caused additional hardship on the Polish people without saving the trade union movement. The Polish crisis demonstrated once again the determination of the Soviets to hold on to their eastern European empire, regardless of what U.S. presidents said or did. Reagan also discovered that sovereign and prosperous NATO countries also felt no compunction about resisting some U.S. anti-Communist initiatives.

Reagan met with frustration again in Europe in 1982, when he tried to block a major economic arrangement between the Soviet Union and western European nations. The Soviets agreed to sell natural gas to the west Europeans if they would build a pipeline to transport the gas. The west Europeans had agreed to purchase the natural gas from Siberia and build the pipeline to transport it. The pipeline required American technology supplied by European corporations. Reagan tried and failed to stop the deal by imposing sanctions against these companies, some of which were partly government owned.

The Reaganauts had more success in stymieing Soviet efforts to crush Afghanistan's *mujahidin* rebels during the early 1980s. The CIA set up a clandestine arms supply operation. Arms were shipped to Pakistan and then smuggled into Afghanistan. The Soviets soon found themselves bogged down in a Vietnam-like quagmire. They unleashed a fearsome arsenal of modern high-tech weaponry against the rebels. Soviet infantry battalions, supported by armor, artillery, and helicopter gunships, tried to sweep the rebels from strategic valleys. The Soviets also tried to interdict the movement of arms and supplies from Pakistan and threatened the Pakistanis if they did not desist—all to no avail. The *mujahidin*, despite absorbing heavy casualties, maintained a determined resistance to Soviet efforts to pacify them. The application of the Reagan Doctrine in Afghanistan succeeded.

Reagan succeeded in implementing Carter's 1979 initiative to place 572 intermediate-range Cruise and Pershing II missiles in western Europe that could strike targets in the western regions of the Soviet Union. These missiles would counter Soviet SS-20 missiles already deployed and aimed at NATO countries. This initiative provoked an angry response from the Soviets, who tried to stop it. It also aroused opposition from leftist political leaders and peace groups in Europe, and from a "nuclear freeze" movement in the United States. In the spring of 1982, nearly a million nuclear freeze supporters gathered in Central Park, the largest political rally in American history.

To offset European and domestic opposition to his plan, Reagan offered two new arms control initiatives. The first, called the "zero option," offered to cancel the proposed deployment of Cruise and Pershing missiles in exchange for Soviet removal of their SS-20 missiles. Second, at a new series of arms talks between American and Soviet negotiators in Geneva, called START, the United States proposed that both sides scrap one-third of their nuclear warheads and permit land-based missiles to have no more than half of the remaining warheads. The Soviets did not take these proposals seriously and quickly rejected both. They had no incentive to remove missiles already in place in exchange for cancellation of weapons not yet deployed. They rejected the second offer because 70 percent of their warheads were on land-based missiles, compared to about one-third for the United States. However, these U.S. arms control proposals reassured nervous Europeans and slowed the nuclear freeze movement. When the new missiles began arriving in Great Britain and West Germany in 1983, the Soviets broke off the START talks.

The United States escalated the arms race in 1983, when Reagan ordered the Pentagon to develop a Strategic Defense Initiative (SDI). The SDI was an immensely complex antimissile defense system that used high-powered, space-based lasers to destroy enemy missiles in flight. The SDI was quickly dubbed "Star Wars" by its critics. Many scientists expressed skepticism that the SDI could work. If it could be built, they estimated that it would take years and cost $1 trillion. If it proved successful, the defense system also posed the danger of destabilizing the arms race because it would force the Soviets to build more missiles and develop an SDI of their own. President Reagan strongly backed the SDI, assuming that it could be built and would free the world from the deadly trap of deterrence based on mutually assured destruction. He clung to his vision of a world free from the threat posed by the nuclear arms race. Whatever his public image or the views of his critics, Ronald Reagan was at heart a passionate antinuclear idealist. His overriding goal was to escape the awful dilemma of Mutually Assured Destruction (MAD) that had kept both sides feverishly building more efficient weapons of mass destruction and had also kept both societies in a state of perpetual angst.

So the costly and dangerous nuclear arms race between the two superpowers roared on. Both sides continued to develop new weapons systems and to refine existing ones. Although both sides observed the unratified SALT II agreement, it placed few curbs on their activities. Arms control negotiations were suspended. The death of Russian leader Leonid Brezhnev, followed by two short tenures of old and sick successors, created a succession crisis for the Soviets. It also made any efforts at negotiations between the Soviets and the Americans difficult. In March 1985, a dynamic new leader emerged in the Soviet Union, Mikhail Gorbachev. Future negotiations on arms control between the two superpowers again became possible. Although he had only a few diplomatic successes against the Soviets, had escalated the arms race, and had intensified the Cold War, Reagan's efforts against the Soviets did restore a measure of American pride and self-confidence. Reagan showed that he had no fear of the Soviet Union and exuded confidence that America would eventually win the long Cold War. His great insight, derived at a time when few defense experts and Sovietologists shared his views, was that the Soviet Union was both evil and weak, and that it could be beaten if Americans kept the faith and increased defense spending. In a speech given in London in 1982, Reagan had predicted the collapse of Communism. Few pundits on either side of the Atlantic took his prediction seriously at the time he made it.

THE PACIFIC RIM

The Reagan administration also gave much attention to U.S. foreign policy interests in the Far East. Asia comprised a vast region of diverse nation states which, many experts believed, was destined to become the center of American diplomatic concerns early in the twenty-first century. The most important nations were China, home to a quarter of the planet's 6 billion inhabitants, and Japan, a nation that had risen from the ashes of total defeat at the end of World War II to become an economic powerhouse by the 1970s. The economies of South Korea, Taiwan, Hong Kong, Maylasia, and Singapore also were thriving in the early 1980s, their prosperity in large measure fueled, like Japan's, on the sale of manufactures to the United States and western Europe.

Washington did not have good relations with China initially, mainly because of Reagan's efforts to bolster the military forces of Taiwan, which the Chinese considered an integral part of their country. In 1984, Sino-American relations improved when Premier Zhao Zivang of the PRC visited the United States and signed agreements pledging cooperation between China and the United States in the crucial areas of industry, science, and technology. Reagan later visited China and signed pacts, pledging renewed cultural exchanges between the two countries. Relations between China and America were cordial by the end of Reagan's first term.

Diplomacy with Japan was the Reagan administration's prime Asian concern. Two major problems strained Japanese–American relations in 1981. The first concerned efforts by the Reagan administration to get Japan to pay a larger share of its defense costs rather than continue to sit comfortably behind the nuclear shield provided by U.S. taxpayers. The Japanese subsequently increased their defense outlays, to about .75 of 1 percent of GDP, less than what the Americans wanted.

The second, more serious problem concerned the growing imbalance in U.S.–Japanese trade that increasingly favored the Japanese. The imbalance had reached $10 billion in 1980 and $16 billion in 1981. The largest part of the imbalance derived from the sale of Japanese cars to U.S. consumers. In 1981, Japanese automakers sold almost 2 million cars to American buyers, hurting domestic automakers, who had lost 25 percent of their market to the Japanese in a decade. U.S. negotiators persuaded the Japanese to voluntarily reduce auto shipments to America for 1982, and they also convinced the Japanese to reduce barriers to the importation of U.S. agricultural commodities. Despite these concessions, the trade imbalance continued to grow in favor of Japan. It reached $20 billion in 1983 and shot up to $35 billion in 1984.

In Southeast Asia, the Vietnamese masses endured a life of poverty and oppression. Their Communist leaders discovered that they were far better equipped to fight American imperialism than they were to provide good government and a prosperous economy for their people. Soviet subsidies kept the backward Vietnamese economy going. Each year, thousands of Vietnamese fled the country to seek a better life for themselves and their families in Taiwan, Hong Kong, France, and the United States. Vietnam also maintained 200,000 troops in Kampuchea to support a puppet regime that the Vietnamese had installed in 1979. The Reagan administration indicated its displeasure with Vietnamese imperialism and also sought an accounting from the Hanoi government of the fate of thousands of American servicemen still missing in action (MIA) from the war. Washington made it clear to the Vietnamese leaders that there could be no improvement in official

American–Vietnamese relations until Vietnam pulled its troops out of Kampuchea and settled the MIA issue to the satisfaction of the concerned families.

DISASTER IN LEBANON

In the Middle East, the Reagan administration tried to continue the peace process, established by Carter, of providing Israel with strategic security and giving the Palestinians a homeland on the West Bank. The larger goal of U.S. Middle Eastern policy continued to be containing Soviet influence in that strategic region. While trying to implement its policies, the United States became embroiled in a civil war going on in Lebanon. Israel continued its policy of gradual annexation of the West Bank, ignoring the national aspirations of the Palestinians. In June 1982, in an effort to destroy the PLO, Israeli forces invaded Lebanon and besieged West Beirut, where refugee camps contained thousands of Palestinians and provided a base for PLO fighters. The PLO and other Muslim factions in Lebanon turned to Syria to counter the Israeli forces.

U.S. policy in Lebanon appeared contradictory. Even as it supported the Israeli invasion, the Reagan administration employed an envoy of Lebanese descent, Philip Habib, who arranged for the Israelis to lift their siege while a UN force supervised the removal of PLO forces. Following the removal of the PLO, the Israelis reoccupied West Beirut. On September 17, 1982, Lebanese Christian militia, working closely with Israeli forces, entered two Palestinian refugee camps and slaughtered hundreds of people in reprisal for the murder three days earlier of a Christian leader. Following the massacre of the Palestinians, the United States sent in troops to try to restore peace in Beirut.

But the U.S. forces came under siege themselves as civil war raged in the streets of Beirut between Christian and Muslim militias. Syrian forces, aided by the Soviets, occupied eastern Lebanon and controlled most of the Muslim factions. Israeli troops remained in southern Lebanon. The 1,500 U.S. Marines, isolated at the Beirut airport, without a clear-cut mission or sufficient force to maintain order, were perceived by the Muslims and their Syrian supporters to be aligned with the Christian forces.

The United States tried unsuccessfully to restore order to Lebanon and to arrange for the Syrians and Israelis to withdraw from that battered country. Early on the morning of October 23, 1983, a yellow Mercedes truck, loaded with explosives and driven by a Muslim terrorist, slammed into the U.S. Marine compound near the Beirut airport and killed 241 Marines who were sleeping inside. Reagan was forced to withdraw the remaining American forces in February 1984, which terminated the U.S. military presence in Lebanon.

The civil war went on. Syria remained the major force in Lebanese affairs. Lebanon became a fertile source of kidnappings and terrorist attacks on American citizens. Moderate Arab states refused to support U.S. Middle East policy, and the peace process appeared hopelessly stalled. Lebanon was a humiliating defeat for

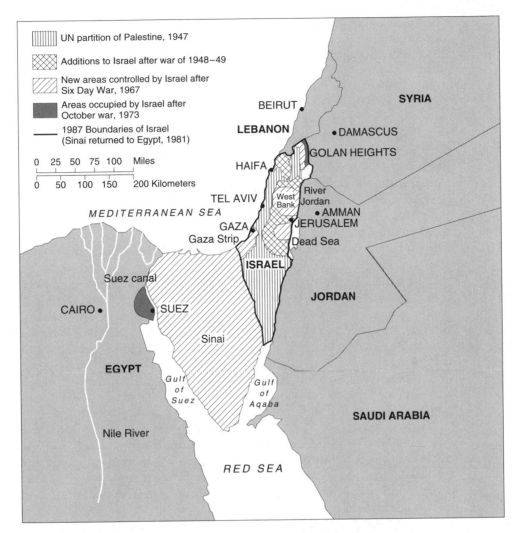

Figure 15.3   The Middle East, 1947–1981.   *Source:* U.S. State Department.

the Reagan administration, and the slaughter of the Marines constituted the worst U.S. military disaster since Vietnam.

POLICING THE WESTERN HEMISPHERE

Reagan administration officials also gave a high priority to Western Hemispheric affairs where the United States had long been the hegemonic power. Canada and America had long been each other's principal trading partner, and the two democratic nations shared the longest unfortified international boundary in the world.

Canada also was the chief supplier of foreign oil to the United States. Even so, relations between the two countries had not been warm in recent years. Canadian nationalists had long resented U.S. domination of many sectors of their economic life, and the two countries often were at odds over trade policies, NATO affairs, fishing rights, disarmament policies, and pollution. Relations between the two nations improved after a new conservative government, headed by Brian Mulroney, came to power in 1984. Mulroney and Reagan soon established a warm, personal relationship. Together they brought about a historic agreement: a treaty removing all barriers to trade between their two countries. The agreement went into effect in December 1988, making the Canadian–U.S. market the largest international free-trade zone in the world. Achievement of free trade with the Canadians was one of the major diplomatic achievements of the Reagan administration.

In addition to its concern with relations with Canada, the Reagan administration involved itself in the internal affairs of Central American countries. Reagan's immediate concern was stopping the spread of Communism in that region. Washington made its top priority overthrowing the Sandinista government in Nicaragua. The Sandinistas were friendly with Marxist leaders in Cuba and the Soviet Union, but they were not Communists. Reagan accused the Sandinistas of suppressing democratic elements within Nicaragua and aiding Marxist rebels in nearby El Salvador. Reagan viewed the Sandinista regime as a serious threat in Central America that must be contained, otherwise it could become another Cuba, using Nicaraguan military bases as staging areas to export Marxist–Leninist revolution to neighboring countries. At the time Reagan assumed the presidency, the CIA estimated that there were about 500 Cuban, Soviet, and east European military advisers, technicians, and intelligence operatives in Nicaragua.

In the spring of 1982, Reagan approved the use of CIA political and paramilitary operations to interdict arms shipments from Nicaragua to El Salvador and to overthrow the Sandinista regime. Washington's chosen instrument for deposing the Sandinistas was to be a "Contra" military force recruited from various groups of anti-Sandinista Nicaraguans, including former supporters of the deposed dictator, Anastasio Somoza Debayle.

Congress, skeptical of Reagan's Central American policy, enacted the Boland Amendment in December 1982, which forbade the CIA or the Pentagon to provide any funds or training to anyone for the purpose "of overthrowing the government of Nicaragua." Reagan appealed to Congress in 1983 for funds to "hold the line against externally supported aggression" in Central America. Congressional Democrats accused him of exaggerating the Cuban and Soviet threats, of relying too heavily upon military solutions, and of ignoring serious social and economic problems within Central American countries that bred rebellion. Public opinion polls revealed much popular opposition to U.S. military involvement in Central America and showed that many Americans feared being drawn into another Vietnam. Congress rejected Reagan's request for $80 million to support CIA covert operations against Nicaragua. Later, Congress reversed itself and approved $24 million for covert operations against the Sandinistas.

Meanwhile, the CIA continued its war on the Sandinistas. Contra forces, trained by the CIA at bases in neighboring Honduras, began operations inside Nicaragua. Other CIA-trained forces attacked various port installations at several sites. In early 1984, helicopters flown by CIA-trained operatives mined three of Nicaragua's major harbors. When Congress learned that CIA-trained forces had mined Nicaraguan harbors and damaged merchant ships, it cut off all American aid for the Contras. The World Court later ruled that the United States had violated international law and that Nicaragua could sue America for damages. With funding of its secret war in Nicaragua cut off by Congress, Washington made a deal with the Saudi Arabians, whereby the United States sold the Saudis 400 Stinger anti-aircraft missiles, in return for which they agreed to provide the Contras with $10 million. The administration also persuaded Israel to aid the Contras, and wealthy Americans also chipped in money. The Iran-Contra scandal originated in these efforts at creative financing to keep Washington's proxy war in Nicaragua afloat and to circumvent the will of Congress.

In El Salvador, the war between left-wing guerrillas and a right-wing government continued. Carter had cut off U.S. aid to the government following the murder of three American nuns by government forces. The Reagan administration restored and increased U.S. assistance and sent in forty-five U.S. military advisers to help government forces. The United States backed a government headed by a moderate democrat, Jose Napoleon Duarte. Duarte defeated the candidate of the extreme Right, Roberto d'Aubisson, in a 1984 election, and he began a reform program. He also tried to curb the excesses of right-wing "death squads" that had murdered thousands of civilians since the war began. But Duarte's forces could not defeat the rebels. The civil war continued.

While the Reagan administration pursued its proxy war against the Sandinistas in Nicaragua and backed the Duarte government in El Salvador, it also fought a brief miniwar for control of Grenada, a small island in the eastern Caribbean. Early on the morning of October 25, 1983, some 1,900 U.S. Marines and Army paratroopers stormed ashore. The U.S. forces invaded Grenada ostensibly to rescue several hundred American citizens studying medicine there. The main purpose of the invasion was to overthrow a Marxist regime headed by General Hudson Austin, who had recently come to power. What most concerned the Reagan administration was the construction of an airport at Point Salines that was capable of accommodating Fidel Castro's air force. The runway also could serve as a refueling station for Soviet aircraft ferrying weapons to the Sandinistas. Within four days, U.S. forces had overwhelmed the small Grenadian army and 784 Cuban construction workers who had been working on the airport. U.S. forces deposed the Austin regime and shipped the Cubans back to their island.

Most Grenadians welcomed the American armed forces as liberators who had rescued them from a tyrannical regime that had taken control of their island and was turning it into an outpost of Cuban and Soviet power. America installed a friendly, interim government and granted it $30 million in military and economic assistance. UN spokesmen, and within the United States, some liberal media pundits and politicians, condemned the Grenada operation as being pointless and immoral. They were drowned out by defenders of Washington's decision to invade the island. Public opinion polls showed that Reagan's actions enjoyed broad popular support. By staging a brief, dramatic, and low-casualty rescue operation only two days after the Marines were blown up in their barracks in Beirut, the Grenada miniwar diverted attention from that horrible tragedy and began to erase bad memories of previous U.S. foreign policy failures.

REAGAN: THE FIRST TERM

Liberal pundits frequently savaged Ronald Reagan. They were offended by both his conservative agenda and his seeming lack of some of the abilities normally associated with occupants of the Oval Office. Historian John Wiltz called Reagan "the least cerebral" of modern presidents. They portrayed him as a kind of ceremonial president: while he looked and acted the part, an inner circle of advisers made policy and ran the country. Reagan tended to disengage himself from the details of his day-to-day administration. On occasion, he dozed off at cabinet meetings while his advisers debated policy options. He often appeared dependent on his wife Nancy for advice and guidance, and the First Lady was fiercely protective of her husband's presidency and image. Reagan sometimes confused events that had transpired in the celluloid world of Hollywood films with political reality. He often was given to misstatements. During his presidency, Reagan's staffers became adept at damage control, at putting the proper "spin" on his more ludicrous remarks. At times, Reagan appeared to be an old actor playing the role of president rather than functioning as chief executive.

Even as his left-wing detractors ridiculed his intellectual and administrative shortcomings, they underated Reagan's remarkable political talents. Elitist intellectuals might have scoffed at the old actor's simplistic ideas, but Reagan understood that average American citizens could care less whether the president of the United States possessed a powerful mind or had mastered all of the facts and details of a policy or program. They wanted a leader, not a policy wonk, in office. Reagan also had a clear vision of the direction in which he wanted to move the country, and he was determined to succeed, to reverse the fifty-year trend whereby the federal government assumed increasing responsibility for underwriting the economic security and general welfare of the population. Reagan wanted to slash taxes and eliminate government regulations that he believed had shackled the entrepreneurial energies of the American people for a half-century. He also was determined to restore American military primacy in the world and to contain Soviet expansionism as Americans had done in the 1940s and 1950s, before the Vietnam debacle sapped their will. And if he could, he would win the Cold War.

In response to a succession of lackluster and failed presidencies, it had become part of the conventional political wisdom to assert that the presidency had gotten too large, had grown too complex, that contemporary problems had become too large and too complex for any mortal to master. Reagan's performance in office disproved such notions. He set out to strengthen the office of the presidency, to prove that he could do the job and do it well. He refurbished executive authority; he reasserted influence over Congress; and he centralized the budget-making process and brought the bureaucracies to heel. Ironically, Reagan became a strong, activist president in order to trim many federal programs. He confronted the dilemma that faced all conservative reformers committed to downsizing government at all levels; they first had to achieve power and assert strong leadership to make government less powerful, instrusive, and expensive.

Reagan largely succeeded in moving Congress and the American people in accordance with his conservative vision. He retained the trust and affection of a large majority of his fellow citizens for most of his presidency. He did not destroy the welfare state, if that was his intent, but he trimmed its sails. The social service state was pared down, and the social contract was attenuated. The economy, after enduring a bitter recession in 1982, rebounded strongly. Inflation was brought under control, and long-term, stable growth for the rest of the decade of the 1980s ensured national prosperity. Reagan strengthened the armed forces, and Americans were treated with a new respect in the world by both friends and foes. Most Americans became more optimistic about both their present conditions and the future of the nation. Reagan's stirring speeches helped lift the malaise that had fastened itself on the nation during the era of limits. Reagan proved to be the most popular and successful president since Eisenhower.

But there was a dark side to the Reagan record. Huge deficits in the federal budget and international trade roared out of control. America found itself becoming the world's largest debtor nation. While yuppies prospered, the number of poor Americans increased. Ronald Reagan presided over a major redistribution of national income, away from the poor and toward the rich. During Reagan's presidency, the rich became richer, while the poor became poorer. The Reagan administration had scant interest in civil rights or ecological concerns. Drugs poured into the country, and crime rates soared.

THE ELECTION OF 1984

Reagan's landslide reelection victory on November 6, 1984, reaffirmed his vast personal popularity. His forty-nine-state sweep expressed voter approval of the strong economic recovery and the country's powerful military buildup. Reagan received 525 electoral votes, the largest total in history. Former Vice President Walter Mondale, the Democratic Party candidate, carried only his home state of Minnesota and the District of Columbia. Reagan got 52.7 million votes (59 percent) to 36.5 million (41 percent) for Mondale. The Republicans gained thirteen seats in the House and won seventeen of thirty-three Senatorial elections, retaining a 54-to-46 majority.

Reagan's smashing reelection victory crossed all regional and most demographic lines. The Democrats appeared to have no remaining regional base of support. In the once-Solid South, every state went for Reagan by decisive majorities. In the West and Southwest, Reagan won easily. The Northeast, once the stronghold of both moderate Republicans and liberal Democrats, also voted for Reagan. He swept the industrial states of the Great Lakes and the Midwestern farm belt, despite continuing economic problems in both of those regions. All age groups voted for him. He did especially well among young, first-time voters, ages eighteen to twenty-one. Baby boomers voted 2 to 1 for Reagan. Half of union members voted for Reagan, even though Mondale's chief backers were the AFL-CIO leadership. Class and ethnic differences were visible in the voting returns. Middle-class and wealthy voters overwhelmingly supported Reagan. Less affluent voters generally supported Mondale. Ninety percent of blacks voted for Mondale, as did 60 percent of Hispanics. Election results showed Hispanics to be an emerging political force, comprising large voting blocs in populous states with large chunks of electoral votes such as California, Texas, and Florida.

At the outset of the election campaign, Reagan had appeared vulnerable to charges that Reaganomics unfairly favored the rich and hurt the poor. His Middle East policy had failed in Lebanon. His Central American policy was controversial, and the Soviets had broken off arms control talks. There had been several scandals involving administration members. But Reagan mounted a buoyant and an energetic campaign. His reelection bid used slick television commercials that emphasized the restoration of the national economy and national pride, while avoiding specific issues. His commercials stressed the themes of redemption, family values, and patriotism. His chief speech writer, Peggy Noonan, wrote the best line of his campaign: "America is back: it's morning again."

Reagan also was helped significantly by what liberal Democratic Congresswoman Pat Schroeder called the "Teflon presidency": the public and most of the established media did not hold Reagan accountable for his failures or for wrongdoing by members of his administration. Reagan, during his first term, enjoyed the most favorable press of any modern president.

Mondale tried to focus the campaign on issues, but he never found one that enabled him to cut into the president's huge lead. Public opinion polls showed that voters disapproved of many of Reagan's specific policies, but they were voting for him because they liked and trusted the man. Given world and national conditions, probably no Democrat could have beaten Reagan in 1984. Mondale also hurt whatever chance he might have had to win by announcing bluntly to American voters at the outset of his campaign that he intended to raise taxes if he won. Polls showed that most Americans believed that they were better off economically in 1984 than they had been in 1980. Mondale came across poorly on television. His droopy-eyed appearance and the nasal twang in his voice projected negativism and pessimism. In contrast, the telegenic Reagan exuded energy, goodwill, and unrelenting optimism.

In defeat, the Democrats made history twice. First, Jesse Jackson, the first serious black candidate for president, conducted a spirited primary campaign,

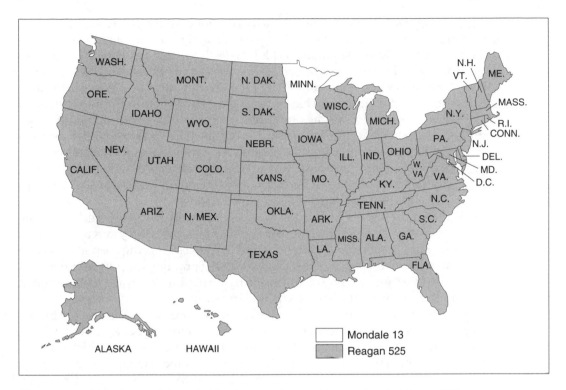

Figure 15.4 The electoral vote, 1984. *Source:* George D. Moss, *Moving On*, p. 337.

getting 18 percent of the vote and winning 373 delegates to the Democratic Convention. Second, Mondale's running mate, Representative Geraldine Ferraro, the first woman vice presidential candidate on a major party ticket, conducted a historic campaign. But Ferraro was on the defensive during much of her campaign because of her violations of campaign spending laws and because of some of her husband's questionable business practices. She neither strengthened a weak Democratic ticket nor enabled Mondale to exploit the "gender gap." Jackson's campaign proved to be too radical and divisive. His promised "rainbow coalition" of all disadvantaged Americans failed to congeal; his political base never reached much beyond the African American community.

THE SECOND TERM

President Reagan began his second term in January 1985, convinced that most Americans endorsed his policies. He reorganized his White House staff with not entirely happy results. His chief of staff, James Baker, switched jobs with Secretary of the Treasury Donald Regan. Regan never developed the rapport with the president that Baker had enjoyed, nor did he have the ability to compensate for or protect Reagan from his shortcomings, as had Baker. Two other personal advisers also departed: Michael Deaver and Edwin Meese, who along with Baker, had formed a "Troika" that was responsible for much of the Reagan administration's legislative successes during the first term. Deever formed a public relations firm to cash in on his White House connections; he promptly ran afoul of laws forbidding influence peddling. Meese became attorney general, where he managed to establish the lowest ethical and legal standards for the nation's top law enforcement office since the days of Warren G. Harding. Meese was in continual difficulty with congressional investigators because of some of his unsavory associations and because of the slipshod manner in which he handled his personal finances.

Reagan made tax reform his top legislative priority for his second term. The federal tax system had become exceedingly complex over the years as Congress had factored in a great many exemptions and loopholes favoring corporations and wealthy individual taxpayers. Polls showed strong popular support for revising a tax structure that former President Carter had called a "disgrace to the human race" and Reagan himself had termed "un-American."

Bipartisan support for tax revision gradually emerged in Congress, led by Democratic Congressman Daniel Rostenkowski and Republican Senator Robert Packwood. In the summer of 1986, Congress passed the Tax Reform Act, which brought the first fundamental overhaul of the modern federal income tax system since its inception during World War II. The act simplified the tax code by eliminating many tax shelters and deductions. It reduced multiple tax brackets on individuals to just three, at rates of 15, 28, and 33 percent. It removed 6 million poor Americans from the federal income tax rolls and lowered the tax burden for a majority of taxpayers. The new law shifted some of the tax burden to the business community by closing loopholes and eliminating write-offs and exemptions. Many corporations that had paid little or no federal income tax would pay more under the new law.

Reagan shared another major achievement when his administration supported a landmark immigration bill passed by Congress in October 1986. The bill revamped the 1965 act, offering legal status to millions of aliens living illegally in the United States. It also required employers to ask for identification, verifying the citizenship of job applicants, and it levied fines on employers who hired illegal aliens.

Another pressing problem to which Reagan was slow to respond was the acquired immunodeficiency syndrome (AIDS) epidemic, which swept the country during the mid-1980s and each year killed thousands of mostly gay males. For years, the administration refused to publicly acknowledge AIDS, and it was, at least in the eyes of those most concerned about fighting the disease, painfully slow to support increased AIDS research and study. Administration officials mainly called for the mandatory testing of categories of people thought to be at risk, or those who held positions of public responsibility. Meanwhile, the disease continued to wreak devastation. AIDS became a worldwide epidemic, and it struck with a special fury among the people of several Central and East African nations.

Reagan came to Washington in 1981, committed to waging a war on drugs and bringing the international drug trade under control. Drug traffic in marijuana, cocaine, and heroin flourished in the mid-1980s. America was the world's major consumer of illicit drugs. The immense costs of America's gargantuan drug habit included thousands of deaths annually, health problems for millions, huge increases in urban crime, corruption in the criminal justice system, and loss of productivity. Efforts to enforce drug laws and American-financed efforts to eradicate drug crops at their sources in Asia and Latin America continued to be ineffective. One of the major reasons for the failure of the Reagan administration's war against drugs, popularized by First Lady Nancy Reagan, was its inability to slow the great American appetite for drugs. All efforts to curtail the supply side of the drug problem were doomed to fail until a measure of control could be imposed on the demand side.

After years of activity and having spent $3 billion, Reagan announced early in 1988 that the war against drugs had been won. His claim was preposterous. According to contemporary surveys, 25 million Americans regularly used marijuana, 6 million regularly used cocaine, particularly "crack," and another million were heroin addicts. Public opinion polls showed that Americans considered the drug epidemic to be the nation's number one domestic problem. Washington's policy of criminalizing drug use and interdicting the supply, either at the source or at the point of entry into this country, was failing as Reagan's presidency ended. Experts suggested that an alternative policy, one that focused on educating people, especially young people, about the hazards of drug use, and one that relied on therapies, counseling, and community support groups to wean people from drug dependencies, promised better results over the long term.

THE "GO-GO" ECONOMY

The economy continued to perform strongly through Reagan's second term. Inflation remained under control, and oil supplies were plentiful. Growth rates averaged 3 percent to 4 percent per annum; many corporations enjoyed record sales and profits, and continually expanded their production. The stock market continued to push through record highs as the Great Bull Market of the 1980s roared on. Consumer spending and consumer confidence remained high.

Despite the economy's strong performance, serious problems plagued the American economy. Individual and corporate indebtedness increased rapidly. The takeover mania that had gripped Wall Street during the 1980s continued. Most of these corporate buyouts were severely "leveraged"; that is, they were financed by a consortia of bankers and brokerage houses that often sold huge portfolios of "junk bonds" (high-yield, high-risk securities issued by companies with low credit ratings) to raise the vast sums of capital needed to buy out shareholders at above-market prices. Once the corporate raiders acquired operating control of the company, they often had to sell off its profitable assets to raise the sums required to meet the huge interest payments on the indebtedness they had contracted to buy out the former stockholders.

Leveraged buyouts (LBOs) usually did not make the economy more productive or competitive; in fact, they often left companies weaker and in serious debt, with no funds for research or the development of new products. Aggregate net capital investment also was not enhanced by these takeovers and mergers. Toward the end of Reagan's presidency, investigations exposed some of the financial wizards who had brokered corporate takeover deals as criminals who had violated laws against insider trading. The two biggest names were high fliers Ivan Boesky and Michael Milken, both of whom served years in jail, paid millions of dollars in fines, and saw their business careers ruined.

Budget deficits continued to grow, exceeding $200 billion in 1986. During Reagan's presidency, the national debt tripled—from $1 trillion to $3 trillion! Paying the annual interest due on the national debt became the third largest item in the federal budget, after social security and defense. The massive indebtedness came about as a result of a tacit agreement between the Reagan White House and the Democrats in Congress. They agreed to support large increases in military spending, modest cuts in social spending, and deep tax cuts.

The national debt became so large during Reagan's presidency that servicing it absorbed much of the net savings accrued by individuals and businesses each year. Pressures on interest rates were eased, because foreign investors, particularly the Germans, Japanese, and Saudi Arabs, bought up about 20 percent of the U.S. debt each year. Even so, the federal government had to take so much money from the private capital markets to fund the debt each year that the money available for investment in research, product development, new technologies, and increased productive capacity was significantly curtailed. Long-term interest rates remained high. There was a link between the huge federal indebtedness and declining American competitiveness in the world's marketplaces. Both the federal government and the private sector became dependent on large annual infusions of foreign capital.

In December 1985, Congress enacted the Gramm-Rudman Act, a measure that required automatic annual reductions in the budget deficit if the president and Congress failed to agree on cuts. The following year, the Supreme Court nullified the law, and the deficit for 1986 came in at a record $226 billion. Congress then enacted a modified version of Gramm-Rudman, but the White House and congressional legislators agreed to accounting procedures that effectively gutted the law. Several large spending programs were declared "off-budget" and not included when figuring the deficit in order to evade Gramm-Rudman limits. It took a record crash of the stock market on October 19, 1987, and fears of an impending recession, to force Reagan and Congress to reduce the budget deficit.

Trade deficits also had expanded rapidly between 1980 and 1985, as imports increased 41 percent while exports decreased slightly. Every week during the Reagan presidency, American consumers spent about $1 billion more buying imported goods than foreigners spent buying American-made products. To offset that imbalance in international trading, huge amounts of American securities, real estate, and factories were purchased by foreign investors who had to recycle their surplus dollars. By the end of Reagan's presidency, U.S. assets in foreign lands totaled less than the U.S. assets owned by foreigners. Until the early 1970s, America had been the world's leading creditor nation. By the end of the Reagan presidency, it had become the world's leading debtor.

Other economic trends alarmed Americans. Increasing numbers of American manufacturing concerns moved their operations overseas to get away from unionized workers and high taxes, and they took thousands of good jobs with them. At the same time, foreign investors continued buying up American assets. By the end of Reagan's presidency, foreign corporations owned American banks, investment houses, fast food restaurants, motion picture studios, landmark skyscrapers, thousands of acres of farm land, publishing firms, and supermarket chains.

While foreigners continued to buy up U.S. properties, other foreign competitors steadily increased their share of American domestic markets for autos, electronic products, cameras, textiles, and shoes. Many of these developments reflected a new reality, that the economic lives of nations were increasingly intertwined. By the mid-1980s, the American economy was intricately plugged in to a global economic system. Henceforth, more and more of the economic and financial activities of Americans would be influenced by decisions made in corporate boardrooms in Tokyo, Riyadh, and Bonn.

Another sign of trouble in America that surfaced in the late 1980s—disasters in the savings and loan industry—was entirely homegrown. The savings and loan (S&L) debacle was an unintended consequence of bipartisan good intentions. Deregulation was a policy idea that was first implemented during the Carter years, in the airline and trucking industries. The Reaganauts embraced and expanded upon deregulation in the name of greater productivity plus economy in government. Under the influence of supply-side economic theory, federal agencies relaxed or abolished rules and regulations affecting the operations of a wide range of American industries. One of these was savings and loan banks. Historically, S&Ls loaned money to individuals to buy homes in local areas where the banks were located. Home mortgages tended to be low-risk, low-profit investments. Savings and loan banks were noted for being safe, sound, and a little dull.

At the urging of the Reagan administration, Congress deregulated the savings and loan industry in 1982. Consequently, S&Ls could offer a much wider range of loans; they could invest depositors' funds in commercial real estate, undeveloped land, in fact, just about any kind of high-risk project imaginable. They also could loan funds for national and even international projects. Even if these high-risk operations went bust and the banks collapsed, the existence of the Federal Savings and Loan Insurance Corporation (FSLIC) meant that the bankers would not incur personal liabilities and that the depositors would get back their money.

In many parts of the nation, especially in the Southwest and West, the new era of deregulation in the S&Ls attracted a generation of incompetent and crooked buccaneers into the banking industry. One wag referred to these financial highfliers as "the morally challenged." They proceeded to invest billions of dollars of depositors' funds in a bewildering variety of dubious projects, knowing that they might reap huge profits from their high-risk undertakings but ran no risk of incurring personal responsibility for any losses because of the existence of the FSLIC. Deregulation of the savings and loan industry eventually reaped a financial disaster that left taxpayers saddled with a tab that ran into hundreds of billions of dollars.

Although the economic expansion of the "go-go" years of the 1980s was real and impressive, it also could be selective and spotty. It excluded large numbers of Americans. The chief regional beneficiaries of the Reagan boom years were the Northeast and California. Both regions were on the cutting edge of the computer revolution, and both had extensive military and aerospace industries. In these areas, good jobs at good salaries abounded; real estate prices for both residential and commercial properties shot upward.

But in the states of the upper Midwest, the site of the traditional smokestack industries, economic conditions deteriorated. Agricultural and energy-producing states also slumped during the 1980s. While the Northeast and the West Coast boomed, much of the rest of the country was mired in a decade-long stagnation and recession. Real wages, adjusted for inflation, continued to stagnate in many parts of the country during the 1980s. Real take-home pay for factory workers declined slightly from 1975 to 1987.

Revenue sharing with state and local governments, enacted by Richard Nixon in 1972, was cut during the Reagan administration. Infrastructure repairs to roads and bridges were neglected. Cities, strapped for funds by shrinking tax bases and increasingly needy populations, were especially hard hit by these losses of federal funds. Social services deteriorated.

During the 1980s, income differentials between upper-income and lower-income families widened. The number of poor women and children increased. One of the main reasons poverty was increasingly feminized was because of a sharp increase in the number of unwed mothers; the rate of children living with a never-married mother increased threefold during the 1980s. By the end of the 1980s, one-fourth of the children born in the United States were born to a never-married mother. The Reagan administration made matters worse for them by cutting funds for the Women-Infants-Children program (WIC), which provided both prenatal and postnatal care to low-income women.

During the 1980s, the poverty rate in America regressed to approximately where it had been in the mid-1960s, about 15 percent. But poverty in America had changed by the mid-1980s. Whereas the elderly had comprised a majority of the poor people of America in the mid-1960s, by the mid-1980s, most of the poor consisted of single mothers, children, and young men with low educational and job skills. A sizeable proportion of the 1980s poor worked full time or part time at minimum-wage levels. Millions of the new jobs that were created during the 1980s were full-time or part-time service sector jobs that paid only minimum wages.

Homeless people constituted a growing proportion of the 1980s poor population. The homeless, the poorest of the poor, came from many backgrounds: the unemployed, the mentally ill, the drug and alcohol abusers, people with serious medical problems, including AIDs victims, racial minorities, runaways, dysfunctional Vietnam veterans, and women fleeing abusive husbands. Many of the homeless struggled to survive, living on the streets of large cities and begging for food and money. If prospering yuppies represented the glittering successes of the Reagan era, the homeless represented the abject failures. In the new Gilded Age, the homeless were the prime victims of recrudescent Social Darwinism. Nobody knew exactly how many homeless there were in America in the 1980s. Estimates ranged from a low of 200,000 up to more than a million. President Reagan, while expressing his personal sympathy for the plight of the homeless, proposed no new federal programs to alleviate their suffering or to get them off of the streets. The assistance that existed for the pathetic armies of the homeless came mostly from local governments, private charities, churches, and compassionate individuals.

THE REAGAN COURT

President Reagan had long opposed most civil rights laws and supported a constitutional amendment outlawing bussing to achieve school integration. The Supreme Court in 1983 blocked attempts by the Justice Department to restore tax benefits to segregated private schools and colleges. When the 1965 Voting Rights Act was up for renewal, Reagan advised Congress to kill it. Congress ignored Reagan's advice and renewed it by large majorities.

In the field of civil liberties, Reagan, like most conservatives, believed that the court system favored the rights of accused criminals over law-abiding citizens who were often victims of violent crimes. During the 1980s, both the Congress and the states, responding to widespread popular concerns, took a stronger law-and-order line. Longer, mandatory sentences were imposed for many crimes. Many states reinstituted the death penalty for heinous crimes. Jail populations rapidly increased, and construction of new prison facilities lagged behind demand. By the end of the 1980s, over a million Americans were incarcerated, the highest rate of incarceration for any country in the world. Each year during the 1980s, many more new prisons were constructed than new schools.

Over the course of his presidency, Reagan appointed over 400 federal judges; these jurists constituted about 60 percent of all sitting federal judges in 1989. The president also appointed a chief justice and three associate justices to the Supreme Court. The administration searched for strict constructionists whose constitutional views also could incorporate right-wing social agenda, including opposition to affirmative action programs, abortion, pornography, and harsher justice for accused criminals. Reaganite judges also were expected to support efforts to restore prayer in public schools and to favor the death penalty.

The president's appointments to the Supreme Court allowed him to gradually reshape that venerable institution. In 1981 he had appointed Sandra Day

O'Connor and in 1986 he had selected Antonin Scalia to be associate justices. Both O'Connor and Scalia were conservatives. Reagan also had replaced retiring Chief Justice Warren Burger with Associate Justice William Rehnquist, the most conservative member of the Court. Reagan's efforts to add a third justice to the High Court in July 1987 proved embarrassing to the elderly chief executive. His first nominee, Appellate Judge Robert Bork, was rejected by the Senate because of his extreme views concerning First Amendment rights. Reagan's second choice, Douglas Ginsburg, had to withdraw his name from consideration after revealing to the press that he had smoked marijuana when he was a student in the 1960s. Reagan's third choice, also a judicial conservative, Anthony Kennedy, was unanimously confirmed by the Senate in February 1988.

Gradually, the Reagan appointees on the Supreme Court shifted the tenor of its decisions in a conservative direction. It chipped away at some of the rights of the accused established in previous decisions. The Reagan court also put some restraints on government affirmative action policies. In *City of Richmond v. J. A. Croson Company* (1989), the Court nullified a government set-aside program that reserved a proportion of government contracts for minority groups.

FOREIGN POLICY

During his second term, President Reagan had to deal with many challenging international problems. Global financial crises threatened as Third World nations sank deeper into debt. The collective debt of Argentina, Brazil, and Mexico approached $250 billion, most of it owed to American and European banks. The possibility of these countries ever repaying their debts appeared nil, and default, which could derange international financial transactions and trade and do serious harm to major U.S. banks, remained a constant danger.

International terrorism was another mounting problem. Between 1981 and 1986, thousands of people were kidnapped, injured, or killed by terrorist attackers. The State Department estimated that approximately 700 major terrorist assaults occurred in the world in 1985. Many terrorists had their roots in the bitter conflicts in Lebanon between Christian and Arab factions, and in the continuing war between Israeli forces and Palestinian fighters. Arab terrorist organizations, dedicated to the destruction of Israel and to attacking its Western supporters, frequently targeted Americans. The slaughter of the American Marines in Beirut in 1983 was the worst of many Muslim terrorist attacks against Americans. In June 1985, Lebanese Muslim terrorists hijacked an American jetliner and held thirty-nine Americans hostage for seventeen days. In October 1985, four members of the Palestinian Liberation Army seized an Italian cruise ship, the *Achille Lauro*, killing a disabled elderly American. In April, 1986, U.S. military installations in West Germany were bombed by Palestinian terrorists supported by Libya. In retaliation, American bombers attacked targets in and near the Libyan capital of Tripoli. Public opinion within the United States supported the air attack, but most of America's European allies, their citizens often the victims of terrorist assaults and kidnappings, called the bombing "counterproductive" and felt that it was likely to provoke further terrorist attacks.

In South Africa, a racist, white minority continued its rule over black, Asian, and mixed-race groups that composed 86 percent of the population. The Reagan administration, following a policy it called "constructive engagement" toward the South African apartheid regime, refrained from public criticism and tried to nudge it toward democracy. The policy produced few results, and South Africa was racked by violence in the mid-1980s as government security forces violently repressed black demonstrators. Angry, frustrated blacks sometimes retaliated with terrorist attacks of their own.

Critics of "constructive engagement" believed that only economic pressure could force the South African government to dismantle apartheid. Fourteen states and forty-one cities passed divestiture laws restricting or prohibiting the investment in South Africa of pension funds and requiring the selling off of current holdings in South African securities. Some universities ordered partial or full divestment. In October 1986, Congress, overriding a presidential veto, imposed economic sanctions on South Africa, including a boycott of South African products and a ban on new U.S. loans and investment in that country. Some U.S. corporations voluntarily sold off their South African operations.

The Reagan administration also had to confront a crisis in the Philippines, the former territory and longtime ally of the United States. For several years, a corrupt military dictator, whom Washington had supported, Ferdinand Marcos, had been losing power. Communist rebels were gaining strength in several regions of the country. Pressure from U.S. officials forced Marcos to permit elections that had been suspended since he took office. In February 1986, he was challenged by Corazon Aquino, the widow of an assassinated political opponent of Marcos. Both sides claimed victory in an election marked by violence and fraud. U.S. officials, worried about the declining Philippine economy and the rising Communist insurgency in a strategically important country, pressured Marcos to resign. He fled Manila in March 1986, and Aquino assumed office. She worked to restore political democracy, revamp the economy, maintain friendly relations with America, and remove the Communist threat. During her first two years in power, Aquino succeeded in restoring political democracy, but she had to survive two coup attempts led by army officers who wanted to restore Marcos to power.

THE IRAQI-IRANIAN WAR

The continuing Iraqi-Iranian war reached menacing proportions in 1987. The stalemated war spilled into the Persian Gulf and threatened vital oil shipments that flowed daily from the Gulf oil fields to Europe, Japan, and the United States. Iraq attacked Iran's oil-export terminals and also struck at Iranian tankers carrying oil from the Gulf. Iran could not strike at Iraqi oil shipments directly because Iraq's oil traveled through pipelines to terminals on the Mediterranean and Black Seas, but the Iranians undertook reprisals by attacking ships hauling oil from Kuwait, a small, oil-rich Arab emirate that was bankrolling Iraq's war against Iran.

Soviet entry into the Gulf, along with both Iraqi and Iranian threats to Gulf oil shipping, caused President Reagan to send a large fleet of U.S. Navy vessels to the region and provide naval escorts for oil convoys. In what amounted to armed intervention into the shipping war, Washington agreed to reflag and escort tankers carrying oil produced by Kuwait. In the summer of 1987, an American guided-missile frigate, stationed in the Gulf, was attacked, apparently by accident, by an Iraqi plane, resulting in the loss of thirty-eight lives. Then, on July 3, 1988, there occurred an even more ghastly accident when a U.S. destroyer, the USS *Vincennes*, fired a missile that brought down an Iranian airliner, killing all 290 people aboard. Crewmen aboard the American destroyer apparently thought that it was an Iranian fighter closing in on their ship for an attack.

The United States feared that a victory by either Saddam Hussein's secular Iraqi regime or Khomeini's Islamic fundamentalist Iranian government would make the winner the dominant power in the Persian Gulf. To prevent either side from winning the war—a victory that could threaten the political stability of Saudi Arabia, Kuwait, and other moderate Arab regimes, and disrupt the flow of oil to the United States and its allies—America, behind an official facade of neutrality, secretly aided whichever side appeared to be losing. In the early years of the war, Washington helped Iran, but after 1986, America aided Saddam. There had been several incidents involving attacks on merchant shipping by Iranian speedboats, and several ships had been damaged by mines lain by Iranians. U.S. ships and helicopter gunships had retaliated for some of the Iranian attacks, sinking speedboats and damaging an Iranian oil platform in the Gulf. In April 1988, there occurred a series of clashes between American and Iranian naval units. As a consequence of American intervention in the Persian Gulf, Iran and the United States were engaged in an undeclared naval war.

The Iraqi–Iranian war ended suddenly in August 1988 when Ayatollah Khomeini accepted a UN-proposed cease-fire. At the time, Iraq had gained the upper hand, and the Iranian enthusiasm for war had subsided after six years of slaughter. Although he had seized the initiative, Saddam, weary of the long war, readily consented to the cease-fire. Mutual exhaustion had brought an end to war. During the war, the Iraqis had used poison gas against the Iranians and were feverishly working to develop nuclear weapons. Despite the ominous indicators, the Reagan administration continued to back Iraq, considering it a necessary counterforce to the Iranians. Washington's support of Saddam in the late 1980s is one of the background causes of the 1991 Persian Gulf War.

As the war between Iraq and Iran ended, the Arab–Israeli conflict took another violent turn. Palestinians living in the West Bank and Gaza took to the streets to protest the continuing Israeli occupation of the two territories. Roving bands of

Palestinian youths, armed with rocks and Molotov cocktails, clashed with Israeli army squads. This Palestinian *intifidah* (uprising) continued intermittently through 1988 and 1989, resulting in the deaths of hundreds of Palestinians and a dozen Israeli soldiers. The Israeli government, headed by Prime Minister Yitzhak Shamir, refused to consider any resolution of the conflict that established a Palestinian state in the territories. He also refused to meet with Yasir Arafat and the PLO, the only organization that represented a majority of the Palestinians. The Reagan administration backed the Shamir government's refusal to meet with PLO leaders, but did favor some kind of political arrangement in the occupied territories that would give the Palestinians autonomy.

CENTRAL AMERICA

The Reagan administration continued its support of the Contra rebels fighting to overthrow Nicaragua's Sandinista regime. In the summer of 1985, Congress narrowly approved $100 million in support of the Contras. Public opinion polls showed a majority of Americans opposed to Contra aid and fearful that American troops would be sent to fight the Sandinistas if the rebels failed. The intermittent civil war went on.

A peaceful alternative to war in Nicaragua surfaced late in 1987, when President Oscar Arias Sanchez of Costa Rica, speaking for the leaders of four Central American republics meeting in Guatemala City, proposed a plan calling for an end to U.S. military backing of the Contras, the restoration of democracy in Nicaragua, and negotiations between the Sandinista government and Contra leaders leading to a cease-fire. Reagan administration officials expressed a willingness to let Arias try to implement his plan, and Nicaraguan leader Daniel Ortega Saavedra appeared willing to accept some of the proposals. In April 1988, both sides agreed to a temporary cease-fire, and Congress voted $48 million for nonlethal humanitarian aid for the Contras. In El Salvador, efforts to get negotiations going between the Duarte government and the Marxist rebels continued to fail, and the civil war in that tormented country went on.

THE IRAN-CONTRA SCANDAL

President Reagan's personal popularity remained high throughout the first half of his second term. But two weeks after the midterm elections in November 1986, the worst political scandal since Watergate erupted in Washington. Americans were shocked to learn that the Reagan administration had entered into secret negotiations with Iranian officials that involved selling them arms in exchange for the release of American hostages held captive in Lebanon by Muslim terrorists. Two weeks after Americans had learned of the arms-for-hostages deals with Iran, Attorney General Edwin Meese told a stunned press conference audience that his investigators had discovered that profits from the Iranian arms sales had been sent to Contra rebels fighting in Nicaragua, even though Congress had enacted legislation forbidding American military aid to the rebel fighters.

At a hastily called press conference, President Reagan gamely denied that he had authorized trading arms for hostages, and he insisted that he had no knowledge of any such transactions. He claimed that an operative with the National Security Council, Marine Lieutenant Colonel Oliver North, was mainly responsible for both the dealings with Iran and the Contra arms sales, and that only North's immediate superior, National Security Adviser Vice Admiral John Poindexter, knew of his activities. For the first time in his presidency, Reagan's integrity and competence were seriously questioned by the citizenry. His public approval rating dropped precipitously, from 67 percent to 46 percent.

The origins of the Iran Contra scandals went back to 1981, when President Reagan ordered CIA Director William Casey to organize an anti-Sandinista force among Nicaraguan exiles living in Honduras. Over the next several years, these Contra forces waged a guerrilla war against the Sandinista forces. Congress, concerned about reports that the Contras had killed many civilians and had also sown mines in Nicaraguan harbors that had damaged merchant ships belonging to other countries, enacted the Boland Amendment. The Boland Amendment forbade the use of any U.S. funds for the purpose of trying to overthrow the Sandinista government.

Reagan, committed to the goal of overthrowing the Sandinistas, instructed the CIA, the National Security Council, and the Pentagon to circumvent congressional restrictions on aiding the Contra forces. In the summer of 1984, Congress, responding to Reagan administration efforts to continue its clandestine proxy war in Nicaragua, tightened the Boland Amendment. It forbade the CIA and any other U.S. government agency from aiding the Contras.

The tighter version of the Boland Amendment failed to deter the president and his men. Casey, National Security Adviser Robert McFarlane, and one of McFarlane's aides, Oliver North, persuaded a handful of U.S. allies to provide funds for the Contras. Nations contributing monetary support for the rebels included Israel, South Africa, Saudi Arabia, South Korea, and Taiwan. Casey, North, and others also solicited additional funds from wealthy American individuals to support the rebels. While President Reagan and his subordinates were circumventing the will of Congress and violating the Boland Amendment by continuing the war in Nicaragua, the administration also began an involvement with Iran aimed at freeing U.S. hostages being held in Lebanon by pro-Iranian Muslim terrorists.

In July 1985, an Iranian arms dealer, Manucher Ghobanifar, met with McFarlane. Ghobanifar claimed to represent a moderate faction within the Iranian government that wanted to improve relations with America. He proposed to McFarlane that the United States, working through Israeli middlemen, arrange for the delivery of TOW antitank missiles to Iran that the Iranians desperately needed for their ongoing war with Iraq. In return, the moderates would work to arrange the release of some of the American hostages. A few months later, Reagan authorized the sale of 100 TOW missiles to Iran. At the time he authorized the sale of the weapons, Reagan clearly understood that the United States was trading arms for hostages. He also knew that it was against the law and contrary to American policy to sell weapons to Iran because of its support of international terrorism.

But no hostages were freed after this transaction. Ghobanifar told McFarlane that the Iranians wanted an additional 400 missiles in exchange for the release of a single hostage. McFarlane arranged for the missiles to be sent, and on September 15, 1986, one of the American hostages, Benjamin Weir, was set free. In November, Ghobanifar was back with another deal: send Iran 100 HAWK surface-to-air missiles and five American hostages would be freed. In December, President Reagan signed a secret document, called a "finding," which approved the proposed sale. The finding described the transaction as an arms-for-hostages deal.

Even though the several arms sales to Iran had yielded only one released hostage, Reagan's enthusiasm for the project remained undiminished. Poindexter, who replaced McFarlane as National Security Adviser in December 1985, working through North, arranged for another shipment of arms to Iran. This time, 3,000 TOW missiles and another 100 HAWKs would be sent in exchange for the remaining six Americans who were still held captive by terrorists in Lebanon. Both Secretary of State George Schultz and Secretary of Defense Caspar Weinberger opposed the arms-for-hostages transactions because they were illegal and did not serve the national interest.

It was Oliver North who came up with the plan to divert the profits from the sale of arms to the Iranians to the Contras. Did President Reagan direct North to send the money to the Contras? Later, in sworn testimony, Reagan could not remember if he had approved the funds; Poindexter testified under oath that the president did approve the funds. In February 1986, a sale of 1,000 TOW missiles to the Iranians netted a profit of about $8 million. North gave the money to retired Air Force Major General Richard Secord to buy arms for the Contras. No hostages were released, but two more Americans in Lebanon were taken hostage. After four arms shipments to the Iranians, more Americans than ever were held hostage.

On July 26, Iran arranged for the release of another American hostage, Lawrence Jenco, a Roman Catholic priest. Another shipment of missiles was sent to Iran, but it resulted in no further prisoners being freed. On November 2, just before the midterm elections, a final arms shipment was sent to Iran through Israeli middlemen, which resulted in the release of another hostage, David Jacobsen.

The cover for the bizarre secret schemes was blown in late October and early November. On October 5, 1986, a plane hauling weapons to the Contras was shot down, and the Sandinistas captured an air crewman, an American named Eugene Hasenfus. Hasenfus confessed to his captors that he was part of a secret American program to aid the Contras. On November 1, the Lebanese magazine *Al Shiraa* ran a story about the U.S. arms-for-hostages deals with Iran. Iranian officials quickly confirmed the story and told the world that the so-called moderates were agents of the Khomeini government. They boasted that they had tricked "The Great Satan" into selling them modern weapons that they urgently needed for their war with the Iraqis. Three weeks later, Edwin Meese made his stunning announcement that money from the sale of arms to Iran had been diverted to the Contra war effort against the Sandinistas.

In some ways, the fallout from the Iran-Contra scandal was worse than Watergate. It severely damaged U.S. foreign policy. The American policy of taking a hard line against terrorism had been exposed as being hypocritical. The Saudis and other moderate Arab states felt an acute sense of betrayal over the news that U.S. officials had sold antitank and antiaircraft missiles to Khomeini's government in the hope of securing the release of seven Americans being held hostage in Lebanon by groups of Islamic fundamentalists controlled by Teheran. At home, conducting a clandestine foreign policy in Central America against the expressed wishes of Congress, contrary to public opinion and the law, weakened Reagan's ability to govern effectively. The essence of the Iran-Contra scandal involved officials within the Reagan administration selling weapons to an outlaw regime to raise money for illegal purposes. Constitutional scholars saw an important principle at stake. By circumventing the congressional ban on aid to the Contras, the architects of the Iran-Contra scandal also had circumvented Article 1 of the Constitution, which vested all control over public moneys in Congress. The Iran-Contra scandal badly wounded the Reagan presidency, eroding both its power and its popularity.

In the aftermath of the revelations about trading arms for hostages and aiding the Contras, there occurred several official investigations of the details. A federal court appointed an independent counsel to investigate the scandals. President Reagan appointed a commission headed by former Senator John Tower to investigate the affair. Congress also appointed committees to examine the scandals. The Tower Commission's report was made public in March 1987. It portrayed Reagan as an out-of-touch president who had surrounded himself with irresponsible advisers pursuing ideologically driven policies that did harm to the national interest.

Reagan responded with a speech to the American people on March 4, in which he tried to restore his faltering hold on events. He acknowledged responsibility for the Iran-Contra affair, but he insisted that it was not his intent to trade arms for hostages and that he knew nothing about using some of the money obtained from Iran to buy arms for the Contras. In effect, he denied all responsibility for any wrongdoing. Reagan's speech neither improved his image nor enabled him to regain the political initiative.

Following the Tower report, the combined congressional committees began holding televised hearings that ran through the summer of 1987. At times, the hearings evoked memories of Watergate as congressmen tried to follow the money trail, find out how the profits from arms sales to Iran were channeled to the Contras, and discover who profited from all of these weird transactions.

Two of the witnesses appearing before the committees, retired Air Force Major General Richard Secord, who was recruited by Colonel North to run the Contra weapons supply system, and former National Security Adviser Robert McFarlane, who had arranged the Iranian arms sales, implicated the president in their testimonies. They insisted that Reagan was repeatedly briefed about the arms sales to Iran and approved of the efforts to get the hostages released. They also implicated the late CIA Director William Casey, who may have been the mastermind behind the Iran-Contra operations and who may have worked through Colonel North and former National Security Adviser Admiral John Poindexter to avoid congressional oversight and public disclosure as required by law. The two key witnesses to appear before the committees, Colonel North and Admiral Poindexter, both insisted that they had kept President Reagan uninformed about the details of the Iranian negotiations and that they never told him of the government's involvement in shipping arms to the Contras. They also admitted that they had deliberately misinformed Congress and the press about their actions—actions which they believed were serving the national interest and accorded with the president's wishes. The flamboyant and unrepentant North was clearly the star of the televised hearings. He passionately defended his actions as being moral and patriotic, even though they did defy Congress and break the law.

The committee hearings were seriously flawed. They were hastily conducted, and investigators lacked crucial documents that would have enabled them to discover the truth about the Iran-Contra scandals. Key witnesses lied or gave evasive answers. The investigating committees clearly did not have the stomach to press their investigation too close to Reagan, nor to consider the possibility of impeaching him, even though they possessed evidence suggesting that he had knowingly and deliberately broken laws and harmed U.S. foreign policy interests. Committee members knew that most Americans could not care less whether funds from arms sales were diverted to the Contras. While resenting the arms sales to Iran, many Americans also could see Reagan's good intentions: he was trying to free the hostages, even though the means chosen were dubious. Lawmakers also feared political reprisals at the hands of the people if they stood guilty once again of regicide. Besides, there was no "smoking gun" in the Iran-Contra scandals that irrefutably implicated the president. Liberal Democrats, who were most outraged by Iran-Contra, given their low estimations of Reagan, could believe that he was an out-of-touch leader who did not know what was happening inside of his own administration.

The committees issued a joint 450-page report on November 18, 1987, that was scathingly critical of the president. The report bluntly accused Reagan of not obeying his oath to uphold the Constitution and the laws of the land, and it said that he bore "the ultimate responsibility" for the wrongdoing of his aides. The congressional report also provided the most accurate accounting to date of how nearly $48 million raised from the arms sales had been distributed. In a sweeping criticism of the officials involved, the report stated that the Iran-Contra affair was "characterized by pervasive dishonesty and inordinate secrecy." It also voiced the suspicion that the president knew more about the arms sales and Contra funding efforts than he acknowledged. And it challenged the credibility of Colonel North's and

Admiral Poindexter's testimony. Without citing specific individual actions or naming specific laws, the report asserted that "laws were broken" in the Iran-Contra affair. The report concluded that the president's protestations of ignorance could not absolve him from responsibility, because the scandal occurred on his watch.

Coming a year after the original revelations, the report failed to elicit much public interest, and White House spokesmen dismissed the report as containing nothing that was new. But the Iran-Contra revelations had severely damaged Reagan's presidency and crippled his crusade to overthrow the Sandinistas. Public opinion polls revealed that a majority of Americans believed that the president knew about the government's involvement in the Contra arms shipments.

In March 1988, independent counsel Lawrence Walsh issued grand jury indictments to four of the most prominent participants in the Iran-Contra scandal, including Colonel North and Admiral Poindexter. All were charged with multiple offenses, including conspiracy, fraud, theft, perjury, and covering up illegal operations. At his trial in 1990, Poindexter repudiated his testimony previously given before the congressional committees. He stated that Reagan was in charge of the Iran-Contra operations from the beginning and had ordered him, North, and others to break the law.

The former president was called to testify at Poindexter's trial. In answers to 127 questions put to him by prosecutors, Reagan frequently gave confused and vague answers, and often he could not recall the names of subordinates or their activities. He reiterated that he was not involved in any wrongdoing and that he did not know what his subordinates were doing, or that they traded arms for hostages or diverted the profits to the Contras. It was a humiliating performance by Reagan. Some observers believed that he was exhibiting the early signs of Alzheimer's disease, which he later contracted. Poindexter was convicted of five felonies, including perjury. North was convicted of obstructing Congress and destroying confidential documents. All convictions of both men were overturned on appeal. The trials of the Iran-Contra conspirators concluded this shabby episode that marred the reputation and undermined the popularity and power of President Reagan.

THE SLEAZE FACTOR

While Iran-Contra investigations raised troubling questions about the integrity and competence of high government figures, other scandals rocked the Reagan administration. In December 1987, former White House adviser Michael Deaver, who operated a political consulting service, was convicted on three counts of perjury for denying that he improperly used his White House connections to help clients. In February 1988, Attorney General Edwin Meese became the latest in a long line of Reagan administration officials to be accused of having a conflict of interest and of conducting himself improperly. The charges against Meese stemmed from his alleged financial relations with a small company that received a defense contract. He came under further attack for his alleged awareness of a proposal to bribe Israeli officials to guarantee that they would not attack a planned oil pipeline construction project in the Middle East. Further problems for Meese developed at the Justice Department when several top officials resigned in April 1988 because they believed that Meese's mounting problems prevented him from exerting strong leadership of the Department. Despite his troubles and declining credibility, Meese continued to enjoy the support of President Reagan, who gave his longtime friend and adviser a strong vote of confidence.

In addition to these revelations of wrongdoing and improprieties at high levels in the White House came the disclosure in 1988 through the memoirs of Donald Regan, Reagan's former chief of staff, that the president, following the attempt on his life, had permitted his wife Nancy, who had consultations with an astrologer, to influence his scheduling. By the end of Reagan's presidency, allegations of illegal and unethical activities tarnished the reputations of more than 100 current and former White House officials.

Reagan administration officials were not the only politicians to be plagued by scandal in 1987 and 1988. The leading contender for the Democratic presidential nomination, Gary Hart, had to abandon his campaign for seven months when a newspaper reporter disclosed that Hart had spent a weekend with an attractive model. When Hart belatedly reentered the race in 1988, he found that he had lost all of his organization and most of his popular support, and he had to abandon his now hopeless candidacy. Another Democratic presidential hopeful, Senator Joseph Biden of Delaware, had to withdraw when reporters learned that he had frequently plagiarized the speeches of other politicians and had falsified his academic record.

THAWING THE COLD WAR

During Reagan's second term, both the United States and the Soviet Union urgently needed to stabilize the nuclear arms race. Ronald Reagan, the quintessential Cold Warrior, alarmed and dismayed most of his conservative supporters when he softened his hard-line approach to the Soviet Union. He authorized the resumption of arms negotiations with the Soviets, which began in March 1985. A dramatic moment in world history occurred when Soviet leader Mikhail Gorbachev and President Reagan met in Geneva from November 24 to November 27, 1985, the first Summit conference since Carter had journeyed to Moscow in 1979. But their six hours of private talks were inconclusive. They achieved no major agreements on arms control. The major block was Reagan's insistence that America would continue its development of the Strategic Defense Initiative (SDI). Gorbachev demanded that the United States abandon the SDI before he would agree to any cuts in nuclear weaponry or sign any arms control agreements. At the Summit's conclusion, Reagan and Gorbachev produced a four and a half page communique pledging to accelerate arms control negotiations.

The Summit was an exercise in global public relations by both sides. But it also was an important breakthrough, giving further diplomacy a needed impetus. A budding friendship between the two world leaders was the main consequence of the meetings. President Reagan toned down his anti-Communist rhetoric, saying Gorbachev was a man with whom he could do business. In the Soviet press, a new image of Reagan as a man who could be reasoned with had replaced a hostile version in which he had often been compared to Hitler. At a hastily called Summit meeting in Reykjavik, Iceland, in October 1986, Gorbachev and Reagan almost reached major agreements on nuclear arms control. But the opportunity for a comprehensive arms control treaty was missed when Gorbachev demanded a limitation on development of the U.S. Strategic Defense Initiative that President Reagan again refused to consider.

During the next year, Reagan replaced many of his hard-line anti-Communist advisers with a new breed of more flexible, pragmatic bureaucrats. Frank Carlucci replaced Weinberger at Defense. Army General Colin Powell became the new head of the National Security Council. Senator Howard Baker replaced Donald Regan as the president's chief of staff. These men favored reaching arms control agreements with the Soviets. First Lady Nancy Reagan, concerned about her husband's place in history in the aftermath of the Iran-Contra scandal, urged him to seek a major arms control agreement with Gorbachev. She wanted an accommodation with the Soviet Union to be the chief legacy of the Reagan presidency.

A year after Iceland, joint arms control efforts finally resulted in a major agreement between the two superpowers. Gorbachev journeyed to the United States, and he and Reagan signed a historic treaty in December 1987 that eliminated an entire class of weapons, intermediate range thermonuclear missiles, which had been located mostly in Europe. Both sides had, in effect, accepted the "zero option" originally proposed by Reagan in 1983. The agreement, known officially as the Intermediate Nuclear Forces (INF) Treaty, was the first nuclear arms control agreement ever reached that required the destruction of deployed nuclear weapons systems. It also provided for inspectors of both nations to observe the dismantling and destruction of the intermediate-range missiles. The INF Treaty and the return of cordial relations with the Soviet Union represented President Reagan's most important diplomatic achievements. The old Cold Warrior was thawing the Cold War.

The signing of the INF Treaty and the return of détente with the Soviets also held out the promise of future agreements cutting strategic weaponry on both sides. Negotiators from both countries continued to work on a Strategic Arms Reduction Treaty (START). The Soviets also announced that they were ending their costly, futile war in Afghanistan. In addition to phasing out the Afghan adventure, Gorbachev undertook a worldwide scaling back of Soviet diplomatic activity. He indicated that the Soviets might end their economic and military support of the Sandinistas. He urged the PLO to recognize Israel's right to exist. He pressured Hanoi to pull its troops out of Kampuchea. He pulled Soviet forces back from the Sino-Soviet border regions, and he urged the Soviet satellites in eastern Europe to reform their economies and become more involved with the nations of western Europe.

The sudden and quite remarkable turnabout in U.S.–Soviet relations culminated in Reagan's triumphant visit to Moscow in June 1988. To anyone familiar with Reagan's long record of fervent anti-Communism, his appearance in the heart of the "evil empire" had to be astonishing. When asked if he still believed that the Soviet Union was the "focus of evil in the modern world," Reagan responded, "They've changed." He spoke to the Soviet people on television and embraced his friend Mikhail Gorbachev at the site of Lenin's tomb. After such acts of reconciliation, no one appeared to care that both nations still had 30,000 thermonuclear warheads aimed at each other. Gorbachev made another visit to America in December 1990. Good pals "Ron"and "Gorby" staged a photo opportunity in front of the Statue of Liberty. Even the First Ladies, Nancy Reagan and Raisa Gorbachev, who had taken a chilly dislike to each other since their first meeting, managed to exchange warm smiles. At the highest political level, the Cold War appeared to be thawing.

IMPORTANT EVENTS

1981	Ronald Reagan is inaugurated as the fortieth president of the United States
	Reaganomics is implemented
	U.S. military buildup begins
1982	Covert aid to Contras in Nicaragua begins
	Congress enacts the Boland Amendment
1983	The United States deploys intermediate-range Pershing missiles in western Europe
	Reagan proposes SDI (Star Wars)
	A Muslim terrorist kills 241 U.S. Marines in Beirut
	The United States invades Grenada
1984	Reagan is reelected by a landslide margin
1985	The Geneva Summit takes place
	The Gramm-Rudman Act is passed
	The United States becomes a debtor nation for the first time since 1915
1986	The Tax Reform Act is passed
	The United States adopts economic sanctions against South Africa
	The Reykjavik Summit occurs
	The Immigration Reform Act is passed
1987	The United States intervenes in the Persian Gulf shipping war
	The Iran-Contra scandal erupts
	The Stock market crashes
	The United States and the Soviet Union sign the INF Treaty
	The Soviet Union begins scaling back its international commitments
1988	President Reagan journeys to Moscow

BIBLIOGRAPHY

A sizeable historical and journalistic literature has already accumulated for the 1980s. F. Clifton White, in *Why Reagan Won: A Narrative History of the Conservative Movement, 1964–1981* tells the story of the conservative movement from the Goldwater debacle to Reagan's successful bid for the presidency in 1980. Haynes Johnson's *Sleepwalking through History: America in the Reagan Years* is a critical look at the Reagan era. The most informative work about the Reagan presidency is Lou Cannon's *President Reagan: The Role of a Lifetime*. President Reagan has written a solid memoir, *An American Life*. A fine recent study is Stephen Vaughn's *Ronald Reagan in Hollywood: Movies and Politics*, which explores the important relationships between Reagan's film and political careers. Two important books that interpret the public career of Ronald Reagan are Garry Wills's *Reagan's America: Innocents at Home* and Michael P. Rogin's *Ronald Reagan: The Movie*. A good account of the early years of the Reagan presidency is Laurence I. Barrett's *Gambling with History: Reagan in the White House*. P.C. Roberts, in *The Supply-Side Revolution*, defends Reaganomics. T.B. Edsall's *The New Politics of Inequality* challenges the president's economic policies. Strobe Talbott, in *Deadly Gambit*, offers a lucid and fascinating analysis of the arcane complexities of arms control. See *Central America: Anatomy of Conflict*, edited by R.S. Leiken, which contains useful essays on that important region. The most thorough account of the Iran-Contra scandal that rocked the Reagan administration in 1986 and 1987 is Theodore Draper's *A Very Thin Line: The Iran-Contra Affairs*. Bob Woodward, in *Veil*, has written an account of the Iran-Contra affair in which he contends that it was masterminded by William Casey. Seth P. Tillman's *The United States and the Middle East: Interests and Obstacles* is a balanced treatment of American policy in that troubled region. Stansfield Turner, in *Terrorism and Democracy*, offers a thoughtful study of one of the most serious and agonizing problems that U.S. presidents have had to deal with in the 1980s and 1990s. Michael Mandelbaum's, *Reagan and Gorbachev* is a good account of their personal diplomacy. Roy Gutman, in *Banana Diplomacy*, offers a critical study of U.S. foreign policy in Nicaragua and El Salvador in the 1980s. Michael Schaller's *Reckoning with Reagan: America and Its President in the 1980s* is a fine study of what happened and why it happened during the Reagan presidency.

16

The 1990s

THE opening of the Berlin wall on November 9, 1989, was the first in a series of stunning events that culminated in the collapse of the Soviet Union and the end of the Cold war that had been the focus of American foreign policy for nearly half a century. As the world's only remaining superpower, the United States suddenly found itself incontestably the most powerful nation on earth. With the demise of the Soviet Union, Americans appeared to inhabit a less dangerous world. While that was true in the sense that the danger of an all-out nuclear war between the superpowers that might have destroyed the planet had vanished, there remained many unstable regions in the world riven with ethnic conflicts, genocidal assaults, and terrorist attacks. As citizens of the only nation with the economic resources, military assets, and political will to intervene in some of these trouble spots, Americans endured periodic involvements in these small but vicious wars that plagued the last decade of the twentieth century. Americans received a horrific reminder that they inhabited a dangerous world on the morning of August 7, 1998, when two powerful car bombs exploded within minutes of each other outside U.S. embassies in Nairobi, Kenya, and Dar es Salaam, Tanzania, killing more than two hundred people and injuring thousands.

At the same time Americans tried to define new strategic roles in the post-Cold War world, they also had to adapt to the rapidly evolving world economy. The contagion of bankruptcies and currency devaluations that collapsed the booming economies of Thailand and Korea during the summer of 1997, spread to other Pacific Rim countries, and then engulfed Russia, and Brazil, highlighted not only the interconnectedness of economic relations, but also the volatility of the new global economy in which loan money could be quickly put into and then pulled out of markets around the world.

As Americans confronted a transformed global situation abroad, at home they had to deal with rapidly changing demographics, a fragmented social order, cultural warfare, and ideologized politics. During the early 1990s, Americans suffered a mild economic recession that probably cost George Bush his chance to be a two-term president. The economy recovered by 1993 and began a sustained period of steady growth and rising prosperity that extended into 1999. The longest and strongest bull market in U.S. financial history carried stocks to record levels. Unemployment and inflation remained low. The prosperous economy annually generated large numbers of well-paying jobs. However, as the American economy was increasingly integrated into the burgeoning global economy, the terms of competition became fiercer. Competitive pressures kept wages down and people had to work harder than ever to keep their jobs.

Within the nation, a searching debate over the role of the state dominated domestic politics during the 1990s. The steady rise of the national state had been one of the major themes of twentieth-century U.S. national history. Ronald Reagan was the first twentieth century president that endeavored to downsize the national government, although his efforts largely failed. But his rhetorical attacks on the welfare state transformed the terms of political debate within this country and prepared the ground for the Republican "earthquake" that followed. With the election of a Republican-controlled Congress in 1994, the conservative assault on the positive state accelerated. Liberal defenders of the welfare state found themselves on the defensive within the most conservative political climate since the 1920s. In his State of the Union Address in January, 1997, President Clinton acknowledged the advent of the new domestic order when he noted that, "The era of big government is over." Beginning January 1998, the debate over the role of the state was displaced by a year-long effort by conservative Republicans to drive Bill Clinton from office for having had an affair with a young White House intern, then lying about it and trying to cover it up. It plunged the nation into a prolonged constitutional crisis that was also part tawdry political theater.

A DEMOGRAPHIC PROFILE FOR THE 1990S

Census takers, combing the country during 1990, discovered that dramatic changes had occurred in the nation's demographic profile during the go-go years of the 1980s. In 1990 the national population totaled 247,000,000, nearly a ten percent increase over 1980. By 1999, the population exceeded 271,000,000 and the median age had reached thirty-five. The proportion of young people (age eighteen and under) in the national population continued to shrink. One of the most important findings of the 1990 census was that the advance wave of baby boomers had entered middle age. The fastest-growing age groups continued to be older Americans.

The Social Security system was increasingly strained. Young workers had to pay higher Social Security taxes to fund pensions paid to an ever-higher proportion of retirees. Many retirees also were drawing generous pensions relative to the

amounts they had contributed to the Social Security system during their working years. Social Security taxes increased by 25 percent during the 1980s. Many young working people in the 1990s remained openly skeptical that Social Security benefits would be there for them when they reached retirement age. By 1998, it was clear that Medicare costs had to be trimmed sharply, or the system would be bankrupt before the end of the century.

The 1990 census confirmed that Americans remained a people on the move. Migration patterns that originated during World War II continued. The Sunbelt states retained their magnetic abilities to attract new residents from the Northeast and Midwest. Population increases in the Sunbelt states stretching from South Carolina to southern California continued to account for most of the nation's population growth in the 1980s. California, fueled by immigration from Mexico and Asia, and the Pacific Islands, added 5 million people and accounted for 25 percent of the total population growth during the decade. In the House of Representatives, which was elected in 1992, California gained seven seats, Florida gained three, and Texas gained two. Several of the older states of the Northeast and Midwest lost representation.

In addition, the 1990 census reflected the growing variety of household living arrangements in America. Nuclear families comprised only about one-fourth of the nation's households in 1990; just as many households were made up of a person living alone. The number of single mothers heading a household increased rapidly during the decade, especially among minority populations. In 1999, there were nearly 14 million single-parent families, most headed by a woman who had never married. And in 1999, approximately 14 percent of American households were poor, about the same proportion that could be found in this country in 1965. The large increase in poor, single-parent families during the 1990s had ominous implications for millions of America's children. In 1998, the rates for teenage eating disorders, drug use, depression, and suicide were all rising. Adolescents were one of the highest-risk groups for contracting AIDS.

THE DECLINE OF THE MIDDLE CLASSES

Many serious, intertwined economic problems, exacerbated by the recession that struck during the early 1990s, vexed the American people. The annual trade deficit ranged between $40 billion and $60 billion. Annual federal deficits continued to run up huge amounts of red ink. The national debt reached $4 trillion in 1992 and was approaching $5 trillion in 1996. That year, annual interest payments on the national debt consumed 16 percent of all federal spending. In 1998, for the first time in nearly thirty years, the federal government, after years of fiscal restraint, tax increases, cuts in military spending, and steady economic growth, managed to produce a small budget surplus.

During the recession, about 9,000,000 workers were without jobs. Housing starts, new car sales, and business investment plummeted. The Federal Reserve

Board slashed interest rates to thirty-year lows, but the economy did not pick up. The first recession to afflict the American people in a decade had two major causes: cuts in military spending in the aftermath of the Cold War and the collapse of commercial real estate markets in the wake of the overexpansion of the 1980s.

More important, the long-term structural weaknesses of the U.S. economy that had first appeared during the early 1970s persisted into the 1990s. The most serious one that has eroded the economic underpinnings of millions of American middle-class families has been the slow rate of economic growth. From 1890 to 1970, the U.S. economy grew at an annual rate of 3.5 percent, adjusted for inflation. That high rate of economic growth, sustained over much of the twentieth century, more than any other single factor created a prosperous middle-class society. Since 1973, including the boom years of the 1980s, the annual rate of growth has averaged 2.2 percent. This sharp decline in growth rates has had devastating impacts on millions of middle-class families. Both real income and the annual share of national income earned by the middle classes has been declining. Slower rates of growth meant declining economic opportunity and lowered social mobility.

By the mid-1990s, the U.S. economy had fully recovered from recession and was performing strongly. From 1995 through 1998, the economy grew at an annual rate of 3.4 percent. By 1996, American industry once again led the world in productive efficiency. U.S. automakers dominated the markets for popular minivans, light trucks, and off-road vehicles. In 1998 and 1999, American-made, powerful, and expensive sports utility vehicles were the vehicles of choice for those who could afford them.

In the late 1990s, American high-tech industries flourished. U.S. electronics companies continued to lead the world in diverse fields such as desktop computers, software applications, and telecommunications. High school and college graduates entered one of the strongest job markets for young people in decades.

In the summer of 1997, Thailand, Hong Kong, South Korea, Indonesia, and several other Asian countries experienced turmoil in their financial markets that abruptly reversed years of robust economic growth and rising prosperity. Asian financial disasters drove stock values down and devalued currencies. It also brought many large banks and corporate conglomerates to the verge of bankruptcy. Several nations received financial assistance from the International Monetary Fund and were forced to implement harsh austerity programs to try to stop the financial hemorrhaging. In Indonesia, mass unrest in the wake of economic decline forced the aging autocrat, Suharto, to resign.

These financial and economic crises deepened the long recession that had already engulfed Japan and threatened to slow the Chinese juggernaut. In September 1998, Russia verged on financial collapse, and its elderly, sick leader, Boris Yeltsin, appeared unable to cope with the crisis that could bring his government down. Even the American powerhouse felt the effects of the Asian meltdown and the Russian collapse. During the summer of 1998, the growth rate of the U.S. economy slowed, stock values plunged by nearly 20 percent, and businesses that sold goods and services on Asian markets were hurt. U.S. farmers who sold grain and

beef to Asians were especially hard hit. The crisis cost 250,000 American jobs. U.S. economic forecasters worried that turbulence in global financial markets could trigger a deflationary spiral and even a world-wide recession. However, continued spending by American consumers enabled the U.S. economy to shake off the recessionary effects of the Asian meltdown and continue its strong performance in 1999. The stock market recovered and continued its record-setting advances.

A NATION OF IMMIGRANTS

During the decade of the 1980s, 6 million legal immigrants entered the country, and hundreds of thousands of illegal immigrants entered annually. Europeans represented only 12 percent of the 1980s immigration. The rate of immigration established during this decade has continued into the 1990s. Most of the immigrants emigrated from a Hispanic country within the Western Hemisphere or from a Pacific Island or an Asian nation.

Most of the 1980s immigrants clustered in a few states and cities. According to the 1990 census, California was the home for two-thirds of the Asian American population and over one-third of the Hispanic American population. In New York, Los Angeles, San Francisco, Chicago, and other great cities, the new Hispanic and Asian populations settled into ethnic neighborhoods. They brought their distinctive cultures, languages, cuisine, dress, music, manners, and styles. America's big cities became home to the most culturally diverse populations in world history.

While cultural diversity brought energy and vitality and made America's big cities the most vibrant urban centers in the world, it also brought tensions, pressures, dislocations, and serious social problems. The huge influx of new people during the 1980s and 1990s triggered an upsurge of nativism. In 1994, California voters approved Proposition 187, a ballot initiative that barred undocumented aliens from access to public schools, health clinics, and all other social services. Federal courts declared most of the initiative's provisions unconstitutional, and it was never enforced.

BLACK AND WHITE, BUT NOT TOGETHER

Festering ethnic tensions exploded in May 1992, when a California jury acquitted four white police officers charged with savagely beating an African American suspect, Rodney King. A bystander had videotaped the incident, and portions of the tape were repeatedly broadcast. To nearly all who observed the gruesome sequences, the television camera presented compelling images of police brutality. The verdict to acquit the four policemen, rendered by a politically conservative suburban jury containing no African American members, ignited the most violent race riot in the nation's history in southcentral Los Angeles. Thousands of businesses were looted and destroyed, and many of them were burned. Fifty-four people were killed and thousands were injured. The Los Angeles police, poorly led and confused, were initially slow to respond to the riot, and events got out of control. National Guard troops were rushed to Los Angeles to quell the rioters.

The riot was reminiscent of the 1965 Watts upheaval, but there were significant differences. The 1965 riot had pitted blacks against whites. The 1992 riot had much more complex ethnic dynamics, reflecting the ethno-racial diversity of the nation's second largest city. Blacks attacked other blacks as well as whites. Hispanics attacked whites. Blacks and Hispanics both attacked Asians. Gangs of African American and Hispanic thugs also engaged in violence and looting. The King verdict obviously triggered the riot, but the underlying causes appeared to be a potent mix of ethno-racial antagonisms, poverty, and neglect, all exacerbated by a severe economic recession that hit poor people, working-class people, and small businessmen especially hard.

In 1995, an ironic sequel to the Rodney King case occurred. From January to October, a former star athlete turned TV sportscaster and film actor, O.J. Simpson, stood trial for the murder of his former wife, Nicole Brown Simpson, and her friend, Ronald Goldman. After a lengthy trial, a jury acquitted Simpson of all charges.

Because of the political and cultural contexts in which the trial occurred, it acquired a significance that far transcended the guilt or innocence of one prominent individual. The O.J. Simpson murder trial became the most famous media event in American history. All of the major media provided constant coverage of the trial for months. Cable TV watchers could catch analyses and perspectives on the trial from ex-prosecutors and ex-defense lawyers. Millions of Americans became personally involved in the "trial of the century." Attorneys for both sides and the judge, Lance Ito, often played to the ever-present television cameras. Due process became judicial theater and Hollywood showbiz. A brutal double murder became prime-time entertainment, a real-life whodunit.

In the eyes of a substantial majority of viewers and expert commentators, the state presented a strong case based on physical evidence that implicated Simpson beyond a reasonable doubt in the two murders. Simpson had no alibi, and the defense presented no credible alternative explanation that challenged the prosecution's claim that Simpson killed both victims. The fact that Simpson, whose resources matched those that Los Angeles County could allocate for the trial, hired a battery of high-priced attorneys to mount a successful defense proved to many Americans the dubious proposition that he was immune to the justice system. Simpson was not held accountable for his murderous actions. His acquittal also reinforced the widely held notion that there was one standard of justice for the rich and another, harsher standard for the poor. The antics of the attorneys on both sides, the often erratic behavior of Judge Ito, and most of all the outcome of the trial suggested to many observers that the American system of criminal justice had produced a terrible miscarriage of justice. The trial raised an ominous question: Could the traditional jury system work in a racially polarized society?

Looming over the trial was the ugly reality of racism. Because the murder victims, Nicole Brown Simpson and Ronald Goldman, were white, and because Simpson was a black celebrity, racial attitudes in this country became central to the outcome of the trial and how people viewed that outcome. The jury, consisting of nine African Americans, eight of them women, a Hispanic male, and two white women, reached a verdict of acquittal within four hours. The jurors rushed to judgment without seriously considering the evidence, much of it quite complex and technical, presented by 133 witnesses who testified during the long trial. Polls showed that 87 percent of black Americans agreed with the jury's verdict; 65 percent of whites believed Simpson was guilty as charged.

The black-white racial chasm that existed in this country was highlighted on October 4, 1995, when the clerk of the court read the jury's verdict. Around the country, wherever crowds of black Americans had gathered to hear the verdict, they cheered loudly and hugged each other at what appeared to them to be a triumphal deliverance. Wherever crowds of whites had gathered to hear the verdict, they stared in disbelief at what appeared to them to be an awful miscarriage of justice. These differential responses dramatically revealed that white and black Americans stared uncomprehendingly at each other from across a vast cultural divide.

Seemingly lost in all of the furor over the verdict of acquittal was the fact that Simpson still faced civil suits brought by the families of the murder victims, accusing him of the "wrongful deaths" of Nicole Brown Simpson and Ronald Goldman. On February 4, 1997, in subsequent civil trials conducted in a West Los Angeles courtroom before a mostly white middle-class jury that did not include a single African American, in which a tough old judge excluded the television cameras and kept a rigid order, Simpson was convicted of being responsible for the "wrongful deaths" of Nicole Brown Simpson and Ronald Goldman. The survivors were awarded a total of $33.4 million in compensatory and punitive damages. Simpson's attorneys promptly appealed both of the verdicts and damage awards. There was far less media coverage of the civil trial, and little noticeable public reaction to the verdicts.

Two weeks after the conclusion of the first Simpson trial, another dramatic event accentuated the black-white racial divide rending the American social fabric. The controversial leader of the Nation of Islam, Louis Farrakhan, led a "Million Man March" on Washington, D.C. About 500,000 black men gathered on the mall in front of the Washington Monument. For the huge gathering of black men, it was a day of atonement and renewal, and an affirmation of their black manhood. For most of the participants, it was a deeply moving experience. The march also demonstrated how far America had yet to travel to achieve Martin Luther King's vision of an individualistic, integrated society, one "in which people were judged not by the color of their skin but by the content of their character."

A FRAGMENTED SOCIETY

During the 1980s and 1990s there occurred a dramatic transformation in the ethnic and racial composition of the American population, the greatest since immigrants from southern and eastern Europe flooded into America during the first fifteen years of the twentieth century. According to the 1990 census, one in four Americans claimed African, Hispanic, Asian, or Native American ancestry. African Americans represented 12 percent, Hispanic Americans 9 percent, Asian Americans 3 percent, and Native Americans 1 percent of the total population of 247,000,000. By 1999, the nation's population had grown to 271,000,000 people; it constituted a pentagonal mosaic of Native Americans, African Americans, Hispanic Americans, Asian Americans, and European Americans. Each of these groups comprised, in turn, an array of subgroups differentiated by region, national origins, religion, education, gender, age, and class. The percentage of foreign-born residents exceeded 10 percent by the late 1990s, the highest since the 1920s.

In 1999, more than 2 million people identified themselves as Native Americans, more than twice the 1970 total. This figure reflected not only a rapid natural increase in the Amerindian population but also the growing numbers of people of mixed-race ancestry eager to affirm their ethnic roots. A network of tribal-controlled colleges and universities provided Native Americans with relevant educations and cultural sustenance. Many tribes energetically pursued various business ventures, from growing wild rice to operating profitable gambling casinos. In August 1998, near New London, Connecticut, on Mashantucket Pequot Tribal Nation land, the 550 surviving Pequots, grown rich on profits from their Foxwood Casino complex, proudly unveiled a magnificent museum and research center. The museum, built at a cost of nearly $200 million, celebrated the resurrection of a once-powerful Native American people who had struggled for centuries to survive at the margins of the dominant European society that had nearly obliterated them during the seventeenth century. The centerpiece of the museum was a recreated Pequot village on a summer day in 1550 on the eve of the European arrival. Fifty-one life-sized figures were shown weaving mats, sharpening arrows, and constructing wigwams.

Fed by continuing high rates of immigration, the Asian American and Pacific Islander populations continued to grow rapidly during the decade of the 1990s. People from Korea, the Philippines, Vietnam, and China continued to come to the United States in large numbers. In 1998, 11 percent of Los Angeles's 3.5 million residents were Asians. Strengthened by family cultures and prizing academic success, Asian Americans showed high rates of college attendance and upward mobility. However, Asian American communities experienced generational tensions as young people got caught between the tug of traditional ways and the lure of American popular culture.

In the mid-1990s, African Americans remained divided along class lines. At one end of the social spectrum, a large and growing class of black professionals and businesspeople enjoyed affluent lifestyles. In 1998, 12 percent of college students were black, roughly equal to their ratio of the general population. In 1998, nearly half of African Americans in the workforce held white-collar, middle-class jobs. At the other end of the spectrum could be found the impoverished inner-city blacks, representing one-third of the African American population of approximately 30,000,000. The poorest of the poor, representing perhaps 10 percent of the African American population in 1998, comprised the "underclass." Although intact families, thriving churches, and other strong institutions could be found in the inner city, this culture of decency often was overwhelmed by a staggering array of social pathologies. As factory jobs once open to urban workers disappeared, inner-city unemployment rates soared. With good jobs no longer available locally, young people faced life on mean streets or held marginal service-sector jobs in car washes or fast food restaurants. Inner-city pathologies such as high crime rates, drug abuse, welfare dependency, and teenage pregnancies derived from more fundamental problems: lack of good educational and job opportunities.

In 1998, the nation's 23,000,000 Hispanics represented America's fastest-growing minority. Hispanic Americans are themselves a diverse group; they include 16 million Mexican Americans concentrated in California and in the American Southwest; 1 million Cuban Americans mostly living in south Florida; and between 1 and 2 million immigrants from the Caribbean region and Central America, living mostly on the East Coast or in California. The Hispanic American population also included 2 million Puerto Ricans, who are American citizens by birth.

Most Hispanics, regardless of their national origins, emigrated to America in search of a better life for themselves and their families. Millions have found success. Family, church, and cultural institutions have sustained hard-working people making it in America. But life remained harsh for millions of Hispanic families. In 1998, 20 percent of Mexican Americans and one-third of Puerto Ricans lived in poverty. Hispanic communities often were devastated by alcohol and drug abuse, soaring crime rates, and high rates of school dropouts and teenage pregnancies.

As American society grew more fragmented in the 1980s and 1990s, the ideal of a common national culture proved to be ever more elusive. Americans appeared to share only consumerist cultural experiences, such as shopping at malls, watching prime-time television programs, and attending sporting events. To many immigrant families, becoming an American was defined primarily in residential and economic terms: reside in the country, get a good education, and then get a well-paying job. Make money, buy a home in the suburbs, provide well for your family, and enjoy the good life based on consumerist values. Questions of politics and culture were ignored or downplayed. Futurists predicted that America would become the world's first post–national political entity in which cultural identities would replace traditional nationalistic and political identities.

CULTURE WARS

In the public arena, debate erupted, as groups hitherto marginalized or excluded from the mainstream of American life demanded cultural as well as political equality. The multiculturalism controversy took many forms. High school and college course offerings became contested arenas. Newly empowered advocates for women, African Americans, Hispanic Americans, Asian Americans, Native Americans, gays and lesbians, and fundamentalist religious groups demanded that high schools and colleges revise their curricula. Multiculturalists challenged course reading lists that continued to privilege DWEMs (dead white European males).

Literary scholars revised reading lists to include works by women, persons of color, and Third World writers. Historians hastened to rewrite textbooks to include previously neglected or excluded nonelite groups.

Culture wars raged on other fronts as well. Congressional conservatives tried to eliminate federal funding for the arts, humanities, and public television. The National Endowment for the Arts and the National Endowment for the Humanities survived the onslaught, but on drastically reduced budgets. The Corporation for Public Broadcasting survived more or less intact.

The multiculturalist reforms provoked a backlash. Traditionalists insisted that these efforts at more inclusive scholarship eroded any sense of a shared national identity. Critics feared that all of that counting by race, ethnicity, gender, sexual preference, age, and religious affiliation could lead to a Balkanization of American society. They worried lest a heedless rush to multiculturalism destroy the basic unity of the most successful pluralistic society in world history. Some professors and teachers expressed dismay at working in repressive environments in which newly empowered champions of multiculturalism and "politically correct" speech imposed a new bureaucratic orthodoxy that stifled academic freedom and encouraged an aggressively litigious culture of victimization.

A number of voices resisted all efforts to polarize Americans into warring factions and insisted that multiculturalism's many positive contributions could be retained, while rejecting its extremist claims. In this view, the cultures carried by ethnically and racially defined communities could be appreciated without expecting individuals to define themselves narrowly as members of the descent-based community into which they were born. David Hollinger, one of the nation's most imminent historians, distinguished sharply between biology and culture, complaining that multiculturalists too often assumed that a person's values and tastes flowed from skin color or facial shape. In a brilliant and timely little book, *Postethnic America: Beyond Multiculturalism,* Hollinger offered his cosmopolitan and inclusive vision of a dynamic, pluralistic society, embracing all people of whatever descent:

> Postethnicity prefers voluntary to prescribed affiliations, appreciates multiple identities, pushes for communities of wide scope, recognizes the constructed character of ethnoracial groups, and accepts the formation of new groups as part of the normal life of a democratic community.[1]

WOMEN AND WORK

By the late 1990s, women had smashed through many sexist barriers to higher education and in the workplace. In many fields that were long virtually closed to women, such as medicine, law, engineering, and business management, large

---

[1]David A. Hollinger, *Postethnic America: Beyond Multiculturalism* (New York: Basic Books, 1995), p. 116.

numbers of women energetically pursued productive careers. In 1998, one-fourth of all doctors and lawyers were women. There also were huge increases in the number of women holding public office in the 1980s and 1990s. President Reagan had appointed Sandra Day O'Connor to the Supreme Court in 1991. President Clinton added Ruth Bader Ginsburg to the Court in 1993. Clinton also appointed several women to cabinet rank, including Madeleine Albright, the first female secretary of state. In 1996, the number of working mothers with children exceeded the number of mothers with children not working outside of the home. By 1999, women constituted almost half of the total workforce.

But as increasing numbers of women moved into formerly male-dominated occupations and professions, disparities continued in the pay women received for performing comparable work. Women who worked full time in 1999 earned about 75 cents for every dollar a man earned. Many working-class women still confronted a segregated job market in the late 1990s. Sixty percent of working women held "pink-collar" jobs.

Many women who had reached managerial positions in business in the late 1990s felt that they were paying too high a personal price for their professional successes. Others complained that they could not fulfill family obligations at home and perform their jobs at the highest levels. Felice Schwartz, the head of a research institute that studied women in business, suggested that these woman might pursue a slower career track in business to have more time for family responsibilities. But feminists claimed that Schwartz's so-called "mommy track" perpetuated the very second-class status of women in business that they were trying to surmount.

Long-term structural changes in the economy adversely affected working women. The rise of service industries and the implementation of new technologies created millions of new jobs for women but also created new limits and liabilities. Automated offices have become the sweatshops of the 1990s. Many businesses, to cut costs, have hired part-time and temporary clerical workers. These contingent workers typically receive less pay and fewer benefits than full timers.

Cultural changes also have accompanied the advent of women into the workplaces of America. Most notable is the change in women's consciousness. Many women in the late 1990s felt that they were equal to men in the marketplace and had greater ambitions and expectations than previous generations of women. But traditional values and stereotypes also exhibited strong staying powers. Advertisers no longer celebrated domesticity as a woman's only appropriate realm but still insisted that the busy career woman had to keep her weight down and look pretty. Women spent far more of their incomes on clothes, beauty aids, and diet and exercise programs than men.

THE ELECTION OF 1988

As candidates in both parties geared up for the 1988 elections, the race for the presidency appeared to be wide open. For the Republicans, the major contenders included Vice President George Bush, Senate Republican leader Robert Dole, and former "televangelist" Pat Robertson. For the Democrats, a large field of candidates sought their party's nomination. They included Congressman Richard Gephardt of Missouri, Senator Albert Gore of Tennessee, Governor Michael Dukakis of Massachusetts, and the charismatic black leader, Jesse Jackson.

When the lengthy primary process finally ran its course in June, the survivors were Reagan's sixty-four-year-old vice president, George Bush, and Massachusetts governor, Michael Dukakis. For the vice presidency, Dukakis chose an elderly conservative senator from Texas, Lloyd Bentsen. Bush easily survived a minicontroversy over his selection of youthful Senator J. Danforth Quayle of Indiana as his vice presidential running mate. Quayle was thought to be too young and inexperienced to be a heartbeat away from the presidency.

The Republicans conducted a richly financed and efficient campaign. The Bush campaign easily won what media analysts have called the "battle of the sound bites," that is, the vivid 10- to 20-second pronouncements uttered daily by the candidates as they campaigned across the nation that would be picked up on the evening television news programs and beamed into millions of living rooms nightly until election day. Bush also found most of the "hot" electoral buttons to push during the contest with Dukakis. He projected a vision of a "kinder, gentler nation," and he encouraged Americans to help one another and shine forth from "a thousand points of light." He pledged "no new taxes," and when questioned about his commitment, responded a la a popular Clint Eastwood movie character, with "read my lips." Bush also waged a long, relentless assault on Dukakis as an exemplar of all that was wrong with contemporary liberalism. He charged that Dukakis was weak on foreign policy and national security matters. The most notorious attack commercial pandered to racist fears by including a mug shot of Willie Horton, a black convicted murderer and rapist who committed another murder while on a weekend furlough from prison. The commercial implied that Dukakis, who was governor when Horton was serving time in a Massachusetts prison, was soft on crime.

Figure 16.1   The Reverend Jesse Jackson campaigning for the presidency in 1988. Jesse Louis Jackson (1941–) founded the Rainbow Coalition and was a candidate for the Democratic presidential nomination in 1984 and 1988. *Source:* Mercantile Library, St. Louis. Used with permission.

Dukakis disdained negative campaigning and even refused to respond to Bush's attacks. Dukakis tried to focus his campaign on the issues. His approach failed, and his campaign never caught fire. He never found a telling issue or a rousing theme that resonated among the voters. During two televised debates between the candidates, Dukakis failed to cut into Bush's lead or even to slow his momentum.

On election day, the Bush–Quayle ticket buried Dukakis and Bentsen, winning 54 percent of the popular vote to 46 percent, 48,000,000 votes for the Republicans to 41,000,000 for the Democrats. Bush carried forty of the fifty states and had a 426-to-112 advantage in the electorate vote. Dukakis's defeat could be attributed in part to the continued flight of white voters, who made up over 80 percent of the electorate. Since 1948, the only Democratic presidential candidate to receive a majority of the white vote was Lyndon Johnson. Dukakis got about 38 percent of the white vote in 1988. The South was now solidly Republican, as was most of the Midwest and West. Millions of blue-collar workers voted for Bush. Despite being beaten in the presidential vote, the Democrats retained control of both houses of Congress.

ECONOMIC AND SOCIAL POLICY

The Bush administration was noteworthy, mainly for the absence of many new initiatives emanating from the White House. Bush clearly lacked Reagan's sense of ideological mission and did not appear capable of articulating a compelling vision that would inspire his fellow citizens or provide them with a sense of direction. His presidency began with a series of political gestures. He met with Democratic leaders to tell them that he wanted a cooperative relationship with Congress rather than continue the partisan confrontational style of his predecessor.

Bush's first budgetary proposals sent to Congress in February 1989 offered a few programs to combat drug abuse and improve the nation's public schools. He also sought additional funding for child care, clean air, AIDS research, and to assist the homeless. In keeping with his campaign promises, he sought no new taxes to pay for these programs; indeed, he proposed a tax cut—he wanted Congress to reduce the capital gains tax by 15 percent. He insisted that, even with his tax cut, his new funding proposals could be paid for, the deficit reduced, and the bankrupt savings and loan banks resuscitated by the increased revenues flowing into the federal treasury from accelerated economic growth. Few economists outside of his administration shared Bush's faith in the miraculous powers of supply-side economics. They feared that the new president might be practicing his own brand of "voodoo economics."

Bush's presidency was dominated by two overriding concerns: the savings and loan crisis and the reduction of huge federal deficits. Bush proposed a rescue plan to either close or sell the bankrupt S&Ls and repay depositors. Congress created a new agency, the Resolution Trust Corporation (RTC), to sell off the assets of the failed thrifts to solvent banks, often on very favorable terms. At the same time,

Figure 16.2   George Bush, forty-first president. He previously served as a Representative from Texas (1967–71), U.S. Ambassador to the UN (1971–72). U.S. Chief liaison to China (1974–75), director of the CIA (1976–77), Vice President of the U.S. (1981–89), and the 41st President of the U.S. (1989–93).   *Source:* The White House Photo Office, neg.# 41.

the FSLIC was folded into the Federal Deposit Insurance Corporation (FDIC) to provide the billions needed to bail out depositors.

Bush acknowledged that "our will is strong, but our wallet is weak," that is, the new president insisted that straitened fiscal circumstances precluded new federal initiatives, however desirable, that cost a lot of money. The Reagan legacy included a prosperous economy, but its prosperity could only be sustained by huge deficit spending—deficit spending by the federal government, by business, and by individual consumers. Reagan's tax cuts had compounded the federal government's enormous debt problems.

In the spring of 1991, Bush, under heavy pressure from Congress to reduce the federal debt, conceded the need to accept some new taxes. His concession promptly outraged his conservative supporters and many citizens who had voted in good faith for Bush and his no-new-taxes promise. This acute sense of betrayal felt by conservatives contributed to Bush's electoral defeat in 1992. In October 1991, the Bush administration and the Democratically controlled Congress finally agreed on a combination of tax hikes and budget cuts that promised modest reductions in the budget deficits over the next four years.

Meanwhile, the economy slipped into a recession, the first in nearly a decade. Despite complaints from many workers who had lost their jobs, congressional Democrats, and even some Republicans, Bush denied for months that the economy had lapsed into recession, and he then appeared unable to devise a program of economic restoratives. The recession, combined with Bush's denials and inept response, seriously undermined his popularity with American voters.

Bush also inherited a host of serious social problems. The most feared pathology was the ongoing AIDS epidemic. By 1990, the disease had claimed over 110,000 lives, and an estimated 1.5 million people had tested HIV-positive. Most of the AIDS-infected cases involved gay males, but in the early 1990s, the proportion of AIDS cases among African American and Hispanic American intravenous drug users grew rapidly. The number of women infected with the AIDS virus also was increasing. Despite the huge sums of money spent on research, there appeared to be no prospect for an early cure or even the development of an effective vaccine, however, some progress occurred in the development of drugs and therapies that suppressed or delayed the onset of AIDS symptoms.

Bush continued the war on drugs begun during Reagan's years. He pushed for more stringent drug testing in the workplaces of America, better enforcement of existing drug laws, and additional measures taken to interdict the flood of illicit drugs pouring into the country from Mexico, Peru, and Colombia. Despite stepped-up efforts on all three fronts, drugs, especially "crack" cocaine, remained popular and widely available within the United States. There also was a connection between widespread crack use and the rising level of violent crime amidst the inner cities of America. Even though the Bush administration spent billions of dollars on its war on drugs, it failed to curb the great American appetite for drugs or slow the illicit traffic.

THE SUPREME COURT IN THE 1990S

By the late 1980s, the Supreme Court had taken a conservative turn. In *Webster v. Reproductive Health Care Services* (1989), the Court, by a five-to-four majority decision, sustained a Missouri statute that restricted abortions. In *Rust v. Sullivan* (1990), the Court upheld a federal law that prohibited personnel at federally funded health clinics from discussing abortion with their clients. In *Planned Parenthood v. Casey* (1992), the Court, by a five to four decision, upheld a Pennsylvania law requiring a twenty-four-hour waiting period and informed consent before an abortion could be performed. Although the conservative Supreme Court placed restrictions on women's access to abortion, they never challenged *Roe v. Wade*, which established that women have a constitutional right to abortion. In other important constitutional areas, the Court adhered to liberal precedents. In *Texas v. Johnson*, a five-to-four majority ruled that burning an American flag as a form of protest was protected as free speech under the First Amendment.

With the retirement from the Court in 1990 and 1991 of William Brennan and Thurgood Marshall, respectively, two elderly liberal associate justices, Bush received opportunities to add additional conservative jurists to the Supreme Court. His first appointment, David Souter, an obscure federal judge from New Hampshire, was quickly confirmed by the Senate with little opposition. Bush's second appointee, Clarence Thomas, a conservative African American jurist, was narrowly confirmed by the Senate in October 1991 by a fifty-two to forty-eight vote.

Judge Thomas had to survive challenges from liberal senators who were dissatisfied with his evasive answers to their questions concerning his views on abortion and other issues. In dramatic televised hearings before the Senate Judiciary Committee, Thomas also had to refute charges brought by an Oklahoma University law professor, Anita Hill, that he had sexually harassed her when she had worked for him at two federal agencies in 1982 and 1983. The nation witnessed three days of often sexually explicit testimony. The close Senate vote to confirm Thomas was not appreciably affected by the hearings; nearly all of the negative votes were cast by senators who would have voted against Thomas, had Hill never made her charges.

The controversy attending Thomas's confirmation hearings brought to the fore the troubling matter of sexual harassment of women in the workforce and political system. The hearings also heightened public disgust with the performance of politicians, and they made people more aware of the seriousness of the problems women face in the workplaces of America.

The insensitive treatment accorded Hill by some male senators bent on discrediting her testimony revived the feminist political movement. Patricia Ireland, a spokeswoman for the National Organization for Women (NOW), vowed that women would seek to replace male office holders with qualified women. Using as their rallying cry, "they still don't get it," woman entered mainstream politics in unprecedented numbers during the 1992 elections.

Figure 16.3   Supreme Court Photo. With the addition of George Bush's nominees, David Souter and Clarence Thomas, the Supreme Court took on a strong, conservative tone. Photographer: Joseph H. Bailey. *Source:* National Geographic Society, neg.# 02935-10.

THE END OF THE COLD WAR

The advent of the Bush presidency coincided with dramatic developments occurring in the international realm that brought about the most fundamental changes in American foreign policy since World War II. The most important of these changes was the decline of Communism, as evidenced by the disintegration of the Soviet empire in eastern Europe and then the collapse of the Soviet Union itself. The Soviet revolution, which had convulsed the world in 1917 and had been one of the most potent shapers of twentieth-century history, disintegrated. The Cold War, which had been the dominant reality of international life for nearly a half-century, suddenly ended. It ended when the Soviet Union had to withdraw from international competition because of severe internal economic weaknesses.

Although conservative spokesmen were quick to say that the rapid American military buildup in the 1980s, the Reagan Doctrine, and Reagan's bold rhetorical attacks on Communism brought about the demise of the Soviet Union, it appeared more likely that Communism had simply imploded. Communism mainly collapsed from within. Washington's aggressive strategies and the pressures of trying to compete with the Americans hastened the Soviet collapse. While the Soviet Union was clearly the ultimate loser in a long struggle for world supremacy, America suffered losses as well. The American people endured secret radiation experiments, spying by their own government, anti-Communist witch-hunts, and fear of nuclear annihilation. During the life of the Cold War, the United States spent $4 trillion on nuclear weapons!

The sudden demise of Communism caught official Washington by complete surprise. Neither the CIA, nor any of the other American intelligence agencies, nor any of the myriad of experts inhabiting prestigious U.S. strategic institutes had the slightest inkling that the Soviet system was on the verge of collapse until it disintegrated. Communism failed, primarily because it did not work. It failed to deliver on its promises of material abundance and social equality. It also failed to transform humanity and reshape society and history. The workers' paradise failed to materialize. The basic failure was economic. Communism's political and ideological failures derived from its economic dysfunctions. It never achieved legitimacy, even among most of the Soviet people, and it finally had to be scrapped, consigned to the dustbin of history.

Mikhail Gorbachev inadvertently destroyed the Soviet Union while trying to save it. He understood that the Achilles heel of the Soviet empire was its stagnating economy and lagging technology, especially in the areas of computer technology and information processing. By the mid-1980s, Gorbachev perceived that the Soviet Union could no longer maintain the arms race with the United States and feed its own people. In an effort to revive a failing system, Gorbachev proclaimed an era of *perestroika* (economic restructuring) and *glasnost* (openness). Economic controls were loosened and censorship was lifted. A civic awakening occurred. An elected parliament supplanted party *aparatchiks*.

Although Soviet politics were reformed, the economy continued to deteriorate. Continuing economic rot forced Gorbachev to pull Soviet troops out of

Afghanistan, ending a nine-year war in that country. In July 1989, Gorbachev repudiated the Brezhnev doctrine that had given Soviet troops the right to intervene in eastern European countries. He cut loose from client governments in Poland, Czechoslovakia, East Germany, Hungary, Bulgaria, and Romania. Once the people of these countries understood that Soviet tanks no longer protected their rulers, they promptly overthrew all of those hated regimes. The dominoes toppled in rapid succession.

The most dramatic event heralding the collapse of the Soviet empire in eastern Europe occurred on November 9, 1989, when the Berlin Wall, which had so long served as a hated symbol of the impasse between East and West, was breached. Thousands of East and West Germans crossed the former barrier as the long-standing division of their country came to an end. With the borders between East and West Germany fully open, the Communist government of East Germany collapsed. A Democratic government quickly replaced it, and on October 3, 1990, East Germany reunited with West Germany. The reunited Germany remained in NATO, and the Warsaw Pact disintegrated. Since disputes over Germany between the Soviets and the Americans were the major causes of the Cold War that originated during the mid-1940s, it was historically appropriate that the reunion of Germany signaled the beginning of the end of the long conflict.

The American leaders, Reagan and his successor George Bush, supported the Gorbachev revolution. Many U.S. corporations quickly penetrated the Soviet Union. McDonald's opened a large restaurant just off of Red Square. But it was the Germans who led the drive to penetrate east European and Soviet markets in the immediate aftermath of the Cold War. Gorbachev and the West Germans cut a deal: the Germans would provide about $30 billion to prop up the Soviet economy, and in return Gorbachev would accept a speedy German reunion and the end of the Warsaw Pact. On August 19, 1991, Stalinist reactionaries among the Red Army, the KGB, and the bureaucrats who controlled the Soviet economy attempted a military coup. It failed, because 40,000 citizens of Moscow defied the putschists and rallied around the courageous leadership of Boris Yeltsin.

THE REAPPEARANCE OF RUSSIA

The death of the Soviet Union was officially proclaimed on December 21, 1991, by Boris Yeltsin and several other leaders who announced the formation of a new federation of sovereign states. The former USSR had mutated into an eleven-republic Commonwealth of Independent States, three independent Baltic nations, and an independent Georgia. On December 26, major European powers and the United States officially recognized the Russian republic under Yeltsin's leadership as the de facto successor to the defunct Soviet Union.

Since its reappearance as a nation, Russia has remained mired in economic stagnation without the institutional base or competitive strategy required to develop a dynamic capitalistic economy. Exogenous factors, such as falling world commodity prices, particularly for oil, and turmoil in Asian financial markets, have hurt Russia. Political instability and the fiscal strategies pursued by the Yeltsin government have been more damaging. Since 1992, Yeltsin has pursued an anti-inflationary program that has three key elements—cutting spending, increasing tax collection, and privatizing the economy by selling off state-owned enterprises; keeping a strong ruble by maintaining exchange rates; and promoting trade and foreign investment in Russia.

The results have all been ruinous. Russia's economy has been decimated. The nation has been in a 1930s'-style depression for most of the decade of the 1990s. Real GDP has fallen 40 percent to 50 percent since 1990; investment has shrunk by 80 percent. Eighty percent of the 150,000,000 Russian people live in poverty. Hyperinflation, especially for basic food commodities, remains a serious problem.

The Russian economy and government are controlled by a capitalist elite, many of them former Communist bureaucrats who acquired ownership of formerly state-owned enterprises for a fraction of their value. This coterie of billionaires concealed income, evaded taxes, and removed an estimated $200 billion in assets offshore. The Yeltsin government has often refused to pay workers or send pensioners their monthly stipends, and the domestic economy is starved for capital. Science and technology have been gutted. Most foreign investment has been channeled into securities, not direct investment. Russia has dropped into the ranks of Third World exporters of raw materials.

Despite pressure from President Clinton, who has been a long-time supporter of Yeltsin, U.S. investors have been reluctant to invest in Russian enterprises. In the summer of 1998, Yeltsin, old and sick, faced another financial crisis that could bring down his sclerotic government and return the Communists to power. Clinton, beset by scandals, could do little to help Yeltsin, except to offer some upbeat rhetoric about staying on the road to democracy and capitalism.

BUSH AND THE POST–COLD WAR WORLD

As the Soviet Union receded from the world stage, Europe, led by a reunified Germany, moved to form a European community free of tariffs, travel restrictions, and monetary impediments. Eleven nations with a population of about 350 million constitute the world's richest market. The euro was launched January 1, 1999; it promised to transform the transatlantic relationship for good by placing Europe on an equal economic footing with the United States.

Along the Pacific Rim, Japan, suffered a series of financial and economic setbacks in the 1990s. America's Asian and Pacific trade in 1998, over half of it with the Japanese, was much larger than its trade with Europe. China, its economy freed from Communist shackles, had the world's fastest-growing major economy. By January 1999, the Chinese Gross Domestic Product (GDP) had reach an estimated

$3.6 trillion, making it the second largest economy in the world. China, with its rich resources, vast population, and dynamic economy, appeared to have an un-bounded future if it could survive the current crises unscathed.

U.S. foreign policy in Latin America also benefited from the end of the Cold War. Gorbachev announced that Soviet aid to prop up the Cuban economy, which had been running at $5 billion per annum, would be drastically curtailed. In the post–Cold War era, Castro appeared to be only an aging caudillo clinging to power in an impoverished insular backwater within a hemisphere that had abandoned dictatorship of either the leftist or rightist variety and had turned instead to U.S.-style liberal democracy.

In Nicaragua, the Sandinistas also felt the impact of the end of the Cold War. The Soviet Union, which had subsidized the Sandinistas to the tune of $500 million a year, turned off the aid spigot. In early 1990, the Sandinista's permitted free elec-tions to take place in Nicaragua. To their dismay, a coalition of anti-Sandinista forces, led by Violetta Chamorro, won. Isolated from their Soviet patron and repudiated by the people of Nicaragua, the Sandinistas surrendered their power. Chamorro be-came Nicaragua's first freely elected president in more than sixty years.

While supporting the spread of Democracy in Nicaragua, the United States also settled some scores in Panama. In December 1989, the U.S. sent military forces into Panama to overthrow dictator Manuel Noriega and to install a pro-American government. Noriega had previously worked with the CIA. He later broke with the Americans, supported the Sandinistas, and became rich as a drug trafficker for the Medellin cartel. Previously, U.S. federal grand juries had indicted Noriega for drug smuggling, gun running, and money laundering. He was captured and brought to the United States for trial. Public opinion polls showed that the Panamanian inter-vention, which was of dubious legality since Panamanian officials had not re-quested U.S. assistance, was overwhelmingly popular with Americans.

China also felt the impact of rising anti-Communism. In April 1989, thou-sands of Chinese students and intellectuals gathered in Beijing's Tiananmen Square to demand democracy for China. The pro-democracy movement spread rapidly, and soon demonstrations sprouted in Nanjing, Shanghai, and other Chi-nese cities. Americans strongly supported the pro-democracy forces. For a time, Chinese authorities appeared uncertain about how to respond to the challenge be-cause of the extensive media coverage the pro-democracy movement received in the world's press. But on the morning of June 4, 1989, Deng ordered the Chinese army to crush the drive for democracy. A brutal massacre ensued that claimed the lives of at least 1,000 people. Dissident Democrats were hunted down and jailed en masse. The nascent pro-democracy movement was violently suppressed. President Bush publicly condemned the Chinese regime's slaughter of its own people, how-ever, he would take no actions that might jeopardize the friendly relations carefully cultivated between the Chinese and American governments since Richard Nixon's historic journey to Beijing in 1972.

While Communist regimes were collapsing in eastern Europe, rightist au-thoritarian regimes also were succumbing to the world Democratic revival. In

Chile, in 1989, General Pinochet's regime gave way to a Democratically elected government. In South Africa, Frederick DeKlerk became prime minister in August 1989. Within a few months, he released African National Conference leader Nelson Mendela from prison, where he had languished for more than twenty-five years. In 1991, as DeKlerk began dismantling apartheid, President Bush lifted American sanctions. In April 1994, there occurred one of the most thrilling moments in modern world history: South Africa held its first elections in which all South Africans could vote. Mendela was elected president, and a multiracial parliament was chosen. Democracy had trumped apartheid.

Elsewhere in Africa, famine threatened millions of people, especially in Somalia, where years of civil war had destroyed any semblance of government. In December 1992, when warring Somali factions diverted UN-sanctioned food relief shipments to black markets, Washington sent in 30,000 American troops to protect food deliveries. Under President Clinton, the American mission expanded to include restoring order and state-building. Eighteen U.S. Marines were killed in fighting the forces of Somali warlord Mohammed Farah Aidid. Yielding to public pressure to bring the troops home, Clinton withdrew all American forces from Somalia in 1994.

WAR IN THE PERSIAN GULF

During January and February 1991, in the first major military action of the new post–Cold War era, America and its allies fought a war in the Persian Gulf against Iraq. The war had a long preparation time, and it derived in part from previous U.S. Middle Eastern diplomatic policies. During the Iraq-Iranian war, America often aided Iraq to prevent an Iranian victory that Washington feared could threaten the oil-rich Saudis. During the late 1980s, American sent the Iraqis nearly a billion dollars' worth of agricultural, economic, and technical aid. These aid packages included high-tech equipment such as advanced computers and lasers that could be used to produce weapons of mass destruction, including nuclear bombs.

Soon after Iraq's war with Iran ended in a draw under the terms of an agreement brokered by UN representatives, Kuwait, which, along with Saudi Arabia, had bankrolled Iraq's war with the Iranians, increased its production of oil in violation of OPEC rules. World oil prices dropped, hurting Saddam Hussein's government, already deeply in debt and dependent on oil revenues for sustaining the Iraqi economy. Saddam also was annoyed by the Kuwaitis and the Saudis over their refusal to forgive Iraq's huge indebtedness to them. He asserted claims to Kuwaiti territory based on maps predating the 1919 political settlement that had created the modern nation-state of Iraq. Saddam may have harbored grandiose ambitions of becoming the dominant power in the Gulf area.

Even as Iraq prepared for war, U.S. leaders did not anticipate military action in the region. Washington was preoccupied with the historic events that brought the Cold War to a sudden end. Its policies in the Gulf region still turned on the notion that Iraq was the major counterweight to Iranian revolutionary aggression. On the eve of Iraq's invasion of Kuwait, the American ambassador to Baghdad, April Gillespie, told Saddam that the United States would not become involved in regional disputes, although America would defend its vital interests. Saddam apparently interpreted Gillespie's remark as a green light for aggression.

On August 2, 1990, Iraqi forces occupied Kuwait and threatened neighboring Saudi Arabia, possessor of more than one-fifth of the world's proven oil reserves. Bush, determined to force Saddam Hussein to withdraw his forces from Kuwait, forged an international coalition under UN auspices to thwart Iraqi aggression. Bush also persuaded Soviet leader Mikhail Gorbachev to abandon his former Iraqi clients and support the UN initiative.

The UN promptly enacted Resolution 661, authorizing a trade embargo against Iraq. The international community clamped a tight economic boycott on Iraq and deployed a military force of some 250,000 troops to defend Saudi Arabia from possible attack. Most of these forces, dubbed Operation DESERT SHIELD, were American troops under the command of U.S. Army General Norman Schwarzkopf. But Schwarzkopf's forces also included a sizable representation from Great Britain, France, and several Arab countries, including Saudi Arabia, Egypt, Syria, and the United Emirates.

Initially, Bush appeared willing to use military force defensively, to protect Saudi Arabia and other possible Iraqi targets from attack and to let economic pressures force Saddam out of Kuwait. But almost from the beginning of Gulf military operations, Pentagon planners were preparing for offensive military action. Bush soon became convinced that the boycott would not work, or that it would take too long. During November, 550,000 soldiers representing some twenty countries gathered in and near Saudi Arabia.

Many liberal Democrats opposed military action against Iraq. They believed that the economic boycott ought to be given a chance to work, and they also did not want America to go to war without congressional approval. The UN enacted Resolution 629 on November 29, which set January 15, 1991, as a deadline for Iraqi withdrawal from Kuwait and authorized the use of force to drive the Iraqis from Kuwait if they did not leave by that date. On January 12, both the House and the Senate enacted resolutions formally approving the use of American military force in the Gulf.

On January 16, 1991, the war in the Persian Gulf, Operation DESERT STORM, commenced when President Bush ordered an Allied air assault on Iraqi targets. Deploying an impressive arsenal of high-tech weaponry, America and its allies waged a destructive five-week air war against the Iraqis. Priority targets included Iraqi chemical, biological, and nuclear production, command and control facilities, and airfields.

On February 23, 1991, General Schwarzkopf ordered his forces, now 700,000 strong, to attack Iraqi positions in Kuwait and southern Iraq. Two hundred thousand American, British, and French armored forces roared across the undefended

Figure 16.4 The former Soviet Union.   *Source:* U.S. State Department.

Iraqi border with Saudi Arabia 200 miles to the west of Kuwait. They smashed into the elite Republican Guard forces and quickly demolished them. Within four days, Allied forces had overwhelmed the Iraqis, whose fighting capabilities had been seriously eroded by the weeks of air attacks that preceded the invasion. President Bush offered a cease-fire, and the Iraqis quickly accepted it. At war's end, the Allied forces occupied Kuwait and held southern Iraq.

Only 148 Americans were killed and 467 wounded during the short war, but an estimated 100,000 Iraqi soldiers and civilians died. In addition to light casualties, the dollar costs of the war to Americans also proved light because its $30 billion tab was picked up by wealthy U.S. allies that did not send combat forces.

Americans erupted in a frenetic celebration of a victory that had been achieved so quickly and at such a low cost. Parades and celebrations, the likes of which had not been seen since 1945, welcomed home the conquering heroes. President Bush's approval ratings soared beyond 90 percent. The Gulf War made a national hero out of General Schwarzkopf, the commander who had led Allied forces to a quick victory. The Gulf War was the most popular one since the Spanish-American War. In the first major crisis of the post–Cold War era, America had asserted its leadership, and the Soviets had followed the U.S. lead.

American home audiences followed the war around the clock on the Cable News Network (CNN). But the U.S. military tightly controlled television reportage, and American TV viewers saw only a sanitized version of the war. Reporters were

Figure 16.5   Post–Cold War Europe, 1992.   *Source:* U.S. State Department.

allowed in the field only with military escorts, who controlled what they saw and who they interviewed. Americans saw little of the gory realities of a war that included civilian casualties and the slaughter of tens of thousands of Iraqi soldiers.

The immediate U.S. policy goal in the Persian Gulf War was liberating Kuwait. Larger American strategic goals included keeping the vast Middle Eastern oil reserves in friendly hands and destroying Saddam Hussein's capacity to wage offensive war or achieve paramountcy in the Persian Gulf region.

Even though the Persian Gulf War was a great success, critics observed that even though the Allied coalition succeeded in driving the Iraqis out of Kuwait, it failed to bring down Saddam Hussein. Bush encouraged ethnic Kurds and Shiite Muslims within Iraq to rebel, but when they did, Washington allowed Saddam to crush them. Bush's reluctance to continue the war derived from Saudi fears that if Saddam were deposed, Iraq would disintegrate. The Saudis preferred a defanged Saddam presiding over a stable Iraq than chaos and civil war on their border. They also feared Iranian hegemony in the region in the wake of an Iraqi collapse.

The short war had a negligible impact on the American economy. Domestic oil prices dropped, but the economy remained mired in recession. Bush's high approval ratings at the time of the war dissipated during the next six months as the U.S. economy remained in the doldrums. There was a poignant aftermath to the war. Hundreds of Persian Gulf veterans developed symptoms, including fatigue, nausea, joint pain, and memory loss, after serving in the combat zone. Medical experts believed that many of these veterans were suffering from the effects of having been exposed to chemical and biological agents released when Allied forces destroyed Iraqi poison gas storage facilities.

Because of the Soviet collapse and the smashing Iraqi defeat, Israel felt more secure than at any other time since the Jewish state was founded. Responding to American pressures, Israeli leaders agreed to participate in an international conference convened in Madrid in December 1991 to try to resolve the Palestinian issue and to achieve a comprehensive Middle East peace treaty. Delegates from several Arab nations and representatives of the Palestinians engaged in dialogues with Israeli envoys. In the spring of 1993, the talks were placed on hold as Israeli security forces fought with Palestinian militants in the occupied territories.

THE ELECTION OF 1992

In the summer of 1990, the economy slid into a recession, the first downturn in eight years, ending the longest period of growth and prosperity in modern American history. Its major causes included a combination of private and public indebtedness, excess productive capacity, and declining consumer confidence. Although the recession was not a severe one, the American people reacted quite negatively to it. It was the slow recovery from the recession, coupled with Bush's political failures, that put the long-term Republican hold on the White House in jeopardy. The state of the economy and jobs for the people became the dominant issues in the 1992 elections.

In the fall of 1991, when Democratic leaders declared their candidacies for their party's 1992 presidential nomination, the most prominent names decided not to run because they had concluded that George Bush was unbeatable. Their withdrawals opened the door for a young, energetic governor, William Jefferson "Bill" Clinton of Arkansas. Clinton, during the 1980s, had been critical of both conservative Republican economic policies and of what he called liberal Democratic "tax-and-spend" alternatives. He had served as chairman of the Democratic Leadership Council, a group of moderate Democratic leaders intent on winning control of the national party.

Early in the primary campaign, Clinton had to respond to allegations that he had had an affair with a woman who had worked in the governor's office in Little Rock, which nearly destroyed his candidacy before it got going. He also acknowledged smoking marijuana while a college student. More seriously, he appeared to have manipulated the selective service system to avoid military service during the Vietnam War era. Another disturbing quality emerged as Clinton campaigned in the early Democratic primaries. His answers and explanations to the myriad of accusations that came his way seemed designed more to evade or appease than to clarify.

Nevertheless, Clinton survived these threats and moved ahead quickly in the Democratic primaries. He rather easily defeated two weak rivals, former Massachusetts Senator Paul Tsongas and former California Governor Jerry Brown. Clinton demonstrated resiliency, an ability to hit back at detractors, and most of all, an impressive grasp of the important issues facing the American people in 1992. At the Democratic Convention, held in Madison Square Garden in New York in July, the delegates proceeded to nominate the first baby-boomer ticket in American political history: forty-five-year-old Bill Clinton for president and forty-two-year-old Albert Gore as vice president. In his crisp acceptance speech, Clinton pronounced an end to spendthrift liberalism and special-interest politics. He called for welfare reform, affordable health care for all Americans, a tax cut for the middle class, higher taxes for rich people, tax breaks for small businesses, and sharp reductions in military spending.

A strong third-party candidate, maverick Texas billionaire populist H. Ross Perot, entered the 1992 campaign. While Bush and Clinton battled their way through the primaries, Perot's electronic grassroots campaign was fueled by voter outrage at a political system that could not address the real problems facing ordinary Americans. The feisty Texan enlivened the political landscape with his presence during the election of 1992. By May, Perot was outpolling both Clinton and Bush in some national surveys. Suddenly, in mid-July, Perot announced that he was withdrawing from the race and threw his support to Bill Clinton, whom, Perot claimed, had taken up his issues.

During the fall campaign, Clinton attacked what he called the "trickle-down" economic policies of the Reagan and Bush administrations, while carefully avoiding the label of "liberal big spender." He portrayed himself as "an agent of change" to appeal to "Perotistas." Clinton called for welfare reform to obtain the votes of Reagan Democrats. He repeated his proposals made at the Democratic Convention—affordable health care for all Americans, taxing the rich, and tax breaks for the middle class.

Bush made a strenuous bid for reelection. He tried to run on his foreign policy record, but in 1992, in the post–Cold War era, the American people considered foreign policy issues secondary or peripheral. Bush blamed the Democratically controlled Congress for political gridlock, the lingering recession, and the runaway deficits. Mostly he concentrated his fire on Bill Clinton. He charged him with being an old-fashioned tax-and-spend liberal disguised as a moderate. He questioned Clinton's character and his judgment. He challenged Clinton's patriotism for being a draft avoider, and he even questioned his loyalty for having visited the Soviet Union. "Who do you trust?" became the focal point of Bush's campaign in its frantic final weeks. Bush's shrill attacks on Clinton had little impact on voter behavior.

In the final month of the campaign, Perot leaped back into the ring. Once again, the election became a three-way contest. The election results confirmed the lead that Clinton had long maintained in the polls. He received 43.7 million votes to 38.1 million for Bush and 19.2 million for Perot. He carried thirty-two states and the District of Columbia, with a total of 370 electoral votes to 168 for Bush and 0 for Perot. For the first time since 1977, the Democrats won control of both the White House and Congress.

Clinton's moderate campaign partially restored the old Democratic coalition that had been ripped to shreds by Nixon and Reagan. Clinton retained the African American vote. Hard times and Bush's failed policies brought a lot of Reagan Democrats home to Clinton's party, especially in the Midwestern industrial states. Clinton probably won the election by carrying Ohio, Illinois, Michigan, and Pennsylvania—all of which had gone to Bush in 1988. Clinton also got a majority of the women's vote and the youth vote. Clinton and Gore, both moderate Southerners, also chipped away at the Solid South, which had been solid for Republicans in recent presidential elections. They carried their home states of Arkansas and Tennessee and also picked up Louisiana and Georgia. In addition, they carried normally Republican California with its huge bloc of 54 electoral votes.

The Democrats picked up one Senate seat, giving them a 58-to-42 edge. The large Democratic majority in the House of Representatives shrank a little, from 266 to 166 to 260 to 174. Although the shift in the relative strength of the major parties was slight, 1992 represented a year of upheaval in congressional voting. Elections for the House were held for the first time under the reapportionment brought about by the 1990 census. Demographic trends underway since World War II continued to prevail. Sunbelt states like California, Arizona, Texas, and Florida were the big winners, gaining many additional seats. The Northeastern states and the old industrial states of the upper Midwest continued to be the big losers, losing the seats that the Southern Rim states gained.

More incumbents resigned or were defeated in primary elections than in any election since 1946. Women, African Americans, Asian Americans, and Hispanics were elected to the House in record numbers. In the Senate, women scored a major breakthrough; five women, all of them Democrats, won seats. Carol Moseley Braun, from Illinois, became the first African American woman to serve in the Senate. California sent two women to the Senate, and Colorado sent a Native American, Ben Nighthorse Campbell.

THE DEMOCRATS RETURN

As in 1960, the 1992 election wrought both a change of party in the White House and a generational shift along the corridors of power. With Clinton and Gore in office, and over 100 new members of Congress in place, the baby boomers assumed national leadership. Clinton made good on his pledge to diversify the upper echelons of the executive branch by selecting many women and minority candidates. Women headed the Environmental Protection Agency and the Council of Economic Advisers. Janet Reno was picked to be the first woman attorney general. Clinton's determination to select women for important offices also reflected the influence of his wife, Hillary Rodham Clinton, an attorney who aspired to be the most influential First Lady since Eleanor Roosevelt.

The new president quickly got embroiled in a controversy with the Pentagon over his proposal to allow openly gay and lesbian people to serve in the armed forces. In July 1993, Clinton announced a compromise policy that had the support of the joint chiefs of staff: the military would no longer ask prospective recruits questions about their sexual orientation and would no longer employ security forces to hound suspected gays and lesbians out of the armed forces. But gays and lesbians serving in the military could not engage in overt homosexual behavior on or off military duty stations; also, open acknowledgment of gay or lesbian preferences would be grounds for dismissal from military service. This "don't ask, don't tell, don't pursue" compromise failed to satisfy gay and lesbian activists, who vowed to continue their campaign to achieve equality within the armed forces in the courts, and it angered those who opposed any change in the anti-gay and lesbian policies of the military services. Evidence also surfaced in the late 1990s that

Figure 16.6   Baby boomers in the White House . . . President Bill Clinton and First Lady Hillary Rodham Clinton. William Jefferson Clinton (1946–) was born William Jefferson Blythe IV. He was governor of Arkansas from (1979–81, 1983–92). He was elected the 42nd President of the U.S. in 1993. Hillary Rodham Clinton (1947–) wrote *It Takes a Village* in 1995.   *Source:* The White House Photo Office.

military security forces continued to harass suspected gay and lesbian personnel, despite the new policy. In 1997 a record number of personnel were discharged from the military for being homosexual.

Clinton also displayed a tendency to abandon or delay many of his campaign commitments, giving rise to the fear that he was less an "agent of change" than a canny politician who exploited hard times and popular resentment against the performance of a lackluster incumbent to get elected. Republicans in the Senate and opposition from his own party leaders in both houses forced him to abandon his proposal to give tax breaks to small businesses and to reduce the size of his promised stimulus package.

Although the recession was clearly over in the spring of 1993, and the economic growth rate exceeded 4 percent per annum, the high rate of unemployment refused to decline. It remained fixed at 7 percent. Thirty-six million Americans lived in poverty. More Americans than ever before were receiving food stamps. In the post–Cold War era, cuts in military and aerospace spending brought massive lay-offs at prime defense contractors such as Boeing, McDonnell-Douglas, and Lockheed. American businesses both large and small were forced to become more efficient to meet the rigors of world economic competition in the 1990s. They laid off workers and mid-level managers to become more cost-effective operations. Companies replaced human workers with computers and computer-driven machines.

The millions who continued to work had to worker harder and longer than ever before. The pressures on workers to be more productive were unrelenting, and they intensified. Record numbers of workers have filed disability claims in the 1990s, their disabilities linked to stress or to disabling injuries caused by spending too many hours on computer terminals. Millions of workers and their families in the cutthroat 1990s suffered serious declines in the quality of their lives. They worked harder than their parents, endured more stress, and were less well compensated.

Figure 16.7   Labor union membership, 1930–1990.   *Source:* Bureau of Labor Statistics, Department of Labor.

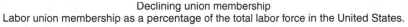

Declining union membership
Labor union membership as a percentage of the total labor force in the United States.

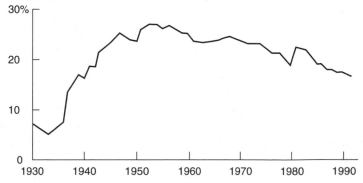

The continued decline of trade unions also contributed to the deteriorating status of working people. In 1999, scarcely 15 percent of American workers belonged to unions, down from a high of 35 percent reached during World War II. Beset by corporate downsizing, the wholesale transfer of jobs overseas, harsh union-busting tactics, and increasingly conservative Congresses that were indifferent or hostile to trade union interests, unions have been powerless to lift the wages of most workers or even to protect their jobs. Adjusted for inflation, wage levels in unionized industries have been stagnant for over twenty years, as productivity and corporate profits have soared.

In August 1993, a Democratic Congress enacted a five-year economic renewal program that incorporated some of Clinton's proposals. It raised the top marginal income tax rates from 31 percent to 36 percent, eased taxes on low-income families, and provided funding for education, retraining, and apprenticeship programs aimed at upgrading workers' skills. The program also brought about modest reductions in the deficits, which continued to exceed $200 billion annually in 1994 and 1995.

Clinton also expected the North American Free Trade Agreement (NAFTA) to boost efforts at economic renewal. Negotiated by the Bush administration, the NAFTA incorporated Mexico into a free-trade zone already created by Canada and the United States during Reagan's presidency. The NAFTA aroused both strong support and fierce opposition. Liberal Democrats and trade union leaders led the opposition, insisting that the NAFTA would send thousands of U.S. jobs south of the border. The NAFTA supporters argued that it would create jobs by opening up Mexican markets to a greater array of U.S. products. With strong support from Republicans, the NAFTA narrowly carried Congress, giving Clinton a political victory over the liberal wing of his own party. Congress also approved a new round of tariff reductions on manufactured goods under the General Agreement on Tariffs and Trade (GATT), which had been in place since the end of World War II. In 1994, Clinton followed these victories by reducing trade barriers with major Pacific Rim nations. In 1995, he became embroiled in a nasty trade dispute with Tokyo over its refusal to allow American companies to sell automotive spare parts to the Japanese. Only after Clinton threatened to impose sanctions that would have severely hurt sales of Japanese luxury automobiles to the United States did the Japanese make concessions.

Polls taken during the 1992 election showed that public concern about the rising tide of crime, especially violent crime, was second only to economic worries. Congress, in 1993, enacted the Handgun Violence Prevention Act. In 1994, it enacted the most costly, far-reaching crime bill in American history. It provided $30 billion to fund increased law enforcement, crime prevention, and prison construction. It extended the death penalty to fifty additional federal crimes, and it banned the sale of certain kinds of assault rifles. Crime rates, especially for violent crimes such as murder, assault, and armed robbery, have steadily declined during the 1990s.

In October 1993, following the lead of Hillary Rodham Clinton, the Clinton administration moved to implement health care reform. Their complex plan had three main goals: to provide coverage for the 45 million Americans who had no health insurance, to hold down costs, and to preserve the high quality of available health care for all Americans. The plan would have drastically restructured the existing health care system. All Americans would be enrolled into large regional health alliances. Individuals could enroll in either a fee-for-service plan, enabling them to choose their own physicians, or in less expensive health maintenance organizations (HMOs), where they would see doctors on the HMO staffs. Employers would pay 80 percent of workers' insurance costs. Self-employed workers would buy their own insurance, and Medicaid would continue to cover the poor. To cover the plan's estimated $100 billion in added costs, Congress would enact large tax increases on tobacco products. The administration's health-care reform proposal instantly attracted legions of critics but had relatively little support. After six grueling months of hearings, the administration conceded defeat on health care reform and settled for some token reforms to contain costs. The big losers were the 45 million Americans who had no health insurance in 1994. These working-class families represented one-fifth of the U.S. population under age sixty-five.

THE REPUBLICAN EARTHQUAKE

The 1994 midterm elections amounted to a popular referendum on Clinton's performance during his first two years in office. A sizeable majority of voters used the occasion to voice their dissatisfaction with the first yuppie president. He brought energy, enthusiasm, and good intentions to the job. He possessed an affable personality and considerable political skills. But he made mistakes, and his image was tarnished by scandals. Most of all, he failed to provide strong leadership or to project a coherent vision for the nation. He also failed to get most of his important programs through a Democratic Congress. There appeared to be two President Clintons—the moderate New Democrat and the paleoliberal committed to

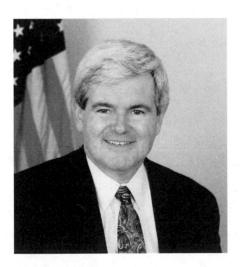

Figure 16.8　Newt Gingrich, the first Republican Speaker of the House of Representatives in more than 40 years.　*Source:* U.S. House of Representatives.

discredited tax-and-spend policies. Clinton also was hurt by popular anger at government and politicians generally, unresolved social issues, cultural conflicts, and continuing economic insecurities and discontents. The elections produced one of the most significant transformations in recent political history. The 1994 midterm elections completed the political transition that had begun with Ronald Reagan's electoral victory in 1980.

The elections brought a Republican Congress to power, the first since 1952. Clinton was the first Democratic president to face a Republican-controlled Congress in a half-century. The shock troops leading this Republican political "earthquake" were a group of seventy-three mostly young conservative reformers, many of whom had strong ties to the religious Right. The new Speaker of the House of Representative, Newt Gingrich, was the leader of the Republican revolt. A controversial politician, Gingrich had for years been the House minority leader. He quickly became the second most powerful politician in Washington.

Gingrich read the election results as a mandate for implementing his "Contract with America," a conservative agenda for the 1990s, with its top priorities being a balanced budget, the phasing out of welfare, and deep tax cuts. In 1995, the most activist Congress in decades enacted legislation that reformed the way the House worked, weakened affirmative action programs, cut foreign aid, cut Medicare, cut taxes, and reduced budget deficits. Following Gingrich's lead, the 104th Congress set out to downsize the federal government and to dismantle the welfare state.

Clinton could only watch passively as the Republicans seized the legislative initiative. The election also forced him to move to the Right. Clinton was forced to adopt a defensive political strategy—of trying to fend off Republican efforts to cut deeply or destroy liberal programs whenever he sensed that he had public opinion on his side, and of trying to position himself to win reelection within an increasingly conservative political environment. Twice in the fall of 1995, Republican enthusiasm for deep tax cuts and achieving a balanced budget by 2002, which Clinton opposed, caused a partial shutdown of the federal government. When Clinton vetoed an appropriations bill, some national parks and museums were forced to shut down, and some recipients reported delays in getting Social Security and Medicare payments. Public anger focused mainly on Republicans, who were seen as ideological zealots and irresponsible politicians whose refusal to compromise caused serious problems for many citizens. Gingrich's and Congress's approval ratings plummeted, while Clinton's soared.

In 1996, both President Clinton and the Republican-controlled Congress sought a centrist middle ground that produced several important new programs and policies. The minimum wage was increased. A major telecommunications bill replaced government regulation of the industry with open competition among telephone and cable TV companies. Congress also transformed federal agricultural policy; it established a program that over seven years gradually removed restrictions on farmers and phased out subsidy payments going back to the New Deal era of the 1930s. The most important legislation enacted by Congress ended the federal welfare program that also dated back to the New Deal. The Welfare Reform Act of 1996 returned the program to the states. According to its provisions, many aid recipients were required to find work and be off of welfare within two years. It also restricted eligibility for welfare to five years during a person's lifetime. The defederalizing of welfare was the most significant downsizing of the federal government in modern times and further attenuated the social contract that was at the heart of what remained of the welfare state. It also signaled that, henceforth, state and local governments would have greater responsibilities and would be required to spend more money for social programs, and that the federal government would have less responsibility and spend less.

THE ELECTION OF 1996

Several prominent Republicans sought their party's presidential nomination in 1996. The contenders included Lamar Alexander, a Southern moderate, and publishing magnate Steve Forbes, who used the family fortune to finance his campaign, promoting a flat tax and a balanced budget. Pat Buchanan pushed his populist attack on the NAFTA and multinational corporations and tried to attract the religious Right with his condemnation of abortion. But Bob Dole, the Senate majority leader, emerged as the party's nominee by capturing a block of key Southern primaries. He ran on a platform intended to attract all Republican factions: deep tax cuts, deregulation, economic growth, a balanced budget, and continued derogation of social programs to the states. He chose former football star Jack Kemp as his running mate.

Bill Clinton ran a well-funded, smoothly orchestrated centrist campaign tailored to appeal to middle-class suburban voters. He went after the "soccer mom" vote, suburban women whose political concerns focused on families and children. Clinton also attracted strong support from segments of the business community—particularly Silicon Valley, Hollywood, telecommunication and multimedia companies. Clinton and Vice President Gore promoted education, job training, and computer literacy as building bridges to the twenty-first-century Information Age. Dole tried to raise the character issue. He called attention to the Whitewater scandals, which involved a failed real estate development and defunct savings and loan bank that occurred in Arkansas when Bill Clinton was governor. Because there was no smoking gun of wrongdoing or lawbreaking by either Bill Clinton or Hillary Rodham Clinton, and because it happened long before Clinton became president, Dole received little political mileage out of raising the matter. Another scandal occurred during the final weeks of the campaign that cost Clinton some votes and perhaps prevented the Democrats from regaining control of the House of Representatives. Evidence surfaced that the Clinton campaign had illegally raised campaign funds from foreign sources, including Chinese officials.

Clinton and Gore nevertheless coasted to an easy victory in November. They received 49 percent of the vote to 41 percent for Dole and 8 percent for maverick

Ross Perot, who was back for another run but this time providing only a colorful footnote to a lackluster campaign. The Democrats accrued 379 electoral votes to 159 for Dole–Kemp, and they carried seven out of the eight most populous states with their huge clusters of electoral votes. Dole and Kemp carried twenty-five states, the same number as Clinton and Gore, but they were mostly Southern, Midwestern, and Mountain states. The Republicans retained control of both branches of Congress, but by reduced majorities.

The election took place within a generally conservative climate of opinion, reminiscent of the 1920s. Apathy and cynicism about politics prevailed, especially among younger citizens who viewed the political process with a mixture of amused contempt and horror. Despite saturation multimedia coverage, scarcely half of the people eligible to vote bothered to do so on election day. It was clear that it simply did not matter to huge numbers of Americans whether Bill Clinton was reelected or replaced by Bob Dole.

THE IMPEACHMENT OF PRESIDENT CLINTON

Political gridlock and endless partisan politicking characterized the first two years of Bill Clinton's second term of office. The Republicans in control of Congress, chastened by adverse public reactions to their antigovernmental zeal and outmaneuvered politically by the president, who co-opted many of their wedge issues, lost momentum. Newt Gingrich was narrowly reelected Speaker of the House of Representatives. He was also reprimanded and fined $300,000 for violating House rules and for "misleading" his colleagues about using tax-exempt donations for political purposes. Clinton was content to propose modest programs to help the middle classes, none of which Congress enacted. Congress failed to enact a $368 billion settlement against the major tobacco companies to recover the costs of treating smoking-related illnesses, which also included fines for concealing from the public scientific evidence in their possession that proved smoking was hazardous to people's health. The one significant achievement of both Congress and the White House came in May 1997, when, after years of political maneuvering, they reached a historic agreement on a balanced budget. With the economy continuing to perform strongly, the federal government produced a balanced budget for the fiscal year 1998, the first in nearly thirty years.

Most of the news out of Washington concerning Clinton's second term focused on a myriad of scandals that plagued the president and at times implicated several cabinet members and Vice President Al Gore. Many of the scandals stemmed from illegal fund-raising practices during the 1996 presidential campaign. Al Gore allegedly solicited funds by making illegal phone calls from the White House. The Vice President denied that these calls violated the law because "no controlling legal authority" forbade the practice. There also was evidence that on April 6, 1996, Gore had knowingly attended a fund-raising luncheon held at a

Buddhist temple in Hacienda Heights, California. Gore admitted attending the luncheon, but he denied that he had known in advance that it was a fund-raiser. In July 1997, the Senate convened a special investigating committee, chaired by Republican Senator Fred Thompson of Tennessee, to hold hearings into potentially illegal fund-raising practices relating to both the 1994 and 1996 electoral campaigns. Specifically, the senators wanted to learn if the Chinese government, through illegal campaign contributions, tried to influence the outcome of the 1996 election.

In January 1998, the fund-raising scandals were relegated to the back pages by sensational discoveries that President Clinton had had an eighteen-month-long sexual relationship with a twenty-one-year-old White House intern, Monica Lewinsky, from Beverly Hills, an affair that had begun in November 1995. The affair attracted the attention of Independent Counsel Kenneth Starr, who for three years had been conducting an investigation into possible improper and illegal activity by both Bill Clinton and Hillary Rodham Clinton, going back to the days of Whitewater and including some White House scandals. Starr received formal authority on January 16 from a federal court to expand his investigation to determine if Clinton had broken any laws during his efforts to conceal the liaison with Lewinsky. On January 27, Starr formally convened a grand jury inquiry into the affair.

Lewinsky herself was in legal jeopardy, because on January 7, 1998, she had denied under oath that she had had sexual relations with the president in a pretrial deposition that she gave in the Paula Jones case. Jones had first surfaced in February 1994, when she stated that in 1991, while she was a state employee, Governor Bill Clinton of Arkansas had invited her to his hotel room and made a crude demand for oral sex. Jones testified that she had refused Clinton's demand and quickly left the room. At the time that Jones came forward with her accusations, President Clinton denied them all. Jones's lawyers then filed a sexual harassment suit against Clinton. The president had also given a deposition at the Jones's pretrial hearing, in which he denied under oath ever having a sexual relationship with Lewinsky. On January 26, President Clinton went on television to deny that he had had a sexual liaison with Lewinsky. Looking the American people squarely in the eye and wagging his finger, he emphatically stated, "I did not have sexual relations with that woman, Ms. Lewinsky." Thereafter, he stonewalled the matter, refusing to answer questions or to discuss it further in public. In April 1998, a judge dismissed Jones's suit, observing that even if her account were true, Clinton's behavior, while tacky and coarse, did not constitute sexual harassment. On November 13, Clinton paid Paula Jones $850,000 and she agreed to drop her efforts to reinstate her lawsuit.

Kenneth Starr, with unlimited resources at his disposal, continued his investigation of the affair. While Starr's team of experienced prosecutors methodically subpoenaed witnesses and compiled evidence, the President ostentatiously went about conducting the public's business as usual. He and his spokespersons publicly proclaimed that they were cooperating with Starr's investigation and that they too wanted the scandal resolved as quickly as possible. Behind-the scenes, for seven months, both Clinton's legal advisers and political operatives did everything they could to thwart, discredit, and delay Starr's investigation. Hillary Clinton, on *Good Morning America,* spoke vaguely of a "vast rightwing conspiracy" out to destroy her husband for partisan and ideological reasons. Clinton's lawyers repeatedly tried to find legal grounds to prevent Secret Service agents and senior aides from testifying before the grand jury. The courts kept quashing the legal arguments and witnesses continued to be compelled to testify. Clinton's power and room for maneuver were both eroded.

As the investigation went forward, polls periodically showed that Clinton's approval rating remained high. The economy remained strong and prosperous, and the nation was at peace. A majority of those polled viewed Clinton as a capable Chief Executive. They separated Clinton's personal character flaws and private life from his public political abilities. The same polls also showed that Kenneth Starr remained unpopular with a majority of voters. They did not think having a sexual relationship with an intern and lying about it, even if proven true, were grounds for impeachment. People also indicated that they were bored by the matter, embarrassed by it, disgusted by it, and sick of it. It had become a distraction, and they wanted the politicians to put it behind them and get on with conducting the nation's business.

On July 17, prosecutors issued a historic subpoena compelling the President's testimony before the grand jury pursuant to a criminal investigation in which he was a suspect. Starr withdrew the subpoena on July 29 when the President agreed to testify from the White House with his lawyers present. On August 6, Lewinsky, granted immunity from prosecution, testified before the grand jury. She told prosecutors that she had had a sexual relationship with the President, contradicting her testimony in the Paula Jones hearing. She also told prosecutors that she and Clinton had discussed how to keep their affair a secret, but that he had never told her to lie nor helped her find a job to keep her quiet.

Clinton testified on August 17. Later that evening, he spoke briefly to the American people.; During his four-minute speech, he admitted that he had had "a relationship that was inappropriate" with Monica Lewinsky. He gave no details and did not say that it was a sexual relationship. He insisted that he had not committed perjury when he denied under oath at the Paula Jones hearing that he had had sexual relations with Lewinsky, although he acknowledged that his testimony was misleading. But half his speech was devoted to an angry attack on Kenneth Starr. The speech proved disastrous for the President. It not only failed to end the matter, it ensured its indefinite perpetuation. Most prominent media editorialists and political leaders, including Democratic supporters of the White House, doubted that the president was sincerely repentant and criticized his attacks on Starr. In the wake of his speech, mainstream media editorialists and leading Democratic senators condemned the President's behavior and his attempts over the past seven months to deceive both Congress and the American people about it.

On September 9, Starr delivered his 445-page report to the House of Representatives containing what he considered "substantial and credible information that may constitute grounds for impeachment of the president of the United States."

Starr's report set the stage for high political drama reminiscent of the days of Watergate when the Senate committee discovered that President Nixon had secretly taped recorded White House conversations. Clinton's stonewall had collapsed.

The most perilous moment of Clinton's presidency had arrived and perhaps the defining episode of his public life. The report landed like a bomb on official Washington for it posed the grave threat that President Clinton could be removed from office. Later that day, two vans pulled up in front of the Capitol carrying 36 boxes of evidence supporting Starr's allegations that Clinton had committed perjury, tampered with witnesses, obstructed justice, and abused his power. On September 10, Congress voted overwhelmingly to make public the Starr report and most of the supporting evidence that his prosecutors had gathered during their seven-months-long investigation. That evening the Starr Report went out over the internet. The next day both the electronic and print media presented the Starr report to the public in its entirety or in edited form with extensive commentary, analysis, and interpretation. On September 21, a videotape of the President's testimony to the grand jury was broadcast to the nation. Clinton's political fate was now in the hands of Congress and public opinion.

After the release of the Starr Report, thousands of pages of supporting testimony, and the videotape, polls showed that two-thirds of Americans still thought Clinton was doing a good job as president and did not want him to be impeached, but his personal ratings had sunk to all-time lows. Clinton the president was praised for a job well done; Clinton the fallible human was condemned for immorality and for dragging the hallowed office of the presidency into the muck.

To live television coverage by all major networks and CNN, the Republican Party leadership in the House set the impeachment process in motion. The Starr report was sent to the House Judiciary Committee, which promptly created a special subcommittee to examine the report. On October 5, by a strict 21-16 party-line vote, the House Judiciary Committee recommended that the House of Representatives open a formal investigation into grounds for impeaching President Clinton. Three days later, the Congress voted 258-176 to authorize a formal impeachment inquiry. In an atmosphere poisoned by intense partisan acrimony, for only the third time in American history, the House Judiciary Committee began hearings to see if there were grounds for impeaching a president.

On November 3, as the House Judiciary Committee prepared to hold its historic hearings, the 1998 midterm elections were held. Given the timing and the dramatic contexts in which these elections occurred, pundits and politicians gave them extraordinary significance; they would amount to a referendum on the impeachment process. The fate of a presidency hung in the balance. The results surprised the experts and confounded the Republican Right that was determined to destroy Clinton if it could. After almost a year dominated by scandals that put the White House in jeopardy and put the Democrats on the defensive, the Democrats made unexpected gains on election day. They picked up five seats in the House and broke even in the Senate. The Republicans retained control of Congress, but by a smaller majority. In contested House districts, where Republicans made Clinton's alleged immoral and criminal behavior the chief issue, Democratic candidates won more often than they lost. For the first time since 1934, a President's party had gained seats at midterm.

Revealing of the disconnect between the American public and the Washington political culture was the fact that only 36% of those eligible to vote turned out on election day. In many states, the turnout was less than 20%. The percentage of young people (ages 18-29) voting was also less than 20%. Voter turnout in 1998 was the lowest since 1942 when the nation was at war. Again defying the conventional wisdom, Democrats capitalized on the low voter turnout. They were particularly successful in persuading blacks, union members, and women to vote. Despite the fact that there were 6 news stories about the scandal for every news story about electoral politics, exit polls revealed that most voters were not interested in the scandal and that it was not a factor in determining how they voted. In all, only about 73 million Americans voted. And the largest number of eligible Americans in history opted not to vote—120 million!

If the election signified anything other than that citizen cynicism and apathy about national politics were worse than ever, it was probably on the whole a victory for incumbents and the status quo. The nation was prosperous and the economy was strong, having survived the Asian meltdown, and the collapse of the Russian and Brazilian currencies. What hurt Republicans the most was their capitulation to Clinton on federal spending priorities. Outmaneuvered and fearful of being blamed if another governmental shutdown occurred, the Republican Congress enacted all of Clinton's budget proposals during the congressional session that ended three weeks before the election. Lacking bold leaders and alternative issues, many Republican voters stayed home on election day. In the immediate aftermath of the election, Newt Gingrich, who had rocketed to power and national prominence with the Republican "earthquake" in 1994, was forced to resign the Speakership of the House. The scandal had claimed its most prominent victim. Ironically, the man who had orchestrated the attacks on Clinton was himself consumed by the fires that he had ignited.

Electoral setbacks did not deter the Republican majority on the House Judiciary committee. Tom DeLay, the Republican House Whip, stepped into the breach left by Gingrich's resignation. The former pest exterminator rallied Republicans to continue the assault on Clinton. On November 18, the House Judiciary Committee, under the leadership of Chairman Henry Hyde, formally convened the impeachment inquiry. Kenneth Starr testified before the Committee the next day. On December 8-10, White House lawyers appeared before the committee to present its defense. On December 11-12, again along strict 21-16 party line votes, the House Judiciary Committee approved four articles of impeachment; The first two articles charged Clinton with perjury, the third article charged Clinton with obstruction of justice, and the fourth article charged Clinton with abuse of power. The Committee, also by a straight party-line vote, rejected a censure resolution proposed by the Democratic members.

The drama built as the full House of Representatives opened formal impeachment hearings on December 18. On the next day, December 19, William Jefferson Clinton became only the second president in American history to be impeached. (The first was Andrew Johnson in 1868.) The House passed two articles of impeachment: Article 1 charged that Clinton had committed perjury in his grand jury testimony of August 17. It passed by a vote of 228-206. Article 2 charged that the President obstructed justice. It passed by a vote of 221-212. Few Democrats voted for either article.

December 19 was one of the weirdest days in the history of the Republic—an enfeebled president took the nation to war on the very day that he was impeached by the Congress! He ordered aircraft and missile attacks on Iraq that began four days of intense aerial warfare aimed at degrading Saddam's command and control facilities, his elite Republican Guard forces, and his capacity to build and use weapons of mass destruction, particularly chemical and biological agents. The previous year, Hollywood had produced a wickedly satiric move, *Wag the Dog,* in which a president, to deflect attention from a sex scandal that might cost him his reelection, arranges to have a prominent Hollywood producer create a fake war on television! Although there was no compelling evidence to support the charge, some prominent politicians and pundits suspected that Clinton had timed the attacks on Iraq to rally public support and to deflect attention from the impeachment proceedings.

On January 7, 1999, the Senate impeachment trial of President Clinton opened, presided over by Chief Justice William Rehnquist, with the Senators themselves impaneled as a 100-person jury to hear the case and render a verdict. Concerned about public opinion, both Senate majority leader, Trent Lott, and the Democratic leader, Tom Daschle, were determined to conduct a prompt, fair trial, and to proceed in a civil and decorous manner in contrast to the impassioned partisanship that had characterized the House debates over impeachment. From January 14 to 16, the 13 Impeachment Managers from the House, led by Henry Hyde, presented their cases. From January 19 to 21, a battery of lawyers representing the president, led by Charles Ruff, presented their defenses. The Impeachment Managers argued that Clinton should be convicted on both articles and removed from office. Clinton's defense team presented a dual line of defense: the president was not guilty of either charge, and even if he were, they did not rise to the level of impeachable offenses under the Constitution. The chief issue that caused conflict during the Senate trial and aroused partisan passions, was whether to call witnesses, particularly Monica Lewinsky. Lott and Daschle worked out a compromise whereby the impeachment managers got to depose three witnesses, Lewinsky, Vernon Jordan, a powerful friend of the President, and Sydney Blumenthal, a White House aide. Both sides then used excerpts from those depositions to bolster their closing arguments.

As the Senate trial went forward, there occurred another bizarre bit of political theater. Clinton appeared before a joint session of Congress to present his State-of-the-Union address. It was Clinton at his best; his speech lasted more than an hour. Ignoring the scandals swirling around him and ignoring the ongoing trial that would determine if he would remain in office to complete his second term, President Clinton offered an extensive array of poll-tested modest programs and initiatives—targeted tax cuts, support for education, and proposals for keeping Social Security and Medicare solvent for the foreseeable future without requiring either tax increases or cuts in benefits. While Democrats cheered, clapped, whistled, and shouted their support, Republicans often sat quietly in their seats, yawned, or twiddled their thumbs. Given the realities of a weakened lame-duck presidency, the intensely partisan atmosphere prevailing in Washington, and most of all, Republican control of Congress, few of Clinton's lengthy laundry list of proposals stood any chance of becoming public policy.

As the five-week long trial in the Senate ran its course, polls consistently showed that two-thirds of Americans did not want President Clinton convicted and removed from office. An even larger percentage consistently showed that they approved of the way he performed his job. Virtually all of the nation's most influential newspapers, led by the *New York Times, Washington Post,* and the *Los Angeles Times,* opposed conviction and removal from office. All Democratic Senators and several Moderate Republican Senators indicated that they would vote to acquit Clinton. Since the Constitution required a two-thirds vote to convict, Clinton's acquittal was a foregone conclusion. The vote, when finally taken, was anti-climatic.

On February 12, 1999, The Senate voted to acquit William Jefferson Clinton. The Senate rejected the perjury charge, 55-45, and it split 50-50 on the obstruction of justice charge. Many Moderate Republican and Democratic Senators were clearly uncomfortable with their votes for acquittal, because they believed that there was considerable evidence to substantiate the charges of perjury and obstruction of justice against President Clinton brought by the House, and by their votes they were acquitting him of all charges. However, they had no choice because they did not want to remove him from the office to which he had been twice elected by the people for criminal behavior that did not threaten the workings of the American government or its Constitutional system. They were voting to save the presidency and the Constitution, not the man whom many distrusted and despised. After the votes were taken, an effort by Senator Dianne Feinstein of California to offer a resolution of censure was quickly defeated.

Shortly after the votes for acquittal, Clinton spoke briefly to the American people. He apologized once more for what he had said and done, for what he had put the American people through, and, for the first time, acknowledged that his words and deeds had contributed to the sordid sequence of events that had disrupted the normal routines of government. The often surreal story that had dismayed and disgusted most Americans for over a year and plunged the nation into a prolonged constitutional crises, had finally played out.

The origins of the impeachment controversy lay in the collision of two essentially irrational forces. First there was Clinton's pattern of dishonest, ruthless, and occasionally illegal political practices stemming from his Arkansas days that carried into the White House. These practices were coupled with his history of philandering. Then there were his conservative Republican political enemies who went after him when his affair with Lewinsky became public knowledge. They believed that he was now vulnerable and could be destroyed via the Constitutional process of impeachment and removal from office. They did not anticipate that a large majority of the American people would rally to Clinton's defense.

There were several sources of conservative hostility towards Clinton. One source of conservative animosity was an expression of the ongoing "culture wars." Conservatives were fighting a battle over the 1960s and its legacy. Clinton was the first baby-boomer president, the first acknowledged pot-smoking, draft-dodging, and affair-having leader to make the White House. Conservatives saw him as a sinister threat to the moral order. Another source of conservative fury directed at Clinton was political; it was a response to his ability to coopt the best parts of the conservative agenda—such issues as crime, welfare reform, and balancing the budget. He maneuvered the Republicans into contending with Democrats over issues where conservative positions were less popular than his, such as social security and troubling issues like abortion and homosexuality. A third, and probably the most potent source of conservative hostility toward Clinton, was personal. To them, he was a con artist, "slick Willie," a clever demagogue, who faked an empathetic concern for the problems of ordinary Americans. They regarded his "I feel your pain" act as exactly that, a fraud, rather than an expression of natural sympathy. Ironically, conservative hatred of Clinton resembled elitist liberal hostility toward Ronald Reagan. Liberal pundits simply could not accept the notion that Reagan's popular appeal might be genuine and issue-based. Generally, liberal intelligentsia chalked up Reagan's broad popular appeal to the mesmeric powers of an old actor tricking the naive and gullible masses. Some conservative intellectuals like William Bennett, with no other way of explaining Clinton's popular appeal, have denounced the American people for having been taken in by a charlatan and for their loss of a capacity for moral outrage.

Because historians will be explaining and assessing these dramatic events for decades to come, any immediate accounting is risky, and must necessarily be tentative and subject to revision. There is a fundamental anomaly—The scandals amounted to a prolonged Constitutional crisis that seemed to have no impact outside the cocooned world of Washington politics. While the President and the Republican majority in Congress were locked in mortal combat, most Americans happily went about their business, and for most Americans, business had never been better. The major electronic and print news media gave the crisis saturation coverage from start to finish, yet most Americans could not care less, or so they said, and denounced the news media for their obsessive devotion to tabloid politics.

One outcome is certain. The first thing all future history texts will say about Bill Clinton is that he is the only elected president ever to be impeached. This fact will be the tin can tied to President Clinton's historical reputation that will rattle and bang through the ages. This fact will be his chief legacy. This singular reality will overpower all other things for which Clinton and his defenders might want to take credit: the most powerful sustained binge of prosperity in American history, spectacular gains in the securities markets, a sharp reduction in violent crime, welfare reform, a balanced budget, crafting a foreign policy that promoted world peace and prosperity, and moving the Democratic Party to the political center where the voters are, thereby displacing the Republicans and marginalizing the liberal troglodytes of his own party.

History will also judge President Clinton to have been irretrievably damaged in the eyes of his family, friends, his supporters, and the nation at large. He has lost all moral authority to lead and he survives in office as a severely wounded lame-duck president. Both his power and the power of the presidency have been substantially eroded. Given the mutual lack of trust, the poisonous partisanship, and the substantive issue differences between them, it is unrealistic to expect that the Republican-controlled Congress and President Clinton can work cooperatively during the remaining two years of his presidency to enact legislation dealing effectively with education, drug abuse, crime, tax cuts, Social Security, Medicare, or the myriad of other pressing problems confronting the nation and its people.

If anything positive can be gleaned from the year-long political train wreck, it is the manifest political maturity and restraint of the American citizenry, a large majority of whom quickly concluded that a capable President should not be removed from office for matters pertaining to his private life, no matter how sordid or repellent. The fact that the national government survived the year-long crisis strong and intact reaffirmed the good sense of the citizenry, the stability of American political institutions, and the fundamental soundness of the U.S. Constitutional system.

CLINTON AND THE POST-COLD WAR WORLD

Upon taking office in January, 1993, Clinton reversed Bush's priorities. For Clinton, an unreconstructed domestic policy wonk, internal affairs took priority over foreign policy issues. In the conduct of foreign affairs, Clinton was handicapped by his lack of experience and his failure to appoint strong leaders to key positions. The Clinton administration also faced the daunting task of developing and implementing effective foreign policies in the post-Cold War era, of redefining America's global role in a new environment without precedents and without guidelines to follow.

Because Clinton and his foreign policy advisers lacked clear objectives and did not have a consistent set of criteria to apply, Washington could never decide when or how much U.S. power and prestige to commit in situations that did not involve vital national interests. A pattern of ad hoc responses to crises as they arose characterized the Clinton's approach to foreign policy. He tried to downplay international politics and the use of military force. He focused U.S. foreign policy on economic issues: on promoting world recovery from recession and stimulating economic growth. In the area of foreign economic policy, he had major achievements. He supported NAFTA, normalized relations with Vietnam, and negotiated trade agreements with Pacific Rim nations.

The shortcomings of the Clinton approach to foreign affairs were glaringly evident in Bosnia and Herzegovina, where the largest war in Europe since World

War II raged on. Vicious ethnic fighting among the Serbs, Bosnian Muslims, and Croats had killed over 100,000 people and generated over 3.5 million refugees. Even though the Bosnian Muslims were clearly the victims of aggression and atrocities, and were hindered in their efforts at self-defense by an arms embargo, Washington appeared more concerned with avoiding significant military involvement and confining the conflict to the petty successor states of the now-defunct Yugoslav federation than aiding the hapless Bosnians. Despite feeble UN efforts to broker a cease-fire and negotiate a settlement that would have divided Bosnia and Herzegovina into a patchwork of ethnic regions, the murderous warfare raged on in 1994 and 1995.

In the fall of 1995, Washington, after years of dithering, finally took action. The initiative was taken by Assistant Secretary of State Richard Holbrooke, who persuaded Clinton and Secretary of State Warren Christopher to come aboard. Holbrooke understood that the United Nations and the Europeans were incapable of effective action in Bosnia. He brought the leaders of the three warring factions to Dayton, Ohio, in December, brokered a cease-fire, and worked out a complex political settlement to be implemented gradually. The settlement involved sending a NATO force of 60,000 troops, 20,000 of which were U.S. combat soldiers, to police the cease-fire and allow the political settlement to gradually take hold. A vocal majority in Congress and among the American public opposed sending U.S. forces to Bosnia, because no vital U.S. interest appeared to be at risk and because prospects for achieving a political solution appeared problematic. Military leaders were reluctant to place American forces in a dangerous and violent region where they could incur casualties.

The NATO military intervention succeeded in maintaining a ceasefire, but as of the summer of 1999, the confederated Bosnia in which the three groups—Croats, Bosnian Muslims, and Serbs—were supposed to live together, had failed completely. Bosnia still had no functioning central government. The country had, in effect, been partitioned. Few refugees had been able to return to their homes. Most prominent war criminals remained ostentatiously at large. The 5,000 U.S. troops that remained in Bosnia had little to do except drink beer, play volleyball, and work out in gyms. Informed observers feared that the uneasy truce would once again explode into ethnic violence if the soldiers were withdrawn.

While Bosnia-Herzegovina endured an uneasy peace, ethnic conflict erupted into war in nearby Kosovo, a Yugoslav province inhabited by 1.8 million ethnic Albanians, who constituted 90 percent of the region's population. The conflict had been building for years. In 1989, the Yugoslav leader, Slobodan Milosevic, revoked the autonomy that the Kosovars had enjoyed since 1974. As the Belgrade regime became more repressive the Kosovars, following the moderate leadership of Ibrahim Rugova, attempted to create a parallel government that would permit at least a semblance of autonomy within the Yugoslav federation. In 1991, more militant Kosovars founded the Kosovo Liberation Army (KLA); its leaders were commited to achieving independence from Yugoslavia and one day uniting with Albania to create a Greater Albanian nation. KLA terrorists sporadically attacked Serbian soldiers and police stationed in Kosovo. The Serbs retaliated brutally, trying to eliminate the KLA and its supporters. They failed; in the spring of 1998, the KLA began a full-scale rebellion against Serb authority. Milosevic responded by escalating the violence against the Kosovars. NATO, led by the United States, attempted to impose a settlement of the conflict along the lines of the Dayton Accords of 1995 that had brought a cease fire to Bosnia-Herzegovina.

On March 22, 1999, efforts by Secretary of State Madeleine Albright to broker a settlement between Milosevic and the KLA at Rambouillet, a suburb of Paris, failed. The proposed agreement called for autonomy for the Kosovars to be guaranteed by the insertion of a NATO peacekeeping force that would include 4,000 U.S. soldiers. Albright made it clear to Milosevic that failure to sign the accord would bring NATO aerial assaults on Yugoslavia. The Yugoslav leader showed his contempt for the agreement by not even bothering to show up; his defiance humiliated and infuriated Albright.

On March 24, NATO, commanded by U.S. Army General Wesley K. Clark, began an aerial war against the Milosevic government to induce him to return to the bargaining table and sign the Rambouillet accords. Albright and Clark clearly underestimated Milosevic. They assumed that a few days of precision bombing with high-tech cruise missiles and laser-guided "smart bombs" against carefully selected targets would persuade the Serb leader to return to the bargaining tables prepared to sign. Instead, the canny and ruthless Milosevic escalated his campaign of "ethnic cleansing" against the hapless Kosovars. He knew that most Serbs regarded Kosovo as sacred soil, and they would support his efforts to retain control over it by standing up to NATO aggression. Milosevic also wanted to maintain control of the massive Trepca mining complex located within Kosovo that annually brought in millions of dollars of hard currency.

Within a few weeks NATO confronted a humanitarian catastrophe of biblical proportions. An estimated 800,000 Kosovars were driven from their homes and forced into exile in neighboring Macedonia, Albania, and the Yugoslav province of Montenegro. The presence of these pitiful refugees threatened to destabilize these small, poor multiethnic countries. Another 600,000 Kosovars were driven from their homes and villages, but remained inside the province, hiding in mountain forests and canyons. They had become refugees within their own country. Thousands, mostly young men, had been murdered, another 100,000 Kosovars were missing, and hundreds of villages, towns, and cities had been razed. NATO, the United Nations, and numerous international aid agencies rushed to provide food, clothing, shelter, and medical care to the Kosovars driven out of their own country.

NATO's gradually escalating air war, OPERATION ALLIED FORCE, wrought serious damage to the Serbian infrastructure and industrial capacity. Accidental bombings, including hitting the Chinese embassy and a hospital, claimed hundreds of civilian casualties. But NATO could not stop the horrid process of ethnic cleansing in Kosovo. In fact, the Allied war effort allowed Milosevic to strengthen his hold on power and to escalate his efforts to rid Kosovo of the Kosovars.

For its duration, Operation Allied Force did not want for critics. Senator John McCain, a Vietnam war hero and a candidate for the Republican presidential nomination in 2000, called for sending ground combat forces to Kosovo. He doubted that air power alone could win the war in Kosovo. However, President Clinton, whose nation furnished the pilots and planes that accounted for 90 percent of the sorties flown during NATO's air war, had ruled out sending in ground combat forces, thus foreclosing that option at the outset of the war. Administration spokesmen would not even acknowledge that NATO was at war. They preferred to think of OPERA-TION ALLIED FORCE as a form of coercive diplomacy that would bring Milosevic to the bargaining table. Domestic politics appeared to drive U.S. foreign policy in southern Europe and limit NATO's strategic options.

While the war raged in Kosovo, questions about its effectiveness abounded. NATO had started the war with minimal contingency planning. When Milosevic refused to buckle after a few days of bombing and missile attacks, NATO strategists appeared to have no operational plan to put in place. The air war quickly took on an ad hoc improvisational quality: as planes became available, fly more sorties and see what happens. It became a pain endurance contest: Who would break first Milosevic or NATO's will?

There was scant legal basis for the military intervention under extant international law. NATO was a defensive military alliance originally created in 1949 to combat the Soviet menace. Serbian forces had committed no acts of aggression against any NATO member. The war violated the United Nations charter, which authorized the use of force only in the case of cross-border attacks. However horrible the results of ethnic cleansing might be, Kosovo was an integral part of the sovereign Yugoslav nation. The war also violated the United States Constitution. Congress had not authorized the use of U.S. forces in combat. The American people had been given no opportunity to debate the pros and cons of a war in southern Europe.

President Clinton and Secretary of State Albright insisted that military intervention in Kosovo was justified on moral grounds and NATO also sought to preserve stability in Europe. But to many expert observers, there appeared to be no vital U.S. economic or geopolitical interests engaged.

Outside NATO's orbit, world public opinion condemned the war. To much of the world, NATO appeared to be a bully—the world's most powerful military alliance trying to impose its will and values on a small nation that refused to be intimidated. Russia, traditionally an ally of the Serbia, denounced the bombing and made a public show of solidarity with Milosevic's government. China, outraged at the attack on its embassy, called for a halt to all bombing and threatened to veto any UN resolution authorizing a peacekeeping force in Kosovo.

The American public, horrified by televised images of the hordes of hapless Kosovars streaming into squalid refugee camps in Macedonia and Albania, initially supported the war. But public support was lukewarm and declined as the war dragged on. The American people gradually disengaged from the war despite massive and mostly favorable media coverage. On April 30, six weeks into the air war, and with the plight of the Kosovars worse than ever, the Republican-controlled Congress defeated a resolution of support for the air war. Within the nation, there were signs of growing antiwar sentiment such as scattered protest demonstrations and full-page ads in major newspapers.

The War in Kosovo ended after 78 days of bombing. A combination of factors brought Milosevic to sign an agreement that differed little from the Rambouillet formula that he had rejected previously. Patient diplomacy conducted by Assistant Secretary of Defense Strobe Talbot persuaded Russian president Boris Yeltsin to align Russia with NATO despite powerful opposition at home. President Martti Ahtisaari of Finland and Russian envoy Viktor Chernomyrdin, meeting with Milosevic, brokered the deal. Increasingly effective tactics by NATO pilots, coordinating their attacks with KLA fighters, inflicted major damage on Yugoslav armed forces fighting in Kosovo. Isolated diplomatically, his army in Kosovo increasingly battered, Milosevic calculated the NATO offer was the best he was likely to get. Besides, he had accomplished his two major goals—consolidating his hold on power in Yugoslavia and ridding Kosovo of much of its indigenous Albanian population.

President Clinton claimed victory for a righteous cause and a stable Europe. NATO's credibility as an aggressive military alliance was maintained. Air power was vindicated. But to many observers, OPERATION ALLIED FORCE appeared to be an unnecessary war with no winners and a lot of losers. NATO blundered into a war that lasted far longer and required a commitment of far more military assets than had been planned—against a pipsqueak power led by a tyrant, who first called NATO's bluff and then embarrassed the leaders of the world's mightiest military alliance by absorbing their best shots for nearly three months.

NATO finally obtained UN sanction for its peacekeeping operations, belatedly giving a fig leaf of legitimacy to the enterprise. 50,000 troops, including 7,000 U.S. soldiers, were deployed in Kosovo as the 40,000 or so Serbian forces exited. As part of the agreement, an undisclosed number of Russian soldiers were also deployed, formally working with the NATO forces, but not under their command. The pro-Serbian Russian troops promised to complicate the staggeringly difficult problems facing the peace keepers in the months ahead.

NATO's postwar goals were to protect and assist the Kosovars as they returned to their homes. But many of the traumatized Kosovars living in makeshift refugee centers in Macedonia, Montenegro, Albania, and elsewhere did not want to return to Kosovo. After ethnic cleansing—with its mass murders, wholesale destruction of their homes and communities, and massive uprootings of a large part of an entire population, the Kosovars would not feel safe, even with UN peacekeepers on hand. A large number of Kosovars, even if they wanted to return or could be persuaded to return, would find no homes, farms, businesses, or villages to return to. Many Kosovars have been radicalized by their horrendous experiences and have turned to the KLA. They have abandoned the moderate strategies of Rugova. Many Kosovars say they will return to Kosovo only if it is independent.

The current agreement does not support independence for the Kosovars, even as a distant goal. NATO leaders have consistently rejected an independent Kosovo because they see it as a prescription for eternal political instability in the Balkans. But the NATO ideal of peaceful multiethnic democratic nations living in harmony with one another appeared increasingly unattainable and divorced from harsh and enduring Balkan realities.

On another front, the hijackings and other terrorist acts that had tormented the presidencies of Carter and Reagan declined during the early 1990s. Suddenly, in February 1993, terrorism struck the United States when a powerful explosion ripped through the World Trade Center in New York City, killing five people and injuring scores of others. In 1995, following a dramatic trial, a militant sheik and four of his Shiite fundamentalist followers were convicted of the bombing. In April 1995, Americans discovered to their horror that they did not have to import terrorists when a car bomb of tremendous explosive power utterly demolished a nine-story federal building in Oklahoma City, killing 168 people in all, many of whom were children enrolled in a preschool housed on the second floor of the structure. The FBI soon arrested Timothy McVeigh and Terry Nichols, who were charged with the crime. Both men had loose ties with the militia movement, an extreme right-wing fringe group that viewed government efforts to impose a measure of gun control as part of a larger conspiracy by the federal government to extinguish freedom in America. Both were convicted of mass murder. McVeigh was sentenced to die for his crimes, and Nichols was given a life sentence without the possibility of parole. In March 1996, FBI agents, acting on a tip from his brother, arrested fifty-three-year-old Theodore Kaczynski, as the suspected Unabomber, a serial killer who had waged a campaign of terror bombing since 1979 that had killed three people and injured twenty-three others in sixteen separate attacks. In 1998, after a trial in federal court in Sacramento, California, Kaczynski, who admitted that he was the Unabomber, was sentenced to life imprisonment without the possibility of parole.

Homegrown terrorist assaults reached new levels of horror in 1998 and 1999 when angry, hateful, and seriously troubled schoolboys gunned down fellow students and teachers in a rash of schoolyard massacres that took place in various cities across the nation. The worst slaughter occurred at Columbine High School in Littleton, Colorado, a prosperous middle class suburb of Denver where most families were living out their version of the American Dream. On Tuesday morning, April 20, 1999, Eric Harris and Dylan Klebold, both seniors, arrived on campus armed with automatic pistols, automatic rifles, sawed-off 12-gauge shotguns, and dozens of pipe bombs. They proceeded to murder 12 students and a teacher in cold blood, wound dozens more of their classmates, and then took their own lives. In the aftermath of the worst school massacre in U.S. history, bewildered, frightened, and grieving survivors and their families struggled to cope with the inexplicable tragedy.

While terrorists recruited from various Middle Eastern countries bombed the Trade Center, Washington's efforts to bring peace to the Middle East World made some progress. Building on the previous efforts of Presidents Reagan and Bush, Clinton's Secretary of State, Warren Christopher, urged Israeli and Palestinian leaders to continue the dialogue begun at Madrid following the smashing Allied victory in the Persian Gulf War. In September 1993, following secret talks, there occurred a startling breakthrough. Israel and the Palestine Liberation Organization (PLO) announced an accord granting the Palestinians limited autonomy in the Gaza Strip and in areas of the West Bank. In return, Yassir Arafat, the PLO leader, renounced terrorism and recognized Israel. On September 13, 1993, in Washington, as a beaming Bill Clinton looked on, Israeli Prime Minister Yitzhak Rabin and Yassir Arafat signed the accord and shook hands. Despite sporadic efforts by Palestinian militants to disrupt the peace process, the Israeli–PLO accord remained in place, and the PLO steadily increased its capacity to govern in the territories. Progress was stalled in 1996 with the election of conservative Israeli Prime Minister Benjamin Netanyahu and the continuing inability of Arafat's security forces to control Palestinian terrorist activity.

On October 20, 1998, a new agreement was hammered out at the Wye Conference Center in Queenstown, Maryland. Israel agreed to turn over additional West Bank land to the Palestinians who agreed to eliminate language in the PLO charter calling for Israel's destruction. Both President Clinton and a mortally ill King Hussein of Jordan played major roles in bringing about the agreement between Netanyahu and Arafat. Netanyahu's government fell in the wake of the Wye Accords. After a contentious election process in Israel, Ehud Barak emerged as the new leader of a center-left coalition of secular parties committed to protecting Israeli security concerns and retaining control of Jerusalem, but apparently more flexible in his approach to negotiations with Arafat's struggling "Palestinian Authority" than Netanyahu. Meanwhile, Arafat struggled to find a modus vivendi with Israel acceptable to most Palestinians and to create a de facto Palestinian state.

While President Clinton provided uncertain leadership in the NATO war against Serbia, U.S. China policy showed signs of serious strain. Since President Nixon opened the gates to improved relations with China in 1972, all subsequent presidents, whether Republicans or Democrats, have followed similar policies toward the emerging giant. They have all attempted to promote trade and cultural exchanges, lectured the Chinese for their human rights violations, and tried to influence Chinese foreign policy—with a very mixed record of results. President Clinton's China policy of constructive engagement came under heavy fire from the Republican-controlled Congress during his second term. There were allegations of illegal efforts by Chinese officials to influence the outcome of the 1996 presidential election. There were allegations of successful Chinese nuclear espionage within the United States over the past twenty years. The Chinese government continued its efforts to suppress political dissent and religious freedom, stamp out the vestiges of traditional Tibetan culture, and intimidate Taiwan. China also continued to pursue foreign policies that challenged U.S. interests in various regions. Because the Chinese leaders pursued all of these controversial activities without suffering reprisals or even serious rebukes from the United States, Clinton's China policy, to many of its critics looked a lot like appeasement of a rogue regime contemptuous of world opinion and international law.

TOWARD THE TWENTY-FIRST CENTURY

Experts concerned about the future of the small planet we inhabit fear that rapid world population increases and severe environmental problems pose far more serious long-term threats to our living standards and general sense of well-being than do political and economic problems. On January 1, 1999, the world's estimated population reached 6 billion. Demographers predict that by 2020, the world's population will reach 8 billion. The consequences of such population growth will be dire. Mass immiseration, especially in Third World countries, will breed extremist political and religious movements that ensure a turbulent future. Surging populations will also use up huge quantities of the earth's finite resources, wipe out millions of acres of rain forests necessary to cool and purify the planet, and extinguish thousands of species of plants and animals. The world's supply of arable farm land and fresh water will continue to diminish. Global warming looms as a serious danger.

As the new millennium arrives, Americans face many challenges at home and abroad. To survive and possibly flourish, they must remain committed to finding new ways of coping with the daunting future that will soon explode among them.

IMPORTANT EVENTS

1988	George H.W. Bush is elected president
1989	The Tiananmen Square massacre takes place
	The Berlin Wall is breached
	The United States invades Panama
1990	Germany is reunited
	Iraq invades Kuwait
1991	The Persian Gulf War occurs
	Clarence Thomas becomes associate justice of the Supreme Court
	The Middle East peace conference occurs
	The Soviet Union disintegrates; the Cold War ends
1992	South Africa votes to end apartheid
	Bill Clinton is elected president
1993	Ruth Bader Ginsberg is appointed to U.S. Supreme Court
	The Israeli–PLO agreement takes place
1994	Republicans win control of Congress
1995	The O.J. Simpson murder trial
	Terrorists bomb the federal building in Oklahoma City
1996	Clinton is reelected president
1997	Tiger (Eldrick) Woods wins the Masters Championship
1998	Terrorists bomb two American embassies in Kenya and Tanzania
	Bill Clinton becomes the first elected president to be impeached
1999	Bill Clinton is tried and acquitted of all charges by the U.S. Senate
	The Kosovo war occurs.

BIBLIOGRAPHY

Recent history is covered best in the *New York Times*, other fine newspapers, and weekly news magazines such as *Time* and *Newsweek*. *The National Review* covers recent history from a conservative perspective, and the *New Republic* covers the same events from a moderate, liberal perspective. Those interested in the troubling world environmental problems of the 1990s will want to read *Crossroads: Environmental Priorities for the Future,* edited by Peter Borrelli. Kevin Phillips, a conservative political analyst, has written *The Politics of Rich and Poor,* which addresses the social inequities deriving from contemporary economic policies. On women's pay issues, see Sara M. Evans's and Barbara J. Nelson's *Wage Justice: Comparable Worth and the Paradox of Technocratic Reform.* There is an extensive literature on the AIDS epidemic. One of the best books about AIDS is Randy Shilts's *And the Band Played On.* For contemporary drug problems plaguing Americans, see Erich Goode's *Drugs in American Society.* Ellis Cose, in *The Rage of a Privileged Class: Why Are Middle-Class Blacks Angry?*, offers an important, disturbing book. See William Wei's *The Asian American Movement* for a study of an important group of Americans that lacks an extensive historical literature. There is a growing literature on all of the historic changes occurring in eastern Europe and the Soviet Union. See *Reform in Russia and the USSR,* edited by Robert O. Crummey, and *Central and Eastern Europe: The Opening Curtain,* edited by William E. Griffith. Two American Sovietologists, Robert Jervis and Seweryn Bailer, eds., present diverse looks at the post–Cold War world in *Soviet-American Relations After the Cold War.* For American–Japanese relations, *The United States and Japan in the Postwar World,* edited by Akira Iriye and Warren I. Cohen, is very good. For recent developments in Central America, consult John A. Booth's and Thomas W. Walker's *Understanding Central America.* Judith Miller and Laurie Mylorie, in *Saddam Hussein,* offer an informative study that sheds light on the motivations of the Iraqi leader and the genesis of the Persian Gulf crisis. *Kosovo: A Short History* by British journalist and scholar Noel Malcolm challenges the notion that Balkan wars are rooted in ancient ethnic hatreds. A recent study that looks to the future of international relations is Paul Kennedy's *Preparing for the Twenty-First Century.*

Appendices

APPENDIX A:
AMENDMENTS TO THE CONSTITUTION ADDED
DURING THE TWENTIETH CENTURY[1]

The Fifteenth Amendment. For nearly a century after it was drafted, the Fifteenth Amendment was evaded by various devices that hindered blacks from registering and voting. The Voting Rights Act of 1965 is the most recent attempt to enforce the amendment by providing federal supervision of voter registration in localities with a history of discrimination.

The Progressive Amendments. The Sixteenth through Nineteenth amenments were the product of the Progressive movement. The Sixteenth was necessitated by a Supreme Court decision in the 1890s that a federal income tax violated the constitutional requirements that direct taxes (as opposed to excises)

Amendment XVI [1913]

The Congress shall have power to lay and collect taxes on incomes, from whatever source derived, without apportionment among the several States, and without regard to any census or enumeration.

Amendment XVII [1916]

The Senate of the United States shall be composed of two Senators from each State, elected by the people thereof, for six years; and each Senator shall have one vote. The electors in each State shall have the qualifications requisite for electors of the most numerous branch of the State legislators.

When vacancies happen in the representation of any State in the Senate, the

[1]From *America: A History of the United States, Volume 2: Since 1865,* by Norman K. Risjord, pp. 933–37. Reprinted with permission of Prentice Hall.

had to be apportioned among the states, which in turn would collect from the people. The Seventeenth Amendment was intended to democratize the "millionaires' club," the U.S. Senate, by requiring that its members be elected directly by the people. The Eighteenth Amendment authorized prohibition, and the Nineteenth women's suffrage.

executive authority of such State shall issue writs of election to fill such vacancies: *Provided,* That the legislature of any State may empower the executive thereof to make temporary appointments until the people fill the vacancies by election as the legislature may direct.

This amendment shall not be so construed as to affect the election or term of any Senator chosen before it becomes valid as part of the Constitution.

Amendment XVIII [1919]

Section 1.   After one year from the ratification of this article the manufacture, sale, or transportation of intoxicating liquors within, the importation thereof into, or the exportation thereof from the United States and all territory subject to the jurisdiction thereof for beverage purposes is hereby prohibited.

Section 2.   The Congress and the several States shall have concurrent power to enforce this article by appropriate legislation.

Section 3.   This article shall be inoperative unless it shall have been ratified as an amendment to the Constitution by the legislatures of the several States, as provided in the Constitution, within seven years from the date of the submission hereof to the States by the Congress.

Amendment XIX [1920]

The right of citizens of the United States to vote shall not be denied or abridged by the United States or by any State on account of sex.

Congress shall have power to enforce this article by appropriate legislation.

The Lame Duck Amendment. The Twentieth Amendment did away with an anomaly created by Article I of the Constitution, the requirement that elections would be held in November but inaugurations delayed until March. This resulted in a "lame duck" session of Congress, lasting from December until March in even-numbered years, when members, many of whom had failed to be reelected and were on their way to private life, were voting on matters of national importance. By moving inauguration day back from March 4 to January 20, the amendment shortens the interval between popular selection and the exercise of presidential and legislative power.

Amendment XX [1933]

Section 1. The terms of the President and Vice President shall end at noon on the 20th day of January, and the terms of Senators and Representatives at noon on the 3rd day of January, of the years in which such terms would have ended if this article had not been ratified; and the terms of their successors shall then begin.

Section 2. The Congress shall assemble at least once in every year, and such meeting shall begin at noon on the 3d day of January, unless they shall by law appoint a different day.

Section 3. If, at the time fixed for the beginning of the term of the President, the President elect shall have died, the Vice President elect shall become President. If a President shall not have been chosen before the time fixed for the beginning of his term, or if the President elect shall have failed to qualify, then the Vice President elect shall act as President until a President shall have qualified; and the Congress may by law provide for the case wherein neither a President elect nor a Vice President elect shall have qualified, declaring who shall then act as President, or the manner in which one who is to act shall be selected, and such person shall act accordingly until a President or Vice President shall have qualified.

Section 4. The Congress may by law provide for the case of the death of any of the persons from whom the House of Representatives may choose a President whenever the right of choice shall have devolved upon them, and for the case of the death of any of the persons from whom the Senate may choose a Vice President whenever the right of choice shall have devolved upon them.

Section 5.   Sections 1 and 2 shall take effect on the 15th day of October following the ratification of this article.

Section 6.   The article shall be inoperative unless it shall have been ratified as an amendment to the Constitution by the legislatures of three-fourths of the several states within seven years from the date of its submission.

The Twenty-first Amendment. The Twenty-first Amendment repealed the Eighteenth, and thereby repealed prohibition. It is the only amendment that provides for its ratification by specially selected conventions, and its is the only one that has been approved in this way.

Amendment XXI [1933]

Section 1.   The eighteenth article of amendment to the Constitution of the United States is hereby repealed.

Section 2.   The transportation or importation into any State, Territory, or possession of the United States for delivery or use therein of intoxicating liquors, in violation of the laws thereof, is hereby prohibited.

Section 3.   This article shall be inoperative unless it shall have been ratified as an amendment to the Constitution by conventions in the several States, as provided in the Constitution, within seven years from the date of the submission hereof to the States by the Congress.

The Twenty-second Amendment. The Twenty-second Amendment, a belated slap at Roosevelt by a Republican-dominated Congress, limits the president to two terms in office. Ironically, the two presidents to which it has applied were Republicans, Dwight D. Eisenhower and Ronald Reagan.

Amendment XXII [1951]

No person shall be elected to the office of the President more than twice, and no person who has held the office of President, or acted as President, for more than two years of a term to which some other person was elected President shall be elected to the office of the President more than once.

But this Article shall not apply to any person holding the office of President when this Article was proposed by the Congress, and shall not prevent any person who may be holding the office of President, or acting as President, during the term within which this Article becomes operative from holding the office of President or acting as President during the remainder of such term.

The Twenty-third Amendment. The Twenty-third Amendment allows residents of the District of Columbia to vote in presidential elections.

Amendment XXIII [1961]

Section 1.   The District constituting the seat of Governor of the United States shall appoint in such manner as the Congress may direct:

A number of electors of President and Vice President equal to the whole number of Senators and Representatives in Congress to which the District would be entitled if it were a State, but in no event more than the least populous State; they shall be in addition to those appointed by the States, but they shall be considered, for the purposes of the election of President and Vice President, to be electors appointed by a state; and they shall meet in the District and perform such duties as provided by the twelfth article of amendment.

Section 2.   The Congress shall have the power to enforce this article by appropriate legislation.

The Poll Tax Amendment.   The Twenty-fourth Amendment prevents the states from making payment of a poll tax a condition for voting. Common at the time among southern states, the poll tax was a capitation (poll, or head) tax on individuals. A poll tax receipt was often required in order to vote. It was designed to prevent uneducated people, especially blacks, who were unaccustomed to saving receipts, from voting.

Amendment XXIV [1964]

Section 1.   The right of citizens of the United States to vote in any primary or other election for President or Vice President, for electors for President or Vice President, or for Senator or Representative in Congress, shall not be denied or abridged by the United States or any State by reason of failure to pay any poll tax or other tax.

Section 2.   The Congress shall have the power to enforce this article by appropriate legislation.

The Twenty-fifth Amendment. The Twenty-fifth Amendment, inspired by President Eisenhower's heart attack and President Johnson's abdominal surgery, provides for the temporary replacement of a president who is unable to discharge the duties of the office.

Amendment XXV [1967]

Section 1. In case of the removal of the President from office or his death or resignation, the Vice President shall become President.

Section 2. Whenever there is a vacancy in the office of the Vice President, the President shall nominate a Vice President who shall take the office upon confirmation by a majority vote of both houses of Congress.

Section 3. Whenever the President transmits to the President pro tempore of the Senate and the Speaker of the House of Representatives his written declaration that he is unable to discharge the powers and duties of his office, and until he transmits to them a written declaration to the contrary, such powers and duties shall be discharged by the Vice President as Acting President.

Section 4. Whenever the Vice President and a majority of either the principal officers of the executive departments, or of such other body as Congress may by law provide, transmit to the President pro tempore of the Senate and the Speaker of the House of Representatives their written declaration that the President is unable to discharge the powers and duties of his office, the Vice President shall immediately assume the powers and duties of the office of Acting President.

Thereafter, when the President transmits to the President pro tempore of the Senate and the Speaker of the House of Representatives his written declaration that no inability exists, he shall resume the powers and duties of his office unless the Vice President and a majority of either the principal officers of the executive departments, or of such other body as Congress may by law provide, transmit within four days to the President pro tempore of the Senate and the speaker of the House of Representatives their written declaration that the President is unable to discharge the powers and duties of his office. Thereupon Congress shall decide the issue, assembling within 48 hours for that purpose if not in session. If the Congress, within 21 days after receipt of the latter written declaration, or, if Congress is not in session, within 21 days after Congress is required to assemble, determines by two thirds vote of both houses that the President is unable to discharge the powers and duties of his office, the Vice President shall continue to discharge the same as Acting President; otherwise, the President shall resume the powers and duties of his office.

The Twenty-sixth Amendment. The Twenty-sixth Amendment corrected a historic injustice: young men could be drafted and sent to war at the age of eighteen, but not allowed to participate in the nation's democratic processes until they were twenty-one. It extended the vote to eighteen-year-olds.

Amendment XXVI [1971]

Section 1. The rights of citizens of the United States, who are 18 yeas of age or older, to vote shall not be denied or abridged by the United States or any state on account of age.

Section 2. The Congress shall have the power to enforce this article by appropriate legislation.

The Twenty-seventh Amendment. Originally proposed by Congress in 1789, it was not ratified by the states until 1992. It was rapidly enacted in the wake of public outrage aimed at Congresspersons who had voted themselves a substantial pay raise.

Amendment XXVII [1992]

No law, varying the compensation for the services of the Senators and Representatives shall take effect, until an election of Representatives shall have intervened.

APPENDIX B:
PRESENTIAL ELECTIONS SINCE 1896

YEAR	CANDIDATES RECEIVING MORE THAN ONE PERCENT OF THE VOTE (PARTIES)	POPULAR VOTE	ELECTORAL VOTE
1896	WILLIAM McKINLEY (Republican)	7,102,246	271
	Wiliam J. Bryan (Democrat)	6,492,559	176
1900	WILLIAM McKINLEY (Republican)	7,218,491	292
	William J. Bryan (Democrat; Populist)	6,356,734	155
	John C. Wooley (Prohibition)	208,914	0
1904	THEODORE ROOSEVELT (Republican)	7,628,461	336
	Alton B. Parker (Democrat)	5,084,223	140
	Eugene V. Debs (Socialist)	402,283	0
	Silas C. Swallow (Prohibition)	258,536	0
1908	WILLIAM H. TAFT (Republican)	7,675,320	321
	William J. Bryan (Democrat)	6,412,294	162
	Eugene V. Debs (Socialist)	420,793	0
	Eugene W. Chafin (Prohibition)	253,840	0
1912	WOODROW WILSON (Democrat)	6,296,547	435
	Theodore Roosevelt (Progressive)	4,118,571	88
	William H. Taft (Republican)	3,486,720	8
	Eugene V. Debs (Socialist)	900,672	0
	Eugene W. Chafin (Prohibition)	206,275	0
1916	WOODROW WILSON (Democrat)	9,127,695	277
	Charles E. Hughes (Republican)	8,533,507	254
	A. L. Benson (Socialist)	585,113	0
	J. Frank Hanly (Prohibition)	220,506	0
1920	WARREN G. HARDING (Republican)	16,143,407	404
	James M. Cox (Democrat)	9,130,328	127
	Eugene V. Debs (Socialist)	919,799	0
	P. P. Christensen (Farmer-Labor)	265,411	0
1924	CALVIN COOLIDGE (Republican)	15,718,211	382
	John W. Davis (Democrat)	8,385,283	136
	Robert M. LaFollette (Progressive)	4,831,289	13
1928	HERBERT C. HOOVER (Republican)	21,391,993	444
	Albert E. Smith (Democrat)	15,016,169	87
1932	FRANKLIN D. ROOSEVELT (Democrat)	22,809,638	472
	Herbert C. Hoover (Republican)	15,758,901	59
	Norman Thomas (Socialist)	881,951	0
1936	FRANKLIN D. ROOSEVELT (Democrat)	27,752,869	523
	Alfred M. Landon (Republican)	16,674,665	8
	William Lemke (Union)	882,479	0
1940	FRANKLIN D. ROOSEVELT (Democrat)	27,307,819	449
	Wendell L. Willkie (Republican)	22,321,018	82
1944	FRANKLIN D. ROOSEVELT (Democrat)	25,606,585	432
	Thomas E. Dewey (Republican)	22,014,745	99
1948	HARRY S. TRUMAN (Democrat)	24,179,345	303
	Thomas E. Dewey (Republican)	21,991,291	189
	J. Strom Thurmond (States' Rights)	1,176,125	39
	Henry Wallace (Progressive)	1,157,326	0

APPENDIX B: *(continued)*

YEAR	CANDIDATES RECEIVING MORE THAN ONE PERCENT OF THE VOTE (PARTIES)	POPULAR VOTE	ELECTORAL VOTE
1952	DWIGHT D. EISENHOWER (Republican)	33,936,234	442
	Adlai E. Stevenson (Democrat)	27,314,992	89
1956	DWIGHT D. EISENHOWER (Republican)	35,590,472	457
	Adlai E. Stevenson (Democrat)	26,022,752	73
1960	JOHN F. KENNEDY (Democrat)	34,226,731	303
	Richard M. Nixon (Republican)	34,108,157	219
1964	LYNDON B. JOHNSON (Democrat)	43,129,566	486
	Barry M. Goldwater (Republican)	27,178,188	52
1968	RICHARD M. NIXON (Republican)	31,785,480	301
	Hubert H. Humphrey (Democrat)	31,275,166	191
	George C. Wallace (American Independent)	9,906,473	46
1972	RICHARD M. NIXON (Republican)	45,631,189	521
	George S. McGovern (Democrat)	28,422,015	17
	John Schmitz (American Independent)	1,080,670	0
1976	JAMES E. CARTER, JR. (Democrat)	40,274,975	297
	Gerald R. Ford (Republican)	38,530,614	241
1980	RONALD W. REAGAN (Republican)	42,968,326	489
	James E. Carter, Jr. (Democrat)	34,731,139	49
	John B. Anderson (Independent)	5,552,349	0
1984	RONALD W. REAGAN (Republican)	53,428,357	525
	Walter F. Mondale (Democrat)	36,930,923	13
1988	GEORGE H. W. BUSH (Republican)	47,917,341	426
	Michael Dukakis (Democrat)	41,013,030	112
1992	WILLIAM J. CLINTON (Democrat)	44,908,254	370
	George H. W. Bush (Republican)	39,102,343	168
	Ross Perot (Independent)	19,741,065	0
1996	WILLIAM J. CLINTON (Democrat)	47,401,185	379
	Robert Dole (Republican)	39,197,469	159
	Ross Perot (Independent)	8,085,294	0

From Irwin Unger, *These United States: The Questions of Our Past, Volume II: Since 1865,* 3rd. ed., pp. 821–22. Reprinted with permission of Prentice Hall.

APPENDIX C:
PRESIDENT, VICE PRESIDENT, AND CABINET OFFICERS, FROM 1897

PRESIDENT AND VICE PRESIDENT	SECRETARY OF STATE	SECRETARY OF TREASURY	SECRETARY OF WAR	SECRETARY OF NAVY	POSMASTER GENERAL	ATTORNEY GENERAL	SECRETARY OF INTERIOR
25. **William McKinley** (1897) Garret A. Hobart (1897) Theodore Roosevelt (1901)	John Sherman (1897) William R. Day (1897) John Hay (1898)	Lyman J. Gage (1897)	Russell A. Alger (1897) Elihu Root (1899)	John D. Long (1897)	James A. Gary (1897) Charles E. Smith (1898)	Joseph McKenna (1897) John W. Griggs (1897) Philander C. Knox (1901)	Cornelius N. Bliss (1897) E. A. Hitchcock (1899)
26. **Theodore Roosevelt** (1901) Charles Fairbanks (1905)	John Hay (1901) Elihu Root (1905) Robert Bacon (1909)	Lyman J. Gage (1901) Leslie M. Shaw (1902) George B. Cortelyou (1907)	Elihu Root (1901) William H. Taft (1904) Luke E. Wright (1908)	John D. Long (1901) William H. Moody (1902) Paul Morton (1904) Charles J. Bonaparte (1905) V. H. Metcalf (1906) T. H. Newberry (1908)	Charles E. Smith (1901) Henry Payne (1902) Robert J. Wynne (1904) George B. Cortelyou (1905) George von L. Meyer (1907)	Philander C. Knox (1901) William H. Moody (1904) Charles J. Bonaparte (1907)	E. A. Hitchcock (1901) James R. Garfield (1907)
27. **William H. Taft** (1909) James S. Sherman (1909)	Philander C. Knox (1909)	Franklin MacVeagh (1909)	Jacob M. Dickinson (1909) Henry L. Stimson (1911)	George von L. Meyer (1909)	Frank H. Hitchcock (1909)	G. W. Wickersham (1909)	R. A. Ballinger (1909) Walter L. Fisher (1911)
28. **Woodrow Wilson** (1913) Thomas R. Marshall (1913)	William J. Bryan (1913) Robert Lansing (1915) Bainbridge Colby (1920)	William G. McAdoo (1913) Carter Glass (1918) David F. Houston (1920)	Lindley M. Garrison (1913) Newton D. Baker (1916)	Josephus Daniels (1913)	Albert S. Burleson (1913)	J. C. McReynolds (1913) T. W. Gregory (1914) A. Mitchell Palmer (1919)	Franklin K. Lane (1913) John B. Payne (1920)
29. **Warren G. Harding** (1921) Calvin Coolidge (1921)	Charles E. Hughes (1921)	Andrew W. Mellon (1921)	John W. Weeks (1921)	Edwin Denby (1921)	Will H. Hays (1921) Hubert Work (1922) Harry S. New (1923)	H. M. Daugherty (1921)	Albert B. Fall (1921) Hubert Work (1923)
30. **Calvin Coolidge** (1923) Charles G. Dawes (1925)	Charles E. Hughes (1923) Frank B. Kellogg (1925)	Andrew W. Mellon (1923)	John W. Weeks (1923) Dwight F. Davis (1925)	Edwin Denby (1923) Curtis D. Wilbur (1924)	Harry S. New (1923)	H. M. Daugherty (1923) Harlan F. Stone (1924) John G. Sargent (1925)	Hubert Work (1923) Roy O. West (1928)
31. **Herbert C. Hoover** (1929) Charles Curtis (1929)	Henry L. Stimson (1929)	Andrew W. Mellon (1929) Ogden L. Mills (1932)	James W. Good (1929) Patrick J. Hurley (1929)	Charles F. Adams (1929)	Walter F. Brown (1929)	W. D. Mitchell (1929)	Ray L. Wilbur (1529)

President / Vice Presidents	Secretary of State	Secretary of the Treasury	Secretary of War / Defense	Secretary of the Navy	Postmaster General	Attorney General	Secretary of the Interior
32. Franklin D. Roosevelt (1933) John Nance Garner (1933) Henry A. Wallace (1941) Harry S. Truman (1945)	Cordell Hull (1933) E. R. Stettinius, Jr. (1944)	William H. Woodin (1933) Henry Morgenthau, Jr. (1934)	George H. Dern (1933) Harry H. Woodring (1936) Henry L. Stimson (1940)	Claude A. Swanson (1933) Charles Edison (1940) Frank Knox (1940) James V. Forrestal (1944)	James A. Farley (1933) Frank C. Walker (1940)	H. S. Cummings (1933) Frank Murphy (1939) Robert Jackson (1940) Francis Biddle (1941)	Harold L. Ickes (1933)
33. Harry S. Truman (1945) Alben W. Barkley (1949)	James F. Byrnes (1945) George C. Marshall (1947) Dean G. Acheson (1949)	Fred M. Vinson (1945) John W. Snyder (1946)	Robert P. Patterson (1945) Kenneth C. Royall (1947) SECRETARY OF DEFENSE James V. Forrestal (1947) Louis A. Johnson (1949) George C. Marshall (1950) Robert A. Lovett (1951)	James V. Forrestal (1945)	R. E. Hannegan (1945) Jesse M. Donaldson (1947)	Tom C. Clark (1945) J. H. McGrath (1949) James P. McGranery (1952)	Harold L. Ickes (1945) Julius A. Krug (1946) Oscar L. Chapman (1949)
34. Dwight D. Eisenhower (1953) Richard M. Nixon (1953)	John Foster Dulles (1953) Christian A. Herter (1959)	George M. Humphrey (1953) Robert B. Anderson (1957)	Charles E. Wilson (1953) Neil H. McElroy (1957) Thomas S. Gates (1959)		A. E. Summerfield (1953)	H. Brownell, Jr. (1953) William P. Rogers (1957)	Douglas McKay (1953) Fred Seaton (1956)
35. John F. Kennedy (1961) Lyndon B. Johnson (1961)	Dean Rusk (1961)	C. Douglas Dillon (1961)	Robert S. McNamara (1961)		J. Edward Day (1961) John A. Gronouski (1963)	Robert F. Kennedy (1961)	Stewart L. Udall (1961)
36. Lyndon B. Johnson (1963) Hubert H. Humphrey (1965)	Dean Rusk (1963)	C. Douglas Dillon (1963) Henry H. Fowler (1965) Joseph W. Barr (1968)	Robert S. McNamara (1963) Clark M. Clifford (1968)		John A. Gronouski (1963) Lawrence F. O'Brien (1965) W. Marvin Watson (1968)	Robert F. Kennedy (1963) N. deB. Katzenbach (1965) Ramsey Clark (1967)	Stewart L. Udall (1963)
37. Richard M. Nixon (1969) Spiro T. Agnew (1969) Gerald R. Ford (1973)	William P. Rogers (1969) Henry A. Kissinger (1973)	David M. Kennedy (1969) John B. Connally (1970) George P. Shultz (1972) William E. Simon (1974)	Melvin R. Laird (1969) Elliot L. Richardson (1973) James R. Schlesinger (1973)		Winton M. Blount (1969)	John M. Mitchell (1969) Richard G. Kleindienst (1972) Elliot L. Richardson (1973) William B. Saxbe (1974)	Walter J. Hickel (1969) Rogers C. B. Morton (1971)

APPENDIX C: (continued)

PRESIDENT AND VICE PRESIDENT	SECRETARY OF STATE	SECRETARY OF TREASURY	SECRETARY OF DEFENSE	ATTORNEY GENERAL	SECRETARY OF INTERIOR
38. **Gerald R. Ford** (1974) Nelson A. Rockefeller (1974)	Henry A. Kissinger (1974)	William E. Simon (1974)	James R. Schlesinger (1974) Donald H. Rumsfeld (1975)	William B. Saxbe (1974) Edward H. Levi (1975)	Rogers C. B. Morton (1974) Stanley K. Hathaway (1975) Thomas D. Kleppe (1975)
39. **James E. Carter, Jr.** (1977) Walter F. Mondale (1977)	Cyrus R. Vance (1977) Edmund S. Muskie (1980)	W. Michael Blumenthal (1977) G. William Miller (1979)	Harold Brown (1977)	Griffin B. Bell (1977) Benjamin R. Civiletti (1979)	Cecil D. Andrus (1977)
40. **Ronald W. Reagan** (1981) George H. W. Bush (1981)	Alexander M. Haig, Jr. (1981) George P. Shultz (1982)	Donald T. Regan (1981)	Caspar W. Weinberger (1981)	William French Smith (1981)	James G. Watt (1981) William Clark (1983) Donald P. Hodel (1985)
41. **Ronald W. Reagan** (1985) George H. W. Bush (1985)	George P. Shultz (1985)	James B. Baker III (1985)	Caspar W. Weinberger (1985)	Edwin Meese III (1985)	
42. **George H. W. Bush** (1989) J. Danforth Quayle (1989)	James B. Baker III (1989)	Nicholas Brady (1989)	Richard Cheney (1989)	Richard Thornburgh (1989)	Manuel Lujan (1989)
43. **William Jefferson Clinton** (1993) Albert Gore (1993)	Warren Christopher (1993) Madeleine K. Albright (1996)	Lloyd Bentsen (1993) Robert E. Rubin (1995)	Les Aspin (1993) William J. Perry (1994) William S. Cohen (1997)	Janet Reno (1993)	Bruce Babbitt (1993)

SECRETARY OF AGRICULTURE	SECRETARY OF VETERAN AFFAIRS	SECRETARY OF COMMERCE	SECRETARY OF LABOR	SECRETARY OF HEALTH AND HUMAN SERVICE	SECRETARY OF EDUCATION	SECRETARY OF HUD	SECRETARY OF TRANSPORTATION
Clayton Yeutter (1989) Mike Espey (1993) Dan Glickman (1995)	Edwin Derwinski (1989) Jesse Brown (1993) Togo West, Jr. (1998)	Robert Mosbacher (1989) Ron Brown (1993) Mickey Kantor (1996) William Daley (1997)	Elizabeth Dole (1989) Robert Reich (1993) Alexis Herman (1997)	Louis W. Sullivan (1989) Donna Shalala (1993)	Richard Riley (1993)	Jack Kemp (1989) Henry Cisneros (1993) Andrew Cuomo (1997)	Samuel K. Skinner (1989) Frederico Peña (1993) Rodney Slater (1997)

SECRETARY OF ENERGY
 James Walters (1989)
 Hazel O'Leary (1993)
 F. Peña (1997)
 Bill Richardson (1998)

Source: From Unger, pp. 826-28. Reprinted with permission of Prentice Hall.

APPENDIX D:
JUSTICES OF THE SUPREME COURT

	TERM OF SERVICE	YEARS OF SERVICE	LIFE SPAN		TERM OF SERVICE	YEARS OF SERVICE	LIFE SPAN
John Jay	1789–1795	5	1745–1829	Lucius Q. C. Lamar	1888–1893	5	1825–1893
John Rutledge	1789–1791	1	1739–1800	*Melville W. Fuller*	1888–1910	21	1833–1910
William Cushing	1789–1810	20	1732–1810	David J. Brewer	1890–1910	20	1837–1910
James Wilson	1789–1798	8	1742–1798	Henry B. Brown	1890–1906	16	1836–1913
John Blair	1789–1796	6	1732–1800	George Shiras, Jr.	1892–1903	10	1832–1924
Robert H. Harrison	1789–1790	—	1745–1790	Howell E. Jackson	1893–1895	2	1832–1895
James Iredell	1790–1799	9	1751–1799	Edward D. White	1894–1910	16	1845–1921
Thomas Johnson	1791–1793	1	1732–1819	Rufus W. Peckham	1895–1909	14	1838–1909
William Patterson	1793–1806	13	1745–1806	Joseph McKenna	1898–1925	26	1843–1926
*John Rutledge**	1795	—	1739–1800	Oliver W. Holmes	1902–1932	30	1841–1935
Samuel Chase	1796–1811	15	1741–1811	William R. Day	1903–1922	19	1849–1923
Oliver Ellsworth	1796–1800	4	1745–1807	William H. Moody	1906–1910	3	1853–1917
Bushrod Washington	1798–1829	31	1762–1829	Horace H. Lurton	1909–1914	4	1844–1914
Alfred Moore	1799–1804	4	1755–1810	Charles E. Hughes	1910–1916	5	1862–1948
John Marshall	1801–1835	34	1755–1835	*Edward D. White*	1910–1921	11	1845–1921
William Johnson	1804–1834	30	1771–1834	Willis Van Devanter	1911–1937	26	1859–1941
H. Brockholst Livingston	1806–1823	16	1757–1823	Joseph R. Lamar	1911–1916	5	1857–1916
Thomas Todd	1807–1826	18	1765–1826	Mahlon Pitney	1912–1922	10	1858–1924
Joseph Story	1811–1845	33	1779–1845	James C. McReynolds	1914–1941	26	1862–1946
Gabriel Duval	1811–1835	24	1752–1844	Louis D. Brandeis	1916–1939	22	1856–1941
Smith Thompson	1823–1835	20	1768–1843	John H. Clarke	1916–1922	6	1857–1945
Robert Trimble	1826–1828	2	1777–1828	William H. Taft	1921–1930	8	1857–1930
John McLean	1829–1861	32	1785–1861	George Sutherland	1922–1938	15	1862–1942
Henry Baldwin	1830–1844	14	1780–1844	Pierce Butler	1922–1939	16	1866–1939
James M. Wayne	1835–1867	32	1790–1867	Edward T. Sanford	1923–1930	7	1865–1930
Roger B. Taney	1836–1864	28	1777–1864	Harlan F. Stone	1925–1941	16	1872–1946
Philip P. Barbour	1836–1841	4	1783–1841	*Charles E. Hughes*	1930–1941	11	1862–1948
John Catron	1837–1865	28	1786–1865	Owen J. Roberts	1930–1945	15	1875–1955
John McKinley	1837–1852	15	1780–1852	Benjamin N. Cardozo	1932–1938	6	1870–1938
Peter V. Daniel	1841–1860	19	1784–1860	Hugo L. Black	1937–1971	34	1886–1971
Samuel Nelson	1845–1872	27	1792–1873	Stanley F. Reed	1938–1957	19	1884–1980
Levi Woodbury	1845–1851	5	1789–1851	Felix Frankfurter	1939–1962	23	1882–1965
Robert C. Grier	1846–1870	23	1794–1870	William O. Douglas	1939–1975	36	1898–1980
Benjamin R. Curtis	1851–1857	6	1809–1874	Frank Murphy	1940–1949	9	1890–1949
John A. Campbell	1853–1861	8	1811–1889	*Harlan F. Stone*	1941–1946	5	1872–1946
Nathan Clifford	1858–1881	23	1803–1881	James F. Byrnes	1941–1942	1	1879–1972
Noah H. Swayne	1862–1881	18	1804–1884	Robert H. Jackson	1941–1954	13	1892–1954
Samuel F. Miller	1862–1890	28	1816–1890	Wiley B. Rutledge	1943–1949	6	1894–1949
David Davis	1862–1877	14	1815–1886	Harold H. Burton	1945–1958	13	1888–1964
Stephen J. Field	1863–1897	34	1816–1899	*Fred M. Vinson*	1946–1953	7	1890–1953
Salmon P. Chase	1864–1873	8	1808–1873	Tom C. Clark	1949–1967	18	1899–1977
William Strong	1870–1880	10	1808–1895	Sherman Minton	1949–1956	7	1890–1965
Joseph P. Bradley	1870–1892	22	1813–1892	*Earl Warren*	1953–1969	16	1891–1974
Ward Hunt	1873–1882	9	1810–1886	John Marshall Harlan	1955–1971	16	1899–1971
Morrison R. Waite	1874–1888	14	1816–1888	William J. Brennan, Jr.	1956–1990	33	1906–
John M. Harlan	1877–1911	34	1833–1911	Charles E. Whittaker	1957–1962	5	1901–1973
William B. Woods	1880–1887	7	1824–1887	Potter Stewart	1958–1981	23	1915–
Stanley Matthews	1881–1889	7	1824–1889	Byron R. White	1962–1993	31	1917–
Horace Gray	1882–1902	20	1828–1902	Arthur J. Goldberg	1962–1965	3	1908–1990
Samuel Blatchford	1882–1893	11	1820–1893	Abe Fortas	1965–1969	4	1910–1982

APPENDIX D: (continued)

	TERM OF SERVICE	YEARS OF SERVICE	LIFE SPAN		TERM OF SERVICE	YEARS OF SERVICE	LIFE SPAN
Thurgood Marshall	1967–1991	24	1908–1993	*William H. Rehnquist*	1986–	—	1924–
Warren C. Burger	1969–1986	17	1907–	Antonin Scalia	1986–	—	1936–
Harry A. Blackmun	1970–1994	24	1908–	Anthony M. Kennedy	1987–	—	1936–
Lewis F. Powell, Jr.	1972–1987	15	1907–	David H. Souter	1990–	—	1939–
William H. Rehnquist	1972–	—	1924–	Clarence Thomas	1991–	—	1948–
John P. Stevens III	1975–	—	1920–	Ruth Bader Ginsburg	1993–	—	1933–
Sandra Day O'Connor	1981–	—	1930–	Stephen G. Breyer	1994–	—	1938–

*Appointed and served one term, but not confirmed by the Senate.
Note: Chief justices are in italics.

APPENDIX E
U.S. TERRITORIAL EXPANSION SINCE 1898

Hawaii	1898
The Philippines	1898–1946
Puerto Rico	1899
Guam	1899
American Somoa	1899
Canal Zone	1904
U.S. Virgin Islands	1917
Pacific Island Trust Territories	1947

APPENDIX F
POPULATION OF THE UNITED STATES, 1890–PRESENT (EST.)

1890	63,000,000
1900	76,000,000
1910	92,000,000
1920	106,000,000
1930	122,000,000
1940	132,000,000
1950	151,000,000
1960	179,000,000
1970	205,000,000
1980	227,000,000
1990	247,000,000
1999 (est.)	271,000,000

APPENDIX G:
MEDIAN LIFE EXPECTANCY (in years)

YEAR	TOTAL POPULATION	WHITE FEMALES	NONWHITE FEMALES	WHITE MALES	NONWHITE MALES
1900	47.3	48.7	33.5	46.6	32.5
1910	50.1	52.0	37.5	48.6	33.8
1920	54.1	55.6	45.2	54.4	45.5
1930	59.7	63.5	49.2	59.7	47.3
1940	62.9	66.6	54.9	62.1	51.5
1950	68.2	72.2	62.9	66.5	59.1
1960	69.7	74.1	66.3	67.4	61.1
1970	70.9	75.6	69.4	68.0	61.3
1980	73.7	78.1	73.6	70.7	65.3
1990	75.4	79.3	76.3	72.6	68.4

APPENDIX H:
RECENT TRENDS IN IMMIGRATION (in thousands)

	1961–1970	1971–1980	1981–1990	1991	PERCENT 1961–1970	PERCENT 1971–1980	PERCENT 1981–1990
All countries	3,321.7	4,493.3	7,338.0	1,827.2	100.0	100.0	100.0
Europe	1,123.5	800.4	761.5	146.7	33.8	17.8	10.4
Austria	20.6	9.5	18.9	3.5	0.6	0.2	0.3
Hungary	5.4	6.6	5.9	0.9	0.2	0.1	0.1
Belgium	9.2	5.3	6.6	0.7	0.3	0.1	0.1
Czechoslovakia	3.3	6.0	5.4	0.6	0.1	0.1	0.1
Denmark	9.2	4.4	2.8	0.6	0.3	0.1	0.1
France	45.2	25.1	92.1	4.0	1.4	0.6	1.3
Germany	190.8	74.4	159.0	10.9	5.7	1.7	2.2
Greece	86.0	92.4	31.9	2.9	2.6	2.1	0.4
Ireland	33.0	11.5	67.2	4.6	1.0	0.3	0.9
Italy	214.1	129.4	12.3	30.3	6.4	2.9	0.2
Netherlands	30.6	10.5	4.2	1.3	0.9	0.2	0.1
Norway	15.5	3.9	83.2	0.6	0.5	0.1	1.1
Poland	53.5	37.2	40.3	17.1	1.6	0.8	0.5
Portugal	76.1	101.7	20.5	4.6	2.3	2.3	0.3
Spain	44.7	39.1	11.1	2.7	1.3	0.9	0.2
Sweden	17.1	6.5	8.0	1.2	0.5	0.1	0.1
Switzerland	18.5	8.2	57.6	1.0	0.6	0.2	0.8
USSR	2.5	39.0	18.7	31.6	0.1	0.9	0.3
United Kingdom	213.8	137.4	159.4	16.8	6.4	3.1	2.2
Yugoslavia	20.4	30.5	37.3	2.8	0.6	0.7	0.5
Other Europe	9.1	18.9	7.7	1.2	0.2	0.2	0.0

APPENDIX H: (continued)

	1961–1970	1971–1980	1981–1990	1991	PERCENT 1961–1970	1971–1980	1981–1990
Asia	427.6	1,588.2	2,738.1	342.2	12.9	35.2	37.3
China	34.8	124.3	298.9	24.0	1.0	2.8	4.1
Hong Kong	75.0	113.5	98.2	15.9	2.3	2.5	1.3
India	27.2	164.1	250.7	42.7	0.8	3.7	3.4
Iran	10.3	45.1	116.0	9.9	0.3	1.0	1.6
Israel	29.6	37.7	44.2	5.1	0.9	0.8	0.6
Japan	40.0	49.8	47.0	5.6	1.2	1.1	0.6
Korea	34.5	267.6	333.8	25.4	1.0	6.0	4.5
Philippines	98.4	355.0	548.7	68.8	3.0	7.9	7.5
Turkey	10.1	13.4	23.4	3.5	0.3	0.3	0.3
Vietnam	4.3	172.8	281.0	14.8	1.1	3.8	3.8
Other Asia	36.5	176.1	631.4	126.4	1.1	3.8	8.6
America	1,716.4	1,982.5	3,615.6	1,297.6	51.7	44.3	49.3
Argentina	49.7	29.9	27.3	4.2	1.5	0.7	0.4
Canada	413.3	169.9	158.0	19.9	12.4	3.8	2.2
Columbia	72.0	77.3	122.9	19.3	2.2	1.7	1.7
Cuba	208.5	264.9	144.6	9.5	6.3	5.9	2.0
Dominican Rep.	93.3	148.1	252.0	42.4	2.8	3.3	3.4
Ecuador	36.8	50.1	56.2	10.0	1.1	1.1	0.8
El Salvador	15.0	34.4	213.5	46.9	0.5	0.8	2.9
Haiti	34.5	56.3	138.4	47.0	1.0	1.3	1.9
Jamaica	74.9	137.6	208.1	23.0	2.3	3.1	2.8
Mexico	453.9	640.3	1,655.7	947.9	13.7	14.3	22.6
Other America	264.4	373.8	639.3	128.4	7.9	8.3	8.7
Africa	29.0	80.8	176.8	33.5	0.9	1.8	2.4
Oceania	25.1	41.2	45.2	7.1	0.8	0.9	0.6

Figures may not add to total due to rounding.

APPENDIX 1:
AMERICAN WORKERS AND FARMERS

YEAR	TOTAL NUMBER OF WORKERS (THOUSANDS)	PERCENT OF WORKERS MALE/FEMALE	PERCENT OF FEMALE WORKERS MARRIED	PERCENT OF WORKERS IN FEMALE POPULATION	PERCENT OF WORKERS IN LABOR UNIONS	FARM POPULATION (THOUSANDS)	FARM POPULATION AS PERCENT OF TOTAL POPULATION
1890	23,318	83/17	13.9	18.9	NA	24,771	42.3
1900	29,073	82/18	15.4	20.6	3	29,875	41.9
1910	38,167	79/21	24.7	25.4	6	32,077	34.9
1920	41,614	79/21	23.0	23.7	12	31,974	30.1
1930	48,830	78/22	28.9	24.8	7	30,529	24.9
1940	53,011	76/24	36.4	27.4	27	30,547	23.2
1950	59,643	72/28	52.1	31.4	25	23,048	15.3
1960	69,877	68/32	59.9	37.7	26	15,635	8.7
1970	82,049	63/37	63.4	43.4	25	9,712	4.8
1980	108,544	58/42	59.7	51.5	23	6,051	2.7
1990	117,914	55/45	58.4	44.3	16	4,591	1.8

APPENDIX: J
THE ECONOMY AND FEDERAL SPENDING

YEAR	GROSS NATIONAL PRODUCT (GNP) (IN BILLIONS)	FOREIGN TRADE (IN MILLION) EXPORTS	FOREIGN TRADE (IN MILLION) IMPORTS	BALANCE OF TRADE	FEDERAL BUDGET (IN BILLIONS)	FEDERAL SURPLUS/DEFICIT (IN BILLIONS)	FEDERAL DEBT (IN BILLIONS)
1890	13.1	910	823	+87	0.318	+0.09	1.2
1900	18.7	1,499	930	+569	0.521	+0.05	1.2
1910	35.3	1,919	1,646	+273	0.694	−0.02	1.1
1920	91.5	8,664	5,784	+2,880	6.357	+0.3	24.3
1930	90.7	4,013	3,500	+513	3.320	+0.7	16.3
1940	100.0	4,030	7,433	−3,403	9.6	−2.7	43.0
1950	286.5	10,816	9,125	+1,691	43.1	−2.2	257.4
1960	506.5	19,600	15,046	+4,556	92.2	+0.3	286.3
1970	992.7	42,700	40,189	+2,511	195.6	−2.8	371.0
1980	2,631.7	220,783	244,871	24,088	590.9	−73.8	907.7
1990	5,524.5	421,730	487,129	−65,399	1,251.8	−220.5	3,233.3

Index